THE WORLD ALMANAC®
OF THE U.S.A.

Allan Carpenter and Carl Provorse
and Editors of The World Almanac

A WORLD ALMANAC BOOK
An Imprint of Funk & Wagnalls Corporation

Library of Congress Catalog Card Number: 93-71729

ISBN: 0-88687-724-5 (hard cover)
ISBN: 0-88687-723-7 (soft cover)

Printed in the United States of America.

A World Almanac® Book
An Imprint of Funk & Wagnalls Corporation
One International Boulevard
Mahwah, NJ 07495-0017

10 9 8 7 6 5

CONTENTS

INTRODUCTION

The World Almanac® of the U.S.A. is the most exhaustive single-volume reference work of its kind. It provides in one source the widest variety of information and statistical data on the fifty states, the District of Columbia, Puerto Rico, and U.S. associated regions.

In Part I, "Portraits of the States," an in-depth profile of each state is provided. Significant physical characteristics, historical milestones, and contemporary facts are interwoven. Traditional data such as state capitals, official nicknames, mottoes, slogans, songs, and symbols are listed. And nontraditional and unusual data such as official beverages, sports, and greetings is offered. Notable personalities, illuminating quotations, and colorful historical details highlight the text.

The factual and statistical data deal with more than 300 different items on geography, climate and environment, major cities, population, vital statistics, health, housing, education, law enforcement, courts and the justice system, religion, personal income, business and the economy, travel and transportation, government and law, arts and culture, and sports.

How do the states compare to one another? In Part II, "The States Compared," readers will discover the relationships of the top five and bottom five states in the most useful categories presented in Part I. Some valuable additional data has been included.

The tables offer users a wealth of useful, intriguing, and even startling information. Where do people live the longest? Where are the most physicians? Which states have the most households lacking complete plumbing or telephones? Where have drug abuse cases increased or decreased? Where are the lowest tuition costs?

Almost every table section catches the eye with revelations such as the greatest changes in population of those over 65 years of age, the largest population of native peoples, the most tornadoes and other disasters, the most endangered species, the highest and lowest rates of weddings and divorce.

Users will find the states with the highest and lowest temperatures, as well as the greatest range of temperature, the state with the largest number of female police officers, the state that spends the most per capita on police protection, the state with the most prisoners under sentence of death, and the state having the highest percentage of males.

Where is there more rental housing than home ownership, the most persons per household, the greatest spending for mental health, the lowest average rent, the least violent crime, the largest percentage enrollment in school, the smallest teacher load? Each table has its own story to tell.

The authors believe that users will find the information in this volume indispensable and enlightening.

The statistical information in *The World Almanac® of the U.S.A.* is based on 1990 figures unless otherwise noted.

Allan Carpenter

Carl Provorse

ACKNOWLEDGMENTS

The authors acknowledge with pleasure the valuable assistance provided by the library and staff of Loyola University, Chicago, and by the many divisions of the Census Bureau, by the other agencies of the U.S. government and the many state and private agencies that have furnished data and other assistance as noted in the sources listed at the tables in "The States Compared" section.

PART I

PORTRAITS OF THE STATES

ALABAMA

"I had no idea Alabama had so much to offer. We have wafted over blue Gulf waters, rustled through venerable historic rooms, lilted across pine-ringed lakes, heard our voices echoed from picturesque mountain tops and resounded through mammoth caverns. We have been transported from the historical lands of the Indians, the Spanish, the French, the English, to the roar of the space age, and we had them all and much more in star-studded Alabama."

Anonymous travel writer

True to its nickname, Alabama is the "Heart of Dixie," where the Confederate constitution was formulated, but it is also a state that looks to the future. As a pioneer in the iron and steel industry, Alabama took an early lead in manufacturing in the South. It became a leader in the Space Age—Huntsville, "Rocket City, U.S.A.," is the center for research on rockets and space vehicles. Alabama is also filled with beauty, from forests rising from the red clay soil in the north, through pine forests and rolling grasslands of the south, to the swamps and bayous in the Mobile Delta on the Gulf of Mexico. This football-mad state (the University of Alabama has won seven national championships) is no longer the rural region it once was—today 60 percent of its residents live in metropolitan areas.

SUPERLATIVES

- Introduced Mardi Gras to the Western Hemisphere.
- Tuscumbia Railroad, the first west of the Alleghenies.
- The first rocket to put men on the moon, built in Huntsville.
- First in cast-iron and steel pipe products.
- The only state to possess all major raw materials to make iron and steel.
- World's first electric trolley system—Montgomery, 1886.

MOMENTS IN HISTORY

- In 1540 the Spanish explorer Hernando de Soto and his large party entered Alabama, killing and enslaving the native peoples as they went.
- The Parish of Mobile was organized in 1704.
- The American Revolution had little effect on what is present-day Alabama, but in 1780 the Spanish captured Mobile Bay from the British and held it for Spain during the war.
- Parts of Alabama came to the United States after the revolution, also following battles with the British during the War of 1812.
- On March 27, 1814, Andrew Jackson's victory at the Battle of Horseshoe Bend brought to an end the power of the formidable Creek Confederacy.
- In 1818 the pioneer smelters near Russellville were forerunners of the state's later leadership in iron and steel.
- The 1830s witnessed the beginning of one of history's saddest episodes as the Five Civilized Tribes were forced to leave their comfortable homes and move west over the "Trail of Tears," and their valuable property was taken over without compensation.
- On January 11, 1861, Alabama seceded from the Union, and on February 4, six states met at Montgomery and formed the Confederate States of America, with Montgomery as the capital.

• The Confederate flag was designed and first flown in Alabama in 1861.

• By April 12, 1865, Selma, Mobile, Tuscaloosa, and Montgomery had fallen to Union forces, and Civil War battles ended in Alabama.

So They Say

"Damn the torpedoes—full speed ahead!"

That order by Union Admiral David Farragut as he moved to capture Mobile Bay has become one of the world's most famous battle cries.

• After the Civil War, Alabama refused to approve the 14th Amendment, and the state suffered many hardships during the Reconstruction period. Federal troops were not withdrawn from Alabama until 1876, and the state then began a slow recovery.

• After the Civil War the condition of the freed slaves had not improved greatly. Then in 1881 Booker T. Washington took over the Tuskegee Institute and was a pioneer in the education of African-Americans.

• Alabama's first steel was produced in 1888.

So They Say

"...progress in the enjoyment of all the privileges that will come to us must be the result of severe and constant struggle rather than of artificial forcing....It is important and right that all privileges of the law be ours, but it is vastly more important that we be prepared for the exercise of those privileges..."

George Washington Carver

• In 1898 an entire battalion of black volunteers joined the state's recruits in the Spanish-American War.

• Alabama was figuratively shaken by a worm in 1910, as the boll weevil threatened the state's mammoth cotton crop, the key factor in its economy, but, although the insect was controlled, peanut growing became more important.

• During World War I, Alabama Seaman Osmond Kelly (O.K.) Ingram, one of the 86,916 Alabamans who saw military service in that conflict, was the first U.S. Navy man to be killed.

• In 1932 the judgment of the Alabama Supreme Court was reversed by the U.S. Supreme Court in the famous Scottsboro case, when nine black men were returned for a new trial because their original trial was deemed prejudiced and unfair. Four were later released, and five were convicted.

• In 1933 the Tennessee Valley Authority (TVA) was established. With its strategic location and pioneer Muscle Shoals dam, Alabama was in an excellent position to benefit from the TVA. Its dams and navigation projects helped to alleviate the severe effects of the Great Depression.

• During World War II, 288,003 Alabamans served in the U.S. armed forces.

• In 1950 Dr. Werner von Braun brought 120 German rocket scientists to the small town of Huntsville. This started it on its way to becoming "Rocket Capital of the World."

• On January 31, 1958, *Explorer One* became the West's first satellite; both the rocket and satellite had been developed at the Army Ballistic Missile Agency at Huntsville, under Werner von Braun.

• On May 15, 1972, while campaigning, Governor George Wallace was shot and partially paralyzed, but he surprised most observers by being elected to a new term as governor in 1974 and by his campaign for the Democratic nomination for the presidency.

• The 1990 census indicated that Alabama's population gained 3.8% over the figure for 1980.

That's Interesting

• An important relic discovered in Russell Cave was the skeleton of a prehistoric man. The tip of the spear that killed him was found lying among his bones.

• When, in 1811, Indian leader Tecumseh became angry with some chiefs, he stamped his foot and threatened to shake down their houses. By strange coincidence, the worst earthquake, ever, struck the area shortly thereafter. As Tecumseh hurried north to join the British forces, one chief exclaimed, "Tecumseh has reached Detroit, feel the earth move with his foot!"

• During the Civil War John H. Wisdom became known as the Paul Revere of the South, after he galloped the 67 mi. between Gadsden, Alabama, and Rome, Georgia, to warn of a Union attack.

• During his 46 yrs. at Tuskeegee Institute, black scientist George Washington Carver discovered 300 new uses for the peanut and 175 for the sweet potato, and made many other important contributions toward feeding the modern world.

• At one time, Alabama claimed to have the "largest representation in Congress." Senator Dixon H. Lewis of Montgomery weighed 500 lbs., and his Senate seat had to be specially made.

• One of the world's most unusual monuments stands at the town of Enterprise—a giant tribute to the boll weevil.

Notable Natives

Henry Louis "Hank" Aaron (Mobile, 1934-), baseball player. **Tallulah Brockman Bankhead** (Huntsville, 1903-1968), actress. **Hugo LaFayette Black** (Harlan, 1886-1971), Supreme Court Justice. **William Crawford Gorgas** (Mobile, 1854-1920), army officer/physician. **William Christopher Handy** (Florence, 1873-1958), musician/composer. **Helen Adams Keller** (Tuscumbia, 1880-1968), author/lecturer. **Joe Louis** (Lexington, 1914-1981), boxer. **Alexander McGillivray** (Alabama, 1759?-1793), Indian leader. **Willie Howard Mays, Jr.** (Fairfield, 1931-), baseball player. **John Hunt Morgan** (Huntsville, 1825-1864), soldier. **Jesse Owens** (Danville, 1913-1980), athlete.

General

Admitted to statehood: Dec. 14, 1819
Origin of name: Indian for tribal town, later a tribe (*Alabamas* or *Alibamons*) of the Creek confederacy
Capital: Montgomery
Nicknames: The Cotton State and The Heart of Dixie
Motto: *"Audemus jura nostra defendere"* ("We dare defend our rights")
Bird: yellowhammer
Fish: tarpon
Flower: camellia
Mineral: red iron ore (Hematite)
Song: "Alabama" (words by Julia S. Tutwiler, music by Edna Gockel Gussen)
Stone: marble
Tree: southern (longleaf) pine

The Land

Area: 52,423 sq. mi., 30th
Land: 50,750 sq. mi., 28th
Water: 1,673 sq. mi., 23rd
Topography: coastal plains including Prairie Black Belt give way to hills, broken terrain
Number of counties: 67
Geographic center: Chilton, 12 mi. SW of Clanton
Length: 330 mi.
Width: 190 mi.
Highest point: 2,405 ft. (Cheaha Mountain), 35th
Lowest point: sea level (Gulf of Mexico), 3rd
Mean elevation: 500 ft., 40th
Coastline: 53 mi., 17th
Shoreline: 607 mi., 19th

Climate and Environment

Temp., highest: 112 deg. on Sept. 5, 1925, at Centerville
lowest: -27 deg. on Jan. 30, 1966, at New Market
Fresh water withdrawn, per capita, per day: 2,140 gal., 14th
Endangered species: mammals, 4—Gray bat, Indiana bat, Alabama beach mouse, Perdido Key beach mouse; birds, 3—American peregrine falcon, wood stock, red-cockaded woodpecker; reptiles, 4; amphibians, none; fishes, 4; invertebrates, 21; plants, 6

Major Cities, Population Percentage Increase (1980-90)

Birmingham, 265,968— -6.49%
Huntsville, 159,789—12.12%
Mobile, 196,278— -2.08%
Montgomery, 187,106—5.20%
Tuscaloosa, 77,759—3.39%

The People

Population: 4,040,587, 22nd
Percent change (1980-90): 3.63%, 33rd
Per sq. mi: 77.08, 25th
Percent in metro. area: 67.39%, 28th

White: 2,975,797—73.65%, 43rd
Black: 1,020,705—25.26%, 6th
Native American: 16,506—0.41%, 26th
Asian, Pacific Isle: 21,979—0.54%, 44th
Other races: 5,782—0.14%,48th
Hispanic origin: 24,629—0.61%, 48th
Percent foreign born: 1.1%, 46th
Percent over 5 yrs. speaking language other than English at home: 2.9%, 46th
Percent males: 47.92%, 49th
Percent females: 52.08%, 3rd
Percent never married: 23.9%, 37th
Marriages per 1,000 (1989): 10.2, 15th
Divorces per 1,000 (1989): 6.1, 9th
Median age: 33
Under 5 years: 283,295—7.01%, 36th
Under 18 years: 1,058,788—26.20%, 22nd
65 years & older: 522,989—12.94%, 23rd
Percent increase among the elderly: 18.9%, 29th

Of Vital Importance

Live births per 1,000 pop.: 16.2, 17th
Infant mortality rate per 1,000 births (1988): 12.1, 6th
Average lifetime (1979-81): 72.53, 45th
Deaths per 100,000 pop. (1988): 953.9, 15th
Causes of death per 100,000 pop. (1988):
Diseases of heart: 323.5, 21st
Malignant neoplasms: 206.2, 18th
Cerebrovascular diseases: 71.2, 12th
Accidents & adverse effects: 54.5, 6th
Chronic obstructive pulmonary diseases: 35.1, 24th
Suicide: 12.1, 29th
HIV infection: 2.2, 29th
Other: 78.7, 17th

Keeping Well

Non-federal physicians per 100,000 pop.: 172, 41st
Dentists per 100,000 (1990-91): 46, 50th
Nurses per 100,000 (1989): 554, 39th
Hospitals per 100,000: 3.4, 19th
Admissions per 100,000: 15,836, 10th
Beds per 100,000: 582.89, 12th
Occupancy rate: 66.4%, 25th
Semiprivate room charges per day: $210, 44th
Average stay: 7.1, 27th
Notifiable diseases per 100,000:
AIDS: 5.9, 33rd
Gonorrhea: 533.7, 4th
Measles: 0.6, 43rd
Syphillis: 77.6, 7th
Tuberculosis (TB): 12.0, 14th
Per capita spending on mental health programs (1987): $28.96, 38th
Pop. without health insur. (1991): 17.9%, 10th

Households by Type

Total households: 1,506,790
Percent change (1980-90): 12.28%, 24th
Family households: 1,103,835
Percent of total: 73.26%, 6th
Nonfamily households: 402,955
Percent of total: 26.74%, 46th
Persons per household: 2.62, 18th
Pop. living in group quarters: 92,402
Percent of pop.: 2.29%, 42nd

Living Quarters

Total housing units: 1,670,379
Persons per unit: 2.42, 22nd
Occupied housing units: 1,506,790
Percent of total units: 90.21%, 20th
Persons per unit: 2.57, 16th
Percent of units with over one person per room: 3.51%, 22nd
Owner-occupied units: 1,061,867
Percent of total units: 63.57%, 8th
Percent of occupied units: 70.47%, 6th
Persons per unit: 2.70, 33rd
Median value: $53,700, 41st
Renter-occupied units: 444,893
Percent of total units: 26.63%, 42nd
Percent of occupied units: 29.53%, 45th
Persons per unit: 2.44, 14th
Median contract rent: $229, 48th
Rental vacancy rate: 9.3%, 19th
Mobile home, trailer & other as a % of occupied housing units: 15.90%, 12th

Crime Index per 100,000

Total: 4,915, 31st
Violent: 709, 15th

Murder and nonnegligent manslaughter: 12, 8th
Aggravated assault: 7,011, 36th
Robbery: 144, 24th
Rape: 33, 32nd
Property: 4,207, 37th
Burglary: 1,103, 27th
Larceny, theft: 2,755, 40th
Motor vehicle theft: 348, 32nd
Drug abuse arrests: 188, 35th

TEACHING AND LEARNING

Literacy (1987): 87%, 31st
Pop. 3 and over enrolled in school: 1,056,402
Percent of pop.: 27.3%, 25th
Public elementary & secondary schools:
Total enrollment: 726,000
Avg. class size (1987): 26, 3rd
Teachers: 39,700
Percent of pop.: 0.98%, 30th
Teachers' avg. salary: $25,500, 39th
Spending per capita: $624, 47th
Spending per pupil in avg. daily attendance: $3,314, 46th
Percent of graduates taking SAT: 8%, 45th
Combined SAT scores: 991, 18th
Percent of pop. over 25 completing:
High school: 66.9%, 47th
College degree/s: 15.7%, 45th
Higher educa., institutions: 87
Per 100,000 pop.: 1.4, 5th
Enroll: 247,117
Percent of pop.: 6.12%, 16th
Public: 225,506
Percent of enroll.: 91.25%, 8th
Private: 21,611
Percent of enroll.: 8.75%, 44th
White non-Hispanic: 40,977
Percent of enroll.: 50.80%, 50th
Black non-Hispanic: 24,770
Percent of enroll.: 30.71%, 1st
Hispanic: 2,406
Percent of enroll.: 2.98%, 12th
Asian/Pacific Islander: 3,222
Percent of enroll.: 3.99%, 9th
Amer. Indian/AK native: 270
Percent of enroll.: 0.33%, 29th
Nonresident alien: 9,024
Percent of enroll.: 11.19%, 1st
Female: 118,688
Percent of enroll.: 48.03%, 51st
Tuition, state university ('90-'91): $1,593, 29th
Public library systems: 206
Books & serial vol. per capita: 1.81, 44th
Govt. expend. per capita: $8.24, 46th
State govt.: $2.11, 36th
Local govts.: $6.12, 44th

LAW ENFORCEMENT, COURTS, AND PRISONS

Police protection expend.: $316,453,000
Per capita: $78.31, 44th
Judicial & legal expend.: $145,070,000
Per capita: $35.90, 38th
Corrections expend.: $212,772,000
Per capita: $52.65, 41st
Police per 10,000 pop. (1990-91): 20.5, 27th
Prisoners (state & fed.) sentenced to over 1 yr., per 100,000 pop.: 370
Percent change (1989-90): 13.19%, 5th
Death penalty: yes, by electrocution
Under sentence of death: 93, 8th
Executed (1989): 4

RELIGION, NUMBER AND PERCENT OF POPULATION

Agnostic: 5,964—0.20%, 42nd
Buddhist: NA
Christian: 2,782,019—93.30%, 5th
Hindu: 2,982—0.10%, 10th
Jewish: 2,982—0.10%, 43rd
Moslem: 5,964—0.20%, 13th
Unitarian: 2,982—0.10%, 31st
Other: 23,854—0.80%, 37th
None: 116,290—3.90%, 44th
Refused to answer: 38,763—1.30%, 45th

MAKING A LIVING

Personal income per capita (1989): $11,486, 40th
Percent increase (1979-'89) (constant 1989 dollars): 16.3%, 21st
Average income per family: $35,253, 42nd
Percent of pop. below poverty level: 18.3%, 7th
Percent 65 and over: 24.0%, 3rd

Cost of living, selected cities
1st qtr., 1991 (U. S. Standard=100)
Decatur-Hartselle 91.5
Birmingham 100.4
Tuscaloosa 102.3

ECONOMY

Civilian labor force : 1,892,000
Percent of tot. pop.: 46.82%, 45th
Percent 65 and over: NA
Percent females: 44.34%, 44th
Percent job growth (1980-90): 18.99%, 26th
Major employer industries:
Agriculture: 49,392—2.80%, 25th
Construction: 86,436—4.90%, 18th
Finance, insurance & real estate: 81,144—4.60%, 39th
Government: 294,588—16.70%, 19th
Manufacturing: 416,304—23.60%, 7th
Mining: 12,265—0.7%, 19th
Service: 276,948—15.70%, 48th
Trade: 313,992—17.80%, 39th
Transportation, communication, & public utilities: 82,908—4.70%, 35th
Wholesale/retail: 354,106—20.3%, 39th
Unemployment rate: 6.77%, 7th
Male: 3.44%, 12th
Female: 3.33%, 4th
Total businesses (1991): 114,123
New business incorp's. (1991): 6,116
Percent of total businesses: 5.36%, 34th
Business failures (1991): 1,022
Percent of total businesses: 0.90%, 21st
Agriculture, farm income
Marketing (1991): $2,977,832,000, 23rd
Net per operation: $25,073, 20th
Net per acre: $116, 11th
Leading products: broilers, cattle, greenhouse, peanuts
Av. value land & build. per acre: $882, 26th
Percent increase (1980-90): 13.08%, 17th
Govt. payments: $66,350,000, 27th
Construction, value of all: $1,648,000,000
Per capita: $407.86, 40th
Percent change 1989-90: 4.83%, 15th
Manufactures:
Value added: : $21,362,000,000
Per capita: $5,286.86, 22nd
Value of shipments: $48,748,000,000
Per capita: $12,064.58, 22nd
Leading products: (1988-89): electronics, cast iron and plastic pipe, fabricated steel prods., ships, paper products, chemicals, steel, mobile homes, fabrics, poultry processing
Mining, min. prod., value (1987): $1,793,000,000, 18th
Leading products: coal, petroleum, nat. gas
Retail sales: $26,373,000,000, 23rd
Per household: $17,435, 40th
Percent increase (1987-90): 19.2%, 16th
Service indust., value (1987): $12,222,000,000, 26th
Per capita: $3,024.81, 43rd
Tourism indus., value (1989): $3,150,000,000, 27th
Foreign exports value: $2,834,000,000, 27th
Per capita: $701.38, 35th
Patents per 1,000 pop.: 11.4, 10th

TRAVEL AND TRANSPORTATION

Motor vehicle registrations: 3,744,491
Per 1,000 pop.: 926, 8th
Motorcycle registrations: 43,871
Per 1,000 pop : 10, 41st
Licensed drivers per 1,000 driving age pop.: 893, 28th
Deaths from motor vehicle accidents per 100,000 pop.: 27.7, 5th
Public roads & streets
Total mileage: 90,672, 20th
Rural mileage: 73,818, 19th
Urban mileage: 16,854, 14th
Interstate mileage: 889, 24th
Annual vehicle-miles of travel per person: 10,480, 5th
Mean travel time for workers 16 + who work away from home: 21.2 min., 20th

GOVERNMENT

Registered voters (1988): 2,451,494
Percentage of voting age pop.: 81.44%, 12th
Voter turnout (1988): 1,378,476
Percentage of registered voters: 56.23%, 48th
Percentage of voting age pop.: 45.80%, 41st
State legislators, total (1992): 140, 28th
Women members (1992): 8

Percentage of legislature: 5.7%, 50th
Dominant party (1992): Democrats
U. S. Congress, House members (1993): 7
Increase 1983-93: 0
Revenues:
State govt.: $9,040,995,000
Per capita: $2,237.54, 35th
State & local govt.: $13,770,020,000
Per capita: $3,407.93, 41st
Indebtedness:
State govt.: $3,979,067,000
Per capita: $984.77, 32nd
State & local govt.: $10,221,000,000
Per capita: $2,529.58, 41st

Laws and Regulations

Legal driving age: 16
Marriage age without parental consent: 18
Divorce residence requirement: 6 mo., qualification—check local statutes

Attractions

Major opera companies (1989): 2, 21st
Per 1 million pop.: 0.49, 34th
Major symphony orchestras (1989): 7, 32nd
Per 1 million pop.: 1.70, 50th
State appropriations for state arts agencies per capita: $0.48, 38th
State Fair in early Oct. at Birmingham.

Sports and Competition

NCAA sports teams, 8: Alabama A & M Univ. Bulldogs, Alabama State Univ. Hornets, Auburn Univ. Tigers, Samford Univ. Bulldogs, Troy State Univ. Trojans, Tuskegee Univ. Golden Tigers, Univ. of Alabama Blazers, Univ. of Alabama Crimson Tide
Professional teams: 3
Baseball: 2—Birmingham Barons (Class AA), Hoover Metropolitan Stadium; Huntsville Stars (Class AA), Joe W. Davis Stadium
Football: 1—Birmingham Fire (World League of American Football), Legion Field

ALASKA

"The future is bound to be a bright and useful one. You are no longer an Arctic frontier. You constitute a bridge to the continent of Asia and all of its people."

Dwight D. Eisenhower

Vast Alaska could swallow up Texas, California, and Montana yet it is the second least populous state. It reaches so far to the west that the international dateline had to be bent around it to keep all the state in the same day. Although it is generally thought of as a "frozen" land, vegetables and fruit can grow two or three times their normal size. Alaska is so large and roads are so few that the airplane becomes the "family car." Alaska is a land where railroads sink into the ground, where the ice barks and huge moose sometimes interfere with golf games. It has been called "a land of promise, America's Last Frontier."

Superlatives

• Largest of all the states, one-fifth as large as all the other states together.

• Only U.S. state extending into the Eastern hemisphere.

• Mt. McKinley is the highest mountain in North America.

• Nation's largest forest acreage.

Moments in History

• Sent by the Russian Czar, Vitus Bering reached Alaska in 1741. Native groups included the Indian, Eskimo, and Aleut, who were decimated by the Russians.

> **So They Say**
>
> "Their (Aleuts) instruments and utensils are all made with amazing beauty and the exactest symmetry....Their boats are infinitely superior to those of any other."
>
> Anonymous early visitor

• Russia's trading headquarters were set up at Kodiak in 1784, the first permanent European settlement in present-day Alaska.

• In 1804 Alexander Baranof routed the Sitka Indians and established Sitka, which soon became the highly civilized capital of Alaska.

• As his hold on Alaska weakened, the Russian Czar decided to sell the territory to the United States. Although most Americans thought of Alaska as a barren frigid waste, on March 30, 1867, the United States bought all of Russian America for $7,200,000.

> **So They Say**
>
> "The mystery is not why Russia wished to sell Alaska but why the United States wanted to buy."
>
> An unnamed journalist

• On October 18, 1867, the Americans present cheered as their flag was raised at Sitka, closing one of the best real estate bargains ever.

• In 1880 prospectors discovered a large gold lode near the headwaters of Gold Creek; in less than a year prospectors and settlers rushed in, and the community was named for prospector Joe Juneau.

• In 1896 thousands of American prospectors crossed Alaska over the treacherous passes to reach the gold discoveries of the Canadian Klondike.

• The gold found exposed on the beaches of Nome in 1899 brought prospectors in near-record numbers. As many as 40,000 scratched for the riches.

• On June 6, 1912, the top of Mt. Katmai exploded with a roar heard 750 miles. The shock has been considered to be the second worst ever recorded.

So They Say

"A mountain has burst near here, so that we are covered with ashes, in some places ten feet deep....Night and day we light lamps...we are expecting death any moment, and we have no water....Here are darkness and hell, thunder and noise. The earth is trembling."

Unamed observer on the explosion of Mt. Katmai

• On July 15, 1923, at the Tanana River bridge, Alaska's first railroad was dedicated by President Warren G. Harding.

• On August 15, 1935, a pontoon plane crashed, and the "world lost two of its most beloved figures" at a place a few miles from Barrow. Dead were the world famed humorist-philosopher Will Rogers and noted aviator Wiley Post.

So They Say

"One man big, have tall boots. Other man short, have sore eye, rag over eye."

Barrow native Okpeasha reporting the crash of Will Rogers and Wiley Post, who wore a patch over one eye

• During World War II, Japanese invaders seized Attu, Kiska, and Agattu islands in 1942, but U.S. forces soon recaptured the Aleutians.

• Alaska became the 49th state on January 3, 1959, the first since 1912.

• One of the most disastrous earthquakes ever to hit North America devastated the Anchorage area on March 27, 1964.

So They Say

"As soon as she heard the first sounds, she grabbed the kids and ran out of the house. A minute later the yard and the house—everything—fell into that hole.

Dr. Richard Sutherland on his wife's experience in the 1959 earthquake

• In 1977 the controversial Trans-Alaska pipeline was completed after three years of work.

• Based on revenues from its oil, by 1985 every Alaskan who applied received a check of about $400.00.

• The grounding of the *Exxon Valdez* oil tanker in Prince William Sound on March 24, 1989, was one of the nation's worst ecological disasters. A vast oil spill killed unknown numbers of marine and shore animals and birds, and affected much of the economy of a vast area. Cleanup costs and damages were staggering.

That's Interesting

• The state of Rhode Island could fit into Alaska 483 times.

• Self-emptying Lake George is the best known curiosity of its kind. A dam of ice forms each winter and the lake backs up behind it. Pressure of the water causes the dam to burst. The lake empties itself and the process begins all over.

• The last shot of the Civil War was fired in the remote region of the Bering Sea. The Confederate cruiser *Shenandoah* fired on a Union whaler on June 22, 1865, not knowing the war was over.

• Juneau's gold made prospector Joe Juneau wealthy, but he felt that he had to spend all his money before he died; he squandered his fortune and soon got his wish, dying penniless in Dawson.

• During Alaska's statehood celebration, Fairbanks attempted to turn the Chena River into gold, as a symbol of the state's gold. However, through some chemical mistake, it turned a lovely green.

• A mapmaker, unfamiliar with the name of an Alaskan community, wrote "name?" on the map. His draftsman misread the notation and entered the word "Nome" at that location, literally putting Nome on the map.

Notable Alaskans

Alexander Baranof (Russia, 1747-1819), trader/public official. **Rex Ellingwood Beach** (Atwood, MI, 1877-1949), author. **Vitus Jonassen Bering** (Denmark, 1681-1741), explorer. **Sheldon Jackson** (Minaville, NY, 1834-1909), missionary. **Jack London** (San Francisco, CA, 1876-1916), author. **John Muir** (Dunbar, Scotland, 1838-1914) naturalist/explorer/conservationist

General

Admitted to statehood: Jan. 3, 1959
Origin of name: Russian version of an Aleutian word, *Alakshak,* for "peninsula," "great lands," or "land that is not an island"
Capital: Juneau
Nicknames: Great Land and The Last Frontier
Motto: "North to the Future"
Bird: willow ptarmigan
Fish: king salmon
Flower: forget-me-not
Gem: jade
Song: "Alaska's Flag"
Tree: Sitka spruce

The Land

Area: 656,424 sq. mi., 1st
Land: 570,374 sq. mi., 1st
Water: 86,051 sq. mi., 1st
Topography: includes Pacific and Arctic mountain systems, central plateau, and Arctic slope. Mt. McKinley, 20,320 ft., is the highest point in North America
Number of counties (called divisions): 25
Geographic center: Approx. 60 mi. NW of Mt. McKinley
Length: 1,480 mi.
Width: 810 mi.
Highest point: 20,320 ft. (Mount McKinley), 1st
Lowest point: sea level (Pacific Ocean), 3rd lowest
Mean elevation: 1,900 ft., 15th
Coastline: 6,640 mi., 1st
Shoreline: 33,904 mi., 1st

Climate and Environment

Temp., highest: 100 deg. on June 27, 1915, at Fort Yukon; lowest: -80 deg. on Jan. 23, 1971, at Prospect Creek Camp
Fresh water withdrawn, per capita, per day: 727 gal., 39th
Endangered species: mammals, none; birds, 3—Eskimo curlew, American peregrine falcon, Aleutian Canada goose; reptiles, none; amphibians, none; fishes, none; invertebrates, none; plants, 1

Major Cities, Population Percentage Increase (1980-90)

Anchorage, 226,338—29.76%
College, 11,249—178.23%
Fairbanks, 30,843—36.20%
Juneau, 26,751—36.99%
Sitka, 8,588—10.06%

The People

Population: 550,043, 50th
Percent change (1980-90): 26.94%, 2nd
Per sq. mi: 0.84, 51st
Percent in metro. area: 41.09%, 41st
Percent foreign born: 4.5%, 19th
White: 415,492—75.54%, 40th
Black: 22,451—4.08%, 31st
Native American: 85,698—15.58%, 1st
Asian, Pacific Isle: 19,728—3.59%, 5th
Other races: 6,674—1.21%, 23rd
Hispanic origin: 17,803—3.24%, 22nd
Percent over 5 yrs. speaking language other than English at home: 12.1%, 15th
Percent males: 52.70%, 1st
Percent females: 47.30%, 51st
Percent never married: 27.2%, 17th
Marriages per 1,000 (1989): 11.0, 9th
Divorces per 1,000 (1989): 6.3, 7th
Median age: 29.4
Under 5 years: 54,897—9.98%, 1st
Under 18 years: 172,344—31.33%, 2nd
65 years & older: 22,369—4.07%, 51st
Percent increase among the elderly: 93.7%, 2nd

Of Vital Importance

Live births per 1,000 pop.: 21.8, 2nd
Infant mortality rate per 1,000 births (1988): 11.6, 8th
Average lifetime (1979-81): 72.24, 46th
Deaths per 100,000 pop. (1988): 393.9, 51st

Causes of death per 100,000 pop. (1988):
Diseases of heart: 88.7, 51st
Malignant neoplasms: 85.7, 51st
Cerebrovascular diseases: 16.4, 51st
Accidents & adverse effects: 74.4, 1st
Chronic obstructive pulmonary diseases: 13.5, 51st
Suicide: 10.5, 42nd
HIV infection: 1.3, 41st
Other: 31.2, 51st

Keeping Well

Non-federal physicians per 100,000 pop.: 141, 51st
Dentists per 100,000 (1990-91): 55, 36th
Nurses per 100,000 (1989): 510, 42nd
Hospitals per 100,000: 4.9, 8th
Admissions per 100,000: 68,192, 1st
Beds per 100,000: 359.24, 47th
Occupancy rate: 51.9%, 50th
Semiprivate room charges per day: $407, 3rd
Average stay: 5.9, 47th
Notifiable diseases per 100,000:
AIDS: 4.5, 41st
Gonorrhea: 193.8, 27th
Measles: 14.5, 5th
Syphillis: 4.7, 40th
Tuberculosis (TB): 12.4, 11th
Per capita spending on mental health programs (1987): $52.69, 10th
Pop. without health insur. (1991): 13.1%, 22nd

Households by Type

Total households: 188,915
Percent change (1980-90): 44.21%, 2nd
Family households: 132,837
Percent of total: 70.32%, 27th
Nonfamily households: 56,078
Percent of total: 29.68%, 25th
Persons per household: 2.80, 3rd
Pop. living in group quarters: 20,701
Percent of pop.: 3.76%, 5th

Living Quarters

Total housing units: 232,608
Persons per unit: 2.36, 34th
Occupied housing units: 188,915
Percent of total units: 81.22%, 49th
Persons per unit: 2.78, 4th
Percent of units with over 1 person per room: 8.58%, 3rd
Owner-occupied units: 105,989
Percent of total units: 45.57%, 50th
Percent of occupied units: 56.10%, 46th
Persons per unit: 2.97, 3rd
Median value: $94,400, 14th
Renter-occupied units: 82,926
Percent of total units: 35.65%, 8th
Percent of occupied units: 43.90%, 7th
Persons per unit: 2.58, 5th
Median contract rent: $503, 6th
Rental vacancy rate: 8.5%, 24th
Mobile home, trailer & other as a % of occupied housing units: 13.08%, 22nd

Crime Index per 100,000

Total: 5,153, 28th
Violent: 525, 26th
Murder and nonnegligent manslaughter: 7, 23rd
Aggravated assault: 9,980, 2nd
Robbery: 77, 38th
Rape: 73, 3rd
Property: 4,628, 27th
Burglary: 894, 36th
Larceny, theft: 3,168, 21st
Motor vehicle theft: 565, 19th
Drug abuse arrests: 101, 45th

Teaching and Learning

Literacy (1987): 93%, 2nd
Pop. 3 and over enrolled in school: 156,357
Percent of pop.: 30.2%, 4th
Public elementary & secondary schools:
Total enrollment: 116,000
Avg. class size (1987): 21, 35th
Teachers: 6,500
Percent of pop.: 1.18%, 7th
Teachers' avg. salary: $43,200, 1st
Spending per capita: $1,566, 1st
Spending per pupil in avg. daily attendance: $7,252, 5th
Percent of graduates taking SAT: 41%, 24th
Combined SAT scores: 920, 29th
Percent of pop. over 25 completing:
High school: 86.6%, 1st

College degree/s: 23.0%, 12th
Higher educa., institutions: 7
Per 100,000 pop.: 0.5, 35th
Enroll: 29,833
Percent of pop.: 5.42%, 27th
Public: 27,792
Percent of enroll.: 93.16%, 5th
Private: 2,041
Percent of enroll.: 6.84%, 47th
White non-Hispanic: 16,132
Percent of enroll.: 30.00%, 51st
Black non-Hispanic: 1,457
Percent of enroll.: 2.71%, 37th
Hispanic: 1,002
Percent of enroll.: 1.86%, 21st
Asian/Pacific Islander: 31,356
Percent of enroll.: 58.31%, 1st
Amer. Indian/AK native: 162
Percent of enroll.: 0.30%, 34th
Nonresident alien: 3,663
Percent of enroll.: 6.81%, 2nd
Female: 17,834
Percent of enroll.: 59.78%, 1st
Tuition, state university ('90-'91): $1,382, 41st
Public library systems: 81
Books & serial vol. per capita: 3.13, 17th
Govt. expend. per capita: $36.18, 1st
State govt.: $10.10, 2nd
Local govts.: $26.07, 2nd

Law Enforcement, Courts, and Prisons

Police protection expend.: $107,756,000
Per capita: $195.92, 2nd
Judicial & legal expend.: $90,108,000
Per capita: $163.83, 2nd
Corrections expend.: $114,904,000
Per capita: $208.92, 2nd
Police per 10,000 pop. (1990-91): 17.5, 36th
Prisoners (state & fed.) sentenced to over 1 yr., per 100,000 pop.: 348
Percent change (1989-90): -2.99%, 50th
Death penalty: no

Religion, Number and Percent of Population

Agnostic: NA
Buddhist: NA
Christian: NA
Hindu: NA
Jewish: NA
Moslem: NA
Unitarian: NA
Other: NA
None: NA
Refused to answer: NA

Making a Living

Personal income per capita (1989): $17,610, 5th
Percent increase (1979-'89) (constant 1989 dollars): 3.1%, 46th
Average income per family: $54,203, 3rd
Percent of pop. below poverty level: 9.0%, 44th
Percent 65 and over: 7.6%, 49th
Cost of living, selected cities
1st qtr., 1991 (U. S. Standard=100)

Fairbanks	133.7
Anchorage	135.0
Kodiak	147.9

Economy

Civilian labor force : 257,000
Percent of tot. pop.: 46.72%, 46th
Percent 65 and over: NA
Percent females: 45.53%, 26th
Percent job growth (1980-90): 40.53%, 4th
Major employer industries:
Agriculture: 1,434—0.60%, 48th
Construction: 9,560—4.00%, 37th
Finance, insurance & real estate: 10,277—4.30%, 42nd
Government: 62,857—26.30%, 2nd
Manufacturing: 9,321—3.90%, 50th
Mining: 8,935—3.6%, 3rd
Service: 44,454—18.60%, 37th
Trade: 42,064—17.60%, 43rd
Transportation, communication, & public utilities: 18,881—7.90%, 1st
Wholesale/retail: 47,046—19.2%, 47th
Unemployment rate: 7.00%, 4th
Male: 3.89%, 3rd
Female: 3.11%, 5th
Total businesses (1991): 19,262
New business incorp's. (1991): 1,250
Percent of total businesses: 6.49%, 19th

Business failures (1991): 143
Percent of total businesses: 0.74%, 34th
Agriculture farm income
Marketing (1991): $26,622,000, 50th
Net per operation: $6,371, 48th
Net per acre: $4, 50th
Leading products: greenhouse, dairy products, hay, potatoes
Av. value land & build. per acre: NA
Percent increase (1980-90): NA
Govt. payments: $1,285,000, 48th
Construction, value of all: $295,000,000
Per capita: $536.32, 26th
Percent change 1989-90: 84.38%, 1st
Manufactures:
Value added: : $1,390,000,000
Per capita: $2,527.08, 43rd
Value of shipments: $3,676,000,000
Per capita: $6,683.11, 40th
Leading products: fish products, lumber and pulp, furs
Mining, min. prod., value (1987): $8,567,000,000, 4th
Leading products: petroleum, nat. gas, sand/gravel
Retail sales: $4,669,000,000, 46th
Per household: $24,533, 3rd
Percent increase (1987-90): 22.7%, 11th
Service indust., value (1987): $2,470,000,000, 46th
Per capita: $4,490.56, 16th
Tourism indus., value (1989): $1,000,000,000, 45th
Foreign exports value: $2,850,000,000, 26th
Per capita: $5,181.41, 1st
Patents per 1,000 pop.: 16.2, 3rd

Travel and Transportation

Motor vehicle registrations: 477,325
Per 1,000 pop.: 867, 12th
Motorcycle registrations: 11,541
Per 1,000 pop.: 20, 21st
Licensed drivers per 1,000 driving age pop.: 801, 48th
Deaths from motor vehicle accidents per 100,000 pop.: 17.3, 30th
Public roads & streets
Total mileage: 13,485, 47th
Rural mileage: 11,936, 45th
Urban mileage: 1,549, 48th
Interstate mileage: 1,089, 14th
Annual vehicle-miles of travel per person: 7,233, 47th
Mean travel time for workers 16 + who work away from home: 16.7 min., 45th

Government

Registered voters (1988): 293,871
Percent of voting age pop.: 76.33%, 17th
Voter turnout (1988): 200,116
Percent of registered voters: 68.10%, 35th
Percent of voting age pop.: 51.98%, 26th
State legislators, total (1992): 60, 49th
Women members (1992): 14
Percent of legislature: 23.3%, 15th
Dominant party (1992): Split
U. S. Congress, House members (1993): 1
Increase 1983-93: 0
Revenues:
State govt.: $5,500,247,000
Per capita: $9,999.67, 1st
State & local govt.: $7,119,136,000
Per capita: $12,942.87, 1st
Indebtedness:
State govt.: $5,535,526,000
Per capita: $10,063.81, 1st
State & local govt.: $10,369,000,000
Per capita: $18,851.25, 1st

Laws and Regulations

Legal driving age: 16
Marriage age without parental consent: 18
Divorce residence requirement: qualification—check local statutes

Attractions

Major opera companies (1989): 1, 30th
Per 1 million pop.: 1.90, 4th
Major symphony orchestras (1989): 5, 40th
Per 1 million pop.: 9.49, 2nd
State appropriations for state arts agencies per capita: $2.29, 5th
State Fair in late Aug.-early Sept. at Palmer

Sports and Competition

NCAA sports teams, 1: Univ. of Alaska Fairbanks Nanooks
Professional teams: none

ARIZONA

"Land of extremes. Land of contrasts. Land of surprises. Land of contradictions. A land that is never to be fully understood but always to be loved....That is Arizona."

Federal Writers Project, Arizona

The last of the contiguous states to be admitted to the union, Arizona is renowned for its natural wonders, with its magnificent deserts, mountains, and plateaus. The most startling area of the state is, of course, the Grand Canyon, which is one of the Seven Natural Wonders of the World. Long ago ancient Indian peoples built on its lands great communal cliff dwellings, whose crumbling adobe walls remain as testimony to their culture. Its capital, Phoenix, was founded on Indian ruins and, like its namesake, the mythical bird, grew swiftly out of the remains. Arizona has continued to grow spectacularly in population as its healthful climate and industrious workers have lured both retired persons and industry.

Superlatives

• The Grand Canyon, one of the world's greatest natural wonders.

• The Arizona trout is found only there.

• Has led the nation in copper production since 1907.

• Leads all the states in value of nonfuel mineral production.

• Hoover Dam impounds the nation's largest artificial body of water.

> So They Say
>
> "The Casa Grande—a four story building as large as a castle and equal to the finest church in these lands of Sonora."
>
> Father Eusebio Kino, describing that monument to Pueblo culture

• Arizona's Navajo Indians form the largest tribe on the largest U.S. reservation.

• Kitts Peak National Observatory, at Sells, operates the world largest solar telescope.

Moments in History

• The Pueblo (Spanish for village) peoples flourished from about 700 A.D. through the late 1200s—a striking civilization.

• In 1539 Franciscan friar Marcos de Niza failed to find the fabled wealth of the Seven Cities of Cibola.

• The enormous expedition of Francisco Vasquez de Coronado entered present-day Arizona in 1540, made many discoveries, but found no wealth.

• Garcia Lopez de Cardenas reached the brink of a great gorge one day in 1540, but failed to realize the wonders of the place now called the Grand Canyon.

> So They Say
>
> "...Ours has been the first and will doubtless be the last party of whites to visit this profitless locality."
>
> Joseph Ives, describing the Grand Canyon

• Little attention was paid to the area until the arrival of the Jesuits in 1692, led by Father Eusebio Francisco Kino. He baptized thousands, taught them how to raise crops and livestock, and explored much of the area.

• In 1752 Tubac, in the Santa Cruz Valley, became the first permanent white settlement in present-day Arizona.

• Arizona continued under Spanish and later Mexican rule until the Mexican War in 1846. That war brought a notable military group. Pioneering the trail from Santa Fe to the West Coast, the renowned Mormon volunteer battalion made the longest infantry march on record.

So They Say

Lieutenant Colonel Philip St. George Cooke, leader of the Mormon Battalion, "...in the evening (Dec 18,1846), camped without water after traveling 30 miles....(Dec. 19) started again ...traveled till a little after dark and still no prospects of water....I was almost choked with thirst and hardly able to stand...passed by many lying on the roadside begging for water. Some of the men finally reached the river...." and brought back water.

• During the gold rush to California, beginning in 1849, 60,000 persons passed across Arizona, suffering many Indian attacks.

• Gold was discovered north of Fort Yuma in 1858; soon Gila City quickly had a population of 1,000, but the boom quickly died.

• In February, 1862, Confederate cavalry took over Tucson. Federal troops then occupied Yuma.

• Phoenix originated in 1866 as a hay camp to supply Camp McDowell's fodder. The next year the town grew as soon as Jack Swilling began to restore the prehistoric irrigation canals.

• The Battle of Apache Pass, July, 1862, was a major struggle in the Indian wars suffered from the 1860s to the early 1870s. Chiefs Cochise and Mangas Coloradas retreated when the troops fired their howitzer, not known to the Indians.

• During the years 1861 to 1880, travelers and peaceful Indians feared the periodic raids of Chief Geronimo. Despite the Indian massacre of his family, powerful warrior Chief Eskiminizin remained friendly to the settlers.

• After several moves the capital was located at Phoenix in 1889.

So They Say

"We would have done well if you hadn't fired wagon wheels at us."

Chief Cochise, commenting on the howitzer fire at the Battle of Apache Pass

• Following earlier attempts, Arizona finally became the 48th state, February 14, 1912.

• In 1916 the already poor relations with Mexico worsened when Mexican revolutionary Pancho Villa was thwarted as he attempted to enter Nogales from Sonora, and this "border war" was soon eclipsed by U.S. entry into World War I in 1917.

• In 1934 Arizona lost the "water war" when the courts awarded a large share of the Colorado River's water to California.

• In the decades from 1960 to 1990, the population grew amazingly, by more than 250%.

That's Interesting

• The bed of the Colorado River at the Grand Canyon lies at about the same level over which it flowed millions of years ago. The canyon was formed as the ground continued to rise and the river continued to carve through it as the force of the water and the sand and boulders cut away at the rising land.

• The great dome of the White Dove of the Desert mission was formed over a lofty mound of earth, piled up by the Indian converts. Learning that many coins had been buried in the earth beneath the dome, the eager Indians cleared away the entire earthen form to dig up those "riches."

• Arizona humorist Dick Wick Hall was noted for his tall tales about the state, such as his story that potatoes were planted so that the onions could be scratched to make the potatoes' eyes water enough to irrigate the rest of the garden.

• Because Arizona's conditions seemed ideal, Edward F. Beale brought in camels, which were used for a time, but camel transport proved impractical. The animals were abandoned, and "wild" camels remained to frighten travelers and their horses until all the camels died out.

• Famed Mission San Xavier at Tucson features a carving of a cat. On the opposite side of the mission is a mouse. According to Indian legend the world will end when that cat catches the mouse.

• Based on the legend of the phoenix bird, which was burned by fire every 500 years then rose from its ashes, the new town that had risen on the "ashes" of the prehistoric Hohokam settlement was named Phoenix.

NOTABLE NATIVES

Cochise (probably in AZ, 1812?-1874), Indian leader. **Geronimo** (in AZ, 1829-1909), Indian leader. **Barry Morris Goldwater** (Phoenix, 1909-), public official. **Morris "Mo" King Udall** (St. Johns, 1922-), public official. **Stewart Lee Udall** (St. Johns, 1920 -), public official.

GENERAL

Admitted to statehood: Feb. 14, 1912
Origin of name: Spanish version of Pima Indian word for "little spring place," or Aztec *arizuma*, meaning "silver-bearing"
Capital: Phoenix
Nickname: Grand Canyon State
Motto: *"Ditat Deus"* ("God Enriches")
Bird: cactus wren
Flower: blossom of the saguaro cactus
Song: "Arizona"
Tree: Palo verde

THE LAND

Area: 114,006 sq. mi., 6th
Land: 113,642 sq. mi., 6th
Water: 364 sq. mi., 48th
Topography: Colorado plateau in the N, containing the Grand Canyon; Mexican Highlands running diagonally NW to SE; Sonoran Desert in the SW
Number of counties: 15
Geographic center: Yavapai, 55 mi. ESE of Prescott
Length: 400 mi.
Width: 310 mi.
Highest point: 12,633 ft. (Humphreys Peak), 12th
Lowest point: 70 ft. (Colorado River), 27th
Mean elevation: 4,100 ft., 7th

CLIMATE AND ENVIRONMENT

Temp., highest: 127 deg. on July 7, 1905, at Parker; lowest: -40 deg. on Jan. 7, 1971, at Hawley Lake
Fresh water withdrawn, per capita, per day: 1,960 gal., 16th
Endangered species: mammals, 6—Sanborn's long-nosed bat, jaguarundi, ocelot, Sonoran pronghorn, Mount Graham red squirrel, Hualapai Mexican vole; birds, 3—masked bobwhite, American peregrine falcon, Yuma clapper rail; reptiles, none; amphibians, none; fishes, 9; invertebrates, none; plants, 9

MAJOR CITIES, POPULATION PERCENTAGE INCREASE (1980-90)

Glendale, 148,134—52.73%
Mesa, 288,091—89.03%
Phoenix, 983,403—24.53%
Tempe, 141,865—32.68%
Tucson, 405,390—22.65%

THE PEOPLE

Population: 3,665,228, 24th
Percent change (1980-90): 25.88%, 3rd
Per sq. mi: 32.15, 38th
Percent in metro. area: 79.01%, 17th
Percent foreign born: 7.6%, 13th
White: 2,963,186—80.85%, 33rd
Black: 110,524—3.02%, 37th
Native American: 203,527—5.55%, 6th
Asian, Pacific Isle: 55,206—1.51%, 20th
Other races: 332,785—9.08%, 4th
Hispanic origin: 688,338—18.78%, 4th
Percent over 5 yrs. speaking language other than English at home: 20.8%, 6th
Percent males: 49.40%, 12th
Percent females: 50.60%, 40th
Percent never married: 25.5%, 26th
Marriages per 1,000 (1989): 10.1, 18th
Divorces per 1,000 (1989): 6.5, 4th
Median age: 32.2
Under 5 years: 292,859—7.99%, 6th
Under 18 years: 918,119—25.05%, 36th
65 years & older: 478,774—13.06%, 21st

Percent increase among the elderly: 55.8%, 4th

Of Vital Importance

Live births per 1,000 pop.: 18.9, 6th
Infant mortality rate per 1,000 births (1988): 9.7, 26th
Average lifetime (1979-81): 74.30, 20th
Deaths per 100,000 pop. (1988): 793.5, 40th
Causes of death per 100,000 pop. (1988):
  Diseases of heart: 251.5, 42nd
  Malignant neoplasms: 180, 39th
  Cerebrovascular diseases: 43.9, 45th
  Accidents & adverse effects: 48.6, 12th
  Chronic obstructive pulmonary diseases: 41.9, 9th
  Suicide: 19.5, 3rd
  HIV infection: 4.3, 16th
  Other: 75.5, 27th

Keeping Well

Non-federal physicians per 100,000 pop.: 224, 19th
Dentists per 100,000 (1990-91): 57, 34th
Nurses per 100,000 (1989): 668, 29th
Hospitals per 100,000: 2.2, 35th
  Admissions per 100,000: 12,526, 38th
  Beds per 100,000: 366.47, 45th
  Occupancy rate: 63.6%, 37th
  Semiprivate room charges per day: $300, 21st
  Average stay: 5.8, 49th
Notifiable diseases per 100,000:
  AIDS: 8.6, 26th
  Gonorrhea: 145.1, 30th
  Measles: 8.5, 10th
  Syphillis: 35.2, 20th
  Tuberculosis (TB): 7.5, 21st
Per capita spending on mental health programs (1987): $19.76, 50th
Pop. without health insur. (1991): 16.9%, 12th

Households by Type

Total households: 1,368,843
  Percent change (1980-90): 43.03%, 3rd
Family households: 940,106
  Percent of total: 68.68%, 41st
Nonfamily households: 428,737
  Percent of total: 31.32%, 11th
Persons per household: 2.62, 18th
Pop. living in group quarters: 80,683
  Percent of pop.: 2.20%, 46th

Living Quarters

Total housing units: 1,659,430
  Persons per unit: 2.21, 46th
Occupied housing units: 1,368,843
  Percent of total units: 82.49%, 46th
  Persons per unit: 2.59, 15th
  Percent of units with over 1 person per room: 7.42%, 7th
Owner-occupied units: 878,561
  Percent of total units: 52.94%, 44th
  Percent of occupied units: 64.18%, 40th
  Persons per unit: 2.71, 29th
  Median value: $80,100, 20th
Renter-occupied units: 490,282
  Percent of total units: 29.55%, 24th
  Percent of occupied units: 35.82%, 14th
  Persons per unit: 2.46, 12th
  Median contract rent: $370, 18th
  Rental vacancy rate: 15.3%, 1st
Mobile home, trailer & other as a % of occupied housing units: 20.08%, 4th

Crime Index per 100,000

Total: 7,889, 3rd
  Violent: 652, 18th
    Murder and nonnegligent manslaughter: 8, 22nd
    Aggravated assault: 7,990, 7th
    Robbery: 161, 20th
    Rape: 41, 22nd
  Property: 7,236, 3rd
    Burglary: 1,670, 5th
    Larceny, theft: 4,703, 2nd
    Motor vehicle theft: 863, 8th
Drug abuse arrests: 383, 10th

Teaching and Learning

Literacy (1987): 88%, 25th
Pop. 3 and over enrolled in school: 991,122
  Percent of pop.: 28.4%, 14th
Public elementary & secondary schools:
  Total enrollment: 641,000
  Avg. class size (1987): 25, 7th
  Teachers: 33,600
    Percent of pop.: 0.92%, 39th

Teachers' avg. salary: $29,400, 24th
Spending per capita: $867, 16th
Spending per pupil in avg. daily attendance: $3,853, 39th
Percent of graduates taking SAT: 26%, 26th
Combined SAT scores: 932, 25th
Percent of pop. over 25 completing:
High school: 78.7%, 20th
College degree/s: 20.3%, 23rd
Higher educa., institutions: 38
Per 100,000 pop.: 0.5, 34th
Enroll: 264,735
Percent of pop.: 7.22%, 3rd
Public: 248,800
Percent of enroll.: 93.98%, 4th
Private: 15,935
Percent of enroll.: 6.02%, 48th
White non-Hispanic: 349,516
Percent of enroll.: 83.44%, 28th
Black non-Hispanic: 18,376
Percent of enroll.: 4.39%, 28th
Hispanic: 12,501
Percent of enroll.: 2.98%, 12th
Asian/Pacific Islander: 16,144
Percent of enroll.: 3.85%, 10th
Amer. Indian/AK native: 1,220
Percent of enroll.: 0.29%, 36th
Nonresident alien: 21,117
Percent of enroll.: 5.04%, 3rd
Female: 141,784
Percent of enroll.: 53.56%, 39th
Tuition, state university ('90-'91): $1,478, 37th
Public library systems: 91
Books & serial vol. per capita: 1.86, 43rd
Govt. expend. per capita: $21.20, 13th
State govt.: $1.73, 40th
Local govts.: $19.47, 10th

Law Enforcement, Courts, and Prisons

Police protection expend.: $559,627,000
Per capita: $152.69, 7th
Judicial & legal expend.: $279,381,000
Per capita: $76.23, 8th
Corrections expend.: $456,535,000
Per capita: $124.57, 7th
Police per 10,000 pop. (1990-91): 20.7, 24th
Prisoners (state & fed.) sentenced to over 1 yr., per 100,000 pop.: 375
Percent change (1989-90): 8.29%, 21st
Death penalty: yes, by lethal gas
Under sentence of death: 86, 10th
Executed (1989): none

Religion, Number and Percent of Population

Agnostic: 29,525—1.10%, 6th
Buddhist: 2,684—0.10%, 17th
Christian: 2,133,867—79.50%, 45th
Hindu: NA
Jewish: 42,946—1.60%, 11th
Moslem: 5,369—0.20%, 13th
Unitarian: 5,368—0.20%, 23rd
Other: 61,735—2.30%, 6th
None: 327,461—12.20%, 6th
Refused to answer: 75,155—2.80%, 12th

Making a Living

Personal income per capita (1989): $13,461, 25th
Percent increase (1979-'89) (constant 1989 dollars): 14.1%, 23rd
Average income per family: $40,170, 27th
Percent of pop. below poverty level: 15.7%, 14th
Percent 65 and over: 10.8%, 30th
Cost of living, selected cities
1st qtr., 1991 (U. S. Standard=100)

Yuma	95.4
Phoenix	102.0
Prescott	109.6

Economy

Civilian labor force : 1,726,000
Percent of tot. pop.: 47.09%, 44th
Percent 65 and over: NA
Percent females: 45.94%, 21st
Percent job growth (1980-90): 48.44%, 3rd
Major employer industries:
Agriculture: 55,556—3.40%, 17th
Construction: 93,138—5.70%, 8th
Finance, insurance & real estate: 116,014—7.10%, 9th
Government: 245,100—15.00%, 28th
Manufacturing: 205,884—12.60%, 38th

Mining: 13,927—0.9%, 16th
Service: 367,650—22.50%, 12th
Trade: 320,264—19.60%, 14th
Transportation, communication, & public utilities: 65,360—4.00%, 48th
Wholesale/retail: 358,390—22.3%, 8th
Unemployment rate: 5.33%, 26th
Male: 3.13%, 22nd
Female: 2.20%, 34th
Total businesses (1991): 146,672
New business incorp's. (1991): 9,832
Percent of total businesses: 6.70%, 16th
Business failures (1991): 2,210
Percent of total businesses: 1.51%, 4th
Agriculture farm income
Marketing (1991): $1,889,907,000, 31st
Net per operation: $64,828, 3rd
Net per acre: $14, 45th
Leading products: cattle, cotton, dairy products, lettuce
Av. value land & build. per acre: $268, 44th
Percent increase (1980-90): 0.37%, 27th
Govt. payments: $40,493,000, 33rd
Construction, value of all: $3,207,000,000
Per capita: $874.98, 5th
Percent change 1989-90: -4.70%, 22nd
Manufactures:
Value added: : $11,916,000,000
Per capita: $3,251.09, 41st
Value of shipments: $22,886,000,000
Per capita: $6,244.09, 43rd
Leading products: electronics, printing and publishing, foods, primary and fabricated metals, aircraft and missiles, apparel
Mining, min. prod., value (1987): $1,752,000,000, 19th
Leading products: nat. gas, petroleum, coal
Retail sales: $26,137,000,000, 24th
Per household: $18,703, 27th
Percent increase (1987-90): 9.8%, 38th
Service indust., value (1987): $15,222,000,000, 23rd
Per capita: $4,153.08, 19th
Tourism indus., value (1989): $4,370,000,000, 20th
Foreign exports value: $3,729,000,000, 22nd
Per capita: $1,017.40, 19th
Patents per 1,000 pop.: 5.0, 34th

Travel and Transportation

Motor vehicle registrations: 2,825,112
Per 1,000 pop.: 770, 31st
Motorcycle registrations: 79,554
Per 1,000 pop.: 21, 19th
Licensed drivers per 1,000 driving age pop.: 869, 37th
Deaths from motor vehicle accidents per 100,000 pop.: 23.7, 13th
Public roads & streets
Total mileage: 51,612, 35th
Rural mileage: 36,945, 38th
Urban mileage: 14,667, 19th
Interstate mileage: 1,169, 12th
Annual vehicle-miles of travel per person: 9,673, 15th
Mean travel time for workers 16 + who work away from home: 21.6 min., 16th

Government

Registered voters (1988): 1,797,714
Percent of voting age pop.: 69.01%, 31st
Voter turnout (1988): 1,171,873
Percent of registered voters: 65.19%, 41st
Percent of voting age pop.: 44.99%, 42nd
State legislators, total (1992): 90, 44th
Women members (1992): 31
Percent of legislature: 34.4%, 1st
Dominant party (1992): Split
U. S. Congress, House members (1993): 6
Increase 1983-93: +1
Revenues:
State govt.: $8,598,443,000
Per capita: $2,345.95, 30th
State & local govt.: $14,902,970,000
Per capita: $4,066.04, 22nd
Indebtedness:
State govt.: $2,192,956,000
Per capita: $598.31, 44th
State & local govt.: $17,566,000,000
Per capita: $4,792.61, 9th

Laws and Regulations

Legal driving age: 18
Marriage age without parental consent: 18
Divorce residence requirement: 90 days

Attractions

Major opera companies (1989): 1, 30th
Per 1 million pop.: 0.28, 43rd
Major symphony orchestras (1989): 13, 23rd
Per 1 million pop.: 3.66, 25th
State appropriations for state arts agencies per capita: $0.70, 26th
State Fair in late Oct.-early Nov. at Phoenix

Sports and Competition

NCAA sports teams: 4—Arizona State Univ. Sun Devils, Grand Canyon Univ. Antelopes, Northern Arizona Univ. Lumberjacks, Univ. of Arizona Wildcats
Professional teams, 5:
Baseball, 2—Tucson Toros (Class AAA), Hi Corbett Field; Phoenix Firebirds (Class AAA), Phoenix Municipal Stadium
Basketball, 1—Phoenix Suns (NBA), Arizona Veterans Memorial Coliseum
Football, 1—Phoenix Cardinals (NFC), Sun Devil Stadium
Hockey, 1—Phoenix Roadrunners (International Hockey League), Veterans Memorial Coliseum

ARKANSAS

"If I could rest anywhere it would be in Arkansaw, where the men are of the real half-horse, half-alligator breed such as grows nowhere else on the face of the universal earth."

Attributed to Davy Crockett

Long known as "a state which should be better known," Arkansas was thrust into national prominence and scrutiny in 1992 as its native son Bill Clinton campaigned for and won the presidency of the United States. It is a beautiful state of mountains, valleys, thick forests, and fertile plains, and tourism is one of its most important industries. Millions of travelers come to the state every year—many of them to visit the hot springs in Eureka Springs and Hot Springs. More than 99% of the people in this westernmost of the southern states are native-born Americans.

SUPERLATIVES

- The continent's only diamond mine is located near Murfreesboro.
- Magnet Cove region claims to possess the world's greatest mineral variety.
- Arkansas produces more than 90% of the nation's bauxite (aluminum).
- Arkansas is one of the country's three leading cotton states.
- Pine Bluff is known as the world center of archery bow production.
- Hattie Carraway was the first woman U.S. Senator.

MOMENTS IN HISTORY

- In 1541 the large party of Spanish explorer Hernando de Soto moved across the Mississippi into present-day Arkansas, and spent the winter at the Indian village of Utiangue on a bluff over the Ouachita River.
- Early explorers found the Quapaw, Osage, and Caddo Indian confederacies; the latter, a notable group, was described by N. Joutel in 1687.

> So They Say
>
> "The cottages...some of them are occupied by fifteen or twenty families...each has its Nook or Corner....They have nothing in common except the fire, which is in the Midst of the Hut, and never goes out."
>
> N. Joutel

- The remarkable party of Father Jacques Marquette and Louis Jolliet reached the mouth of the Arkansas River in 1673.
- The French explorer La Salle entered present-day Arkansas in 1682.

> So They Say
>
> "...we came upon a village (Quapaw)...were well treated...took possession of the land in the name of his Christian majesty....these savages were the best of all we had ever seen..."
>
> Henri de Tonti, La Salle's lieutenant

- Under Henri de Tonti, stragglers from La Salle's party founded Arkansas Post, the first permanent European settlement in the lower Mississippi Valley, for 80 years the only outpost in a vast region.

• After the United States bought the huge Louisiana Territory from France, U.S. troops took over Arkansas Post in 1804.

• The earthquake that shook the Mississippi Valley in 1811 has been called the strongest ever to strike the continent.

> So They Say
>
> "The agitation which convulsed the earth and the waters of the mighty Missisippi filled every living creature with horror. The earth on the shores opened up in wide fissures...threw water, sand and mud in huge jets higher than the tops of trees."
>
> Anonymous account of the 1811 earthquake

• Despite the opposition to a new slave state, Arkansas became a state on June 15, 1836.

• Arkansas Governor Henry M. Rector seized Fort Smith, and Arkansas joined the Confederacy in 1861.

• When the Civil War ended in 1865, returning Confederate troops found their farms in ruin, no mules or plows to put in new crops, and their credit gone.

• Arkansas was put under U.S. military rule in 1867.

• After Arkansas adopted a new constitution in 1874, the state returned to civil rule.

• Fort Smith became a principal outfitting post for travelers to the West, and with the rush of the 1849 gold seekers, it became a "rip-roaring" frontier settlement.

• Until Federal Judge Isaac C. Parker took over at Fort Smith in 1875, the region to the west was lawless. For the next 21 years Judge Parker dispensed stern justice on the frontier.

• Large reserves of bauxite were found in 1887, later providing the nation with an important source of aluminum's basic raw material.

• In 1906 diamonds were found near Murfreesboro. This proved to be the only "diamond mine" on the continent, but only modest numbers of the stones have been taken out over the years.

• With the beginning of World War I in 1917, Arkansas became one of the major centers for war training camps, such as Camp Pike.

• In 1919 the state's first oil well was brought in near Stephens, and the state continues its oil and gas production.

• By the end of World War II, more than 200,000 Arkansas men and women had gone into the armed services.

• In the 1957 struggle over school integration, Pres. Dwight Eisenhower sent federal troops to Little Rock to enforce a court integration order.

• Republican Winthrop Rockefeller became governor in 1967, gaining national attention as the second Rockefeller brother to govern a state.

• In 1986 Arkansas mounted a yearlong celebration of its 150 years of statehood.

• The 1990 census found Arkansas's population had reached 2,351,000, an increase of 2.8% over 1980.

• Gov. Bill Clinton was elected as first U.S. president from Arkansas in November 1992.

That's Interesting

• During a battle of Chicasaw vs. Quapaw, the Chicasaw ran out of ammunition. The Quawpaws gave half of their gunpowder to the enemy, and the battle continued.

• The Brooks—Baxter War, a dispute between two candidates for governor, actually became so fierce that ten persons were killed in the squabble.

• A newly rich oil family at El Dorado bought a home at a high price. When the owners started to take down the family portraits, the buyer shouted: "Oh no you don't; pitchers is furniture!"

• The farm of John M. Huddleston was so poor that he was about to give up on it when he discovered the continent's only diamond mine on his property.

• Some Arkansas rivers were so shallow that steamboats were designed to operate in as little as a foot of water.

• Sam Walton founded his Wal-Mart Stores merchandizing empire in Bentonville and became the nation's richest man.

Notable Natives

Bill Clinton (Hope, 1946-), U.S. president. **Dizzy Dean** (Lucas, 1911-1976), baseball player. **Orval**

Faubus (Combs, 1910-), politician. **John Johnson** (Arkansas City, 1918-), publisher. **Scott Joplin** (Texarkana, 1868-1917), musician/composer. **Douglas MacArthur** (Little Rock, 1880-1964), soldier/statesman. **Edward Durell Stone** (Fayetteville, 1862-1978), architect.

General

Admitted to statehood: June 15, 1836
Origin of name: French variant of *Quapaw* , a Siouan term meaning "downstream people"
Capital: Little Rock
Nicknames: Land of Opportunity and Razorback State
Motto: *"Regnat Populus" ("The People Rule")*
Bird: mockingbird
Insect: honeybee
Flower: apple blossom
Song: "Arkansas"
Gemstone: diamond
Tree: pine

The Land

Area: 53,182 sq. mi., 29th
Land: 52,075 sq. mi., 27th
Water: 1,107 sq. mi., 31st
Topography: delta and prairie in the E; lowland forests in the S; and highland in the NW, which includes the Ozark plateaus
Number of counties: 75
Geographic center: Pulaski, 12 miles NW of Little Rock.
Length: 260 mi.
Width: 240 mi.
Highest point: 2,753 ft. (Magazine Mountain), 34th
Lowest point: 55 ft. (Ouachita River), 26th
Mean elevation: 650 ft., 36th.

Climate and Environment

Temp., highest: 120 deg. on Aug. 10, 1936, at Ozark; lowest: -29 deg. on Feb. 13, 1905, at Pond
Fresh water withdrawn, per capita, per day: 2,500 gal., 9th
Endangered species: mammals, 3—gray bat, Indiana bat, Ozark big-eared bat; birds, 3—American peregrine falcon, least tern, red-cockaded woodpecker; reptiles, none; amphibians, none; fishes, 1; invertebrates, 4; plants, 1

Major Cities, Population Percentage Increase (1980-90)

Fort Smith, 72,798—1.64%
Jonesboro, 46,535—47.59%
Little Rock, 175,795—10.45%
North Little Rock, 61,741— -4.11%
Pine Bluff, 57,140—0.89%

The People

Population: 2,350,725, 33rd
Percent change (1980-90): 2.74%, 34th
Per sq. mi: 44.20, 36th
Percent in metro. area: 40.12%, 43rd
Percent foreign born: 1.1%, 46th
White: 1,944,744—82.73%, 31st
Black: 373,912—15.91%, 12th
Native American: 12,773—0.54%, 22nd
Asian, Pacific Isle: 12,530—0.53%, 47th
Other races: 6,766—0.29%, 40th
Hispanic origin: 19,876—0.85%, 42nd
Percent over 5 yrs. speaking language other than English at home: 2.8%, 48th
Percent males: 48.20%, 39th
Percent females: 51.80%, 13th
Percent never married: 20.7%, 51st
Marriages per 1,000 (1989): 14.4, 4th
Divorces per 1,000 (1989): 6.8, 3rd
Median age: 33.8
Under 5 years: 164,667—7.00%, 37th
Under 18 years: 621,131—26.42%, 18th
65 years & older: 350,058—14.89%, 6th
Percent increase among the elderly: 12.0%, 44th

Of Vital Importance

Live births per 1,000 pop.: 14.7, 43rd
Infant mortality rate per 1,000 births (1988): 10.7, 16th
Average lifetime (1979-81): 73.72, 28th
Deaths per 100,000 pop. (1988): 1,039.8, 5th
Causes of death per 100,000 pop. (1988):
Diseases of heart: 359.4, 7th
Malignant neoplasms: 225.8, 7th

Cerebrovascular diseases: 88.9, 1st
Accidents & adverse effects: 51.7, 8th
Chronic obstructive pulmonary diseases: 36.2, 21st
Suicide: 12.6, 24th
HIV infection: 2.2, 29th
Other: 85.5, 6th

KEEPING WELL

Non-federal physicians per 100,000 pop.: 169, 44th
Dentists per 100,000 (1990-91): 47, 47th
Nurses per 100,000 (1989): 500, 43rd
Hospitals per 100,000: 4.1, 13th
Admissions per 100,000: 15,971, 8th
Beds per 100,000: 547.36, 19th
Occupancy rate: 64.8%, 31st
Semiprivate room charges per day: $170, 50th
Average stay: 6.7, 36th
Notifiable diseases per 100,000:
AIDS: 8.8, 24th
Gonorrhea: 362.1, 12th
Measles: 2.3, 34th
Syphillis: 55.3, 15th
Tuberculosis (TB): 13.7, 7th
Per capita spending on mental health programs (1987): $26.54, 41st
Pop. without health insur. (1991): 15.7%, 14th

HOUSEHOLDS BY TYPE

Total households: 891,179
Percent change (1980-90): 9.21%, 34th
Family households: 651,555
Percent of total: 73.11%, 7th
Nonfamily households: 239,624
Percent of total: 26.89%, 45th
Persons per household: 2.57, 31st
Pop. living in group quarters: 58,332
Percent of pop.: 2.48%, 34th

LIVING QUARTERS

Total housing units: 1,000,667
Persons per unit: 2.35, 36th
Occupied housing units: 891,179
Percent of total units: 89.06%, 29th
Persons per unit: 2.55, 20th
Percent of units with over 1 person per room: 3.73%, 20th
Owner-occupied units: 619,938
Percent of total units: 61.95%, 12th
Percent of occupied units: 69.56%, 14th
Persons per unit: 2.61, 48th
Median value: $46,300, 48th
Renter-occupied units: 271,241
Percent of total units: 27.11%, 38th
Percent of occupied units: 30.44%, 38th
Persons per unit: 2.48, 11th
Median contract rent: $230, 47th
Rental vacancy rate: 10.4%, 14th
Mobile home, trailer & other as a % of occupied housing units: 15.87%, 13th

CRIME INDEX PER 100,000

Total: 4,867, 32nd
Violent: 532, 24th
Murder and nonnegligent manslaughter: 10, 16th
Aggravated assault: 7,005, 37th
Robbery: 113, 31st
Rape: 43, 19th
Property: 4,335, 33rd
Burglary: 1,211, 19th
Larceny, theft: 2,834, 35th
Motor vehicle theft: 289, 36th
Drug abuse arrests: 256, 24th

TEACHING AND LEARNING

Literacy (1987): 85%, 40th
Pop. 3 and over enrolled in school: 582,405
Percent of pop.: 25.8%, 43rd
Public elementary & secondary schools:
Total enrollment: 435,000
Avg. class size (1987): 22, 28th
Teachers: 25,500
Percent of pop.: 1.08%, 15th
Teachers' avg. salary: $22,000, 50th
Spending per capita: $621, 48th
Spending per pupil in avg. daily attendance: $3,272, 48th
Percent of graduates taking SAT: 6%, 46th
Combined SAT scores: 1005, 11th
Percent of pop. over 25 completing:

High school: 66.3%, 48th
College degree/s: 13.3%, 50th
Higher educa., institutions: 35
Per 100,000 pop.: 0.9, 17th
Enroll: 90,425
Percent of pop.: 3.85%, 51st
Public: 78,645
Percent of enroll.: 86.97%, 17th
Private: 11,780
Percent of enroll.: 13.03%, 35th
White non-Hispanic: 145,797
Percent of enroll.: 87.49%, 19th
Black non-Hispanic: 2,153
Percent of enroll.: 1.29%, 42nd
Hispanic: 2,990
Percent of enroll.: 1.79%, 24th
Asian/Pacific Islander: 6,321
Percent of enroll.: 3.79%, 11th
Amer. Indian/AK native: 1,694
Percent of enroll.: 1.02%, 14th
Nonresident alien: 7,686
Percent of enroll.: 4.61%, 4th
Female: 51,721
Percent of enroll.: 57.20%, 4th
Tuition, state university ('90-'91): $1,418, 39th
Public library systems: 37
Books & serial vol. per capita: 1.97, 39th
Govt. expend. per capita: $7.25, 50th
State govt.: $2.51, 27th
Local govts.: $4.74, 47th

Law Enforcement, Courts, and Prisons

Police protection expend.: $144,939,000
Per capita: $61.65, 50th
Judicial & legal expend.: $56,008,000
Per capita: $23.82, 51st
Corrections expend.: $100,953,000
Per capita: $42.94, 47th
Police per 10,000 pop. (1990-91): 15.5, 43rd
Prisoners (state & fed.) sentenced to over 1 yr., per 100,000 pop.: 277
Percent change (1989-90): 6.53%, 29th
Death penalty: yes, by lethal injection or given choice of electrocution if crime commited before July 4, 1983
Under sentence of death: 31, 20th
Executed (1989): none

Religion, Number and Percent of Population

Agnostic: 3,459—0.20%, 42nd
Buddhist: 3,459—0.20%, 11th
Christian: 1,549,716—89.60%, 14th
Hindu: NA
Jewish: 1,730—0.10%, 43rd
Moslem: NA
Unitarian: 3,459—0.20%, 23rd
Other: 12,107—0.70%, 43rd
None: 100,317—5.80%, 35th
Refused to answer: 55,347—3.20%, 6th

Making a Living

Personal income per capita (1989): $10,520, 50th
Percent increase (1979-'89) (constant 1989 dollars): 11.8%, 26th
Average income per family: $31,499, 49th
Percent of pop. below poverty level: 19.1%, 5th
Percent 65 and over: 22.9%, 4th
Cost of living, selected cities
1st qtr., 1991 (U. S. Standard=100)

Jonesboro	90.8
Little Rock	95.9

Economy

Civilian labor force : 1,133,000
Percent of tot. pop.: 48.20%, 42nd
Percent 65 and over: 2.47%, 34th
Percent females: 46.96%, 9th
Percent job growth (1980-90): 18.13%, 30th
Major employer industries:
Agriculture: 55,968—5.30%, 10th
Construction: 39,072—3.70%, 42nd
Finance, insurance & real estate: 40,128—3.80%, 49th
Government: 156,288—14.80%, 29th
Manufacturing: 217,536—20.60%, 14th
Mining: 4,010—0.4%, 22nd
Service: 172,128—16.30%, 47th
Trade: 187,968—17.80%, 37th
Transportation, communication, & public utilities: 66,528—6.30%, 11th
Wholesale/retail: 211,893—21.3%, 30th

Unemployment rate: 6.88%, 5th
Male: 3.44%, 11th
Female: 3.44%, 2nd
Total businesses (1991): 79,276
New business incorp's. (1991): 5,326
Percent of total businesses: 6.72%, 15th
Business failures (1991): 477
Percent of total businesses: 0.60%, 45th
Agriculture farm income
Marketing (1991): $4,310,724,000, 12th
Net per operation: $30,981, 13th
Net per acre: $92, 12th
Leading products: broilers, cattle, soybeans, rice
Av. value land & build. per acre: $776, 30th
Percent increase (1980-90): -15.47%, 37th
Govt. payments: $352,750,000, 8th
Construction, value of all: $804,000,000
Per capita: $342.02, 43rd
Percent change 1989-90: 11.36%, 13th
Manufactures:
Value added: : $12,468,000,000
Per capita: $5,303.90, 21st
Value of shipments: $30,493,000,000
Per capita: $12,971.74, 16th
Leading products: food prods., chemicals, lumber, paper, electric motors, furniture, home appliances, auto components, airplane parts, apparel, machinery, petroleum prods.
Mining, min. prod., value (1987): $1,232,000,000, 23rd
Leading products: petroleum, nat. gas, bromine
Retail sales: $15,386,000,000, 32nd
Per household: $17,205, 43rd
Percent increase (1987-90): 24.3%, 8th
Service indust., value (1987): $6,046,000,000, 35th
Per capita: $2,571.97, 50th
Tourism indus., value (1989): $2,065,000,000, 36th
Foreign exports value: $920,000,000, 39th
Per capita: $391.37, 46th
Patents per 1,000 pop.: 15.9, 4th

Travel and Transportation

Motor vehicle registrations: 1,447,660
Per 1,000 pop.: 615, 49th
Motorcycle registrations: 14,556
Per 1,000 pop.: 6, 50th
Licensed drivers per 1,000 driving age pop.: 962, 7th
Deaths from motor vehicle accidents per 100,000 pop.: 25.7, 9th
Public roads & streets
Total mileage: 77,085, 25th
Rural mileage: 69,408, 22nd
Urban mileage: 7,677, 32nd
Interstate mileage: 542, 39th
Annual vehicle-miles of travel per person: 8,938, 27th
Mean travel time for workers 16 + who work away from home: 19.0 min., 38th

Government

Registered voters (1988): 1,203,016
Percent of voting age pop.: 68.31%, 32nd
Voter turnout (1988): 827,738
Percent of registered voters: 68.81%, 33rd
Percent of voting age pop.: 47.00%, 39th
State legislators, total (1992): 135, 31st
Women members (1992): 10
Percent of legislature: 7.4%, 46th
Dominant party (1992): Democrats
U. S. Congress, House members (1993): 4
Increase 1983-93: 0
Revenues:
State govt.: $4,511,017,000
Per capita: $1,918.99, 45th
State & local govt.: $6,346,952,000
Per capita: $2,700.00, 51st
Indebtedness:
State govt.: $1,747,048,000
Per capita: $743.20, 41st
State & local govt.: $4,612,000,000
Per capita: $1,961.95, 49th

Laws and Regulations

Legal driving age: 16
Marriage age without parental consent: 18
Divorce residence requirement: 60 days

Attractions

Major opera companies (1989): 1, 30th
Per 1 million pop.: 0.42, 36th

Major symphony orchestras (1989): 7, 32nd
Per 1 million pop.: 2.91, 35th
State appropriations for state arts agencies per capita: $0.43, 43rd
State Fair in late Sept.-Early Oct. at Little Rock

Sports and Competition

NCAA sports teams: 3—Arkansas State Univ. Indians, Univ. of Arkansas at Fayetteville Razorbacks, Univ. of Arkansas at Little Rock Trojans
Professional teams, 1:
Baseball, 1—Arkansas Travelers (Class AA), Ray Winder Field

CALIFORNIA

"This is one of the most favored spots of the earth."

John Muir

"Why! It is even worth the expense of a trip across the continent"

John D. Rockefeller, Sr.

The most populous state, California is a land of contrasts, with its high mountains, rocky cliffs, sandy beaches, redwood forests, and barren deserts. This state, with its vast vineyards in the north, its glitter in Hollywood and Beverly Hills in the south, its tremendous farms and ranches almost everywhere, combines the Old World charm of San Francisco and the unusual lifestyles of Los Angeles to maintain its image as a truly unique part of the country. First in manufacturing, first in agriculture, it also contains some of the largest cities in the nation. If famed naturalist John Muir were alive today, he would be even more convinced that he had been very right when he wrote that "California is the most favored spot on earth!" Millions of visitors have agreed.

Superlatives

- First in population
- World's largest landlocked harbor—San Francisco Bay
- Lowest point in the western hemisphere—Death Valley, 282 ft. below sea level
- Hottest recorded temperature in the United States, Death Valley: 134° F.
- Most life zones in the nation—six
- World's most fertile valley
- Most national sites of any state
- Largest living tree—Gen. Sherman tree, trunk 101.6 ft. circ., Sequoia National Park
- The oldest living thing, a bristlecone pine, appr. 4,600 yrs. old, Inyo National Forest

Moments in History

- Nine major tribes were found by earliest Europeans, beginning circa 1540.
- In 1540 Hernando de Alarcon may have touched California at the Colorado River.
- Sir Franics Drake explored the coast in 1579 and claimed the area for Queen Elizabeth.
- In 1769 Gaspar de Portola and Father Junipero Serra founded San Diego.
- San Francisco was founded in 1776.
- Sleepy El Pueblo de Nuestra Senora la Reina de Los Angeles de Porciuncula (Los Angeles) was founded in 1781.
- At the missions, Indians became Christianized and, some say, harshly treated.

So They Say

The mission "...treatment of the Indians is the most cruel I have ever read in history."—Father Antonio Horra—

"There never were enough Franciscans, even reinforced by soldiers, to coerce the Indian population of California in such a manner as charged."

W.H. Hutchinson

- In 1812 Russia established Fort Ross, adding to its Alaskan fur trade.
- In 1825 Mexico took over California, with the capital at Monterey.

• The first overland wagon train to California arrived in the San Joaquin Valley on November 4, 1841.

> **So They Say**
> "To this gate I gave the name of Chrysolpylae, or Golden Gate....The form... and its advantages for commerce, Asiatic inclusive, suggested to me the name..."
>
> John Charles Fremont (1844)

• With the 1848 Treaty of Guadaloupe Hidalgo, Mexico gave up California.

• A pea-sized metal pellet from Sutter's Millrace changed the course of history when it proved to be gold.

> **So They Say**
> "Sir: I have to report to the state department one of the most astonishing excitements...now existing in this country...a placer, a vast tract of land containing gold...."
>
> Thomas O. Larkin, to Pres. James Buchanan

• News of the gold discovery sparked a record rush to the gold fields. In 1849, thousands of 49ers braved danger and death, for riches.

• Congress hesitated to welcome a new free state, but California was at last admitted on September 9, 1850.

• During the Civil War, loyal California's gold helped to support the Union.

• In a last heroic but unsuccessful fight for their rights, the Modoc Indians went to war (1872-1873).

• Land booms, growth of agriculture, and the discovery of oil at Bakersfield in 1899 brought people and prosperity.

• Before the ruins of the earthquake and fire of 1906 had cooled, devastated San Francisco had begun to rebuild.

• A Republican dispute gave Woodrow Wilson California's 1916 election vote, just enough to put him over the top for the White House.

• World War I found California far removed from the conflict, but great numbers of Californians crossed the continent and the sea to serve.

> **So They Say**
> "Of a sudden we had found ourselves staggering and reeling...a sickening swaying of the earth....a great cornice crushed a man as if he were a maggot..."
>
> P. Barrett, San Francisco Examiner, April 19, 1906

• California was particularly hard hit by the Great Depression. However, despite the depression, San Francisco's great bridges were opened in 1936-1937, and in 1939 the city celebrated with the Golden Gate International Exposition.

• Thought to be a security threat in World War II, Japanese Americans were sent to relocation camps where they endured many hardships.

• In 1945 the United Nations was founded at San Francisco.

• Big league baseball came to California in 1957 with the Dodgers at Los Angeles.

• By 1963, California could claim to be the nation's most populous state.

• In 1969 Richard Nixon became California's only native U.S. president.

• Los Angeles hosted the financially successful Olympic games of 1984.

• California's 1980s drought was one of its worst in history; some relief started in 1992.

• Striking just minutes before the start of the third game of the World Series, the 1989 San Francisco earthquake was a major disaster, causing at least 59 deaths and massive property damage.

That's Interesting

• In the Mexican War, the "Paul Revere of the West," John Brown (Lean John), rode horseback from Los Angeles to San Francisco to warn of approaching Mexican troops, making the 500 mi. in only five days.

• An 1849 gold rush miner asked Levi Strauss to make a pair of pants. Lacking suitable thread, he stapled the pants at stress points, and "Levis" have been popular ever since.

• Beginning at San Diego in 1769, Father Junipero Serra established nine thriving missions, centers of civilization in the wilderness, and he become known as the "Father of California."

• 1849 gold rush bar owners hired bartenders with large hands. Drinks sold for a pinch of gold dust—the larger the hands the bigger the pinch.

• The 1916 drought at San Diego was so severe that the city hired the famous rainmaker, Charles Hatfield. Shortly after he set up his rainmaking towers so much rain fell that disastrous floods were caused, and the city refused to pay Hatfield his $10,000 fee.

• Told by a medium that she would never die as long as she kept building her house in San Jose, wealthy widow Mrs. Sara Winchester kept Carpenters busy creating 1,660 rooms, secret passageways, 40 stairways, blind chimneys, and other novel arrangements. Despite spending $5.5 million, she could not forestall her death in 1922.

Notable Natives

Robert Frost (San Francisco, 1874-1963), poet. **Lillian Moller Gilbreth** (Oakland, 1878-1972), consulting engineer. **Richard Nixon** (Yorba Linda, 1913-), U.S. president. **William Saroyan** (Fresno, 1908-1981), author. **John Steinbeck** (Salinas, 1902-1968), author. **Earl Warren** (Los Angeles, 1891-1974), jurist, U.S. chief justice.

General

Admitted to statehood: Sept. 9, 1850

Origin of name: Bestowed by the Spanish conquistadors (possibly by Cortez). It was the name of an imaginary island, an earthly paradise, in "Las Serges de Esplandian," a Spanish romance written by Montalvo in 1510. Baha California (Lower California, in Mexico) was first visited by the Spanish in 1533. The present U.S. state was called Alta (Upper) California.

Capital: Sacramento

Nickname: Golden State

Motto: *"Eureka"* ("I have found it")

Animal: California grizzly bear

Bird: California valley quail

Fish: California golden trout

Flower: golden poppy

Song: "I Love You, California"

Stone: serpentine

Tree: redwood

The Land

Area: 163,707 sq. mi., 3rd

Land: 155,973 sq. mi., 3rd

Water: 7,734 sq. mi., 6th

Topography: long mountainous coastline, central valley, Sierra Nevada on the E, desert basins of the S interior, rugged mountains of the N

Number of counties: 58

Geographic center: 38 mi. E of Madera

Length: 770 mi.

Width: 250 mi.

Highest point: 14,494 ft. (Mt. Whitney), 2nd

Lowest point: -282 ft. (Death Valley), 1st

Mean elevation: 2,900 ft., 11th

Coastline: 840 mi., 3rd

Shoreline: 3,427 mi., 5th

Climate and Environment

Temp., highest: 134 deg. on July 10, 1913, at Greenland Ranch; lowest: -45 deg. on Jan. 20, 1937, at Boca

Fresh water withdrawn, per capita, per day: 1,420 gal., 21st

Endangered species: mammals, 8—San Joaquin kit fox, salt marsh harvest mouse, Fresno kangaroo rat, giant kangaroo rat, Morro Bay kangaroo rat, Stephen's kangaroo rat, Tipton kangaroo rat, Amargosa vole; birds, 10—California condor, American peregrine falcon, Aleutian Canada goose, brown pelican, California clapper rail, light-footed clapper rail, Yuma clapper rail, San Clemente loggerhead shrike, California least tern, least Bell's vireo; reptiles, 3; amphibians, 2; fishes, 10; invertebrates, 10; plants, 29

Major Cities, Population Percentage Increase (1980-90)

Long Beach, 429,433—18.79%

Los Angeles, 3,485,398—17.41%

San Diego, 1,110,549—26.84%

San Francisco, 723,959—6.63%
San Jose, 782,248—24.28%

THE PEOPLE

Population: 29,760,021, 1st
Percent change (1980-90): 20.47%, 5th
Per sq. mi: 181.79, 13th
Percent in metro. area: 95.74%, 3rd
Percent foreign born: 21.7%, 1st
White: 20,524,327—68.97%, 47th
Black: 2,208,801—7.42%, 25th
Native American: 242,164—0.81%, 18th
Asian, Pacific Isle: 2,845,659—9.56%, 2nd
Other races: 3,939,070—13.24%, 1st
Hispanic origin: 7,687,938—25.83%, 2nd
Percent over 5 yrs. speaking language other than English at home: 31.5%, 2nd
Percent males: 50.06%, 4th
Percent females: 49.94%, 48th
Percent never married: 30.1%, 4th
Marriages per 1,000 (1989): 8.1, 42nd
Divorces per 1,000 (1989): 4.3, 31st
Median age: 31.5
Under 5 years: 2,397,715—8.06%, 5th
Under 18 years: 7,750,725—26.04%, 24th
65 years & older: 3,135,552—10.54%, 45th
Percent increase among the elderly: 29.9%, 15th

OF VITAL IMPORTANCE

Live births per 1,000 pop.: 20.7, 4th
Infant mortality rate per 1,000 births (1988): 8.6, 39th
Average lifetime (1979-81): 74.57, 19th
Deaths per 100,000 pop. (1988): 761.1, 44th
Causes of death per 100,000 pop. (1988):
Diseases of heart: 249.5, 43rd
Malignant neoplasms: 168.5, 43rd
Cerebrovascular diseases: 56.5, 36th
Accidents & adverse effects: 37.4, 35th
Chronic obstructive pulmonary diseases: 34.2, 27th
Suicide: 13.7, 12th
HIV infection: 11.2, 5th
Other: 78.7, 17th

KEEPING WELL

Non-federal physicians per 100,000pop.: 263, 9th
Dentists per 100,000 (1990-91): 74, 13th
Nurses per 100,000 (1989): 578, 36th
Hospitals per 100,000: 1.8, 48th
Admissions per 100,000: 11,146, 47th
Beds per 100,000: 354.10, 48th
Occupancy rate: 67.5%, 21st
Semiprivate room charges per day: $453, 2nd
Average stay: 6.1, 46th
Notifiable diseases per 100,000:
AIDS: 24.7, 5th
Gonorrhea: 185.2, 28th
Measles: 41.9, 1st
Syphillis: 54.9, 16th
Tuberculosis (TB): 16.4, 4th
Per capita spending on mental health programs (1987): $36.89, 23rd
Pop. without health insur. (1991): 18.7%, 6th

HOUSEHOLDS BY TYPE

Total households: 10,381,206
Percent change (1980-90): 20.29%, 15th
Family households: 7,139,394
Percent of total: 68.77%, 40th
Nonfamily households: 3,241,812
Percent of total: 31.23%, 12th
Persons per household: 2.79, 4th
Pop. living in group quarters: 751,860
Percent of pop.: 2.53%, 32nd

LIVING QUARTERS

Total housing units: 11,182,882
Persons per unit: 2.66, 3rd
Occupied housing units: 10,381,206
Percent of total units: 92.83%, 5th
Persons per unit: 2.79, 3rd
Percent of units with over 1 person per room: 12.29%, 2nd
Owner-occupied units: 5,773,943
Percent of total units: 51.63%, 46th
Percent of occupied units: 55.62%, 47th
Persons per unit: 2.84, 8th
Median value: $195,500, 2nd
Renter-occupied units: 4,607,263
Percent of total units: 41.20%, 4th
Percent of occupied units: 44.38%, 6th
Persons per unit: 2.74, 2nd
Median contract rent: $561, 2nd
Rental vacancy rate: 5.9%, 46th

Mobile home, trailer & other as a % of occupied housing units: 6.55%, 40th

Crime Index per 100,000

Total: 6,604, 7th
Violent: 1,045, 4th
Murder and nonnegligent manslaughter: 12, 6th
Aggravated assault: 8,057, 6th
Robbery: 377, 5th
Rape: 43, 20th
Property: 5,558, 10th
Burglary: 1,345, 12th
Larceny, theft: 3,198, 20th
Motor vehicle theft: 1,016, 3rd
Drug abuse arrests: 839, 2nd

Teaching and Learning

Literacy (1987): 86%, 33rd
Pop. 3 and over enrolled in school: 8,300,046
Percent of pop.: 29.3%, 9th
Public elementary & secondary schools:
Total enrollment: 5,042,000
Avg. class size (1987): 28, 1st
Teachers: 207,300
Percent of pop.: 0.70%, 50th
Teachers' avg. salary: $36,400, 6th
Spending per capita: $811, 25th
Spending per pupil in avg. daily attendance: $4,598, 24th
Percent of graduates taking SAT: 47%, 22nd
Combined SAT scores: 897, 34th
Percent of pop. over 25 completing:
High school: 76.2%, 28th
College degree/s: 23.4%, 10th
Higher educa., institutions: 310
Per 100,000 pop.: 0.5, 47th
Enroll: 1,771,746
Percent of pop.: 5.95%, 17th
Public: 1,556,427
Percent of enroll.: 87.85%, 13th
Private: 215,319
Percent of enroll.: 12.15%, 39th
White non-Hispanic: 753,074
Percent of enroll.: 72.38%, 44th
Black non-Hispanic: 112,173
Percent of enroll.: 10.78%, 14th
Hispanic: 74,835
Percent of enroll.: 7.19%, 7th
Asian/Pacific Islander: 49,171
Percent of enroll.: 4.73%, 4th
Amer. Indian/AK native: 3,914
Percent of enroll.: 0.38%, 26th
Nonresident alien: 47,317
Percent of enroll.: 4.55%, 5th
Female: 955,711
Percent of enroll.: 53.94%, 37th
Tuition, state university ('90-'91): $1,220, 46th
Public library systems: 168
Books & serial vol. per capita: 1.95, 40th
Govt. expend. per capita: $18.75, 18th
State govt.: $1.69, 42nd
Local govts.: $17.07, 16th

Law Enforcement, Courts, and Prisons

Police protection expend.: $4,914,911,000
Per capita: $165.15, 4th
Judicial & legal expend.: $2,619,101,000
Per capita: $88.01, 5th
Corrections expend.: $4,368,817,000
Per capita: $146.80, 5th
Police per 10,000 pop. (1990-91): 20.5, 26th
Prisoners (state & fed.) sentenced to over 1 yr., per 100,000 pop.: 311
Percent change (1989-90): 11.60%, 7th
Death penalty: yes, by lethal gas
Under sentence of death: 247, 3rd
Executed (1989): none

Religion, Number and Percent of Population

Agnostic: 264,112—1.20%, 2nd
Buddhist: 154,065—0.70%, 1st
Christian: 16,947,158—77.00%, 48th
Hindu: 22,009—0.10%, 10th
Jewish: 506,214—2.30%, 7th
Moslem: 132,056—0.60%, 2nd
Unitarian: 88,037—0.40%, 8th
Other: 418,177—1.90%, 12th
None: 2,861,209—13.00%, 5th
Refused to answer: 616,260—2.80%, 12th

Making a Living

Personal income per capita (1989): $16,409, 8th
Percent increase (1979-'89) (constant 1989 dollars): 18.0%, 19th

Average income per family: $51,198, 8th
Percent of pop. below poverty level: 12.5%, 24th
Percent 65 and over: 7.6%, 49th
Cost of living, selected cities
1st qtr., 1991 (U. S. Standard=100)

Blythe	105.1
Los Angeles-Long Beach	120.0
San Diego	131.4

ECONOMY

Civilian labor force : 14,670,000
Percent of tot. pop.: 49.29%, 33rd
Percent 65 and over: 2.41%, 36th
Percent females: 43.54%, 48th
Percent job growth (1980-90): 32.26%, 10th
Major employer industries:
Agriculture: 429,226—3.10%, 19th
Construction: 733,838—5.30%, 13th
Finance, insurance & real estate: 899,990—6.50%, 11th
Government: 1,924,594—13.90%, 35th
Manufacturing: 2,256,898—16.30%, 25th
Mining: 39,542—0.3%, 26th
Service: 2,866,122—20.70%, 18th
Trade: 2,533,818—18.30%, 29th
Transportation, communication, & public utilities: 650,762—4.70%, 37th
Wholesale/retail: 2,922,338—20.9%, 35th
Unemployment rate: 5.61%, 21st
Male: 3.23%, 17th
Female: 2.39%, 27th
Total businesses (1991): 1,097,465
New business incorp's. (1991): 36,561
Percent of total businesses: 3.33%, 48th
Business failures (1991): 14,466
Percent of total businesses: 1.32%, 8th
Agriculture farm income
Marketing (1991): $17,886,698,000, 1st
Net per operation: $67,531, 2nd
Net per acre: $185, 8th
Leading products: dairy products, greenhouse, cattle, grapes
Av. value land & build. per acre: $1,753, 10th
Percent increase (1980-90): 23.10%, 13th
Govt. payments: $260,825,000, 13th
Construction, value of all: $24,480,000,000
Per capita: $822.58, 9th
Percent change 1989-90: -40.10%, 49th
Manufactures:
Value added: : $149,578,000,000
Per capita: $5,026.14, 27th
Value of shipments: $293,190,000,000
Per capita: $9,851.81, 31st
Leading products: foods, printed material, primary and fabricated metals, machinery, electric and electronic equipment, transportation equipment instruments
Mining, min. prod., value (1987): $8,693,000,000, 3rd
Leading products: petroleum, nat. gas, cement
Retail sales: $225,066,000,000, 1st
Per household: $21,245, 9th
Percent increase (1987-90): 16.8%, 24th
Service indust., value (1987): $175,670,000,000, 1st
Per capita: $5,902.89, 5th
Tourism indus., value (1989): $38,241,000,000, 1st
Foreign exports value: $44,520,000,000, 1st
Per capita: $1,495.97, 10th
Patents per 1,000 pop.: 3.8, 44th

TRAVEL AND TRANSPORTATION

Motor vehicle registrations: 21,925,878
Per 1,000 pop.: 736, 36th
Motorcycle registrations: 640,554
Per 1,000 pop.: 21, 20th
Licensed drivers per 1,000 driving age pop.: 878, 36th
Deaths from motor vehicle accidents per 100,000 pop.: 17.4, 27th
Public roads & streets
Total mileage: 163,574, 2nd
Rural mileage: 89,652, 10th
Urban mileage: 73,922, 2nd
Interstate mileage: 2,399, 2nd
Annual vehicle-miles of travel per person: 8,700, 33rd
Mean travel time for workers 16 + who work away from home: 24.6 min., 6th

GOVERNMENT

Registered voters (1988): 14,004,873
Percent of voting age pop.: 67.09%, 34th
Voter turnout (1988): 9,887,065
Percent of registered voters: 70.60%, 29th

Percent of voting age pop.: 47.36%, 37th
State legislators, total (1992): 120, 37th
Women members (1992): 22
Percent of legislature: 18.3%, 25th
Dominant party (1992): Democrats
U. S. Congress, House members (1993): 52
Increase 1983-93: +7
Revenues:
State govt.: $88,703,877,000
Per capita: $2,980.64, 10th
State & local govt.: $147,714,787,000
Per capita: $4,963.53, 6th
Indebtedness:
State govt.: $28,866,306,000
Per capita: $969.97, 35th
State & local govt.: $93,358,000,000
Per capita: $3,137.03, 30th

Laws and Regulations

Legal driving age: 18
Marriage age without parental consent: 18
Divorce residence requirement: 6 mo.

Attractions

Major opera companies (1989): 23, 2nd
Per 1 million pop.: 0.79, 20th
Major symphony orchestras (1989): 93, 1st
Per 1 million pop.: 3.20, 31st
State appropriations for state arts agencies per capita: $0.56, 32nd
State Fair in late Aug.-early Sept. at Sacramento

Sports and Competition

NCAA sports teams, 24: California Poly State Univ. Mustangs, California State Poly Univ. Broncos, California State Univ. Toros, California State Univ. Titans, California State Univ. 49ers, California State Univ. Matadors, California State Univ. Hornets, California State Univ.-Fresno Bulldogs, Loyola Marymount Univ. Lions, Pepperdine Univ. Waves, San Diego State Univ. Aztecs, San Jose State Univ. Spartans, Santa Clara Univ. Broncos, Saint Mary's College Gaels, Stanford Univ. Cardinals, Univ. of California Golden Bears, Univ. of California Aggies, Univ. of California Anteaters, Univ. of California Bruins, Univ. of California Gauchos, Univ. of the Pacific Tigers, Univ. of San Diego Toreros, Univ. of San Francisco Dons, Univ. of Southern California

Professional teams, 30:

Baseball, 14—California Angels (AL West), Anaheim Stadium; Stockton Ports (California League Class A), Billy Herbert Field; San Francisco Giants (NL West), Candlestick Park; Los Angeles Dodgers (NL West), Dodger Stadium; San Bernardino Spirit (California League, Class A), Fiscalini Field; Modesto A's (California League, Class A), John Thurman Field; High Desert Mavericks (California League, Class A), Maverick Stadium; Oakland Athletics (AL West), Oakland Coliseum; Palm Springs Angels (California League, Class A), Palm Springs Angel Stadium; Visalia Oaks (California League, Class A), Recreation Park; Salinas Spurs (California League, Class A), Salinas Municipal Stadium/Chet Chesholm Field; Bakersfield Dodgers (California League, Class A), Sam Lynn Ballpark; San Diego Padres (NL West), San Diego Jack Murphy Stadium; San Jose Giants (California League, Class A), San Jose Municipal Stadium

Basketball, 5—Sacramento Kings (NBA), Arco Arena; Los Angeles Clippers (NBA), LA Memorial Sports Arena; Golden State Warriors (NBA), Oakland Coliseum Arena; San Jose Jammers (Continental Basketball Association, National Conference), San Jose State Arena; Los Angeles Lakers (NBA), The Great Western Forum

Football, 5—Los Angeles Rams (NFC), Anaheim Stadium; San Francisco 49ers (NFC), Candlestick Park; Sacramento Surge (World League of American Football), Hughes Stadium; Los Angeles Raiders (AFC), Los Angeles Memorial Coliseum; San Diego Chargers (AFC), San Diego Jack Murphy Stadium

Hockey, 3—San Jose Sharks (NHL), Cow Palace; San Diego Gulls (International Hockey League), San Diego Sports Arena; Los Angeles Kings (NHL), The Great Western Forum

Soccer, 3—San Francisco Bay Blackhawks (American Professional Soccer League), Newark Memorial Stadium; San Diego Sockers (Major Soccer League), San Diego Sports Arena; Real California (American Professional Soccer League), to be announced

COLORADO

"Passing through your wonderful mountains and canyons I realize that this state is going to be more and more the playground for the whole republic....You will see this the real Switzerland of America."

Theodore Roosevelt

A skier's paradise, Colorado is the nation's loftiest state. Its mountain reaches provide some of the nation's most dramatic and beautiful scenery — Colorado vistas inspired "America the Beautiful." From those same mountains flow much of the nation's river waters. It is a center for vacationers, with its cool, pleasant summer climate and its winter supply of powdered snow. But it is also the leading manufacturing area in the Rocky Mountain states, and a major agricultural and mining state. Indeed, the story of its gold- and silver-mining boom days has become the theme of two popular musicals— *The Unsinkable Molly Brown* and *The Ballad of Baby Doe* .

Superlatives

• Highest mean altitude of the states.

• More mountains at 14,000 or more feet than any other state.

• Grand Mesa, the world's largest flat top mountain.

• Three of the nation's greatest river systems rise in Colorado.

• Colorado oil shales are thought to contain five times more oil than all the present reserves of the world combined.

• 60% of world molybdenum is produced in Colorado.

• Highest suspension bridge in the world, 1,053 feet over the Arkansas River.

Moments in History

• Though others may have been there before, the first known written record of the Colorado area was left by Diego de Vargas in 1694 as he pursued Indians who had escaped from Taos Pueblo in New Mexico.

• No Spanish or Mexican settlements were made in present-day Colorado.

• After the Louisiana Purchase in 1803, the Spanish continued to claim portions of Colorado.

• The party of U.S. Lt. Zebulon Pike explored present-day Colorado in 1806, discovering the mountain that bears Pike's name.

> **So They Say**
>
> "...so remarkable as to be known to all savage nations for hundreds of miles around, to be spoken of with admiration by the Spaniards of New Mexico, and to be the bounds of their travel northwest,"
>
> Zebulon Pike, on sighting Pike's Peak

• In 1832 William Bent completed the construction of massive Fort Bent, with walls as thick as four feet; this stronghold became the center of trade of a vast region.

• Settlers from Mexican lands to the south in 1851 founded San Luis, the oldest continuously occupied community in Colorado.

• In 1858, thousands rushed to the gold at Cherry Creek, spurred by the slogan "Pike's Peak or bust!"

• By June of 1858 the "bust" had come. Little easy-to-reach gold had been found and thousands of disappointed fortune hunters turned back in despair.

• In November, 1858, promoter William Larimer and his son William H.H. Larimer came to Cherry Creek and founded Denver, named in honor of the governor of the territory.

• In May, 1859, a real gold find was discovered by John Gregory, and Gregory Gulch soon became bustling Central City.

• In 1860 Abe Lee discovered gold in the canyon where the community of Leadville soon developed.

• Actual battles of the Civil war bypassed Colorado, but Indian warfare plagued the region from 1861 to 1871.

• Retaliating for a ranch massacre, in 1864 a group of irregulars surprised and massacred a group of Indians in a slaughter known as the Battle of Sand Creek.

So They Say

"The slaughter was continuous. No Indian, old or young, male or female, was spared. It was reported that one toddler became the object of target practice."

Los Angeles County Museum of Natural History

• Enraged over the Sand Creek massacre and other complaints, the Indians attacked, spreading terror but much of the Indian power was broken in the Battle of Beecher Island, and the last battle with the Indians in Colorado was the Battle of Summit Springs on July 11, 1869. Pawnee Chief Traveling Bear was awarded the Medal of Honor for his support of federal forces in that battle.

• After three tries Colorado was made a state on August 1, 1876.

• Just as Colorado's gold appeared to be running out, new wealth came from the silver found at Leadville in 1877.

• In 1891 gold brought Cripple Creek to world attention. The overall value of gold taken from the Cripple Creek region has been called second only to that from the Witwatersrand mines in South Africa.

• Women of Colorado won the right to vote in 1893.

• World War I called 43,000 to service from Colorado.

• Royal Gorge was spanned in 1929, becoming the world's highest suspension bridge.

• The Great Depression was made even more tragic in the 1930s by the worst drought and dust storms in history.

So They Say

"Part of my farm blew off into Kansas yesterday, so I guess I'll have to pay taxes there, too."

An unnamed farmer, responding to the drought and duststorms

• Beginning in 1942 nearly 10,000 persons of Japanese-American descent were brought to "resettlement camps" at Arkansas Valley near Grenada because of the fear that they might somehow be loyal to Japan during World War II. Those fears proved groundless.

• The U.S. Air Force Academy opened in 1955 and moved to its permanent location near Colorado Springs in 1958.

• Deep within Cheyenne Mountain, the North American Air Defense Command headquarters commenced operations in 1965.

• Despite statewide increases in the 1990 census, Denver had a loss of 5.1% in population.

That's Interesting

• Many explanations have been given for the decline of the Pueblo culture. According to one of the most interesting, the people ground their grain in stone grinders; fine stone mixed with the meal, and their teeth were ground down until they no longer could eat.

• In 1936 in a unique ceremony Middle Park officially became a part of the United States. This was said to have been necessary because the area supposedly had never been included in any of the cessions of territory to the federal government.

• Mining tycoon Auguste Rische was asked to donate a large chandelier to a church he financed. He refused, saying that he could not play a chandelier, and he thought no one else in the congregation could do so.

• One of the passengers who escaped the sinking of the liner *Titanic* was Mrs. James J. (Molly) Brown, socialite wife of a mining tycoon. She became famous as "The Unsinkable Molly Brown" in the Broadway hit of that name. Her home is now a Denver museum.

NOTABLE NATIVES

William Harrison "Jack" Dempsey (Manassa, 1895-1984), boxer. **Douglas Fairbanks** (Denver, 1883-1939), actor. **Byron Raymond White** (Fort Collins, 1917-) U.S. Supreme Court justice. **Paul Whiteman** (Denver, 1890-1967), musician/conductor.

GENERAL

Admitted to statehood: Aug. 1, 1876
Origin of name: Spanish, "color red," first applied to Colorado River
Capital: Denver, founded 1858
Nickname: Centennial State
Motto: *"Nil Sine Numine"* ("Nothing Without Providence")
Animal: Rocky Mountain bighorn sheep
Bird: Lark bunting
Colors: blue and white
Flower: Rocky Mountain columbine
Song: "Where the Columbines Grow"
Stone: aquamarine
Tree: Colorado blue spruce

THE LAND

Area: 104,100 sq. mi., 8th
Land: 103,730 sq. mi., 8th
Water: 371 sq. mi., 46th
Topography: E, dry high plains; hilly to mountainous central plateau; W, Rocky Mountains of high ranges, alternating with broad valleys and deep, narrow canyons
Number of counties: 63
Geographic center: park 30 mi. NW of Pike's Peak
Length: 380 mi.
Width: 280 mi.
Highest point: 14,433 ft. (Mt. Elbert), 3rd
Lowest point: 3,350 ft. (Arkansas River), 51st
Mean elevation: 6,800 ft., 1st

CLIMATE AND ENVIRONMENT

Temp., highest: 118 deg. on July 11, 1888, at Bennett; lowest: -61 deg. on Feb. 1, 1985, at Maybell
Fresh water withdrawn, per capita, per day: 4,190 gal., 5th
Endangered species: mammals, 1—black-footed ferret; birds, 3—Whooping crane, American peregrine falcon, least tern; reptiles, none; amphibians, none; fishes, 3; invertebrates, none; plants, 7

MAJOR CITIES, POPULATION PERCENTAGE INCREASE (1980-90)

Aurora, 222,103—40.05%
Colorado Springs, 281,140—30.70%
Denver, 467,610— -5.09%
Lakewood, 126,481—11.14%
Pueblo, 98,640— -3.00%

THE PEOPLE

Population: 3,294,394, 26th
Percent change (1980-90): 12.28%, 14th
Per sq. mi: 31.65, 39th
Percent in metro. area: 81.53%, 15th
Percent foreign born: 4.3%, 20th
White: 2,905,474—88.19%, 23rd
Black: 133,146—4.04%, 32nd
Native American: 27,776—0.84%, 17th
Asian, Pacific Isle: 59,862—1.82%, 17th
Other races: 168,136—5.10%, 6th
Hispanic origin: 424,302—12.88%, 5th
Percent over 5 yrs. speaking language other than English at home: 10.5%, 16th
Percent males: 49.52%, 11th
Percent females: 50.48%, 41st
Percent never married: 25.8%, 24th
Marriages per 1,000 (1989): 9.6, 25th
Divorces per 1,000 (1989): 5.6, 12th
Median age: 32.5
Under 5 years: 252,893—7.68%, 11th
Under 18 years: 861,266—26.14%, 23rd
65 years & older: 329,443—10.00%, 49th
Percent increase among the elderly: 33.2%, 12th

OF VITAL IMPORTANCE

Live births per 1,000 pop.: 16.0, 19th
Infant mortality rate per 1,000 births (1988): 9.6, 28th
Average lifetime (1979-81): 73.30, 38th
Deaths per 100,000 pop. (1988): 646.8, 48th

Causes of death per 100,000 pop. (1988):
- Diseases of heart: 196.2, 46th
- Malignant neoplasms: 134.9, 49th
- Cerebrovascular diseases: 40.1, 48th
- Accidents & adverse effects: 34.4, 43rd
- Chronic obstructive pulmonary diseases: 39.3, 16th
- Suicide: 18.1, 4th
- HIV infection: 5.1, 14th
- Other: 65.9, 43rd

KEEPING WELL

Non-federal physicians per 100,000 pop.: 231, 16th

Dentists per 100,000 (1990-91): 80, 7th

Nurses per 100,000 (1989): 704, 25th

Hospitals per 100,000: 2.6, 30th
- Admissions per 100,000: 11,798, 42nd
- Beds per 100,000: 413.46, 41st
- Occupancy rate: 67.2%, 23rd
- Semiprivate room charges per day: $321, 17th
- Average stay: 7.2, 25th

Notifiable diseases per 100,000:
- AIDS: 11.0, 20th
- Gonorrhea: 105.2, 34th
- Measles: 4.2, 26th
- Syphillis: 6.1, 37th
- Tuberculosis (TB): 2.2, 45th

Per capita spending on mental health programs (1987): $35.81, 27th

Pop. without health insur. (1991): 10.1%, 39th

HOUSEHOLDS BY TYPE

Total households: 1,282,489
- Percent change (1980-90): 20.88%, 14th

Family households: 854,214
- Percent of total: 66.61%, 49th

Nonfamily households: 428,275
- Percent of total: 33.39%, 3rd

Persons per household: 2.51, 48th

Pop. living in group quarters: 79,472
- Percent of pop.: 2.41%, 37th

LIVING QUARTERS

Total housing units: 1,477,349
- Persons per unit: 2.23, 43rd

Occupied housing units: 1,282,489
- Percent of total units: 86.81%, 38th
- Persons per unit: 2.46, 44th
- Percent of units with over 1 person per room: 2.97%, 25th

Owner-occupied units: 798,277
- Percent of total units: 54.03%, 41st
- Percent of occupied units: 62.24%, 43rd
- Persons per unit: 2.66, 40th
- Median value: $82,700, 18th

Renter-occupied units: 484,212
- Percent of total units: 32.78%, 14th
- Percent of occupied units: 37.76%, 11th
- Persons per unit: 2.25, 39th
- Median contract rent: $362, 20th
- Rental vacancy rate: 11.4%, 10th

Mobile home, trailer & other as a % of occupied housing units: 7.97%, 32nd

CRIME INDEX PER 100,000

Total: 6,054, 13th
- Violent: 526, 25th
  - Murder and nonnegligent manslaughter: 4, 37th
  - Aggravated assault: 7,676, 12th
  - Robbery: 91, 36th
  - Rape: 46, 16th
- Property: 5,528, 11th
  - Burglary: 1,209, 20th
  - Larceny, theft: 3,891, 8th
  - Motor vehicle theft: 428, 27th

Drug abuse arrests: 228, 29th

TEACHING AND LEARNING

Literacy (1987): 92%, 4th

Pop. 3 and over enrolled in school: 896,144
- Percent of pop.: 28.5%, 13th

Public elementary & secondary schools:
- Total enrollment: 585,000
- Avg. class size (1987): 23, 20th
- Teachers: 3,200
  - Percent of pop.: 0.10%, 51st
- Teachers' avg. salary: $30,800, 19th
- Spending per capita: $787, 29th
- Spending per pupil in avg. daily attendance: $4,580, 26th

Percent of graduates taking SAT: 29%, 25th
- Combined SAT scores: 959, 23rd

Percent of pop. over 25 completing:
High school: 84.4%, 3rd
College degree/s: 27.0%, 4th
Higher educa., institutions: 57
Per 100,000 pop.: 0.8, 18th
Enroll: 231,547
Percent of pop.: 7.03%, 6th
Public: 205,069
Percent of enroll.: 88.56%, 12th
Private: 26,478
Percent of enroll.: 11.44%, 40th
White non-Hispanic: 155,204,
Percent of enroll.: 91.02%, 10th
Black non-Hispanic: 4,044
Percent of enroll.: 2.37%, 40th
Hispanic: 1,587
Percent of enroll.: 0.93%, 37th
Asian/Pacific Islander: 2,430
Percent of enroll.: 1.43%, 33rd
Amer. Indian/AK native: 441
Percent of enroll.: 0.26%, 39th
Nonresident alien: 6,809
Percent of enroll.: 3.99%, 6th
Female: 120,857
Percent of enroll.: 52.20%, 48th
Tuition, state university ('90-'91): $1,919, 21st
Public library systems: 124
Books & serial vol. per capita: 2.62, 24th
Govt. expend. per capita: $18.87, 17th
State govt.: $1.33, 45th
Local govts.: $17.54, 15th

Law Enforcement, Courts, and Prisons

Police protection expend.: $406,925,000
Per capita: $123.54, 17th
Judicial & legal expend.: $185,802,000
Per capita: $56.41, 18th
Corrections expend.: $370,581,000
Per capita: $112.50, 10th
Police per 10,000 pop. (1990-91): 23.5, 11th
Prisoners (state & fed.) sentenced to over 1 yr., per 100,000 pop.: 209
Percent change (1989-90): 1.59%, 44th
Death penalty: yes, by Lethal injection.
Under sentence of death: 3, 31st
Executed (1989): none

Religion, Number and Percent of Population

Agnostic: 26,764—1.10%, 6th
Buddhist: 2,433—0.10%, 17th
Christian: 1,944,069—79.90%, 43rd
Hindu: 4,866—0.20%, 3rd
Jewish: 43,796—1.80%, 9th
Moslem: NA
Unitarian: 17,032—0.70%, 4th
Other: 48,663—2.00%, 10th
None: 277,377—11.40%, 8th
Refused to answer: 68,128—2.80%, 12th

Making a Living

Personal income per capita (1989): $14,821, 17th
Percent increase (1979-'89) (constant 1989 dollars): 10.6%, 30th
Average income per family: $43,321, 19th
Percent of pop. below poverty level: 11.7%, 29th
Percent 65 and over: 11.0%, 29th
Cost of living, selected cities
1st qtr., 1991 (U. S. Standard=100)

Loveland	86.2
Denver	101.6
Glenwood Springs	111.5

Economy

Civilian labor force : 1,756,000
Percent of tot. pop.: 53.30%, 8th
Percent 65 and over: 2.05%, 43rd
Percent females: 47.89%, 3rd
Percent job growth (1980-90): 24.50%, 19th
Major employer industries:
Agriculture: 41,725—2.50%, 27th
Construction: 66,760—4.00%, 37th
Finance, insurance & real estate: 106,816—6.40%, 12th
Government: 288,737—17.30%, 13th
Manufacturing: 210,294—12.60%, 39th
Mining: 20,438—1.3%, 12th
Service: 348,821—20.90%, 17th
Trade: 320,448—19.20%, 19th
Transportation, communication, & public utilities: 106,816—6.40%, 10th
Wholesale/retail: 357,581—21.9%, 18th
Unemployment rate: 4.95%, 35th

Male: 2.28%, 44th
Female: 2.62%, 18th
Total businesses (1991): 156,891
New business incorp's. (1991): 13,583
Percent of total businesses: 8.66%, 10th
Business failures (1991): 1,944
Percent of total businesses: 1.24%, 11th
Agriculture farm income
Marketing (1991): $3,761,320,000, 18th
Net per operation: $27,397, 17th
Net per acre: $22, 40th
Leading products: cattle, corn, wheat, dairy products
Av. value land & build. per acre: $369, 41st
Percent increase (1980-90): -4.65%, 31st
Govt. payments: $217,102,000, 14th
Construction, value of all: $2,536,000,000
Per capita: $769.79, 13th
Percent change 1989-90: 19.57%, 7th
Manufactures:
Value added: : $13,819,000,000
Per capita: $4,194.70, 35th
Value of shipments: $27,701,000,000
Per capita: $8,408.53, 37th
Leading products: computer equipment, instruments, foods, machinery, aerospace products
Mining, min. prod., value (1987): $2,591,000,000, 15th
Leading products: petroleum, nat. gas, coal
Retail sales: $24,383,000,000, 25th
Per household: $18,864, 26th
Percent increase (1987-90): 15.2%, 26th
Service indust., value (1987): $16,816,000,000, 21st
Per capita: $5,104.43, 10th
Tourism indus., value (1989): $4,844,000,000, 18th
Foreign exports value: $2,274,000,000, 29th
Per capita: $690.26, 36th
Patents per 1,000 pop.: 4.0, 41st

Travel and Transportation

Motor vehicle registrations: 3,155,371
Per 1,000 pop.: 957, 6th
Motorcycle registrations: 108,433
Per 1,000 pop.: 32, 7th
Licensed drivers per 1,000 driving age pop.: 810, 47th
Deaths from motor vehicle accidents per 100,000 pop.: 16.5, 35th
Public roads & streets
Total mileage: 77,680, 24th
Rural mileage: 66,408, 25th
Urban mileage: 11,272, 25th
Interstate mileage: 942, 18th
Annual vehicle-miles of travel per person: 8,249, 40th
Mean travel time for workers 16 + who work away from home: 20.7 min., 24th

Government

Registered voters (1988): 2,029,518
Percent of voting age pop.: 81.54%, 11th
Voter turnout (1988): 1,372,394
Percent of registered voters: 67.62%, 37th
Percent of voting age pop.: 55.14%, 15th
State legislators, total (1992): 100, 42nd
Women members (1992): 31
Percent of legislature: 31.0%, 5th
Dominant party (1992): Republicans
U. S. Congress, House members (1993): 6
Increase 1983-93: 0
Revenues:
State govt.: $7,526,860,000
Per capita: $2,284.75, 34th
State & local govt.: $14,092,653,000
Per capita: $4,277.77, 16th
Indebtedness:
State govt.: $2,421,555,000
Per capita: $735.05, 42nd
State & local govt.: $13,354,000,000
Per capita: $4,053.55, 15th

Laws and Regulations

Legal driving age: 21
Marriage age without parental consent: 18
Divorce residence requirement: 90 days

Attractions

Major opera companies (1989): 3, 15th
Per 1 million pop.: 0.90, 11th
Major symphony orchestras (1989): 16, 19th
Per 1 million pop.: 4.82, 12th
State appropriations for state arts agencies per capita: $0.40, 47th
State Fair in the last week in Aug. at Pueblo

Sports and Competition

NCAA sports teams, 6: Colorado College Tigers, Colorado School of Mines Miners, Colorado State Univ. Rams, U.S. Air Force Academy Falcons, Univ. of Colorado Buffaloes, Univ. of Denver Pioneers

Professional teams, 5:

Baseball, 2—Denver Zephyrs (American Association, Class AAA), Mile High Stadium; Colorado Springs Sky Sox (Pacific Coast League, Class AAA), Sky Box Stadium

Basketball, 1—Denver Nuggets (NBA), McNichols Sports Arena

Football, 1—Denver Broncos (AFC), Denver Mile High Stadium

Soccer, 1—Colorado Foxes (American Professional Soccer League), Jefferson County Stadium

CONNECTICUT

"The warm, very warm heart of 'New England at its best,' such a vast abounding arcadia of mountains, broad vales and great rivers and large lakes and white villages embowered in prodigious elms and maples. It is extraordinarily graceful and idyllic."

Henry James

Although Connecticut is the third smallest of the states, it must rank among the greatest in its contributions to the nation and the world. The state gave the world its "first workable written constitution," and introduced mass production, which paved the way for modern manufacture. Its inventors and manufacturers introduced a wide variety of inexpensive products. "Y ankee pedlars" and the masters of the Yankee clippers carried these products around the nation and the world. It has long led in the insurance field and in the production of helicopters, jet aircraft engines, submarines, pins and needles, silverware, small firearms, and thread.

SUPERLATIVES

• The first tax-supported library in the United States was opened at Salisbury.

• Modern manufacturing methods were first developed by Eli Terry and Eli Whitney.

• The first woman to receive a U.S. patent was Mary Kies of South Killingly, for a machine to weave silk and straw.

• America's first cigars, machine-made combs, factory hats, plows, friction matches, tacks, and many other products were made in Connecticut.

• The nation's first commercial telephone exchange opened in New Haven.

• Naugatuck Valley manufacturers founded America's first trade association.

• first in insurance written.

MOMENTS IN HISTORY

• Adriaen Block, a Dutch explorer, discovered and entered the Connecticut River in 1614.

• In 1633 the Dutch built a fort at present-day Hartford. The British countered with a fortified trading post where Windsor now stands.

• Wetherfield was founded in 1634, becoming the oldest permanent European settlement in Connecticut.

• To counter the threat of Indian attack, a force under Captain John Mason attacked and destroyed the Indian encampment of Pequot in 1637.

> So They Say
>
> "The greatness and the violence of the fire... the shrieks and yells of men and women and children....It was a fearful sight to see them frying in the fire and the streams of blood quenching the same."
>
> Cotton Mather, describing the destruction of Pequot

• The three towns of Connecticut in 1639 grouped themselves into a commonwealth; they were governed by a covenant known as the Fundamental Orders, sometimes called the first constitution. This document was the first to declare that "The foundation of authority is in the free consent of the people," a forerunner of the U.S. Constitution.

• The charter granted Connecticut by the king in 1662 was amazingly liberal. It legalized almost every act previously taken in the Connecticut colony, including the Fundamental Orders.

• In 1687 King James II revoked the Connecticut charter. Royal governor Sir Edmund Andros attempted to seize the charter, but Joseph Wadsworth stole away with it. Tradition says it was hidden in the hollow of an oak on Samuel Wyllys' property. This "Charter Oak" became a famous landmark.

• Six years before the national Declaration of Independence, in 1770 Lebanon freemen drafted a declaration of rights and liberties, and Old Lyme launched its own little "Tea Party" by burning the tea sacks of a traveling peddler.

• During the American Revolution, Connecticut is said to have "furnished more men and money than any other colony except Massachusetts."

• Revolutionary Stonington was attacked in 1775; Danbury was burned and looted in 1777, New Haven in 1779, and Bridgeport and New London in 1781.

• On January 9, 1788, Connecticut became the fifth state, after dropping its claim to extend to the west coast, except for what became the "Western Reserve," now the area of Cleveland, OH.

• Connecticut adopted "universal manhood suffrage in 1845," extending the vote to all men, but not to women.

• Beginning in 1861, the state's quota of Civil War volunteers was met five times over. Of the 57,379 Connecticut men and women serving in the war, more than a third (20,573) were killed or missing in action.

• The nation's first code of law for registering airplanes and licensing pilots was inaugurated in Connecticut in 1911.

• During World War I, beginning in 1917, Connecticut led all the states in production per person.

• In 1954 the Groton shipyards produced the world's first atomic powered submarine, the *Nautilus.*

• County government was abolished in Connecticut in 1960, the first such step taken by any state. Local government was transferred to an extension of the township system.

• Ella T. Grasso was elected governor in 1975, becoming the first woman to be elected governor without previously having been preceded by her husband as governor.

• Despite the damage of Hurricane Gloria in 1985, the state went on to celebrate its 350th anniversary.

That's Interesting

• Early Hartford was known for its strict religious law, described as a Puritan theocracy. Its "blue laws" called for the death penalty to any son who cursed or struck his parents. Elder Malbone flogged his daughter Martha on the green for going on a date with a young gentleman.

• The great charter of 1662 extended Connecticut west even to the Pacific Ocean, which would have included present-day Cleveland, Chicago, Des Moines, Omaha, Ogden, and Crescent City.

• During the American Revolution, Lime Rock metal workers forged a huge chain that was stretched across the Hudson River to keep British ships from sailing up that strategic waterway. Each link was three feet long.

• During the American Revolution, at the age of 15, Samuel Smedley of Fairfield became a captain of a privateer ship. By war's end he had captured more enemy prize ships than any other captain, surpassing even the small U.S. navy.

• Connecticut's Charter Oak gained such fame that it became fashionable to own a product supposedly made from its trunk. It was said that Charter Oak products included a walking stick, dog collar, needlecase, three-legged stools, bootjack, dinner table, tenpin alley, toothpicks, and enough Charter Oak to build a plank road from Hartford to Salt Lake City.

Notable Natives

Ethan Allen (Litchfield, 1738-1789), Revolutionary soldier. **Phineas Taylor Barnum** (Bethel, 1810-1891), showman. **Samuel Colt** (Hartford, 1814-1862), inventor. **John Fitch** (Hartford County, 1743-1798), inventor. **Charles Goodyear** (1800-1860), inventor/manufacturer. **Nathan Hale** (Coventry, 1755-1776), Revolutionary soldier. **Katharine Hepburn** (Hartford, 1907-), actress. **Collis Potter Huntington** (Harwinton, 1821-1900), railroad builder. **J. Pierpont Morgan**

(Hartford, 1837-1913), financier. **Harriet Beecher Stowe** (Litchfield, 1811-1896), author. **Eli Terry** (East Windsor, 1772-1852), clock manufacturer. **John Trumbull** (Lebanon, 1756-1843), painter. **Jonathan Trumbull,** (Lebanon, 1710-1785), public official. **Emma Hart Willard** (Berlin, 1787-1870), educator.

GENERAL

Admitted to statehood: Jan. 9, 1788
Origin of name: From Mohican and other Algonquin words meaning "Long river place"
Capital: Hartford
Nicknames: The Constitution State and The Nutmeg State
Motto: *"Qui Transtulit Sustinet"* ("He Who Transplanted Still Sustains")
Animal: sperm whale
Bird: American robin
Flower: mountain laurel
Insect: praying mantis
Mineral: garnet
Ship: USS *Nautilus* (SSN571)
Song: "Yankee Doodle"
Tree: white oak

THE LAND

Area: 5,544 sq. mi., 48th
Land: 4,845 sq. mi., 48th
Water: 698 sq. mi., 37th
Topography: Wupland, the Berkshires; in the NW, highest elevation; narrow central lowland N-S; hilly E upland drained by rivers
Number of counties: 8
Geographic center: Hartford, at East Berlin
Length: 110 mi.
Width: 70 mi.
Highest point: 2,380 ft. (Mt. Fissell on S slope), 36th
Lowest point: sea level (Long Island Sound), 3rd
Mean elevation: 500 ft., 41st
Coastline: 0 mi., 24th
Shoreline: 618 mi., 18th

CLIMATE AND ENVIRONMENT

Temp., highest: 105 deg. on July 22, 1926, at Waterbury; lowest: -32 deg. on Feb. 16, 1943, at Falls Village
Fresh water withdrawn, per capita, per day: 375 gal., 46th
Endangered species: mammals, none; birds, 2—American peregrine falcon, roseate tern; reptiles, 2; amphibians, none; fishes, none; invertebrates, none; plants, 2

MAJOR CITIES, POPULATION PERCENTAGE INCREASE (1980-90)

Bridgeport, 141,686— –0.60%
Hartford, 139,739—2.45%
New Haven, 130,474—3.48%
Stamford, 108,056—5.46%
Waterbury, 108,961—5.51%

THE PEOPLE

Population: 3,287,116, 27th
Percent change (1980-90): 5.46%, 26th
Per sq. mi: 592.91, 4th
Percent in metro. area: 92.42%, 6th
Percent foreign born: 8.5%, 11th
White: 2,859,353—86.99%, 26th
Black: 274,269—8.34%, 22nd
Native American: 6,654—0.20%, 44th
Asian, Pacific Isle: 50,698—1.54%, 19th
Other races: 69,142—2.10%, 17th
Hispanic origin: 213,116—6.48%, 12th
Percent over 5 yrs. speaking language other than English at home: 15.2%, 10th
Percent males: 48.46%, 33rd
Percent females: 51.54%, 19th
Percent never married: 29.0%, 9th
Marriages per 1,000 (1989): 8.2, 41st
Divorces per 1,000 (1989): 3.1, 48th
Median age: 34.4
Under 5 years: 228,356—6.95%, 41st
Under 18 years: 749,581—22.80%, 47th
65 years & older: 445,907—13.57%, 14th
Percent increase among the elderly: 22.2%, 22nd

OF VITAL IMPORTANCE

Live births per 1,000 pop.: 16.1, 18th
Infant mortality rate per 1,000 births (1988): 8.9, 34th
Average lifetime (1979-81): 75.12, 11th
Deaths per 100,000 pop. (1988): 883.9, 27th
Causes of death per 100,000 pop. (1988):

Diseases of heart: 318.8, 25th
Malignant neoplasms: 211.9, 16th
Cerebrovascular diseases: 53.9, 40th
Accidents & adverse effects: 30.7, 47th
Chronic obstructive pulmonary diseases: 29.3, 41st
Suicide: 10.3, 44th
HIV infection: 6.2, 8th
Other: 74.2, 29th

Keeping Well

Non-federal physicians per 100,000 pop.: 325, 5th
Dentists per 100,000 (1990-91): 91, 3rd
Nurses per 100,000 (1989): 869, 8th
Hospitals per 100,000: 1.9, 46th
Admissions per 100,000: 11,483, 43rd
Beds per 100,000: 442.12, 35th
Occupancy rate: 80.1%, 5th
Semiprivate room charges per day: $456, 1st
Average stay: 8.6, 11th
Notifi able diseases per 100,000:
AIDS: 12.9, 15th
Gonorrhea: 251.3, 21st
Measles: 6.0, 17th
Syphilis: 56.6, 14th
Tuberculosis (TB): 5.0, 33rd
Per capita spending on mental health programs (1987): $68.02, 4th
Pop. without health insur. (1991): 7.5%, 50th

Households by Type

Total households: 1,230,479
Percent change (1980-90): 12.48%, 23rd
Family households: 864,493
Percent of total: 70.26%, 28th
Nonfamily households: 365,986
Percent of total: 29.74%, 24th
Persons per household: 2.59, 26th
Pop. living in group quarters: 101,167
Percent of pop.: 3.08%, 14th

Living Quarters

Total housing units: 1,320,850
Persons per unit: 2.49, 9th
Occupied housing units: 1,230,479
Percent of total units: 93.16%, 3rd
Persons per unit: 2.52, 26th
Percent of units with over 1 person per room: 2.29%, 38th
Owner-occupied units: 807,481
Percent of total units: 61.13%, 18th
Percent of occupied units: 65.62%, 34th
Persons per unit: 2.74, 22nd
Median value: $177,800, 3rd
Renter-occupied units: 422,998
Percent of total units: 32.02%, 15th
Percent of occupied units: 34.38%, 19th
Persons per unit: 2.30, 32nd
Median contract rent: $510, 4th
Rental vacancy rate: 6.9%, 42nd
Mobile home, trailer & other as a % of occupied housing units: 2.52%, 48th

Crime Index per 100,000

Total: 5,387, 23rd
Violent: 554, 22nd
Murder and nonnegligent manslaughter: 5, 30th
Aggravated assault: 6,947, 41st
Robbery: 235, 12th
Rape: 28, 41st
Property: 4,833, 23rd
Burglary: 1,228, 18th
Larceny, theft: 2,874, 32nd
Motor vehicle theft: 731, 10th
Drug abuse arrests: 571, 6th

Teaching and Learning

Literacy (1987): 88%, 25th
Pop. 3 and over enrolled in school: 805,486
Percent of pop.: 25.6%, 44th
Public elementary & secondary schools:
Total enrollment: 485,000
Avg. class size (1987): 20, 41st
Teachers: 34,800
Percent of pop.: 1.06%, 20th
Teachers' avg. salary: $40,500, 2nd
Spending per capita: $1,129, 3rd
Spending per pupil in avg. daily attendance: $7,934, 3rd
Percent of graduates taking SAT: 81%, 1st
Combined SAT scores: 897, 34th
Percent of pop. over 25 completing:

High school: 79.2%, 17th
College degree/s: 27.2%, 2nd
Higher educa., institutions: 47
Per 100,000 pop.: 0.7, 24th
Enroll: 169,480
Percent of pop.: 5.16%, 32nd
Public: 110,432
Percent of enroll.: 65.16%, 44th
Private: 59,048
Percent of enroll.: 34.84%, 8th
White non-Hispanic: 110,150
Percent of enroll.: 90.81%, 12th
Black non-Hispanic: 661
Percent of enroll.: 0.54%, 49th
Hispanic: 2,233
Percent of enroll.: 1.84%, 23rd
Asian/Pacific Islander: 2,243
Percent of enroll.: 1.85%, 23rd
Amer. Indian/AK native: 1,322
Percent of enroll.: 1.09%, 13th
Nonresident alien: 4,694
Percent of enroll.: 3.87%, 7th
Female: 95,401
Percent of enroll.: 56.29%, 11th
Tuition, state university ('90-'91): $2,313, 12th
Public library systems: 194
Books & serial vol. per capita: 3.42, 12th
Govt. expend. per capita: $28.10, 3rd
State govt.: $4.72, 9th
Local govts.: $23.38, 3rd

Law Enforcement, Courts, and Prisons

Police protection expend.: $457,735,000
Per capita: $139.26, 10th
Judicial & legal expend.: $196,265,000
Per capita: $59.71, 13th
Corrections expend.: $323,302,000
Per capita: $98.36, 15th
Police per 10,000 pop. (1990-91): 21.5, 19th
Prisoners (state & fed.) sentenced to over 1 yr., per 100,000 pop.: 238
Percent change (1989-90): 23.17%, 1st
Death penalty: yes, by electrocution
Under sentence of death: 1, 34th
Executed (1989): none

Religion, Number and Percent of Population

Agnostic: 12,688—0.50%, 27th
Buddhist: 5,075—0.20%, 11th
Christian: 2,167,055—85.40%, 29th
Hindu: 2,538—0.10%, 10th
Jewish: 60,901—2.40%, 6th
Moslem: 2,538—0.10%, 22nd
Unitarian: 7,613—0.30%, 15th
Other: 32,988—1.30%, 24th
None: 147,177—5.80%, 35th
Refused to answer: 98,964—3.90%, 3rd

Making a Living

Personal income per capita (1989): $20,189, 1st
Percent increase (1979-'89) (constant 1989 dollars): 41.5%, 1st
Average income per family: $61,458, 1st
Percent of pop. below poverty level: 6.8%, 50th
Percent 65 and over: 7.2%, 51st
Cost of living, selected cities
2nd qtr., 1989 (U. S. Standard=100)
Meriden 123.1
Hartford 125.8

Economy

Civilian labor force : 1,789,000
Percent of tot. pop.: 54.42%, 4th
Percent 65 and over: 3.75%, 6th
Percent females: 45.28%, 29th
Percent job growth (1980-90): 18.58%, 28th
Major employer industries:
Agriculture: 10,188—0.60%, 50th
Construction: 79,806—4.70%, 23rd
Finance, insurance & real estate: 156,216—9.20%, 1st
Government: 188,478—11.10%, 51st
Manufacturing: 378,654—22.30%, 10th
Mining: 2,081—0.1%, 38th
Service: 402,426—23.70%, 5th
Trade: 283,566—16.70%, 49th
Transportation, communication, & public utilities: 79,806—4.70%, 36th
Wholesale/retail: 331,204—19.6%, 45th
Unemployment rate: 5.09%, 33rd

Male: 3.30%, 15th
Female: 1.79%, 47th
Total businesses (1991): 139,462
New business incorp's. (1991): 8,501
Percent of total businesses: 6.10%, 23rd
Business failures (1991): 898
Percent of total businesses: 0.64%, 42nd
Agriculture farm income
Marketing (1991): $463,372,000, 43rd
Net per operation: $49,714, 6th
Net per acre: $462, 2nd
Leading products: greenhouse, eggs, dairy products, tobacco
Av. value land & build. per acre: $4,463, 3rd
Percent increase (1980-90): 86.97%, 4th
Govt. payments: $1,351,000, 47th
Construction, value of all: $1,602,000,000
Per capita: $487.36, 30th
Percent change 1989-90: -38.10%, 48th
Manufactures:
Value added: : $23,826,000,000
Per capita: $7,248.30, 5th
Value of shipments: $39,898,000,000
Per capita: $12,137.69, 21st
Leading products: aircraft engines and parts, submarines, helicopters, instruments, machinery & computer equipment, electronics & electrical equipment
Mining, min. prod., value (1987): $130,000,000, 43rd
Leading products: sand & gravel, stone, limestone, feldspar
Retail sales: $27,729,000,000, 22nd
Per household: $22,435, 7th
Percent increase (1987-90): 3.3%, 51st
Service indust., value (1987): $18,642,000,000, 18th
Per capita: $5,671.23, 6th
Tourism indus., value (1989): $3,022,000,000, 29th
Foreign exports value: $4,356,000,000, 19th
Per capita: $1,325.17, 12th
Patents per 1,000 pop.: 2.2, 50th

Travel and Transportation

Motor vehicle registrations: 2,622,966
Per 1,000 pop.: 797, 23rd
Motorcycle registrations: 51,443
Per 1,000 pop.: 15, 30th
Licensed drivers per 1,000 driving age pop.: 851, 40th
Deaths from motor vehicle accidents per 100,000 pop.: 11.7, 47th
Public roads & streets
Total mileage: 19,991, 44th
Rural mileage: 9,086, 47th
Urban mileage: 10,905, 26th
Interstate mileage: 341, 45th
Annual vehicle-miles of travel per person: 8,001, 42nd
Mean travel time for workers 16 + who work away from home: 21.1 min., 22nd

Government

Registered voters (1988): 1,795,419
Percent of voting age pop.: 72.05%, 24th
Voter turnout (1988): 1,443,394
Percent of registered voters: 80.39%, 2nd
Percent of voting age pop.: 57.92%, 13th
State legislators, total (1992): 187, 9th
Women members (1992): 43
Percent of legislature: 23.0%, 16th
Dominant party (1992): Democrats
U. S. Congress, House members (1993): 6
Increase 1983-93: 0
Revenues:
State govt.: $9,590,710,000
Per capita: $2,917.67, 12th
State & local govt.: $14,555,281,000
Per capita: $4,427.98, 13th
Indebtedness:
State govt.: $10,987,665,000
Per capita: $3,342.65, 4th
State & local govt.: $14,392,000,000
Per capita: $4,378.31, 11th

Laws and Regulations

Legal driving age: 18
Marriage age without parental consent: 18
Divorce residence requirement: 1 yr., qualification—check local statutes

Attractions

Major opera companies (1989): 3, 15th
Per 1 million pop.: 0.93, 10th

Major symphony orchestras (1989): 23, 13th
Per 1 million pop.: 7.10, 4th
State appropriations for state arts agencies per capita: $0.66, 27th

Sports and Competition

NCAA sports teams, 12: Central Connecticut State Blue Devils, Fairfield Univ. Stags, Sacred Heart Univ. Pioneers, Southern Connecticut State Univ. Owls, Trinity College, U.S. Coast Guard Academy, Univ. of Bridgeport Purple Knights, Univ. of Connecticut Huskies, Univ. of Hartford Hawks, Univ. of New Haven Chargers, Wesleyan Univ. Cardinals, Yale Univ. Bulldogs.
Professional teams; 3:
Baseball, 1—New Britain Red Sox (Eastern League, Class AA), Beehive field
Hockey, 2—Hartford Whalers (NHL, Wales Conference), Hartford Civic Center Coliseum; New Haven Nighthawks (American Hockey League), New Haven Veterans Memorial Coliseum

DELAWARE

"Delaware is like a diamond, diminutive, but having within it inherent value."
John Lofland, poet and author

The distinguished history of the second smallest state extends over more than 300 yrs. Delaware is proud to be known as the first State, the first to accept the new U.S. Constitution. It was the only colony to have been claimed by Sweden, Holland, and England. The lotus plants found there have led some specialists to believe that the region may have been visited by early Egyptian explorers. Swedish settlers in present-day Delaware introduced the log cabin to American shores, and the nation's first steam railroad was operated there. Today, it is both a farming and an industrial region, and leads the nation in the production of chemicals. More corporations are headquartered in Delaware than elsewhere, due to its corporate laws.

> So They Say
>
> He "...did there trade with the inhabitants....Furs, Robes and other skins....He hath found the said Country full of trees.....Bucks and does, turkeys and partridges."
>
> Cornelius Hendricksen, writing about the exploration of Cornelius Jacobsen Mey in 1613.

SUPERLATIVES

• The nation's first steam railroad began operations out of New Castle in 1831.

• At one time Delaware was the nation's flour industry center, and the price of wheat was set in Wilmington

MOMENTS IN HISTORY

• Henry Hudson sailed his storied ship, the *Half Moon,* up Delaware Bay in 1609, to become the first known European to visit in the area.

• In 1613 another explorer, Cornelius Jacobsen Mey, explored and traded in the area.

• Dutch leader Peter Minuit, employed by Sweden, brought settlers in two ships to present-day Wilmington in 1638, and they landed on "The Rocks," known as the "Plymouth Rock" of Delaware.

• In 1655 New York Governor Peter Stuyvesant brought a large fleet to the area, captured all of New Sweden, and ended Swedish rule in America.

• In 1682 William Penn, new proprietor of present-day Delaware and Pennsylvania, sailed up the Delaware River past flourishing Christina (Wilmington) on his way to his new capital, Philadelphia, from which Delaware would be governed until it became a British crown colony in 1704.

• In 1776, although he was dying of cancer, Caesar Rodney, a member of the Continental Congress, made a famous ride from Wilmington to Philadelphia in order to cast the deciding vote for the Declaration of Independence.

• On August 27, 1776, Delaware's first Regiment played a key role in the important Battle of Long Island.

• Delaware gained distinction as The First State when it ratified the U.S. Constitution on December 7, 1787.

• During the War of 1812, Delaware's Captain Thomas MacDonough's victory in the Battle of Lake Champlain became a "turning point" of that conflict.

> So They Say
>
> "Sir: The Almighty has been pleased to grant us a signal victory on Lake Champlain in the capture of one frigate, one brig, and two sloops of war of the enemy."
>
> In reporting to his commander, Capt. Thomas MacDonough modestly neglected that he had brought the entire British fleet into his hands.

• In the Civil War Battle of Antietam on September 17, 1862, almost half of the Delaware men who took part were killed, emphasizing the small state's sacrifices during that war.

• During the great storm of 1889, 40 ships were destroyed off Lewes and 70 lives were lost.

• The U.S. Battleship *Delaware* was commissioned in 1910.

• The disastrous Pocomoke Swamp fire of 1930 burned the underlying peat for eight months.

• The Delaware Memorial Bridge went into service in 1951, paying tribute to the 800 Delaware men and women who lost their lives during World War II.

• The 1978 order of the U.S. Supreme Court permitted the busing of children from Wilmington to the suburbs to promote racial integration. The decision was a landmark for the establishment of this practice.

That's Interesting

• Johan Prinz, capable governor of New Sweden from 1643 to 1653, was the "greatest" of all colonial governors. He weighed 400 lbs. and was called the "Big Tub."

• When a ship carrying peas wrecked on a sandbar, the peas grew and collected so much sand that a new island formed, now Pea Patch Island.

• When one of the DuPont men saw sparks flying from a machine in their blasting powder plant, he dipped his tall silk hat in water and put out the fire, before a tremendous explosion could occur.

• One of the most curious exhibits at the Delaware Historical Society is a cigar store white man, a carving of George Washington.

• When Shadrach Cannon of Seaford was bitten by a rabid dog, some of the town's best citizens were selected to smother him to death between two feather beds, in an early mercy killing.

Notable Natives

James Asheton Bayard (Wilmington, 1799-1880), politician. **Henry Sidell Canby** (Wilmington, 1878-1961), author/publisher. **Annie Jump Cannon** (Dover, 1863-1941), astronomer. **John Middleton Clayton** (Dagsborough, 1796-1856), jurist/statesman. **Alfred Irenee Du Pont** (near Wilmington, 1864-1965), industrialist/philanthropist. **Henry Du Pont** (Wilmington, 1812-1889), industrialist/philanthropist. **Henry Algernon Du Pont** (near Wilmington, 1838-1926), politician/industrialist. **Pierre Samuel Du Pont** (Wilmington, 1870-1954), industrialist. **Jacob Jones** (near Smyrna, 1768-1850), naval officer. **Thomas MacDonough** (MacDonough, 1783-1825), naval officer. **John Phillips Marquand** (Wilmington, 1893-1960), author. **Howard Pyle** (Wilmington, 1853-1911), author/artist. **Caesar Rodney** (near Dover, 1728-1784), patriot/statesman.

General

Admitted to statehood: Dec. 7, 1787

Origin of name: Named for Lord De La Warr, early governor of Virginia; first applied to river, then to Indian tribe (Lenni-Lenape), and the state

Capital: Dover

Nicknames: The Diamond State, First State, and Blue Hen State

Motto: "Liberty and Independence"

Beverage: milk

Bird: blue hen chicken

Colors: colonial blue and buff

Fish: weakfish (Cynoscion regalis)

Flower: peach blossom

Insect: ladybug

Mineral: sillimanite

Song: "Our Delaware"

Tree: American holly

The Land

Area: 2,489 sq. mi., 49th

Land: 1,955 sq. mi., 49th

Water: 535 sq. mi., 40th
Topography: Piedmont plateau to the N, sloping to a near sea-level plain
Number of counties: 3
Geographic center: Kent, 11 mi. S of Dover
Length: 100 mi.
Width: 30 mi.
Highest point: 442 ft., Ebrigth Road, New Castle County; 49th
Lowest point: sea level (Atlantic Ocean), 3rd
Mean elevation: 60 ft., 51st
Coastline: 28 mi., 21st
Shoreline: 381 mi., 21st

Climate and Environment

Temp., highest: 110 deg. on July 21, 1930, at Millsboro; lowest: -17 deg. on Jan. 17, 1893, at Millsboro
Fresh water withdrawn, per capita, per day: 222 gal., 50th
Endangered species: mammals, 1—Delmarva peninsula fox squirrel; birds, 1—American peregrine falcon; reptiles, 2; amphibians, none; fishes, none; invertebrates, none; plants, 1

Major Cities, Population Percentage Increase (1980-90)

Brookside, 15,307—0.34%
Dover, 27,630—17.54%
Newark, 25,098— -0.59%
Pike Creek, 10,163—NA
Wilmington, 71,529—1.90%

The People

Population: 666,168, 46th
Percent change (1980-90): 10.78%, 17th
Per sq. mi: 267.64, 8th
Percent in metro. area: 66.35%, 29th
Percent foreign born: 3.3%, 24th
White: 535,094—80.32%, 34th
Black: 112,460—16.88%, 10th
Native American: 2,019—0.30%, 32nd
Asian, Pacific Isle: 9,057—1.36%, 21st
Other races: 7,538—1.13%, 24th
Hispanic origin: 15,820—2.37%, 26th
Percent over 5 yrs. speaking language other than English at home: 6.9%, 27th
Percent males: 48.48%, 32nd
Percent females: 51.52%, 20th
Percent never married: 27.6%, 12th
Marriages per 1,000 (1989): 8.8, 33rd
Divorces per 1,000 (1989): 4.4, 29th
Median age: 32.9
Under 5 years: 483,824—7.33%, 29th
Under 18 years: 163,341—24.52%, 40th
65 years & older: 80,735—12.12%, 32nd
Percent increase among the elderly: 36.4%, 9th

Of Vital Importance

Live births per 1,000 pop.: 17.1, 11th
Infant mortality rate per 1,000 births (1988): 11.8, 7th
Average lifetime (1979-81): 73.21, 40th
Deaths per 100,000 pop. (1988): 874.1, 28th
Causes of death per 100,000 pop. (1988):
Diseases of heart: 309.8, 27th
Malignant neoplasms: 217.7, 11th
Cerebrovascular diseases: 44.7, 44th
Accidents & adverse effects: 43.8, 19th
Chronic obstructive pulmonary diseases: 30.2, 39th
Suicide: 13.2, 20th
HIV infection: 3.9, 20th
Other: 65.4, 45th

Keeping Well

Non-federal physicians per 100,000 pop.: 218, 21st
Dentists per 100,000 (1990-91): 51, 42nd
Nurses per 100,000 (1989): 899, 7th
Hospitals per 100,000: 2.0, 45th
Admissions per 100,000: 13,827, 21st
Beds per 100,000: 425.87, 39th
Occupancy rate: 78.1%, 7th
Semiprivate room charges per day: $385, 4th
Average stay: 6.7, 38th
Notifiable diseases per 100,000:
AIDS: 14.1, 11th
Gonorrhea: 506.3, 5th
Measles: 1.4, 37th
Syphillis: 59.3, 12th
Tuberculosis (TB): 5.7, 30th
Per capita spending on mental health programs (1987): $128.61, 2nd
Pop. without health insur. (1991): 13.2%, 21st

Households by Type

Total households: 247,497
  Percent change (1980-90): 19.56%, 18th
Family households: 175,867
  Percent of total: 71.06%, 22nd
Nonfamily households: 71,630
  Percent of total: 28.94%, 30th
Persons per household: 2.61, 21st
Pop. living in group quarters: 20,071
  Percent of pop.: 3.01%, 17th

Living quarters

Total housing units: 289,919
  Persons per unit: 2.30, 40th
Occupied housing units: 247,497
  Percent of total units: 85.37%, 42nd
  Persons per unit: 2.55, 20th
  Percent of units with over 1 person per room: 2.27%, 39th
Owner-occupied units: 173,813
  Percent of total units: 59.95%, 23rd
  Percent of occupied units: 70.23%, 9th
  Persons per unit: 2.71, 29th
  Median value: $100,100, 11th
Renter-occupied units: 73,684
  Percent of total units: 25.42%, 47th
  Percent of occupied units: 29.77%, 43rd
  Persons per unit: 2.38, 22nd
  Median contract rent: $425, 12th
  Rental vacancy rate: 7.8%, 32nd
Mobile home, trailer & other as a % of occupied housing units: 14.98%, 14th

Crime Index per 100,000

Total: 5,360, 24th
  Violent: 655, 17th
    Murder and nonnegligent manslaughter: 5, 31st
    Aggravated assault: 72,628, 1st
    Robbery: 165, 19th
    Rape: 88, 1st
  Property: 4,705, 26th
    Burglary: 970, 33rd
    Larceny, theft: 3,291, 17th
    Motor vehicle theft: 444, 25th
Drug abuse arrests: 334, 14th

Teaching and Learning

Literacy (1987): 89%, 17th
Pop. 3 and over enrolled in school: 171,219
  Percent of pop.: 26.9%, 30th
Public elementary & secondary schools:
  Total enrollment: 101,000
  Avg. class size (1987): 23, 20th
  Teachers: 6,000
    Percent of pop.: 0.90%, 40th
  Teachers' avg. salary: $33,400, 11th
  Spending per capita: $835, 20th
  Spending per pupil in avg. daily attendance: $5,848, 9th
Percent of graduates taking SAT: 61%, 13th
  Combined SAT scores: 892, 37th
Percent of pop. over 25 completing:
  High school: 77.5%, 23rd
  College degree/s: 21.4%, 17th
Higher educa., institutions: 10
  Per 100,000 pop.: 0.8, 22nd
  Enroll: 42,004
    Percent of pop.: 6.31%, 12th
  Public: 34,252
    Percent of enroll.: 81.54%, 28th
  Private: 7,752
    Percent of enroll.: 18.46%, 24th
  White non-Hispanic: 241,666
    Percent of enroll.: 74.60%, 40th
  Black non-Hispanic: 33,113
    Percent of enroll.: 10.22%, 15th
  Hispanic: 21,642
    Percent of enroll.: 6.68%, 9th
  Asian/Pacific Islander: 14,340
    Percent of enroll.: 4.43%, 6th
  Amer. Indian/AK native: 776
    Percent of enroll.: 0.24%, 43rd
  Nonresident alien: 12,410
    Percent of enroll.: 3.83%, 8th
  Female: 23,801
    Percent of enroll.: 56.66%, 7th
  Tuition, state university ('90-'91): $2,910, 4th
Public library systems: 29
  Books & serial vol. per capita: 1.68, 47th
  Govt. expend. per capita: $10.02, 40th
    State govt.: $2.93, 19th
    Local govts.: $7.09, 42nd

Law Enforcement, Courts, and Prisons

Police protection expend.: $86,191,000
Per capita: $129.42, 14th
Judicial & legal expend.: $51,688,000
Per capita: $77.61, 7th
Corrections expend.: $71,181,000
Per capita: $106.88, 11th
Police per 10,000 pop. (1990-91): 23.2, 12th
Prisoners (state & fed.) sentenced to over 1 yr., per 100,000 pop.: 321
Percent change (1989-90): -2.32%, 48th
Death penalty: yes, by lethal injection
Under sentence of death: 7, 29th
Executed (1989): none

Religion, Number and Percent of Population

Agnostic: NA
Buddhist: NA
Christian: 429,414—85.40%, 29th
Hindu: NA
Jewish: 7,040—1.40%, 14th
Moslem: NA
Unitarian: NA
Other: 1,509—0.30%, 48th
None: 36,204—7.20%, 20th
Refused to answer: 28,661—5.70%, 1st

Making a Living

Personal income per capita (1989): $15,854, 10th
Percent increase (1979-'89) (constant 1989 dollars): 27.0%, 11th
Average income per family: $47,653, 11th
Percent of pop. below poverty level: 8.7%, 46th
Percent 65 and over: 10.1%, 40th
Cost of living, selected cities
1st qtr., 1991 (U. S. Standard=100)

Dover	107.2
Wilmington	112.8

Economy

Civilian labor force : 362,000
Percent of tot. pop.: 54.34%, 5th
Percent 65 and over: 2.49%, 33rd
Percent females: 46.96%, 8th
Percent job growth (1980-90): 35.15%, 7th
Major employer industries:
Agriculture: 6,536—1.90%, 37th
Construction: 21,328—6.20%, 5th
Finance, insurance & real estate: 30,960—9.00%, 2nd
Government: 44,032—12.80%, 43rd
Manufacturing: 71,896—20.90%, 13th
Mining: 427—0.1%, 39th
Service: 72,928—21.20%, 16th
Trade: 61,920—18.00%, 33rd
Transportation, communication, & public utilities: 15,136—4.40%, 43rd
Wholesale/retail: 66,067—19.7%, 44th
Unemployment rate: 5.25%, 29th
Male: 3.04%, 26th
Female: 2.21%, 32nd
Total businesses (1991): 21,542
New business incorp's. (1991): 29,887
Percent of total businesses: 138.74%, 1st
Business failures (1991): 158
Percent of total businesses: 0.73%, 35th
Agriculture farm income
Marketing (1991): $619,536,000, 40th
Net per operation: $60,296, 4th
Net per acre: $307, 3rd
Leading products: broilers, soybeans, corn, greenhouse
Av. value land & build. per acre: $2,334, 6th
Percent increase (1980-90): 29.81%, 12th
Govt. payments: $2,676,000, 44th
Construction, value of all: $572,000,000
Per capita: $858.64, 6th
Percent change 1989-90: -20.11%, 37th
Manufactures:
Value added: : $4,512,000,000
Per capita: $6,773.07, 8th
Value of shipments: $12,901,000,000
Per capita: $19,365.99, 1st
Leading products: nylon, apparel, luggage, foods, autos, processed meats and vegetables, railroad and aircraft equipment
Mining, min. prod., value (DE, DC) (1987): $17,000,000, 49th
Leading products: magnesium compds., sand/gravel
Retail sales: $6,041,000,000, 43rd
Per household: $24,145, 4th
Percent increase (1987-90): 9.9%, 37th

Service indust., value (1987): $3,043,000,000, 44th
Per capita: $4,567.92, 14th
Tourism indus., value (1989): $748,000,000, 48th
Foreign exports value: $1,344,000,000, 36th
Per capita: $2,017.51, 5th
Patents per 1,000 pop.: 1.5, 51st

TRAVEL AND TRANSPORTATION

Motor vehicle registrations: 526,089
Per 1,000 pop.: 789, 25th
Motorcycle registrations: 8,867
Per 1,000 pop.: 13, 34th
Licensed drivers per 1,000 driving age pop.: 938, 12th
Deaths from motor vehicle accidents per 100,000 pop.: 20.7, 20th
Public roads & streets
Total mileage: 5,444, 49th
Rural mileage: 3,829, 48th
Urban mileage: 1,615, 47th
Interstate mileage: 41, 50th
Annual vehicle-miles of travel per person: 9,829, 11th
Mean travel time for workers 16 + who work away from home: 20.0 min., 30th

GOVERNMENT

Registered voters (1988): 318,362
Percent of voting age pop.: 64.97%, 38th
Voter turnout (1988): 249,891
Percent of registered voters: 78.49%, 7th
Percent of voting age pop.: 51.00%, 28th
State legislators, total (1992): 62, 48th
Women members (1992): 8
Percent of legislature: 12.9%, 36th
Dominant party (1992): Split
U. S. Congress, House members (1993): 1
Increase 1983-93: 0
Revenues:
State govt.: $2,315,578,000
Per capita: $3,475.97, 5th
State & local govt.: $2,949,672,000
Per capita: $4,427.82, 14th
Indebtedness:
State govt.: $2,978,014,000
Per capita: $4,470.36, 2nd
State & local govt.: $3,960,000,000
Per capita: $5,944.45, 3rd

LAWS AND REGULATIONS

Legal driving age: 18
Marriage age without parental consent: 18
Divorce residence requirement: 6 mo.

ATTRACTIONS

Major opera companies (1989): 1, 30th
Per 1 million pop.: 1.49, 6th
Major symphony orchestras (1989): 2, 48th
Per 1 million pop.: 2.97, 34th
State appropriations for state arts agencies per capita: $1.62, 9th
State Fair in the end of July at Harrisburg

SPORTS AND COMPETITION

NCAA sports teams, 2: Delaware State College Hornets, Univ. of Delaware Fightin' Blue Hens
Professional teams: none

DISTRICT OF COLUMBIA

"I went to Washington the other day...and I felt that the sun in all its course could not look down upon a better sight than that majestic home of the Republic that had taught the world its best lessons in liberty."

Henry W. Grady, journalist and author

The city of Washington and the District of Columbia—"the district," as residents call it—are one and the same. The site was selected as the nation's capital on December 1, 1800, and over the years the District has brought together the nation's most famous statesmen and politicians. It was burned in the War of 1812, and its capture was threatened in the Civil War. Events that affect the nation and the world have occurred with regularity in its legislative, executive, and judicial halls. Washington has been the center of national mourning, where martyred presidents were honored. The grandeur of its buildings and monuments and the glamor of its world figures attract tourists from home and abroad. Washington has become an international metropolis in every sense of the word!

MOMENTS IN HISTORY

• In 1790 a bill was passed to locate a new capital along the Potomac River.

> So They Say
>
> "No nation ever before had the opportunity offered them of deliberately deciding upon the spot where their capital city should be fixed."
>
> Pierre Charles L'Enfant

• The cornerstone of the capitol was laid in 1793 by George Washington, who was a mason.

• In 1800 the federal government moved to Washington, with 300 clerks, 138 members of Congress, the Supreme Court and Circuit Court, all crowded into a part of the unfinished capitol. The East Room of the uncompleted president's house was used by Mrs. John Adams for drying laundry.

• The British burned Washington during the War of 1812, and Dolley Madison escaped carrying only a portrait of Washington, some official papers and a few valuables.

• The Marquis de Lafayette visited Washington in 1824, received a gift of the "incredible sum" of $200,000 and was the first foreign dignitary to address the full Congress.

> So They Say
>
> Washington "...the central star of the constellation which enlightens the whole world!"
>
> Marquis de Lafayette

• Washington might have been captured by the Confederates if they had followed up on their victory after the first Battle of Bull Run, July 21, 1861.

• Abraham Lincoln was assassinated at Ford's Theater on April 15, 1865, and Washington mourned its leader, martyred on the threshold of Civil War victory.

• President James Garfield died on September 19, 1881, the victim of assassination in a Washington rail station.

• Protesting unemployment, in 1894 Jacob Coxey "invaded" Washington with 300 followers. Accused of walking on the grass, Coxey was arrested, and his followers dispersed.

• In March, 1952, the complete restoration of the White House was finished.

• Under a new home rule charter Washington's mayor and city council took office in 1975.

• In 1990, Mayor Marion S. Barry was sentenced to jail for six months for cocaine possession.

That's Interesting

• Roosevelt Island in the Potomac River at Theodore Roosevelt Memorial Bridge "grows" about 20 acres every hundred years, as new land forms around the brush and branches that have floated down the river.

• In the competition for the design of the Capitol, one plan called for the structure to be topped by the statue of an enormous rooster.

• The name of the performance playing when President Abraham Lincoln was shot was *Our American Cousin.*

• House Speaker Joe Cannon gave Congress one of its cherished traditions when he commanded that his famous bean soup be served every day in the capitol. It has been on the menu since 1907.

• Sudden rises of temperature in the Washington Monument cause the moisture to condense, and "rain" falls inside.

General

Not yet a state, but statehood often considered.
Origin of name: "For Columbus," 1791
Capital: Washington
Nicknames: The Nation's Capital and America's first City
Motto: *"Justitia Omnibus"* ("Justice for All")
Bird: wood thrush
Flag: based on George Washington's coat of arms
Flower: American beauty rose
Tree: scarlet oak

The Land

Area: 68 sq. mi., 51st
Land: 61 sq. mi., 51st
Water: 7 sq. mi., 51st
Topography: The natural contour is roughly like a great amphitheater. Low hills rise toward the N and slope to the S. The largest part of the District rises away from the Potomac River on a series of terraces of what is called the Atlantic Coastal Plain. The Capitol rises on the most noticeable of these terraces
Number of counties: none
Geographic center: near 4th and L Streets, NW.; the District was roughly 10 mi square until the Virginia portion was returned to that state
Highest point: 410 ft. (Tenleytown), 50th
Lowest point: 1 ft. (Potomac River), 25th
Mean elevation: 150 ft., 48th

Climate and Environment

Temp., highest: 106 deg. on July 20, 1930, at Washington; lowest: -15 deg. on Feb. 11, 1988, at Washington
Fresh water withdrawn, per capita, per day: 556 gal., 42nd
Endangered species: mammals, none; birds, 1—American peregrine falcon; reptiles, none; amphibians, none; fishes, none; invertebrates, 1; plants, none

Major Cities, Population Percentage Increase (1980-90)

Washington, 606,900— -4.94%

The People

Population: 606,900, 48th
Percent change (1980-90): -5.20%, 50th
Per sq. mi: 8,925.00, 1st
Percent in metro. area: 100.00%, 1st
Percent foreign born: 9.7%, 6th
White: 179,667—29.60%, 51st
Black: 399,604—65.84%, 1st
Native American: 1,466—0.24%, 38th
Asian, Pacific Isle: 11,214—1.85%, 15th
Other races: 14,949—2.46%, 13th
Hispanic origin: 32,710—5.39%, 14th
Percent over 5 yrs. speaking language other than English at home: 12.5%, 14th

Percent males: 46.63%, 51st
Percent females: 53.37%, 1st
Percent never married: 47.6%, 1st
Marriages per 1,000 (1989): 7.9, 43rd
Divorces per 1,000 (1989): 4.0, 35th
Median age: 33.5
Under 5 years: 37,351—6.15%, 50th
Under 18 years: 117,092—19.29%, 51st
65 years & older: 77,847—12.83%, 24th
Percent increase among the elderly: 4.8%, 51st

Of Vital Importance

Live births per 1,000 pop.: 36.8, 1st
Infant mortality rate per 1,000 births (1988): 23.2, 1st
Average lifetime (1979-81): 69.20, 51st
Deaths per 100,000 pop. (1988): 1242.1, 1st
Causes of death per 100,000 pop. (1988):
Diseases of heart: 355.9, 11th
Malignant neoplasms: 263.9, 1st
Cerebrovascular diseases: 64.5, 22nd
Accidents & adverse effects: 39.1, 28th
Chronic obstructive pulmonary diseases: 23.5, 48th
Suicide: 7.8, 49th
HIV infection: 40, 1st
Other: 155.0, 1st

Keeping Well

Non-federal physicians per 100,000 pop.: 647, 1st
Dentists per 100,000 (1990-91): 151, 1st
Nurses per 100,000 (1989): 1575, 1st
Hospitals per 100,000: 2.8, 28th
Admissions per 100,000: 32,912, 2nd
Beds per 100,000: 1324.93, 1st
Occupancy rate: 79.1%, 6th
Semiprivate room charges per day: $325, 16th
Average stay: 8.3, 13th
Notifiable diseases per 100,000:
AIDS: 122.1, 1st
Gonorrhea: 2,419.7, 1st
Measles: 4.0, 27th
Syphillis: 488.5, 1st
Tuberculosis (TB): 26.9, 1st
Per capita spending on mental health programs (1987): $57.41, 7th
Pop. without health insur. (1991): 25.7%, 1st

Households by Type

Total households: 249,634
Percent change (1980-90): -1.33%, 51st
Family households: 122,087
Percent of total: 48.91%, 51st
Nonfamily households: 127,547
Percent of total: 51.09%, 1st
Persons per household: 2.26, 51st
Pop. living in group quarters: 41,717
Percent of pop.: 6.87%, 1st

Living Quarters

Total housing units: 278,489
Persons per unit: 2.18, 48th
Occupied housing units: 249,634
Percent of total units: 89.64%, 25th
Persons per unit: 2.31, 51st
Percent of units with over 1 person per room: 8.25%, 4th
Owner-occupied units: 97,108
Percent of total units: 34.87%, 51st
Percent of occupied units: 38.90%, 51st
Persons per unit: 2.50, 50th
Median value: $123,900, 9th
Renter-occupied units: 152,526
Percent of total units: 54.77%, 1st
Percent of occupied units: 61.10%, 1st
Persons per unit: 2.12, 50th
Median contract rent: $441, 10th
Rental vacancy rate: 7.9%, 30th
Mobile home, trailer & other as a % of occupied housing units: 1.14%, 51st

Crime Index per 100,000

Total: 10,774, 1st
Violent: 2,458, 1st
Murder and nonnegligent manslaughter: 78, 1st
Aggravated assault: 6,154, 50th
Robbery: 1,214, 1st
Rape: 50, 10th
Property: 8,316, 1st
Burglary: 1,983, 2nd
Larceny, theft: 4,997, 1st
Motor vehicle theft: 1,336, 1st

Drug abuse arrests: 1,647, 1st

Teaching and Learning

Literacy (1987): 84%, 47th
Pop. 3 and over enrolled in school: 151,248
Percent of pop.: 25.9%, 41st
Public elementary & secondary schools:
Total enrollment: 83,000
Avg. class size (1987): not available
Teachers: 6,500
Percent of pop.: 1.07%, 17th
Teachers' avg. salary: $38,000, 4th
Spending per capita: $945, 8th
Spending per pupil in avg. daily attendance: $7,407, 4th
Percent of graduates taking SAT: 71%, 6th
Combined SAT scores: 840, 50th
Percent of pop. over 25 completing:
High school: 73.1%, 39th
College degree/s: 33.3%, 1st
Higher educa., institutions: 17
Per 100,000 pop.: 0.3, 49th
Enroll: 80,669
Percent of pop.: 13.29%, 1st
Public: 12,595
Percent of enroll.: 15.61%, 51st
Private: 68,074
Percent of enroll.: 84.39%, 1st
White non-Hispanic: 1,131,741
Percent of enroll.: 63.88%, 48th
Black non-Hispanic: 114,804
Percent of enroll.: 6.48%, 23rd
Hispanic: 222,749
Percent of enroll.: 12.57%, 3rd
Asian/Pacific Islander: 215,416
Percent of enroll.: 12.16%, 2nd
Amer. Indian/AK native: 21,005
Percent of enroll.: 1.19%, 12th
Nonresident alien: 66,031
Percent of enroll.: 3.73%, 9th
Female: 42,960
Percent of enroll.: 53.25%, 43rd
Tuition, state university ('90-'91): $664, 51st
Public library systems: 1
Books & serial vol. per capita: 2.77, 21st
Govt. expend. per capita: $32.16, 2nd
State govt.: $0.00, 51st
Local govts.: $32.16, 1st

Law Enforcement, Courts, and Prisons

Police protection expend.: $275,728,000
Per capita: $454.25, 1st
Judicial & legal expend.: $122,207,000
Per capita: $201.33, 1st
Corrections expend.: $400,710,000
Per capita: $660.15, 1st
Police per 10,000 pop. (1990-91): 74.2, 1st
Prisoners (state & fed.) sentenced to over 1 yr., per 100,000 pop.: 1,125
Percent change (1989-90): -1.11%, 46th
Death penalty: no

Religion, Number and Percent of Population

Agnostic: 2,449—0.50%, 27th
Buddhist: 1,469—0.30%, 8th
Christian: 417,806—85.30%, 31st
Hindu: NA
Jewish: 11,266—2.30%, 7th
Moslem: 2,939—0.60%, 2nd
Unitarian: NA
Other: 12,245—2.50%, 4th
None: 30,858—6.30%, 30th
Refused to answer: 10,776—2.20%, 23rd

Making a Living

Personal income per capita (1989): $18,881, 2nd
Percent increase (1979-'89) (constant 1989 dollars): 25.7%, 12th
Average income per family: $53,049, 5th
Percent of pop. below poverty level: 16.9%, 9th
Percent 65 and over: 17.2%, 12th
Cost of living, selected cities
1st qtr., 1989 (U. S. Standard=100)
Washington 129.8

Economy

Civilian labor force : 298,000
Percent of tot. pop.: 49.10%, 38th
Percent 65 and over: 2.68%, 28th
Percent females: 49.33%, 1st
Percent job growth (1980-90): 11.01%, 43rd
Major employer industries:
Agriculture: 556—0.20%, 51st
Construction: 9,174—3.30%, 48th

Finance, insurance & real estate: 20,294—7.30%, 8th
Government: 86,458—31.10%, 1st
Manufacturing: 8,896—3.20%, 51st
Mining: 102—0.0%, 50th
Service: 92,018—33.10%, 2nd
Trade: 28,634—10.30%, 51st
Transportation, communication, & public utilities: 10,564—3.80%, 50th
Wholesale/retail: 36,190—11.9%, 51st
Unemployment rate: 6.71%, 8th
Male: 3.69%, 4th
Female: 3.02%, 7th
Total businesses (1991): 28,638
New business incorp's. (1991): 2,256
Percent of total businesses: 7.88%, 12th
Business failures (1991): 198
Percent of total businesses: 0.69%, 39th
Agriculture farm income
Marketing (1991): NA
Net per operation: NA
Net per acre: NA
Leading products: NA
Av. value land & build. per acre: NA
Percent increase (1980-90): NA
Govt. payments: NA
Construction, value of all: $170,000,000
Per capita: $280.11, 48th
Percent change 1989-90: 22.30%, 6th
Manufactures:
Value added: : $1,573,000,000
Per capita: $2,591.86, 42nd
Value of shipments: $2,152,000,000
Per capita: $3,545.89, 50th
Leading products: NA
Mining, min. prod., value (DE, DC) (1987): $17,000,000, 49th
Leading products: NA
Retail sales: $3,815,000,000, 50th
Per household: $15,360, 49th
Percent increase (1987-90): 12.8%, 33rd
Service indust., value (1987): $14,128,000,000, 25th
Per capita: $23,278.96, 1st
Tourism indus., value (1989): $2,714,000,000, 31st
Foreign exports value: $321,000,000, 46th
Per capita: $528.92, 43rd
Patents per 1,000 pop.: 12.6, 7th

Travel and Transportation

Motor vehicle registrations: 261,931
Per 1,000 pop.: 431, 51st
Motorcycle registrations: 2,560
Per 1,000 pop.: 4, 51st
Licensed drivers per 1,000 driving age pop.: 860, 39th
Deaths from motor vehicle accidents per 100,000 pop.: 7.9, 51st
Public roads & streets
Total mileage: 1,102, 51st
Rural mileage: NA, 51st
Urban mileage: 1,102, 51st
Interstate mileage: 12, 51st
Annual vehicle-miles of travel per person: 5,613, 51st
Mean travel time for workers 16 + who work away from home: 27.1 min., 2nd

Government

Registered voters (1988): 299,757
Percent of voting age pop.: 61.30%, 45th
Voter turnout (1988): 192,877
Percent of registered voters: 64.34%, 43rd
Percent of voting age pop.: 39.44%, 49th
State legislators, total (1992): NA, 51st
Women members (1992): NA
Percent of legislature: NA
Dominant party (1992): NA
U. S. Congress, House members (1993):
Increase 1983-93: 0
Revenues:
State govt.: NA
Local govt.: $4,926,602,000
Per capita: $8,117.65, 2nd
Indebtedness:
State govt.: NA
Local govt.: $4,420,000,000
Per capita: $7,282.91, 2nd

Laws and Regulations

Legal driving age: 18
Marriage age without parental consent: 18
Divorce residence requirement: 6 mo.

Attractions

Major opera companies (1989): 2, 21st
Per 1 million pop.: 3.31, 1st

Major symphony orchestras (1989): 7, 32nd
Per 1 million pop.: 11.59, 1st
State appropriations for state arts agencies per capita: $4.61, 2nd

Sports and Competition

NCAA sports teams, 4: American Univ. Eagles, George Washington Univ. Colonials, Georgetown Univ. Hoyas, Howard Univ. Bisons
Professional teams, 1:
Football, 1—Washington Redskins (NFC), Robert F. Kennedy Stadium

FLORIDA

"Florida is today to the United States what the United States was to Europe 100 yrs. ago—a melting pot, a frontier, a place to improve your health or your luck."

Budd Schulberg

Florida is the nation's most rapidly growing state, and it boasts the nation's oldest European settlement in continuous occupation. A land of sunshine and flowers, Florida has become one of the world's tourist magnets, with Walt Disney World leading the way. The state's gleaming beaches, crystal springs, sophisticated cities, and other recreation opportunities have made it a leading center for retired persons as well as tourists. The quality of its labor and its moderate climate have brought rapidly increasing numbers of industry and business. To winter-weary northerners, Florida is an Eden where they might still find Ponce De Leon's legendary fountain of youth.

Superlatives

- St. Augustine is the oldest continuously occupied European settlement in North America.
- Florida's population was the nation's fastest growing in 1980-1990.
- Commercial aviation came to the United States when Pan American flew from Key West to Cuba.
- Florida citrus production is first in the United States.
- Florida leads the nation in phosphate production.
- Walt Disney World in Orlando lures more visitors than any other single attraction anywhere.
- Florida has more than a fourth of all the country's major springs.

Moments in History

- Juan Ponce de Leon sighted present-day Florida on March 27, 1513. Although others knew of the area before, his is the first record of the place.
- The 1502 map by Alberto Cantino clearly shows the distinctive Florida outline, but it apparently was not known to Ponce de Leon.
- Panfilo de Narvaez and his large force entered Tampa Bay in 1528. Only four of his 400 men survived hurricanes and other disasters.
- The huge expedition of Hernando De Soto landed at present-day Tampa on May 30, 1539. His letter to the King of Spain is thought to be the first letter mailed from what is today the United States.

> **So They Say**
>
> "...a country of rivers, havens and islands of such surpassing fruitfulness as cannot by the tongue be expressed."
>
> Jean Ribaut describing the St. Johns River area, 1562

- Pedro Menendez de Aviles entered a harbor on St. Augustine's day. The place he founded there in 1565 took the saint's name, and St. Augustine remains the oldest continuing settlement in the country.
- Englishman Sir Francis Drake captured St. Augustine in 1586 and burned it to the ground, but the Spanish rebuilt the town.
- In 1763 the English returned captured Cuba to Spain and received Florida in trade.

• Florida remained faithful to Britain during the American Revolution, but Spain gave the British the Bahamas and Gibraltar in return for Florida.

• On July 17, 1821, Andrew Jackson received the transfer of Florida from Spain to the United States. The stars and stripes then flew over Castillo de San Marcos at St. Augustine, which had never been captured in battle.

• A costly seven-year war with the Seminole Indians began in 1836. It is said that this was the only Indian war never won by the United States, and the $20 million cost was enormous for the time.

• Florida became a state on March 3, 1845, a move delayed by the reluctance of Congress to admit another slave state.

• When the issue of slavery finally led to the Civil War, Florida joined the Confederacy on January 10, 1861.

• Union forces lost the Battle of Olustee on February 20, 1864, the largest battle of the war on Florida soil.

• Florida forces repelled a Union attack on Tallahassee in the Battle of Natural Bridge, March 6, 1865.

So They Say

"From boys of fourteen to men of seventy, from the humble woodsmen to the highest civil dignitaries, all came to the defense of their country."

Gen. William Miller on the Civil War Battle of Natural Bridge

• Much of Florida's wealth was destroyed by the Civil War, but new development began in earnest in 1881 when Hamilton Disston paid the state $1 million for 4 million acres of state land.

• Florida became the main point of embarkation for troops and supplies in the Spanish American War in 1898, expanding business there.

• Florida promoter Henry Flagler built a railroad from Miami to Key West, going "out to sea" on a series of bridges built from island to island in the Florida Keys. The first train reached Key West in 1912.

So They Say

The college was founded "...with five girls, a small cabin, $1.50 and a million dollars' worth of faith. We used charred splinters as pencils. For ink we mashed up elderberries."

Mary McLeod Bethune on the founding of Bethune-Cookman College in 1904

• The great Florida land boom that began in 1919 was the largest in the country to that time. Carl Fisher founded Miami Beach in that year, and other promoters brought hosts of investors to the state.

So They Say

"...It is the dream of my life to see this wilderness (Miami) turned into prosperous country and where this tangled mass of vines, brush, trees and rocks now are, to see homes, surrounded by beautiful grassy lawns."

Julia D. Tuttle, an associate of Henry Flagler, 1890

• The hurricane of 1926 brought 16 hours of destruction to the Miami area.

• In 1933 at Miami, President-elect Franklin D. Roosevelt escaped assassination, but Mayor Anton Cermak of Chicago was killed in the attack.

• During World War II Florida became one of the greatest wartime military and transportation centers ever known.

• In 1962 John Glenn soared into space from Cape Canaveral, becoming the first American in orbit.

• The early 1980s posed great problems for the state in accommodating the Cuban boat people, refugees from the troubles of their homeland.

• On January 28, 1986, the tragic explosion of the shuttle *Challenger* brought death to the seven persons aboard, including Christa McAuliffe, who was to have been the first teacher in space.

• In August, 1992, Hurricane Andrew, perhaps the worst natural disaster to strike the United States, devastated southern Florida, claiming 30 lives and wreaking damage estimated as high as $20 billion.

That's Interesting

• During the hurricane of 1926 the barometer at Miami reached the country's record low, causing hundreds to faint due to lack of oxygen.

• When a British captain's ear was cut off in a war between Spain and England, the conflict, which was waged in Florida, became known as "The War of Jenkins' Ear."

• The demand was so great for Florida property during the great land boom that investors paid up to $25,000 for lots that had not yet been dredged up from the ocean.

• Once endangered, alligators increased to become something of a nuisance, sometimes swallowing poodles and other pets. The stomach of one contained a pickle jar, dog collar, and several golf balls.

• After fishing, Florida's anhinga, or water turkey, must dry its feathers in the sun. They lie in groups with wings outspread, looking much like a washing out to dry.

Notable Floridians

John James Audobon (Haiti, 1785-1851), ornithologist/artist. **Henry Morrison Flagler** (Hopewell, NY, 1830-1913), capitalist/promoter. **John Gorrie** (Charleston, SC, 1803-1855), physician/inventor. **Edmund Kirby-Smith** (St. Augustine, FL, 1824-1893), army officer. **Alexander McGillivray** (Alabama, 1758?-1793), Indian leader. **Osceola** (Georgia, 1804?-1838), Indian leader. **Henry Bradley Plant** (Branford, CT, 1899-1899), transportation official.

General

Admitted to statehood: March 3, 1845
Origin of name: named by Ponce de Leon as *Pascua Florida*, "flowery Easter," on Easter Sunday, 1513
Capital: Tallahassee
Nickname: The Sunshine State
Motto: "In God We Trust"
Beverage: orange juice
Bird: mockingbird
Flower: orange blossom
Gem: moonstone
Shell: horse conch
Song: "Swanee River" ("Old Folks at Home")
Tree: Sabal palmetto palm

The Land

Area: 65,758 sq. mi., 22nd
Land: 52,997 sq. mi., 26th
Water: 11,761 sq. mi., 3rd
Topography: land is flat or rolling to highest point in the NW
Number of counties: 67
Geographic center: Hernando County, 12 mi. NNW of Brooksville
Length: 500 mi.
Width: 160 mi.
Highest point: 345 ft. Sec. 30, T6N, R20W, Walton County; 51st
Lowest point: sea level (Atlantic Ocean), 3rd
Mean elevation: 100 ft., 49th
Coastline: 1,350 mi., 2nd
Shoreline: 8,426 mi., 2nd

Climate and Environment

Temp., highest: 109 deg. on June 29, 1931, at Monticello; lowest: -2 deg. on Feb. 13, 1899, at Tallahassee
Fresh water withdrawn, per capita, per day: 554 gal., 43rd
Endangered species: mammals, 11—Gray bat, Indiana bat, Key deer, West Indian manatee, Anastasia Island beach mouse, Choctawhatchee beach mouse, Key Largo cotton mouse, Perdido Key beach mouse, Florida panther, Lower Keys rabbit, Key Largo woodrat; birds, 7—American peregrine falcon, Everglade snail kite, piping plover, Cape Sable seaside sparrow, Florida grasshopper sparrow, wood stock, red-cockaded woodpecker; reptiles, 5; amphibians, none; fishes, 1; invertebrates, 1; plants, 31

Major Cities, Population Percentage Increase (1980-90)

Hialeah, 188,004—29.43%
Jacksonville, 635,230—17.44%
Miami, 358,548—3.42%

Saint Petersburg, 238,629— –0.01%
Tampa, 280,015—3.11%

The People

Population: 12,937,926, 4th
Percent change (1980-90): 24.66%, 4th
Per sq. mi: 196.75, 12th
Percent in metro. area: 90.85%, 8th
Percent foreign born: 12.9%, 4th
White: 10,749,285—83.08%, 29th
Black: 1,759,534—13.60%, 16th
Native American: 36,335—0.28%, 34th
Asian, Pacific Isle: 154,302—1.19%, 23rd
Other races: 238,407—1.84%, 20th
Hispanic origin: 1,574,143—12.17%, 7th
Percent over 5 yrs. speaking language other than English at home: 17.3%, 8th
Percent males: 48.40%, 37th
Percent females: 51.60%, 15th
Percent never married: 22.6%, 44th
Marriages per 1,000 (1989): 10.9, 10th
Divorces per 1,000 (1989): 6.3, 7th
Median age: 36.4
Under 5 years: 849,596—6.57%, 49th
Under 18 years: 2,866,237—22.15%, 50th
65 years & older: 2,369,431—18.31%, 1st
Percent increase among the elderly: 40.4%, 6th

Of Vital Importance

Live births per 1,000 pop.: 15.3, 35th
Infant mortality rate per 1,000 births (1988): 10.6, 18th
Average lifetime (1979-81): 74.00, 22nd
Deaths per 100,000 pop. (1988): 1062.4, 2nd
Causes of death per 100,000 pop. (1988):
Diseases of heart: 380.4, 3rd
Malignant neoplasms: 253, 2nd
Cerebrovascular diseases: 71.5, 10th
Accidents & adverse effects: 43.7, 20th
Chronic obstructive pulmonary diseases: 43.1, 6th
Suicide: 16.7, 9th
HIV infection: 11.7, 4th
Other: 81.9, 9th

Keeping Well

Non-federal physicians per 100,000 pop.: 243, 12th
Dentists per 100,000 (1990-91): 58, 32nd
Nurses per 100,000 (1989): 664, 30th
Hospitals per 100,000: 2.2, 40th
Admissions per 100,000: 13,675, 24th
Beds per 100,000: 484.90, 25th
Occupancy rate: 63.7%, 34th
Semiprivate room charges per day: $271, 25th
Average stay: 7.0, 29th
Notifiable diseases per 100,000:
AIDS: 31.3, 4th
Gonorrhea: 328.1, 15th
Measles: 4.7, 23rd
Syphillis: 115.9, 4th
Tuberculosis (TB): 14.2, 5th
Per capita spending on mental health programs (1987): $33.75, 30th
Pop. without health insur. (1991): 18.6%, 8th

Households by Type

Total households: 5,134,869
Percent change (1980-90): 37.15%, 4th
Family households: 3,511,825
Percent of total: 68.39%, 44th
Nonfamily households: 1,623,044
Percent of total: 31.61%, 8th
Persons per household: 2.46, 49th
Pop. living in group quarters: 307,461
Percent of pop.: 2.38%, 39th

Living Quarters

Total housing units: 6,100,262
Persons per unit: 2.12, 49th
Occupied housing units: 5,134,869
Percent of total units: 84.17%, 44th
Persons per unit: 2.44, 48th
Percent of units with over 1 person per room: 5.79%, 12th
Owner-occupied units: 3,452,160
Percent of total units: 56.59%, 36th
Percent of occupied units: 67.23%, 27th
Persons per unit: 2.49, 51st
Median value: $77,100, 21st
Renter-occupied units: 1,682,709
Percent of total units: 27.58%, 35th
Percent of occupied units: 32.77%, 25th
Persons per unit: 2.39, 18th
Median contract rent: $402, 15th
Rental vacancy rate: 12.4%, 6th

Mobile home, trailer & other as a % of occupied housing units: 15.99%, 11th

CRIME INDEX PER 100,000

Total: 8,811, 2nd
Violent: 1,244, 2nd
Murder and nonnegligent manslaughter: 11, 12th
Aggravated assault: 6,567, 49th
Robbery: 417, 3rd
Rape: 52, 8th
Property: 7,566, 2nd
Burglary: 2,171, 1st
Larceny, theft: 4,570, 3rd
Motor vehicle theft: 826, 9th
Drug abuse arrests: 506, 8th

TEACHING AND LEARNING

Literacy (1987): 85%, 40th
Pop. 3 and over enrolled in school: 2,926,662
Percent of pop.: 23.5%, 51st
Public elementary & secondary schools:
Total enrollment: 1,878,000
Avg. class size (1987): 26, 3rd
Teachers: 104,100
Percent of pop.: 0.80%, 48th
Teachers' avg. salary: $28,800, 26th
Spending per capita: $787, 30th
Spending per pupil in avg. daily attendance: $5,051, 19th
Percent of graduates taking SAT: 48%, 21st
Combined SAT scores: 882, 41st
Percent of pop. over 25 completing:
High school: 74.4%, 37th
College degree/s: 18.3%, 30th
Higher educa., institutions: 101
Per 100,000 pop.: 0.3, 51st
Enroll: 538,389
Percent of pop.: 4.16%, 49th
Public: 439,818
Percent of enroll.: 81.69%, 27th
Private: 98,571
Percent of enroll.: 18.31%, 25th
White non-Hispanic: 143,116
Percent of enroll.: 87.54%, 18th
Black non-Hispanic: 6,798
Percent of enroll.: 4.16%, 29th
Hispanic: 3,538
Percent of enroll.: 2.16%, 16th
Asian/Pacific Islander: 2,717
Percent of enroll.: 1.66%, 27th
Amer. Indian/AK native: 1,969
Percent of enroll.: 1.20%, 11th
Nonresident alien: 5,340
Percent of enroll.: 3.27%, 10th
Female: 295,918
Percent of enroll.: 54.96%, 25th
Tuition, state university ('90-'91): $1,337, 43rd
Public library systems: 119
Books & serial vol. per capita: 1.54, 49th
Govt. expend. per capita: $13.88, 29th
State govt.: $2.06, 37th
Local govts.: $11.82, 25th

LAW ENFORCEMENT, COURTS, AND PRISONS

Police protection expend.: $1,904,096,000
Per capita: $147.17, 8th
Judicial & legal expend.: $793,540,000
Per capita: $61.33, 11th
Corrections expend.: $1,466,698,000
Per capita: $113.36, 9th
Police per 10,000 pop. (1990-91): 23.7, 10th
Prisoners (state & fed.) sentenced to over 1 yr., per 100,000 pop.: 336
Percent change (1989-90): 11.06%, 9th
Death penalty: yes, by electrocution
Under sentence of death: 294, 1st
Executed (1989): 2

RELIGION, NUMBER AND PERCENT OF POPULATION

Agnostic: 100,717—1.00%, 10th
Buddhist: 10,072—0.10%, 17th
Christian: 8,480,362—84.20%, 38th
Hindu: 10,072—0.10%, 10th
Jewish: 362,581—3.60%, 3rd
Moslem: 10,072—0.10%, 22nd
Unitarian: 30,215—0.30%, 15th
Other: 130,932—1.30%, 24th
None: 725,162—7.20%, 20th
Refused to answer: 211,506—2.10%, 28th

MAKING A LIVING

Personal income per capita (1989): $14,698, 18th
Percent increase (1979-89) (constant 1989 dollars): 20.8%, 16th

Average income per family: $41,860, 21st
Percent of pop. below poverty level: 12.7%, 23rd
Percent 65 and over: 10.8%, 30th
Cost of living, selected cities
1st qtr., 1991 (U. S. Standard=100)

Ocala	94.2
Miami/Dade County	113.9
Boca Raton	116.5

Economy

Civilian labor force : 6,365,000
Percent of tot. pop.: 49.20%, 36th
Percent 65 and over: 3.25%, 13th
Percent females: 46.36%, 14th
Percent job growth (1980-90): 50.14%, 2nd
Major employer industries:
Agriculture: 143,688—2.40%, 30th
Construction: 365,207—6.10%, 6th
Finance, insurance & real estate: 437,051—7.30%, 5th
Government: 880,089—14.70%, 31st
Manufacturing: 646,596—10.80%, 40th
Mining: 11,095—0.2%, 33rd
Service: 1,353,062—22.60%, 10th
Trade: 1,317,140—22.00%, 1st
Transportation, communication, & public utilities: 323,298—5.40%, 23rd
Wholesale/retail: 1,405,861—24.2%, 1st
Unemployment rate: 5.94%, 14th
Male: 3.00%, 27th
Female: 2.95%, 10th
Total businesses (1991): 415,975
New business incorp's. (1991): 81,083
Percent of total businesses: 19.49%, 3rd
Business failures (1991): 5,180
Percent of total businesses: 1.25%, 10th
Agriculture farm income
Marketing (1991): $6,140,999,000, 8th
Net per operation: $68,018, 1st
Net per acre: $259, 6th
Leading products: oranges, greenhouse, tomatoes, sugar
Av. value land & build. per acre: $2,125, 8th
Percent increase (1980-90): 53.87%, 9th
Govt. payments: $40,786,000, 32nd
Construction, value of all: $12,007,000,000
Per capita: $928.05, 4th
Percent change 1989-90: -29.52%, 42nd
Manufactures:
Value added: : $29,793,000,000
Per capita: $2,302.76, 45th
Value of shipments: $60,750,000,000
Per capita: $4,695.50, 47th
Leading products: electric & electronic equip., transportation equipment, food, printing & publishing, machinery
Mining, min. prod., value (1987): $1,479,000,000, 20th
Leading products: phosphate, petroleum, stone
Retail sales: $105,304,000,000, 4th
Per household: $20,056, 14th
Percent increase (1987-90): 8.9%, 41st
Service indust., value (1987): $60,872,000,000, 4th
Per capita: $4,704.93, 12th
Tourism indus., value (1989): $24,437,000,000, 2nd
Foreign exports value: $11,634,000,000, 9th
Per capita: $899.22, 23rd
Patents per 1,000 pop.: 6.8, 26th

Travel and Transportation

Motor vehicle registrations: 10,949,806
Per 1,000 pop.: 846, 17th
Motorcycle registrations: 205,827
Per 1,000 pop.: 15, 29th
Licensed drivers per 1,000 driving age pop.: 894, 27th
Deaths from motor vehicle accidents per 100,000 pop.: 22.4, 16th
Public roads & streets
Total mileage: 108,085, 15th
Rural mileage: 60,051, 29th
Urban mileage: 48,034, 3rd
Interstate mileage: 1,426, 7th
Annual vehicle-miles of travel per person: 8,502, 35th
Mean travel time for workers 16 + who work away from home: 21.8 min., 15th

Government

Registered voters (1988): 6,047,347
Percent of voting age pop.: 62.90%, 43rd
Voter turnout (1988): 4,302,313
Percent of registered voters: 71.14%, 26th
Percent of voting age pop.: 44.75%, 44th

State legislators, total (1992): 160, 18th
Women members (1992): 30
Percent of legislature: 18.8%, 21st
Dominant party (1992): Democrats
U. S. Congress, House members (1993): 23
Increase 1983-93: +4
Revenues:
State govt.: $23,868,131,000
Per capita: $1,844.82, 47th
State & local govt.: $47,069,843,000
Per capita: $3,638.13, 36th
Indebtedness:
State govt.: $9,950,071,000
Per capita: $769.06, 39th
State & local govt.: $53,464,000,000
Per capita: $4,132.35, 14th

Laws and Regulations

Legal driving age: 16
Marriage age without parental consent: 18
Divorce residence requirement: 6 mo.

Attractions

Major opera companies (1989): 7, 6th
Per 1 million pop.: 0.55, 33rd
Major symphony orchestras (1989): 32, 8th
Per 1 million pop.: 2.53, 40th
State appropriations for state arts agencies per capita: $1.83, 7th
State Fair in early to mid-Feb. at Tampa

Sports and Competition

NCAA sports teams, 9—Bethune-Cookman College Wildcats, Florida A&M Univ. Rattlers, Florida International Univ. Golden Panthers, Jacksonville Univ. Dolphins, Stetson Univ. Hatters, Univ. of Central Florida Knights, Univ. of Florida Gators, Univ. of Miami Hurricanes, Univ. of South Florida Bulls
Professional teams, 27:
Baseball, 16—St. Petersburg Cardinals (FL State League, Class A), Al Lang Stadium; Baseball City Royals (FL State League, Class A), Baseball City Sports Complex; Winterhaven Red Sox (FL State League, Class A), Chain O'Lakes Park; Charlotte Rangers (FL State League, Class A), Charlotte County Stadium; Ft. Lauderdale Yankees (FL State League, Class A), City of Ft. Lauderdale Yankee Stadium; Dunedin Blue Jays (FL State League, Class A), Dunedin Stadium at Grant Field; Sarasota White Sox (FL State League, Class A), Ed Smith Stadium; Vero Beach Dodgers (FL State League, Class A), Holman Stadium; Clearwater Phillies (FL State League, Class A), Jack Russell Memorial Stadium; Lakeland Tigers (FL State League, Class A), Joker Marchant Stadium; Osceola Astros (FL State League, Class A), Osceola County Stadium; Miami Miracle (FL State League, Class A), Pompano Beach Municipal Stadium; St. Lucie Mets (FL State League, Class A), Thomas J. White Stadium; Orlando SunRays (Southern League, Class AA), Tinker Field; West Palm Beach Expos (FL State League, Class A), West Palm Beach Municipal Stadium; Jacksonville Suns (Southern League, Class AA), Wolfson Park
Basketball, 4—Florida Jades (World Basketball League), Florida Atlantic Univ. Gymnasium; Orlando Magic (NBA), Orlando Arena; Pensacola Tornados (Continental Basketball Association), Pensacola Civic Center; Miami Heat (NBA), The Miami Arena
Football, 3—Orlando Thunder (World League of American Football), Florida Citrus Bowl; Miami Dolphins (AFC), Joe Robbie Stadium; Tampa Bay Buccaneers (AFC), Tampa Stadium
Hockey, 1—Tampa Bay Lightning (NHL), to be announced
Soccer, 3—Ft. Lauderdale Strikers (American Professional Soccer League), Lockhart Stadium; Miami Freedom (American Professional Soccer League), Miami Orange Bowl; Tampa Bay Rowdies (American Professional Soccer League), Tampa Stadium

GEORGIA

"...the transportation, manufacturing, and marketing hub of the Deep South...the charm of the South as symbolized by Greek porticos, Doric columns, and romantic traditions. Here is a land where modern fortresses (Air Force bases) are not far from communities where sacred harp singing is still carried on...a land of forested mountains, deep lakes, and clear mountain streams, contrasted with miles of sunny beaches and sun-drenched isles, with still further contrast in the misty swamps where alligators splash and exotic tropical birds preen their elaborate plumage."

James E. (Jimmy) Carter

Today the commercial leader of its region, Georgia was the only colony to be founded as a refuge for poor and deserving people. Invented in Georgia, the cotton gin revolutionized the South. The state ranks first in the production of peanuts and pecans, lima beans, and pimiento peppers. It leads the nation in production of fine china clays. Savannah is the nation's foremost cotton port, and is often called "the nation's most beautiful city." Atlanta has become the leading transportation center of the Southeast, and in 1996 will host the Summer Olympics. Perhaps of more personal interest, Georgia gave Coca Cola to the world and Atlanta native Margaret Mitchell was the author of one of the world's best-known novels, *Gone with the Wind.*

Superlatives

• First steamship to cross the Atlantic, the *City of Savannah* sailed from Georgia

• Site of first U.S. gold rush at Dahlonga

• Home of the cotton gin

• First U.S. source of aluminum

Moments in History

• In 1540 the great expedition of Hernando de Soto entered present-day Georgia and may have spent a month at the site of Rome. The visit left a never-forgiven legacy of cruelty to the Indians.

• Beginning in 1565 Spaniard Pedro Menendez de Aviles established forts and missions.

• English and French pirates plagued the Spanish settlements beginning in 1670.

• The pirate Blackbeard made his headquarters on Blackbeard Island in 1716, becoming a de facto lord of the area.

• On February 12, 1733, James Oglethorpe arrived at present-day Savannah to claim and settle the land he called Georgia in honor of the King of England.

> **So They Say**
>
> The Georgia charter provided a grant for "...the land lying between the Savannah and Altamaha rivers and westward from the sources to the South Sea...for settling poor persons of London"

• Oglethorpe reached his colony on February 12, 1733. He and 125 colonists pitched their tents and next day founded the last of the original thirteen British colonies.

• In 1736 Oglethorpe arrived with a large group of colonists in "The Great Embarkation." They laid out the city, including the neat pattern of square parks that still distinguish Savannah.

• When the Spanish attempted to take the

colony, Oglethorpe's forces won the "Battle of Bloody Marsh," July 7, 1742. This small struggle has been called "one of the decisive battles of world history," because it kept the Spanish from pressing their claims northward on the coast.

• In 1752 Georgia became a crown colony.

• During the Revolution, on December 29, 1778, the British captured Savannah in a surprise attack.

• On July 11, 1782, Savannah was recaptured by American General Anthony Wayne, and the Revolution was over in Georgia.

• Georgia unanimously ratified the U.S. Constitution and became the fourth state on January 2, 1788.

• After the War of 1812, Georgia entered its "Golden Age of Prosperity."

• In 1838 the Indians remaining in Georgia were forced from their lands and sent West over the Trail of Tears, a great injustice to the tribes involved.

• On January 19, 1861, Georgia joined the Confederacy.

• During the Civil War one of the most important Union aims was to retake the state. After many unsuccessful efforts, Union General William Tecumseh Sherman, "marching through Georgia," captured and burned Atlanta and left almost complete destruction in his subsequent path to the sea, capturing Savannah on December 22, 1864.

• After a long, harsh Reconstruction period, Georgia was readmitted to the Union on July 15, 1870.

• More than 3,000 Georgia men volunteered to serve in the Spanish-American War in 1898.

• Although Atlanta suffered a disastrous fire in 1917, the area remained a major military training center during World War I.

• Georgia continued as a center of World War II activity, and the state drew world attention with the death of President F.D. Roosevelt at Warm Springs on April 12, 1945.

• Jimmy Carter was inaugurated in 1977, the first U.S. president from the state.

That's Interesting

• Rivalry between Indian tribes did not always lead to war. Some disputes between Cherokee and Creek groups were settled in favor of the winner of a ball game.

• In the 1740s, Mary Jones was the skillful and successful captain of Fort Wimberley during a Spanish attack.

• Youthful polio victim Franklin D. Roosevelt often visited and enjoyed the waters of Warm Springs. That small community gained world fame when he became President.

• The sculpture created by Gutzon Borglum on the side of Stone Mountain was so grand that Borglum once hosted twenty guests at breakfast on the shoulder of the Robert E. Lee carving. The work was later destroyed to make way for a smaller monument.

> **So They Say**
>
> "The only fitting memorial to the South of 1861-65 is (to carve) the great characters of those days, and in colossal proportions...in scale with the mountain."
>
> Gutzon Borglum, on his Stone Mountain memorial

• One of the famed incidents of the Civil War was later known as "The Great Locomotive Chase," when Confederate forces pursued and retook a captured locomotive.

Notable Natives

Asa Griggs Candler (near Villa Rica, 1851-1929), businessman/philanthropist. **Jimmy Carter** (Plains, 1924-), U.S. president. **Tyrus Raymond "Ty" Cobb** (Narrows, 1886-1961), baseball player. **John C. Fremont** (Savannah, 1813-1890), soldier. **Joel Chandler Harris** (Eatonton, 1848-1908), journalist/author. **Bobby Jones** (Atlanta, 1902-1971), golfer. **Martin Luther King, Jr.** (1929-1968), religious leader/social reformer. **Sidney Lanier** (Macon, 1842-1881), poet/critic. **Crawford Williamson Long** (Danielsville, 1815-1878), surgeon. **Margaret Mitchell** (Atlanta, 1900-1949), author. **Jack Roosevelt "Jackie" Robinson** (Cairo, 1919-1972), baseball player. **Alexander Hamilton Stephens** (Wilkes County, later Taliaferro County, 1812-1883), statesman

GENERAL

Admitted to statehood: Jan. 2, 1788
Origin of name: for King George II of England, by James Oglethorpe, colonial administator, 1732
Capital: Atlanta
Nicknames: The Empire State of the South and The Peach State
Motto: "Wisdom, Justice and Moderation"
Bird: brown thrasher
Fish: largemouth bass
Flower: Cherokee rose
Song: "Georgia on My Mind"
Tree: live oak

THE LAND

Area: 59,441 sq. mi., 24th
Land: 57,919 sq. mi., 21st
Water: 1,522 sq. mi., 24th
Topography: most southerly of the Blue Ridge Mtns. cover NE and N central, central Piedmont, extending to the fall line of rivers, coastal plain levels to the coast flatlands
Number of counties: 159
Geographic center: Twiggs, 18 mi. SE of Macon
Length: 300 mi.
Width: 230 mi.
Highest point: 4,784 ft., Brasstown Bald; 25th
Lowest point: sea level (Atlantic Ocean), 3rd
Mean elevation: 600 ft., 37th
Coastline: 100 mi., 16th
Shoreline: 2,344 mi., 12th

CLIMATE AND ENVIRONMENT

Temp., highest: 112 deg. on July 24, 1953, at Louisville; lowest: -17 deg. on Jan. 27, 1940, at CCC Camp F-16
Fresh water withdrawn, per capita, per day: 899 gal., 35th
Endangered species: mammals, 3—Gray bat, Indiana bat, West Indian manatee; birds, 3—American peregrine falcon, wood stock, red-cockaded woodpecker; reptiles, 3; amphibians, none; fishes, 2; invertebrates, none; plants, 12

MAJOR CITIES, POPULATION PERCENTAGE INCREASE (1980-90)

Albany, 78,122— –5.7%
Atlanta, 394,017— –7.29%
Columbus, 178,681— –5.45%
Macon, 106,612— –8.78%
Savannah, 137,560— –2.89%

THE PEOPLE

Population: 6,478,216, 11th
  Percent change (1980-90): 15.67%, 8th
  Per sq. mi: 108.99, 19th
  Percent in metro. area: 65.02%, 31st
  Percent foreign born: 2.7%, 29th
White: 4,600,148—71.01%, 44th
Black: 1,746,565—26.96%, 5th
Native American: 13,348—0.21%, 41st
Asian, Pacific Isle: 75,781—1.17%, 24th
Other races: 42,374—0.65%, 32nd
Hispanic origin: 108,922—1.68%, 33rd
Percent over 5 yrs. speaking language other than English at home: 4.8%, 39th
Percent males: 48.54%, 28th
Percent females: 51.46%, 24th
Percent never married: 26.2%, 22nd
Marriages per 1,000 (1989): 9.8, 23rd
Divorces per 1,000 (1989): 4.7, 24th
Median age: 31.6
Under 5 years: 495,535—7.65%, 14th
Under 18 years: 1,727,303—26.66%, 15th
65 years & older: 654,270—10.10%, 48th
Percent increase among the elderly: 26.6%, 19th

OF VITAL IMPORTANCE

Live births per 1,000 pop.: 17.6, 10th
Infant mortality rate per 1,000 births (1988): 12.6, 2nd
Average lifetime (1979-81): 72.22, 47th
Deaths per 100,000 pop. (1988): 814.0, 37th
Causes of death per 100,000 pop. (1988):
  Diseases of heart: 266.7, 38th
  Malignant neoplasms: 171.2, 42nd
  Cerebrovascular diseases: 63.7, 25th
  Accidents & adverse effects: 49.6, 9th

Chronic obstructive pulmonary diseases: 29, 43rd
Suicide: 13.4, 15th
HIV infection: 7.5, 6th
Other: 68.7, 39th

Keeping Well

Non-federal physicians per 100,000 pop.: 184, 37th
Dentists per 100,000 (1990-91): 50, 44th
Nurses per 100,000 (1989): 556, 38th
Hospitals per 100,000: 3.1, 24th
Admissions per 100,000: 15,274, 14th
Beds per 100,000: 535.35, 20th
Occupancy rate: 67.9%, 19th
Semiprivate room charges per day: $198, 48th
Average stay: 6.7, 37th
Notifiable diseases per 100,000:
AIDS: 18.9, 8th
Gonorrhea: 756.7, 2nd
Measles: 5.6, 19th
Syphillis: 142.2, 2nd
Tuberculosis (TB): 12.3, 12th
Per capita spending on mental health programs (1987): $35.83, 26th
Pop. without health insur. (1991): 14.1%, 18th

Households by Type

Total households: 2,366,615
Percent change (1980-90): 26.42%, 6th
Family households: 1,713,072
Percent of total: 72.38%, 12th
Nonfamily households: 653,543
Percent of total: 27.62%, 40th
Persons per household: 2.66, 14th
Pop. living in group quarters: 173,633
Percent of pop.: 2.68%, 29th

Living Quarters

Total housing units: 2,638,418
Persons per unit: 2.46, 14th
Occupied housing units: 2,366,615
Percent of total units: 89.70%, 24th
Persons per unit: 2.63, 11th
Percent of units with over 1 person per room: 4.05%, 16th
Owner-occupied units: 1,536,759
Percent of total units: 58.25%, 30th
Percent of occupied units: 64.93%, 37th
Persons per unit: 2.76, 20th
Median value: $71,300, 23rd
Renter-occupied units: 829,856
Percent of total units: 31.45%, 17th
Percent of occupied units: 35.07%, 17th
Persons per unit: 2.49, 10th
Median contract rent: $344, 23rd
Rental vacancy rate: 12.2%, 7th
Mobile home, trailer & other as a % of occupied housing units: 13.85%, 18th

Crime Index per 100,000

Total: 6,764, 5th
Violent: 756, 12th
Murder and nonnegligent manslaughter: 12, 7th
Aggravated assault: 7,649, 15th
Robbery: 263, 9th
Rape: 54, 7th
Property: 6,007, 5th
Burglary: 1,619, 6th
Larceny, theft: 3,714, 10th
Motor vehicle theft: 674, 13th
Drug abuse arrests: 272, 22nd

Teaching and Learning

Literacy (1987): 86%, 33rd
Pop. 3 and over enrolled in school: 1,643,859
Percent of pop.: 26.6%, 32nd
Public elementary & secondary schools:
Total enrollment: 1,173,000
Avg. class size (1987): 25, 7th
Teachers: 66,500
Percent of pop.: 1.03%, 23rd
Teachers' avg. salary: $27,900, 30th
Spending per capita: $796, 27th
Spending per pupil in avg. daily attendance: $4,456, 28th
Percent of graduates taking SAT: 62%, 12th
Combined SAT scores: 844, 48th
Percent of pop. over 25 completing:
High school: 70.9%, 42nd
College degree/s: 19.3%, 26th
Higher educa., institutions: 95

Per 100,000 pop.: 0.8, 21st
Enroll: 251,810
Percent of pop.: 3.89%, 50th
Public: 196,413
Percent of enroll.: 78.00%, 35th
Private: 55,397
Percent of enroll.: 22.00%, 17th
White non-Hispanic: 140,865
Percent of enroll.: 81.32%, 33rd
Black non-Hispanic: 11,816
Percent of enroll.: 6.82%, 22nd
Hispanic: 2,635
Percent of enroll.: 1.52%, 28th
Asian/Pacific Islander: 2,904
Percent of enroll.: 1.68%, 25th
Amer. Indian/AK native: 9,609
Percent of enroll.: 5.55%, 4th
Nonresident alien: 5,392
Percent of enroll.: 3.11%, 11th
Female: 137,197
Percent of enroll.: 54.48%, 33rd
Tuition, state university ('90-'91): $1,680, 28th
Public library systems: 53
Books & serial vol. per capita: 1.70, 46th
Govt. expend. per capita: $8.13, 47th
State govt.: $6.68, 3rd
Local govts.: $1.45, 50th

LAW ENFORCEMENT, COURTS, AND PRISONS

Police protection expend.: $656,059,000
Per capita: $101.27, 28th
Judicial & legal expend.: $238,502,000
Per capita: $36.82, 37th
Corrections expend.: $681,289,000
Per capita: $105.17, 13th
Police per 10,000 pop. (1990-91): 26.3, 5th
Prisoners (state & fed.) sentenced to over 1 yr., per 100,000 pop.: 327
Percent change (1989-90): 10.12%, 11th
Death penalty: yes, by electrocution
Under sentence of death: 102, 6th
Executed (1989): 1

RELIGION, NUMBER AND PERCENT OF POPULATION

Agnostic: 14,253—0.30%, 37th
Buddhist: 4,751—0.10%, 17th
Christian: 4,328,082—91.10%, 7th
Hindu: 9,502—0.20%, 3rd
Jewish: 23,755—0.50%, 27th
Moslem: 14,253—0.30%, 9th
Unitarian: 4,751—0.10%, 31st
Other: 66,513—1.40%, 20th
None: 218,542—4.60%, 43rd
Refused to answer: 66,513—1.40%, 44th

MAKING A LIVING

Personal income per capita (1989): $13,631, 22nd
Percent increase (1979-'89) (constant 1989 dollars): 27.5%, 10th
Average income per family: $41,539, 22nd
Percent of pop. below poverty level: 14.7%, 16th
Percent 65 and over: 20.4%, 8th
Cost of living, selected cities
1st qtr., 1991 (U. S. Standard=100)
Moultrie 88.3
Savannah 96.3
Atlanta 100.9

ECONOMY

Civilian labor force : 3,216,000
Percent of tot. pop.: 49.64%, 31st
Percent 65 and over: 2.08%, 42nd
Percent females: 46.61%, 11th
Percent job growth (1980-90): 36.84%, 5th
Major employer industries:
Agriculture: 76,025—2.50%, 28th
Construction: 124,681—4.10%, 31st
Finance, insurance & real estate: 179,419—5.90%, 17th
Government: 477,437—15.70%, 23rd
Manufacturing: 577,790—19.00%, 17th
Mining: 8,890—0.3%, 27th
Service: 574,749—18.90%, 34th
Trade: 574,749—18.90%, 23rd
Transportation, communication, & public utilities: 209,829—6.90%, 3rd
Wholesale/retail: 665,699—21.5%, 25th

Unemployment rate: 5.44%, 24th
Male: 2.67%, 36th
Female: 2.77%, 12th
Total businesses (1991): 191,583
New business incorp's. (1991): 18,098
Percent of total businesses: 9.45%, 8th
Business failures (1991): 3,367
Percent of total businesses: 1.76%, 2nd
Agriculture farm income
Marketing (1991): $3,978,361,000, 13th
Net per operation: $31,979, 12th
Net per acre: $122, 10th
Leading products: broilers, peanuts, eggs, cattle
Av. value land & build. per acre: $1,053, 19th
Percent increase (1980-90): 17.52%, 14th
Govt. payments: $97,675,000, 23rd
Construction, value of all: $4,730,000,000
Per capita: $730.14, 16th
Percent change 1989-90: -19.09%, 36th
Manufactures:
Value added: : $36,423,000,000
Per capita: $5,622.38, 18th
Value of shipments: $83,997,000,000
Per capita: $12,966.07, 17th
Leading products: (1990): textiles, apparel, food, transportation equipment, printing and publishing
Mining, min. prod., value (1987): $1,193,000,000, 25th
Leading products: clays, stone, cement
Retail sales: $46,748,000,000, 12th
Per household: $19,417, 22nd
Percent increase (1987-90): 6.5%, 47th
Service indust., value (1987): $25,775,000,000, 12th
Per capita: $3,978.72, 24th
Tourism indus., value (1989): $7,054,000,000, 11th
Foreign exports value: $5,763,000,000, 15th
Per capita: $889.60, 26th
Patents per 1,000 pop.: 9.0, 16th

Travel and Transportation

Motor vehicle registrations: 5,489,144
Per 1,000 pop.: 847, 16th
Motorcycle registrations: 74,463
Per 1,000 pop.: 11, 37th
Licensed drivers per 1,000 driving age pop.: 919, 15th
Deaths from motor vehicle accidents per 100,000 pop.: 24.1, 12th
Public roads & streets
Total mileage: 109,601, 14th
Rural mileage: 87,873, 12th
Urban mileage: 21,728, 10th
Interstate mileage: 1,245, 8th
Annual vehicle-miles of travel per person: 11,229, 2nd
Mean travel time for workers 16 + who work away from home: 22.7 min., 9th

Government

Registered voters (1988): 2,934,487
Percent of voting age pop.: 62.90%, 43rd
Voter turnout (1988): 1,809,672
Percent of registered voters: 61.67%, 45th
Percent of voting age pop.: 38.79%, 51st
State legislators, total (1992): 236, 3rd
Women members (1992): 34
Percent of legislature: 14.4%, 34th
Dominant party (1992): Democrats
U. S. Congress, House members (1993): 11
Increase 1983-93: +1
Revenues:
State govt.: $13,107,914,000
Per capita: $2,023.38, 43rd
State & local govt.: $24,059,769,000
Per capita: $3,713.95, 30th
Indebtedness:
State govt.: $3,117,366,000
Per capita: $481.21, 47th
State & local govt.: $17,397,000,000
Per capita: $2,685.46, 38th

Laws and Regulations

Legal driving age: 21
Marriage age without parental consent: 16
Divorce residence requirement: 6 mo.

Attractions

Major opera companies (1989): 2, 21st
Per 1 million pop.: 0.31, 42nd
Major symphony orchestras (1989): 16, 19th
Per 1 million pop.: 2.49, 42nd

State appropriations for state arts agencies per capita: $0.53, 33rd

Sports and Competition

NCAA sports teams, 8: Augusta College Jaguars, Emory Univ., Georgia Southern College Eagles, Georgia State Univ. Crimson Panthers, Georgia Tech Yellow Jackets, Mercer Univ. Bears, Morris Brown College Wolverines, Univ. of Georgia Bulldogs.

Professional teams, 5:

Baseball, 3—Atlanta Braves (NL), Atlanta-Fulton County Stadium; Savannah Cardinals (South Atlantic League, Class A), Grayson Stadium; Augusta Pirates (South Atlantic League, Class A), Heaton Stadium

Basketball, 1—Atlanta Hawks (NBA), The Omni

Football, 1—Atlanta Falcons (NFC), Atlanta-Fulton county Stadium

HAWAII

"The loveliest fleet of islands that lies anchored in any ocean....No other land could so longingly and bewitchingly haunt me, sleeping and waking, through half a lifetime, as that one has done."

Mark Twain

In some ways Hawaii is the nation's most unusual state. "Hawaii rests like a water lily on the swelling bosom of the Pacific," as the first king described his realm. It is the only state ever governed directly by monarchs who were recognized by international law. The nation's only island state, it forms the world's longest island chain. The climate in the only tropical state "sweetens one's bones," as Robert Louis Stevenson described it. Consequently the language of Hawaii has no word for weather. Stupendous Waimea Canyon rivals that of the Colorado River. The island chain was the home of unique prehistoric peoples who left mysterious evidence of their culture. They were followed by native peoples noted for their traditional wisdom, strength, bravery, and loyalty. In its "...most fortunate location," Hawaii is master of the Pacific.

SUPERLATIVES

- World's most active volcano—the crater of Kilauea on Mauna Loa.
- World's bulkiest mountain—Mauna Loa.
- "The wettest place on earth"—Mt. Waialeale.
- Only state with an official native language.
- King Kalakakaua was the first reigning monarch ever to visit the United States.
- World's most diverse population mix.
- Leader in pineapple production.

MOMENTS IN HISTORY

- As early as 500 B.C., expert navigators arrived in present-day Hawaii in their double-hulled canoes, bringing evidence of their Indo-Malay culture.
- In 1778 native Hawaiians were astonished to see two "floating islands" carrying strange white-skinned men. Captain James Cook had arrived at Kauai, and he named the archipelago the "Sandwich Islands."
- On the Big Island (Hawaii) Cook was killed in 1789 in revenge for the many injustices he and his men had committed against the islanders.
- In 1795 King Kamehameha I conquered Oahu and soon extended his rule across the islands, acquiring the title of "The Great."
- The first American missionaries arrived in 1820 aboard the *Thaddeus*, in a move that was to transform the islands.

> **So They Say**
>
> "It is no small thing to say of the missionaries...that in less than 40 years they have taught this whole people to read and to write, to cipher, and to sew. They have given them an alphabet, grammar, and dictionary, preserved their language...given it a literature, and translated into it the Bible and works of devotion, science, and entertainment, etc...."
>
> Richard Henry Dana

- During the reign of Kamehameha II, the feudal system was changed into a constitutional monarchy in 1840.

• The new constitution of 1852 created a two-house legislature and courts of law. Religious freedom was guaranteed.

So They Say

"This is a blessed country....There is not a locked door in Hilo, and nobody makes anybody else afraid....I never saw such healthy bright complexions...or such sparkling smiles....The population at Cook's time may have been 300,000 in 1779. In 1872 it was only 49,000. It is a pity the race is dying out. It has shown a singular aptitude for politics and civilization."

British travel writer Isabella Bird, describing the Hawaii of the 1870s

• Queen Liliuokalani, the last Hawaiian monarch, was overthrown and a temporary republic set up in 1893.

• In 1898, the Hawaiian republic transferred sovereignty to the United States by a treaty accepted on both sides.

• In 1900 Hawaii became a U.S. territory, with all residents U.S. citizens.

• In 1903 the first Hawaiian pineapple was packed, and the islands' commerce increased so rapidly that many Asian immigrants were brought in as workers.

• Beginning in 1917, World War I brought many Hawaiians into service.

• Hawaiian isolation became a thing of the past after the first flight arrived from the mainland in 1927, and radio-telephone communication came in 1931.

• During the 1930s Hawaii felt little effect of the Great Depression, due partly to the enormous military buildup.

• The Japanese bombing of Pearl Harbor on December 7, 1941, was a "day of infamy" never to be forgotten. Hawaii then became the principal Pacific fortress of the war, the greatest arsenal the world had ever known.

• The eruption of Mauna Loa in 1950 proved to be one of the largest in historic times.

• The first proposal for Hawaiian statehood was made during the time of Kamehameha II. That finally occurred on August 21, 1959, and the United States had its 50th state.

• The 1990 census revealed that Hawaii's population had increased almost 15% in the past decade. The population is composed of perhaps the world's greatest racial and ethnic mixture, with more than 60 different racial combinations, all living together in harmony.

That's Interesting

• As many as 100 people often crowded into a single Polynesian double-hulled canoe as the seaworthy ships sailed the thousands of stormy ocean miles from the South Pacific to populate Hawaii.

• When the Hawaiians killed Captain Cook, they prepared his body as they would have their own great chief, removing the flesh from the bones before burial.

• In 1825 Hawaii chiefess Kapiolani defied the volcano goddess Pele and ate the sacred ohelo berries to prove that the old religion was no longer effective.

• Hawaiian kings were noted for their great size and strength. Kamehamha I once moved a 4,500 pound stone. His Queen, Kaahumanu, weighed 300 pounds.

• The Robinson family, owners of the Island of Niihau, have for years done everything in their power to preserve the ways of early Hawaii, making the island an off-limits place of mystery.

Notable Natives

Sanford Ballard Dole (Honolulu, 1844-1926), public official. **Don Ho** (Kakaaho, Oahu, 1922-), singer. **Daniel K. Inouye** (Honolulu, 1924-), public official. **Kamehameha I** (Hawaii Island, 1738-1819), King of Hawaii. **Kamehameha II** (Hawaii Island, 1797-1824), King of Hawaii. **Kamehameha III** (Oahu, 1814-1854), King of Hawaii. **Kamehameha IV** (Oahu, 1834-1863), King of Hawaii. **Kamehameha V** (Oahu,1831-1872), King of Hawaii. **Lilioukalani** (Oahu, 1838-1917), Queen of Hawaii.

General

Admitted to statehood: Aug. 21, 1959
Origin of name: Possibly derived from native word for homeland, *Hawaiki* or *Owyhyhee*
Capital: Honolulu
Nickname: Aloha State
Motto: *"Ua Mau Ke Ea O Ka Aina I Ka Pono"* ("The Life of the Land Is Perpetuated in Righteousness")
Bird: Hawaiian goose *(Nene)*
Flower: red hibiscus
Song: *"Hawaii Ponoi"*
Tree: candlenut *(Kukui)*

The Land

Area: 10,932 sq. mi., 43rd
Land: 6,423 sq. mi., 47th
Water: 4,508 sq. mi., 13th
Topography: Islands are the tops of a chain of submerged volcanic mountains, active volcanoes Mauna Loa, Kilauea
Number of counties: 5
Geographic center: Hawaii, 20"15'N, 156"20'W, off Maui Island
Highest point: 13,796 ft. (Mauna Kea), 6th
Lowest point: sea level (Pacific Ocean), 3rd
Mean elevation: 3,030 ft., 10th
Coastline: 750 mi., 4th
Shoreline: 1,052 mi., 17th

Climate and Environment

Temp., highest: 100 deg. on April 27, 1931, at Pahala; lowest: 12 deg. on May 17, 1979, at Mauna Kea
Fresh water withdrawn, per capita, per day: 1,100 gal., 31st
Endangered species: mammals, 1—Hawaiian hoary bat; birds, 29—Hawaii 'akepa, Maui 'akepa, Kauai 'akialoa, 'akiapolaau, Hawaiian coot, Hawaiian creeper, Molokai creeper, Oahu creeper, Hawaiian crow, Hawaiian duck, Laysan duck, Laysan finch, Nihoa finch, Hawaiian goose, Hawaiian hawk, crested honeycreeper, Nihoa millerbird, Hawaiian common moorhen, Nukupu'u, Kauai 'o'o, Hawaiian 'o'u, Palila, Maui parrotbill, Hawaiian dark-rumped petrel, Po'ouli, Hawaiian stilt, large Kauai thrush, Molokai thrush, small Kauai thrush; reptiles, 2; amphibians, none; fishes, none; invertebrates, 1; plants, 19

Major Cities, Population Percentage Increase (1980-90)

Hilo, 37,800—7.18%
Honolulu, 365,272—0.06%
Kailua, 36,818—2.81%
Kaneohe, 35,448—18.48%
Pearl City, 30,993— -27.20%

The People

Population: 1,108,229, 41st
Percent change (1980-90): 12.95%, 13th
Per sq. mi: 101.37, 21st
Percent in metro. area: 75.44%, 20th
Percent foreign born: 14.7%, 3rd
White: 369,616—33.35%, 50th
Black: 27,195—2.45%, 38th
Native American: 5,099—0.46%, 24th
Asian, Pacific Isle: 685,236—61.83%, 1st
Other races: 21,083—1.90%, 19th
Hispanic origin: 81,390—7.34%, 11th
Percent over 5 yrs. speaking language other than English at home: 24.8%, 4th
Percent males: 50.88%, 3rd
Percent females: 49.12%, 49th
Percent never married: 29.8%, 5th
Marriages per 1,000 (1989): 16.2, 2nd
Divorces per 1,000 (1989): 5.1, 16th
Median age: 32.6
Under 5 years: 83,223—7.51%, 21st
Under 18 years: 280,126—25.28%, 33rd
65 years & older: 125,005—11.28%, 38th
Percent increase among the elderly: 64.2%, 3rd

Of Vital Importance

Live births per 1,000 pop.: 18.1, 8th
Infant mortality rate per 1,000 births (1988): 7.2, 50th
Average lifetime (1979-81): 77.02, 1st
Deaths per 100,000 pop. (1988): 553.3, 49th
Causes of death per 100,000 pop. (1988):
Diseases of heart: 167.3, 50th

Malignant neoplasms: 139.3, 48th
Cerebrovascular diseases: 39.2, 50th
Accidents & adverse effects: 28.7, 50th
Chronic obstructive pulmonary diseases: 17.5, 50th
Suicide: 7.9, 48th
HIV infection: 5.6, 10th
Other: 45.2, 50th

KEEPING WELL

Non-federal physicians per 100,000 pop.: 253, 11th
Dentists per 100,000 (1990-91): 87, 4th
Nurses per 100,000 (1989): 533, 40th
Hospitals per 100,000: 2.4, 37th
Admissions per 100,000: 10,666, 50th
Beds per 100,000: 369.33, 44th
Occupancy rate: 83.0%, 2nd
Semiprivate room charges per day: $348, 9th
Average stay: 8.5, 12th
Notifiable diseases per 100,000:
AIDS: 14.1, 11th
Gonorrhea: 54.5, 41st
Measles: 3.7, 28th
Syphillis: 3.0, 42nd
Tuberculosis (TB): 17.7, 3rd
Per capita spending on mental health programs (1987): $24.68, 43rd
Pop. without health insur. (1991): 7.0%, 51st

HOUSEHOLDS BY TYPE

Total households: 356,267
Percent change (1980-90): 21.18%, 13th
Family households: 263,456
Percent of total: 73.95%, 3rd
Nonfamily households: 92,811
Percent of total: 26.05%, 49th
Persons per household: 3.01, 2nd
Pop. living in group quarters: 37,632
Percent of pop.: 3.40%, 9th

LIVING QUARTERS

Total housing units: 389,810
Persons per unit: 2.84, 2nd
Occupied housing units: 356,267
Percent of total units: 91.40%, 14th
Persons per unit: 2.99, 2nd
Percent of units with over 1 person per room: 15.92%, 1st
Owner-occupied units: 191,911
Percent of total units: 49.23%, 47th
Percent of occupied units: 53.87%, 49th
Persons per unit: 3.19, 2nd
Median value: $245,300, 1st
Renter-occupied units: 164,356
Percent of total units: 42.16%, 3rd
Percent of occupied units: 46.13%, 3rd
Persons per unit: 2.78, 1st
Median contract rent: $599, 1st
Rental vacancy rate: 5.4%, 48th
Mobile home, trailer & other as a % of occupied housing units: 1.71%, 50th

CRIME INDEX PER 100,000

Total: 6,107, 11th
Violent: 281, 42nd
Murder and nonnegligent manslaughter: 4, 39th
Aggravated assault: 7,510, 22nd
Robbery: 91, 35th
Rape: 32, 34th
Property: 5,826, 7th
Burglary: 1,228, 17th
Larceny, theft: 4,217, 6th
Motor vehicle theft: 381, 30th
Drug abuse arrests: 325, 15th

TEACHING AND LEARNING

Literacy (1987): 85%, 40th
Pop. 3 and over enrolled in school: 290,578
Percent of pop.: 27.4%, 23rd
Public elementary & secondary schools:
Total enrollment: 179,000
Avg. class size (1987): 26, 3rd
Teachers: 9,300
Percent of pop.: 0.84%, 46th
Teachers' avg. salary: $32,000, 15th
Spending per capita: $710, 38th
Spending per pupil in avg. daily attendance: $4,504, 27th
Percent of graduates taking SAT: 55%, 18th
Combined SAT scores: 883, 40th
Percent of pop. over 25 completing:
High school: 80.1%, 13th
College degree/s: 22.9%, 13th
Higher educa., institutions: 15

Per 100,000 pop.: 0.8, 20th
Enroll: 53,772
Percent of pop.: 4.85%, 39th
Public: 43,064
Percent of enroll.: 80.09%, 31st
Private: 10,708
Percent of enroll.: 19.91%, 21st
White non-Hispanic: 34,380
Percent of enroll.: 90.77%, 13th
Black non-Hispanic: 246
Percent of enroll.: 0.65%, 47th
Hispanic: 195
Percent of enroll.: 0.51%, 44th
Asian/Pacific Islander: 285
Percent of enroll.: 0.75%, 45th
Amer. Indian/AK native: 1,616
Percent of enroll.: 4.27%, 6th
Nonresident alien: 1,156
Percent of enroll.: 3.05%, 12th
Female: 28,640
Percent of enroll.: 53.26%, 42nd
Tuition, state university ('90-'91): $1,290, 44th
Public library systems: 1
Books & serial vol. per capita: 2.15, 34th
Govt. expend. per capita: $19.81, 16th
State govt.: $19.44, 1st
Local govts.: $0.38, 51st

LAW ENFORCEMENT, COURTS, AND PRISONS

Police protection expend.: $137,656,000
Per capita: $124.24, 16th
Judicial & legal expend.: $111,489,000
Per capita: $100.62, 3rd
Corrections expend.: $80,117,000
Per capita: $72.31, 27th
Police per 10,000 pop. (1990-91): 23.8, 9th
Prisoners (state & fed.) sentenced to over 1 yr., per 100,000 pop.: 150
Percent change (1989-90): -2.51%, 49th
Death penalty: no

RELIGION, NUMBER AND PERCENT OF POPULATION

Agnostic: NA
Buddhist: NA
Christian: NA
Hindu: NA
Jewish: NA
Moslem: NA
Unitarian: NA
Other: NA
None: NA
Refused to answer: NA

MAKING A LIVING

Personal income per capita (1989): $15,770, 11th
Percent increase (1979-'89) (constant 1989 dollars): 21.6%, 15th
Average income per family: $52,363, 7th
Percent of pop. below poverty level: 8.3%, 48th
Percent 65 and over: 8.0%, 48th
Cost of living, selected cities
1st qtr., 1991 (U. S. Standard=100)
Hilo 135.4

ECONOMY

Civilian labor force : 539,000
Percent of tot. pop.: 48.64%, 40th
Percent 65 and over: 3.53%, 8th
Percent females: 48.05%, 2nd
Percent job growth (1980-90): 25.55%, 18th
Major employer industries:
Agriculture: 18,340—3.50%, 15th
Construction: 33,536—6.40%, 3rd
Finance, insurance & real estate: 33,012—6.30%, 14th
Government: 102,704—19.60%, 8th
Manufacturing: 26,200—5.00%, 47th
Mining: 323—0.1%, 40th
Service: 123,140—23.50%, 6th
Trade: 106,372—20.30%, 6th
Transportation, communication, & public utilities: 34,060—6.50%, 8th
Wholesale/retail: 121,627—23.0%, 3rd
Unemployment rate: 2.78%, 50th
Male: 1.67%, 50th
Female: 1.11%, 50th
Total businesses (1991): 31,188
New business incorp's. (1991): 3,792
Percent of total businesses: 12.16%, 4th
Business failures (1991): 72
Percent of total businesses: 0.23%, 50th
Agriculture farm income
Marketing (1991): $596,925,000, 41st
Net per operation: $16,455, 31st

Net per acre: $44, 30th
Leading products: Sugar, pineapples, greenhouse, macadamia nuts
Av. value land & build. per acre: NA
Percent increase (1980-90): NA
Govt. payments: $906,000, 49th
Construction, value of all: $2,116,000,000
Per capita: $1,909.35, 1st
Percent change 1989-90: 18.68%, 9th
Manufactures:
Value added: : $1,558,000,000
Per capita: $1,405.85, 50th
Value of shipments: $4,203,000,000
Per capita: $3,792.54, 48th
Leading products: sugar, canned pineapple, clothing, foods, printing and publishing
Mining, min. prod., value (1987): $31,000,000, 47th
Leading products: stone, cement, sand/gravel
Retail sales: $11,204,000,000, 35th
Per household: $31,121, 1st
Percent increase (1987-90): 29.4%, 2nd
Service indust., value (1987): $6,124,000,000, 34th
Per capita: $5,525.93, 8th
Tourism indus., value (1989): $5,492,000,000, 16th
Foreign exports value: $179,000,000, 51st
Per capita: $161.52, 51st
Patents per 1,000 pop.: 13.2, 5th

Travel and Transportation

Motor vehicle registrations: 771,478
Per 1,000 pop.: 696, 43rd
Motorcycle registrations: 20,424
Per 1,000 pop.: 18, 24th
Licensed drivers per 1,000 driving age pop.: 797, 49th
Deaths from motor vehicle accidents per 100,000 pop.: 16.0, 36th
Public roads & streets
Total mileage: 4,099, 50th
Rural mileage: 2,587, 49th
Urban mileage: 1,512, 49th
Interstate mileage: 43, 49th
Annual vehicle-miles of travel per person: 7,278, 46th
Mean travel time for workers 16 + who work away from home: 23.8 min., 8th

Government

Registered voters (1988): 443,742
Percent of voting age pop.: 53.85%, 49th
Voter turnout (1988): 354,461
Percent of registered voters: 79.88%, 4th
Percent of voting age pop.: 43.02%, 48th
State legislators, total (1992): 76, 46th
Women members (1992): 21
Percent of legislature: 27.6%, 8th
Dominant party (1992): Democrats
U. S. Congress, House members (1993): 2
Increase 1983-93: 0
Revenues:
State govt.: $4,325,531,000
Per capita: $3,903.10, 3rd
State & local govt.: $5,661,258,000
Per capita: $5,108.38, 5th
Indebtedness:
State govt.: $3,395,949,000
Per capita: $3,064.30, 6th
State & local govt.: $4,429,000,000
Per capita: $3,996.47, 16th

Laws and Regulations

Legal driving age: 18
Marriage age without parental consent: 18
Divorce residence requirement: 6 mo., qualification—check local statutes

Attractions

Major opera companies (1989): 1, 30th
Per 1 million pop.: 0.90, 11th
Major symphony orchestras (1989): 2, 48th
Per 1 million pop.: 1.80, 49th
State appropriations for state arts agencies per capita: $7.92, 1st
State Fair in late May to mid-June at Honolulu

Sports and Competition

NCAA sports teams, 1: Univ. of Hawaii Rainbows.
Professional teams: none

IDAHO

Dice 'em, hash 'em, boil 'em, mash 'em! Idaho, Idaho, Idaho!

An Idaho football cheer

Idaho is a land of dramatic natural features, with towering, snow-capped mountain ranges, swirling white rapids, deep canyons, and peaceful lakes ranked among the world's most beautiful. The Snake River rushes through Hell's Canyon, which is deeper than the Grand Canyon. Shoshone Falls on the Snake River are higher than Niagara Falls. Known the world around for its potatoes, the state also possesses vast and unique mineral and forest reserves. Idahoans believe that they live in a state where life is unmatched for serenity and harmony.

SUPERLATIVES

- The tiny Malad River is said to be the shortest river in the world.
- Largest prehistoric art work in the United States is near Nampa.
- World's largest stands of white pine.
- World's largest reserves of phosphate.
- First in silver production.
- Two-thirds of all U.S. processed potatoes produced in Idaho.

MOMENTS IN HISTORY

- The great exploration of Lewis and Clark provided the first record of the area as the explorers crossed the present-day state in 1805.
- Waiting for the snows to melt on their way home in 1806, Lewis and Clark performed many kindnesses to the Indians.
- Representing the Hudson Bay Company, noted explorer David Thompson set up the first trading post in present-day Idaho in 1809, Kullyspell House on Pend Oreille Lake.

So They Say

"...after brakfast I began to administer eye water and in a few minits had near 40 applicants with sore eyes and maney others with other complaints most common rhumatic disorders & weaknesses in the back and loins perticularly the womin."

William Clark

- In 1810 Andrew Henry built Fort Henry, the first American trading post in the Pacific Northwest, but the post was later abandoned.
- In 1818-1819 Donald Mackenzie firmly established the Idaho fur trade and began a great annual fur rendezvous, attracting some of the most rowdy gatherings of the West.

So They Say

"I have again to repeat to you the advice which I before gave you not to come with a small party to the American rendezvous. There are here a great collection of scoundrels."

Nathaniel Wyeth

- Fort Hall on the Snake River was built by Nathaniel Wyeth in 1834 and sold two years later to Dr. John McLaughlin, "ruler" of the Hudson Bay Company in the region.
- In 1834 the first missionaries arrived, and the Rev. Jason Lee conducted at Fort Hall the first Christian religious service in present-day Idaho.

• The Rev. and Mrs. Henry H. Spalding established Lapwai Mission in Nez Perce country near Lewiston in 1836, and he served his Indian congregation until his death in 1874.

• By the mid-1840s a stream of settlers was crossing over the Oregon trail, and many turned off to settle in present-day Idaho.

• Beginning in 1849, more thousands crossed the region on their way to California gold.

• Indian wars followed until 1855, when the tribes agreed to move to other tracts.

• Franklin, the first permanent European-style town in Idaho, was founded by the Mormons on April 14, 1860.

• Also in 1860 gold discoveries led to a boom, and the town that sprang up at the site was named for E.D. Pierce, a pioneer gold prospector.

• On June 17, 1877, the long-time friendship of the Nez Perce with the whites ended in the Battle of White Bird Canyon, during which the government forces lost a third of their men.

• Then, under the superb leadership of Chief Joseph, the Nez Perce tribe began its bitter flight from its ancestral lands.

• With the defeat of the Sheepeater tribe in 1879, Indian wars ended in Idaho.

• The 1870s brought rich gold strikes.

• Even greater was the strike of 1883 in silver, lead, and zinc in the Coeur d' Alene district.

• Idaho became a state on July 3, 1890.

• The miners' strike of 1899 was particularly bitter.

• In December, 1905, Frank Steunenberg, governor at the time of the miners' strike, was killed in a bomb explosion, and his murder trial gained international prominence.

• Craters of the Moon National Monument became a reality in 1924.

• Development of Sun Valley began in 1936.

• During World War II, the mammoth naval training base of Farragut Park was one of the principal centers of its kind.

• The world's first usable atomic-powered electricity was generated in 1951 at the National Reactor Testing Station.

• More than 460 miles from the sea, remote inland Lewiston became an "ocean port" with the opening of the Snake River Navigation Project in 1975.

• The collapse of the Teton Dam in June 1976 caused vast property damage, particularly to the cattle industry.

• The grasshopper infestation of 1985 devasted farmlands already hard hit by depressed agriculture.

That's Interesting

• Thirsty travelers on the brink of Hell's Canyon could look down on the waters of the Snake River but had no way to get down to drink.

• Wood River is known as the "Upside Down River." At one place it flows through a gorge 4 ft. wide and 104 ft. deep. At another point the gorge is 104 ft. wide and the river 4 ft. deep.

• A pioneer family of Palouse country once gave an Indian family a meal. From that time on the pioneer family found a large salmon left at their door at the same time each year.

• During the gold boom in the early 1860s, Idaho City was a large rip-roaring boom town, where crime and "frontier justice" ran rampant. Of the 200 people buried in the pioneer cemetery of Idaho City, only 28 died of natural causes.

• A unique Idaho attraction is Thousand Springs. Each spring spouts out from the side of a single cliff.

• The eruption of Mt. St. Helens in Washington State brought great clouds of ash to Idaho, and the Palouse crop the next year increased 30%.

Idaho Notables

William Borah (Fairfield, IL, 1865-1940), public official/political leader. **William "Big Bill" Haywood** (Salt Lake City, UT, 1869-1928), labor leader. **Chief Joseph** (Wallowa Valley? 1840?-1904), Indian leader. **Ezra Pound** (Hailey, 1885-1972), poet. **Sacajawea** (eastern Idaho? 1787?-1812?), Indian guide.

General

Admitted to statehood: July 3, 1890

Origin of name: a combined name with an invented Indian meaning: "gem of the mountains"; originally suggested for the Pike's Peak mining territory (Colorado), then applied to the new mining territory of the Pacific Northwest; another theory suggests Idaho may be a Kiowa Apache term for the Comanche

Capital: Boise
Nickname: Gem State
Motto: *"Esto Perpetua"* ("It Is Perpetual")
Bird: mountain bluebird
Flower: syringa
Gemstone: star garnet
Song: "Here We Have Idaho"
Tree: white pine

THE LAND

Area: 83,574 sq. mi., 14th
Land: 82,751 sq. mi., 11th
Water: 823 sq. mi., 33rd
Topography: Snake River plains in the S; central region of mountains, canyons, gorges (Hell's Canyon 7,900 ft., deepest in N.A.); subalpine N region
Number of counties: 44
Geographic center: Custer, SW of Challis
Length: 570 mi.
Width: 300 mi.
Highest point: 12,662 ft. (Borah Peak), 11th
Lowest point: 710 ft. (Snake River), 44th
Mean elevation: 5,000 ft., 6th

CLIMATE AND ENVIRONMENT

Temp., highest: 118 deg. on July 28, 1934, at Orofino; lowest: -60 deg. on Jan. 16, 1943, at Island Park Dam
Fresh water withdrawn, per capita, per day: 22,200 gal., 1st
Endangered species: mammals, 2—woodland caribou, Northern Rocky Mountain gray wolf; birds, 2—whooping crane, American peregrine falcon; reptiles, none; amphibians, none; fishes, none; invertebrates, none; plants, 1

MAJOR CITIES, POPULATION PERCENTAGE INCREASE (1980-90)

Boise, 125,738—22.97%
Idaho Falls, 43,929—10.54%
Lewiston, 28,082—0.34%
Nampa, 28,365—12.95%
Pocatello, 46,080— -0.56%

THE PEOPLE

Population: 1,006,749, 42nd
Percent change (1980-90): 6.22%, 23rd
Per sq. mi: 12.05, 45th
Percent in metro. area: 20.46%, 51st
Percent foreign born: 2.9%, 28th
White: 950,451—94.41%, 7th
Black: 3,370—0.33%, 50th
Native American: 13,780—1.37%, 12th
Asian, Pacific Isle: 9,365—0.93%, 31st
Other races: 29,783—2.96%, 10th
Hispanic origin: 52,927–5.26%, 15th
Percent over 5 yrs. speaking language other than English at home: 6.4%, 30th
Percent males: 49.76%, 7th
Percent females: 50.24%, 45th
Percent never married: 21.2%, 49th
Marriages per 1,000 (1989): 12.9, 7th
Divorces per 1,000 (1989): 6.0, 10th
Median age: 31.5
Under 5 years: 80,193—7.97%, 7th
Under 18 years: 308,405—30.63%, 3rd
65 years & older: 121,265—12.05%, 33rd
Percent increase among the elderly: 29.4%, 16th

OF VITAL IMPORTANCE

Live births per 1,000 pop.: 16.0, 19th
Infant mortality rate per 1,000 births (1988): 8.8, 36th
Average lifetime (1979-81): 75.19, 8th
Deaths per 100,000 pop. (1988): 767.8, 43rd
Causes of death per 100,000 pop. (1988):
Diseases of heart: 237.1, 45th
Malignant neoplasms: 158.8, 44th
Cerebrovascular diseases: 60.1, 29th
Accidents & adverse effects: 54.6, 5th
monary diseases: 40.2, 14th
Suicide: 17.8, 6th
HIV infection: 1.1, 44th
Other: 69.0, 38th

KEEPING WELL

Non-federal physicians per 100,000 pop.: 143, 50th
Dentists per 100,000 (1990-91): 62, 25th
Nurses per 100,000 (1989): 526, 41st
Hospitals per 100,000: 5.0, 7th

Admissions per 100,000: 10,273, 51st
Beds per 100,000: 386.69, 43rd
Occupancy rate: 60.7%, 44th
Semiprivate room charges per day: $259, 28th
Average stay: 6.6, 41st
Notifiable diseases per 100,000:
AIDS: 2.8, 46th
Gonorrhea: 15.7, 48th
Measles: 2.6, 32nd
Syphillis: 2.7, 44th
Tuberculosis (TB): 1.4, 50th
Per capita spending on mental health programs (1987): $16.74, 51st
Pop. without health insur. (1991): 17.8%, 11th

Households by Type

Total households: 360,723
Percent change (1980-90): 11.33%, 26th
Family households: 263,194
Percent of total: 72.96%, 8th
Nonfamily households: 97,529
Percent of total: 27.04%, 44th
Persons per household: 2.73, 8th
Pop. living in group quarters: 21,490
Percent of pop.: 2.13%, 47th

Living Quarters

Total housing units: 413,327
Persons per unit: 2.44, 17th
Occupied housing units: 360,723
Percent of total units: 87.27%, 36th
Persons per unit: 2.67, 9th
Percent of units with over 1 person per room: 4.21%, 14th
Owner-occupied units: 252,734
Percent of total units: 61.15%, 17th
Percent of occupied units: 70.06%, 10th
Persons per unit: 2.82, 10th
Median value: $58,200, 38th
Renter-occupied units: 107,989
Percent of total units: 26.13%, 43rd
Percent of occupied units: 29.94%, 42nd
Persons per unit: 2.51, 9th
Median contract rent: $261, 41st
Rental vacancy rate: 7.3%, 38th
Mobile home, trailer & other as a % of occupied housing units: 16.70%, 8th

Crime Index per 100,000

Total: 4,057, 43rd
Violent: 276, 43rd
Murder and nonnegligent manslaughter: 3, 44th
Aggravated assault: 7,966, 8th
Robbery: 15, 48th
Rape: 27, 42nd
Property: 3,781, 43rd
Burglary: 813, 39th
Larceny, theft: 2,803, 38th
Motor vehicle theft: 165, 47th
Drug abuse arrests: 175, 38th

Teaching and Learning

Literacy (1987): 92%, 4th
Pop. 3 and over enrolled in school: 295,638
Percent of pop.: 30.8%, 3rd
Public elementary & secondary schools:
Total enrollment: 215,000
Avg. class size (1987): 24, 15th
Teachers: 11,100
Percent of pop.: 1.10%, 14th
Teachers' avg. salary: $23,900, 45th
Spending per capita: $668, 42nd
Spending per pupil in avg. daily attendance: $3,037, 50th
Percent of graduates taking SAT: 18%, 30th
Combined SAT scores: 968, 22nd
Percent of pop. over 25 completing:
High school: 79.7%, 16th
College degree/s: 17.7%, 35th
Higher educa., institutions: 11
Per 100,000 pop.: 0.6, 32nd
Enroll: 51,881
Percent of pop.: 5.15%, 33rd
Public: 41,315
Percent of enroll.: 79.63%, 32nd
Private: 10,566
Percent of enroll.: 20.37%, 20th
White non-Hispanic: 397,880
Percent of enroll.: 73.90%, 42nd
Black non-Hispanic: 53,400
Percent of enroll.: 9.92%, 17th
Hispanic: 58,490
Percent of enroll.: 10.86%, 5th
Asian/Pacific Islander: 10,871

Percent of enroll.: 2.02%, 20th
Amer. Indian/AK native: 1,616
Percent of enroll.: 0.30%, 34th
Nonresident alien: 16,132
Percent of enroll.: 3.00%, 13th
Female: 28,144
Percent of enroll.: 54.25%, 35th
Tuition, state university ('90-'91): $1,189, 47th
Public library systems: 107
Books & serial vol. per capita: 3.37, 15th
Govt. expend. per capita: $12.33, 35th
State govt.: $2.45, 28th
Local govts.: $9.89, 34th

Law Enforcement, Courts, and Prisons

Police protection expend.: $90,423,000
Per capita: $89.79, 33rd
Judicial & legal expend.: $37,169,000
Per capita: $36.91, 36th
Corrections expend.: $52,151,000
Per capita: $51.79, 42nd
Police per 10,000 pop. (1990-91): 20.1, 29th
Prisoners (state & fed.) sentenced to over 1 yr., per 100,000 pop.: 201
Percent change (1989-90): 12.19%, 6th
Death penalty: yes, by firing squad or lethal injection
Under sentence of death: 16, 24th
Executed (1989): none

Religion, Number and Percent of Population

Agnostic: 7,682—1.10%, 6th
Buddhist: 1,397—0.20%, 11th
Christian: 571,944—81.90%, 41st
Hindu: NA
Jewish: NA
Moslem: NA
Unitarian: 2,793—0.40%, 8th
Other: 9,777—1.40%, 20th
None: 83,103—11.90%, 7th
Refused to answer: 21,649—3.10%, 7th

Making a Living

Personal income per capita (1989): $11,457, 41st
Percent increase (1979-'89) (constant 1989 dollars): 9.4%, 36th
Average income per family: $35,832, 40th
Percent of pop. below poverty level: 13.3%, 19th
Percent 65 and over: 11.5%, 27th
Cost of living, selected cities
1st qtr., 1991 (U. S. Standard=100)

Pocatello	91.6
Boise	99.8
Idaho Falls	100.9

Economy

Civilian labor force : 496,000
Percent of tot. pop.: 49.27%, 34th
Percent 65 and over: 2.42%, 35th
Percent females: 43.35%, 49th
Percent job growth (1980-90): 16.89%, 33rd
Major employer industries:
Agriculture: 37,360—8.00%, 6th
Construction: 21,949—4.70%, 23rd
Finance, insurance & real estate: 20,081—4.30%, 40th
Government: 72,852—15.60%, 25th
Manufacturing: 70,517—15.10%, 31st
Mining: 3,638—0.8%, 18th
Service: 77,522—16.60%, 44th
Trade: 89,664—19.20%, 20th
Transportation, communication, & public utilities: 21,482—4.60%, 40th
Wholesale/retail: 97,961—22.1%, 10th
Unemployment rate: 5.85%, 15th
Male: 3.23%, 18th
Female: 2.62%, 17th
Total businesses (1991): 46,787
New business incorp's. (1991): 1,944
Percent of total businesses: 4.16%, 43rd
Business failures (1991): 390
Percent of total businesses: 0.83%, 27th
Agriculture farm income
Marketing (1991): $2,615,946,000, 25th
Net per operation: $34,625, 11th
Net per acre: $55, 28th
Leading products: cattle, potatoes, dairy products, wheat
Av. value land & build. per acre: $685, 33rd
Percent increase (1980-90): -1.86%, 28th
Govt. payments: $141,250,000, 21st
Construction, value of all: $824,000,000

Per capita: $818.48, 10th
Percent change 1989-90: 32.48%, 3rd
Manufactures:
Value added: : $3,928,000,000
Per capita: $3,901.67, 36th
Value of shipments: $9,184,000,000
Per capita: $9,122.43, 33rd
Leading products: processed foods, lumber and wood products, chemical products, primary metals, fabricated metal products, machinery, electronic components
Mining, min. prod., value (1987): $243,000,000, 37th
Leading products: silver, phosphate, gold
Retail sales: $6,004,000,000, 44th
Per household: $16,591, 47th
Percent increase (1987-90): 17.6%, 20th
Service indust., value (1987): $2,949,000,000, 45th
Per capita: $2,929.23, 45th
Tourism indus., value (1989): $1,179,000,000, 41st
Foreign exports value: $898,000,000, 40th
Per capita: $891.98, 25th
Patents per 1,000 pop.: 5.3, 30th

Travel and Transportation

Motor vehicle registrations: 1,053,538
Per 1,000 pop.: 1,046, 2nd
Motorcycle registrations: 41,974
Per 1,000 pop.: 41, 4th
Licensed drivers per 1,000 driving age pop.: 956, 8th
Deaths from motor vehicle accidents per 100,000 pop.: 24.2, 10th
Public roads & streets
Total mileage: 62,435, 32nd
Rural mileage: 60,006, 30th
Urban mileage: 2,429, 42nd
Interstate mileage: 605, 35th
Annual vehicle-miles of travel per person: 9,782, 12th
Mean travel time for workers 16 + who work away from home: 17.3 min., 43rd

Government

Registered voters (1988): 572,430
Percent of voting age pop.: 81.66%, 10th
Voter turnout (1988): 408,968
Percent of registered voters: 71.44%, 25th
Percent of voting age pop.: 58.34%, 11th
State legislators, total (1992): 126, 36th
Women members (1992): 36
Percent of legislature: 28.6%, 7th
Dominant party (1992): Split
U. S. Congress, House members (1993): 2
Increase 1983-93: 0
Revenues:
State govt.: $2,417,006,000
Per capita: $2,400.80, 28th
State & local govt.: $3,372,524,000
Per capita: $3,349.92, 44th
Indebtedness:
State govt.: $977,171,000
Per capita: $970.62, 34th
State & local govt.: $1,528,000,000
Per capita: $1,517.76, 51st

Laws and Regulations

Legal driving age: 16
Marriage age without parental consent: 18
Divorce residence requirement: 6 wks

Attractions

Major opera companies (1989): 1, 30th
Per 1 million pop.: 0.99, 9th
Major symphony orchestras (1989): 7, 32nd
Per 1 million pop.: 6.90, 6th
State appropriations for state arts agencies per capita: $0.42, 45th
State Fair in late Aug. at Boise and in early Sept. at Blackfoot

Sports and Competition

NCAA sports teams, 3: Boise State Univ. Broncos, Idaho State Univ. Bengals, Univ. of Idaho Vandals.
Professional teams, 3:
Baseball, 3—Pocatello Pioneers (Pioneer League, Advanced Rookie Class), Halliwell Park; Idaho Falls Braves (Pioneer League, Advanced Rookie Class), McDermott Field; Boise Hawks (Northwest League, Class A), Memorial Stadium

ILLINOIS

"Illinois is perhaps the most American of all the states. It's the U.S. in capsule....The capacity for greatness is as limitless as the sweep of the undulating corn fields."

Clyde Brion Davis, journalist, author

The Land of Lincoln nourished the future president and gave him his start toward world fame. The state is rich in archaeological treasures, including the unique Piasa bird and the largest primitive earthworks anywhere. Because of its location, Illinois has the world's greatest concentration of transportation facilities by land, water, and air. The Chicago area continues to rank as the nation's major center of manufacture, and the state often leads the nation in production of foodstuffs, particularly corn and soybeans. Three of the world's five tallest buildings rise above a Chicago skyline that has been praised as the world's most beautiful. That skyline contains architectural masterpieces that have given Chicago its international reputation in the field.

> So They Say
>
> "Most beautiful and suitable for settlement...a settler would not there spend ten years in cutting down and burning trees; on the very day of his arrival, he could put his plow into the ground. Thus he would easily find in the country his food and clothing."
>
> Louis Jolliet

Superlatives

- World center of transportation.
- World's busiest airport.
- World's first skyscraper.
- World's tallest building— Sears Tower
- Leads in fluorospar production.
- Principal center of printing.
- Pioneer in commercial television.
- Leader in mail order sales.

Moments in History

- The expedition of Louis Jolliet and Father Jacques Marquette brought the first Europeans to Illinois in 1673.
- French priests founded Cahokia in 1699, and it is the oldest European settlement in the state.
- After the French surrendered North America, their flag at Fort de Chartres in 1765 was the last to be lowered on the continent.
- From 1765 to 1778, British rule was weak, and Illinois became a lawless "wild west."
- During the Revolution, George Rogers Clark and 175 men captured Kaskaskia on July 4, 1778.
- In 1809 the Territory of Illinois was created, with popular Ninian Edwards as governor.
- During the War of 1812, tiny Fort Dearborn (Chicago) was ordered evacuated, and the people were massacred by the Potawatomi Indians.
- On December 3, 1818, Illinois became the 21st state.

> So They Say
>
> "We will enter upon a state government with better prospects than any state ever did—the best soil in the world, a mild climate, a large state with the most ample funds to educate every child in the state."
>
> Nathaniel Pope, Illinois territorial delegate to Congress

• When Chief Black Hawk of the Sauk and Fox tried to reclaim the tribal lands in 1832, the Black Hawk War began. His forces won the small Battle of Stillman's Run in April, but he was later defeated in Wisconsin.

• Chicago was incorporated in 1837 with a population of 4,000.

• Nauvoo was the largest city in Illinois when Joseph Smith, the Mormon leader, was killed in 1844. The Mormons left for the West, and Nauvoo became a ghost town.

• By 1845 the Galena area had become the nation's leading supplier of lead, and Galena had become the largest city in the state. The mining boom had almost died out by 1850.

• In 1858 Abraham Lincoln and Stephen Douglas engaged in a series of debates that gave Lincoln national prominence.

• In 1861 President-elect Lincoln left Springfield for the last time.

• Only days after Lee had surrendered at Appomatox, victorious President Lincoln was assassinated on February 12, 1865, and his body was returned to a sorrowing Springfield.

• Galena's U.S. Grant was elected president in 1868 and reelected in 1872.

• The great Chicago fire of 1871 destroyed much of the city, but rebuilding began before the ashes had died down.

• In 1893 the magnificent World's Columbian Exposition at Chicago dazzled visitors from around the world.

• In one of the great engineering feats of all time, in 1900 the Chicago River was reversed to dispose of sewage and to create a water route from the Great Lakes to the Gulf of Mexico.

• Beginning in 1917, 351,153 Illinoisans served in U.S. armed forces in World War I.

• On December 2, 1942, during World War II, the power of the atom was mastered at Chicago, and the course of history was to be changed by that event.

• Riots at the Democratic National Convention at Chicago in 1968 brought the city notoriety.

• On November 25, 1987, Harold Washington, the city's first black mayor, died of a heart attack at his desk.

That's Interesting

• Before statehood, the northern border of Illinois was set at the southern extremity of Lake Michigan. If this had not been moved northward, Illinois would have had no Lake Michigan shoreline.

• One of the most mysterious of all prehistoric remains is the huge figure of a monster, known as the Piasa Bird, painted high on the bluff near Alton. Its origin has never been determined.

• Lincoln, Illinois, was the only town named for Abraham Lincoln during his lifetime. Invited to dedicate the town, he christened it with watermelon juice and provided watermelon for the crowd.

• When a gang of counterfeiters attempted to steal Abraham Lincoln's body from his tomb in exchange for a jailed member's freedom, this bizarre ransom try was foiled by quick Secret Service work.

Notable Natives

Jane Addams (Cedarville, 1860-1935), social reformer. **Jack Benny** (Chicago, 1894-1974), comedian. **Black Hawk** (near Rockford, 1767-1838), Indian leader. **Ernest Hemingway** (Oak Park, 1899-1961), author. **James Butler "Wild Bill" Hickock** (Troy Grove, 1837-1876), scout, frontiersman. **Ronald Wilson Reagan** (Tampico, 1911-), U.S. President. **Carl Sandburg** (Galesburg, 1878-1967), poet. **Charles Rudolph Walgreen** (Knox County, 1873-1939), pharmacist/merchant.

General

Admitted to statehood: Dec. 3, 1818
Origin of name: French for the *Illini* Indians or land of Illini, Algonquin word meaning "men" or "warriors"
Capital: Springfield
Nickname: Prairie State
Motto: "State Sovereignty, National Union"
Bird: cardinal
Fish: bluegill
Flower: native violet
Insect: Monarch butterfly

Mineral: fluorite
Slogan: "Land of Lincoln"
Song: "Illinois"
Tree: white oak

THE LAND

Area: 57,918 sq. mi., 25th
Land: 55,593 sq. mi., 24th
Water: 2,325 sq. mi., 20th
Topography: prairies and fertile plains throughout, open hills in the S region
Number of counties: 102
Geographic center: Logan, 28 mi. NE of Springfield
Length: 390 mi.
Width: 210 mi.
Highest point: 1,235 ft. (Charles Mound), 45th
Lowest point: 279 ft. (Mississippi River), 33rd
Mean elevation: 600 ft., 38th

CLIMATE AND ENVIRONMENT

Temp., highest: 117 deg. on July 14, 1954, at E. St. Louis; lowest: -35 deg. on Jan. 22, 1930, at Mount Carroll
Fresh water withdrawn, per capita, per day: 1,250 gal., 25th
Endangered species: mammals, 2—gray bat, Indiana bat; birds, 3—American peregrine falcon, piping plover, least tern; reptiles, none; amphibians, none; fishes, 1; invertebrates, 8; plants, 1

MAJOR CITIES, POPULATION PERCENTAGE INCREASE (1980-90)

Aurora, 99,581—22.50%
Chicago, 2,783,726— -7.37%
Peoria, 113,504— -8.58%
Rockford, 139,426—0.20%
Springfield, 105,227—5.17%

THE PEOPLE

Population: 11,430,602, 6th
  Percent change (1980-90): 0.03%, 46th
  Per sq. mi: 197.36, 11th
  Percent in metro. area: 82.67%, 12th
  Percent foreign born: 8.3%, 12th
White: 8,952,978—78.32%, 36th
Black: 1,694,273—14.82%, 14th
Native American: 21,836—0.19%, 47th
Asian, Pacific Isle: 285,311—2.50%, 10th
Other races: 476,204—4.17%, 8th
Hispanic origin: 904,446—7.91%, 10th
Percent over 5 yrs. speaking language other than English at home: 14.2%, 12th
Percent males: 48.57%, 26th
Percent females: 51.43%, 26th
Percent never married: 28.8%, 10th
Marriages per 1,000 (1989): 7.2, 49th
Divorces per 1,000 (1989): 4.0, 35th
Median age: 32.8
Under 5 years: 848,141—7.42%, 24th
Under 18 years: 2,946,366—25.78%, 29th
65 years & older: 1,436,545—12.57%, 27th
Percent increase among the elderly: 13.8%, 37th

OF VITAL IMPORTANCE

Live births per 1,000 pop.: 16.4, 15th
Infant mortality rate per 1,000 births (1988): 11.3, 9th
Average lifetime (1979-81): 73.37, 36th
Deaths per 100,000 pop. (1988): 906.2, 22nd
Causes of death per 100,000 pop. (1988):
  Diseases of heart: 340.8, 16th
  Malignant neoplasms: 202.3, 20th
  Cerebrovascular diseases: 59.9, 30th
  Accidents & adverse effects: 37.9, 32nd
  monary diseases: 30.4, 36th
  Suicide: 10.8, 40th
  HIV infection: 4, 19th
  Other: 78.6, 19th

KEEPING WELL

Non-federal physicians per 100,00 pop.: 233, 15th
Dentists per 100,000 (1990-91): 76, 10th
Nurses per 100,000 (1989): 717, 21st
Hospitals per 100,000: 2.2, 43rd
  Admissions per 100,000: 14,075, 20th
  Beds per 100,000: 507.90, 22nd
  Occupancy rate: 68.9%, 16th
  Semiprivate room charges per day: $300, 21st
  Average stay: 7.2, 23rd
Notifiable diseases per 100,000:
  AIDS: 11.2, 19th
  Gonorrhea: 334.5, 14th

Measles: 11.9, 6th
Syphillis: 36.1, 19th
Tuberculosis (TB): 9.8, 16th
Per capita spending on mental health programs (1987): $24.48, 44th
Pop. without health insur. (1991): 11.5%, 31st

Households by Type

Total households: 4,202,240
Percent change (1980-90): 3.89%, 47th
Family households: 2,924,880
Percent of total: 69.60%, 34th
Nonfamily households: 1,277,360
Percent of total: 30.40%, 17th
Persons per household: 2.65, 15th
Pop. living in group quarters: 286,956
Percent of pop.: 2.51%, 33rd

Living Quarters

Total housing units: 4,506,275
Persons per unit: 2.54, 5th
Occupied housing units: 4,202,240
Percent of total units: 93.25%, 2nd
Persons per unit: 2.59, 14th
Percent of units with over 1 person per room: 3.97%, 17th
Owner-occupied units: 2,699,182
Percent of total units: 59.90%, 24th
Percent of occupied units: 64.23%, 39th
Persons per unit: 2.81, 12th
Median value: $80,900, 19th
Renter-occupied units: 1,503,058
Percent of total units: 33.35%, 13th
Percent of occupied units: 35.77%, 15th
Persons per unit: 2.37, 24th
Median contract rent: $369, 19th
Rental vacancy rate: 8.0%, 29th
Mobile home, trailer & other as a % of occupied housing units: 4.50%, 44th

Crime Index per 100,000

Total: 5,935, 16th
Violent: 967, 6th
Murder and nonnegligent manslaughter: 10, 15th
Aggravated assault: 7,420, 25th
Robbery: 394, 4th
Rape: 39, 24th
Property: 4,968, 19th
Burglary: 1,063, 30th
Larceny, theft: 3,262, 18th
Motor vehicle theft: 643, 14th
Drug abuse arrests: 101, 46th

Teaching and Learning

Literacy (1987): 86%, 33nd
Pop. 3 and over enrolled in school: 3,031,673
Percent of pop.: 27.8%, 19th
Public elementary & secondary schools:
Total enrollment: 1,811,000
Avg. class size (1987): 23, 20th
Teachers: 105,900
Percent of pop.: 0.93%, 38th
Teachers' avg. salary: $32,800, 13th
Spending per capita: $728, 34th
Spending per pupil in avg. daily attendance: $4,853, 21st
Percent of graduates taking SAT: 16%, 32nd
Combined SAT scores: 1006, 10th
Percent of pop. over 25 completing:
High school: 76.2%, 29th
College degree/s: 21.0%, 20th
Higher educa., institutions: 170
Per 100,000 pop.: 0.5, 39th
Enroll: 729,246
Percent of pop.: 6.38%, 11th
Public: 551,333
Percent of enroll.: 75.60%, 39th
Private: 177,913
Percent of enroll.: 24.40%, 13th
White non-Hispanic: 195,079
Percent of enroll.: 73.65%, 43rd
Black non-Hispanic: 44,582
Percent of enroll.: 16.83%, 8th
Hispanic: 5,026
Percent of enroll.: 1.90%, 20th
Asian/Pacific Islander: 11,694
Percent of enroll.: 4.42%, 7th
Amer. Indian/AK native: 852
Percent of enroll.: 0.32%, 31st
Nonresident alien: 7,629
Percent of enroll.: 2.88%, 14th
Female: 397,920

Percent of enroll.: 54.57%, 31st
Tuition, state university ('90-'91): $2,465, 10th
Public library systems: 603
Books & serial vol. per capita: 3.13, 18th
Govt. expend. per capita: $22.15, 11th
State govt.: $5.48, 6th
Local govts.: $16.66, 18th

Law Enforcement, Courts, and Prisons

Police protection expend.: $1,522,440,000
Per capita: $133.19, 13th
Judicial & legal expend.: $535,596,000
Per capita: $46.85, 28th
Corrections expend.: $743,524,000
Per capita: $65.04, 33rd
Police per 10,000 pop. (1990-91): 25.7, 8th
Prisoners (state & fed.) sentenced to over 1 yr., per 100,000 pop.: 234
Percent change (1989-90): 11.35%, 8th
Death penalty: yes, by lethal injection
Under sentence of death: 120, 4th
Executed (1989): none

Religion, Number and Percent of Population

Agnostic: 50,905—0.60%, 19th
Buddhist: 8,484—0.10%, 17th
Christian: 7,262,506—85.60%, 27th
Hindu: 16,969—0.20%, 3rd
Jewish: 127,264—1.50%, 13th
Moslem: 33,937—0.40%, 5th
Unitarian: 33,937—0.40%, 8th
Other: 118,779—1.40%, 20th
None: 593,897—7.00%, 23rd
Refused to answer: 237,559—2.80%, 12th

Making a Living

Personal income per capita (1989): $15,201, 14th
Percent increase (1979-'89) (constant 1989 dollars): 12.5%, 24th
Average income per family: $47,259, 12th
Percent of pop. below poverty level: 11.9%, 27th
Percent 65 and over: 10.7%, 34th
Cost of living, selected cities
1st qtr., 1991 (U. S. Standard=100)

Decatur	93.9
Rockford	103.8
Chicago (Schaumburg)	128.7

Economy

Civilian labor force : 6,029,000
Percent of tot. pop.: 52.74%, 12th
Percent 65 and over: 2.82%, 24th
Percent females: 44.98%, 34th
Percent job growth (1980-90): 13.49%, 40th
Major employer industries:
Agriculture: 118,818—2.10%, 34th
Construction: 231,978—4.10%, 31st
Finance, insurance & real estate: 413,034—7.30%, 6th
Government: 752,514—13.30%, 40th
Manufacturing: 1,086,336—19.20%, 16th
Mining: 20,899—0.4%, 23rd
Service: 1,239,102—21.90%, 15th
Trade: 1,075,020—19.00%, 21st
Transportation, communication, & public utilities: 345,138—6.10%, 13th
Wholesale/retail: 1,158,062—21.4%, 28th
Unemployment rate: 6.15%, 12th
Male: 3.42%, 13th
Female: 2.74%, 13th
Total businesses (1991): 441,411
New business incorp's. (1991): 29,068
Percent of total businesses: 6.59%, 18th
Business failures (1991): 3,027
Percent of total businesses: 0.69%, 40th
Agriculture farm income
Marketing (1991): $7,508,777,000, 5th
Net per operation: $14,018, 38th
Net per acre: $40, 33rd
Leading products: Corn, soybeans, hogs, cattle
Av. value land & build. per acre: $1,416, 12th
Percent increase (1980-90): -30.62%, 46th
Govt. payments: $441,407,000, 6th
Construction, value of all: $6,711,000,000
Per capita: $587.11, 21st
Percent change 1989-90: -18.55%, 35th
Manufactures:
Value added: : $70,784,000,000
Per capita: $6,192.50, 11th
Value of shipments: $156,675,000,000

Per capita: $13,706.63, 13th
Leading products: machinery, electric and electronic equipment, primary and fabricated metals, chemical products, printing and publishing, food and kindred products
Mining, min. prod., value (1987): $3,026,000,000, 12th
Leading products: coal, petroleum, stone
Retail sales: $83,479,000,000, 5th
Per household: $19,840, 17th
Percent increase (1987-90): 21.8%, 12th
Service indust., value (1987): $55,943,000,000, 5th
Per capita: $4,894.14, 11th
Tourism indus., value (1989): $10,865,000,000, 5th
Foreign exports value: $12,965,000,000, 8th
Per capita: $1,134.24, 17th
Patents per 1,000 pop.: 3.9, 42nd

Travel and Transportation

Motor vehicle registrations: 7,873,189
Per 1,000 pop.: 688, 44th
Motorcycle registrations: 179,962
Per 1,000 pop.: 15, 31st
Licensed drivers per 1,000 driving age pop.: 826, 45th
Deaths from motor vehicle accidents per 100,000 pop.: 13.9, 43rd
Public roads & streets
Total mileage: 135,944, 3rd
Rural mileage: 103,941, 5th
Urban mileage: 32,003, 5th
Interstate mileage: 1,961, 3rd
Annual vehicle-miles of travel per person: 7,290, 45th
Mean travel time for workers 16 + who work away from home: 25.1 min., 5th

Government

Registered voters (1988): 6,356,940
Percent of voting age pop.: 74.35%, 19th
Voter turnout (1988): 4,559,120
Percent of registered voters: 71.72%, 24th
Percent of voting age pop.: 53.32%, 22nd
State legislators, total (1992): 177, 13th
Women members (1992): 33
Percent of legislature: 18.6%, 22nd
Dominant party (1992): Democrats
U. S. Congress, House members (1993): 20
Increase 1983-93: -2
Revenues:
State govt.: $24,313,085,000
Per capita: $2,127.02, 39th
State & local govt.: $43,541,366,000
Per capita: $3,809.19, 28th
Indebtedness:
State govt.: $15,262,397,000
Per capita: $1,335.22, 21st
State & local govt.: $32,027,000,000
Per capita: $2,801.86, 35th

Laws and Regulations

Legal driving age: 18
Marriage age without parental consent: 18
Divorce residence requirement: 90 days

Attractions

Major opera companies (1989): 8, 5th
Per 1 million pop.: 0.69, 24th
Major symphony orchestras (1989): 38, 6th
Per 1 million pop.: 3.26, 30th
State appropriations for state arts agencies per capita: $0.94, 20th
State Fair in early Aug. at Springfield and in late Aug. at DuQuoin

Sports and Competition

NCAA sports teams, 16: Bradley Univ. Braves, Chicago State Univ. Cougars, De Paul Univ. Blue Demons, Eastern Illinois Univ. Panthers, Illinois State Univ. Redbirds, Lake Forest College Foresters, Loyola Univ. Ramblers, Northeastern Illinois Golden Eagles, Northwestern Univ. Wildcats, Rockford College Regents, Southern Illinois Univ. Salukis, Trinity Christian College Trolls, Univ. of Chicago Maroons, Univ. of Illinois fighting Illini, Univ. of Illinois flames, Western Illinois Univ. Leathernecks.
Professional teams, 12:
Baseball, 6—Chicago White Sox (AL), Comiskey Park; Kane County Cougars (Midwest League, Class A), Kane County Events Center; Springfield Cardinals (Midwest

League, Class A), Lanphier Park; Rockford Expos (Midwest League, Class A), Marinelli field; Peoria Chiefs (Midwest League, Class A), Meinen Field; Chicago Cubs (NL), Wrigley Field

Basketball, 3—Chicago Bulls (NBA), Chicago Stadium; Rockford Lightning (Continental Basketball Association), Rockford Metrocentre; Quad City Thunder (Continental Basketball Association), Wharton Fieldhouse

Football, 1—Chicago Bears (NFC), Soldier Field

Hockey, 2—Chicago Blackhawks (NHL), Chicago Stadium; Peoria Rivermen (International Hockey League), Peoria Civic Center

INDIANA

"Blest Indiana....Find here the best retreat on earth."

John Finley, explorer

The Hoosier State provided a natural route between Canada and Louisiana for French explorers, trappers, and traders. Captured by the United States in the Revolution and secured by the War of 1812, Indiana soon greeted large numbers of settlers, who came floating down the Ohio River in flatboats. The area has nurtured an extraordinary number of notables, including Indian leaders, future presidents, and four vice-presidents. An impressive number of U.S. literary figures, musicians, inventors, industrialists, and other personalities have enjoyed "My Indiana Home." It is also the premier basketball state in the nation.

SUPERLATIVES

• Wabash was the first electrically lighted city.

• The first U.S. industrial union was founded by Eugene Debs at Terre Haute.

• National leader in production of musical instruments.

• Produces 80% of the nation's dimensional limestone.

MOMENTS IN HISTORY

• In 1673 Robert Cavelier, Sieur de La Salle, entered the St. Joseph River near present-day Benton Harbor, the first recorded European visit.

• Records are unclear, but it is thought that Vincennes took shape between 1727 and 1732, when French fur trappers and traders plied their trade.

• In 1749 Pierre Joseph, Celeron de Bienville, led a colorful expedition down the Ohio River. He buried a series of lead plates along the way as evidence of French ownership of the region.

• In 1763 the British took over.

• During the American Revolution in 1779 George Rogers Clark, with only a handful of men, captured Vincennes and its hated leader, Henry Hamilton, the "Hair Buyer."

> So They Say
>
> "The capture of Vincennes by George Rogers Clark has been called ...one of the most heroic episodes in U.S. history...one of the greatest exploits of American arms."
>
> Anonymous

• The Northwest Ordinance of 1787 paved the way for settlement in Indiana.

• Alarmed at the prospect of losing their lands, the Indians took up arms, but Revolutionary hero General "Mad Anthony" Wayne overcame Indian resistance and in 1795 forced the Indian leaders to sign a treaty giving up much of the region.

• After a period of relative peace, the Indians led by Chief Tecumseh and his brother, The Prophet, again threatened the growing settlements. On November 7, 1811, territorial governor William Henry Harrison decisively defeated the Indian confederation at their Prophetstown headquarters near present-day Lafayette in the Battle of Tippecanoe.

• With the Indian threat diminished, the population quickly exceeded 60,000, and Indiana became the 19th state, on December 11, 1816.

• In 1825, four wagons moved the government of Indiana to the new capital at Indianapolis, still much in its wilderness condition.

> **So They Say**
> The area of Buffaloville was "...a wild region with bears and other wild animals still in the woods. The clearing away of surplus wood was the great task ahead."
> Abraham Lincoln, 1816

• Slavery in the state was no longer an issue by 1843, and many Indiana cities became "stations" on the "Underground Railroad." More than 2,000 slaves found refuge at Levi Coffin's house in Fountain City on their way to freedom in Canada.

> **So They Say**
> "...A gentle rap at the door....Outside in the cold or rain, there would be a two horse wagon loaded with fugitives, perhaps the greater part of them women and children...the cold and hungry fugitives would be made comfortable."
> Levi Coffin

• Civil War reached Indiana in 1863 when Confederate raider John Hunt Morgan swept through the state.

• The state capitol was completed in 1878.

• In 1917 James Gresham of Evansville was one of the first three U.S. World War I casualties; the war called 130,670 from Indiana into service.

• The worst Ohio River floods in history occurred in 1937.

• World War II called 338,000 Indiana men and women into service.

• Burns Harbor opened for shipping in 1970, giving Indiana a much-needed major Great Lakes shipping port.

• In 1976 Indiana Dunes National Lakeshore was substantially expanded.

THAT'S INTERESTING

• British governor of Indiana, Henry Hamilton, was known as the "Hair Buyer" because he encouraged Indians friendly to the British to take American scalps, for which they were paid.

• Indiana's Lost River travels 22 miles underground.

• Indiana General Ambrose Burnside's bushy whiskers were called "burnsides," and now are called "sideburns."

• Indiana is known for its unusual place names, such as Gnaw Bone and Bean Blossom.

• The Indiana capitol is probably the only major public building in the nation to have been built within its budget.

NOTABLE NATIVES

George Ade ((Kentland, 1866-1944), humorist/playwright. **Charles Austin Beard** (near Knightstown, 1874-1948), political scientist/historian. **Albert Jeremiah Beveridge** (Highland County, 1862-1927), public official/historian. **Ambrose Everett Burnside** (Liberty, 1824-1881), soldier/public official. **Theodore Dreiser** (Terre Haute, 1871-1943), author. **Edward Eggleston** (Vevay, 1837-1902), religious leader/historian. **John Milton Hay** (Salem, 1838-1905), diplomat/author. **Robert Staughton Lind** (New Albany, 1892-1970), sociologist. **Thomas Riley Marshall** (North Manchester, 1854-1925), U.S. vice-president. **John Tinney McCutcheon** (Tippecanoe County, 1870-1949), cartoonist. **Oliver Perry Morton** (Salisbury, 1823-1877), public official. **Cole Porter** (Peru, 1893-1964), lyricist/composer. **Gene Stratton Porter** (Wabash County, 1863-1924), author. **Ernest Taylor Pyle** (Dana, 1900-1945), journalist. **J. Danforth "Dan" Quayle** (Indianapolis, 1947-), U.S. vice-president. **James Whitcomb Riley** (Greenfield, 1849-1916), poet. **Booth Tarkington** (Indianapolis, 1869-1946), author. **Lew(is) Wallace** (Brookville, 1827-1905), U.S. general/diplomat/author. **Wendell Wilkie** (Elwood, 1892-1944), industrialist/political leader. **Wilbur Wright** (Millville, 1867-1912), inventor/pioneer aviator.

GENERAL

Admitted to statehood: Dec. 11, 1816
Origin of name: from the Latin meaning "land of the Indians"
Capital: Indianapolis
Nickname: Hoosier State
Motto: "The Crossroads of America"
Bird: cardinal
Flower: peony

Song: "On the Banks of the Wabash, Far Away"
Stone: limestone
Tree: tulip poplar

The Land

Area: 36,420 sq. mi., 38th
Land: 35,870 sq. mi., 38th
Water: 550 sq. mi., 39th
Topography: hilly S region; fertile rolling plains of central region; flat, heavily glaciated N; dunes along Lake Michigan shore
Number of counties: 92
Geographic center: Boone, 14 mi. NNW of Indianapolis
Length: 270 mi.
Width: 140 mi.
Highest point: 1,257 ft. (Franklin Twp., Wayne County), 44th
Lowest point: 320 ft. (Ohio River), 35th
Mean elevation: 700 ft., 34th

Climate and Environment

Temp., highest: 116 deg. on July 14, 1936, at Collegeville; lowest: -35 deg. on Feb. 2, 1951, at Greensburg
Fresh water withdrawn, per capita, per day: 1,470 gal., 20th
Endangered species: mammals, 2—gray bat, Indiana bat; birds, 3—American peregrine falcon, piping plover, least tern; reptiles, none; amphibians, none; fishes, none; invertebrates, 6; plants, 2

Major Cities, Population Percentage Increase (1980-90)

Evansville, 126,272— –3.24%
Fort Wayne, 173,072—0.40%
Gary, 116,646— –23.24%
Indianapolis, 731,327—4.35%
South Bend, 105,511— –3.84%

The People

Population: 5,544,159, 14th
Percent change (1980-90): 0.97%, 38th
Per sq. mi: 152.23, 14th
Percent in metro. area: 68.47%, 24th
Percent foreign born: 1.7%, 37th
White: 5,020,700—90.56%, 18th
Black: 432,092—7.79%, 23rd
Native American: 12,720—0.23%, 40th
Asian, Pacific Isle: 37,617—0.68%, 38th
Other races: 41,030—0.74%, 31st
Hispanic origin: 98,788—1.78%, 32nd
Percent over 5 yrs. speaking language other than English at home: 4.8%, 39th
Percent males: 48.49%, 31st
Percent females: 51.51%, 21st
Percent never married: 24.3%, 35th
Marriages per 1,000 (1989): 9.9, 20th
Divorces per 1,000 (1989): NA
Median age: 32.8
Under 5 years: 398,656—7.19%, 33rd
Under 18 years: 1,455,964—26.26%, 21st
65 years & older: 696,196—12.56%, 28th
Percent increase among the elderly: 18.9%, 30th

Of Vital Importance

Live births per 1,000 pop.: 15.1, 38th
Infant mortality rate per 1,000 births (1988): 11.0, 12th
Average lifetime (1979-81): 73.84, 26th
Deaths per 100,000 pop. (1988): 900.6, 23rd
Causes of death per 100,000 pop. (1988):
Diseases of heart: 318, 26th
Malignant neoplasms: 204.3, 19th
Cerebrovascular diseases: 70, 15th
Accidents & adverse effects: 39, 29th
monary diseases: 37.4, 18th
Suicide: 11.6, 32nd
HIV infection: 2, 36th
Other: 77.1, 23rd

Keeping Well

Non-federal physicians per 100,000 pop.: 172, 42nd
Dentists per 100,000 (1990-91): 54, 37th
Nurses per 100,000 (1989): 678, 27th
Hospitals per 100,000: 2.4, 36th
Admissions per 100,000: 13,599, 26th
Beds per 100,000: 478.00, 27th
Occupancy rate: 63.6%, 36th
Semiprivate room charges per day: $258, 29th
Average stay: 6.8, 34th
Notifiable diseases per 100,000:
AIDS: 5.1, 38th

Gonorrhea: 205.0, 24th
Measles: 7.3, 13th
Syphillis: 6.6, 36th
Tuberculosis (TB): 4.9, 34th
Per capita spending on mental health programs (1987): $43.94, 18th
Pop. without health insur. (1991): 13.0%, 26th

HOUSEHOLDS BY TYPE

Total households: 2,065,355
Percent change (1980-90): 7.18%, 38th
Family households: 1,480,351
Percent of total: 71.68%, 16th
Nonfamily households: 585,004
Percent of total: 28.32%, 36th
Persons per household: 2.61, 21st
Pop. living in group quarters: 161,992
Percent of pop.: 2.92%, 22nd

LIVING QUARTERS

Total housing units: 2,246,046
Persons per unit: 2.47, 12th
Occupied housing units: 2,065,355
Percent of total units: 91.96%, 9th
Persons per unit: 2.52, 28th
Percent of units with over 1 person per room: 2.20%, 40th
Owner-occupied units: 1,450,898
Percent of total units: 64.60%, 3rd
Percent of occupied units: 70.25%, 8th
Persons per unit: 2.73, 26th
Median value: $53,900, 40th
Renter-occupied units: 614,457
Percent of total units: 27.36%, 37th
Percent of occupied units: 29.75%, 44th
Persons per unit: 2.30, 32nd
Median contract rent: $291, 32nd
Rental vacancy rate: 8.3%, 26th
Mobile home, trailer & other as a % of occupied housing units: 8.53%, 30th

CRIME INDEX PER 100,000

Total: 4,683, 34th
Violent: 474, 30th
Murder and nonnegligent manslaughter: 6, 26th
Aggravated assault: 7,191, 33rd
Robbery: 101, 33rd
Rape: 38, 25th
Property: 4,209, 36th
Burglary: 943, 34th
Larceny, theft: 2,827, 36th
Motor vehicle theft: 439, 26th
Drug abuse arrests: 110, 44th

TEACHING AND LEARNING

Literacy (1987): 89%, 17th
Pop. 3 and over enrolled in school: 1,436,188
Percent of pop.: 27.1%, 26th
Public elementary & secondary schools:
Total enrollment: 957,000
Avg. class size (1987): 23, 20th
Teachers: 54,700
Percent of pop.: 0.99%, 28th
Teachers' avg. salary: $30,500, 22nd
Spending per capita: $728, 35th
Spending per pupil in avg. daily attendance: $4,126, 36th
Percent of graduates taking SAT: 57%, 16th
Combined SAT scores: 865, 47th
Percent of pop. over 25 completing:
High school: 75.6%, 31st
College degree/s: 15.6%, 46th
Higher educa., institutions: 80
Per 100,000 pop.: 0.5, 41st
Enroll: 283,015
Percent of pop.: 5.10%, 36th
Public: 222,929
Percent of enroll.: 78.77%, 33rd
Private: 60,086
Percent of enroll.: 21.23%, 19th
White non-Hispanic: 144,265
Percent of enroll.: 85.12%, 24th
Black non-Hispanic: 9,952
Percent of enroll.: 5.87%, 25th
Hispanic: 5,648
Percent of enroll.: 3.33%, 11th
Asian/Pacific Islander: 4,362
Percent of enroll.: 2.57%, 14th
Amer. Indian/AK native: 433
Percent of enroll.: 0.26%, 39th
Nonresident alien: 4,820

Percent of enroll.: 2.84%, 15th
Female: 149,109
Percent of enroll.: 52.69%, 47th
Tuition, state university ('90-'91): $2,067, 17th
Public library systems: 238
Books & serial vol. per capita: 3.39, 13th
Govt. expend. per capita: $22.43, 10th
State govt.: $1.15, 47th
Local govts.: $21.28, 6th

Law Enforcement, Courts, and Prisons

Police protection expend.: $480,834,000
Per capita: $86.73, 36th
Judicial & legal expend.: $169,675,000
Per capita: $30.61, 46th
Corrections expend.: $318,716,000
Per capita: $57.49, 38th
Police per 10,000 pop. (1990-91): 15.7, 42nd
Prisoners (state & fed.) sentenced to over 1 yr., per 100,000 pop.: 223
Percent change (1989-90): 3.23%, 40th
Death penalty: yes, by electrocution
Under sentence of death: 50, 14th
Executed (1989): none

Religion, Number and Percent of Population

Agnostic: 12,265—0.30%, 37th
Buddhist: 4,088—0.10%, 17th
Christian: 3,577,171—87.50%, 21st
Hindu: NA
Jewish: 12,265—0.30%, 35th
Moslem: 4,089—0.10%, 22nd
Unitarian: 4,088—0.10%, 31st
Other: 77,676—1.90%, 12th
None: 302,526—7.40%, 17th
Refused to answer: 94,029—2.30%, 21st

Making a Living

Personal income per capita (1989): $13,149, 29th
Percent increase (1979-'89) (constant 1989 dollars): 9.9%, 33rd
Average income per family: $40,096, 28th
Percent of pop. below poverty level: 10.7%, 37th
Percent 65 and over: 10.8%, 30th
Cost of living, selected cities
1st qtr., 1991 (U. S. Standard=100)

Richmond	90.6
Indianapolis	97.77
Warsaw	104.6

Economy

Civilian labor force : 2,832,000
Percent of tot. pop.: 51.08%, 25th
Percent 65 and over: 2.26%, 39th
Percent females: 46.26%, 18th
Percent job growth (1980-90): 17.67%, 32nd
Major employer industries:
Agriculture: 75,096—2.80%, 26th
Construction: 136,782—5.10%, 17th
Finance, insurance & real estate: 144,828—5.40%, 24th
Government: 316,476—11.80%, 49th
Manufacturing: 651,726—24.30%, 5th
Mining: 8,765—0.3%, 28th
Service: 463,986—17.30%, 42nd
Trade: 563,220—21.00%, 4th
Transportation, communication, & public utilities: 131,418—4.90%, 29th
Wholesale/retail: 562,041—21.4%, 28th
Unemployment rate: 5.30%, 27th
Male: 2.65%, 37th
Female: 2.61%, 19th
Total businesses (1991): 160,619
New business incorp's. (1991): 10,205
Percent of total businesses: 6.35%, 20th
Business failures (1991): 1,723
Percent of total businesses: 1.07%, 14th
Agriculture farm income
Marketing (1991): $4,474,513,000, 11th
Net per operation: $7,155, 47th
Net per acre: $29, 35th
Leading products: corn, soybeans, hogs, cattle
Av. value land & build. per acre: $1,288, 14th
Percent increase (1980-90): -30.86%, 47th
Govt. payments: $210,055,000, 15th
Construction, value of all: $3,453,000,000
Per capita: $622.82, 20th
Percent change 1989-90: -7.43%, 27th

Manufactures:
Value added: : $44,924,000,000
Per capita: $8,102.94, 2nd
Value of shipments: $98,619,000,000
Per capita: $17,787.91, 2nd
Leading products: primary and fabricated metals, transportation equipment, electrical and electronic equipment, non-electrical machinery, plastics, chemical products, foods
Mining, min. prod., value (1987): $1,118,000,000, 27th
Leading products: coal, petroleum, stone
Retail sales: $37,574,000,000, 14th
Per household: $18,153, 33rd
Percent increase (1987-90): 8.1%, 43rd
Service indust., value (1987): $17,994,000,000, 19th
Per capita: $3,245.58, 37th
Tourism indus., value (1989): $3,493,000,000, 26th
Foreign exports value: $5,273,000,000, 16th
Per capita: $951.09, 21st
Patents per 1,000 pop.: 5.3, 31st

Travel and Transportation

Motor vehicle registrations: 4,365,760
Per 1,000 pop.: 787, 27th
Motorcycle registrations: 96,712
Per 1,000 pop.: 17, 25th
Licensed drivers per 1,000 driving age pop.: 845, 41st
Deaths from motor vehicle accidents per 100,000 pop.: 18.9, 24th
Public roads & streets
Total mileage: 91,908, 19th
Rural mileage: 74,040, 18th
Urban mileage: 17,868, 13th
Interstate mileage: 1,148, 13th
Annual vehicle-miles of travel per person: 9,685, 14th
Mean travel time for workers 16 + who work away from home: 20.4 min., 29th

Government

Registered voters (1988): 2,865,852
Percent of voting age pop.: 70.45%, 26th
Voter turnout (1988): 2,168,621
Percent of registered voters: 75.67%, 14th
Percent of voting age pop.: 53.31%, 23rd
State legislators, total (1992): 150, 20th
Women members (1992): 26
Percent of legislature: 17.3%, 26th
Dominant party (1992): Split
U. S. Congress, House members (1993): 10
Increase 1983-93: 0
Revenues:
State govt.: $11,456,232,000
Per capita: $2,066.36, 42nd
State & local govt.: $18,168,008,000
Per capita: $3,276.96, 45th
Indebtedness:
State govt.: $4,140,038,000
Per capita: $746.74, 40th
State & local govt.: $10,883,000,000
Per capita: $1,962.97, 48th

Laws and Regulations

Legal driving age: 18
Marriage age without parental consent: 18
Divorce residence requirement: 6 mo., qualification—check local statutes

Attractions

Major opera companies (1989): 2, 21st
Per 1 million pop.: 0.36, 40th
Major symphony orchestras (1989): 25, 12th
Per 1 million pop.: 4.47, 17th
State appropriations for state arts agencies per capita: $0.42, 44th
State Fair in mid-Aug. at Indianapolis

Sports and Competition

NCAA sports teams, 10: Ball State Univ. Cardinals, Butler Univ. Bulldogs, Indiana State Univ. Sycamores, Indiana Univ. Fightin' Hoosiers, Indiana Univ.-Purdue Univ. Mastodons, Purdue Univ. Boilermakers, St. Joseph's College Pumas, Univ. of

Evansville Aces, Univ. of Notre Dame Fighting Irish, Valparaiso Univ. Crusaders.

Professional teams, ,7:

Baseball, 2,—Indianapolis Indians (American Association, Class AAA), Owen J. Bush Stadium; South Bend White Sox (Midwest League Class AAA), Stanley Coveleski Regional Stadium

Basketball, 2—Fort Wayne Fury (Continental Basketball Association), Allen County War Memorial Coliseum; Indiana Pacers (NBA), Market Square arena

Football, 1—Indianapolis Colts (NFL), Hoosier Dome

Hockey, 2—Fort Wayne Komets (International Hockey League), Allen County Memorial Coliseum; Indianapolis Ice (International Hockey League), Indiana State Fairgrounds

IOWA

"The people who have lived on the land between the two great rivers have fought, struggled, labored, laughed, and grown in wealth and culture through the years. No other similar area has produced so much to feed the world—Iowa, an often neglected treasure!"

Allan Carpenter, native of Waterloo, Iowa

Many think of Iowa as a land of huge farms and small cities populated by people right out of Meredith Willson's *The Music Man.* True, it is one of the greatest farming states in the country, producing about one-fifth of the nation's corn supply and containing about a quarter of the country's richest farmlands. But it is also a leader in manufacturing cereals, tractors, and washing machines. Iowa also is the state with the highest literacy rate in the nation, one of the finest writing schools in the country (the University of Iowa), and among its notables are many authors and artists, including Grant Wood. The state is known as the "Hartford of the West" because of its many insurance company headquarters.

So They Say

"The Indians treated the exploring party (Marquette and Jolliet) with great respect, preparing a huge feast of dog meat and other delicacies. The hosts, as a sign of honor, insisted on placing the food in the mouths of the guests, much to the visitors' discomfort."

The Palimpsest

SUPERLATIVES

• Herbert Hoover, first U.S. president born west of the Mississippi River, was from Iowa.

• The first state ever to produce a billion-dollar harvest from a single crop.

• Produced the first "traction machine" (tractor).

• World's largest tractor plant is at Waterloo.

• The mechanical washing machine was first manufactured in Iowa.

MOMENTS IN HISTORY

• In 1763 European explorers first glimpsed present-day Iowa as Father Jacques Marquette and Louis Jolliet marvelled at the Iowa bluffs soaring above the Mississippi River.

• The French claimed the region, and explorer Joseph Des Noyelles fought a little-known battle with the Fox and Sauk Indians in 1735, at the junction of the Raccoon and Des Moines rivers.

• In 1762 France turned over to Spain its claims west of the Mississippi, including Iowa.

• In 1788 Julian Dubuque settled at Catfish Creek on the Missisippi, founding the community of Dubuque, where he mined the plentiful lead of the region.

• The Louisiana Purchase of 1803 brought Iowa to the United States.

• In 1804 Sergean Floyd of the famed Lewis and Clark expedition died at the site of Sioux City, the only member of the party to die on the journey, and he was buried there.

• At present-day Burlington, explorer Zebulon Pike hoisted the first U.S. flag to fly over Iowa, in 1805. The bluff near McGregor was named Pike's Peak.

• In 1819 the first steamer, the *Western Engineer,*

reached the area of Council Bluffs on the Missouri River.

• On December 28, 1846, Iowa became the first free state in the old Louisiana Territory.

• In 1856 the bridge between Davenport and Rock Island was the first to span the mighty Mississippi River.

• Progress continued rapidly with the first state fair, at Fairfield in 1854, at the University of Iowa at Iowa City in 1855, and at the new capital at Des Moines in 1856.

• Notorious abolitionist John Brown headquarted for a time at Tabor as he helped slaves escape to freedom over the "Underground Railroad."

• Iowa Civil War troops were especially prominent in the battle of Wilson's Creek (Aug. 20, 1861) and Iuka (Sept. 19, 1862)

So They Say

"We fixed our sword bayonets on our good Whitney rifles and sat down to wait the coming foe....We hear their very tramp. We think of Iowa. She shall not be dishonored; rather every man at Iuka die than that."

Iowa poet, S.H.M. Byers

• In 1869 Council Bluffs became the central terminal of the first transcontinental railroad.

• In 1889 Grinnell College and the University of Iowa played the first intercollegiate football game west of the Mississippi.

• In the 1890s the small city of Independence became internationally famous as a center for trotting races.

• In 1917 Iowa serviceman Merle Hay was one of the first three Americans to be killed during World War I. Iowan J.C. Sabin is said to have fired the first U.S. shot of that war.

• In 1932, for the first time since before the Civil War, the Democratic Party gained complete control of Iowa government.

• During World War II 260,000 Iowans served, and 8,398 lost their lives.

• The 1980s brought increasing problems to Iowa farmers, with rising costs, falling prices and values, and overextended debt, but the early 1990s brought an increasing upturn for Iowa agriculture in a state which nearly every year produces more foodstuffs than any other.

That's Interesting

• When the Fox Indians refused to do a favor for Julian Dubuque, he threatened to burn the Mississippi. At the mouth of Catfish Creek, Dubuque set fire to oil poured into the creek upstream by an assistant. The frightened Indians quickly came to terms, and Dubuque called on the fire to die just as the oil gave out.

• The honey trees of a region disputed between Iowa and Missouri were so prized as a source of sweetening that the two states almost came to blows in a territorial dispute called the "Honey War."

• Iowa's Civil War Greybeard Regiment, made up of men over the legal age of 45, was the only one of its kind ever authorized.

• The first "road" in Iowa consisted of a furrow plowed by Lyman Dillon from Dubuque to Iowa City, thought to be the longest continuous furrow ever plowed.

• James "Tama Jim" Wilson of Traer holds the all-time record for cabinet service in any cabinet office—16 yrs. as secretary of agriculture.

• Famed composer Antonin Dvorak spent a summer in Iowa and one day jotted a musical inspiration on his shirt cuff. He managed to rescue the shirt just before it went to the wash, and his "Indian Lament" was the result.

• One Iowan traveling in Scotland was so taken with the local oatmeal that he ordered a barrel of it sent to him in Iowa. When it arrived from Scotland, it bore the legend, "Quaker Oats, made in Cedar Rapids, Iowa."

• The popular Delicious apple originated in Iowa.

Notable Natives

Adrian Constantine "Cap" Anson (Marshalltown, 1851-1922), baseball player/manager. **William Frederick "Buffalo Bill" Cody** (Scott County, 1846-1917), frontiersman/showman. **James Norman Hall** (Colfax, 1887-1951), author. **Herbert Clark Hoover** (West Branch, 1874-

1964), U.S. president. **Emerson Hough** (Newton, 1857-1923), author. **MacKinlay Kantor** (Webster City, 1904-1977), author. **Phil Stong** (Pittsburgh, IA, 1899-1957), author. **William Ashley "Billy" Sunday** (1862-1935), baseball player/evangelist. **James Van Allen** (Mount Pleasant, 1914-), astrophysicist. **Henry Agard Wallace** (Adair County, 1888-1965), U.S. vice-president. **John Wayne** (winterset, 1907-1979), actor. **Margaret Wilson** (Traer, 1882-1976), Pulitzer-Prize-winning author. **Grant Wood** (near Anamosa, 1892-1942), artist.

General

Admitted to statehood: Dec. 28, 1846
Origin of name: Indian word variously translated as "one who puts to sleep" or "beautiful land"
Capital: Des Moines
Nickname: The Hawkeye State
Motto: "Our liberties we prize and our rights we will maintain"
Bird: Eastern goldfinch
Flower: wild rose
Song: "Song of Iowa"
Stone: geode
Tree: oak

The Land

Area: 56,276 sq. mi., 26th
Land: 55,875 sq. mi., 23rd
Water: 401 sq. mi., 44th
Topography: watershed from NW to SE, soil especially rich and land level in the N central counties
Number of counties: 99
Geographic center: Story County, 5 mi. NE of Ames
Length: 310 mi.
Width: 200 mi.
Highest point: 1,670 ft. (Sec. 29, T100N, R41W, Osceola County), 42nd
Lowest point: 480 ft. (Mississippi River), 38th
Mean elevation: 1,100 ft., 22nd

Climate and Environment

Temp., highest: 118 deg. on July 20, 1934, at Keokuk; lowest: -47 deg. on Jan. 12, 1912, at Washta
Fresh water withdrawn, per capita, per day: 960 gal., 33rd
Endangered species: mammals, 1—Indiana bat; birds, 2—American peregrine falcon, least tern; reptiles, none; amphibians, none; fishes, 1; invertebrates, 3; plants, 1

Major Cities, Population Percentage Increase (1980-90)

Cedar Rapids, 108,751— –1.35%
Davenport, 95,333— –7.68%
Des Moines, 193,187—1.14%
Sioux City, 80,505— –1.83%
Waterloo, 66,467— –12.53%

The People

Population: 2,776,755, 30th
Percent change (1980-90): -4.94%, 49th
Per sq. mi: 49.34, 34th
Percent in metro. area: 44.04%, 40th
Percent foreign born: 1.6%, 41st
White: 2,683,090—96.63%, 4th
Black: 48,090—1.73%, 41st
Native American: 7,349—0.26%, 36th
Asian, Pacific Isle: 25,476—0.92%, 32nd
Other races: 12,750—0.46%, 37th
Hispanic origin: 32,647—1.18%, 38th
Percent over 5 yrs. speaking language other than English at home: 3.9%, 42nd
Percent males: 48.43%, 35th
Percent females: 51.57%, 17th
Percent never married: 23.7%, 39th
Marriages per 1,000 (1989): 8.5, 34th
Divorces per 1,000 (1989): 3.5, 42nd
Median age: 34
Under 5 years: 193,203—6.96%, 40th
Under 18 years: 718,880—25.89%, 26th
65 years & older: 426,106—15.35%, 3rd
Percent increase among the elderly: 9.9%, 48th

Of Vital Importance

Live births per 1,000 pop.: 13.9, 48th
Infant mortality rate per 1,000 births (1988): 8.7, 37th
Average lifetime (1979-81): 75.18, 9th
Deaths per 100,000 pop. (1988): 983.4, 8th

Causes of death per 100,000 pop. (1988):
- Diseases of heart: 359.2, 9th
- Malignant neoplasms: 218.4, 10th
- Cerebrovascular diseases: 78.1, 2nd
- Accidents & adverse effects: 41.4, 24th
- Chronic obstructive pulmonary diseases: 42.5, 7th
- Suicide: 11.2, 38th
- HIV infection: 0.8, 47th
- Other: 86.9, 4th

KEEPING WELL

Non-federal physicians per 100,000 pop.: 170, 43rd
Dentists per 100,000 (1990-91): 64, 23rd
Nurses per 100,000 (1989): 813, 12th
Hospitals per 100,000: 4.8, 9th
- Admissions per 100,000: 14,556, 17th
- Beds per 100,000: 621.26, 9th
- Occupancy rate: 65.4%, 27th
- Semiprivate room charges per day: $221, 39th
- Average stay: 7.6, 16th

Notifiable diseases per 100,000:
- AIDS: 2.5, 47th
- Gonorrhea: 83.9, 38th
- Measles: 0.9, 41st
- Syphillis: 5.3, 38th
- Tuberculosis (TB): 2.6, 42nd

Per capita spending on mental health programs (1987): $32.46, 32nd
Pop. without health insur. (1991): 8.8%, 45th

HOUSEHOLDS BY TYPE

Total households: 1,064,325
- Percent change (1980-90): 1.08%, 49th

Family households: 740,819
- Percent of total: 69.60%, 35th

Nonfamily households: 323,506
- Percent of total: 30.40%, 18th

Persons per household: 2.52, 46th
Pop. living in group quarters: 99,520
- Percent of pop.: 3.58%, 7th

LIVING QUARTERS

Total housing units: 1,143,669
- Persons per unit: 2.43, 19th

Occupied housing units: 1,064,325
- Percent of total units: 93.06%, 4th
- Persons per unit: 2.44, 48th
- Percent of units with over 1 person per room: 1.50%, 51st

Owner-occupied units: 745,377
- Percent of total units: 65.17%, 2nd
- Percent of occupied units: 70.03%, 11th
- Persons per unit: 2.63, 44th
- Median value: $15,900, 51st

Renter-occupied units: 318,948
- Percent of total units: 27.89%, 31st
- Percent of occupied units: 29.97%, 41st
- Persons per unit: 2.25, 39th
- Median contract rent: $216, 50th
- Rental vacancy rate: 6.4%, 45th

Mobile home, trailer & other as a % of occupied housing units: 6.43%, 41st

CRIME INDEX PER 100,000

Total: 4,101, 42nd
- Violent: 300, 40th
  - Murder and nonnegligent manslaughter: 2, 49th
  - Aggravated assault: 6,958, 40th
  - Robbery: 39, 42nd
  - Rape: 18, 50th
- Property: 3,801, 42nd
  - Burglary: 808, 40th
  - Larceny, theft: 2,823, 37th
  - Motor vehicle theft: 170, 46th

Drug abuse arrests: 116, 43rd

TEACHING AND LEARNING

Literacy (1987): 90%, 14th
Pop. 3 and over enrolled in school: 737,729
- Percent of pop.: 27.7%, 22nd

Public elementary & secondary schools:
- Total enrollment: 466,000
- Avg. class size (1987): 21, 35th
- Teachers: 30,900
  - Percent of pop.: 1.11%, 13th
- Teachers' avg. salary: $26,700, 37th
- Spending per capita: $777, 31st
- Spending per pupil in avg. daily attendance: $4,590, 25th

Percent of graduates taking SAT: 5%, 48th
- Combined SAT scores: 1093, 1st

Percent of pop. over 25 completing:

High school: 80.1%, 14th
College degree/s: 16.9%, 41st
Higher educa., institutions: 58
Per 100,000 pop.: 0.6, 27th
Enroll: 170,515
Percent of pop.: 6.14%, 13th
Public: 117,834
Percent of enroll.: 69.10%, 43rd
Private: 52,681
Percent of enroll.: 30.90%, 9th
White non-Hispanic: 617,626
Percent of enroll.: 68.52%, 47th
Black non-Hispanic: 80,458
Percent of enroll.: 8.93%, 18th
Hispanic: 148,296
Percent of enroll.: 16.45%, 2nd
Asian/Pacific Islander: 27,907
Percent of enroll.: 3.10%, 13th
Amer. Indian/AK native: 3,006
Percent of enroll.: 0.33%, 29th
Nonresident alien: 24,144
Percent of enroll.: 2.68%, 16th
Female: 91,011
Percent of enroll.: 53.37%, 40th
Tuition, state university ('90-'91): $1,880, 23rd
Public library systems: 500
Books & serial vol. per capita: 3.82, 8th
Govt. expend. per capita: $18.55, 19th
State govt.: $2.25, 30th
Local govts.: $16.30, 19th

Law Enforcement, Courts, and Prisons

Police protection expend.: $232,868,000
Per capita: $83.86, 39th
Judicial & legal expend.: $136,300,000
Per capita: $49.08, 24th
Corrections expend.: $124,582,000
Per capita: $44.86, 45th
Police per 10,000 pop. (1990-91): 15.5, 44th
Prisoners (state & fed.) sentenced to over 1 yr., per 100,000 pop.: 139
Percent change (1989-90): 10.69%, 10th
Death penalty: no

Religion, Number and Percent of Population

Agnostic: 22,637—1.10%, 6th
Buddhist: NA
Christian: 1,837,682—89.30%, 15th
Hindu: 2,058—0.10%, 10th
Jewish: NA
Moslem: NA
Unitarian: 2,058—0.10%, 31st
Other: 41,158—2.00%, 10th
None: 121,415—5.90%, 34th
Refused to answer: 30,868—1.50%, 42nd

Making a Living

Personal income per capita (1989): $12,422, 35th
Percent increase (1979-'89) (constant 1989 dollars): 3.9%, 44th
Average income per family: $37,227, 36th
Percent of pop. below poverty level: 11.5%, 31st
Percent 65 and over: 11.2%, 28th
Cost of living, selected cities
1st qtr., 1991 (U. S. Standard=100)

Waterloo-Cedar Falls	94.7
Marshalltown	99.6
Des Moines (1st Qtr., 1989)	104.9

Economy

Civilian labor force : 1,496,000
Percent of tot. pop.: 53.88%, 7th
Percent 65 and over: 4.34%, 3rd
Percent females: 45.52%, 27th
Percent job growth (1980-90): 7.04%, 47th
Major employer industries:
Agriculture: 140,434—9.80%, 3rd
Construction: 47,289—3.30%, 48th
Finance, insurance & real estate: 78,815—5.50%, 22nd
Government: 243,610—17.00%, 15th
Manufacturing: 246,476—17.20%, 22nd
Mining: 1,889—0.1%, 41st
Service: 250,775—17.50%, 41st
Trade: 249,342—17.40%, 45th
Transportation, communication, & public utilities: 57,320—4.00%, 47th
Wholesale/retail: 294,229—22.0%, 14th

Unemployment rate: 4.21%, 46th
Male: 2.34%, 43rd
Female: 1.87%, 45th
Total businesses (1991): 168,153
New business incorp's. (1991): 4,531
Percent of total businesses: 2.69%, 49th
Business failures (1991): 288
Percent of total businesses: 0.17%, 51st
Agriculture farm income
Marketing (1991): $10,179,249,000, 3rd
Net per operation: $22,462, 21st
Net per acre: $68, 21st
Leading products: hogs, corn, cattle, soybeans
Av. value land & build. per acre: $1,130, 17th
Percent increase (1980-90): -38.59%, 48th
Govt. payments: $644,955,000, 3rd
Construction, value of all: $1,249,000,000
Per capita: $449.81, 38th
Percent change 1989-90: 6.57%, 14th
Manufactures:
Value added: : $19,503,000,000
Per capita: $7,023.67, 6th
Value of shipments: $45,927,000,000
Per capita: $16,539.81, 5th
Leading products: tires, farm machinery, electronic products, appliances, office furniture, chemicals, fertilizers, auto accessories
Mining, min. prod., value (1987): $196,000,000, 39th
Leading products: stone, cement, sand/gravel
Retail sales: $18,818,000,000, 30th
Per household: $17,724, 37th
Percent increase (1987-90): 25.5%, 5th
Service indust., value (1987): $8,758,000,000, 32nd
Per capita: $3,154.04, 41st
Tourism indus., value (1989): $2,341,000,000, 33rd
Foreign exports value: $2,189,000,000, 30th
Per capita: $788.33, 31st
Patents per 1,000 pop.: 7.2, 25th

TRAVEL AND TRANSPORTATION

Motor vehicle registrations: 2,631,973
Per 1,000 pop.: 947, 7th
Motorcycle registrations: 173,367
Per 1,000 pop.: 62, 1st
Licensed drivers per 1,000 driving age pop.: 867, 38th
Deaths from motor vehicle accidents per 100,000 pop.: 16.7, 33rd
Public roads & streets
Total mileage: 112,541, 10th
Rural mileage: 103,755, 6th
Urban mileage: 8,786, 29th
Interstate mileage: 782, 28th
Annual vehicle-miles of travel per person: 8,280, 39th
Mean travel time for workers 16 + who work away from home: 16.2 min., 46th

GOVERNMENT

Registered voters (1988): 1,690,093
Percent of voting age pop.: 81.73%, 9th
Voter turnout (1988): 1,225,614
Percent of registered voters: 72.52%, 21st
Percent of voting age pop.: 59.27%, 8th
State legislators, total (1992): 150, 20th
Women members (1992): 22
Percent of legislature: 14.7%, 31st
Dominant party (1992): Democrats
U. S. Congress, House members (1993): 5
Increase 1983-93: -1
Revenues:
State govt.: $6,727,704,000
Per capita: $2,422.87, 27th
State & local govt.: $10,511,043,000
Per capita: $3,785.37, 29th
Indebtedness:
State govt.: $1,875,183,000
Per capita: $675.31, 43rd
State & local govt.: $5,456,000,000
Per capita: $1,964.88, 47th

LAWS AND REGULATIONS

Legal driving age: 18
Marriage age without parental consent: 18
Divorce residence requirement: 1 yr., qualification—check local statutes

ATTRACTIONS

Major opera companies (1989): 1, 30th
Per 1 million pop.: 0.35, 41st
Major symphony orchestras (1989): 18, 17th
Per 1 million pop.: 6.34, 7th

State appropriations for state arts agencies per capita: $0.52, 34th

State Fair in mid-Aug. at Des Moines

Sports and Competition

NCAA sports teams, 7: Drake Univ. Bulldogs, Iowa State Univ. Cyclones, Simpson College Flames, Univ. of Dubuque Spartans, Univ. of Iowa Hawkeyes, Univ. of Northern Iowa Panthers, William Penn College Statesmen.

Professional teams, 7:

Baseball, 6—Burlington Astros (Midwest League, Class A), Community Field; Quad City Angels (Midwest League, Class A), John O'Donnell Stadium; Waterloo Diamonds (Midwest League, Class A), Municipal Stadium; Clinton Giants (Midwest League, Class A), Riverview Stadium; Iowa Cubs (American Association, Class AAA), Sec Taylor Stadium; Cedar Rapids Reds (Midwest League, Class A), Veterans Memorial Ballpark

Basketball, 1—Cedar Rapids Silver Bullets (Continental Basketball Association), Five Seasons Center

KANSAS

"There is no monument under heaven on which I would rather have my name inscribed than on this goodly state of Kansas."

Henry Ward Beecher

"To understand why people say 'Dear old Kansas!' is to understand that Kansas is no mere geographical expression, but a state of mind, a religion and a philosophy in one."

Carl Becker

Kansas is the world's breadbasket, producing far more wheat than any other region of its size, and Hutchison is a world grain center. By contrast, the state is also a world center of aviation manufacture, with Wichita the leader in private aircraft production. Its historic trails were critical in the opening of the West. Dodge City, "the cowboy capital of the world," was once the world's largest cattle-market town—a dusty, brawling crossroads that was home to Wyatt Earp, Bat Masterson, and Wild Bill Hickock. Perhaps unexpectedly this prairie state is also a world center of psychiatric study and practice, thanks to the Menninger family of Topeka.

Superlatives

• A point in Kansas near Osborne is the geodetic center of the United States.

• World's greatest salt deposits, at Hutchison.

• First in wheat production.

• World's largest primary hard wheat market.

• Pony Express founded at Leavenworth.

• Claims more newspapers per capita than any other state.

• World leader in personal aircraft production.

Moments in History

• In 1541, Spanish explorer Francisco Vasquez de Coronado came overland from Mexico, reaching what is now Junction City, before turning back.

> **So They Say**
> "The plains are full of crooked necked oxen."
> Coronado's description of the buffalo

• In 1719 French explorer Claude du Tisne crossed the southeastern border of present-day Kansas, but aside from a few other explorers Kansas remained Indian country.

• Explorer Zebulon Pike crossed the length of Kansas in 1806. At a "grand council" with the Pawnees, he raised the U.S. flag for the first time in Kansas territory.

> **So They Say**
> "...I stood on a hill and in one view below me saw buffalo, elk, deer, cabrie (antelope) and panthers....I prevented the men shooting at the game, not merely because of the scarcity of ammunition, but, as I conceived, the laws of morality forbade it also."
> Zebulon Pike

• In 1822 Captain W.H. Becknell pioneered the Santa Fe Trail, and before long thousands of wagons used the trail, crossing 500 mi. of Kansas to carry on very profitable trade with New Mexico. Fortunes were sometimes made in a single round trip.

• In 1824 Benton Pixley established a mission to the Osage Indians in present Neosho County, and in the years that followed the Kansas plains were dotted with mission stations of many denominations.

• Fort Leavenworth was established in 1827.

• In 1854 Kansas was opened to settlement by the Kansas-Nebraska Act. This act permitted the residents of the territory to decide whether the territory would be free or slave, setting the stage for a frantic period when both sides came to blows over slavery, and Kansas became "Bloody Kansas."

• The population grew and Kansas became a free state on January 29, 1861.

• During the war, Confederate raiders made many attacks on Kansas communities. Notorious raider William Clarke Quantrill raided Lawrence on August 21, 1863, burned 200 buildings, and killed 150 innocent civilians.

> **So They Say**
>
> "...During all this time citizens were being murdered everywhere. Germans and Negroes...were shot immediately....In many instances (women) placed themselves between their husbands and fathers...when the drunken fiends held cocked pistols at them."
>
> A Kansas newspaper reporting on Quantrill's raid on Lawrence

• In the Battle of Mine Creek, October 25, 1864, Union forces were victorious, and the threat of Confederate invasion was ended. Kansas sent to the war the highest percentage of its eligible men of all the states and suffered the most casualties in proportion to population.

• In 1867 the first cattle were driven up the Chisholm Trail to Abilene, where the railroad had arrived.

• As the railroad moved west, other communities became the principal cow towns, including famed Dodge City, which was established in 1872.

• In 1887 Susanna Salter was elected mayor of Argonia, said to be the first woman mayor in the United States.

• Kansas sent four regiments into the Spanish-American War in 1898.

• During World War I thousands of Kansas acres were plowed for the first time to provide food, but later during the drought of the 1930s, dirt from these fields was carried up into terrible duststorms.

• During 1951 Kansas experienced great floods, with damage amounting to $2.5 billion.

• Kansas' adopted son, Dwight David Eisenhower, won the 1952 presidential election.

• In 1954 the U.S. Supreme Court decided against the segregation policies of the Topeka school system in a famed and far-reaching decision.

• In 1987 Alf Landon celebrated his 100th birthday, but within a few weeks Kansas lost its beloved centenarian.

That's Interesting

• The legendary lawmen of Dodge City, such as Bat Masterson and Wyatt Earp, were not always as heroic as they have been portrayed. On one occasion, Wyatt Earp was said to have "amateurishly loaded all six chambers of his revolver and blasted a hole through his coat."

• Pioneering the Santa Fe Trail, the Becknell party almost died of thirst on the dry bed of the Cimarron River until they discovered by accident that the river was "flowing" beneath the sand.

• With the slaughter of the buffalo, the scattered bones became so valuable that they were collected by the tons, and Dodge City bankers and businesses accepted them as legal tender.

Notable Natives

Walter Percy Chrysler (Wamego, 1875-1940), automobile manufacturer. **John Steuart Curry** (Jefferson County, 1897-1946), painter. **Charles Curtis** (Topeka, 1860-1936), U.S. vice-president. **Amelia Mary Earhart** (Atchison, 1897-1937), aviator. **William Inge** (Independence, 1913-1973), playwright. **Edgar Lee Masters** (Garnett, 1869-1950), poet and biographer. **Carl Menninger** (Topeka, 1893-1990), psychiatrist. **Damon Run-**

yan (Manhattan, KS, 1884-1946), journalist and author.

General

Admitted to statehood: Jan. 29, 1861
Origin of name: Sioux word for "south wind people"
Capital: Topeka, founded 1854
Nicknames: Sunflower State and Jayhawk State
Motto: *"Ad Astra per Aspera"* ("To the Stars through Difficulties")
Animal: American buffalo
Bird: Western meadowlark
Flower: wild native sunflower (Helianthus)
Insect: honeybee
March: "The Kansas March"
Song: "Home on the Range"
Tree: Cottonwood

The Land

Area: 82,282 sq. mi., 15th
Land: 81,823 sq. mi., 13th
Water: 459 sq. mi., 43rd
Topography: hilly Osage plains in the E, central region level prairie and hills, high plains in the W
Number of counties: 105
Geographic center: Barton, 15 mi. NE of Great Bend
Length: 400 mi.
Width: 210 mi.
Highest point: 4,039 ft. (Mount Sunflower), 28th
Lowest point: 679 ft. (Verdigris River), 43rd
Mean elevation: 2,000 ft., 14th

Climate and Environment

Temp., highest: 121 deg. on July 24, 1936 near Alton; lowest: -40 deg. on Feb. 13, 1905, at Lebanon
Fresh water withdrawn, per capita, per day: 2,310 gal., 12th
Endangered species: mammals, 2—gray bat, Indiana bat; birds, 5—whooping crane, Eskimo curlew, American peregrine falcon, least tern, black-capped vireo; reptiles, none; amphibians, none; fishes, 1; invertebrates, none; plants, 2

Major Cities, Population Percentage Increase (1980-90)

Kansas City, 149,767— –7.06%
Lawrence, 65,608—24.40%
Overland Park, 111,790—36.69%
Topeka, 119,883—1.01%
Wichita, 304,011—8.64%

The People

Population: 2,477,574, 32nd
Percent change (1980-90): 4.57%, 29th
Per sq. mi: 30.11, 40th
Percent in metro. area: 53.80%, 36th
Percent foreign born: 2.5%, 31st
White: 2,231,986—90.09%, 19th
Black: 143,076—5.77%, 28th
Native American: 21,965—0.89%, 16th
Asian, Pacific Isle: 31,750—1.28%, 22nd
Other races: 48,797—1.97%, 18th
Hispanic origin: 93,670—3.78%, 21st
Percent over 5 yrs. speaking language other than English at home: 5.7%, 33rd
Percent males: 49.03%, 19th
Percent females: 50.97%, 33rd
Percent never married: 22.7%, 43rd
Marriages per 1,000 (1989): 9.3, 26th
Divorces per 1,000 (1989): 5.0, 20th
Median age: 32.9
Under 5 years: 188,390—7.60%, 16th
Under 18 years: 661,614—26.70%, 13th
65 years & older: 342,571—13.83%, 11th
Percent increase among the elderly: 11.9%, 45th

Of Vital Importance

Live births per 1,000 pop.: 15.4, 34th
Infant mortality rate per 1,000 births (1988): 8.0, 45th
Average lifetime (1979-81): 75.31, 7th
Deaths per 100,000 pop. (1988): 921.5, 21st
Causes of death per 100,000 pop. (1988):
Diseases of heart: 322.8, 22nd
Malignant neoplasms: 199.6, 25th
Cerebrovascular diseases: 71.3, 11th
Accidents & adverse effects: 40.2, 26th
Chronic obstructive pulmonary diseases: 40.4, 13th

Suicide: 12.3, 28th
HIV infection: 2.2, 29th
Other: 79.1, 16th

Keeping Well

Non-federal physicians per 100,000 pop.: 196, 32nd
Dentists per 100,000 (1990-91): 60, 28th
Nurses per 100,000 (1989): 715, 22nd
Hospitals per 100,000: 6.5, 6th
Admissions per 100,000: 13,530, 27th
Beds per 100,000: 651.40, 6th
Occupancy rate: 61.3%, 40th
Semiprivate room charges per day: $256, 30th
Average stay: 7.6, 17th
Notifiable diseases per 100,000:
AIDS: 5.5, 36th
Gonorrhea: 195.6, 26th
Measles: 9.4, 8th
Syphillis: 7.1, 35th
Tuberculosis (TB): 3.1, 38th
Per capita spending on mental health programs (1987): $43.51, 19th
Pop. without health insur. (1991): 11.4%, 32nd

Households by Type

Total households: 944,726
Percent change (1980-90): 8.34%, 35th
Family households: 658,600
Percent of total: 69.71%, 32nd
Nonfamily households: 286,126
Percent of total: 30.29%, 20th
Persons per household: 2.53, 42nd
Pop. living in group quarters: 82,765
Percent of pop.: 3.34%, 13th

Living Quarters

Total housing units: 1,044,112
Persons per unit: 2.37, 32nd
Occupied housing units: 944,726
Percent of total units: 90.48%, 19th
Persons per unit: 2.48, 38th
Percent of units with over 1 person per room: 2.51%, 36th
Owner-occupied units: 641,762
Percent of total units: 61.46%, 14th
Percent of occupied units: 67.93%, 22nd
Persons per unit: 2.64, 43rd
Median value: $52,200, 42nd
Renter-occupied units: 302,964
Percent of total units: 29.02%, 27th
Percent of occupied units: 32.07%, 30th
Persons per unit: 2.31, 30th
Median contract rent: $285, 33rd
Rental vacancy rate: 11.1%, 12th
Mobile home, trailer & other as a % of occupied housing units: 8.30%, 31st

Crime Index per 100,000

Total: 5,193, 27th
Violent: 448, 31st
Murder and nonnegligent manslaughter: 4, 40th
Aggravated assault: 7,604, 17th
Robbery: 118, 29th
Rape: 40, 23rd
Property: 4,745, 25th
Burglary: 1,167, 21st
Larceny, theft: 3,244, 19th
Motor vehicle theft: 335, 34th
Drug abuse arrests: 223, 30th

Teaching and Learning

Literacy (1987): 91%, 9th
Pop. 3 and over enrolled in school: 668,365
Percent of pop.: 28.2%, 15th
Public elementary & secondary schools:
Total enrollment: 437,000
Avg. class size (1987): 20, 41st
Teachers: 28,700
Percent of pop.: 1.16%, 9th
Teachers' avg. salary: $28,700, 28th
Spending per capita: $819, 24th
Spending per pupil in avg. daily attendance: $4,706, 22nd
Percent of graduates taking SAT: 10%, 41st
Combined SAT scores: 1039, 4th
Percent of pop. over 25 completing:
High school: 81.3%, 10th
College degree/s: 21.1%, 19th
Higher educa., institutions: 53
Per 100,000 pop.: 1.2, 6th
Enroll: 163,478
Percent of pop.: 6.60%, 9th
Public: 149,220
Percent of enroll.: 91.28%, 7th

Private: 14,258
Percent of enroll.: 8.72%, 45th
White non-Hispanic: 48,024
Percent of enroll.: 92.57%, 7th
Black non-Hispanic: 310
Percent of enroll.: 0.60%, 48th
Hispanic: 1,004
Percent of enroll.: 1.94%, 19th
Asian/Pacific Islander: 706
Percent of enroll.: 1.36%, 35th
Amer. Indian/AK native: 485
Percent of enroll.: 0.93%, 16th
Nonresident alien: 1,352
Percent of enroll.: 2.61%, 17th
Female: 89,941
Percent of enroll.: 55.02%, 24th
Tuition, state university ('90-'91): $1,569, 32nd
Public library systems: 318
Books & serial vol. per capita: 4.04, 6th
Govt. expend. per capita: $12.42, 34th
State govt.: $1.71, 41st
Local govts.: $10.70, 30th

Law Enforcement, Courts, and Prisons

Police protection expend.: $228,452,000
Per capita: $92.19, 32nd
Judicial & legal expend.: $120,651,000
Per capita: $48.69, 26th
Corrections expend.: $210,011,000
Per capita: $84.75, 20th
Police per 10,000 pop. (1990-91): 21.5, 21st
Prisoners (state & fed.) sentenced to over 1 yr., per 100,000 pop.: 227
Percent change (1989-90): 2.87%, 41st
Death penalty: no

Religion, Number and Percent of Population

Agnostic: 10,896—0.60%, 19th
Buddhist: 5,448—0.30%, 8th
Christian: 1,632,548—89.90%, 12th
Hindu: 1,816.0—0.10%, 10th
Jewish: 5,448—0.30%, 35th
Moslem: 1,816—0.10%, 22nd
Unitarian: 7,264—0.40%, 8th
Other: 16,344—0.90%, 35th
None: 103,510—5.70%, 37th
Refused to answer: 30,871—1.70%, 35th

Making a Living

Personal income per capita (1989): $13,300, 27th
Percent increase (1979-'89) (constant 1989 dollars): 8.0%, 38th
Average income per family: $40,040, 29th
Percent of pop. below poverty level: 11.5%, 30th
Percent 65 and over: 12.0%, 24th
Cost of living, selected cities
1st qtr., 1991 (U. S. Standard=100)

Salina	86.5
Wichita	95.2
Hays	96.7

Economy

Civilian labor force : 1,300,000
Percent of tot. pop.: 52.47%, 15th
Percent 65 and over: 4.46%, 2nd
Percent females: 44.85%, 38th
Percent job growth (1980-90): 14.47%, 38th
Major employer industries:
Agriculture: 77,066—6.20%, 8th
Construction: 49,720—4.00%, 37th
Finance, insurance & real estate: 70,851—5.70%, 19th
Government: 211,310—17.00%, 14th
Manufacturing: 198,880—16.00%, 26th
Mining: 11,554—1.0%, 14th
Service: 231,198—18.60%, 36th
Trade: 226,226—18.20%, 31st
Transportation, communication, & public utilities: 62,150—5.00%, 27th
Wholesale/retail: 243,899—20.8%, 37th
Unemployment rate: 4.38%, 42nd
Male: 2.46%, 41st
Female: 2.00%, 41st
Total businesses (1991): 107,489
New business incorp's. (1991): 3,930
Percent of total businesses: 3.66%, 46th
Business failures (1991): 995
Percent of total businesses: 0.93%, 18th
Agriculture farm income
Marketing (1991): $6,934,986,000, 7th
Net per operation: $13,293, 41st
Net per acre: $19, 42nd
Leading products: cattle, wheat, corn, hogs
Av. value land & build. per acre: $473, 39th
Percent increase (1980-90): -19.42%, 40th

Govt. payments: $697,895,000, 2nd
Construction, value of all: $1,185,000,000
Per capita: $478.29, 34th
Percent change 1989-90: -11.17%, 30th
Manufactures:
Value added: : $12,998,000,000
Per capita: $5,246.26, 24th
Value of shipments: $36,349,000,000
Per capita: $14,671.21, 9th
Leading products: transportation equipment, industrial machinery, food and kindred products, printing and publishing
Mining, min. prod., value (1987): $3,566,000,000, 11th
Leading products: petroleum, nat. gas, cement
Retail sales: $16,656,000,000, 31st
Per household: $17,540, 38th
Percent increase (1987-90): 19.7%, 15th
Service indust., value (1987): $8,384,000,000, 33rd
Per capita: $3,383.96, 33rd
Tourism indus., value (1989): $2,176,000,000, 34th
Foreign exports value: $2,113,000,000, 31st
Per capita: $852.85, 30th
Patents per 1,000 pop.: 7.6, 22nd

Travel and Transportation

Motor vehicle registrations: 2,012,353
Per 1,000 pop.: 812, 20th
Motorcycle registrations: 75,696
Per 1,000 pop.: 30, 10th
Licensed drivers per 1,000 driving age pop.: 906, 20th
Deaths from motor vehicle accidents per 100,000 pop.: 17.9, 25th
Public roads & streets
Total mileage: 133,578, 4th
Rural mileage: 124,473, 2nd
Urban mileage: 9,105, 28th
Interstate mileage: 872, 25th
Annual vehicle-miles of travel per person: 9,222, 23rd
Mean travel time for workers 16 + who work away from home: 17.2 min., 44th

Government

Registered voters (1988): 1,265,958
Percent of voting age pop.: 69.22%, 30th
Voter turnout (1988): 993,044
Percent of registered voters: 78.44%, 8th
Percent of voting age pop.: 54.29%, 20th
State legislators, total (1992): 165, 17th
Women members (1992): 45
Percent of legislature: 27.3%, 9th
Dominant party (1992): Split
U. S. Congress, House members (1993): 4
Increase 1983-93: -1
Revenues:
State govt.: $5,135,621,000
Per capita: $2,072.84, 41st
State & local govt.: $9,050,852,000
Per capita: $3,653.11, 35th
Indebtedness:
State govt.: $306,297,000
Per capita: $123.63, 50th
State & local govt.: $6,961,000,000
Per capita: $2,809.60, 34th

Laws and Regulations

Legal driving age: 16
Marriage age without parental consent: 18
Divorce residence requirement: 60 days

Attractions

Major opera companies (1989): 1, 30th
Per 1 million pop.: 0.40, 38th
Major symphony orchestras (1989): 11, 26th
Per 1 million pop.: 4.38, 18th
State appropriations for state arts agencies per capita: $0.50, 37th
State Fair starts Friday after Labor Day at Hutchinson

Sports and Competition

NCAA sports teams, 4: Fort Hays State Univ. Tigers, Kansas State Univ. Wildcats, Univ. of Kansas Jayhawks, Wichita State Univ. Shockers
Professional teams, 2:
Baseball, 1—Wichita Wranglers (Texas League, Class AA), Lawrence-Dumont Stadium
Soccer, 1—Wichita Wings (Major Soccer League), Kansas Coliseum

KENTUCKY

"The moonlight is the softest in Kentucky.
Summer days come oftenest.
Love's fire glows the longest,
Yet a wrong is always wrongest in Kentucky."

James H. Mulligan

The Bluegrass State is famed for its fine horses, the renowned Kentucky Derby, its bourbon, and its fine tobacco, but it deserves greater fame for the extraordinary personalities who have been associated with it and for a state park system that has been called "the finest in the nation." Louisville's symphony is renowned as a leader in first performances of classical music, and the baseball world could not survive without "Louisville Slugger" bats. Among the numerous natural attractions, Mammoth Cave contains three rivers, two lakes, and one "sea." Millions around the world sing of the joys of "My Old Kentucky Home." When Henry Clay stood at Cumberland Gap he said, "I am listening to the tread of the coming millions," and they have indeed followed in his footsteps.

SUPERLATIVES

- Kentucky's Cave Region is world unique.
- First in pedigreed horses.
- World's largest loose leaf tobacco market.
- First in fine grass seed.
- World's largest producer of bourbon.
- Leader in fluorspar production.
- First in bituminous coal production.
- First daily newspaper west of the Alleghenies.

MOMENTS IN HISTORY

- The first recorded exploration was made by Virginia Colonel Abram Wood in 1654.
- By 1690 most of the native Indian people had been driven from the region by the Iroquois Indians. Then a few scattered groups returned.
- The whole vast region west of the Allegheny Mountains was claimed by France, and around 1729 Lower Shawneetown was begun by French traders and groups of Delaware, Shawnee, and Mingo tribes, then abandoned before the French and Indian War.
- The British did not recognize French claims, and in 1750 Dr. Thomas Walker explored the region for the British Loyal Land Company of Virginia.
- In 1751 noted explorer Christopher Gist traveled the Ohio River country and visited Lower Shawneetown, as he noted in his journal.
- The British were triumphant in the French and Indian War in 1763.
- In 1769 John Findley and Daniel Boone crossed the pass now known as the Cumberland Gap.

> So They Say
>
> "...returned to my family, being determined to reside in Kentucky which I esteemed a second paradise."
>
> Daniel Boone, 1771

- Despite the King's ban on settlement, James Harrod and a group of 31 settlers founded present-day Harrodsburg in 1774. It is the state's oldest permanent European settlement.
- After leading a party over "Boone's Trace," on April 5, 1775, Boone and 30 men began to build Fort Boonesborough.

• As the Revolutionary War approached, the British stirred up the Indians of the region against the settlers, and in July 1776 Indians attacked Boonesborough and captured Daniel Boone's daughter and two other young women. They were rescued by a party led by Daniel Boone.

• Indian attacks continued after the Revolution, but settlement grew and on June 1, 1792, Kentucky became the first state to be carved from the great wilderness west.

• In 1799 a hunter tracking a wounded animal discovered Mammoth Cave.

> **So They Say**
>
> "...200 acres of second-rate land lying on the Green River, including two petre caves."
>
> A land grant described the Mammoth Cave region

• The terrible earthquake of 1811 shook western Kentucky, but progress came that year with the arrival of the first steamboat on the Ohio River.

• In 1833 Kentucky prohibited the importation of slaves.

• With the 1850 repeal of the slave ban, Kentucky became an important center of the slave trade.

• The state was bitterly divided over slavery during the Civil War. By 1862 Union forces controlled the state, but costly guerrilla warfare continued. At war's end in 1865, 90,000 from Kentucky had served in Union forces; 45,000 fought for the Confederacy.

• The Ohio was bridged in 1866 by the nation's first great suspension bridge, between Covington, KY, and Cincinnati.

• The Kentucky Derby began at Louisville in 1875.

• In 1900 William Goebel, candidate for governor, was murdered, and the mystery of his death was never solved.

• During World War I, 75,043 Kentuckians served, and Breathitt County was the only one in the United States in which no one was drafted.

• In 1937 the Ohio River floods were the worst in the river's history.

• Fort Knox was a major training center for tank operations during World War II.

• The terrible supper club fire at Southgate in 1977 took 164 lives.

• Frankfort celebrated its 200th anniversary in 1986.

That's Interesting

• Captured by the Indians at Boonesborough, Elizabeth Calloway broke off pieces of brush and twigs and pieces of her clothing to leave a trail for possible rescue. Following this trail, a party led by Daniel Boone caught up with the captives, and the Indians fled.

• Prehistoric animal bones were not so highly regarded in 1773 when explorer James Douglas used the ribs of mastodons for tent poles.

• Confederate President Jefferson Davis and Union President Abraham Lincoln were both Kentucky natives.

• The admirers of a large sycamore tree at Pippa Passes bought 36 square ft. of land on which it stood, and registered the tree as the landowner.

• U.S. Senate candidate John Pope received one man's vote because "He has only one arm to thrust into the treasury."

• Because Mammoth Cave has a constant 54-deg.-F temperature, it "breathes" in when the outside temperature is high and "exhales" when the temperature is lower.

Notable Natives

Muhammad Ali (Louisville, 1942-), boxer. **Alben William Barkley** (Graves County, 1877-1956), U.S. vice-president. **Louis Dembitz Brandeis** (Louisville, 1856-1941), U.S. Supreme Court justice. **Jefferson Davis** (Fairview, 1808-1889), president of the Confederate States of America. **Abraham Lincoln** (near Hodgenville, 1809-1865), U.S. president. **Carry Amelia Nation** (Gerrard County, 1846-1911), social reformer. **Frederick Moore Vinson** (Louisa, 1890-1953), U.S. chief justice.

General

Admitted to statehood: June 1, 1792

Origin of name: Indian word variously translated as "dark and bloody ground," "meadow land," and "land of tomorrow"

Capital: Frankfort
Nickname: The Bluegrass State
Motto: "United We Stand, Divided We Fall"
Bird: cardinal
Fish: bass
Flower: goldenrod
Song: "My Old Kentucky Home"
Tree: Kentucky coffee tree

The Land

Area: 40,411 sq. mi., 37th
Land: 39,732 sq. mi., 36th
Water: 679 sq. mi., 38th
Topography: mountainous in E; rounded hills of the Knobs in the N; bluegrass, heart of state; wooded rocky hillsides of the Pennyroyal; W coal field, the fertile Purchase in the SW
Number of counties: 120
Geographic center: Marion, 3 mi. NNW of Lebanon
Length: 380 mi.
Width: 140 mi.
Highest point: 4,139 ft. (Black Mountain), 27th
Lowest point: 257 ft. (Mississippi River), 32nd
Mean elevation: 750 ft., 33rd

Climate and Environment

Temp., highest: 114 deg. on July 28, 1930, at Greensburg; lowest: -34 deg. on Jan. 28, 1963, at Cynthiana
Fresh water withdrawn, per capita, per day: 1,130 gal., 30th
Endangered species: mammals, 3—gray bat, Indiana bat, Virginia big-eared bat; birds, 3—American peregrine falcon, least tern, red-cockaded woodpecker; reptiles, none; amphibians, none; fishes, 1; invertebrates, 16; plants, 3

Major Cities, Population Percentage Increase (1980-90)

Bowling Green, 40,641—0.47%
Covington, 43,264— -12.75%
Lexington-Fayette, 225,366—10.38%
Louisville, 269,063— -9.92%
Owensboro, 53,549— -1.65%

The People

Population: 3,685,296, 23rd
Percent change (1980-90): 0.68%, 40th
Per sq. mi: 91.20, 23rd
Percent in metro. area: 46.51%, 39th
Percent foreign born: 0.9%, 49th
White: 3,391,832—92.04%, 15th
Black: 262,907—7.13%, 26th
Native American: 5,769—0.16%, 49th
Asian, Pacific Isle: 17,812—0.48%, 49th
Other races: 6,976—0.19%, 45th
Hispanic origin: 21,984—0.60%, 49th
Percent over 5 yrs. speaking language other than English at home: 2.5%, 51st
Percent males: 48.44%, 34th
Percent females: 51.56%, 18th
Percent never married: 22.6%, 44th
Marriages per 1,000 (1989): 13.5, 5th
Divorces per 1,000 (1989): 5.5, 13th
Median age: 33
Under 5 years: 2,50,871—6.81%, 46th
Under 18 years: 9,54,094—17.75%, 27th
65 years & older: 466,845—12.67%, 26th
Percent increase among the elderly: 13.9%, 36th

Of Vital Importance

Live births per 1,000 pop.: 15.2, 36th
Infant mortality rate per 1,000 births (1988): 10.7, 16th
Average lifetime (1979-81): 73.06, 41st
Deaths per 100,000 pop. (1988): 955.6, 12th
Causes of death per 100,000 pop. (1988):
Diseases of heart: 338, 18th
Malignant neoplasms: 215.3, 13th
Cerebrovascular diseases: 68.9, 19th
Accidents & adverse effects: 46.1, 15th
Chronic obstructive pulmonary diseases: 41.1, 10th
Suicide: 12.6, 24th
HIV infection: 1.2, 42nd
Other: 83.5, 7th

Keeping Well

Non-federal physicians per 100,000 pop.: 182, 39th
Dentists per 100,000 (1990-91): 60, 29th
Nurses per 100,000 (1989): 495, 45th
Hospitals per 100,000: 3.3, 20th

Admissions per 100,000: 15,743, 11th
Beds per 100,000: 511.36, 21st
Occupancy rate: 65.0%, 28th
Semiprivate room charges per day: $242, 33rd
Average stay: 6.8, 33rd
Notifiable diseases per 100,000:
AIDS: 5.1, 38th
Gonorrhea: 15.7, 48th
Measles: 1.2, 39th
Syphillis: 7.8, 34th
Tuberculosis (TB): 9.8, 16th
Per capita spending on mental health programs (1987): $22.97, 46th
Pop. without health insur. (1991): 13.1%, 22nd

Households by Type

Total households: 1,379,782
Percent change (1980-90): 9.25%, 33rd
Family households: 1,015,998
Percent of total: 73.63%, 5th
Nonfamily households: 363,784
Percent of total: 26.37%, 47th
Persons per household: 2.60, 25th
Pop. living in group quarters: 101,176
Percent of pop.: 2.75%, 25th

Living Quarters

Total housing units: 1,506,845
Persons per unit: 2.45, 16th
Occupied housing units: 1,379,782
Percent of total units: 91.57%, 12th
Persons per unit: 2.54, 22nd
Percent of units with over 1 person per room: 2.60%, 33rd
Owner-occupied units: 960,469
Percent of total units: 63.74%, 7th
Percent of occupied units: 69.61%, 13th
Persons per unit: 2.69, 35th
Median value: $50,500, 44th
Renter-occupied units: 419,313
Percent of total units: 27.83%, 33rd
Percent of occupied units: 30.39%, 39th
Persons per unit: 2.39, 18th
Median contract rent: $250, 45th
Rental vacancy rate: 8.2%, 27th
Mobile home, trailer & other as a % of occupied housing units: 14.46%, 17th

Crime Index per 100,000

Total: 3,299, 48th
Violent: 390, 34th
Murder and nonnegligent manslaughter: 7, 24th
Aggravated assault: 6,807, 46th
Robbery: 69, 39th
Rape: 29, 40th
Property: 2,909, 48th
Burglary: 767, 41st
Larceny, theft: 1,943, 49th
Motor vehicle theft: 199, 43rd
Drug abuse arrests: 315, 16th

Teaching and Learning

Literacy (1987): 85%, 40th
Pop. 3 and over enrolled in school: 918,315
Percent of pop.: 26.0%, 40th
Public elementary & secondary schools:
Total enrollment: 621,000
Avg. class size (1987): 24, 15th
Teachers: 35,800
Percent of pop.: 0.97%, 32nd
Teachers' avg. salary: $26,300, 38th
Spending per capita: $629, 44th
Spending per pupil in avg. daily attendance: $3,824, 40th
Percent of graduates taking SAT: 11%, 38th
Combined SAT scores: 993, 17th
Percent of pop. over 25 completing:
High school: 64.6%, 50th
College degree/s: 13.6%, 49th
Higher educa., institutions: 62
Per 100,000 pop.: 0.6, 31st
Enroll: 177,852
Percent of pop.: 4.83%, 40th
Public: 147,095
Percent of enroll.: 82.71%, 24th
Private: 30,757
Percent of enroll.: 17.29%, 28th
White non-Hispanic: 205,676
Percent of enroll.: 77.69%, 36th
Black non-Hispanic: 7,585
Percent of enroll.: 2.87%, 35th
Hispanic: 29,618
Percent of enroll.: 11.19%, 4th
Asian/Pacific Islander: 6,116

Percent of enroll.: 2.31%, 18th
Amer. Indian/AK native: 8,845
Percent of enroll.: 3.34%, 7th
Nonresident alien: 6,895
Percent of enroll.: 2.60%, 18th
Female: 103,250
Percent of enroll.: 58.05%, 2nd
Tuition, state university ('90-'91): $1,444, 38th
Public library systems: 115
Books & serial vol. per capita: 1.87, 42nd
Govt. expend. per capita: $9.69, 42nd
State govt.: $3.12, 16th
Local govts.: $6.57, 43rd

LAW ENFORCEMENT, COURTS, AND PRISONS

Police protection expend.: $263,835,000
Per capita: $71.60, 47th
Judicial & legal expend.: $128,821,000
Per capita: $34.96, 39th
Corrections expend.: $233,474,000
Per capita: $63.36, 36th
Police per 10,000 pop. (1990-91): 15.4, 45th
Prisoners (state & fed.) sentenced to over 1 yr., per 100,000 pop.: 241
Percent change (1989-90): 8.86%, 15th
Death penalty: yes, by electrocution
Under sentence of death: 28, 21st
Executed (1989): none

RELIGION, NUMBER AND PERCENT OF POPULATION

Agnostic: 8,194—0.30%, 37th
Buddhist: 2,731—0.10%, 17th
Christian: 2,452,619—89.80%, 13th
Hindu: NA
Jewish: 5,462—0.20%, 40th
Moslem: NA
Unitarian: 5,462—0.20%, 23rd
Other: 32,774—1.20%, 29th
None: 177,528—6.50%, 25th
Refused to answer: 46,430—1.70%, 35th

MAKING A LIVING

Personal income per capita (1989): $11,153, 44th
Percent increase (1979-'89) (constant 1989 dollars): 11.4%, 28th
Average income per family: $33,386, 46th
Percent of pop. below poverty level: 19.0%, 6th
Percent 65 and over: 20.6%, 6th
Cost of living, selected cities
1st qtr., 1991 (U. S. Standard=100)

Murray	85.6
Louisville	96.2
Lexington	97.5

ECONOMY

Civilian labor force : 1,767,000
Percent of tot. pop.: 47.95%, 43rd
Percent 65 and over: 2.77%, 25th
Percent females: 46.07%, 19th
Percent job growth (1980-90): 18.85%, 27th
Major employer industries:
Agriculture: 66,560—4.00%, 12th
Construction: 64,896—3.90%, 41st
Finance, insurance & real estate: 69,888—4.20%, 44th
Government: 261,248—15.70%, 24th
Manufacturing: 272,896—16.40%, 24th
Mining: 37,595—2.4%, 7th
Service: 302,848—18.20%, 39th
Trade: 324,480—19.50%, 15th
Transportation, communication, & public utilities: 103,168—6.20%, 12th
Wholesale/retail: 333,805—21.3%, 30th
Unemployment rate: 5.83%, 16th
Male: 3.11%, 24th
Female: 2.72%, 14th
Total businesses (1991): 111,784
New business incorp's. (1991): 6,782
Percent of total businesses: 6.07%, 24th
Business failures (1991): 1,221
Percent of total businesses: 1.09%, 13th
Agriculture farm income
Marketing (1991): $3,178,704,000, 21st
Net per operation: $11,777, 43rd
Net per acre: $76, 18th
Leading products: tobacco, cattle, horses, dairy products
Av. value land & build. per acre: $1,034, 22nd
Percent increase (1980-90): 5.94%, 23rd
Govt. payments: $73,416,000, 25th
Construction, value of all: $1,424,000,000
Per capita: $386.40, 41st
Percent change 1989-90: -3.98%, 21st

Manufactures:
Value added: : $23,629,000,000
Per capita: $6,411.70, 9th
Value of shipments: $53,777,000,000
Per capita: $14,592.31, 10th
Leading products: nonelectrical machinery, food products, electrical & electronic products, apparel, printing and publishing
Mining, min. prod., value (1987): $5,957,000,000, 6th
Leading products: coal, petroleum, stone
Retail sales: $23,861,000,000, 26th
Per household: $17,283, 42nd
Percent increase (1987-90): 18.4%, 17th
Service indust., value (1987): $9,922,000,000, 30th
Per capita: $2,692.32, 48th
Tourism indus., value (1989): $2,901,000,000, 30th
Foreign exports value: $3,175,000,000, 23rd
Per capita: $861.53, 29th
Patents per 1,000 pop.: 11.9, 9th

Travel and Transportation

Motor vehicle registrations: 2,909,408
Per 1,000 pop.: 789, 26th
Motorcycle registrations: 34,509
Per 1,000 pop.: 9, 45th
Licensed drivers per 1,000 driving age pop.: 845, 42nd
Deaths from motor vehicle accidents per 100,000 pop.: 23.0, 14th
Public roads & streets
Total mileage: 69,668, 29th
Rural mileage: 61,976, 28th
Urban mileage: 7,692, 31st
Interstate mileage: 763, 29th
Annual vehicle-miles of travel per person: 9,127, 25th
Mean travel time for workers 16 + who work away from home: 20.7 min., 24th

Government

Registered voters (1988): 2,026,307
Percent of voting age pop.: 73.79%, 21st
Voter turnout (1988): 1,322,517
Percent of registered voters: 65.27%, 40th
Percent of voting age pop.: 48.16%, 35th
State legislators, total (1992): 138, 30th
Women members (1992): 8
Percent of legislature: 5.8%, 49th
Dominant party (1992): Democrats
U. S. Congress, House members (1993): 6
Increase 1983-93: -1
Revenues:
State govt.: $8,592,819,000
Per capita: $2,331.65, 31st
State & local govt.: $11,791,869,000
Per capita: $3,199.71, 47th
Indebtedness:
State govt.: $5,295,370,000
Per capita: $1,436.89, 17th
State & local govt.: $13,321,000,000
Per capita: $3,614.64, 23rd

Laws and Regulations

Legal driving age: 18
Marriage age without parental consent: 18
Divorce residence requirement: 180 days

Attractions

Major opera companies (1989): 1, 30th
Per 1 million pop.: 0.27, 44th
Major symphony orchestras (1989): 9, 28th
Per 1 million pop.: 2.41, 47th
State appropriations for state arts agencies per capita: $0.65, 29th

Sports and Competition

NCAA sports teams, 7: Eastern Kentucky Univ. Colonels, Kentucky State Univ. Thorobreds, Morehead State Univ. Eagles, Murray State Univ. Racers, Univ. of Kentucky Wildcats, Univ. of Louisville Cardinals, Western Kentucky Univ. Hilltoppers
Professional teams, 2:
Baseball, 1—Louisville Redbirds (American Association, Class AAA), Cardinal Stadium
Hockey, 1—Louisville Ice Hawks (East Coast Hockey League), Broadbent Arena

LOUISIANA

"But where is that favored Land?—It is in this great continent.—It is, reader, Louisiana that these bounties of nature are in the greatest perfection."

John James Audubon

Louisiana is the home of the famous Mardi Gras held in New Orleans, that charming old city with its rich French heritage. Many people from southern Louisiana are descended from the French settlers who left the Acadia region of eastern Canada. Louisiana is one of the nation's busiest commercial areas. Shipping is important, as are fishing, petroleum production, and farming. White-columned mansions, built before the Civil War, symbolize Louisiana's past glory. Louisiana has been called "an unparalleled combination of beauty, historic charm, and bountiful resources."

Superlatives

• Claimed at one time by more nations than any other.

• Birthplace of jazz.

• Nation's leading port.

• Four major deep-water harbors.

• Largest U.S. iron ore reserves.

• First in sulphur production.

• First in production of fur pelts.

Moments in History

• In 1519 Spanish explorer Alvarez de Pineda claimed to have reached the mouth of the Mississippi, calling it Rio del Espiritu Santo (River of the Holy Spirit).

• Despite Pineda's claims, Hernando de Soto is generally thought of as the Mississippi's discoverer in his 1541-1542 expedition, the first Europeans to reach present-day Louisiana.

• Few visitors touched the present state until 1682 when the Sieur de La Salle claimed the entire Mississippi watershed for France and named it for King Louis XIV.

• In 1699 explorations of the brothers Sieur d'Iberville and Sieur de Bienville strengthened French claims, and France made Louisiana a crown colony that year.

• Juchereau de St. Denis founded present-day Natchitoches in 1714, the first permanent European settlement in Louisiana.

• Bienville founded New Orleans in 1718.

• In 1743 Marquis de Veudreuil became governor of French Louisiana.

• In 1672 King Louis XV gave his cousin Charles II of Spain all the land west of the Mississippi, to keep it out of British hands.

• In 1768 colonists of Louisiana rebelled against Spanish rule and governed an independent republic for almost a year. This was the first North American rebellion against European rule.

So They Say

"They (the Houma Indians) gave a formal ball for us. They brought...drums...a short time afterward there came 20 young people...of the prettiest young girls magnificently adorned...Many had pieces of copper...fastened to their belts...which made a noise and assisted in marking the time. They danced like that for three hours in a very active and sprightly manner.

Sieur d'Iberville

> **So They Say**
>
> "His administration...was for Louisiana...what the reign of Louis XIV had been for France...He loved to keep up a miniature court, a distant imitation of that of Versailles...old people were fond of talking of the exquisitely refined manner, the magnificent balls, the splendidly uniformed troops...and many other unparalleled things they had seen in the day of the great Marquis."
>
> Charles Gayarre on the Marquis de Vaudreuil

• Spanish rule was reestablished in 1769.

• On Good Friday 1788 much of the city of New Orleans was destroyed by fire.

• The Treaty of San Ildefonso in 1801 returned Louisiana to France.

• On November 30, 1803, the United States took over the Cabildo (capitol) at New Orleans, after buying the entire Louisiana territory, in one of history's best real estate deals.

• Spain continued to claim eastern Louisiana, but this was taken by the United States in 1810.

• Despite eastern fears of the "foreigners" in Louisiana, that territory became the 18th state on April 30, 1812.

• On January 8, 1815, Andrew Jackson won the enormously important Battle of New Orleans. He had not heard that the war had already ended.

• The 1840 census showed New Orleans to be the nation's fourth largest city, informal capital of the great plantation region.

• One of the states most dependent on slavery, Louisiana moved quickly to join the Confederacy on January 26, 1861.

• On April 29, 1862, Union Admiral David Farragut captured New Orleans.

• When Confederate General Kirby-Smith surrendered at Shreveport on June 2, 1865, his was the last major army of the South to lay down arms.

• Chaos reigned in Lousiaiana for twelve years after war's end. Then in 1877 state control was returned.

• In 1892 New Orleans was hit by a general strike, first in the nation.

• In 1901 the state's first oil flowed from a "monster" well near Jennings.

• In 1915 New Orleans jazz spread to Chicago and was soon popularized around the world.

• Huey Long first assumed the governorship in 1928 and soon became one of the nation's best-known and most powerful politicians.

• Seven years after he became governor, in 1935 Huey Long was assassinated on the steps of the state capitol.

• Of the 260,000 Louisianans who served in World War II, 5,015 died.

That's Interesting

• When the Bonnet Carre Spillway was completed, 6,000 goats were put to work keeping the grass down so that flood waters could flow without resistance.

• Shipwrecked explorer Marcos de Mena was wounded by the Indians and buried alive; a small airhole permitted him to breathe; after his followers were killed, he managed to wriggle out and make his way back to Mexico.

• Jean Lafitte and his pirate crew were pardoned as reward for their services in the War of 1812, but they soon returned to their pirate ways.

• Huey Long was noted for his brilliant mind. He could quote much of the Bible, Shakespeare, and other works, and often spellbound his opponents with apt quotations from innumerable sources, related with his great eloquence.

• Membership in the Live Oak Society was limited to the trees themselves. There was a senior membership of trees 100 years old, and there was a junior society. The society died out with its founder's death, a man, not a tree.

• The Indians painted a conspicuous tree bright red as a marker. The French called this tree "baton rouge" (red stick), giving the Louisiana capitol its name.

Notable Natives

Louis Daniel Armstrong (New Orleans, 1900-1971), musician. **Pierre Gustave Toutant Beauregard** (New Orleans, 1818-1893), soldier. **Truman Capote** (New Orleans, 1924-1984), author. **Louis Moreau Gottschalk** (New Orleans, 1829-1869), pianist/ composer. **Lillian Hellman**

(New Orleans, 1905-1984), playwright. **Huddie "Leadbelly" Ledbetter** (near Shreveport, 1888?-1949), folk singer/composer. **Huey Long** (Winnfield, 1893-1935), public official. **Edward Douglass White** (Lafourche Parish, Nov. 3, 1845-1921), Supreme Court justice.

GENERAL

Admitted to statehood: April 30, 1812
Origin of name: Part of territory called Louisiana by Sieur de La Salle for French King Louis XIV
Capital: Baton Rouge
Nicknames: The Pelican State and The Creole State
Motto: "Union, Justice and Confidence"
Bird: Eastern (Louisiana) brown pelican
Dog: Catahoula leopard dog
Flower: magnolia bloom
Insect: honeybee
Songs: "Give Me Louisiana" and "You Are My Sunshine"
Tree: bald cypress

THE LAND

Area: 51,843 sq. mi., 31st
Land: 43,566 sq. mi., 33rd
Water: 8,277 sq. mi., 5th
Topography: lowlands of the marshes and Mississippi River flood plain, Red River Valley lowlands
Number of counties (called parishes): 64
Geographic center: Avoyelles, 3 mi. SE of Marksville
Length: 380 mi.
Width: 130 mi.
Highest point: 535 ft. (Driskill Mountain), 48th
Lowest point: -8 ft. (New Orleans), 2nd
Mean elevation: 100 ft., 50th
Coastline: 397 mi., 5th
Shoreline: 7,721 mi., 3rd

CLIMATE AND ENVIRONMENT

Temp., highest: 114 deg. on Aug. 10, 1936, at Plain Dealing; lowest: -16 deg. on Feb. 13, 1899, at Minden
Fresh water withdrawn, per capita, per day: 2,210 gal., 13th
Endangered species: mammals, 1—West Indian manatee; birds, 4—American peregrine falcon, brown pelican, least tern, red-cockaded woodpecker; reptiles, 3; amphibians, none; fishes, 1; invertebrates, 1; plants, 1

MAJOR CITIES, POPULATION PERCENTAGE INCREASE (1980-90)

Baton Rouge, 219,531— –0.39%
Lafayette, 94,440—17.19%
Metairie, 149,428— –8.97%
New Orleans, 496,938— –10.93%
Shreveport, 198,525— –3.62%

THE PEOPLE

Population: 4,219,973, 21st
  Percent change (1980-90): 0.33%, 44th
  Per sq. mi: 81.40, 24th
  Percent in metro. area: 69.55%, 22nd
  Percent foreign born: 2.1%, 34th
White: 2,839,138—67.28%, 48th
Black: 1,299,281—30.79%, 3rd
Native American: 18,541—0.44%, 25th
Asian, Pacific Isle: 41,099—0.97%, 29th
Other races: 21,914—0.52%, 34th
Hispanic origin: 93,044—2.20%, 28th
Percent over 5 yrs. speaking language other than English at home: 10.1%, 17th
Percent males: 48.14%, 43rd
Percent females: 51.86%, 9th
Percent never married: 27.4%, 14th
Marriages per 1,000 (1989): 8.9, 32nd
Divorces per 1,000 (1989): NA
Median age: 31
Under 5 years: 334,650—7.93%, 8th
Under 18 years: 1,277,269—30.27%, 4th
65 years & older: 468,991—11.11%, 40th
Percent increase among the elderly: 16.0%, 32nd

OF VITAL IMPORTANCE

Live births per 1,000 pop.: 16.5, 14th
Infant mortality rate per 1,000 births (1988): 11.0, 12th
Average lifetime (1979-81): 71.74, 49th
Deaths per 100,000 pop. (1988): 853.0, 30th
Causes of death per 100,000 pop. (1988):
  Diseases of heart: 303, 29th

Malignant neoplasms: 190.8, 34th
Cerebrovascular diseases: 58.4, 32nd
Accidents & adverse effects: 44.5, 17th
Chronic obstructive pulmonary diseases: 25.9, 46th
Suicide: 13.1, 21st
HIV infection: 5.6, 10th
Other: 71.9, 35th

Keeping Well

Non-federal physicians per 100,000 pop.: 206, 26th
Dentists per 100,000 (1990-91): 52, 39th
Nurses per 100,000 (1989): 427, 51st
Hospitals per 100,000: 4.1, 12th
Admissions per 100,000: 15,597, 12th
Beds per 100,000: 566.12, 16th
Occupancy rate: 60.2%, 48th
Semiprivate room charges per day: $203, 47th
Average stay: 6.5, 42nd
Notifiable diseases per 100,000:
AIDS: 16.7, 9th
Gonorrhea: 312.8, 16th
Measles: 0.2, 47th
Syphillis: 125.1, 3rd
Tuberculosis (TB): 8.7, 18th
Per capita spending on mental health programs (1987): $25.09, 42nd
Pop. without health insur.(1991): 20.7%, 4th

Households by Type

Total households: 1,499,269
Percent change (1980-90): 6.18%, 43rd
Family households: 1,089,882
Percent of total: 72.69%, 10th
Nonfamily households: 409,387
Percent of total: 27.31%, 42nd
Persons per household: 2.74, 6th
Pop. living in group quarters: 112,578
Percent of pop.: 2.67%, 30th

Living Quarters

Total housing units: 1,716,241
Persons per unit: 2.46, 13th
Occupied housing units: 1,499,269
Percent of total units: 87.36%, 35th
Persons per unit: 2.70, 6th
Percent of units with over 1 person per room: 5.95%, 10th
Owner-occupied units: 987,919
Percent of total units: 57.56%, 33rd
Percent of occupied units: 65.89%, 33rd
Persons per unit: 2.83, 9th
Median value: $58,500, 36th
Renter-occupied units: 511,250
Percent of total units: 29.79%, 23rd
Percent of occupied units: 34.10%, 20th
Persons per unit: 2.57, 6th
Median contract rent: $260, 42nd
Rental vacancy rate: 12.5%, 5th
Mobile home, trailer & other as a % of occupied housing units: 14.51%, 16th

Crime Index per 100,000

Total: 6,487, 8th
Violent: 898, 8th
Murder and nonnegligent manslaughter: 17, 2nd
Aggravated assault: 7,930, 9th
Robbery: 270, 8th
Rape: 42, 21st
Property: 5,588, 9th
Burglary: 1,438, 9th
Larceny, theft: 3,549, 11th
Motor vehicle theft: 602, 15th
Drug abuse arrests: 309, 17th

Teaching and Learning

Literacy (1987): 84%, 47th
Pop. 3 and over enrolled in school: 1,185,759
Percent of pop.: 29.5%, 8th
Public elementary & secondary schools:
Total enrollment: 796,000
Avg. class size (1987): 24, 15th
Teachers: 44,000
Percent of pop.: 1.04%, 21st
Teachers' avg. salary: $24,300, 44th
Spending per capita: $620, 49th
Spending per pupil in avg. daily attendance: $3,457, 45th
Percent of graduates taking SAT: 9%, 43rd
Combined SAT scores: 994, 16th
Percent of pop. over 25 completing:
High school: 68.3%, 44th
College degree/s: 16.1%, 43rd
Higher educa., institutions: 36

Per 100,000 pop.: 0.5, 45th
Enroll: 186,599
Percent of pop.: 4.42%, 47th
Public: 158,290
Percent of enroll.: 84.83%, 21st
Private: 28,309
Percent of enroll.: 15.17%, 31st
White non-Hispanic: 69,974
Percent of enroll.: 89.40%, 16th
Black non-Hispanic: 2,558
Percent of enroll.: 3.27%, 33rd
Hispanic: 1,606
Percent of enroll.: 2.05%, 18th
Asian/Pacific Islander: 1,891
Percent of enroll.: 2.42%, 16th
Amer. Indian/AK native: 222
Percent of enroll.: 0.28%, 37th
Nonresident alien: 2,022
Percent of enroll.: 2.58%, 19th
Female: 105,746
Percent of enroll.: 56.67%, 6th
Tuition, state university ('90-'91): $1,791, 26th
Public library systems: 64
Books & serial vol. per capita: 2.03, 37th
Govt. expend. per capita: $12.56, 33rd
State govt.: $0.53, 50th
Local govts.: $12.03, 24th

Law Enforcement, Courts, and Prisons

Police protection expend.: $469,677,000
Per capita: $111.30, 23rd
Judicial & legal expend.: $186,466,000
Per capita: $44.19, 30th
Corrections expend.: $291,250,000
Per capita: $69.02, 31st
Police per 10,000 pop. (1990-91): 26.2, 6th
Prisoners (state & fed.) sentenced to over 1 yr., per 100,000 pop.: 427
Percent change (1989-90): 7.78%, 24th
Death penalty: yes, by electrocution
Under sentence of death: 39, 19th
Executed (1989): none

Religion, Number and Percent of Population

Agnostic: NA
Buddhist: 2,993—0.10%, 17th
Christian: 2,834,091—94.70%, 1st
Hindu: NA
Jewish: 5,985—0.20%, 40th
Moslem: 2,993—0.10%, 22nd
Unitarian: NA
Other: 23,942—0.80%, 37th
None: 86,788—2.90%, 46th
Refused to answer: 35,912—1.20%, 46th

Making a Living

Personal income per capita (1989): $10,635, 48th
Percent increase (1979-'89) (constant 1989 dollars): -1.2%, 50th
Average income per family: $33,613, 44th
Percent of pop. below poverty level: 23.6%, 2nd
Percent 65 and over: 24.1%, 2nd
Cost of living, selected cities
1st qtr., 1991 (U. S. Standard=100)

Lake Charles	91.6
New Orleans	97.7

Economy

Civilian labor force : 1,874,000
Percent of tot. pop.: 44.41%, 50th
Percent 65 and over: 2.93%, 19th
Percent females: 44.08%, 47th
Percent job growth (1980-90): 2.46%, 49th
Major employer industries:
Agriculture: 49,224—2.80%, 24th
Construction: 110,754—6.30%, 4th
Finance, insurance & real estate: 68,562—3.90%, 47th
Government: 293,586—16.70%, 17th
Manufacturing: 179,316—10.20%, 41st
Mining: 52,329—3.2%, 4th
Service: 339,294—19.30%, 28th
Trade: 344,568—19.60%, 11th
Transportation, communication, & public utilities: 116,028—6.60%, 6th
Wholesale/retail: 361,074—22.0%, 14th
Unemployment rate: 6.24%, 10th
Male: 3.47%, 8th
Female: 2.77%, 11th
Total businesses (1991): 127,163
New business incorp's. (1991): 8,973
Percent of total businesses: 7.06%, 14th
Business failures (1991): 1,101
Percent of total businesses: 0.87%, 25th

Agriculture farm income
Marketing (1991): $1,792,907,000, 32nd
Net per operation: $18,690, 28th
Net per acre: $64, 23rd
Leading products: Cotton, cattle, sugar, soybeans
Av. value land & build. per acre: $940, 25th
Percent increase (1980-90): -25.16%, 44th
Govt. payments: $174,605,000, 18th
Construction, value of all: $1,101,000,000
Per capita: $260.90, 49th
Percent change 1989-90: -11.99%, 31st
Manufactures:
Value added: : $22,617,000,000
Per capita: $5,359.51, 20th
Value of shipments: $65,807,000,000
Per capita: $15,594.18, 8th
Leading products (1990): chemical products, foods, transportation equipment, electronic equipment, petroleum products, lumber, wood and paper
Mining, min. prod., value (1987): $24,630,000,000, 2nd
Leading products: petroleum, nat. gas, sulfur
Retail sales: $28,778,000,000, 21st
Per household: $19,260, 25th
Percent increase (1987-90): 36.2%, 1st
Service indust., value (1987): $14,917,000,000, 24th
Per capita: $3,534.86, 32nd
Tourism indus., value (1989): $4,161,000,000, 22nd
Foreign exports value: $14,199,000,000, 6th
Per capita: $3,364.71, 3rd
Patents per 1,000 pop.: 8.4, 19th

Travel and Transportation

Motor vehicle registrations: 2,994,763
Per 1,000 pop.: 709, 41st
Motorcycle registrations: 30,065
Per 1,000 pop.: 7, 49th
Licensed drivers per 1,000 driving age pop.: 826, 46th
Deaths from motor vehicle accidents per 100,000 pop.: 22.7, 15th
Public roads & streets
Total mileage: 58,620, 33rd
Rural mileage: 46,330, 34th
Urban mileage: 12,290, 22nd
Interstate mileage: 844, 26th
Annual vehicle-miles of travel per person: 8,925, 28th
Mean travel time for workers 16 + who work away from home: 22.3 min., 11th

Government

Registered voters (1988): 2,231,857
Percent of voting age pop.: 70.29%, 27th
Voter turnout (1988): 1,628,202
Percent of registered voters: 72.95%, 20th
Percent of voting age pop.: 51.28%, 27th
State legislators, total (1992): 144, 27th
Women members (1992): 10
Percent of legislature: 6.9%, 47th
Dominant party (1992): Democrats
U. S. Congress, House members (1993): 7
Increase 1983-93: -1
Revenues:
State govt.: $10,096,284,000
Per capita: $2,392.50, 29th
State & local govt.: $15,561,600,000
Per capita: $3,687.61, 31st
Indebtedness:
State govt.: $12,770,321,000
Per capita: $3,026.16, 7th
State & local govt.: $21,560,000,000
Per capita: $5,109.04, 6th

Laws and Regulations

Legal driving age: 17
Marriage age without parental consent: 18
Divorce residence requirement: 1 yr., qualification—check local statutes

Attractions

Major opera companies (1989): 3, 15th
Per 1 million pop.: 0.69, 24th
Major symphony orchestras (1989): 9, 28th
Per 1 million pop.: 2.08, 48th
State appropriations for state arts agencies per capita: $0.21, 49th
State Fair in Oct. at Shreveport

Sports and Competition

NCAA sports teams, 13: Centenary College Gentlemen, Grambling State Univ. Tigers, Louisiana State Univ. Fighting Tigers,

Louisiana Tech Univ., McNeese State Univ. Cowboys, Nicholls State Univ. Colonels, Northeast Louisiana Univ. Indians, Northwestern Louisiana Univ. Demons, Southeastern Louisiana Univ. Lions, Southern Univ. & A&M Jaguars, Tulane Univ. Green Wave, Univ. of New Orleans Privateers, Univ. of Southwestern Louisiana Ragin' Cajuns

Professional teams, 2:

Baseball, 1—Shreveport Captains (Texas League, Class AA), Fairgrounds Field

Football, 1—New Orleans Saints (NFC), Louisiana Superdome

MAINE

"Did you ever see a place that looks like it was built just to enjoy? Well this whole state of Maine looks that way."

Will Rogers

Potatoes, lobsters, and submarines make an unusual combination, but Maine has been famous for all of these. The seacoast of "hundred-harbor Maine," with its lighthouses, sandy beaches, quiet fishing villages, and thousands of off-shore islands, is one of the world's most notable for its beauty, the tremendous catches of fish, the many outstanding ports and for shipbuilding, including the first ship built in the Western Hemisphere. Although not primarily farming land, Maine's farms are world famous for the wonderful white potatoes grown there. The lack of natural resources has been overcome by the courage, ingenuity, and persistence of the Maine character.

SUPERLATIVES

- World's highest tides.
- First ship launched in the Western Hemisphere.
- First atomic submarine, the *Swordfish,* built in Maine.
- Leader in canoe manufacture.
- Holds clipper ship sailing record.
- First sawmill in the United States.
- Produces a fourth of U.S. feldspar.
- Leader in lobster catch.
- World's first steel sailing vessel.

MOMENTS IN HISTORY

- In 1604 Pierre du Guast of France landed at Dochet Island and began a place he called St. Croix.
- In 1607 the primeval forests of Maine provided timber; the 120 settlers at the mouth of the Kennebec River provided the labor, and the *Virginia,* the first ship ever to be launched in the hemisphere, went down the primitive ways.
- Captain John Smith visited present-day Maine in 1614.

> **So They Say**
>
> "Those barren Isles are so furnished with good woods, springs, fruits, fish and foule, that it makes me think though the coast be rocky, and thus affrightable, the valleys, plains, and interior parts may well be very fertile."
>
> Captain John Smith

- In 1622 Maine's first permanent European settlement, Monhegan, was established.
- Present-day Maine came under the control of Massachusetts in 1652.
- During King Philip's War, Saco was attacked on September 18, 1675, and a long period of war with the Indians continued in Maine.
- Peace came to Maine in 1760 in a treaty made with the Indians during the French and Indian War.
- The British king had claimed most of the area's best trees for masts. In 1775, when a British ship attempted to take the trees, the people of Machiasport rose up under Foster and Jeremiah O'Brien, captured the boat, and killed the commander. This engagement has been called the "first naval battle of the Revolution," and it took place just five days before the battle of Bunker Hill.
- During the Revolution, the coastal towns of

Maine endured much destruction, but the British were not able to remove the needed mast trees, and their navy was greatly hampered.

• Maine suffered again during the War of 1812. Bangor was captured, and Britain seized sizeable portions of Maine, but Maine's boundaries remained unchanged after the war.

• Based on an ancient map by Champlain, the border with Canada was decided in Maine's favor in 1815, keeping much of present-day eastern Maine in U.S. hands.

• Maine became the 23rd state on May 15, 1820.

• Another boundary dispute was settled by the Webster-Ashburton Treaty of 1842, with Canada receiving a substantial area claimed by the United States.

• There never had been much slavery in Maine. In 1857 Republican Hannibal Hamlin became governor on an anti-slave platform.

• By the end of the Civil War in 1865, a fifth of all Maine residents had served in the military, and 8,800 lost their lives.

• Portland suffered a destructive fire in 1866.

• Of the 35,000 from Maine who saw World War I service, special tribute for heroism was awarded to Passamaquody Indian Charles Nola.

> So They Say
>
> "I have been in Portland since the fire. Desolation, desolation, desolation! It reminds me of Pompeii."
>
> Henry Wadsworth Longfellow

• In 1948 Margaret Chase Smith became the first Republican woman elected to the U.S. Senate, where she had a distinguished career.

• Shipbuilding in Maine played a prominent part in World War II, in which 95,000 men and women served in U.S. forces.

• Little Samantha Smith of Maine gained world fame when she wrote a letter to Soviet leader Yuri Andropov, expressing her fear of nuclear war, and then visited Russian leaders at their invitation. She died tragically on August 25, 1985, in a private plane crash.

That's Interesting

• The first European settlers in Maine brought timber in their ships to build houses and were astonished that their new home had its own magnificent forests.

• Because Cushnoc Island in the Kennebec River at Augusta was a navigation hazard, the people there hitched 200 oxen to the island, but failed to move it an inch.

• Thanksgiving in Maine predated the Pilgrims. The Etchimin Indians celebrated for two weeks in autumn. Their feasts included turkey, cranberries, popcorn, and other familiar delicacies.

• Barney Beal of Beal's Island was a noted strongman who could knock out a horse with one blow and who once bested 15 men in a tavern dispute.

• During the Revolution, 19-yr.-old Aaron Burr fell in love with Indian Princess Jacataqua, but Burr moved on to later fame and notoriety.

• Samuel Francis Smith of Waterville gave the nation *America,* which many believe should be the national anthem.

Notable Natives

Cyrus H.K. Curtis (Portland, 1850-1933), publisher. **Melville Weston Fuller** (Augusta, 1833-1910), U.S. Chief Justice. **Hannibal Hamlin** (Paris Hill, 1809-1891), U.S. vice-president. **Stephen King** (Portland, 1947-), author. **Henry Wadsworth Longfellow** (Portland, 1807-1882) poet. **Hiram Stevens Maxim** (near Sangerville, 1840-1916), inventor. **Edna St. Vincent Millay** (Rockland, 1892-1950), poet. **Lillian Nordica** (Farmington, 1857-1914), opera singer. **John Knowles Paine** (Portland, 1839-1906), composer/educator. **Sir William Phips** (Maine, 1651-1695) colonial governor. **Thomas Brackett Reed** (Portland, 1839-1902), public official. **Kenneth Lewis Roberts** (Kennebunkport, 1885-1957), author. **Edwin Arlington Robinson** (Head Tide, 1869-1935), poet. **Nathaniel Parker Willis** (Portland, 1806-1867), poet.

General

Admitted to statehood: March 15, 1820

Origin of name: from Maine, ancient French province. Also descriptive, referring to

the mainland as distinct from the many coastal islands
Capital: Augusta
Nickname: The Pine Tree State.
Motto: *"Dirigo"* ("I Direct")
Bird: chickadee (parus atricapillus)
Fish: landlocked salmon
Flower: white pine cone and tassel
Mineral: tourmaline
Song: "State of Maine Song"
Tree: Eastern white pine

The Land

Area: 35,387 sq. mi., 39th
Land: 30,865 sq. mi., 39th
Water: 4,523 sq. mi., 12th
Topography: Appalachian Mtns. extend through state, W borders have rugged terrain, long sand beaches on S coast, N coast mainly rocky promontories, peninsulas, fjords
Number of counties: 16
Geographic center: Piscataquis, 18 mi. N of Dover
Length: 320 mi.
Width: 190 mi.
Highest point: 5,267 ft. (Mount Katahdin), 22nd
Lowest point: sea level (Atlantic Ocean), 3rd
Mean elevation: 600 ft., 39th
Coastline: 228 mi., 9th
Shoreline: 3,478 mi., 4th

Climate and Environment

Temp., highest: 105 deg. on July 10, 1911, at North Bridgeton; lowest: -48 deg. on Jan. 19, 1925, at Van Buren
Fresh water withdrawn, per capita, per day: 733 gal., 38th
Endangered species: mammals, none; birds, 2—American peregrine falcon, roseate tern; reptiles, none; amphibians, none; fishes, none; invertebrates, none; plants, 2

Major Cities, Population Percentage Increase (1980-90)

Auburn, 24,309—5.11%
Bangor, 33,181—4.86%
Lewiston, 39,757— –1.79%
Portland, 64,358—4.52%
South Portland, 23,163—1.99%

The People

Population: 1,227,928, 38th
Percent change (1980-90): 8.38%, 20th
Per sq. mi: 34.70, 37th
Percent in metro. area: 35.91%, 45th
Percent foreign born: 3.0%, 27th
White: 1,208,360—98.41%, 2nd
Black: 5,138—0.42%, 48th
Native American: 5,998—0.49%, 23rd
Asian, Pacific Isle: 6,683—0.54%, 43rd
Other races: 1,749—0.14%, 49th
Hispanic origin: 6,829—0.56%, 50th
Percent over 5 yrs. speaking language other than English at home: 9.2%, 18th
Percent males: 48.69%, 24th
Percent females: 51.31%, 28th
Percent never married: 24.0%, 36th
Marriages per 1,000 (1989): 10.2, 15th
Divorces per 1,000 (1989): 4.7, 24th
Median age: 33.9
Under 5 years: 85,722—6.98%, 38th
Under 18 years: 309,002—25.16%, 34th
65 years & older: 163,373—13.30%, 19th
Percent increase among the elderly: 15.9%, 33rd

Of Vital Importance

Live births per 1,000 pop.: 13.1, 50th
Infant mortality rate per 1,000 births (1988): 7.9, 47th
Average lifetime (1979-81): 74.59, 18th
Deaths per 100,000 pop. (1988): 955.9, 11th
Causes of death per 100,000 pop. (1988):
Diseases of heart: 330.4, 19th
Malignant neoplasms: 226.6, 6th
Cerebrovascular diseases: 64.5, 22nd
Accidents & adverse effects: 39.5, 27th
Chronic obstructive pulmonary diseases: 46.1, 4th
Suicide: 13.4, 15th
HIV infection: 1.4, 40th
Other: 80.3, 13th

Keeping Well

Non-federal physicians per 100,000 pop.: 205, 27th
Dentists per 100,000 (1990-91): 58, 33rd

Nurses per 100,000 (1989): 834, 10th
Hospitals per 100,000: 3.6, 18th
Admissions per 100,000: 12,697, 36th
Beds per 100,000: 458.98, 31st
Occupancy rate: 73.8%, 12th
Semiprivate room charges per day: $335, 14th
Average stay: 7.8, 15th
Notifiable diseases per 100,000:
AIDS: 5.5, 36th
Gonorrhea: 16.3, 47th
Measles: 2.4, 33rd
Syphillis: 1.7, 47th
Tuberculosis (TB): 2.8, 40th
Per capita spending on mental health programs (1987): $52.58, 11th
Pop. without health insur.(1991): 11.1%, 34th

HOUSEHOLDS BY TYPE

Total households: 465,312
Percent change (1980-90): 17.80%, 20th
Family households: 328,685
Percent of total: 70.64%, 26th
Nonfamily households: 136,627
Percent of total: 29.36%, 26th
Persons per household: 2.56, 34th
Pop. living in group quarters: 37,169
Percent of pop.: 3.03%, 16th

LIVING QUARTERS

Total housing units: 587,045
Persons per unit: 2.09, 50th
Occupied housing units: 465,312
Percent of total units: 79.26%, 50th
Persons per unit: 2.46, 44th
Percent of units with over 1 person per room: 1.72%, 48th
Owner-occupied units: 327,888
Percent of total units: 55.85%, 38th
Percent of occupied units: 70.47%, 7th
Persons per unit: 2.71, 29th
Median value: $87,400, 17th
Renter-occupied units: 137,424
Percent of total units: 23.41%, 50th
Percent of occupied units: 29.53%, 46th
Persons per unit: 2.20, 47th
Median contract rent: $358, 21st
Rental vacancy rate: 8.4%, 25th
Mobile home, trailer & other as a % of occupied housing units: 14.62%, 15th

CRIME INDEX PER 100,000

Total: 3,698, 45th
Violent: 143, 48th
Murder and nonnegligent manslaughter: 2, 46th
Aggravated assault: 6,981, 38th
Robbery: 25, 45th
Rape: 20, 49th
Property: 3,555, 44th
Burglary: 823, 38th
Larceny, theft: 2,555, 42nd
Motor vehicle theft: 177, 45th
Drug abuse arrests: 187, 36th

TEACHING AND LEARNING

Literacy (1987): 89%, 17th
Pop. 3 and over enrolled in school: 304,868
Percent of pop.: 25.9%, 41st
Public elementary & secondary schools:
Total enrollment: 216,000
Avg. class size (1987): 20, 41st
Teachers: 14,200
Percent of pop.: 1.16%, 10th
Teachers' avg. salary: $26,900, 36th
Spending per capita: $974, 6th
Spending per pupil in avg. daily attendance: $5,577, 12th
Percent of graduates taking SAT: 64%, 10th
Combined SAT scores: 879, 44th
Percent of pop. over 25 completing:
High school: 78.8%, 18th
College degree/s: 18.8%, 28th
Higher educa., institutions: 31
Per 100,000 pop.: 1.1, 9th
Enroll: 57,186
Percent of pop.: 4.66%, 43rd
Public: 41,500
Percent of enroll.: 72.57%, 40th
Private 15,686
Percent of enroll.: 27.43%, 12th
White non-Hispanic: 251,389
Percent of enroll.: 88.83%, 17th
Black non-Hispanic: 15,323
Percent of enroll.: 5.41%, 26th
Hispanic: 4,380
Percent of enroll.: 1.55%, 27th

Asian/Pacific Islander: 3,913
Percent of enroll.: 1.38%, 34th
Amer. Indian/AK native: 720
Percent of enroll.: 0.25%, 42nd
Nonresident alien: 7,290
Percent of enroll.: 2.58%, 19th
Female: 33,115
Percent of enroll.: 57.91%, 3rd
Tuition, state university ('90-'91): $2,263, 15th
Public library systems: 238
Books & serial vol. per capita: 4.88, 1st
Govt. expend. per capita: $12.20, 36th
State govt.: $2.92, 20th
Local govts.: $9.28, 35th

LAW ENFORCEMENT, COURTS, AND PRISONS

Police protection expend.: $93,467,000
Per capita: $76.11, 45th
Judicial & legal expend.: $40,541,000
Per capita: $33.01, 43rd
Corrections expend.: $79,657,000
Per capita: $64.87, 35th
Police per 10,000 pop. (1990-91): 15.3, 46th
Prisoners (state & fed.) sentenced to over 1 yr., per 100,000 pop.: 118
Percent change (1989-90): 3.35%, 39th
Death penalty: no

RELIGION, NUMBER AND PERCENT OF POPULATION

Agnostic: 8,270—0.90%, 14th
Buddhist: 919—0.10%, 17th
Christian: 780,168—84.90%, 35th
Hindu: 919—0.10%, 10th
Jewish: 3,676—0.40%, 31st
Moslem: NA
Unitarian: 5,514—0.60%, 5th
Other: 7,351—0.80%, 37th
None: 91,893—10.00%, 11th
Refused to answer: 20,216—2.20%, 23rd

MAKING A LIVING

Personal income per capita (1989): $12,957, 31st
Percent increase (1979-'89) (constant 1989 dollars): 34.1%, 5th
Average income per family: $38,374, 33rd
Percent of pop. below poverty level: 10.8%, 36th
Percent 65 and over: 14.0%, 19th
Cost of living, selected cities
1st qtr., 1991 (U. S. Standard=100)
not available

ECONOMY

Civilian labor force : 635,000
Percent of tot. pop.: 51.71%, 19th
Percent 65 and over: 3.15%, 17th
Percent females: 46.30%, 16th
Percent job growth (1980-90): 29.08%, 14th
Major employer industries:
Agriculture: 10,251—1.70%, 39th
Construction: 33,768—5.60%, 12th
Finance, insurance & real estate: 31,959—5.30%, 28th
Government: 93,465—15.50%, 26th
Manufacturing: 104,319—17.30%, 21st
Mining: 533—0.1%, 42nd
Service: 120,600—20.00%, 23rd
Trade: 100,098—16.60%, 50th
Transportation, communication, & public utilities: 27,135—4.50%, 42nd
Wholesale/retail: 126,130—22.1%, 10th
Unemployment rate: 5.20%, 32nd
Male: 2.99%, 28th
Female: 2.20%, 33rd
Total businesses (1991): 45,619
New business incorp's. (1991): 2,326
Percent of total businesses: 5.10%, 37th
Business failures (1991): 392
Percent of total businesses: 0.86%, 26th
Agriculture farm income
Marketing (1991): $444,601,000, 44th
Net per operation: $45,350, 33rd
Net per acre: $77, 17th
Leading products: Potatoes, eggs, dairy products, aquaculture
Av. value land & build. per acre: $1,029, 23rd
Percent increase (1980-90): 73.23%, 5th
Govt. payments: $6,066,000, 39th
Construction, value of all: $569,000,000
Per capita: $463.38, 37th
Percent change 1989-90: -35.05%, 47th
Manufactures:
Value added: $5,886,000,000
Per capita: $4,793.44, 31st

Value of shipments: $12,477,000,000
Per capita: $10,161.02, 28th
Leading products: paper and wood products, leather goods
Mining, min. prod., value (1987): $8,000,000, 51st
Leading products: sand/gravel cement stone
Retail sales: $10,399,000,000, 37th
Per household: $22,149, 8th
Percent increase (1987-90): 9.8%, 38th
Service indust., value (1987): $3,986,000,000, 43rd
Per capita: $3,246.12, 36th
Tourism indus., value (1989): $1,357,000,000, 40th
Foreign exports value: $870,000,000, 41st
Per capita: $708.51, 34th
Patents per 1,000 pop.: 10.9, 12th

Travel and Transportation

Motor vehicle registrations: 976,610
Per 1,000 pop.: 795, 24th
Motorcycle registrations: 37,795
Per 1,000 pop.: 30, 11th
Licensed drivers per 1,000 driving age pop.: 926, 14th
Deaths from motor vehicle accidents per 100,000 pop.: 17.3, 29th
Public roads & streets
Total mileage: 22,389, 43rd
Rural mileage: 19,895, 40th
Urban mileage: 2,494, 40th
Interstate mileage: 366, 44th
Annual vehicle-miles of travel per person: 9,667, 16th
Mean travel time for workers 16 + who work away from home: 19.0 min., 39th

Government

Registered voters (1988): 854,764
Percent of voting age pop.: 95.72%, 1st
Voter turnout (1988): 555,035
Percent of registered voters: 64.93%, 42nd
Percent of voting age pop.: 62.15%, 3rd
State legislators, total (1992): 186, 10th
Women members (1992): 60
Percent of legislature: 32.3%, 3rd
Dominant party (1992): Democrats
U. S. Congress, House members (1993): 2
Increase 1983-93: 0
Revenues:
State govt.: $3,246,033,000
Per capita: $2,643.50, 19th
State & local govt.: $4,520,883,000
Per capita: $3,681.72, 34th
Indebtedness:
State govt.: $2,125,146,000
Per capita: $1,730.68, 16th
State & local govt.: $3,398,000,000
Per capita: $2,767.26, 37th

Laws and Regulations

Legal driving age: 17
Marriage age without parental consent: 18
Divorce residence requirement: 6 mo., qualification—check local statutes

Attractions

Major opera companies (1989): NA
Per 1 million pop.: NA
Major symphony orchestras (1989): 3, 45th
Per 1 million pop.: 2.45, 45th
State appropriations for state arts agencies per capita: $0.60, 31st
State Fair in mid-Aug. at Skowhegan

Sports and Competition

NCAA sports teams, 1: Univ. of Maine Black Bears
Professional teams: 1
Hockey, 1—Maine Mariners (American Hockey League), Cumberland County Civic Center

M A R Y L A N D

"...a delightsome land!"

Captain John Smith

"America in miniature — a small state, it offers a large part of the variety of attractions found in the United States as a whole."

Theodore McKeldin

Chesapeake Bay, which divides Maryland into two parts, furnishes the state with several excellent harbors, as well as fine seafood, especially crabs. The defense of Fort McHenry in the War of 1812 inspired the national anthem, "The Star Spangled Banner," and some experts believe that the success there indeed "preserved us a nation," as the anthem proclaims. Maryland was given to the lords Baltimore for the annual rent of two Indian arrows a year plus complete loyalty to the king. Although Maryland was a slave-holding Southern state, it remained loyal to the Union during the Civil War. Among its many contributions, it donated the site of the national capital.

So They Say

"Smyth Fales...abundance of fish, lying so thick with their heads above the waters, as for want of nets...we attempted to catch them with a frying pan...neither better fish, more plentyous nor more varietie for small fish had any of us ever seen in any place, but they could not be catched with frying pans."

Captain John Smith

Superlatives

- Narrowest width of any state.
- Most navigable rivers of any state.
- One of the foremost sources of marine fossils.
- First military highway in the United States.
- First railway locomotive in the United States.
- World's first telegraph line—Baltimore—Washington, D.C.
- First U.S. manufacture of umbrellas.

Moments in History

- In 1524 Giovanni de Verrazano described an estuary believed to be Chincoteague Bay.
- The first recorded European visit to present-day Maryland was made by Captain John Smith in 1608.
- William Claiborne's trading post on Kent Island in 1622 became the first permanent European settlement in Maryland.
- Cecil Calvert, the second Lord Baltimore, arrived on November 22, 1633, to take possession of his great grant.
- Conflicting claims made unsettled times during the Cromwell period, but in 1660 the new king, Charles II, affirmed the Baltimore lords' titles.
- In 1692 a royal governor took over the Maryland colony.
- The capital was moved to newly incorporated Annapolis in 1694.
- Baltimore was founded in 1729, and the colony's boundaries with Pennsylvania and Maryland were settled that year.
- Fort Mt. Pleasant was begun in 1754 by a youthful George Washington, to discourage French claims in the western area.

• In 1774, Maryland had its own "tea party" protesting the mother country's tax on tea, and delegates were chosen for the Continental Congress.

• On August 27, 1776, Maryland troops played a key role in the Battle of Long Island, saving Washington's forces from destruction.

• During the Revolution the Maryland navy also had a key role, and in 1778 Count Casimir Pulaski organized his "legion" at Baltimore.

• Because of mob action at Philadelphia, the capital of the infant United States was moved to Annapolis on November 26, 1783.

• Maryland became the seventh state on April 28, 1788.

• During the War of 1812 the bells of Baltimore warned that a British fleet was approaching. They attacked Fort McHenry with advanced weapons, including their new rockets. Their defeat outside of Baltimore was a turning point in the war.

So They Say

"Sir—I have the honor of informing you that the enemy...appears to be retiring. We have a force hanging on their rear....P.S. The enemy's vessels in the Patapsco are all under way going down the river."

U.S. commander Samuel Smith at the Battle of Baltimore

• Baltimore became a center of the slave trade, but there also was much opposition to slavery, especially in the west.

• When the Civil War came, President Abraham Lincoln placed Maryland under military control.

• The Battle of Antietam Creek near Sharpsburg is known as the most costly single day of battle in the country, with 23,000 dead or wounded.

• In 1872 the Radical Republicans held their national convention at Baltimore.

• In 1889 the Johns Hopkins Hospital opened there.

• A disastrous fire swept Baltimore in 1904, bringing fire companies from as far away as New York City.

• Woodrow Wilson was nominated for president at the Democratic National Convention of 1912 in Baltimore.

• World War I brought 62,568 Marylanders into the armed services.

• In 1927 Maryland created the nation's first permanent interracial commission.

• World War II took a toll of 6,454 of the 250,787 Marylanders who served in that conflict.

• In 1984 Maryland celebrated the 350th anniversary of its founding.

That's Interesting

• Near the town of Hancock, Maryland is only about 1 mi. wide, the narrowest part of any state.

• The British attack on Fort McHenry during the War of 1812, with its "rockets' red glare," inspired onlooker Francis Scott Key to write the poem that is now the national anthem.

• Jan Frazier of the Cumberland area was expecting a child when she was captured by the Indians. The Indians raided another settlement to get clothes for the infant, who died, and the mother escaped, walking for 300 miles and living on herbs and bark until she reached a house of friends, only to find her husband had remarried.

• One of the king's colonial grants was known as the "Thumb Grant," because the grantee was given as much land as his thumb could cover on a map.

• Maryland is the only state to have developed a distinct breed of dog — the Chesapeake Bay retriever.

• Maryland has the only official state sport — jousting.

Notable Natives

Benjamin Bannecker (Ellicott, 1731-1806), mathematician. **Anna Ellis Carroll** (Pocomoke City, 1815-1893), political science writer. **Charles Carroll** (Annapolis, 1737-1832), Revolutionary leader/public official. **Samuel Chase** (Somerset County, 1741-1811), U.S. Supreme Court justice. **Stephen Decatur** (Sineppuxent, 1779-1820), naval officer. **Frederick Douglass** (Tuckahoe, 1817-1895), social reformer. **John Hanson** (Charles County, 1721-1783), first president under the Articles of Confederation. **Francis Scott Key** (Carroll County), lawyer/poet. **Henry Louis Mencken** (Baltimore, 1880-1956), journalist/editor/critic. **Charles Willson Peale** (Queen Anne's County, 1741-1827), artist/naturalist. **James Rumsey** (Cecil County, 1743-1792), inventor. **George Herman "Babe" Ruth** (Baltimore, 1895-1948), baseball player. **Upton Sinclair** (Baltimore, 1878-1968), author/social reformer. **Roger Brooke Taney** (Calvert County, 1777-1864), U.S. chief justice. **Harriet Tubman** (Dorchester County, 1820?-1913), abolitionist. **Leon Uris** (Baltimore, 1924-), author. **Mason Locke "Parson" Weems** (Anne Arundel County, 1759-1825), author.

GENERAL

Admitted to statehood: April 28, 1788
Origin of name: for Queen Henrietta Maria, wife of Charles I of England
Capital: Annapolis
Nicknames: The Old Line State and Free State—Pine Tree State—Lumber State
Motto: *"Fatti Maschii, Paeole Femine"* ("Manly deeds, womanly words")
Animal: Chesapeake Bay retriever (unique among states)
Bird: Baltimore oriole
Fish: rockfish and striped bass
Flower: black-eyed susan
Insect: Baltimore checkerspot butterfly
Song: "Maryland, My Maryland"
Sport (unique among states): Jousting
Tree: white oak (Wye Oake, Wyle Mills)

THE LAND

Area: 12,407 sq. mi., 42nd
Land: 9,775 sq. mi., 42nd
Water: 2,633 sq. mi., 18th
Topography: E shore of coastal plain and Maryland Main of coastal plain, Piedmont plateau, and the Blue Ridge Mts., separated by Chesapeake Bay.
Number of counties: 23
Geographic center: Prince George's, 4.5 mi. NW of Davidsonville
Length: 250 mi.
Width: 90 mi.
Highest point: 3,360 ft. (Backbone Mt.), 32nd
Lowest point: sea level (Atlantic Ocean), 3rd
Mean elevation: 350 ft., 43rd
Coastline: 31 mi., 20th
Shoreline: 3,190 mi., 9th

CLIMATE AND ENVIRONMENT

Temp., highest: 109 deg. on July 10, 1936, at Cumberland & Frederick; lowest: -40 deg. on Jan. 13, 1912, at Oakland
Fresh water withdrawn, per capita, per day: 321 gal., 47th
Endangered species: mammals, 2—Indiana bat, Delmarva peninsula fox squirrel; birds, 1—American peregrine falcon; reptiles, 2; amphibians, none; fishes, 1; invertebrates, 1; plants, 4

MAJOR CITIES, POPULATION PERCENTAGE INCREASE (1980-90)

Baltimore, 736,014— –6.45%
Bethesda, 62,936—0.32%
Dundalk, 65,800— –7.70%
Silver Spring, 76,046—4.33%
Wheaton/Glenmont, 53,720—10.54%

THE PEOPLE

Population: 4,781,468, 19th
Percent change (1980-90): 11.81%, 15th
Per sq. mi: 385.38, 6th
Percent in metro. area: 92.84%, 4th
Percent foreign born: 6.6%, 14th
White: 3,393,964—70.98%, 45th
Black: 1,189,899—24.89%, 7th
Native American: 12,972—0.27%, 35th
Asian, Pacific Isle: 139,719—2.92%, 8th
Other races: 44,914—0.94%, 28th
Hispanic origin: 125,102—2.62%, 24th
Percent over 5 yrs. speaking language other than English at home: 8.9%, 20th
Percent males: 48.49%, 29th
Percent females: 51.51%, 23rd
Percent never married: 29.1%, 7th
Marriages per 1,000 (1989): 10.1, 18th
Divorces per 1,000 (1989): 3.3, 44th
Median age: 33
Under 5 years: 357,818—7.48%, 23rd
Under 18 years: 1,162,241—24.31%, 42nd

65 years & older: 517,482—10.82%, 41st
Percent increase among the elderly: 30.8%, 14th

Of Vital Importance

Live births per 1,000 pop.: 15.9, 24th
Infant mortality rate per 1,000 births (1988): 11.3, 9th
Average lifetime (1979-81): 73.32, 37th
Deaths per 100,000 pop. (1988): 836.3, 35th
Causes of death per 100,000 pop. (1988):
  Diseases of heart: 276.2, 36th
  Malignant neoplasms: 201, 24th
  Cerebrovascular diseases: 51.3, 41st
  Accidents & adverse effects: 33.3, 44th
  Chronic obstructive pulmonary diseases: 30.4, 36th
  Suicide: 11.3, 35th
  HIV infection: 5.4, 12th
  Other: 71.4, 36th

Keeping Well

Non-federal physicians per 100,000 pop.: 350, 3rd
Dentists per 100,000 (1990-91): 75, 11th
Nurses per 100,000 (1989): 715, 22nd
Hospitals per 100,000: 1.7, 49th
  Admissions per 100,000: 13,182, 30th
  Beds per 100,000: 431.58, 38th
  Occupancy rate: 75.1%, 10th
  Semiprivate room charges per day: $266, 27th
  Average stay: 7.0, 30th
Notifiable diseases per 100,000:
  AIDS: 21.0, 6th
  Gonorrhea: 489.7, 6th
  Measles: 4.5, 25th
  Syphillis: 66.4, 9th
  Tuberculosis (TB): 8.0, 19th
Per capita spending on mental health programs (1987): $53.76, 9th
Pop. without health insur. (1991): 13.1%, 22nd

Households by Type

Total households: 1,748,991
  Percent change (1980-90): 19.71%, 16th
Family households: 1,245,814
  Percent of total: 71.23%, 19th
Nonfamily households: 503,177
  Percent of total: 28.77%, 33rd
Persons per household: 2.67, 12th
Pop. living in group quarters: 113,856
  Percent of pop.: 2.38%, 38th

Living Quarters

Total housing units: 1,891,917
  Persons per unit: 2.53, 6th
Occupied housing units: 1,748,991
  Percent of total units: 92.45%, 6th
  Persons per unit: 2.62, 12th
  Percent of units with over 1 person per room: 3.04%, 24th
Owner-occupied units: 1,137,296
  Percent of total units: 60.11%, 22nd
  Percent of occupied units: 65.03%, 36th
  Persons per unit: 2.79, 15th
  Median value: $116,500, 10th
Renter-occupied units: 661,695
  Percent of total units: 34.97%, 9th
  Percent of occupied units: 37.83%, 10th
  Persons per unit: 2.45, 13th
  Median contract rent: $473, 8th
  Rental vacancy rate: 6.8%, 44th
Mobile home, trailer & other as a % of occupied housing units: 3.20%, 45th

Crime Index per 100,000

Total: 5,830, 17th
  Violent: 919, 7th
    Murder and nonnegligent manslaughter: 12, 9th
    Aggravated assault: 7,483, 24th
    Robbery: 364, 6th
    Rape: 46, 17th
  Property: 4,912, 21st
    Burglary: 1,120, 25th
    Larceny, theft: 3,083, 23rd
    Motor vehicle theft: 709, 12th
Drug abuse arrests: 599, 5th

Teaching and Learning

Literacy (1987): 88%, 25th
Pop. 3 and over enrolled in school: 1,212,333
  Percent of pop.: 26.6%, 32nd
Public elementary & secondary schools:
  Total enrollment: 740,000
  Avg. class size (1987): 25, 7th
  Teachers: 40,700

Percent of pop.: 0.85%, 44th
Teachers' avg. salary: $36,600, 5th
Spending per capita: $891, 11th
Spending per pupil in avg. daily attendance: $5,887, 8th
Percent of graduates taking SAT: 64%, 10th
Combined SAT scores: 904, 33rd
Percent of pop. over 25 completing:
High school: 78.4%, 22nd
College degree/s: 26.5%, 5th
Higher educa., institutions: 57
Per 100,000 pop.: 0.7, 25th
Enroll: 264,862
Percent of pop.: 5.54%, 25th
Public: 225,945
Percent of enroll.: 85.31%, 20th
Private 38,917
Percent of enroll.: 14.69%, 32nd
White non-Hispanic: 482,201
Percent of enroll.: 86.77%, 20th
Black non-Hispanic: 45,270
Percent of enroll.: 8.15%, 19th
Hispanic: 5,467
Percent of enroll.: 0.98%, 36th
Asian/Pacific Islander: 7,356
Percent of enroll.: 1.32%, 36th
Amer. Indian/AK native: 1,422
Percent of enroll.: 0.26%, 39th
Nonresident alien: 13,986
Percent of enroll.: 2.52%, 21st
Female: 147,448
Percent of enroll.: 55.67%, 16th
Tuition, state university ('90-'91): $2,287, 14th
Public library systems: 24
Books & serial vol. per capita: 2.34, 30th
Govt. expend. per capita: $23.84, 6th
State govt.: $5.60, 5th
Local govts.: $18.24, 12th

Law Enforcement, Courts, and Prisons

Police protection expend.: $663,521,000
Per capita: $138.78, 11th
Judicial & legal expend.: $290,502,000
Per capita: $60.76, 12th
Corrections expend.: $628,394,000
Per capita: $131.44, 6th
Police per 10,000 pop. (1990-91): 27.2, 4th
Prisoners (state & fed.) sentenced to over 1 yr., per 100,000 pop.: 347
Percent change (1989-90): 8.49%, 19th
Death penalty: yes, by lethal gas.
Under sentence of death: 19, 23rd
Executed (1989): none

Religion, Number and Percent of Population

Agnostic: 25,335—0.70%, 17th
Buddhist: 3,619—0.10%, 17th
Christian: 3,069,105—84.80%, 36th
Hindu: 7,239—0.20%, 3rd
Jewish: 101,338—2.80%, 5th
Moslem: 7,239—0.20%, 13th
Unitarian: 10,858—0.30%, 15th
Other: 50,669—1.40%, 20th
None: 260,584—7.20%, 20th
Refused to answer: 83,242—2.30%, 21st

Making a Living

Personal income per capita (1989): $17,730, 4th
Percent increase (1979-'89) (constant 1989 dollars): 27.6%, 9th
Average income per family: $53,846, 4th
Percent of pop. below poverty level: 8.3%, 47th
Percent 65 and over: 10.5%, 38th
Cost of living, selected cities
1st qtr., 1991 (U. S. Standard=100)

Cumberland	97.5
Baltimore (1st qtr., 1989)	107.3
St. Mary's County	111.0

Economy

Civilian labor force : 2,535,000
Percent of tot. pop.: 53.02%, 10th
Percent 65 and over: 2.64%, 29th
Percent females: 47.50%, 5th
Percent job growth (1980-90): 31.22%, 11th
Major employer industries:
Agriculture: 26,587—1.10%, 44th
Construction: 166,773—6.90%, 2nd
Finance, insurance & real estate: 154,688—6.40%, 13th
Government: 567,995—23.50%, 3rd
Manufacturing: 234,449—9.70%, 42nd
Mining: 3,535—0.1%, 42nd
Service: 587,331—24.30%, 4th

Trade: 406,056—16.80%, 48th
Transportation, communication, & public utilities: 125,684—5.20%, 25th
Wholesale/retail: 467,357—18.8%, 50th
Unemployment rate: 4.65%, 41st
Male: 2.21%, 47th
Female: 2.45%, 24th
Total businesses (1991): 148,454
New business incorp's. (1991): 16,463
Percent of total businesses: 11.09%, 5th
Business failures (1991): 1,314
Percent of total businesses: 0.89%, 23rd
Agriculture farm income
Marketing (1991): $1,332,494,000, 35th
Net per operation: $25,186, 19th
Net per acre: $172, 9th
Leading products: Broilers, greenhouse, dairy products, soybeans
Av. value land & build. per acre: $2,512, 5th
Percent increase (1980-90): 12.24%, 18th
Govt. payments: $15,342,000, 38th
Construction, value of all: $3,623,000,000
Per capita: $757.72, 14th
Percent change 1989-90: -26.72%, 40th
Manufactures:
Value added: $15,724,000,000
Per capita: $3,288.53, 40th
Value of shipments: $30,679,000,000
Per capita: $6,416.23, 42nd
Leading products: electric and electronic equipment, food and kindred products, chemicals and allied products
Mining, min. prod., value (1987): $371,000,000, 34th
Leading products: coal, stone, cement
Retail sales: $36,837,000,000, 15th
Per household: $20,790, 11th
Percent increase (1987-90): 5.2%, 49th
Service indust., value (1987): $24,939,000,000, 13th
Per capita: $5,215.76, 9th
Tourism indus., value (1989): $4,273,000,000, 21st
Foreign exports value: $2,592,000,000, 28th
Per capita: $542.09, 42nd
Patents per 1,000 pop.: 5.4, 28th

Travel and Transportation

Motor vehicle registrations: 3,606,520
Per 1,000 pop.: 754, 33rd
Motorcycle registrations: 56,124
Per 1,000 pop.: 11, 38th
Licensed drivers per 1,000 driving age pop.: 902, 24th
Deaths from motor vehicle accidents per 100,000 pop.: 14.3, 41st
Public roads & streets
Total mileage: 28,752, 42nd
Rural mileage: 16,462, 41st
Urban mileage: 12,290, 22nd
Interstate mileage: 400, 42nd
Annual vehicle-miles of travel per person: 8,477, 38th
Mean travel time for workers 16 + who work away from home: 27.0 min., 3rd

Government

Registered voters (1988): 2,310,080
Percent of voting age pop.: 66.17%, 36th
Voter turnout (1988): 1,714,358
Percent of registered voters: 74.21%, 17th
Percent of voting age pop.: 49.11%, 32nd
State legislators, total (1992): 188, 8th
Women members (1992): 44
Percent of legislature: 23.4%, 14th
Dominant party (1992): Democrats
U. S. Congress, House members (1993): 8
Increase 1983-93: 0
Revenues:
State govt.: $12,194,598,000
Per capita: $2,550.39, 21st
State & local govt.: $19,527,566,000
Per capita: $4,084.01, 21st
Indebtedness:
State govt.: $6,643,753,000
Per capita: $1,389.48, 18th
State & local govt.: $16,288,000,000
Per capita: $3,406.49, 26th

Laws and Regulations

Legal driving age: 18
Marriage age without parental consent: 18
Divorce residence requirement: 1 yr.

Attractions

Major opera companies (1989): 4, 11th
Per 1 million pop.: 0.85, 15th

Major symphony orchestras (1989): 14, 21st
Per 1 million pop.: 2.98, 33rd
State appropriations for state arts agencies per capita: $1.32, 12th
State Fair in late Aug.-early Sept. at Timonium

Sports and Competition

NCAA sports teams, 11: Coppin State College, Johns Hopkins Univ. Blue Jays, Loyola College Greyhounds, Morgan State Univ. Golden Bears, Mount St. Mary's College Mountaineers, Towson State Univ. Tigers, U. S. Naval Academy Mids, Univ. of Maryland Retrievers, Univ. of Maryland Terrapins, Univ. of Maryland Hawks, Western Maryland College Terrors

Professional teams, 8:
Baseball, 3—Frederick Keys (Carolina League, Class A), Harry Grove Stadium; Baltimore Orioles (AL), Memorial Stadium; Hagerstown Suns (Eastern League, Class AA), Municipal Stadium
Basketball, 1—Washington Bullets (NBA), Capital Centre
Hockey, 2—Baltimore Skipjacks (American Hockey League), Baltimore Arena; Washington Capitals (NHL), Capital Centre
Soccer, 2—Baltimore Blast (Major Soccer League), Baltimore Arena; Maryland Bays (American Professional Soccer League), Cedar Lane Park

MASSACHUSETTS

"A spirit that's as American as apple pie. For the spirit of Massachusetts truly is the spirit of America."

Michael S. Dukakis

"Massachusetts—the cornerstone of a nation!"

Henry Wadsworth Longfellow

"I shall enter on no encomium upon Massachusetts; she needs none. There she is. Behold her and judge for yourselves."

Daniel Webster

Even though it is the 45th state in terms of area, the commonwealth of Massachusetts has always been a national leader. The first printing press, newspaper, library, college, and secondary school in the country were established here. Massachusetts has also given the nation four presidents. It has long been one of our top manufacturing states. The historic city of Boston is a major seaport and airline terminal, and the many universities in and around Boston make this area one of the world's greatest educational, research, and cultural centers. The Revolutionary War really began in Massachusetts with the Boston Massacre, the Boston Tea Party, and the battles of Lexington, Concord, and Bunker Hill.

Superlatives

- Mayflower Compact, model for future governments.
- First popular U.S. election.
- Institution of the town meeting.
- First Thanksgiving.
- Birthplace of the iron/steel industry.
- First integrated U.S. textile plant.
- First U.S. public school.
- Home to Harvard University, the oldest American college/university.
- Oldest U.S. private secondary school, the Mather School in Boston.
- Oldest boys' boarding school, Phillips Academy in Andover.
- First pipe organ in America.

Moments in History

- On his voyage of 1497-1498, John Cabot made the first record of European presence in present Massachusetts.
- In 1602 Bartholomew Gosnold noted so many codfish in the area that he named the nearby land Cape Cod.
- Church of England dissenters landed at Cape Cod near present Provincetown on November 11, 1620, to become the Pilgrims in this new land. A month later they reached their new home and named it Plymouth.
- In April, 1621, the Pilgrims and the Wampanoag chief Massasoit made a treaty regarding the settlement, kept by the chief for the rest of his life.
- In the fall of 1621 the Pilgrims and their Indian friends celebrated the first Thanksgiving.

• The Royal Charter of 1629 provided the foundation for democratic government in the Bay Colony.

• Boston was founded by a Puritan group in 1630.

• Only five years later Harvard was founded.

• Beginning in 1662, King Philip's War brought a long period of conflict with the Indians.

So They Say

"Your patent from King James is but idle parchment. James has no more right to give away or sell Massasoit's lands...than Massasoit has to sell King James' kingdom..."

Roger Williams

• The terrible witchcraft hysteria reached its darkest period about 1692 with the trials at Salem, with 19 hanged and one crushed to death.

• By the mid-1700s the colony prospered with fishing and trade in lumber, carried by ships built locally, manned by local sailors.

• Increasing laws and regulations imposed on the colony by Britain brought growing resistance. On March 5, 1770, British troops fired on a Boston mob and five died in the "Boston Massacre."

• Protesting the British tax on tea, a group of Bostonians dressed as Indians boarded a tea ship and threw its cargo into the harbor in December 1773—the famed "Boston Tea Party."

• Alerted by Paul Revere and others, beginning on April 19, 1775, patriots harried British troops in the region of Lexington and Concord and the "shots heard 'round the world" heralded the coming Revolution.

• On June 17, 1775, one of the first Revolutionary struggles took place on Breed's Hill, mistakenly called the Battle of Bunker Hill.

So They Say

"Here once the embattled farmers stood, and fired the shot heard round the world."

Ralph Waldo Emerson, on the encounter at Concord Bridge

• The British laid siege to Boston, but on March 17, 1776, they were forced to withdraw, in the first great American victory of the war.

So They Say

"Stand your ground. Don't fire unless fired upon. But if they mean to have war, let it begin here."

John Parker

• Massachusetts became a state on February 6, 1788.

• In 1796 John Adams of Massachusetts was elected president, and the famed Adams family contributed John Quincy Adams to the presidency in 1824.

• As early as 1832 an antislavery society was founded in Boston.

• The Civil War called 160,000 to service from Massachusetts.

• There was a continuing growth in industry and commerce, which was accelerated by World War I.

• His handling of the Boston police strike of 1919 brought fame to Gov. Calvin Coolidge, who became the third president from Massachusetts in 1923.

• The depression of 1929 was followed by a recovery that was stimulated by World War II, in which 556,000 went into service from the state.

• In 1961 Massachusetts celebrated its fourth U.S. president and all too soon mourned the death in 1963 of John Fitzgerald Kennedy.

• In 1986 Harvard University celebrated its 350th anniversary.

That's Interesting

• Chief Massasoit brought 94 of his people to the first Thanksgiving, but they also brought much food. The men played games, while five Pilgrim women and a few girls labored over the feast of venison, geese, turkey, clam chowder, oysters, lobsters, fish and eels, dried fruits and berries, corn biscuits, Indian pudding and probably popcorn balls.

• Silversmith Paul Revere made some fine false teeth of silver.

• The lake with the Indian name Chargoggargoggagoggmanchuaggagoggchubunagung-amaugg gives the English language its longest word.

• The first cargo ship sent out by the colony was seized by the French as a prize of war.

• The only artists' "model" owned by any community was the little red fish house at Rockport.

• Several religious movements were founded in the Bay State. Mary Baker Eddy founded the Church of Christ Scientist in 1879. Following the lead of William Ellery Channing, the American Unitarian Association was organized in 1825. Dwight L. Moody established his evangelistic headquarters at Northfield in the late 1870s .

NOTABLE NATIVES

John Adams (Braintree, later Quincy, 1735-1826), U.S. president. **John Quincy Adams** (Braintree, 1767-1848), U.S. president. **Clara Barton** (Oxford, 1821-1912), founder of the American Red Cross. **Katharine Lee Bates** (Falmouth, 1859-1929), educator and author. **William Cullen Bryant** (Cummington, 1794-1878), poet/editor. **Bette Davis** (Lowell, 1908-1990), actress. **Emily Dickinson** (Amherst, 1830-1886), poet. **Ralph Waldo Emerson** (Boston, 1803-1882), poet/essayist. **Benjamin Franklin** (Boston, 1706-1790), public official/diplomat/scientist. **John Hancock** (Braintree, 1737-1793), merchant/public official. **Nathaniel Hawthorne** (Salem, 1804-1864), author. **Oliver Wendell Holmes** (Cambridge, 1809-1894) physician/author/educator. **Oliver Wendell Holmes** (Boston, 1841-1935), U.S. Supreme Court justice. **Winslow Homer** (Boston, 1836-1910), painter. **Elias Howe** (Spencer, 1819-1967), inventor. **John Fitzgerald Kennedy** (Brookline, 1917-1963), U.S. president. **Jack Lemmon** (Boston, 1925-), actor. **Horace Mann** (Franklin, 1796-1859), educator. **Dwight Lyman Moody** (Northfield, 1837-1899), evangelist. **Samuel Finley Breese Morse** (Charlestown, 1791-1872), artist/inventor. **George Peabody** (South Danvers, 1795-1869), merchant/philanthropist. **Edgar Allan Poe** (Boston, 1809-1849), poet/critic. **Paul Revere** (Boston, 1735-1818), patriot/silversmith. **Henry David Thoreau** (Concord, 1817-1862), philosopher/naturalist. **James Abbott McNeill Whistler** (Lowell, 1834-1903), artist. **John Greenleaf Whittier** (Haverhill, 1807-1892), poet/abolitionist.

GENERAL

Admitted to statehood: Feb. 6, 1788
Origin of name: from Indian tribe named after "large hill place" identified by Capt. John Smith as being near Milton
Capital: Boston
Nicknames: The Bay State and The Old Colony State.
Motto: *"Ense Petit Placidam Sub Libertate Quietem"* ("By the Sword We Seek Peace, but Peace Only under Liberty")
Animal: Morgan horse
Beverage: cranberry juice
Bird: chickadee
Dog: Boston terrier
Fish: cod
Flower: mayflower, or trailing arbutus
Folk song: "Massachusetts"
Fossil: theropod dinosaur tracks
Gem: rhodonite
Insect: ladybug
Marine mammal: Right whale
Mineral: Babingtonite
Poem: "Blue Hills of Massachusetts"
Song: "All Hail to Massachusetts"
Tree: American elm

THE LAND

Area: 10,555 sq. mi., 44th
Land: 7,838 sq. mi., 45th
Water: 2,717 sq. mi., 17th
Topography: jagged indented coast from Rhode Island around Cape Cod; flat land yields to stony upland pastures near central region and gentle hill country in W; except in W, land is rocky, sandy, and not fertile
Number of counties: 14
Geographic center: Worcester, N part of city
Length: 190 mi.
Width: 50 mi.

Highest point: 3,487 ft. (Mt. Greylock), 31st
Lowest point: sea level (Atlantic Ocean), 3rd
Mean elevation: 500 ft., 42nd
Coastline: 192 mi., 10th
Shoreline: 1,519 mi., 15th

Climate and Environment

Temp., highest: 107 deg. on Aug. 2, 1975, at Chester and New Bedford; lowest: -35 deg. on Jan. 12, 1981, at Chester
Fresh water withdrawn, per capita, per day: 1,070 gal., 32nd
Endangered species: mammals, none; birds, 2—American peregrine falcon, roseate tern; reptiles, 3; amphibians, none; fishes, none; invertebrates, 2; plants, 2

Major Cities, Population Percentage Increase (1980-90)

Boston, 574,283—2.01%
Lowell, 103,439—11.93%
New Bedford, 99,922—1.47%
Springfield, 156,983—3.06%
Worcester, 169,759—4.92%

The People

Population: 6,016,425, 13th
  Percent change (1980-90): 4.64%, 28th
  Per sq. mi: 570.01, 5th
  Percent in metro. area: 90.39%, 9th
  Percent foreign born: 9.5%, 7th
White: 5,405,374—89.84%, 20th
Black: 300,130—4.99%, 30th
Native American: 12,241—0.20%, 43rd
Asian, Pacific Isle: 143,392—2.38%, 12th
Other races: 155,288—2.58%, 11th
Hispanic origin: 287,549—4.78%, 17th
Percent over 5 yrs. speaking language other than English at home: 15.2%, 10th
Percent males: 48.01%, 45th
Percent females: 51.99%, 7th
Percent never married: 32.8%, 2nd
Marriages per 1,000 (1989): 9.0, 29th
Divorces per 1,000 (1989): 2.6, 49th
Median age: 33.6
Under 5 years: 412,473—6.86%, 44th
Under 18 years: 1,353,075—22.49%, 49th
65 years & older: 819,284—13.62%, 13th
Percent increase among the elderly: 12.8%, 41st

Of Vital Importance

Live births per 1,000 pop.: 16.0, 19th
Infant mortality rate per 1,000 births (1988): 7.9, 47th
Average lifetime (1979-81): 75.01, 12th
Deaths per 100,000 pop. (1988): 959.1, 10th
Causes of death per 100,000 pop. (1988):
  Diseases of heart: 343.9, 15th
  Malignant neoplasms: 223.4, 9th
  Cerebrovascular diseases: 63.5, 26th
  Accidents & adverse effects: 29.7, 48th
  Chronic obstructive pulmonary diseases: 34.4, 25th
  Suicide: 8.6, 47th
  HIV infection: 5.4, 12th
  Other: 85.9, 5th

Keeping Well

Non-federal physicians per 100,000 pop.: 357, 2nd
Dentists per 100,000 (1990-91): 83, 5th
Nurses per 100,000 (1989): 1150, 2nd
Hospitals per 100,000: 2.6, 31st
  Admissions per 100,000: 14,499, 18th
  Beds per 100,000: 563.52, 18th
  Occupancy rate: 77.3%, 8th
  Semiprivate room charges per day: $351, 8th
  Average stay: 10.7, 7th
Notifiable diseases per 100,000:
  AIDS: 14.0, 13th
  Gonorrhea: 125.3, 31st
  Measles: 0.5, 45th
  Syphillis: 28.3, 23rd
  Tuberculosis (TB): 7.3, 24th
Per capita spending on mental health programs (1987): $61.69, 6th
Pop. without health insur.(1991): 10.9%, 35th

Households by Type

Total households: 2,247,110
  Percent change (1980-90): 10.53%, 28th
Family households: 1,514,746
  Percent of total: 67.41%, 48th
Nonfamily households: 732,364
  Percent of total: 32.59%, 4th
Persons per household: 2.58, 29th

Pop. living in group quarters: 214,307
Percent of pop.: 3.56%, 8th

Living Quarters

Total housing units: 2,472,711
Persons per unit: 2.43, 18th
Occupied housing units: 2,247,110
Percent of total units: 90.88%, 17th
Persons per unit: 2.53, 23rd
Percent of units with over 1 person per room: 2.52%, 35th
Owner-occupied units: 1,331,493
Percent of total units: 53.85%, 42nd
Percent of occupied units: 59.25%, 45th
Persons per unit: 2.82, 10th
Median value: $162,800, 4th
Renter-occupied units: 915,617
Percent of total units: 37.03%, 6th
Percent of occupied units: 40.75%, 8th
Persons per unit: 2.24, 42nd
Median contract rent: $506, 5th
Rental vacancy rate: 6.9%, 42nd
Mobile home, trailer & other as a % of occupied housing units: 2.27%, 49th

Crime Index per 100,000

Total: 5,298, 26th
Violent: 736, 13th
Murder and nonnegligent manslaughter: 4, 38th
Aggravated assault: 6,856, 44th
Robbery: 217, 14th
Rape: 34, 31st
Property: 4,562, 28th
Burglary: 1,113, 26th
Larceny, theft: 2,525, 45th
Motor vehicle theft: 924, 6th
Drug abuse arrests: 254, 25th

Teaching and Learning

Literacy (1987): 89%, 17th
Pop. 3 and over enrolled in school: 1,530,134
Percent of pop.: 26.5%, 35th
Public elementary & secondary schools:
Total enrollment: 842,000
Avg. class size (1987): 21, 35th
Teachers: 59,000
Percent of pop.: 0.98%, 31st
Teachers' avg. salary: $34,200, 10th
Spending per capita: $826, 23rd
Spending per pupil in avg. daily attendance: $6,170, 7th
Percent of graduates taking SAT: 79%, 2nd
Combined SAT scores: 896, 36th
Percent of pop. over 25 completing:
High school: 80.0%, 15th
College degree/s: 27.2%, 3rd
Higher educa., institutions: 116
Per 100,000 pop.: 0.5, 40th
Enroll: 418,874
Percent of pop.: 6.96%, 7th
Public: 184,672
Percent of enroll.: 44.09%, 50th
Private 234,202
Percent of enroll.: 55.91%, 2nd
White non-Hispanic: 475,505
Percent of enroll.: 83.45%, 27th
Black non-Hispanic: 56,786
Percent of enroll.: 9.97%, 16th
Hispanic: 9,094
Percent of enroll.: 1.60%, 25th
Asian/Pacific Islander: 10,693
Percent of enroll.: 1.88%, 22nd
Amer. Indian/AK native: 2,547
Percent of enroll.: 0.45%, 24th
Nonresident alien: 14,178
Percent of enroll.: 2.49%, 22nd
Female: 230,771
Percent of enroll.: 55.09%, 22nd
Tuition, state university ('90-'91): $2,580, 9th
Public library systems: 374
Books & serial vol. per capita: 4.32, 2nd
Govt. expend. per capita: $23.71, 7th
State govt.: $3.55, 13th
Local govts.: $20.16, 7th

Law Enforcement, Courts, and Prisons

Police protection expend.: $809,202,000
Per capita: $134.51, 12th
Judicial & legal expend.: $352,685,000
Per capita: $58.62, 15th
Corrections expend.: $694,292,000
Per capita: $115.41, 8th
Police per 10,000 pop. (1990-91): 22.4, 15th

Prisoners (state & fed.) sentenced to over 1 yr., per 100,000 pop.: 132
Percent change (1989-90): 8.68%, 18th
Death penalty: no

Religion, Number and Percent of Population

Agnostic: 46,634—1.00%, 10th
Buddhist: 18,653—0.40%, 5th
Christian: 3,837,937—82.30%, 40th
Hindu: 4,663—0.10%, 10th
Jewish: 163,217—3.50%, 4th
Moslem: 18,653—0.40%, 5th
Unitarian: 37,307—0.80%, 3rd
Other: 51,297—1.10%, 32nd
None: 340,425—7.30%, 19th
Refused to answer: 144,564—3.10%, 7th

Making a Living

Personal income per capita (1989): $17,224, 6th
Percent increase (1979-'89) (constant 1989 dollars): 37.8%, 2nd
Average income per family: $53,017, 6th
Percent of pop. below poverty level: 8.9%, 45th
Percent 65 and over: 9.4%, 43rd
Cost of living, selected cities
1st qtr., 1991 (U. S. Standard=100)

Fitchburg-Leominster	115.2
Springfield	117.9

Economy

Civilian labor force : 3,166,000
Percent of tot. pop.: 52.62%, 13th
Percent 65 and over: 3.06%, 18th
Percent females: 46.94%, 10th
Percent job growth (1980-90): 17.77%, 31st
Major employer industries:
Agriculture: 26,793—0.90%, 47th
Construction: 122,057—4.10%, 31st
Finance, insurance & real estate: 217,321—7.30%, 7th
Government: 372,125—12.50%, 44th
Manufacturing: 544,791—18.30%, 19th
Mining: 2,682—0.1%, 44th
Service: 779,974—26.20%, 3rd
Trade: 544,791—18.30%, 28th
Transportation, communication, & public utilities: 142,896—4.80%, 33rd
Wholesale/retail: 615,606—20.3%, 39th
Unemployment rate: 5.97%, 13th
Male: 3.44%, 10th
Female: 2.53%, 20th
Total businesses (1991): 201,385
New business incorp's. (1991): 11,706
Percent of total businesses: 5.81%, 26th
Business failures (1991): 2,806
Percent of total businesses: 1.39%, 6th
Agriculture farm income
Marketing (1991): $475,540,000, 42nd
Net per operation: $27,674, 16th
Net per acre: $281, 4th
Leading products: greenhouse, cranberries, dairy products, eggs
Av. value land & build. per acre: $3,802, 4th
Percent increase (1980-90): 136.44%, 1st
Govt. payments: $1,494,000, 45th
Construction, value of all: $2,889,000,000
Per capita: $480.19, 33rd
Percent change 1989-90: -34.30%, 45th
Manufactures:
Value added: $35,102,000,000
Per capita: $5,834.36, 16th
Value of shipments: $63,796,000,000
Per capita: $10,603.64, 27th
Leading products: (1990): electric and electronic equipment, machinery, industrial machinery and equipment, printing and publishing, fabricated metal products
Mining, min. prod., value (1987): $178,000,000, 41st
Leading products: stone, sand/gravel, lime
Retail sales: $50,757,000,000, 10th
Per household: $22,488, 6th
Percent increase (1987-90): 7.6%, 44th
Service indust., value (1987): $41,367,000,000, 9th
Per capita: $6,875.68, 3rd
Tourism indus., value (1989): $6,252,000,000, 14th
Foreign exports value: $9,501,000,000, 10th
Per capita: $1,579.18, 8th
Patents per 1,000 pop.: 2.8, 48th

Travel and Transportation

Motor vehicle registrations: 3,725,798
Per 1,000 pop.: 619, 48th
Motorcycle registrations: 55,730
Per 1,000 pop.: 9, 46th

Licensed drivers per 1,000 driving age pop.: 880, 34th
Deaths from motor vehicle accidents per 100,000 pop.: 10.1, 49th
Public roads & streets
  Total mileage: 34,076, 41st
    Rural mileage: 13,230, 42nd
    Urban mileage: 20,846, 11th
    Interstate mileage: 567, 37th
Annual vehicle-miles of travel per person: 7,667, 43rd
Mean travel time for workers 16 + who work away from home: 22.7 min., 9th

Government

Registered voters (1988): 3,274,777
  Percent of voting age pop.: 72.21%, 23rd
Voter turnout (1988): 2,632,801
  Percent of registered voters: 80.40%, 1st
  Percent of voting age pop.: 58.06%, 12th
State legislators, total (1992): 200, 6th
  Women members (1992): 37
    Percent of legislature: 18.5%, 23rd
  Dominant party (1992): Democrats
U. S. Congress, House members (1993): 10
  Increase 1983-93: -1
Revenues:
  State govt.: $17,034,053,000
    Per capita: $2,831.26, 14th
  State & local govt.: $26,068,621,000
    Per capita: $4,332.91, 15th
Indebtedness:
  State govt.: $18,714,704,000
    Per capita: $3,110.60, 5th
  State & local govt.: $26,976,000,000
    Per capita: $4,483.73, 10th

Laws and Regulations

Legal driving age: 18
Marriage age without parental consent: 18
Divorce residence requirement: 1 yr., qualification—check local statutes

Attractions

Major opera companies (1989): 6, 8th
  Per 1 million pop.: 1.01, 8th
Major symphony orchestras (1989): 31, 9th
  Per 1 million pop.: 5.24, 9th
State appropriations for state arts agencies per capita: $2.06, 6th

Sports and Competition

NCAA sports teams, 12: Boston College Eagles, Boston Univ. Terriers, Brandeis Univ. Judges, Harvard Univ. Crimson, Holy Cross College Crusaders, Nichols College Bisons, Northeastern Univ. Huskies, Springfield College Chiefs, Univ. of Massachusetts-Amherst Minutemen, Univ. of Massachusetts-Boston Beacons, Williams College Ephs, Worcester Polytechnic Institute Engineers
Professional teams, 6:
  Baseball, 2—Boston Red Sox (AL), Fenway Park; Pittsfield Mets (New York-Penn League, Class A), Wahconah Park
  Basketball, 1—Boston Celtics (NBA), Boston Garden
  Football, 1—New England Patriots (AFC), Foxboro Stadium
  Hockey, 2—Boston Bruins (NHL), Boston Garden; Springfield Indians (American Hockey League), Springfield Civic Center

MICHIGAN

"Michigan, handsome as a well made woman, and dressed and jewelled. It seemed to me that the earth was generous and outgoing here in the heartland, and, perhaps its people took a cue from it."

John Steinbeck

Michigan extends as far east as parts of South Carolina. A good part of Canada, the "northern" neighbor, lies south of Michigan. Michigan is the only state that is divided into two peninsulas — Upper and Lower. The Upper Peninsula is sparsely populated and quite rural, whereas the Lower Peninsula contains all the large cities and most of the industry and agriculture. Michigan is a state in which almost half its area is fresh water; with water and land combined it is the largest state east of the Mississippi River. Michigan had the imagination to create a capital in the wilderness, and the courage to elect the youngest governor to serve anywhere in the United States. The world automobile industry was established there, and it still leads the United States in auto production.

SUPERLATIVES

- Longest siege in Indian warfare.
- First in U.S. automobile production.
- World's busiest ship canal.
- Detroit River carries world's greatest tonnage.
- Most million-ton ports in the United States.
- Largest U.S. producer of salt, mint, navy beans, and sour cherries.
- First in baby food and carpet sweepers.
- Greatest variety of trees in the United States.
- Largest copper reserve in the United States.
- First university established by a state.

MOMENTS IN HISTORY

- Explorers from French Canada, Etienne Brule and Grenoble, reached present-day Michigan during their journeys of 1618-1622.
- In 1668 Father Jacques Marquette and Father Claude Dablon founded the first permanent European settlement in present-day Michigan, Sault Sainte Marie, at the Soo.
- In 1679 the Sieur de La Salle constructed the first French fort in lower Michigan, where St. Joseph now stands.
- Detroit was begun in 1701 by Antoine de la Mothe Cadillac, and now ranks as the first major city founded in the Midwest.
- In 1760 Major Robert Rogers and his Royal English Rangers captured Detroit without a struggle, and French rule came to an end.
- Angered by British mistreatment, Chief Pontiac laid siege to Detroit in 1763; lasting for 175 days, it was the longest siege in Indian warfare, but he failed to take the city.
- The Treaty of Paris in 1783 gave Michigan to the young United States, but the British continued to occupy most of the area until General Anthony "Mad Anthony" Wayne asserted American control, confirmed by the Jay Treaty of 1794.
- In 1805 much of Detroit was destroyed by fire.
- During the War of 1812, the British retook Detroit, but the Americans returned in September 1813.
- The cholera epidemic of 1832 took many lives, including that of the beloved priest, Father Gabriel Richard.
- In a "border war" both Michigan and Ohio claimed the area now occupied by Toledo. finally

Michigan accepted the entire Upper Peninsula in exchange for giving up its claim.

> **So They Say**
>
> "Father Gabriel Richard ...might be seen clothed in the robes of his high calling, pale and emaciated...going from house to house ...encouraging the well, and administering spiritual consolation to the sick and dying.
>
> Anonymous

• Michigan became the 26th state on January 26, 1837.

• In 1840 the rich copper lands in the Upper Peninsula were discovered.

• In 1847 the legislature chose an unoccupied woodland site as the state capital, and Lansing, the "capital in the forest," was begun.

• A Republican party was created at Jackson on July 6, 1854, and Michigan claims to be the site of the founding of the national party, although other states make the same claim.

• In 1854 Michigan became the first state to elect a Republican governor.

• During the Civil War the Michigan Cavalry Brigade played a key role in the Battle of Gettysburg.

• By strange coincidence a terrible fire roared through Holland and other areas of Michigan on the same day of the great Chicago fire, October 8, 1871.

• Around the turn of the century, Detroit began its rise as the principal center of automobile production.

• In World War I, the 32nd Division, with many Michigan troops, was the first from America to reach German soil.

• During World War II, Michigan factories manufactured an eighth of all war materiel produced in the nation.

• In 1957 Big Mac, the bridge, linked the Upper and Lower peninsulas for the first time.

• The riots of 1967 destroyed much of the inner city of Detroit.

• During the late 1980s and early 1990s, Michigan auto industries were greatly concerned by the competition of Japanese automobiles. However, they were encouraged by a gain in U.S. vehicle production of about 25% during the period from 1986 through 1990.

• In early 1992, scientists announced that the largest living thing in the world was a fungus, *Armillaria bulbosa*, growing beneath 37 acres near Crystal Falls.

That's Interesting

• Chief Black Hawk passed through Detroit after the Black Hawk War, and the whole city turned out to see the well-dressed leader in a Fourth of July celebration.

• Michigan history took a peculiar turn when Mormon leader James Strang proclaimed himself King of Beaver Island. He was assassinated in 1856, and mainland forces took over the Mormon properties.

• Disguised as a man, Sarah Emma Edmonds fought through four major Civil War campaigns before her identity was discovered.

• Michigan's shoreline of 3,177 mi. is second only to that of Alaska.

• Ann Arbor's name came from the habit of two wives named Ann chatting under a grape arbor. Their husbands named the town for them.

Notable Natives

Ralph Johnson Bunche (Detroit, 1904-1971), diplomat. **Thomas Edmund Dewey** (Owosso, 1902-1971), lawyer/public official. **Edna Ferber** (Kalamazoo, 1887-1968), author. **Henry Ford** (near Dearborn, 1863-1947), industrialist/philanthropist. **Will Keith Kellogg** (Battle Creek, 1860-1951), businessman. **Ring Lardner** (Niles, 1885-1933), journalist/author. **Charles Augustus Lindbergh** (Detroit, 1902-1974), aviator. **Glenn Theodore Seaborg** (Ishpeming, 1912-), chemist.

General

Admitted to statehood: Jan. 26, 1837

Origin of name: from Chippewa words *mici gama* meaning "great water," after the lake of the same name

Capital: Lansing

Nicknames: The Wolverine State, The Great Lake State, and Water Wonderland

Motto: *"Si Quaeris Peninsulam Amoenam Circumspice"* ("If You Seek a Pleasant Peninsula, Look about You")
Bird: robin
Fish: brook trout
Flower: apple blossom
Gem: Isle royal greenstone (chlorastrolite)
Song: "Michigan, My Michigan"
Stone: Petoskey stone
Tree: white pine

The Land

Area: 96,810 sq. mi., 11th
Land: 56,809 sq. mi., 22nd
Water: 40,001 sq. mi., 2nd
Topography: low rolling hills give way to northern tableland of hilly belts in Lower Peninsula. Upper Peninsula is level in the E, with swampy areas; W region is higher and more rugged.
Number of counties: 83
Geographic center: Wexford, 5 mi. NNW of Cadillac
Length: 490 mi.
Width: 240 mi.
Highest point: 1,979 ft. (Mt. Arvon), 38th
Lowest point: 572 ft. (Lake Erie), 40th
Mean elevation: 900 ft., 29th

Climate and Environment

Temp., highest: 112 deg. on July 13, 1936, at Mio; lowest: -51 deg. on Feb. 9, 1934, at Vanderbilt
Fresh water withdrawn, per capita, per day: 1,270 gal., 23rd
Endangered species: mammals, 2—Indiana bat, Eastern timber wolf; birds, 3—American peregrine falcon, piping plover, Kirtland's warbler; reptiles, none; amphibians, none; fishes, none; invertebrates, none; plants, 2

Major Cities, Population Percentage Increase (1980-90)

Detroit, 1,027,974— –14.58%
Flint, 140,761— –11.81%
Grand Rapids, 189,126—4.01%
Lansing, 127,321— –2.37%
Warren, 144,864— –10.10%

The People

Population: 9,295,297, 8th
  Percent change (1980-90): 0.36%, 43rd
  Per sq. mi: 96.02, 22nd
  Percent in metro. area: 80.11%, 16th
  Percent foreign born: 3.8%, 21st
White: 7,756,086—83.44%, 28th
Black: 1,291,706—13.90%, 15th
Native American: 55,638—0.60%, 21st
Asian, Pacific Isle: 104,983—1.13%, 26th
Other races: 86,884—0.93%, 29th
Hispanic origin: 201,596—2.17%, 29th
Percent over 5 yrs. speaking language other than English at home: 6.6%, 28th
Percent males: 48.55%, 27th
Percent females: 51.45%, 25th
Percent never married: 27.8%, 11th
Marriages per 1,000 (1989): 8.4, 35th
Divorces per 1,000 (1989): 4.3, 31st
Median age: 32.6
Under 5 years: 702,554—7.56%, 19th
Under 18 years: 2,458,765—26.45%, 17th
65 years & older: 1,108,461—11.92%, 34th
Percent increase among the elderly: 21.5%, 23rd

Of Vital Importance

Live births per 1,000 pop.: 16.9, 12th
Infant mortality rate per 1,000 births (1988): 11.1, 11th
Average lifetime (1979-81): 73.67, 30th
Deaths per 100,000 pop. (1988): 867.4, 29th
Causes of death per 100,000 pop. (1988):
  Diseases of heart: 372.2, 5th
  Malignant neoplasms: 193.8, 30th
  Cerebrovascular diseases: 56.8, 35th
  Accidents & adverse effects: 35.1, 38th
  Chronic obstructive pulmonary diseases: 31.4, 32nd
  Suicide: 11.8, 31st
  HIV infection: 2.3, 28th
  Other: 81.7, 10th

Keeping Well

Non-federal physicians per 100,000 pop.: 200, 30th

Dentists per 100,000 (1990-91): 72, 18th
Nurses per 100,000 (1989): 678, 27th
Hospitals per 100,000: 2.2, 41st
  Admissions per 100,000: 12,006, 41st
  Beds per 100,000: 441.08, 36th
  Occupancy rate: 66.7%, 24th
  Semiprivate room charges per day: $337, 13th
  Average stay: 13.2, 2nd
Notifiable diseases per 100,000:
  AIDS: 6.2, 31st
  Gonorrhea: 336.0, 13th
  Measles: 5.1, 21st
  Syphillis: 28.2, 24th
  Tuberculosis (TB): 5.4, 31st
Per capita spending on mental health programs (1987): $66.94, 5th
Pop. without health insur. (1991): 9.0%, 44th

Households by Type

Total households: 3,419,331
  Percent change (1980-90): 7.02%, 39th
Family households: 2,439,171
  Percent of total: 71.33%, 18th
Nonfamily households: 980,160
  Percent of total: 28.67%, 34th
Persons per household: 2.66, 13th
Pop. living in group quarters: 211,692
  Percent of pop.: 2.28%, 43rd

Living Quarters

Total housing units: 3,847,926
  Persons per unit: 2.42, 23rd
Occupied housing units: 3,419,331
  Percent of total units: 88.86%, 30th
  Persons per unit: 2.56, 19th
  Percent of units with over 1 person per room: 2.65%, 32nd
Owner-occupied units: 2,427,643
  Percent of total units: 63.09%, 9th
  Percent of occupied units: 71.00%, 4th
  Persons per unit: 2.80, 13th
  Median value: $60,600, 33rd
Renter-occupied units: 991,688
  Percent of total units: 25.77%, 45th
  Percent of occupied units: 29.00%, 48th
  Persons per unit: 2.31, 30th
  Median contract rent: $343, 25th
  Rental vacancy rate: 7.2%, 40th
Mobile home, trailer & other as a % of occupied housing units: 6.69%, 39th

Crime Index per 100,000

Total: 5,995, 15th
  Violent: 790, 9th
    Murder and nonnegligent manslaughter: 10, 14th
    Aggravated assault: 7,558, 20th
    Robbery: 234, 13th
    Rape: 78, 2nd
  Property: 5,204, 14th
    Burglary: 1,143, 23rd
    Larceny, theft: 3,347, 15th
    Motor vehicle theft: 714, 11th
Drug abuse arrests: 297, 18th

Teaching and Learning

Literacy (1987): 89%, 17th
Pop. 3 and over enrolled in school: 2,581,042
  Percent of pop.: 29.1%, 10th
Public elementary & secondary schools:
  Total enrollment: 1,609,000
  Avg. class size (1987): 25, 7th
  Teachers: 78,100
    Percent of pop.: 0.84%, 45th
  Teachers' avg. salary: $36,000, 8th
  Spending per capita: $888, 12th
  Spending per pupil in avg. daily attendance: $5,073, 18th
Percent of graduates taking SAT: 11%, 38th
  Combined SAT scores: 980, 20th
Percent of pop. over 25 completing:
  High school: 76.8%, 25th
  College degree/s: 17.4%, 37th
Higher educa., institutions: 97
  Per 100,000 pop.: 0.5, 46th
  Enroll: 569,803
    Percent of pop.: 6.13%, 14th
  Public: 487,359
    Percent of enroll.: 85.53%, 19th
  Private 82,444
    Percent of enroll.: 14.47%, 33rd
  White non-Hispanic: 130,361
    Percent of enroll.: 69.86%, 45th
  Black non-Hispanic: 44,738
    Percent of enroll.: 23.98%, 3rd
  Hispanic: 3,448
    Percent of enroll.: 1.85%, 22nd
  Asian/Pacific Islander: 2,683

Percent of enroll.: 1.44%, 32nd
Amer. Indian/AK native: 856
Percent of enroll.: 0.46%, 23rd
Nonresident alien: 4,513
Percent of enroll.: 2.42%, 23rd
Female: 313,728
Percent of enroll.: 55.06%, 23rd
Tuition, state university ('90-'91): $2,635, 7th
Public library systems: 376
Books & serial vol. per capita: 2.43, 28th
Govt. expend. per capita: $14.03, 28th
State govt.: $2.99, 17th
Local govts.: $11.05, 28th

LAW ENFORCEMENT, COURTS, AND PRISONS

Police protection expend.: $1,169,958,000
Per capita: $125.87, 15th
Judicial & legal expend.: $538,973,000
Per capita: $57.99, 17th
Corrections expend.: $958,387,000
Per capita: $103.11, 14th
Police per 10,000 pop. (1990-91): 20.4, 28th
Prisoners (state & fed.) sentenced to over 1 yr., per 100,000 pop.: 366
Percent change (1989-90): 8.31%, 20th
Death penalty: no

RELIGION, NUMBER AND PERCENT OF POPULATION

Agnostic: 34,183—0.50%, 27th
Buddhist: 6,837—0.10%, 17th
Christian: 5,790,543—84.70%, 37th
Hindu: 13,673—0.20%, 3rd
Jewish: 54,692—0.80%, 20th
Moslem: 20,510—0.30%, 9th
Unitarian: 20,510—0.30%, 15th
Other: 157,240—2.30%, 6th
None: 594,778—8.70%, 13th
Refused to answer: 143,567—2.10%, 28th

MAKING A LIVING

Personal income per capita (1989): $14,154, 20th
Percent increase (1979-'89) (constant 1989 dollars): 9.8%, 34th
Average income per family: $43,561, 18th
Percent of pop. below poverty level: 13.1%, 20th
Percent 65 and over: 10.8%, 30th
Cost of living, selected cities
1st qtr., 1991 (U. S. Standard=100)
Muskegon 99.7
Lansing 105.8

ECONOMY

Civilian labor force : 4,578,000
Percent of tot. pop.: 49.25%, 35th
Percent 65 and over: 2.14%, 41st
Percent females: 44.32%, 45th
Percent job growth (1980-90): 18.31%, 29th
Major employer industries:
Agriculture: 46,227—1.90%, 36th
Construction: 85,155—3.50%, 47th
Finance, insurance & real estate: 119,217—4.90%, 31st
Government: 340,620—14.00%, 34th
Manufacturing: 605,817—24.90%, 4th
Mining: 10,818—0.3%, 29th
Service: 472,002—19.40%, 26th
Trade: 501,198—20.60%, 5th
Transportation, communication, & public utilities: 99,753—4.10%, 45th
Wholesale/retail: 915,561—22.0%, 14th
Unemployment rate: 7.51%, 2nd
Male: 4.50%, 2nd
Female: 3.01%, 8th
Total businesses (1991): 320,693
New business incorp's. (1991): 20,099
Percent of total businesses: 6.27%, 22nd
Business failures (1991): 2,273
Percent of total businesses: 0.71%, 37th
Agriculture farm income
Marketing (1991): $3,081,072,000, 22nd
Net per operation: $14,149, 37th
Net per acre: $71, 20th
Leading products: Dairy products, corn, cattle, soybeans
Av. value land & build. per acre: $1,060, 18th
Percent increase (1980-90): -4.59%, 30th
Govt. payments: $123,691,000, 22nd
Construction, value of all: $5,075,000,000
Per capita: $545.98, 25th
Percent change 1989-90: -16.97%, 33rd
Manufactures:
Value added: $64,799,000,000
Per capita: $6,971.16, 7th
Value of shipments: $153,386,000,000

Per capita: $16,501.46, 6th
Leading products: transportation equipment, machinery, fabricated metals, primary metals, food products, rubber and plastic
Mining, min. prod., value (1987): $2,426,000,000, 16th
Leading products: petrol., iron ore, nat. gas, clay
Retail sales: $67,785,000,000, 8th
Per household: $19,765, 18th
Percent increase (1987-90): 14.9%, 27th
Service indust., value (1987): $37,401,000,000, 10th
Per capita: $4,023.65, 23rd
Tourism indus., value (1989): $6,427,000,000, 12th
Foreign exports value: $18,474,000,000, 5th
Per capita: $1,987.46, 6th
Patents per 1,000 pop.: 3.4, 45th

Travel and Transportation

Motor vehicle registrations: 7,209,217
Per 1,000 pop.: 775, 29th
Motorcycle registrations: 176,524
Per 1,000 pop.: 18, 23rd
Licensed drivers per 1,000 driving age pop.: 904, 22nd
Deaths from motor vehicle accidents per 100,000 pop.: 16.8, 32nd
Public roads & streets
Total mileage: 117,449, 7th
Rural mileage: 90,773, 9th
Urban mileage: 26,676, 8th
Interstate mileage: 1,227, 9th
Annual vehicle-miles of travel per person: 8,723, 32nd
Mean travel time for workers 16 + who work away from home: 21.2 min., 20th

Government

Registered voters (1988): 5,952,513
Percent of voting age pop.: 87.65%, 4th
Voter turnout (1988): 3,669,163
Percent of registered voters: 61.64%, 46th
Percent of voting age pop.: 54.03%, 21st
State legislators, total (1992): 148, 25th
Women members (1992): 22
Percent of legislature: 14.9%, 30th
Dominant party (1992): Split
U. S. Congress, House members (1993): 16
Increase 1983-93: -2
Revenues:
State govt.: $23,405,004,000
Per capita: $2,517.94, 22nd
State & local govt.: $37,183,968,000
Per capita: $4,000.30, 25th
Indebtedness:
State govt.: $9,169,639,000
Per capita: $986.48, 31st
State & local govt.: $21,414,000,000
Per capita: $2,303.75, 44th

Laws and Regulations

Legal driving age: 18
Marriage age without parental consent: 18
Divorce residence requirement: 180 days

Attractions

Major opera companies (1989): 4, 11th
Per 1 million pop.: 0.43, 35th
Major symphony orchestras (1989): 35, 7th
Per 1 million pop.: 3.77, 22nd
State appropriations for state arts agencies per capita: $1.34, 11th
State Fair in mid-Aug. at Escanaba for the Upper Peninsula and in late Aug.-early Sept. at Detroit

Sports and Competition

NCAA sports teams, 9: Central Michigan Univ. Chippewas, Eastern Michigan Univ. Hurons, Ferris State Univ. Bulldogs, Hillsdale College Chargers, Michigan State Univ. Spartans, Northern Michigan Univ. Wildcats, Univ. of Detroit Titans, Univ. of Michigan Wolverines, Western Michigan Univ. Broncos
Professional teams, 7:
Baseball, 1—Detroit Tigers (AL), Tiger Stadium
Basketball, 2—Detroit Pistons (NBA), The Palace of Auburn Hills; Grand Rapids Hoops (Continental Basketball Associaiton), Welsh Auditorium
Football, 1—Detroit Lions (NFC), Pontiac Silver Dome
Hockey, 3—Detroit Red Wings (NHL), Joe Louis Sports Arena; Muskegon Lumberjacks (International Hockey League), L.C. Walker Sports Arena; Kalamazoo Wings (International Hockey League), Wings Stadium

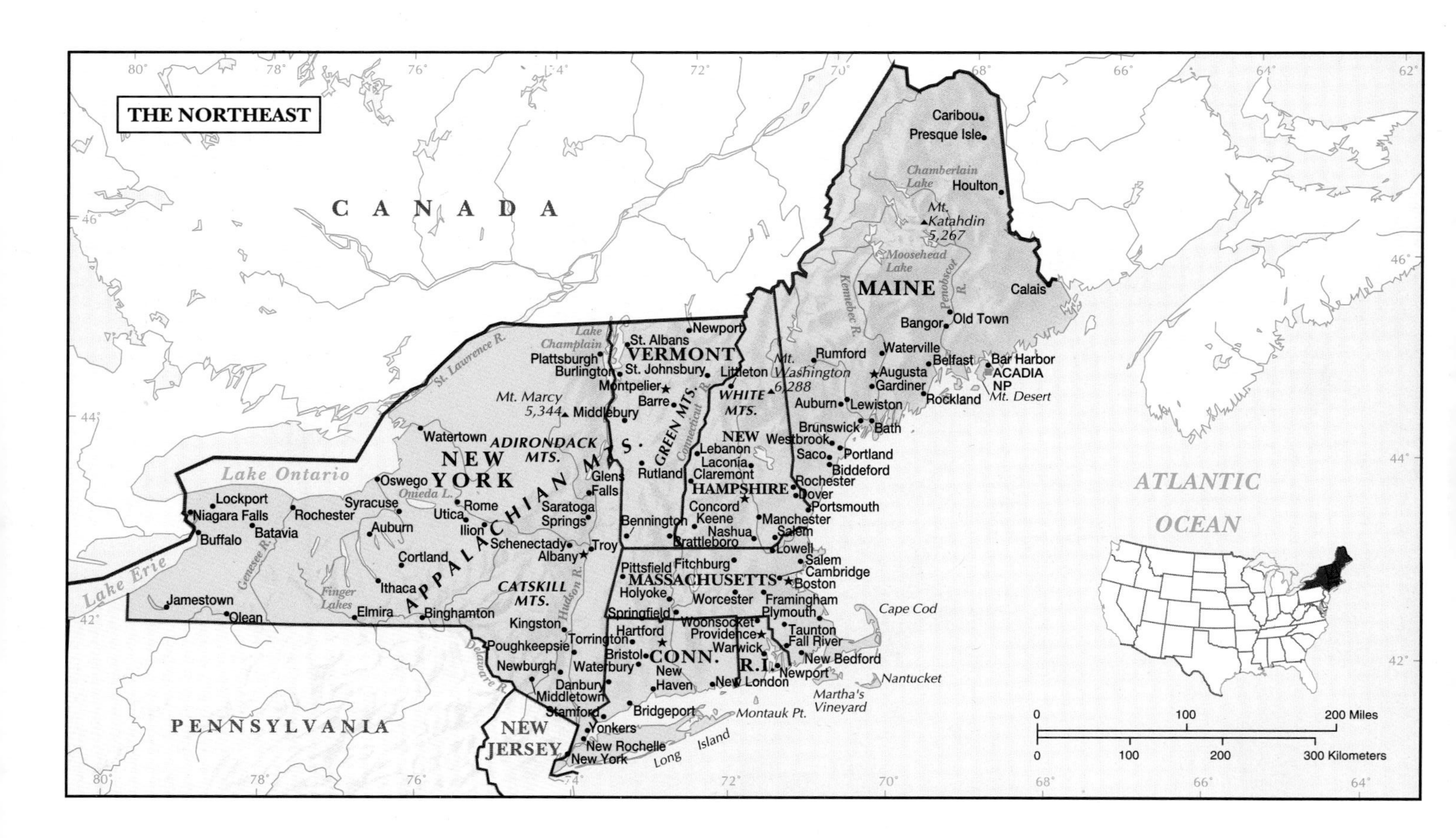
THE NORTHEAST
CANADA
ATLANTIC OCEAN
MAINE
VERMONT
NEW HAMPSHIRE
NEW YORK
MASSACHUSETTS
CONN.
R.I.
NEW JERSEY
PENNSYLVANIA
ADIRONDACK MTS.
APPALACHIAN MTS.
GREEN MTS.
WHITE MTS.
CATSKILL MTS.
Mt. Katahdin 5,267
Mt. Washington 6,288
Mt. Marcy 5,344
Lake Ontario
Lake Erie
Lake Champlain
Chamberlain Lake
Moosehead Lake
Omeda L.
Finger Lakes
St. Lawrence R.
Kennebec R.
Penobscot R.
Connecticut R.
Hudson R.
Delaware R.
Genesee R.
Caribou
Presque Isle
Houlton
Calais
Bangor
Old Town
Waterville
Belfast
Bar Harbor
ACADIA NP
Mt. Desert
Augusta
Gardiner
Rockland
Rumford
Auburn
Lewiston
Brunswick
Bath
Westbrook
Portland
Saco
Biddeford
Rochester
Dover
Portsmouth
Littleton
Lebanon
Laconia
Claremont
Concord
Keene
Manchester
Nashua
Salem
Newport
St. Albans
St. Johnsbury
Burlington
Plattsburgh
Montpelier
Barre
Middlebury
Rutland
Bennington
Brattleboro
Glens Falls
Saratoga Springs
Troy
Albany
Schenectady
Watertown
Oswego
Syracuse
Rome
Utica
Ilion
Auburn
Rochester
Lockport
Niagara Falls
Batavia
Buffalo
Cortland
Ithaca
Elmira
Binghamton
Jamestown
Olean
Kingston
Poughkeepsie
Newburgh
Middletown
Yonkers
New Rochelle
New York
Lowell
Salem
Cambridge
Boston
Pittsfield
Fitchburg
Holyoke
Worcester
Framingham
Springfield
Plymouth
Woonsocket
Providence
Warwick
Taunton
Fall River
New Bedford
Newport
Cape Cod
Nantucket
Martha's Vineyard
Hartford
Torrington
Bristol
Waterbury
Danbury
New Haven
New London
Bridgeport
Stamford
Montauk Pt.
Long Island
0 100 200 Miles
0 100 200 300 Kilometers
80° 78° 76° 74° 72° 70° 68° 66° 64° 62°
46° 44° 42°

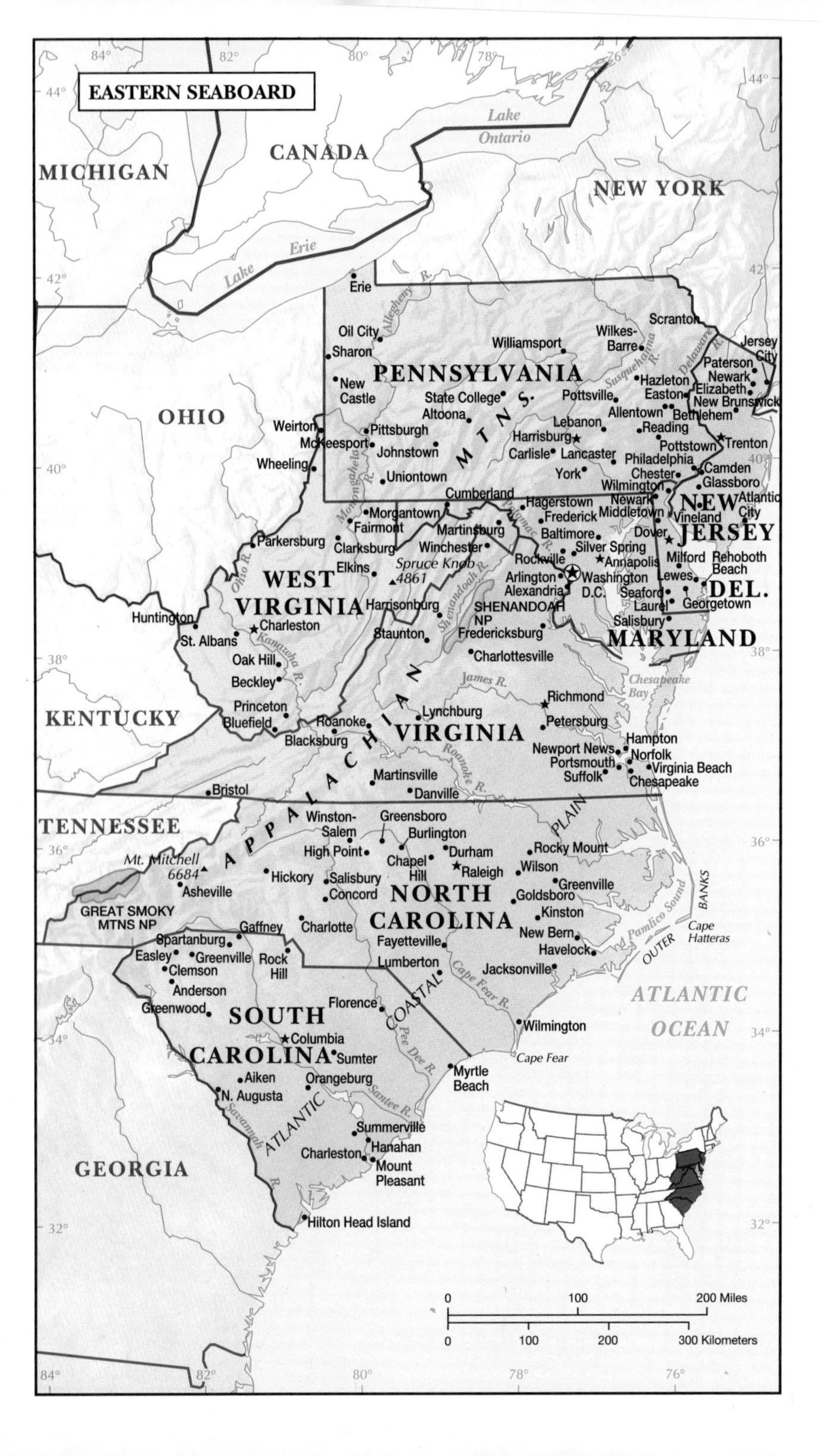

EASTERN SEABOARD
CANADA
MICHIGAN
Lake Ontario
Lake Erie
NEW YORK
PENNSYLVANIA
OHIO
WEST VIRGINIA
KENTUCKY
VIRGINIA
TENNESSEE
NORTH CAROLINA
SOUTH CAROLINA
GEORGIA
MARYLAND
NEW JERSEY
DEL.
ATLANTIC OCEAN
APPALACHIAN MTNS.
ATLANTIC COASTAL PLAIN
OUTER BANKS
Cape Hatteras
Cape Fear
Pamlico Sound
Chesapeake Bay
Erie
Oil City
Sharon
New Castle
Williamsport
Wilkes-Barre
Scranton
Hazleton
Easton
Allentown
Bethlehem
Pottsville
State College
Altoona
Lebanon
Reading
Harrisburg
Carlisle
Lancaster
York
Pottstown
Philadelphia
Chester
Wilmington
Newark
Middletown
Dover
Weirton
Pittsburgh
McKeesport
Johnstown
Wheeling
Uniontown
Cumberland
Hagerstown
Frederick
Baltimore
Silver Spring
Annapolis
Rockville
Washington D.C.
Arlington
Alexandria
Martinsburg
Winchester
Morgantown
Fairmont
Clarksburg
Elkins
Spruce Knob 4861
Parkersburg
Harrisonburg
Staunton
SHENANDOAH NP
Fredericksburg
Charlottesville
Huntington
St. Albans
Charleston
Oak Hill
Beckley
Princeton
Bluefield
Roanoke
Blacksburg
Lynchburg
Richmond
Petersburg
Hampton
Newport News
Norfolk
Portsmouth
Virginia Beach
Suffolk
Chesapeake
Martinsville
Danville
Bristol
Jersey City
Paterson
Newark
Elizabeth
New Brunswick
Trenton
Camden
Glassboro
Atlantic City
Vineland
Milford
Rehoboth Beach
Lewes
Seaford
Laurel
Georgetown
Salisbury
Winston-Salem
Greensboro
Burlington
High Point
Durham
Chapel Hill
Raleigh
Rocky Mount
Wilson
Greenville
Goldsboro
Kinston
New Bern
Havelock
Jacksonville
Wilmington
Hickory
Salisbury
Concord
Charlotte
Fayetteville
Lumberton
Mt. Mitchell 6684
Asheville
GREAT SMOKY MTNS NP
Gaffney
Spartanburg
Easley
Greenville
Clemson
Anderson
Rock Hill
Greenwood
Florence
Columbia
Sumter
Myrtle Beach
Aiken
N. Augusta
Orangeburg
Summerville
Hanahan
Charleston
Mount Pleasant
Hilton Head Island
Allegheny R.
Susquehanna R.
Delaware R.
Monongahela R.
Potomac R.
Shenandoah R.
Ohio R.
Kanawha R.
James R.
Roanoke R.
Cape Fear R.
Pee Dee R.
Santee R.
Savannah R.
84°
82°
80°
78°
76°
44°
42°
40°
38°
36°
34°
32°
0
100
200 Miles
0
100
200
300 Kilometers

FLORIDA
MISS.
ALA.
GEORGIA
LA.
FLORIDA
Pensacola
Tallahassee
Panama City
Apalachicola R.
Suwannee R.
St. Johns R.
Jacksonville
St. Augustine
Gainesville
Ocala
Lake George
Daytona Beach
Orlando
Titusville
Cape Canaveral
Melbourne
Palm Bay
Lakeland
Clearwater
Largo
Tampa
St. Petersburg
Tampa Bay
Bradenton
Sarasota
Lake Kissimmee
Kissimmee R.
Fort Pierce
Lake Okeechobee
Cape Coral
Fort Myers
Naples
West Palm Beach
Boca Raton
Pompano Beach
Fort Lauderdale
Hollywood
Hialeah
Miami
Miami Beach
BISCAYNE NP
EVERGLADES NP
Cape Sable
Key West
Florida Keys
Straits of Florida
Gulf of Mexico
ATLANTIC OCEAN
THE BAHAMAS
0 100 200 Miles
0 100 200 300 Kilometers
PUERTO RICO
Aguadilla
Arecibo
San Juan
Bayamón
Carolina
El Toro 3,254
Caguas
Mayagüez
CORDILLERA CENTRAL
Ponce
Mona
Culebra
Vieques
Caribbean Sea
0 25 50 Miles
0 25 50 75 Kilometers

LOWER MIDWEST
CANADA
S.D.
NEBRASKA
KANSAS
OKLAHOMA
ARKANSAS
TENNESSEE
N.C.
VIRGINIA
WEST VIRGINIA
PA.
MICHIGAN
WISCONSIN
IOWA
MISSOURI
ILLINOIS
INDIANA
OHIO
KENTUCKY
Lake Michigan
Lake Erie
OZARK PLATEAU
CUMBERLAND PLATEAU
Taum Sauk Mtn. 1,772
Black Mtn. 4,145
MAMMOTH CAVE NP
Lake of the Ozarks
Kentucky Lake
Lake Barkley
Lake Cumberland
Mississippi River
Missouri River
Illinois River
Kaskaskia River
Wabash River
Ohio River
Scioto River
Des Moines River
Green River
Cumberland River
Osage R.
Black R.
Sioux City
Council Bluffs
Mason City
Fort Dodge
Cedar Falls
Waterloo
Dubuque
Ames
Marshalltown
Marion
Cedar Rapids
Des Moines
Newton
Iowa City
Davenport
Muscatine
Ottumwa
Burlington
Clinton
Bettendorf
Moline
Rock Island
Freeport
Rockford
Waukegan
Elgin
Evanston
De Kalb
Naperville
Aurora
Chicago
Joliet
Gary
Hammond
Galesburg
Kankakee
Peoria
Bloomington
Champaign
Danville
Urbana
Decatur
Springfield
Carbondale
East St. Louis
Belleville
St. Joseph
Kirksville
Hannibal
Moberly
Kansas City
Independence
Marshall
Columbia
Warrensburg
Sedalia
St. Charles
St. Louis
Jefferson City
Rolla
Farmington
Springfield
Joplin
Cape Girardeau
Sikeston
Poplar Bluff
La Porte
South Bend
Elkhart
Michigan City
Fort Wayne
Marion
Lafayette
Kokomo
Anderson
Muncie
Lawrence
Indianapolis
Richmond
Greenwood
Terre Haute
Bloomington
Columbus
Evansville
New Albany
Toledo
Bowling Green
Sandusky
Cleveland
Ashtabula
Youngstown
Akron
Alliance
Canton
Findlay
Lima
Mansfield
Wooster
Marion
Steubenville
Newark
Columbus
Zanesville
Springfield
Dayton
Lancaster
Middletown
Athens
Chillicothe
Cincinnati
Covington
Portsmouth
Ashland
Louisville
Frankfort
Pleasure Ridge Park
Lexington
Radcliff
Winchester
Henderson
Owensboro
Elizabethtown
Danville
Richmond
Madisonville
Somerset
Bowling Green
Glasgow
Hopkinsville
Paducah
Murray
Middlesboro
0 100 200 Miles
0 100 200 300 Kilometers

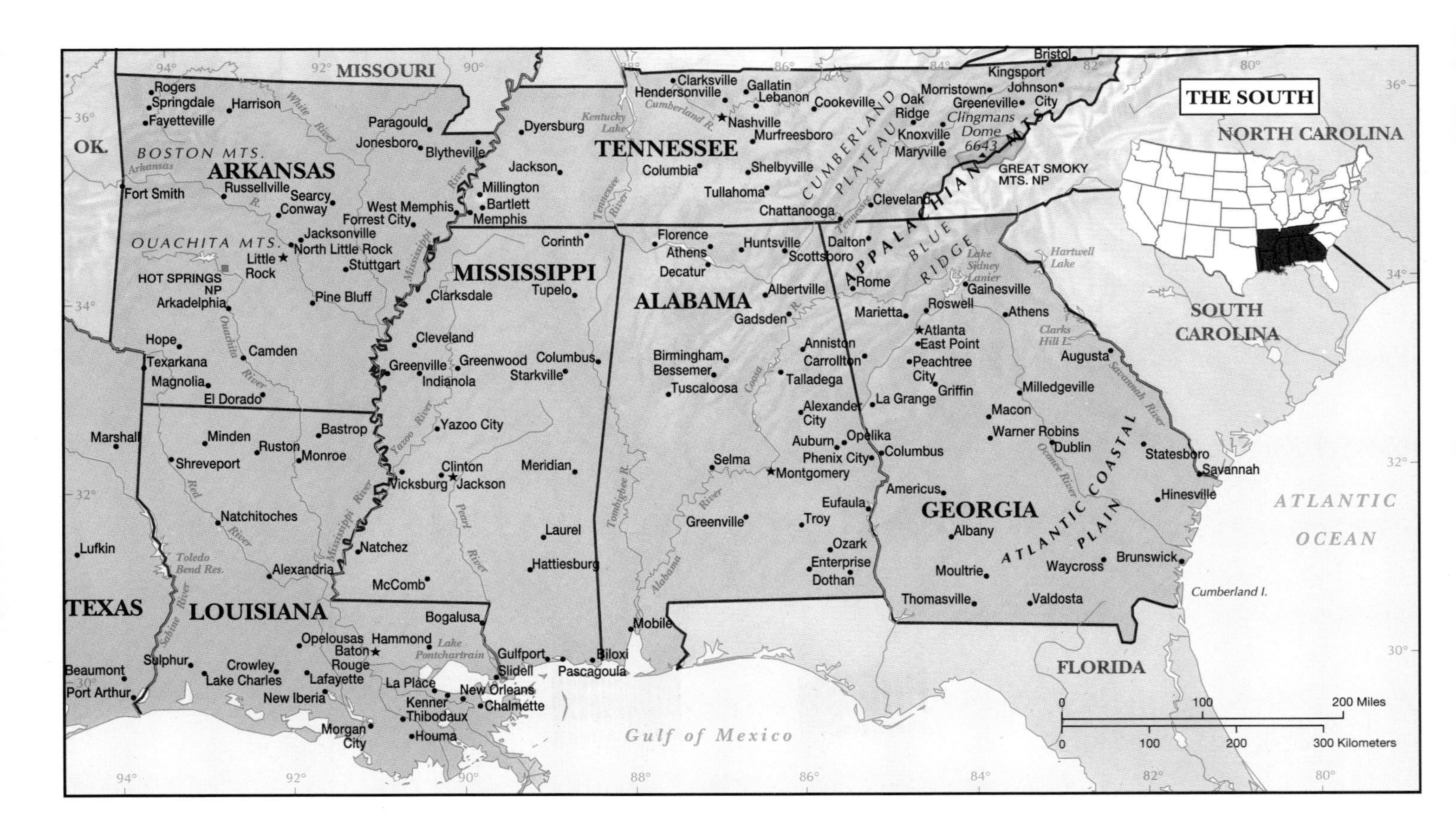
THE SOUTH
NORTH CAROLINA
SOUTH CAROLINA
TENNESSEE
ARKANSAS
MISSISSIPPI
ALABAMA
GEORGIA
LOUISIANA
TEXAS
FLORIDA
MISSOURI
OK.
ATLANTIC OCEAN
Gulf of Mexico
BOSTON MTS.
OUACHITA MTS.
HOT SPRINGS NP
CUMBERLAND PLATEAU
APPALACHIAN MTS.
BLUE RIDGE
ATLANTIC COASTAL PLAIN
GREAT SMOKY MTS. NP
Clingmans Dome 6643
Rogers
Springdale
Fayetteville
Harrison
Fort Smith
Russellville
Searcy
Conway
Jacksonville
North Little Rock
Little Rock
Stuttgart
Pine Bluff
Arkadelphia
Hope
Texarkana
Camden
Magnolia
El Dorado
Paragould
Jonesboro
Blytheville
West Memphis
Forrest City
Dyersburg
Jackson
Millington
Bartlett
Memphis
Clarksville
Hendersonville
Gallatin
Lebanon
Nashville
Murfreesboro
Cookeville
Columbia
Shelbyville
Tullahoma
Chattanooga
Cleveland
Oak Ridge
Knoxville
Maryville
Morristown
Greeneville
Johnson City
Kingsport
Bristol
Corinth
Tupelo
Clarksdale
Cleveland
Greenville
Indianola
Greenwood
Columbus
Starkville
Yazoo City
Clinton
Jackson
Vicksburg
Meridian
Laurel
Hattiesburg
Natchez
McComb
Gulfport
Biloxi
Pascagoula
Florence
Athens
Decatur
Huntsville
Scottsboro
Albertville
Gadsden
Birmingham
Bessemer
Tuscaloosa
Anniston
Talladega
Alexander City
Auburn
Opelika
Phenix City
Montgomery
Selma
Greenville
Troy
Eufaula
Ozark
Enterprise
Dothan
Mobile
Dalton
Rome
Marietta
Roswell
Gainesville
Athens
Atlanta
East Point
Carrollton
Peachtree City
Griffin
La Grange
Columbus
Macon
Warner Robins
Milledgeville
Augusta
Dublin
Statesboro
Savannah
Hinesville
Americus
Albany
Moultrie
Thomasville
Valdosta
Waycross
Brunswick
Cumberland I.
Marshall
Lufkin
Beaumont
Port Arthur
Minden
Shreveport
Ruston
Monroe
Bastrop
Natchitoches
Alexandria
Opelousas
Baton Rouge
Hammond
Bogalusa
Slidell
Lafayette
Crowley
Lake Charles
Sulphur
New Iberia
La Place
Kenner
New Orleans
Chalmette
Thibodaux
Houma
Morgan City
Toledo Bend Res.
Lake Pontchartrain
Lake Sidney Lanier
Hartwell Lake
Clarks Hill L.
Kentucky Lake
Arkansas
White River
Ouachita River
Red River
Sabine River
Mississippi River
Yazoo River
Pearl River
Tombigbee R.
Alabama
Coosa
Tennessee River
Tennessee R.
Cumberland R.
Savannah River
Oconee River
0 100 200 Miles
0 100 200 300 Kilometers
94°
92°
90°
88°
86°
84°
82°
80°
36°
34°
32°
30°

UPPER MIDWEST
CANADA
NORTH DAKOTA
SOUTH DAKOTA
MINNESOTA
WISCONSIN
MICHIGAN
UPPER PENINSULA
IOWA
ILLINOIS
INDIANA
OHIO
NEB.
MESABI RANGE
Eagle Mtn. 2,301
VOYAGEURS NP
ISLE ROYALE NP
Lake Superior
Lake Michigan
Lake Huron
Lake Erie
Lake of the Woods
Upper Red Lake
Lower Red Lake
Leech Lake
Mille Lacs L.
Burt Lake
Mullett Lake
Houghton Lake
Petenwell Lake
L. Winnebago
Red River
Minnesota R.
Mississippi
St. Croix R.
Flambeau R.
Wisconsin R.
Wisconsin River
Au Sable R.
Muskegon River
Grand River
International Falls
Bemidji
Hibbing
Virginia
Grand Rapids
Moorhead
Duluth
Superior
Fergus Falls
Brainerd
St. Cloud
Anoka
Coon Rapids
Willmar
Brooklyn Park
Plymouth
Minneapolis
Bloomington
St. Paul
Burnsville
Red Wing
Faribault
Northfield
New Ulm
Mankato
Owatonna
Winona
Rochester
Albert Lea
Austin
La Crosse
Menomonie
Eau Claire
Wausau
Marshfield
Stevens Point
Wisconsin Rapids
Green Bay
Appleton
Oshkosh
Fond du Lac
Manitowoc
Sheboygan
West Bend
Beaver Dam
Watertown
Madison
Waukesha
Whitewater
Janesville
Beloit
Milwaukee
Racine
Kenosha
Marinette
Houghton
Marquette
Iron Mountain
Sault Ste. Marie
Alpena
Traverse City
Mount Pleasant
Midland
Bay City
Saginaw
Muskegon
Flint
Port Huron
Owasso
Lansing
Grand Rapids
Holland
Kalamazoo
Battle Creek
Jackson
Benton Harbor
St. Joseph
Adrian
Monroe
Detroit
0 100 200 Miles
0 100 200 300 Kilometers
98° 96° 94° 92° 90° 88° 86° 84° 82° 80°
48° 46° 44° 42°

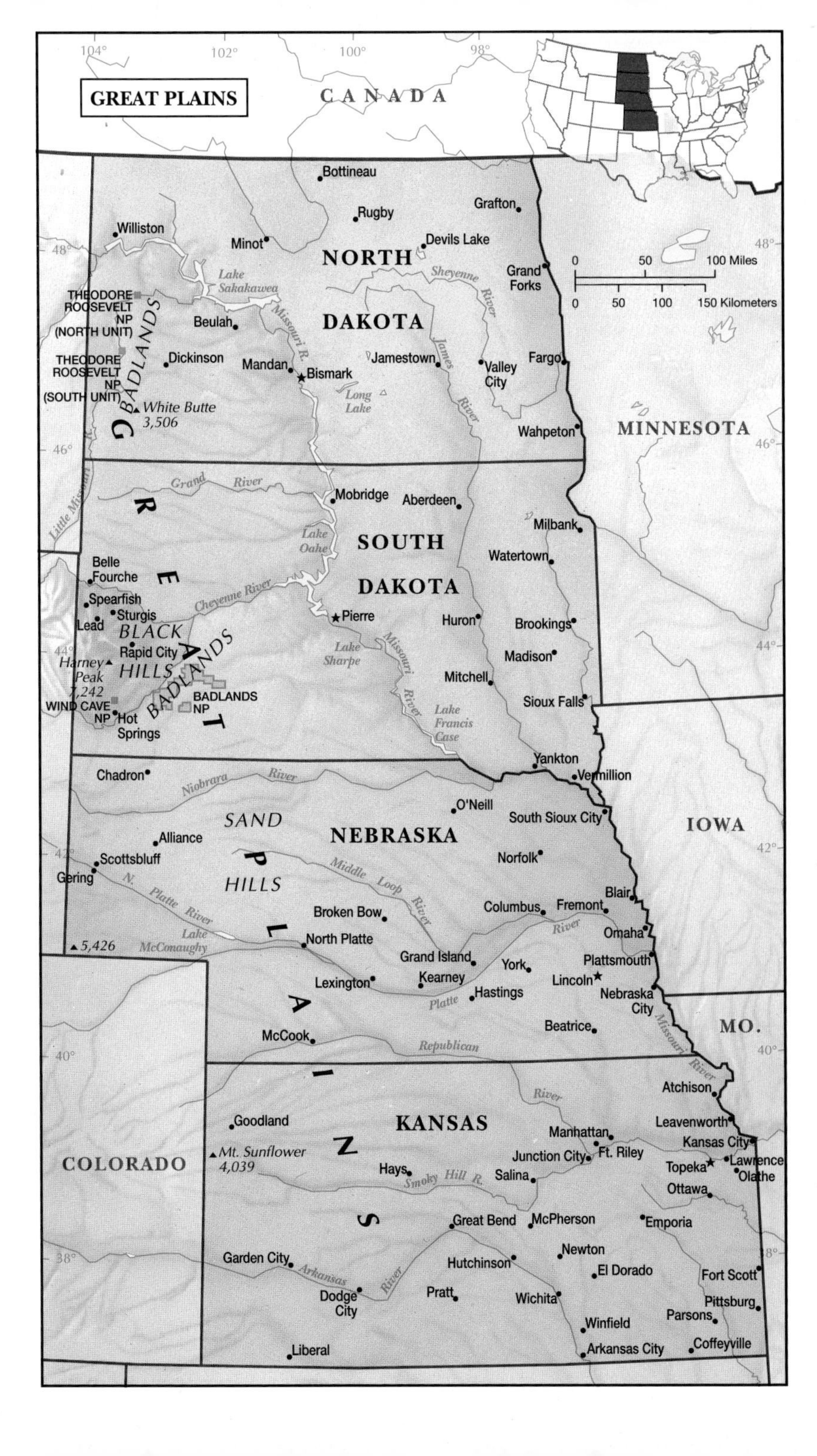
GREAT PLAINS
CANADA
NORTH DAKOTA
SOUTH DAKOTA
NEBRASKA
KANSAS
MINNESOTA
IOWA
MO.
COLORADO
GREAT PLAINS
0 50 100 Miles
0 50 100 150 Kilometers
Bottineau
Rugby
Grafton
Williston
Minot
Devils Lake
Grand Forks
Lake Sakakawea
Sheyenne River
THEODORE ROOSEVELT NP (NORTH UNIT)
THEODORE ROOSEVELT NP (SOUTH UNIT)
BADLANDS
Beulah
Dickinson
Mandan
Bismark
Missouri R.
Jamestown
James River
Valley City
Fargo
Long Lake
White Butte 3,506
Wahpeton
Little Missouri R.
Grand River
Mobridge
Aberdeen
Milbank
Lake Oahe
Watertown
Belle Fourche
Spearfish
Sturgis
Lead
Cheyenne River
Pierre
Huron
Brookings
BLACK HILLS
Rapid City
Harney Peak 7,242
Lake Sharpe
Madison
Missouri River
Mitchell
BADLANDS NP
WIND CAVE NP
Hot Springs
Sioux Falls
Lake Francis Case
Yankton
Vermillion
Chadron
Niobrara River
O'Neill
South Sioux City
SAND HILLS
Alliance
Scottsbluff
Gering
N. Platte River
Middle Loop River
Norfolk
Blair
Broken Bow
Columbus
Fremont
Omaha
Lake McConaughy
5,426
North Platte
Grand Island
York
Plattsmouth
Lexington
Kearney
Lincoln
Hastings
Platte River
Nebraska City
Beatrice
McCook
Republican River
Missouri River
Atchison
Goodland
Manhattan
Leavenworth
Mt. Sunflower 4,039
Ft. Riley
Kansas City
Junction City
Topeka
Lawrence
Hays
Smoky Hill R.
Salina
Olathe
Ottawa
Great Bend
McPherson
Emporia
Newton
Garden City
Arkansas River
Hutchinson
El Dorado
Fort Scott
Dodge City
Pratt
Wichita
Pittsburg
Parsons
Winfield
Liberal
Arkansas City
Coffeyville
104°
102°
100°
98°
48°
46°
44°
42°
40°
38°

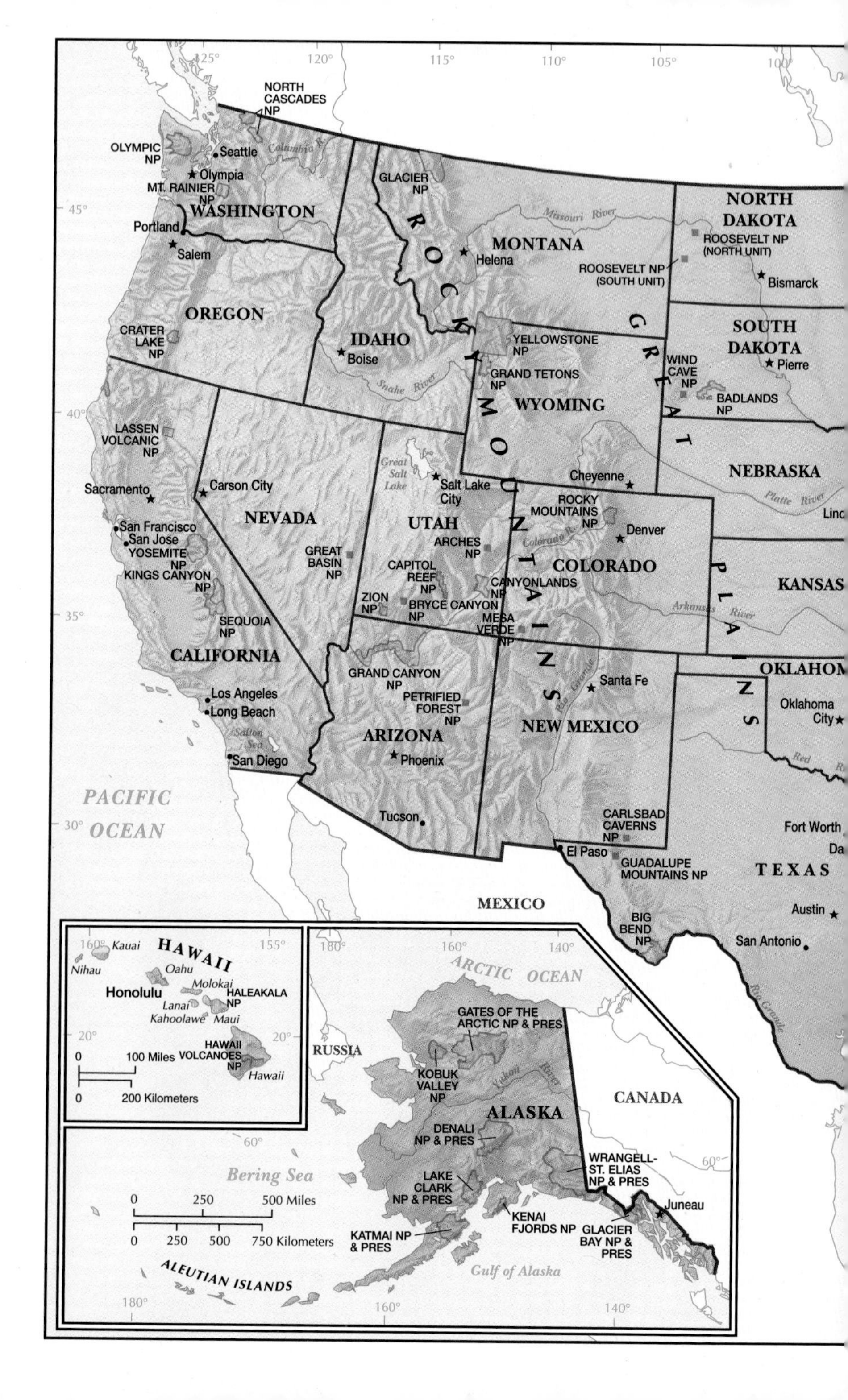

NORTH CASCADES NP
OLYMPIC NP
Seattle
Olympia
MT. RAINIER NP
WASHINGTON
Portland
Salem
Columbia R.
GLACIER NP
ROCKY MOUNTAINS
MONTANA
Helena
Missouri River
NORTH DAKOTA
ROOSEVELT NP (NORTH UNIT)
ROOSEVELT NP (SOUTH UNIT)
Bismarck
OREGON
CRATER LAKE NP
IDAHO
Boise
Snake River
YELLOWSTONE NP
GRAND TETONS NP
WYOMING
GREAT PLAINS
SOUTH DAKOTA
Pierre
WIND CAVE NP
BADLANDS NP
LASSEN VOLCANIC NP
Sacramento
Carson City
NEVADA
Great Salt Lake
Salt Lake City
UTAH
Cheyenne
NEBRASKA
Platte River
Linc
San Francisco
San Jose
YOSEMITE NP
KINGS CANYON NP
GREAT BASIN NP
ARCHES NP
CAPITOL REEF NP
ZION NP
BRYCE CANYON NP
CANYONLANDS NP
ROCKY MOUNTAINS NP
Denver
Colorado R.
COLORADO
KANSAS
Arkansas River
SEQUOIA NP
MESA VERDE NP
CALIFORNIA
OKLAHOM
GRAND CANYON NP
PETRIFIED FOREST NP
Santa Fe
Rio Grande
Oklahoma City
Los Angeles
Long Beach
Salton Sea
ARIZONA
NEW MEXICO
San Diego
Phoenix
Red
PACIFIC OCEAN
Tucson
CARLSBAD CAVERNS NP
Fort Worth
Da
El Paso
GUADALUPE MOUNTAINS NP
TEXAS
MEXICO
Austin
BIG BEND NP
San Antonio
HAWAII
Kauai
Nihau
Oahu
Honolulu
Molokai
HALEAKALA NP
Lanai
Kahoolawe
Maui
HAWAII VOLCANOES NP
Hawaii
0 100 Miles
0 200 Kilometers
ARCTIC OCEAN
GATES OF THE ARCTIC NP & PRES
RUSSIA
KOBUK VALLEY NP
Yukon River
CANADA
ALASKA
DENALI NP & PRES
Bering Sea
WRANGELL-ST. ELIAS NP & PRES
LAKE CLARK NP & PRES
0 250 500 Miles
0 250 500 750 Kilometers
Juneau
KENAI FJORDS NP
GLACIER BAY NP & PRES
KATMAI NP & PRES
Gulf of Alaska
ALEUTIAN ISLANDS

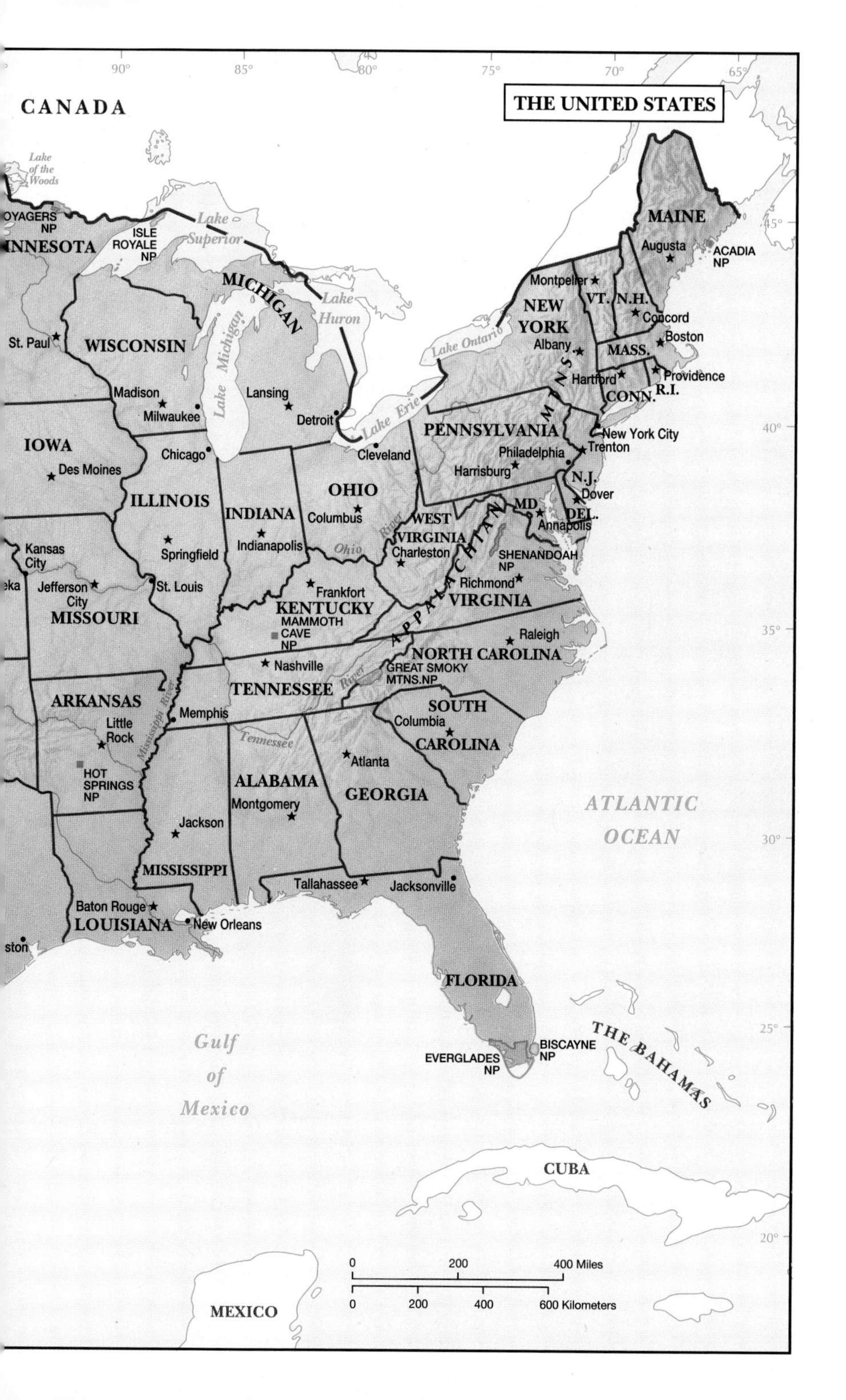
THE UNITED STATES
CANADA
Lake of the Woods
VOYAGERS NP
MINNESOTA
ISLE ROYALE NP
Lake Superior
MICHIGAN
Lake Huron
Lake Michigan
St. Paul
WISCONSIN
Madison
Milwaukee
Lansing
Detroit
Lake Ontario
Lake Erie
IOWA
Des Moines
Chicago
ILLINOIS
Springfield
INDIANA
Indianapolis
OHIO
Columbus
Cleveland
PENNSYLVANIA
Harrisburg
Philadelphia
NEW YORK
Albany
New York City
MAINE
Augusta
ACADIA NP
Montpelier
VT.
N.H.
Concord
Boston
MASS.
Hartford
Providence
CONN.
R.I.
Trenton
N.J.
Dover
DEL.
MD.
Annapolis
WEST VIRGINIA
Charleston
Ohio River
SHENANDOAH NP
Richmond
VIRGINIA
APPALACHIAN MTNS.
Kansas City
Jefferson City
St. Louis
MISSOURI
Frankfort
KENTUCKY
MAMMOTH CAVE NP
Raleigh
NORTH CAROLINA
GREAT SMOKY MTNS.NP
Nashville
TENNESSEE
Tennessee River
Memphis
ARKANSAS
Little Rock
HOT SPRINGS NP
Mississippi River
SOUTH CAROLINA
Columbia
Atlanta
GEORGIA
ALABAMA
Montgomery
Jackson
MISSISSIPPI
Tallahassee
Jacksonville
Baton Rouge
New Orleans
LOUISIANA
FLORIDA
ATLANTIC OCEAN
BISCAYNE NP
EVERGLADES NP
THE BAHAMAS
Gulf of Mexico
CUBA
MEXICO
90°
85°
80°
75°
70°
65°
45°
40°
35°
30°
25°
20°
0
200
400 Miles
0
200
400
600 Kilometers

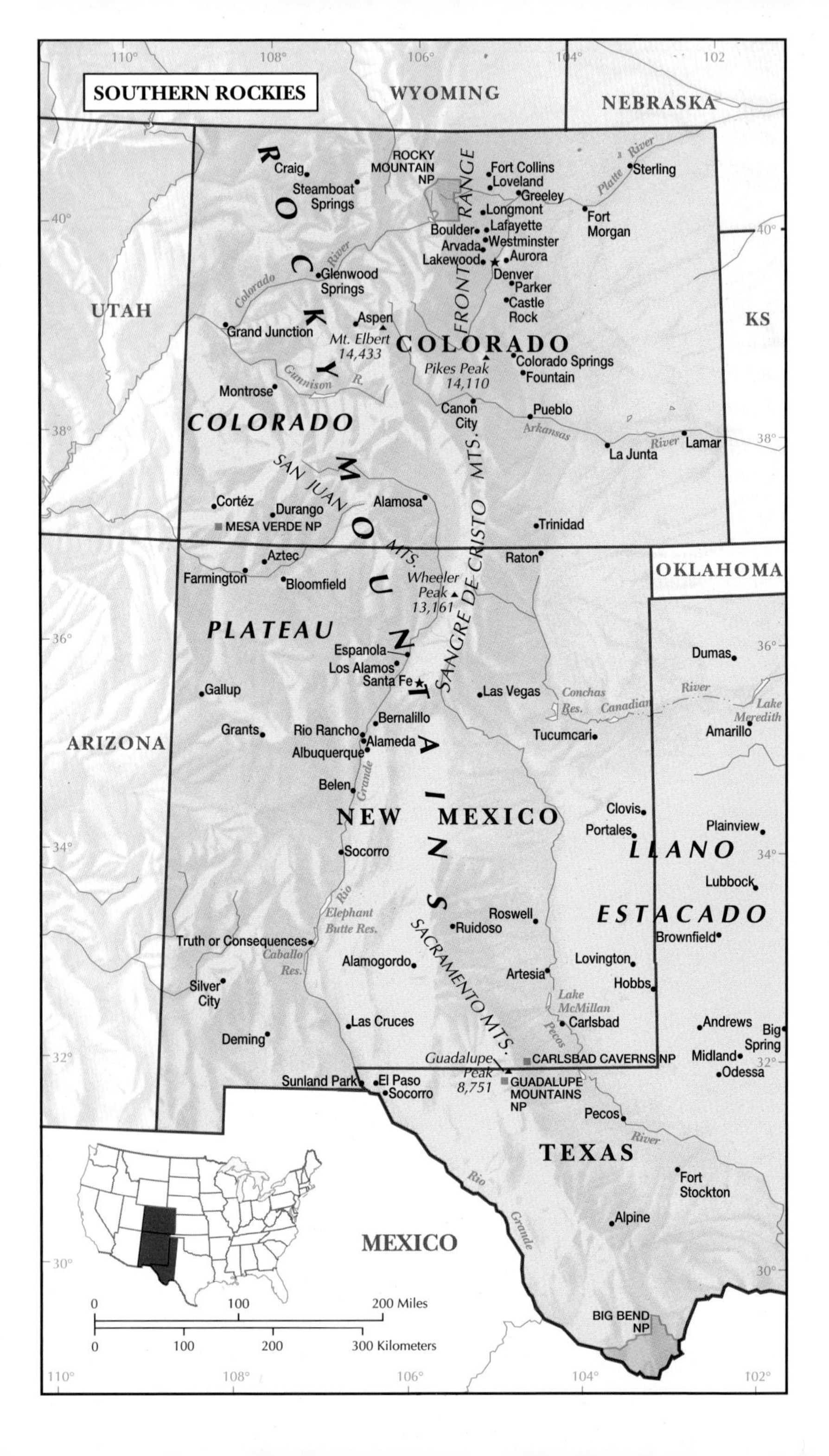

SOUTHERN ROCKIES
WYOMING
NEBRASKA
UTAH
KS
COLORADO
OKLAHOMA
ARIZONA
NEW MEXICO
TEXAS
MEXICO
ROCKY MOUNTAINS
COLORADO PLATEAU
LLANO ESTACADO
FRONT RANGE
SAN JUAN MTS.
SANGRE DE CRISTO MTS.
SACRAMENTO MTS.
ROCKY MOUNTAIN NP
MESA VERDE NP
CARLSBAD CAVERNS NP
GUADALUPE MOUNTAINS NP
BIG BEND NP
Mt. Elbert 14,433
Pikes Peak 14,110
Wheeler Peak 13,161
Guadalupe Peak 8,751
Craig
Steamboat Springs
Fort Collins
Loveland
Greeley
Sterling
Longmont
Fort Morgan
Boulder
Lafayette
Arvada
Westminster
Lakewood
Aurora
Denver
Parker
Castle Rock
Glenwood Springs
Aspen
Grand Junction
Colorado Springs
Fountain
Montrose
Canon City
Pueblo
La Junta
Lamar
Cortéz
Durango
Alamosa
Trinidad
Aztec
Farmington
Bloomfield
Raton
Espanola
Los Alamos
Santa Fe
Gallup
Las Vegas
Dumas
Bernalillo
Grants
Rio Rancho
Alameda
Albuquerque
Tucumcari
Amarillo
Belen
Clovis
Portales
Plainview
Socorro
Lubbock
Roswell
Ruidoso
Brownfield
Truth or Consequences
Alamogordo
Artesia
Lovington
Hobbs
Silver City
Carlsbad
Las Cruces
Deming
Andrews
Big Spring
Midland
Odessa
Sunland Park
El Paso
Socorro
Pecos
Fort Stockton
Alpine
Platte River
Colorado River
Gunnison R.
Arkansas River
Conchas Res.
Canadian River
Lake Meredith
Rio Grande
Elephant Butte Res.
Caballo Res.
Lake McMillan
Pecos River
0 100 200 Miles
0 100 200 300 Kilometers
110° 108° 106° 104° 102°
40° 38° 36° 34° 32° 30°

SOUTHERN PLAINS
KANSAS
MO.
ARK.
GREAT PLAINS
OKLAHOMA
TEXAS
LLANO ESTACADO
EDWARDS PLATEAU
OUACHITA MTS
MEXICO
Gulf of Mexico
Guymon
Woodward
Enid
Ponca City
Bartlesville
Miami
Claremore
Tulsa
Stillwater
Broken Arrow
Sapulpa
Muskogee
Okmulgee
Edmond
Oklahoma City
El Reno
Clinton
Shawnee
Norman
Chickasha
McAlester
Ada
Altus
Lawton
Duncan
Ardmore
Durant
Dumas
Pampa
Amarillo
Plainview
Lubbock
Brownfield
Wichita Falls
Sherman
Denison
Paris
Texarkana
Denton
Greenville
Plano
Garland
Irving
Dallas
Fort Worth
Arlington
Mesquite
Marshall
Longview
Tyler
Andrews
Big Spring
Abilene
Midland
Odessa
Corsicana
Nacogdoches
Lufkin
San Angelo
Waco
Killeen
Temple
Fort Stockton
Bryan
College Station
Huntsville
Round Rock
Austin
San Marcos
New Braunfels
Seguin
San Antonio
Houston
Baytown
Pasadena
Texas City
Galveston
Del Rio
BIG BEND NP
Eagle Pass
Victoria
Alice
Corpus Christi
Laredo
Kingsville
Padre Island
Edinburg
Mission
McAllen
Pharr
Harlingen
San Benito
Weslaco
Brownsville
Arkansas R.
Neosho R.
Keystone Lake
Canadian River
Lake Meredith
Robert S. Kerr Lake
Eufaula Lake
Lake Texoma
Red River
Sabine River
Colorado River
Brazos River
Pecos River
Sam Rayburn Res.
Lake Livingston
Amistad Res.
Galveston Bay
Matagorda Bay
Nueces River
Rio Grande
Falcon Res.
100°
98°
96°
94°
36°
34°
32°
30°
28°
26°
102°
0
100
200 Miles
0
100
200
300 Kilometers

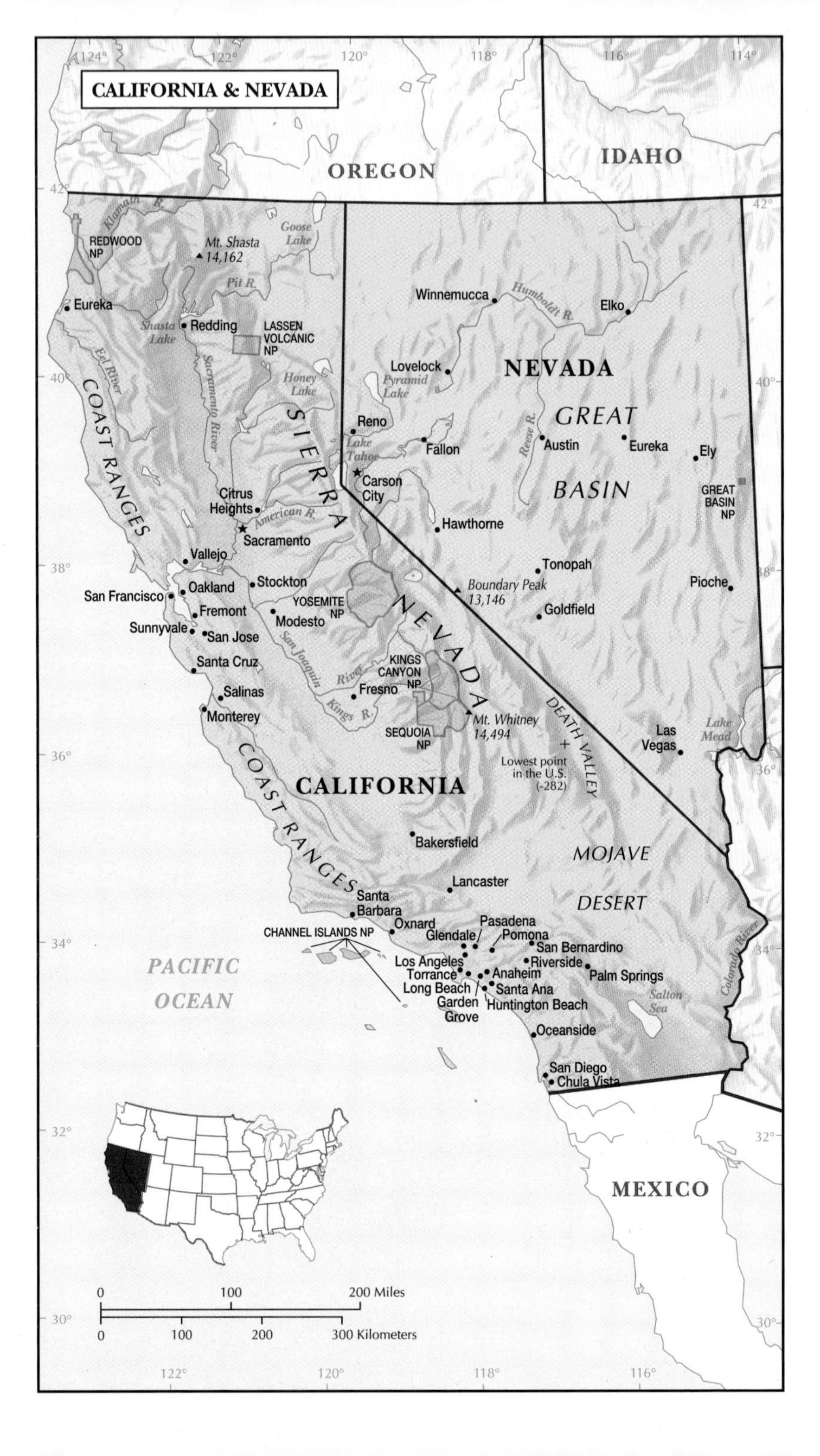

CALIFORNIA & NEVADA
OREGON
IDAHO
NEVADA
CALIFORNIA
MEXICO
PACIFIC OCEAN
GREAT BASIN
MOJAVE DESERT
SIERRA NEVADA
COAST RANGES
COAST RANGES
DEATH VALLEY
REDWOOD NP
LASSEN VOLCANIC NP
YOSEMITE NP
KINGS CANYON NP
SEQUOIA NP
GREAT BASIN NP
CHANNEL ISLANDS NP
Mt. Shasta 14,162
Boundary Peak 13,146
Mt. Whitney 14,494
Lowest point in the U.S. (-282)
Klamath R.
Goose Lake
Pit R.
Shasta Lake
Eel River
Sacramento River
Honey Lake
Pyramid Lake
Lake Tahoe
American R.
Humboldt R.
Reese R.
San Joaquin River
Kings R.
Lake Mead
Colorado River
Salton Sea
Eureka
Redding
Winnemucca
Elko
Lovelock
Reno
Fallon
Austin
Eureka
Ely
Carson City
Citrus Heights
Sacramento
Hawthorne
Vallejo
Tonopah
Oakland
Stockton
San Francisco
Pioche
Fremont
Modesto
Goldfield
Sunnyvale
San Jose
Santa Cruz
Salinas
Fresno
Monterey
Las Vegas
Bakersfield
Lancaster
Santa Barbara
Oxnard
Pasadena
Glendale
Pomona
San Bernardino
Los Angeles
Riverside
Torrance
Anaheim
Palm Springs
Long Beach
Santa Ana
Garden Grove
Huntington Beach
Oceanside
San Diego
Chula Vista
124°
122°
120°
118°
116°
114°
42°
40°
38°
36°
34°
32°
30°
0
100
200 Miles
0
100
200
300 Kilometers

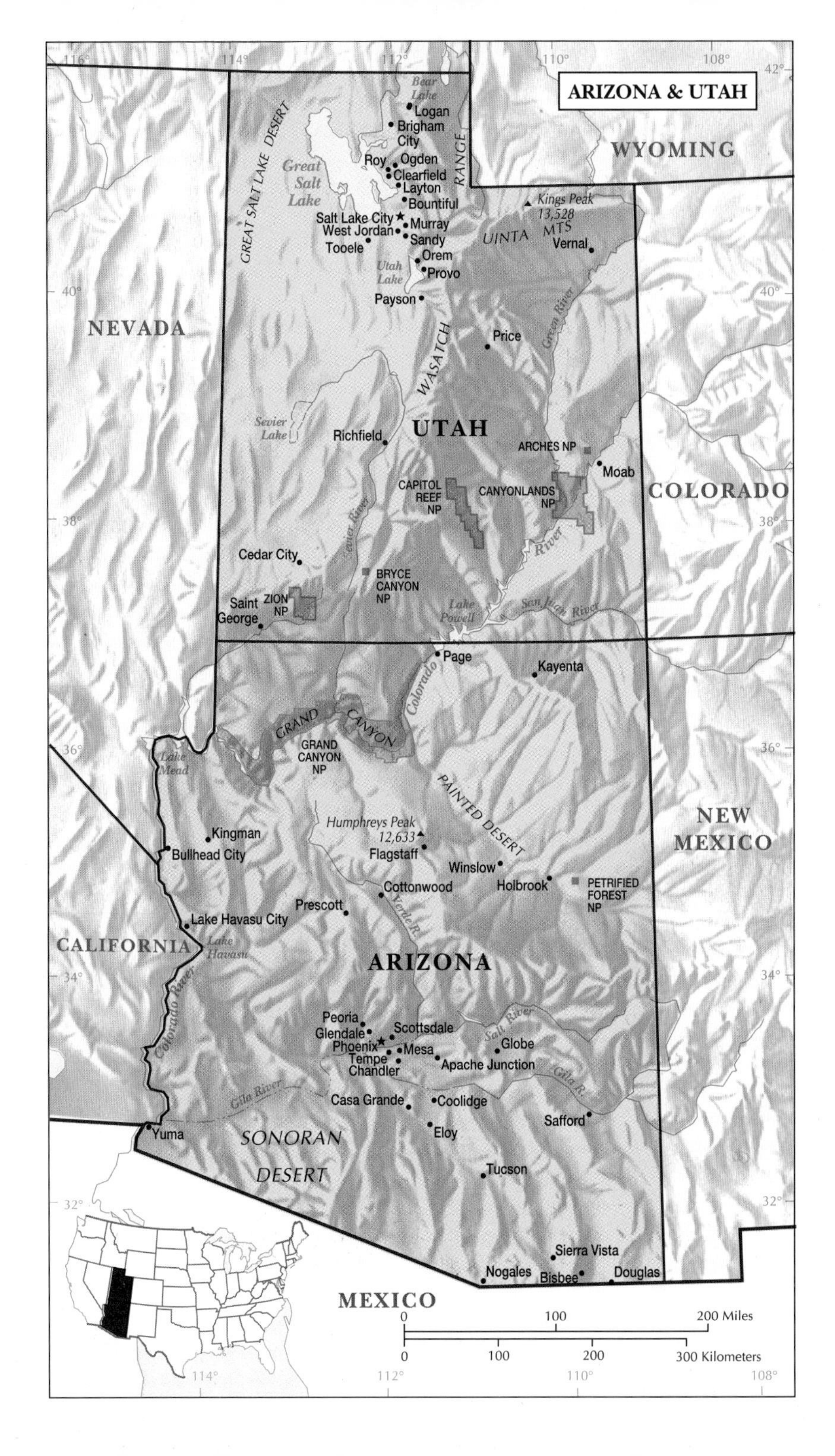

ARIZONA & UTAH
WYOMING
NEVADA
UTAH
COLORADO
ARIZONA
CALIFORNIA
NEW MEXICO
MEXICO
Bear Lake
Logan
Brigham City
Roy
Ogden
Clearfield
Layton
Bountiful
Great Salt Lake
GREAT SALT LAKE DESERT
RANGE
Salt Lake City
West Jordan
Murray
Sandy
Tooele
Orem
Provo
Utah Lake
Payson
Kings Peak 13,528
UINTA MTS
Vernal
Green River
WASATCH
Price
Sevier Lake
Richfield
ARCHES NP
Moab
CAPITOL REEF NP
CANYONLANDS NP
Sevier River
River
Cedar City
BRYCE CANYON NP
Saint George
ZION NP
Lake Powell
San Juan River
Page
Kayenta
Colorado
GRAND CANYON
GRAND CANYON NP
Lake Mead
PAINTED DESERT
Humphreys Peak 12,633
Kingman
Bullhead City
Flagstaff
Winslow
Holbrook
PETRIFIED FOREST NP
Cottonwood
Prescott
Verde R.
Lake Havasu City
Lake Havasu
Colorado River
Peoria
Glendale
Scottsdale
Phoenix
Mesa
Tempe
Chandler
Apache Junction
Globe
Salt River
Gila R.
Gila River
Casa Grande
Coolidge
Safford
Yuma
Eloy
SONORAN DESERT
Tucson
Sierra Vista
Nogales
Bisbee
Douglas
0 100 200 Miles
0 100 200 300 Kilometers
116° 114° 112° 110° 108°
42° 40° 38° 36° 34° 32°

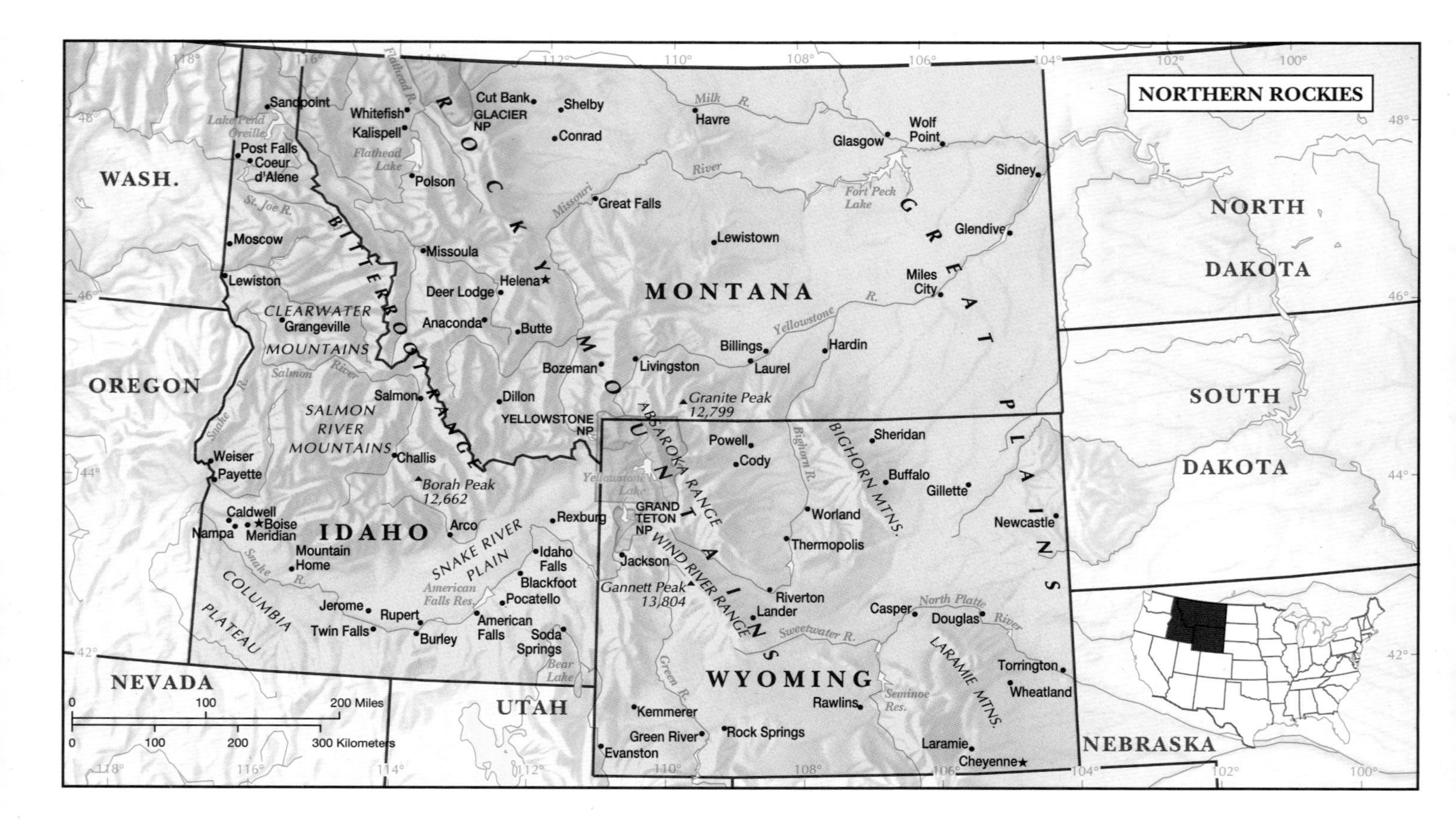

NORTHERN ROCKIES
WASH.
OREGON
NEVADA
UTAH
NEBRASKA
NORTH DAKOTA
SOUTH DAKOTA
MONTANA
IDAHO
WYOMING
ROCKY MOUNTAINS
GREAT PLAINS
BITTERROOT RANGE
CLEARWATER MOUNTAINS
SALMON RIVER MOUNTAINS
SNAKE RIVER PLAIN
COLUMBIA PLATEAU
ABSAROKA RANGE
BIGHORN MTNS.
WIND RIVER RANGE
LARAMIE MTNS.
Sandpoint
Lake Pend Oreille
Post Falls
Coeur d'Alene
St. Joe R.
Moscow
Lewiston
Grangeville
Salmon River
Snake R.
Weiser
Payette
Caldwell
Boise
Nampa
Meridian
Mountain Home
Jerome
Twin Falls
Rupert
Burley
American Falls Res.
American Falls
Pocatello
Blackfoot
Idaho Falls
Rexburg
Arco
Soda Springs
Bear Lake
Salmon
Challis
Borah Peak 12,662
Flathead R.
Whitefish
Kalispell
Flathead Lake
Polson
Missoula
Deer Lodge
Anaconda
Butte
Helena
Dillon
Bozeman
Cut Bank
GLACIER NP
Shelby
Conrad
Missouri
Great Falls
Milk R.
Havre
River
Lewistown
Glasgow
Wolf Point
Fort Peck Lake
Sidney
Glendive
Miles City
Yellowstone R.
Billings
Laurel
Hardin
Livingston
Granite Peak 12,799
YELLOWSTONE NP
Yellowstone Lake
GRAND TETON NP
Jackson
Gannett Peak 13,804
Powell
Cody
Bighorn R.
Worland
Thermopolis
Riverton
Lander
Sheridan
Buffalo
Gillette
Newcastle
Casper
North Platte River
Douglas
Sweetwater R.
Torrington
Wheatland
Seminoe Res.
Rawlins
Green R.
Kemmerer
Green River
Rock Springs
Evanston
Laramie
Cheyenne
0
100
200 Miles
0
100
200
300 Kilometers
118°
116°
114°
112°
110°
108°
106°
104°
102°
100°
48°
46°
44°
42°

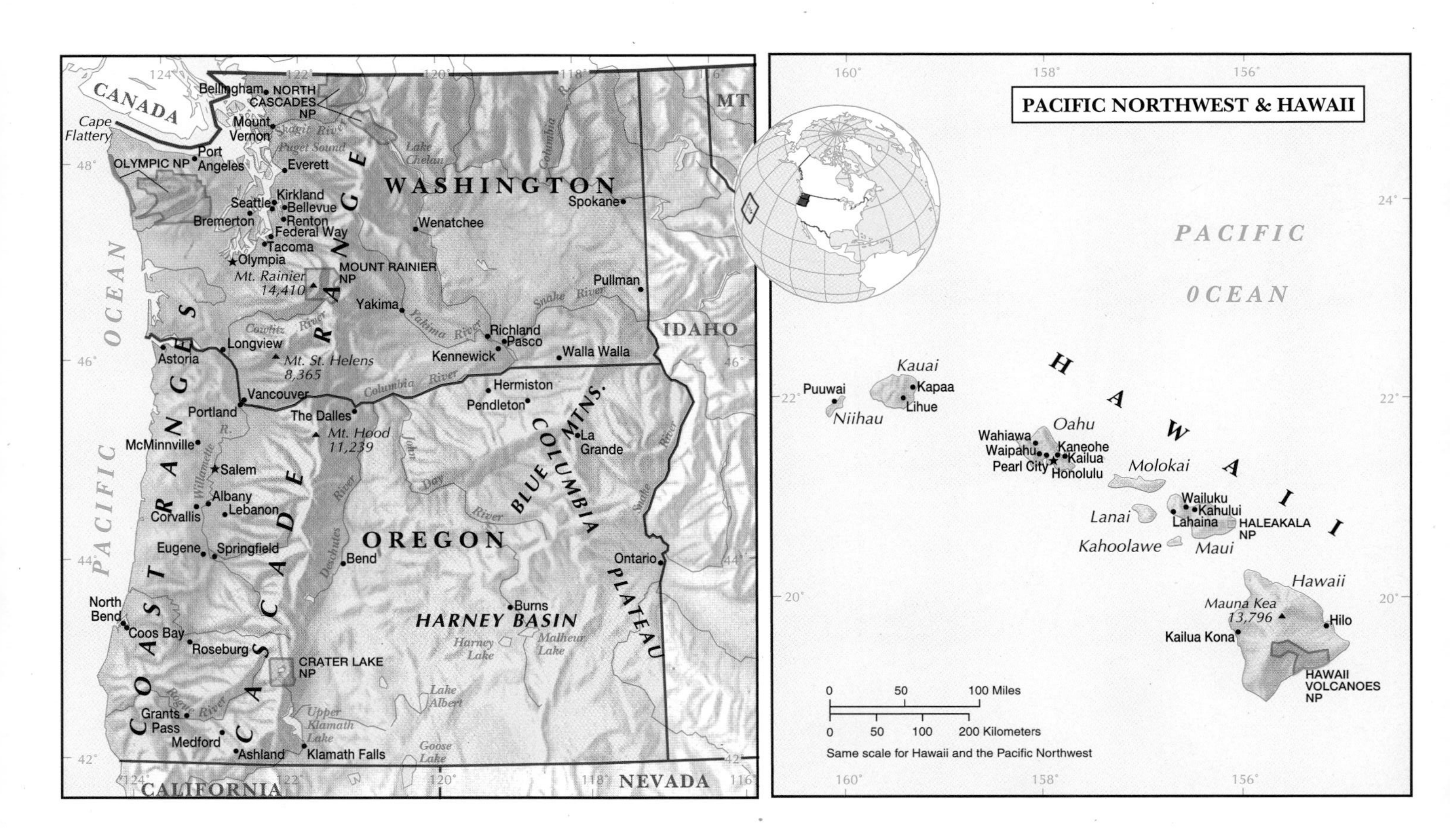

PACIFIC NORTHWEST & HAWAII
CANADA
Cape Flattery
OLYMPIC NP
Port Angeles
Bellingham
NORTH CASCADES NP
Mount Vernon
Skagit River
Puget Sound
Everett
Lake Chelan
WASHINGTON
Spokane
Kirkland
Seattle
Bellevue
Bremerton
Renton
Federal Way
Tacoma
Olympia
Wenatchee
Mt. Rainier 14,410
MOUNT RAINIER NP
Pullman
Snake River
Yakima
Yakima River
Cowlitz River
Richland
Pasco
Kennewick
Walla Walla
IDAHO
MT
Columbia
Longview
Astoria
Mt. St. Helens 8,365
Columbia River
Vancouver
Portland
The Dalles
Mt. Hood 11,239
Hermiston
Pendleton
BLUE MTNS.
La Grande
COLUMBIA PLATEAU
McMinnville
Willamette R.
Salem
Albany
Corvallis
Lebanon
John Day River
Deschutes River
OREGON
Eugene
Springfield
Bend
Ontario
North Bend
Coos Bay
Roseburg
Burns
HARNEY BASIN
Harney Lake
Malheur Lake
CRATER LAKE NP
Lake Albert
Rogue River
Grants Pass
Medford
Ashland
Upper Klamath Lake
Klamath Falls
Goose Lake
COAST RANGES
CASCADE RANGE
PACIFIC OCEAN
CALIFORNIA
NEVADA
124°
122°
120°
118°
116°
48°
46°
44°
42°
160°
158°
156°
24°
22°
20°
PACIFIC OCEAN
HAWAII
Kauai
Kapaa
Lihue
Puuwai
Niihau
Oahu
Wahiawa
Waipahu
Pearl City
Kaneohe
Kailua
Honolulu
Molokai
Lanai
Wailuku
Kahului
Lahaina
HALEAKALA NP
Kahoolawe
Maui
Hawaii
Mauna Kea 13,796
Hilo
Kailua Kona
HAWAII VOLCANOES NP
0
50
100 Miles
0
50
100
200 Kilometers
Same scale for Hawaii and the Pacific Northwest

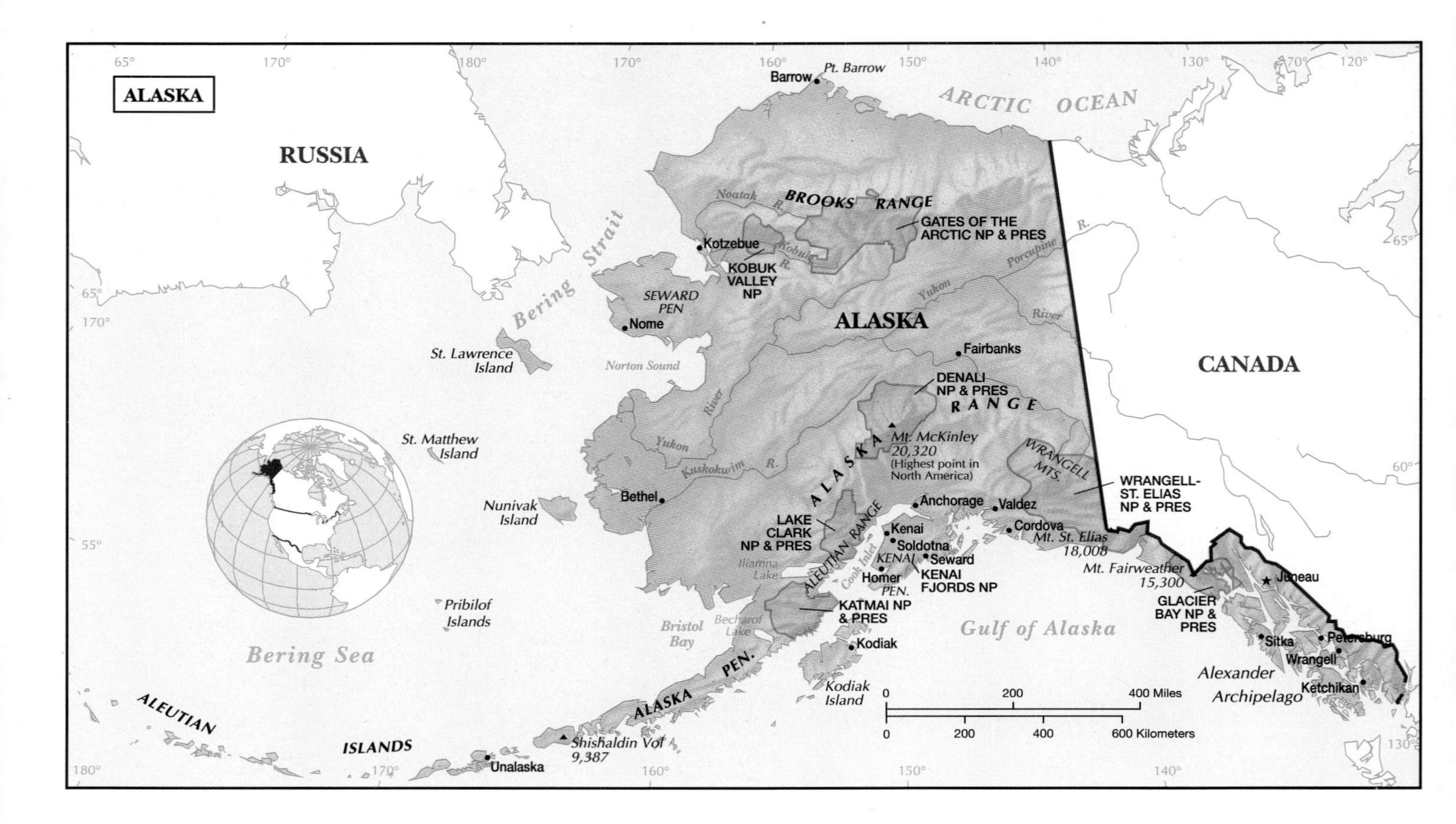

ALASKA
RUSSIA
CANADA
ARCTIC OCEAN
Bering Strait
Bering Sea
Gulf of Alaska
Norton Sound
Bristol Bay
Barrow
Pt. Barrow
Kotzebue
Nome
SEWARD PEN
BROOKS RANGE
Noatak R.
Kobuk R.
GATES OF THE ARCTIC NP & PRES
KOBUK VALLEY NP
Porcupine
Yukon
River
Fairbanks
DENALI NP & PRES
ALASKA RANGE
Mt. McKinley 20,320 (Highest point in North America)
WRANGELL MTS.
WRANGELL-ST. ELIAS NP & PRES
Kuskokwim R.
Bethel
Anchorage
Valdez
Cordova
Mt. St. Elias 18,008
Mt. Fairweather 15,300
LAKE CLARK NP & PRES
ALEUTIAN RANGE
Iliamna Lake
Cook Inlet
Kenai
Soldotna
KENAI PEN.
Seward
Homer
KENAI FJORDS NP
KATMAI NP & PRES
Becharof Lake
Kodiak
Kodiak Island
ALASKA PEN.
Shishaldin Vol 9,387
Unalaska
ALEUTIAN ISLANDS
St. Lawrence Island
St. Matthew Island
Nunivak Island
Pribilof Islands
Juneau
GLACIER BAY NP & PRES
Sitka
Petersburg
Wrangell
Ketchikan
Alexander Archipelago
0 200 400 Miles
0 200 400 600 Kilometers

MINNESOTA

"Minnesotans are just different, that's all...with the wind chill hovering at fifty-seven below...there were all these Minnesotans running around outdoors, happy as lambs in the spring."

Charles Kuralt

Minnesota modestly boasts of its 10,000 lakes, but in reality there are more than 15,000. Its history is said by some experts to hark back to Viking explorers in the 1300s, and the state has long been a haven for Scandanavian immigrants. It is a dairy state, and almost three million cattle graze on its rich pastures. The state makes more butter than any other, and it is a leader in milk and cheese production. It cherishes a world-renowned center of medical care and research, and its state university system ranks among the largest and best. It is a principal world center of milling concerns. Today, the Twin Cities of Minneapolis and St. Paul are a leading center of music, theater, and shopping. Minneapolis has been ranked as the nation's most liveable city.

Superlatives

- Source of the Mississippi River.
- Only state with source of three main river systems (Mississippi, St. Lawrence, Red River of the North).
- Principal U.S. source of manganese.
- Lady's slipper, unique among state flowers.
- Pioneer in open-pit mining.
- Pioneer in overland bus travel.

Moments in History

- Some experts believe European explorers reached Minnesota in 1362. This belief is based on a carving called the Kensington Runestone found near Kensington. Although some Norse implements of the 1300s have been found in Minnesota, other experts call this find a hoax.

> So They Say
>
> "We had a camp by two islands. We were out fishing one day. When we returned home, we found ten men red of blood and dead...Save us from evil."
>
> From a translation of the Kensington Runestone.

- The first authenticated record of European visitors was made by explorer Daniel Greysolon, Sieur de Lhut (Duluth) in 1679.
- Beginning in 1727 French trading posts were established, and in 1763 the British took control from the French.
- The Northwest Territory Act of 1787 included most of eastern Minnesota, and the Louisiana Purchase of 1803 brought most of the western region under U.S. control.
- In 1805 Zebulon Pike raised the U.S. flag over Minnesota for the first time, but the British paid little attention to U.S. claims.
- The War of 1812 finally settled the ownership of Minnesota.
- In 1820 Colonel Josiah Snelling started the fort bearing his name at the site where the Minnesota and Mississippi rivers join.
- In 1832 Henry R. Schoolcraft discovered the long-sought source of the Mississippi River and named it Lake Itasca.

> **So They Say**
>
> "...Unexpectedly, the outlet (source of the Mississippi) proved quite a brisk brook....Ten feet wide in most places, reached from bank, and the depth would probably average over a foot.
>
> Henry R. Schoolcraft

- In 1838 both St. Paul and Minneapolis were begun separately.
- Most of Minnesota's northern boundary was established by the Webster-Ashburton Treaty of 1842.
- On May 11, 1858, Minnesota became the 32nd state, with Henry H. Sibley as first governor.
- During the Civil War, Minnesota was the first state to offer troops, and the first Minnesota Regiment played a key role in the Battle of Gettysburg.
- In 1862 the Sioux Indians went on a rampage. The warfare finally was put down by H.S. Sibley, taking about 2,000 prisoners.
- The boundary line of the Lake of the Woods, extending into Canada, was not settled until 1873.
- The capitol was dedicated in 1905 and boasts the world's largest unsupported marble dome.
- World War I found 123,325 Minnesotans in uniform.
- The election of 1936 brought a dramatic victory to the Farmer-Labor party.
- More than 300,000 from Minnesota served in World War II, and over 6,000 lost their lives.
- The opening of the St. Lawrence Seaway in 1959 brought ocean traffic to the great port of Duluth.
- From 1965 to 1969, beloved Minnesota political figure Hubert H. Humphrey served as vice-president under Lyndon B. Johnson.
- In 1977 Minnesota's Walter F. Mondale became the U.S. vice-president.

That's Interesting

- There are so many lakes in Minnesota that novel names are scarce. There are 91 Long Lakes, and other bodies of water also have identical names.
- In 1838 an unsavory character built a cabin at present-day Saint Paul and called the place Pig's Eye. Fortunately, Father Lucian Galtier built a chapel there in 1841 and dedicated the place to St. Paul.
- The execution of 37 Sioux for their part in the Sioux War was the largest official wholesale execution in U.S. history. The Indians went to the scaffold singing a war song.
- The Falls of St. Anthony have "traveled." Their waters have continued to cut into the soft limestone until they have moved upstream about 4 mi. since their discovery.
- Charles Mayo, of the famed Mayo medical family, began his career at age nine by administering ether during operations.
- The great Cuyuna iron range was named for Cuyler Adams and his dog Una (Cuy-Una).
- The red-colored stone of Pipestone National Monument is found nowhere else. It was a sacred place to the Indians, who carved their pipes of peace from its soft redstone.

Notable Natives

William Orville Douglas (Maine, MN, 1898-1980), U.S. Supreme Court justice/author. **F. Scott Fitzgerald** (St. Paul, 1896-1940), author. **James Earle Fraser** (Winona, 1876-1953), sculptor. **Judy Garland** (Grand Rapids, MN, 1922-1969), actress/singer. **Garrison Keillor** (Anoka, 1942-), humorist. **Sinclair Lewis** (Sauk Centre, 1885-1951), author. **William James Mayo** (Le Sueur, 1861-1939) and **Charles Horace Mayo** (Rochester, 1865-1939), physicians. **Charles Monroe Schultz** (Minneapolis, 1922-), cartoonist. **Harold Edward Stassen** (West St. Paul, 1907-) public official.

General

Admitted to statehood: May 11, 1858

Origin of name: From Dakota Sioux word meaning "cloudy water" or "sky-tinted water" or the Minnesota River

Capital: Saint Paul

Nicknames: North Star State and Gopher State

Motto: *"L'Etoile du Nord"* ("The Star of the North")

Bird: common loon

Fish: walleye
Flower: Pink and white lady's slipper
Gemstone: Lake Superior agate
Slogan: Land of 10,000 Lakes
Song: "Hail! Minnesota"
Tree: red pine (Norway)

The Land

Area: 86,943 sq. mi., 12th
Land: 79,617 sq. mi., 14th
Water: 7,326 sq. mi., 7th
Topography: central hill and lake region covering approximately half the state; to the NE, rocky ridges and deep lakes; to the NW, flat plain; to the S, rolling plains and deep river valleys
Number of counties: 87
Geographic center: Crow Wing, 10 mi. SW of Brainerd
Length: 400 mi.
Width: 250 mi.
Highest point: 2,301 ft. (Eagle Mt., Cook County), 37th
Lowest point: 602 ft. (Lake Superior), 42nd
Mean elevation: 1,200 ft., 21st

Climate and Environment

Temp., highest: 114 deg. on July 6, 1936, at Moorhead; lowest: -59 deg. on Feb. 16, 1903, at Pokegama Dam
Fresh water withdrawn, per capita, per day: 676 gal., 41st
Endangered species: mammals, none; birds, 2—American peregrine falcon, piping plover; reptiles, none; amphibians, none; fishes, none; invertebrates, 1; plants, 1

Major Cities, Population Percentage Increase (1980-90)

Bloomington, 86,335—5.50%
Brooklyn Park, 56,381—30.11%
Duluth, 85,493— -7.88%
Minneapolis, 368,383— -0.69%
Rochester, 70,745—22.17%
Saint Paul, 272,235—0.74%

The People

Population: 4,375,099, 20th
Percent change (1980-90): 6.84%, 22nd
Per sq. mi: 50.32, 33rd
Percent in metro. area: 67.66%, 25th
Percent foreign born: 2.6%, 30th
White: 4,130,395—94.41%, 8th
Black: 94,944—2.17%, 39th
Native American: 49,909—1.14%, 15th
Asian, Pacific Isle: 77,886—1.78%, 18th
Other races: 21,965—0.50%, 35th
Hispanic origin: 53,884—1.23%, 36th
Percent over 5 yrs. speaking language other than English at home: 5.6%, 35th
Percent males: 49.03%, 18th
Percent females: 50.97%, 34th
Percent never married: 27.4%, 14th
Marriages per 1,000 (1989): 7.9, 43rd
Divorces per 1,000 (1989): 3.6, 39th
Median age: 32.5
Under 5 years: 336,800—7.70%, 10th
Under 18 years: 1,166,783—26.67%, 14th
65 years & older: 546,934—12.50%, 29th
Percent increase among the elderly: 14.0%, 35th

Of Vital Importance

Live births per 1,000 pop.: 15.5, 32nd
Infant mortality rate per 1,000 births (1988): 7.8, 49th
Average lifetime (1979-81): 76.15, 2nd
Deaths per 100,000 pop. (1988): 823.0, 36th
Causes of death per 100,000 pop. (1988):
Diseases of heart: 276.5, 35th
Malignant neoplasms: 188.2, 36th
Cerebrovascular diseases: 69.9, 16th
Accidents & adverse effects: 34.7, 41st
Chronic obstructive pulmonary diseases: 30.1, 40th
Suicide: 11.3, 35th
HIV infection: 1.7, 38th
Other: 68.1, 42nd

Keeping Well

Non-federal physicians per 100,000 pop.: 239, 13th
Dentists per 100,000 (1990-91): 77, 9th
Nurses per 100,000 (1989): 788, 14th
Hospitals per 100,000: 3.8, 15th

Admissions per 100,000: 12,807, 35th
Beds per 100,000: 564.90, 17th
Occupancy rate: 68.2%, 18th
Semiprivate room charges per day: $282, 23rd
Average stay: 10.3, 8th
Notifiable diseases per 100,000:
AIDS: 4.7, 40th
Gonorrhea: 95.6, 36th
Measles: 10.6, 7th
Syphillis: 4.8, 39th
Tuberculosis (TB): 2.6, 42nd
Per capita spending on mental health programs (1987): $54.47, 8th
Pop. without health insur. (1991): 9.3%, 43rd

Households by Type

Total households: 1,647,853
Percent change (1980-90): 14.04%, 22nd
Family households: 1,130,683
Percent of total: 68.62%, 42nd
Nonfamily households: 517,170
Percent of total: 31.38%, 10th
Persons per household: 2.58, 29th
Pop. living in group quarters: 117,621
Percent of pop.: 2.69%, 28th

Living Quarters

Total housing units: 1,848,445
Persons per unit: 2.37, 33rd
Occupied housing units: 1,647,853
Percent of total units: 89.15%, 28th
Persons per unit: 2.43, 50th
Percent of units with over 1 person per room: 2.07%, 42nd
Owner-occupied units: 1,183,673
Percent of total units: 64.04%, 6th
Percent of occupied units: 71.83%, 2nd
Persons per unit: 2.78, 17th
Median value: $74,000, 22nd
Renter-occupied units: 464,180
Percent of total units: 25.11%, 48th
Percent of occupied units: 28.17%, 50th
Persons per unit: 2.08, 51st
Median contract rent: $348, 22nd
Rental vacancy rate: 7.9%, 32nd
Mobile home, trailer & other as a % of occupied housing units: 6.77%, 38th

Crime Index per 100,000

Total: 4,539, 35th
Violent: 306, 38th
Murder and nonnegligent manslaughter: 3, 45th
Aggravated assault: 7,698, 11th
Robbery: 93, 34th
Rape: 34, 30th
Property: 4,233, 34th
Burglary: 907, 35th
Larceny, theft: 2,960, 30th
Motor vehicle theft: 366, 31st
Drug abuse arrests: 126, 41st

Teaching and Learning

Literacy (1987): 91%, 9th
Pop. 3 and over enrolled in school: 1,175,027
Percent of pop.: 28.1%, 17th
Public elementary & secondary schools:
Total enrollment: 755,000
Avg. class size (1987): 25, 7th
Teachers: 43,100
Percent of pop.: 0.99%, 29th
Teachers' avg. salary: $32,200, 14th
Spending per capita: $933, 9th
Spending per pupil in avg. daily attendance: $5,114, 16th
Percent of graduates taking SAT: 12%, 34th
Combined SAT scores: 1023, 7th
Percent of pop. over 25 completing:
High school: 82.4%, 6th
College degree/s: 21.8%, 16th
Higher educa., institutions: 78
Per 100,000 pop.: 0.8, 19th
Enroll: 253,789
Percent of pop.: 5.80%, 20th
Public: 199,211
Percent of enroll.: 78.49%, 34th
Private 54,578
Percent of enroll.: 21.51%, 18th
White non-Hispanic: 523,157
Percent of enroll.: 86.61%, 22nd
Black non-Hispanic: 44,009
Percent of enroll.: 7.29%, 21st
Hispanic: 7,709
Percent of enroll.: 1.28%, 32nd
Asian/Pacific Islander: 13,588
Percent of enroll.: 2.25%, 19th

Amer. Indian/AK native: 1,011
Percent of enroll.: 0.17%, 50th
Nonresident alien: 14,586
Percent of enroll.: 2.41%, 24th
Female: 139,444
Percent of enroll.: 54.94%, 26th
Tuition, state university ('90-'91): $2,216, 16th
Public library systems: 130
Books & serial vol. per capita: 2.58, 25th
Govt. expend. per capita: $18.42, 20th
State govt.: $1.39, 44th
Local govts.: $17.04, 17th

Law Enforcement, Courts, and Prisons

Police protection expend.: $449,893,000
Per capita: $102.83, 26th
Judicial & legal expend.: $229,471,000
Per capita: $52.45, 20th
Corrections expend.: $239,391,000
Per capita: $54.72, 39th
Police per 10,000 pop. (1990-91): 15.1, 47th
Prisoners (state & fed.) sentenced to over 1 yr., per 100,000 pop.: 72
Percent change (1989-90): 2.35%, 42nd
Death penalty: no

Religion, Number and Percent of Population

Agnostic: 19,250—0.60%, 19th
Buddhist: 3,208—0.10%, 17th
Christian: 2,865,026—89.30%, 15th
Hindu: 3,208—0.10%, 10th
Jewish: 25,667—0.80%, 20th
Moslem: 3,208—0.10%, 22nd
Unitarian: 12,833—0.40%, 8th
Other: 25,667—0.80%, 37th
None: 179,666—5.60%, 38th
Refused to answer: 70,583—2.20%, 23rd

Making a Living

Personal income per capita (1989): $14,389, 19th
Percent increase (1979-'89) (constant 1989 dollars): 15.2%, 22nd
Average income per family: $43,843, 15th
Percent of pop. below poverty level: 10.2%, 40th
Percent 65 and over: 12.1%, 23rd
Cost of living, selected cities
1st qtr., 1991 (U. S. Standard=100)

Moorhead	91.4
Rochester	98.5
Minneapolis-St. Paul	98.8

Economy

Civilian labor force : 2,404,000
Percent of tot. pop.: 54.95%, 2nd
Percent 65 and over: 2.41%, 36th
Percent females: 46.05%, 20th
Percent job growth (1980-90): 19.26%, 24th
Major employer industries:
Agriculture: 128,128—5.60%, 9th
Construction: 93,808—4.10%, 31st
Finance, insurance & real estate: 157,872—6.90%, 10th
Government: 308,880—13.50%, 38th
Manufacturing: 366,080—16.00%, 26th
Mining: 7,761—0.4%, 24th
Service: 503,360—22.00%, 14th
Trade: 416,416—18.20%, 30th
Transportation, communication, & public utilities: 123,552—5.40%, 20th
Wholesale/retail: 484,247—22.1%, 10th
Unemployment rate: 4.83%, 39th
Male: 2.91%, 30th
Female: 1.91%, 43rd
Total businesses (1991): 176,738
New business incorp's. (1991): 9,564
Percent of total businesses: 5.41%, 33rd
Business failures (1991): 1,566
Percent of total businesses: 0.89%, 22nd
Agriculture farm income
Marketing (1991): $6,936,001,000, 6th
Net per operation: $21,362, 24th
Net per acre: $63, 24th
Leading products: corn, dairy products, soybeans, cattle
Av. value land & build. per acre: $831, 28th
Percent increase (1980-90): -23.48%, 42nd
Govt. payments: $435,819,000, 7th
Construction, value of all: $3,628,000,000
Per capita: $829.24, 8th
Percent change 1989-90: -6.69%, 25th
Manufactures:
Value added: $25,804,000,000
Per capita: $5,897.92, 14th
Value of shipments: $55,244,000,000
Per capita: $12,626.91, 19th

Leading products: food processing, non-electrical machinery, chemicals, paper, electric and electronic equipment, printing and publishing, instruments, fabricated metal products.
Mining, min. prod., value (1987): $999,000,000, 28th
Leading products: iron ore, sand/gravel, stone
Retail sales: $33,315,000,000, 19th
Per household: $20,050, 15th
Percent increase (1987-90): 14.0%, 29th
Service indust., value (1987): $18,977,000,000, 17th
Per capita: $4,337.50, 18th
Tourism indus., value (1989): $3,587,000,000, 25th
Foreign exports value: $5,091,000,000, 18th
Per capita: $1,163.63, 16th
Patents per 1,000 pop.: 3.0, 47th

Travel and Transportation

Motor vehicle registrations: 3,507,337
Per 1,000 pop.: 801, 21st
Motorcycle registrations: 122,476
Per 1,000 pop.: 27, 13th
Licensed drivers per 1,000 driving age pop.: 754, 50th
Deaths from motor vehicle accidents per 100,000 pop.: 12.9, 45th
Public roads & streets
Total mileage: 129,397, 5th
Rural mileage: 115,189, 3rd
Urban mileage: 14,208, 21st
Interstate mileage: 905, 23rd
Annual vehicle-miles of travel per person: 8,901, 29th
Mean travel time for workers 16 + who work away from home: 19.1 min., 36th

Government

Registered voters (1988): 2,916,957
Percent of voting age pop.: 92.28%, 2nd
Voter turnout (1988): 2,096,790
Percent of registered voters: 71.88%, 23rd
Percent of voting age pop.: 66.33%, 1st
State legislators, total (1992): 201, 5th
Women members (1992): 42
Percent of legislature: 20.9%, 17th
Dominant party (1992): Democrats
U. S. Congress, House members (1993): 8
Increase 1983-93: 0
Revenues:
State govt.: $13,161,868,000
Per capita: $3,008.36, 9th
State & local govt.: $21,098,505,000
Per capita: $4,822.41, 7th
Indebtedness:
State govt.: $3,764,071,000
Per capita: $860.34, 38th
State & local govt.: $17,351,000,000
Per capita: $3,965.85, 17th

Laws and Regulations

Legal driving age: 19
Marriage age without parental consent: 18
Divorce residence requirement: 180 days

Attractions

Major opera companies (1989): 3, 15th
Per 1 million pop.: 0.69, 24th
Major symphony orchestras (1989): 18, 17th
Per 1 million pop.: 4.14, 19th
State appropriations for state arts agencies per capita: $0.96, 19th
State Fair in late Aug. to early Sept. at Saint Paul

Sports and Competition

NCAA sports teams, 3—Bethel College Royals, Univ. of Minnesota Golden Gophers, Univ. of St. Thomas Tommies.
Professional teams, 4:
Baseball, 1—Minnesota Twins (AL), Hubert H. Humphrey Metrodome
Basketball, 1—Minnesota Timberwolves (NBA), Target Center
Football, 1—Minnesota Vikings (NFC), Hubert H. Humphrey Metrodome
Hockey, 1—Minnesota North Stars (NHL), Met Center

MISSISSIPPI

"It is in Mississippi, more than any other state, that the character of the old South remains apparent today. Once the very heartland of plantation society, the state remains the leading cotton producer of the states that once relied on such a one-crop economy....As a result Misissippi has yet to show the effects of urbanization which have changed the character of the neighboring states."

Robert O'Brien

Mississippi is a land where a beetle (the boll weevil) changed the way of life. Before the Civil War the planters of Mississippi, with their "Little Cotton Kingdoms" and mansions, enjoyed the brilliant plantation culture, which was based on slave labor. During that war the state suffered the "first modern total warfare," with the greatest number killed in proportion to the population. It suffered still more during the brutal period of Reconstruction. At one time Mississippi was the home of one of the largest Indian populations, people who were known for their civilized lifestyle and who were forced to leave their property to travel west over a "Trail of Tears." As the native state of some of the nation's best-known authors, composers, and playwrights, Mississippi has a well-earned reputation for culture.

Superlatives

- First European settlement in the southern Mississippi Valley — Ocean Springs.
- One of the earliest and best reforestation programs.
- Natchez boasts more than 500 pre-Civil War mansions.
- A record eight flags have flown over Biloxi.
- Celebrated the first "Decoration Day," now Memorial Day.
- First U.S. state-operated university for women, at Columbus.
- Pioneer in state system of junior colleges.

Moments in History

- In 1540 Hernando deSoto and his great expedition entered present-day Mississippi near where Columbus now stands, and his party may have been the first Europeans to see the Mississippi River. Their cruelty to the Indians was responsible for the decline of many tribes of the area.
- In 1682 Robert Rene Cavelier, Sieur de La Salle, claimed the vast region drained by the Mississippi for the king of France.
- The first European settlement in the entire Mississippi Valley, Fort Maurepas, now Ocean Springs, was founded in 1699 by Pierre Lemoyne, Sieur d'Iberville.
- At the command of King Louis, in 1720 John Law was sent with 200 settlers to the Pascagoula area. Although other settlers arrived, Law's "Mississippi Bubble" burst, and the failure almost brought France to financial collapse.
- After years of Indian attacks, in 1736 French forces under Bienville were defeated by the Chickasaw, hastening the French decline in North America.
- With the French withdrawal in 1763, the British made their headquarters at present-day Natchez, and most of the area now Mississippi became part of British West Florida. During the American Revolution, the Spanish attacked the area, and by 1781 they had seized British West Florida.

• After a long dispute with Spain over the ownership of the region, in 1789 Spanish forces left the upper area, and Congress created the Mississippi Territory with the capital at Natchez. It also included much of Alabama.

• On December 10, 1817, Mississippi was admitted as the 20th state.

• By 1832 the last of the Indian tribes had their substantial property seized. Forced to leave the state, they trudged in desperation over the "Trail of Tears" on their way to western lands.

• The great plantations of Mississippi depended on their slave labor, and on January 9, 1861, Mississippi became the second state to secede from the Union.

• The 47-day siege of Vicksburg during the war ended on July 4, 1863, and the battle for that city was one of the most crucial of the entire conflict. The Union success cut the Confederacy in two and opened the entire Mississippi to Union forces.

• Civil war battles raged across the state, ending with the Battle of Tupelo in early 1865. Altogether, the state lost 60,000, the largest percentage dead of any state of those in Confederate service.

• Mississippi was readmitted to the Union in 1870, but the terrible hardships of Reconstruction endured until about 1875.

• An epidemic of yellow fever swept the state in 1878, and thousands died.

• In 1904 James K. Vardaman became governor with the support of small farmers and others, ending the control of the plantation "planter class."

• During World War I, 66,000 men and women served in the armed forces, and Camp Shelby was a principal training center.

• The Mississippi River floods of 1927 were the worst in memory.

• During World War II, more Mississippians won the Medal of Honor than those of any other state, and 4,187 servicemen and women died.

• In 1967 the space age came to the state with the opening of what became the National Space Technology Laboratories.

• In 1977 Mississippi celebrated its bicentennial of Statehood.

• The 1990 census indicated that Mississippi continued a slow increase in population.

That's Interesting

• Among geographic curiosities is the Singing River, the Pascagoula. It sometimes makes a sound like the humming of bees, and this has never been explained.

• When Hernando de Soto died, his followers were so afraid of the Indians that they slipped his body into the Mississipi in the dead of night, at a spot thought to have been near present-day Natchez.

• The mother-daughter combination of Maria and Miranda Younghans manned the landmark Biloxi lighthouse for a total of 62 years.

• The five sons of the William Henry Cox family all died tragic deaths; among the tragedies were the son who was killed riding his horse up a stairway, one who killed his bride and committed suicide, another who died in a wagon as it crashed over a cliff.

•Only state where the state flower is the blossom of the state tree.

Notable Natives

Theodore Bilbo (near Poplarville, 1877-1947), public official. **Jefferson Davis** (present Fairview, 1808-1889), president of the Confederate States of America. **William Faulkner** (New Albany, 1897-1962), author. **Elvis Presley** (Tupelo, 1935-1977), entertainer. **Leontyne Price** (Laurel, 1927-), opera singer. **William Grant Still** (Woodville, 1895-1978), composer. **Eudora Welty** (Jackson, 1909-), author. **Tennessee Williams** (Columbus, 1911-1983), playwright.

General

Admitted to statehood: Dec. 10, 1817
Origin of name: probably Chippewa, *mici zibi* , "great river" or "gathering in of all the waters"; also, Algonquin word, *Messipi* "
Capital: Jackson
Nickname: The Magnolia State
Motto: "*Virtute et Armis*" ("By Valor and Arms")
Bird: mockingbird
Flower: magnolia
Song: "Go, Mississippi"
Tree: magnolia

The Land

Area: 48,434 sq. mi., 32nd
Land: 46,914 sq. mi., 31st
Water: 1,520 sq. mi., 25th
Topography: low, fertile delta between the Yazoo and Mississippi rivers, loess bluffs stretching around delta border, sandy gulf coastal terraces followed by piney woods and prairie, prairie belt; Pontotoc Ridge and flatwoods into the N central highlands
Number of counties: 82
Geographic center: Leake, 9 mi. WNW of Carthage.
Length: 340 mi.
Width: 170 mi.
Highest point: 806 ft. (Woodall Mt.), 47th
Lowest point: sea level (Gulf of Mexico), 3rd
Mean elevation: 300 ft., 45th
Coastline: 44 mi., 18th
Shoreline: 359 mi., 22nd

Climate and Environment

Temp., highest: 115 deg. on July 29, 1930, at Holly Springs; lowest: -19 deg. on Jan. 30, 1966, at Corinth
Fresh water withdrawn, per capita, per day: 885 gal., 36th
Endangered species: mammals, 2—Indiana bat, West Indian manatee; birds, 5—Mississippi sandhill crane, American peregrine falcon, brown pelican, least tern, red-cockaded woodpecker; reptiles, 3; amphibians, none; fishes, 1; invertebrates, 5; plants, 1

Major Cities, Population Percentage Increase (1980-90)

Biloxi, 46,319— –6.07%
Greenville, 45,226—11.36%
Hattisburg, 41,882—2.58%
Jackson, 196,637— –3.08%
Meridian, 41,036— –11.90%

The People

Population: 2,573,216, 31st
  Percent change (1980-90): 2.04%, 36th
  Per sq. mi: 53.13, 32nd
  Percent in metro. area: 30.16%, 46th
  Percent foreign born: 0.8%, 51st
White: 1,633,461—63.48%, 49th
Black: 915,057,—35.56%, 2nd
Native American: 8,525—0.33%, 31st
Asian, Pacific Isle: 13,016—0.51%, 48th
Other races: 3,157—0.12%, 50th
Hispanic origin: 15,931—0.62%, 47th
Percent over 5 yrs. speaking language other than English at home: 2.8%, 48th
Percent males: 47.82%, 50th
Percent females: 52.18%, 2nd
Percent never married: 26.7%, 20th
Marriages per 1,000 (1989): 9.3, 26th
Divorces per 1,000 (1989): 4.9, 22nd
Median age: 31.2
Under 5 years: 195,365—7.59%, 17th
Under 18 years: 746,734—29.02%, 7th
65 years & older: 321,284—12.49%, 30th
Percent increase among the elderly: 11.0%, 46th

Of Vital Importance

Live births per 1,000 pop.: 16.4, 15th
Infant mortality rate per 1,000 births (1988): 12.3, 4th
Average lifetime (1979-81): 71.98, 48th
Deaths per 100,000 pop. (1988): 947.9, 14th
Causes of death per 100,000 pop. (1988):
  Diseases of heart: 352.7, 13th
  Malignant neoplasms: 201.4, 22nd
  Cerebrovascular diseases: 76.1, 4th
  Accidents & adverse effects: 54.8, 4th
  Chronic obstructive pulmonary diseases: 30.7, 35th
  Suicide: 11.3, 35th
  HIV infection: 2.8, 26th
  Other: 73.5, 31st

Keeping Well

Non-federal physicians per 100,000 pop.: 146, 49th
Dentists per 100,000 (1990-91): 41, 51st
Nurses per 100,000 (1989): 465, 49th
Hospitals per 100,000: 4.5, 10th
  Admissions per 100,000: 16,873, 5th
  Beds per 100,000: 666.52, 5th
  Occupancy rate: 64.6%, 32nd
  Semiprivate room charges per day: $167, 51st

Average stay: 7.0, 28th
Notifiable diseases per 100,000:
AIDS: 10.8, 21st
Gonorrhea: 555.8, 3rd
Measles: 1.1, 40th
Syphillis: 96.5, 5th
Tuberculosis (TB): 14.1, 6th
Per capita spending on mental health programs (1987): $21.81, 48th
Pop. without health insur. (1991): 18.9%, 5th

Households by Type

Total households: 911,374
Percent change (1980-90): 10.20%, 30th
Family households: 674,378
Percent of total: 74.00%, 2nd
Nonfamily households: 236,996
Percent of total: 26.00%, 50th
Persons per household: 2.75, 5th
Pop. living in group quarters: 69,717
Percent of pop.: 2.71%, 27th

Living Quarters

Total housing units: 1,010,423
Persons per unit: 2.55, 4th
Occupied housing units: 911,374
Percent of total units: 90.20%, 21st
Persons per unit: 2.72, 5th
Percent of units with over 1 person per room: 5.80%, 11th
Owner-occupied units: 651,587
Percent of total units: 64.49%, 4th
Percent of occupied units: 71.50%, 3rd
Persons per unit: 2.78, 17th
Median value: $45,600, 49th
Renter-occupied units: 259,787
Percent of total units: 25.71%, 46th
Percent of occupied units: 28.50%, 49th
Persons per unit: 2.65, 4th
Median contract rent: $215, 51st
Rental vacancy rate: 9.5%, 18th
Mobile home, trailer & other as a % of occupied housing units: 16.38%, 9th

Crime Index per 100,000

Total: 3,869, 44th
Violent: 340, 36th
Murder and nonnegligent manslaughter: 12, 5th
Aggravated assault: 7,592, 18th
Robbery: 86, 37th
Rape: 44, 18th
Property: 3,529, 45th
Burglary: 1,251, 16th
Larceny, theft: 2,070, 48th
Motor vehicle theft: 208, 42nd
Drug abuse arrests: 178, 37th

Teaching and Learning

Literacy (1987): 84%, 47th
Pop. 3 and over enrolled in school: 727,486
Percent of pop.: 29.6%, 7th
Public elementary & secondary schools:
Total enrollment: 498,000
Avg. class size (1987): 24, 15th
Teachers: 27,500
Percent of pop.: 1.07%, 18th
Teachers' avg. salary: $24,400, 43rd
Spending per capita: $626, 46th
Spending per pupil in avg. daily attendance: $3,151, 49th
Percent of graduates taking SAT: 4%, 51st
Combined SAT scores: 997, 13th
Percent of pop. over 25 completing:
High school: 64.3%, 51st
College degree/s: 14.7%, 48th
Higher educa., institutions: 46
Per 100,000 pop.: 1.1, 10th
Enroll: 122,883
Percent of pop.: 4.78%, 41st
Public: 109,038
Percent of enroll.: 88.73%, 11th
Private 13,845
Percent of enroll.: 11.27%, 41st
White non-Hispanic: 189,189
Percent of enroll.: 75.13%, 39th
Black non-Hispanic: 49,199
Percent of enroll.: 19.54%, 5th
Hispanic: 2,740
Percent of enroll.: 1.09%, 35th
Asian/Pacific Islander: 4,241
Percent of enroll.: 1.68%, 25th
Amer. Indian/AK native: 548
Percent of enroll.: 0.22%, 47th

Nonresident alien: 5,893
Percent of enroll.: 2.34%, 25th
Female: 69,424
Percent of enroll.: 56.50%, 9th
Tuition, state university ('90-'91): $1,927, 20th
Public library systems: 46
Books & serial vol. per capita: 1.88, 41st
Govt. expend. per capita: $5.73, 51st
State govt.: $2.25, 31st
Local govts.: $3.48, 48th

LAW ENFORCEMENT, COURTS, AND PRISONS

Police protection expend.: $166,883,000
Per capita: $64.86, 48th
Judicial & legal expend.: $61,948,000
Per capita: $24.08, 50th
Corrections expend.: $105,875,000
Per capita: $41.15, 49th
Police per 10,000 pop. (1990-91): 14.9, 49th
Prisoners (state & fed.) sentenced to over 1 yr., per 100,000 pop.: 311
Percent change (1989-90): 6.22%, 31st
Death penalty: yes, by lethal gas convicted after July 1, 1984. Lethal injection convicted before July 1, 1984.
Under sentence of death: 45, 16th
Executed (1989): 1

RELIGION, NUMBER AND PERCENT OF POPULATION

Agnostic: 9,132—0.50%, 27th
Buddhist: NA
Christian: 1,720,521—94.20%, 3rd
Hindu: NA
Jewish: 10,959—0.60%, 25th
Moslem: NA
Other: 23,744—1.30%, 24th
None: 51,141—2.80%, 47th
Unitarian: NA
Refused to answer: 10,959—0.60%, 49th

MAKING A LIVING

Personal income per capita (1989): $9,648, 51st
Percent increase (1979-'89) (constant 1989 dollars): 11.1%, 29th
Average income per family: $30,769, 51st
Percent of pop. below poverty level: 25.2%, 1st
Percent 65 and over: 29.4%, 1st
Cost of living, selected cities
1st qtr., 1991 (U. S. Standard=100)
Gulfport 89.4
Laurel 93.4

ECONOMY

Civilian labor force : 1,184,000
Percent of tot. pop.: 46.01%, 48th
Percent 65 and over: 2.36%, 38th
Percent females: 46.54%, 12th
Percent job growth (1980-90): 8.85%, 45th
Major employer industries:
Agriculture: 35,040—3.20%, 18th
Construction: 47,085—4.30%, 29th
Finance, insurance & real estate: 50,370—4.60%, 36th
Government: 185,055—16.90%, 16th
Manufacturing: 233,235—21.30%, 12th
Mining: 8,890—0.3%, 26th
Service: 164,250—15.00%, 51st
Trade: 206,955—18.90%, 24th
Transportation, communication, & public utilities: 62,415—5.70%, 17th
Wholesale/retail: 204,822—19.9%, 43rd
Unemployment rate: 7.43%, 3rd
Male: 3.21%, 20th
Female: 4.22%, 1st
Total businesses (1991): 79,509
New business incorp's. (1991): 3,602
Percent of total businesses: 4.53%, 40th
Business failures (1991): 520
Percent of total businesses: 0.65%, 41st
Agriculture farm income
Marketing (1991): $2,422,070,000, 28th
Net per operation: $19,352, 27th
Net per acre: $57, 26th
Leading products: corn, broilers, cattle, soybeans
Av. value land & build. per acre: $754, 31st
Percent increase (1980-90): -7.94%, 33rd
Govt. payments: $176,298,000, 17th
Construction, value of all: $592,000,000
Per capita: $230.06, 50th
Percent change 1989-90: -25.25%, 39th
Manufactures:
Value added: $12,793,000,000
Per capita: $4,971.60, 29th

Value of shipments: $30,313,000,000
Per capita: $11,780.20, 23rd
Leading products: apparel, furniture, lumber and wood products, foods and kindred products, electrical machinery and equipment, transportation equipment.
Mining, min. prod., value (1987): $1,128,000,000, 26th
Leading products: petrol., nat. gas, sand/gravel
Retail sales: $13,803,000,000, 33rd
Per household: $15,131, 50th
Percent increase (1987-90): 17.5%, 21st
Service indust., value (1987): $5,624,000,000, 37th
Per capita: $2,185.59, 51st
Tourism indus., value (1989): $1,821,000,000, 38th
Foreign exports value: $1,605,000,000, 33rd
Per capita: $623.73, 37th
Patents per 1,000 pop.: 19.9, 1st

TRAVEL AND TRANSPORTATION

Motor vehicle registrations: 1,875,445
Per 1,000 pop.: 728, 38th
Motorcycle registrations: 26,090
Per 1,000 pop.: 10, 44th
Licensed drivers per 1,000 driving age pop.: 990, 4th
Deaths from motor vehicle accidents per 100,000 pop.: 29.0, 2nd
Public roads & streets
Total mileage: 72,520, 27th
Rural mileage: 65,164, 26th
Urban mileage: 7,356, 33rd
Interstate mileage: 684, 32nd
Annual vehicle-miles of travel per person: 9,481, 19th
Mean travel time for workers 16 + who work away from home: 20.6 min., 27th

GOVERNMENT

Registered voters (1988): 1,595,826
Percent of voting age pop.: 85.48%, 7th
Voter turnout (1988): 931,527
Percent of registered voters: 58.37%, 47th
Percent of voting age pop.: 49.89%, 31st
State legislators, total (1992): 174, 14th
Women members (1992): 12
Percent of legislature: 6.9%, 47th
Dominant party (1992): Democrats
U. S. Congress, House members (1993): 5
Increase 1983-93: 0
Revenues:
State govt.: $5,343,972,000
Per capita: $2,076.77, 40th
State & local govt.: $8,150,934,000
Per capita: $3,167.61, 48th
Indebtedness:
State govt.: $1,342,623,000
Per capita: $521.77, 46th
State & local govt.: $4,769,000,000
Per capita: $1,853.32, 50th

LAWS AND REGULATIONS

Legal driving age: 16
Marriage age without parental consent: Male, 17; female, 15, notice to parents if under 21
Divorce residence requirement: 6 mo.

ATTRACTIONS

Major opera companies (1989): 2, 21st
Per 1 million pop.: 0.76, 22nd
Major symphony orchestras (1989): 7, 32nd
Per 1 million pop.: 2.67, 39th
State appropriations for state arts agencies per capita: $0.19, 50th
State Fair in the fall at Jackson

SPORTS AND COMPETITION

NCAA sports teams, 6—Alcorn State Univ. Braves, Jackson State Univ. Tigers, Mississippi State Univ. Bulldogs, Mississippi Valley State Univ. Delta Devils, Univ. of Mississippi Ole Miss Rebels, Univ. of Southern Mississippi Golden Eagles
Professional teams, 1:
Baseball, 1—Jackson Generals (Texas League, Class AA), Smith-Willis Stadium

MISSOURI

"I come from a state that raises corn and cotton and cockleburrs and Democrats, and frothy eloquence neither convinces nor satisfies me. I am from Missouri. You have got to show me."

Willard D. Vandiver

Missouri is the "Show Me" state, a nickname that stands for intelligent skepticism. It came into being when Missouri Congressman Willard Duncan Vandiver said, in 1899, in a speech in Philadelphia: "Frothy eloquence neither convinces nor satisfies me. I am from Missouri. You have got to show me." Missouri is a center of transportation. The nation's two greatest rivers, the Mississippi on the eastern border and the Missouri winding through the state, lend themselves to shipping. Fifteen major railroads and many transcontinental airlines service Missouri. The state is sometimes called "The Mother of the West" because it supplied so many of the pioneers who moved on to settle the land between the Missouri and the Pacific Ocean.

Superlatives

- Nation's tallest monument, the Gateway Arch in St. Louis.
- Founded in Columbia in 1839, The University of Missouri was the first state university west of the Mississippi. In 1908 it was the world's first college to grant a journalism degree.
- First in U.S. production of lead.
- Center of U.S. barite mining.
- World's largest shoe manufacturing center, St. Louis.
- First newspaper published west of the Mississippi.
- Home of the Missouri mule.
- First pony express run.
- World's first all-steel railroad bridge.

Moments in History

- Father Pierre Marquette and Louis Jolliet floated down the Mississippi in 1673, and found the mouth of the Missouri. They were the first Europeans of record to pass Missouri shores.
- In 1682 the Sieur de La Salle claimed the entire Mississippi Valley watershed in the name of France.
- In 1735 Ste. Genvieve was founded, the first permanent European settlement in present-day Missouri.
- St. Louis was begun in March, 1764, by Auguste Chouteau.

> So They Say
>
> "...the first boat reached the mouth of the gully at the head of which were the marked trees....I put the men to work....They commenced the shed, and the little cabins for the men were built in the vicinity."
>
> Auguste Chouteau, on the founding of St. Louis.

- After France relinquished the area to Spain in 1764, French settlers flocked to St. Louis, and the fur trade flourished.
- In 1780, 50 defenders of St. Louis held off more than 1,000 Indians and 24 white traders, keeping the vital Mississippi open to the United States.
- Spain returned the Louisiana territory to France. After France again took over, the entire

Louisiana territory was bought by the United States in 1803.

• On May 14, 1804, the great Lewis and Clark expedition left St. Louis to explore the country's new territory.

• On December 16, 1811, the area for hundreds of miles around New Madrid was rocked by what has been said to have been the strongest earthquake in North American history.

• Indian wars occurred between 1811 and 1815, but Missouri defenders held out.

• In 1819 the *Western Engineer* was the first steamboat to sail up the Missouri River.

• Missouri was admitted as a slave state on August 10, 1821, after an agreement known as the Missouri Compromise.

• After William Bicknell blazed the Santa Fe trail in 1822, fortunes were made in the New Mexico trade.

> So They Say
>
> "If the mud does not quite get over your boot tops when you sit in the saddle, they call it a middling good road."
>
> Anonymous traveler on the Santa Fe Trail

• By the 1840s thousands of immigrants began their trips to the far west from various Missouri cities, principally St. Louis, the "Gateway to the West."

• In 1831 Mormon leader Joseph Smith and his followers arrived. They founded the towns of Salem and Far West, becoming so powerful that they were persecuted and fled the state in 1839. Far West was destroyed, and its site is now a country field; the town of Salem remains.

• In the conflict over slavery, many from Missouri moved to Kansas in an effort to make it a slave state; they fought with free-state settlers until about 1858.

• Missouri refused to join the Confederacy in the Civil War, and many bloody battles were fought there for this critical state. The last major conflict, the Battle of Westport, was won by the Union, October 13, 1864. But Missouri was the center of raids by Confederate guerrillas.

> So They Say
>
> "The guerrilla warfare...was a war of terror, surprise, sabotage, and arson...a total war,...cold-blooded...hit-and-run."
>
> Anonymous

• By the war's end Missouri counted 1,100 battles and skirmishes.

• On January 11, 1865, Missouri became the first slave state to free its slaves.

• Former guerrillas turned bandits, robbed banks, held up trains, and plagued the Midwest until about 1882.

• A border dispute between Missouri and Iowa was settled by the U.S. Supreme Court in 1896.

• In 1904 St. Louis held the Louisiana Purchase Exposition, a great world's fair, celebrating that event a hundred years later.

• Missouri native John J. Pershing led the U.S. expeditionary force during World War I.

• On the death of Pres. F.D. Roosevelt, Missouri's Harry S. Truman became president on April 12, 1945.

• World War II ended in the Pacific when the Japanese signed the surrender on the Battleship *Missouri*, September 2, 1945.

• Kansas City became Missouri's largest city in the 1980s.

That's Interesting

• From the first steamboat on the Missouri River, smoke poured out of a stack made like a dragon's head to frighten the Indians.

• St. Louis is perhaps the only major city to have been founded by a 14-year-old boy, Auguste Chouteau, who did the job at the request of his patron, Pierre Laclede Liguest.

• The ice cream cone is said to have originated at the St. Louis World's Fair of 1904.

Notable Natives

Josephine Baker (St. Louis, 1906-1974), entertainer. **Thomas Hart Benton** (Neosho, 1889-1975), painter. **Omar Nelson Bradley** (Clark, 1893-1981), soldier. **Martha Jane "Calamity Jane" Canary Burk** (Princeton, 1852?-1903), frontier figure. **Dale Carnegie** (Maryville, 1888-

1935), author/teacher of public speaking. **George Washington Carver** (near Diamond Grove, 1864?-1943), agronomist/chemist. **Winston Churchill** (St. Louis, 1871-1947), novelist. **Samuel Langhorne "Mark Twain" Clemens** (Florida, MO, 1835-1910), humorist/author. **Walter Leland Cronkite**, Jr. (St. Joseph, 1916-), journalist/commentator. **Thomas Stearns "T.S." Eliot** (St. Louis, 1888-1965), poet. **Eugene Field** (St. Louis, 1850-1895), author/poet. **George Hearst** (near Sullivan, 1820-1891), businessman/public official. **Langston Hughes** (Joplin, 1902-1967), author. **James Cash Penney** (Hamilton, 1875-1971) merchant. **John Joseph Pershing** (Laclede, 1860-1948), soldier. **Harry S. Truman** (Lamar, 1884-1972), U.S. president.

General

Admitted to statehood: Aug. 10, 1821
Origin of name: Algonquin Indian tribe named after Missouri River, meaning "muddy water"
Capital: Jefferson City
Nickname: The Show Me State
Motto: "*Salus Populi Suprema Les Esto*" ("The Welfare of the People Shall Be the Supreme Law")
Bird: Eastern bluebird
Flower: hawthorn blossom
Mineral: galena (lead)
Song: "Missouri Waltz"
Stone: mozarkite
Tree: flowering dogwood

The Land

Area: 69,709 sq. mi., 21st
Land: 68,898 sq. mi., 18th
Water: 811 sq. mi., 34th
Topography: Rolling hills, open, fertile plains, and well-watered prairie N of the Missouri R.; S of the river land is rough and hilly with deep, narrow valleys; alluvial plain in the SE; low elevation in the W
Number of counties: 114
Geographic center: Miller, 20 mi. SW of Jefferson City
Length: 300 mi.
Width: 240 mi.
Highest point: 1,772 ft. (Taum Sauk Mt.), 41st
Lowest point: 230 ft. (St. Francis River), 30th
Mean elevation: 800 ft., 32nd

Climate and Environment

Temp., highest: 118 deg. on July 14, 1954, at Warsaw and Union; lowest: -40 deg. on Feb. 13, 1905, at Warsaw
Fresh water withdrawn, per capita, per day: 1,210 gal., 27th
Endangered species: mammals, 3—gray bat, Indiana bat, Ozark big-eared bat; birds, 3—American peregrine falcon, least tern, Alabama beach mouse; reptiles, none; amphibians, none; fishes, 1; invertebrates, 4; plants, 3

Major Cities, Population Percentage Increase (1980-90)

Saint Joseph, 71,852— -6.31%
Independence, 112,301—0.45%
Kansas City, 435,146— -2.88%
Saint Louis, 396,685— -12.39%
Springfield, 140,494—5.54%

The People

Population: 5,117,073, 15th
Percent change (1980-90): 3.91%, 30th
Per sq. mi: 73.41, 28th
Percent in metro. area: 66.19%, 30th
Percent foreign born: 1.6%, 41st
White: 4,486,228—87.67%, 25th
Black: 584,208—11.42%, 19th
Native American: 19,835—0.39%, 29th
Asian, Pacific Isle: 41,277—0.81%, 35th
Other races: 21,525—0.42%, 39th
Hispanic origin: 61,702—1.21%, 37th
Percent over 5 yrs. speaking language other than English at home: 3.8%, 44th
Percent males: 48.16%, 42nd
Percent females: 51.84%, 10th
Percent never married: 23.9%, 37th
Marriages per 1,000 (1989): 9.9, 20th
Divorces per 1,000 (1989): 5.1, 16th
Median age: 33.5
Under 5 years: 369,244—7.22%, 31st
Under 18 years: 1,314,826—25.69%, 30th

65 years & older: 717,681—14.03%, 10th
Percent increase among the elderly: 10.7%, 47th

Of Vital Importance

Live births per 1,000 pop.: 16.0, 19th
Infant mortality rate per 1,000 births (1988): 10.1, 21st
Average lifetime (1979-81): 73.84, 26th
Deaths per 100,000 pop. (1988): 988.9, 6th
Causes of death per 100,000 pop. (1988):
Diseases of heart: 359.3, 8th
Malignant neoplasms: 212.7, 14th
Cerebrovascular diseases: 71.1, 13th
Accidents & adverse effects: 43.6, 21st
Chronic obstructive pulmonary diseases: 40.5, 12th
Suicide: 13.3, 19th
HIV infection: 3.6, 22nd
Other: 78.1, 20th

Keeping Well

Non-federal physicians per 100,000 pop.: 210, 24th
Dentists per 100,000 (1990-91): 60, 27th
Nurses per 100,000 (1989): 754, 16th
Hospitals per 100,000: 3.1, 25th
Admissions per 100,000: 15,520, 13th
Beds per 100,000: 577.97, 13th
Occupancy rate: 64.8%, 30th
Semiprivate room charges per day: $268, 26th
Average stay: 7.5, 18th
Notifiable diseases per 100,000:
AIDS: 11.4, 18th
Gonorrhea: 391.2, 10th
Measles: 2.0, 35th
Syphillis: 11.7, 31st
Tuberculosis (TB): 6.1, 28th
Per capita spending on mental health programs (1987): $31.41, 33rd
Pop. without health insur. (1991): 12.2%, 30th

Households by Type

Total households: 1,961,206
Percent change (1980-90): 9.38%, 32nd
Family households: 1,368,334
Percent of total: 69.77%, 31st
Nonfamily households: 592,872
Percent of total: 30.23%, 21st
Persons per household: 2.54, 39th
Pop. living in group quarters: 145,397
Percent of pop.: 2.84%, 24th

Living Quarters

Total housing units: 2,199,129
Persons per unit: 2.33, 37th
Occupied housing units: 1,961,206
Percent of total units: 89.18%, 27th
Persons per unit: 2.46, 44th
Percent of units with over 1 person per room: 2.46%, 37th
Owner-occupied units: 1,348,746
Percent of total units: 61.33%, 15th
Percent of occupied units: 68.77%, 16th
Persons per unit: 2.67, 38th
Median value: $59,800, 34th
Renter-occupied units: 612,460
Percent of total units: 27.85%, 32nd
Percent of occupied units: 31.23%, 36th
Persons per unit: 2.24, 42nd
Median contract rent: $282, 35th
Rental vacancy rate: 10.7%, 13th
Mobile home, trailer & other as a % of occupied housing units: 9.28%, 29th

Crime Index per 100,000

Total: 5,121, 29th
Violent: 715, 14th
Murder and nonnegligent manslaughter: 9, 20th
Aggravated assault: 7,216, 31st
Robbery: 216, 15th
Rape: 32, 33rd
Property: 4,405, 29th
Burglary: 1,066, 29th
Larceny, theft: 2,800, 39th
Motor vehicle theft: 539, 20th
Drug abuse arrests: 269, 23rd

Teaching and Learning

Literacy (1987): 88%, 25th
Pop. 3 and over enrolled in school: 1,292,623
Percent of pop.: 26.4%, 37th
Public elementary & secondary schools:
Total enrollment: 825,000
Avg. class size (1987): 22, 28th
Teachers: 51,200
Percent of pop.: 1.00%, 27th
Teachers' avg. salary: $27,200, 33rd

Spending per capita: $676, 41st
Spending per pupil in avg. daily attendance: $4,226, 32nd
Percent of graduates taking SAT: 12%, 34th
Combined SAT scores: 1002, 12th
Percent of pop. over 25 completing:
High school: 73.9%, 38th
College degree/s: 17.8%, 33rd
Higher educa., institutions: 93
Per 100,000 pop.: 0.5, 37th
Enroll: 289,407
Percent of pop.: 5.66%, 23rd
Public: 200,093
Percent of enroll.: 69.14%, 42nd
Private 89,314
Percent of enroll.: 30.86%, 10th
White non-Hispanic: 250,758
Percent of enroll.: 86.65%, 21st
Black non-Hispanic: 23,050
Percent of enroll.: 7.96%, 20th
Hispanic: 3,434
Percent of enroll.: 1.19%, 33rd
Asian/Pacific Islander: 4,487
Percent of enroll.: 1.55%, 31st
Amer. Indian/AK native: 1,132
Percent of enroll.: 0.39%, 25th
Nonresident alien: 6,546
Percent of enroll.: 2.26%, 26th
Female: 158,542
Percent of enroll.: 54.78%, 28th
Tuition, state university ('90-'91): $1,733, 27th
Public library systems: 155
Books & serial vol. per capita: 3.38, 14th
Govt. expend. per capita: $12.58, 32nd
State govt.: $1.09, 48th
Local govts.: $11.50, 26th

Law Enforcement, Courts, and Prisons

Police protection expend.: $494,270,000
Per capita: $96.59, 31st
Judicial & legal expend.: $171,437,000
Per capita: $33.50, 42nd
Corrections expend.: $264,819,000
Per capita: $51.75, 43rd
Police per 10,000 pop. (1990-91): 18.6, 32nd
Prisoners (state & fed.) sentenced to over 1 yr., per 100,000 pop.: 287
Percent change (1989-90): 7.17%, 27th
Death penalty: yes, by lethal gas or lethal injection.
Under sentence of death: 73, 12th
Executed (1989): 1

Religion, Number and Percent of Population

Agnostic: 15,209—0.40%, 34th
Buddhist: 3,802—0.10%, 17th
Christian: 3,372,593—88.70%, 17th
Hindu: NA
Jewish: 22,814—0.60%, 25th
Moslem: NA
Unitarian: 7,605—0.20%, 23rd
Other: 49,429—1.30%, 24th
None: 247,146—6.50%, 25th
Refused to answer: 83,650—2.20%, 23rd

Making a Living

Personal income per capita (1989): $12,989, 30th
Percent increase (1979-'89) (constant 1989 dollars): 12.1%, 25th
Average income per family: $38,856, 32nd
Percent of pop. below poverty level: 13.3%, 18th
Percent 65 and over: 14.8%, 16th
Cost of living, selected cities
2nd qtr., 1989 (U. S. Standard=100)

Kennett	83.6
Kansas City (MO-KS)	94.6
St. Louis (MO-IL)	97.8
St. Charles	102.1

Economy

Civilian labor force : 2,634,000
Percent of tot. pop.: 51.47%, 21st
Percent 65 and over: 2.62%, 30th
Percent females: 45.94%, 22nd
Percent job growth (1980-90): 19.25%, 25th
Major employer industries:
Agriculture: 86,905—3.50%, 16th
Construction: 106,769—4.30%, 29th
Finance, insurance & real estate: 129,116—5.20%, 29th
Government: 290,511—11.70%, 50th
Manufacturing: 471,770—19.00%, 17th
Mining: 31,396—0.6%, 20th
Service: 509,015—20.50%, 20th

Trade: 528,879—21.30%, 3rd
Transportation, communication, & public utilities: 161,395—6.50%, 7th
Wholesale/retail: 514,671—21.7%, 21st
Unemployment rate: 5.73%, 17th
Male: 3.45%, 9th
Female: 2.32%, 30th
Total businesses (1991): 172,165
New business incorp's. (1991): 9,521
Percent of total businesses: 5.53%, 29th
Business failures (1991): 1,575
Percent of total businesses: 0.91%, 20th
Agriculture farm income
Marketing (1991): $3,861,179,000, 16th
Net per operation: $7,568, 46th
Net per acre: $27, 38th
Leading products: cattle, soybeans, hogs, corn
Av. value land & build. per acre: $706, 32nd
Percent increase (1980-90): -21.73%, 41st
Govt. payments: $268,615,000, 12th
Construction, value of all: $2,522,000,000
Per capita: $492.86, 29th
Percent change 1989-90: -10.79%, 29th
Manufactures:
Value added: $30,255,000,000
Per capita: $5,912.56, 13th
Value of shipments: $67,355,000,000
Per capita: $13,162.80, 15th
Leading products: transportation equipment, food and related products, electrical and electronic equipment, chemicals
Mining, min. prod., value (1987): $636,000,000, 31st
Leading products: lead, cement, stone
Retail sales: $36,032,000,000, 17th
Per household: $18,281, 32nd
Percent increase (1987-90): 12.2%, 35th
Service indust., value (1987): $21,251,000,000, 14th
Per capita: $4,152.96, 20th
Tourism indus., value (1989): $5,393,000,000, 17th
Foreign exports value: $3,103,000,000, 25th
Per capita: $606.40, 38th
Patents per 1,000 pop.: 7.3, 24th

Travel and Transportation

Motor vehicle registrations: 3,904,679
Per 1,000 pop.: 763, 32nd
Motorcycle registrations: 67,751
Per 1,000 pop.: 13, 35th
Licensed drivers per 1,000 driving age pop.: 930, 13th
Deaths from motor vehicle accidents per 100,000 pop.: 21.4, 18th
Public roads & streets
Total mileage: 120,527, 6th
Rural mileage: 105,488, 4th
Urban mileage: 15,039, 18th
Interstate mileage: 1,177, 11th
Annual vehicle-miles of travel per person: 9,943, 9th
Mean travel time for workers 16 + who work away from home: 21.6 min., 16th

Government

Registered voters (1988): 2,943,024
Percent of voting age pop.: 77.02%, 16th
Voter turnout (1988): 2,093,713
Percent of registered voters: 71.14%, 26th
Percent of voting age pop.: 54.79%, 18th
State legislators, total (1992): 197, 7th
Women members (1992): 31
Percent of legislature: 15.7%, 28th
Dominant party (1992): Democrats
U. S. Congress, House members (1993): 9
Increase 1983-93: 0
Revenues:
State govt.: $9,343,485,000
Per capita: $1,825.94, 48th
State & local govt.: $15,412,201,000
Per capita: $3,011.92, 50th
Indebtedness:
State govt.: $5,249,856,000
Per capita: $1,025.95, 30th
State & local govt.: $10,110,000,000
Per capita: $1,975.74, 46th

Laws and Regulations

Legal driving age: 15
Marriage age without parental consent: 18
Divorce residence requirement: 90 days

Attractions

Major opera companies (1989): 2, 21st
Per 1 million pop.: 0.39, 39th

Major symphony orchestras (1989): 13, 23rd
Per 1 million pop.: 2.52, 41st
State appropriations for state arts agencies per capita: $0.98, 17th
State Fair in the 3rd week in Aug. at Sedalia

Sports and Competition

NCAA sports teams, 5—Lincoln State Univ. Blue Tigers, Southwest Baptist Univ. Bearcats, Southwest Missouri State Univ. Bears, Univ. of Missouri Tigers, Univ. of Missouri Kangaroos

Professional teams, 7:
Baseball, 2—St. Louis Cardinals (NL), Busch Stadium; Kansas City Royals (AL), Royals Stadium
Football, 1—Kansas City Chiefs (AFC), Arrowhead Stadium
Hockey, 2—Kansas City Blades (International Hockey League), Kemper Arena; St. Louis Blues (NHL), St. Louis Arena
Soccer, 2—Kansas City Comets (Major Soccer League), Kemper Arena; St. Louis Storm (Major Soccer League), St. Louis Arena

MONTANA

"I am in love with Montana. Montana seems to me to be what a small boy would think Texas is like from hearing Texans."

John Steinbeck

Montana is "Big Sky Country," a land of tall, rugged mountains in the west and broad plains in the east. The mountains have produced a great wealth of gold and silver, and some of the peaks in Glacier National Park are so steep and remote that they have never been climbed. On the prairies, huge herds of cattle graze. Montana's history recounts one of the nation's most memorable events, the Battle of Little Bighorn. Tourists feel close to the old frontier days in Montana when they visit the mountains, the battlefields, the old gold-mining camps, and the vast, lonely plains. The Indians knew the area as the Shining Land, and it lives up to that reputation today.

SUPERLATIVES

- "Birthplace" of the Missouri River.
- First woman in U.S. House—Jeannette Rankin, 1917.
- Site of Custer's Last Stand.

MOMENTS IN HISTORY

- The Verendrye brothers, Francis and Louis, came to Montana in 1742, and they are the first Europeans known to have visited the area.
- James Mackay paid a visit to the region about 1795 and named the Yellowstone River.
- Little was known about the area until the great exploration of Lewis and Clark reached the present-day state in 1805.
- On July 25, 1805, Lewis and Clark made a dramatic discovery. After much searching and discussion they concluded that the place where three rivers met was the long-sought "ultimate source of the Missouri River."

> **So They Say**
>
> "We were now about to penetrate a country at least two thousand miles in width, on which the foot of civilized man had never trodden."
>
> Merriwether Lewis

- On their way back to St. Louis, Lewis and Clark again entered and passed through present-day Montana on June 29, 1806.
- Many traders took advantage of the explorers' discoveries. In 1807 Manuel Lisa built a trading post fort where the Yellowstone and Big Horn rivers meet.
- The first steamboat reached Fort Union in 1832.
- By means of infected blankets, the white "civilization" deliberately brought a terrible small-pox epidemic to the Indians in 1837.
- St. Mary's Mission was founded in 1842.
- The main beaver trapping period lasted until about 1843.
- In 1858 John Mullan began the Mullan Road, and it became the first wagon road over the northern Rockies.
- The mid-1850s found some disappointed miners from the California gold fields coming to Montana in search of possible rich finds there.
- John White made the first real gold discovery in July of 1862, and camp Bannack reached a population of 500 within a few days. A number of other gold discoveries were made as time went on.
- Montana territory was created on May 26, 1864.

> So They Say
> "Out there every prairie dog hole is a gold mine; every hill a mountain; every creek a river, and everybody you meet is a liar."
> Anonymous

• Butte was founded in 1864, after it started as a gold camp.

• The best known battle with the Indians in the nation's history took place at the Little Bighorn River on June 25, 1876. Civil War hero George Armstrong Custer led his troops into a massacre. He and his entire force were killed, and the exact course of events still remains a mystery. One horse was the lone survivor of the Custer forces.

> So They Say
> "Every man kept fighting to the last. There were no cowards on either side....Long Hair was not scalped. He was a great chief. My people did not want his scalp."
> Chief Sitting Bull

• Another Indian battle with an entirely different ending occurred on August 7, 1877. Brave and brilliant Chief Joseph of the Nez Perce tribe surrendered after the Battle of Big Hole Prairie.

> So They Say
> "Our chiefs are dead; the little children are freezing. My people have no blankets, no food. From where the sun now stands, I will fight no more, forever."
> Chief Joseph

• The Northern Pacific Railroad arrived on July 5, 1881.

• Statehood was achieved on Nov. 8, 1889.

• The U.S. and Canada cooperated to create the International Peace Park in 1932, with Glacier National Park as the U.S. portion.

• On August 17, 1959, a severe earthquake caused damage over a wide area. A mountainside collapsed across the Madison River, creating Earthquake Lake.

• The state adopted a new constitution in 1978.

• In 1985 Glacier National Park celebrated its 75th anniversary.

That's Interesting

• On the present site of Helena, a little party of gold miners agreed that they had reached their "last chance" to find wealth. Then they made a strike on what is now the city's main street, Last Chance Gulch.

• Montana's territorial governor, Francis Meagher, a hero of the Civil War, boarded a Missouri River steamboat at Fort Benton, went to his stateroom and was never seen again.

• Montana Indians believed that stealing a horse was a man's best way to show his bravery.

• Early visitors to Montana prairies noted the many mounds of earth covered with flowers and were startled to learn that these were the sod houses of the settlers.

• In a house near Frenchtown four brothers were born, but each was born in a different territory. Before statehood Montana had been a part of five territories.

• Montana shepherds spent many lonely hours piling rocks into high stacks called cairns. Some can still be seen.

Notable Natives

Gary Cooper (Helena, 1901-1961), actor. **Chet Huntley** (Cardwell, 1911-1974), news commentator. **Myrna Loy** (Radersburg, 1911-), actress. **Jeannette Rankin** (near Missoula, 1880-1973), suffragist, first woman member of Congress. **Sacagawea** (either western Montana or eastern Idaho, 1787?-1812?), Indian guide for Lewis and Clark.

General

Admitted to statehood: Nov. 8, 1889
Origin of name: Latin or Spanish for "mountainous"
Capital: Helena, settled 1864
Nickname: Treasure State
Motto: *"Oro y Plata"* ("Gold and Silver")
Bird: Western meadowlark

Flower: bitterroot
Song: "Montana"
Stones: sapphire and agate
Tree: ponderosa pine

THE LAND

Area: 147,046 sq. mi., 4th
Land: 145,556 sq. mi., 4th
Water: 1,490 sq. mi., 26th
Topography: Rocky Mtns. in W third of the state, E two-thirds gently rolling northern Great Plains
Number of counties: 56
Geographic center: Fergus, 11 mi. W of Lewiston
Length: 630 mi.
Width: 280 mi.
Highest point: 12,799 ft. (Granite Peak), 10th
Lowest point: 1,800 ft. (Kootenal River), 47th
Mean elevation: 3,400 ft., 8th

CLIMATE AND ENVIRONMENT

Temp., highest: 117 deg. on July 5, 1937, at Medicine Lake; lowest: -7 deg. on Jan. 20, 1954, at Rogers Pass
Fresh water withdrawn, per capita, per day: 10,500 gal., 3rd
Endangered species: mammals, 2—black-footed ferret, Northern Rocky Mountain gray wolf; birds, 3—whooping crane, American peregrine falcon, least tern; reptiles, none; amphibians, none; fishes, 1; invertebrates, none; plants, none

MAJOR CITIES, POPULATION PERCENTAGE INCREASE (1980-90)

Billings, 81,151—21.46%
Butte, 33,336— -10.40%
Great Falls, 55,097— -3.14%
Helena, 24,569—2.64%
Missoula, 42,918—28.69%

THE PEOPLE

Population: 799,065, 44th
Percent change (1980-90): 1.55%, 37th
Per sq. mi: 5.43, 49th
Percent in metro. area: 23.90%, 49th
Percent foreign born: 1.7%, 37th
White: 741,111,—92.75%, 13th
Black: 2,381—0.30%, 51st
Native American: 47,679—5.97%, 5th
Asian, Pacific Isle: 4,259—0.53%, 46th
Other races: 3,635—0.45%, 38th
Hispanic origin: 12,174—1.52%, 34th
Percent over 5 yrs. speaking language other than English at home: 5.0%, 37th
Percent males: 49.53%, 10th
Percent females: 50.47%, 42nd
Percent never married: 22.3%, 46th
Marriages per 1,000 (1989): 8.3, 36th
Divorces per 1,000 (1989): 5.1, 16th
Median age: 33.8
Under 5 years: 59,257—7.42%, 25th
Under 18 years: 222,104—27.80%, 10th
65 years & older: 106,497—13.33%, 17th
Percent increase among the elderly: 25.9%, 20th

OF VITAL IMPORTANCE

Live births per 1,000 pop.: 14.2, 45th
Infant mortality rate per 1,000 births (1988): 8.7, 37th
Average lifetime (1979-81): 73.93, 24th
Deaths per 100,000 pop. (1988): 842.4, 33rd
Causes of death per 100,000 pop. (1988):
Diseases of heart: 257.3, 40th
Malignant neoplasms: 191.7, 33rd
Cerebrovascular diseases: 57, 33rd
Accidents & adverse effects: 46.7, 14th
Chronic obstructive pulmonary diseases: 47.6, 3rd
Suicide: 18, 5th
HIV infection: 0.6, 49th
Other: 75.8, 26th

KEEPING WELL

Non-federal physicians per 100,000 pop.: 182, 38th
Dentists per 100,000 (1990-91): 71, 20th
Nurses per 100,000 (1989): 656, 31st
Hospitals per 100,000: 7.8, 3rd
Admissions per 100,000: 14,270, 19th
Beds per 100,000: 623.73, 8th
Occupancy rate: 61.2%, 41st
Semiprivate room charges per day: $318, 18th
Average stay: 18.7, 1st
Notifiable diseases per 100,000:
AIDS: 2.1, 48th
Gonorrhea: 30.8, 44th

Measles: 0.1, 49th
Syphillis: 1.3, 48th
Tuberculosis (TB): 3.3, 37th
Per capita spending on mental health programs (1987): $35.63, 28th
Pop. without health insur. (1991): 12.7%, 27th

Households by Type

Total households: 306,163
Percent change (1980-90): 7.80%, 36th
Family households: 211,666
Percent of total: 69.14%, 36th
Nonfamily households: 94,497
Percent of total: 30.86%, 16th
Persons per household: 2.53, 42nd
Pop. living in group quarters: 23,747
Percent of pop.: 2.97%, 20th

Living Quarters

Total housing units: 361,155
Persons per unit: 2.21, 45th
Occupied housing units: 306,163
Percent of total units: 84.77%, 43rd
Persons per unit: 2.47, 42nd
Percent of units with over 1 person per room: 2.90%, 27th
Owner-occupied units: 205,899
Percent of total units: 57.01%, 35th
Percent of occupied units: 67.25%, 26th
Persons per unit: 2.65, 42nd
Median value: $56,600, 39th
Renter-occupied units: 100,264
Percent of total units: 27.76%, 34th
Percent of occupied units: 32.75%, 26th
Persons per unit: 2.28, 35th
Median contract rent: $251, 44th
Rental vacancy rate: 9.6%, 16th
Mobile home, trailer & other as a % of occupied housing units: 19.13%, 5th

Crime Index per 100,000

Total: 4,502, 36th
Violent: 159, 47th
Murder and nonnegligent manslaughter: 5, 33rd
Aggravated assault: 7,416, 26th
Robbery: 22, 46th
Rape: 24, 46th
Property: 4,343, 31st
Burglary: 709, 47th
Larceny, theft: 3,391, 14th
Motor vehicle theft: 243, 39th
Drug abuse arrests: 129, 40th

Teaching and Learning

Literacy (1987): 92%, 4th
Pop. 3 and over enrolled in school: 215,759
Percent of pop.: 28.2%, 15th
Public elementary & secondary schools:
Total enrollment: 152,000
Avg. class size (1987): 20, 41st
Teachers: 9,600
Percent of pop.: 1.20%, 5th
Teachers' avg. salary: $25,100, 40th
Spending per capita: $801, 26th
Spending per pupil in avg. daily attendance: $4,147, 34th
Percent of graduates taking SAT: 22%, 28th
Combined SAT scores: 982, 19th
Percent of pop. over 25 completing:
High school: 81.0%, 11th
College degree/s: 19.8%, 25th
Higher educa., institutions: 19
Per 100,000 pop.: 1.8, 3rd
Enroll: 35,876
Percent of pop.: 4.49%, 46th
Public: 31,865
Percent of enroll.: 88.82%, 10th
Private 4,011
Percent of enroll.: 11.18%, 42nd
White non-Hispanic: 235,231
Percent of enroll.: 92.69%, 6th
Black non-Hispanic: 4,143
Percent of enroll.: 1.63%, 41st
Hispanic: 1,936
Percent of enroll.: 0.76%, 40th
Asian/Pacific Islander: 4,948
Percent of enroll.: 1.95%, 21st
Amer. Indian/AK native: 2,002
Percent of enroll.: 0.79%, 18th
Nonresident alien: 5,529
Percent of enroll.: 2.18%, 27th
Female: 18,974
Percent of enroll.: 52.89%, 45th
Tuition, state university ('90-'91): $1,553, 33rd

Public library systems: 82
Books & serial vol. per capita: 3.01, 20th
Govt. expend. per capita: $11.71, 38th
State govt.: $2.97, 18th
Local govts.: $8.74, 36th

LAW ENFORCEMENT, COURTS, AND PRISONS

Police protection expend.: $64,348,000
Per capita: $80.54, 42nd
Judicial & legal expend.: $32,564,000
Per capita: $40.76, 35th
Corrections expend.: $34,227,000
Per capita: $42.84, 48th
Police per 10,000 pop. (1990-91): 16.3, 39th
Prisoners (state & fed.) sentenced to over 1 yr., per 100,000 pop.: 174
Percent change (1989-90): 6.10%, 33rd
Death penalty: yes, by hanging or lethal injection
Under sentence of death: 10, 27th
Executed (1989): none

RELIGION, NUMBER AND PERCENT OF POPULATION

Agnostic: 3,462—0.60%, 19th
Buddhist: NA
Christian: 490,417—85.00%, 33rd
Hindu: NA
Jewish: NA
Moslem: NA
Unitarian: 1,731—0.30%, 15th
Other: 6,924—1.20%, 29th
None: 58,850—10.20%, 10th
Refused to answer: 15,578—2.70%, 16th

MAKING A LIVING

Personal income per capita (1989): $11,213, 43rd
Percent increase (1979-'89) (constant 1989 dollars): 1.5%, 49th
Average income per family: $33,358, 47th
Percent of pop. below poverty level: 16.1%, 11th
Percent 65 and over: 12.5%, 20th
Cost of living, selected cities
1st qtr., 1991 (U. S. Standard=100)
Bozeman 97.4

ECONOMY

Civilian labor force : 402,000
Percent of tot. pop.: 50.31%, 27th
Percent 65 and over: 3.98%, 5th
Percent females: 45.27%, 30th
Percent job growth (1980-90): 9.42%, 44th
Major employer industries:
Agriculture: 34,489—9.10%, 5th
Construction: 14,023—3.70%, 42nd
Finance, insurance & real estate: 14,023—3.70%, 50th
Government: 76,937—20.30%, 7th
Manufacturing: 23,877—6.30%, 45th
Mining: 5,537—1.6%, 10th
Service: 71,252—18.80%, 35th
Trade: 73,905—19.50%, 16th
Transportation, communication, & public utilities: 22,740—6.00%, 14th
Wholesale/retail: 81,084—23.1%, 2nd
Unemployment rate: 5.72%, 18th
Male: 3.48%, 7th
Female: 2.49%, 21st
Total businesses (1991): 43,961
New business incorp's. (1991): 1,572
Percent of total businesses: 3.58%, 47th
Business failures (1991): 159
Percent of total businesses: 0.36%, 49th
Agriculture farm income
Marketing (1991): $1,531,169,000, 33rd
Net per operation: $20,866, 25th
Net per acre: $9, 46th
Leading products: cattle, wheat, barley, hay
Av. value land & build. per acre: $243, 45th
Percent increase (1980-90): 3.40%, 25th
Govt. payments: $320,133,000, 9th
Construction, value of all: $282,000,000
Per capita: $352.91, 42nd
Percent change 1989-90: 84.31%, 2nd
Manufactures:
Value added: $1,190,000,000
Per capita: $1,489.24, 48th
Value of shipments: $4,040,000,000
Per capita: $5,055.91, 45th
Leading products: food products, wood and paper products, primary metals, printing and publishing, petroleum & coal products
Mining, min. prod., value (1987): $1,432,000,000, 22nd
Leading products: petroleum, coal, nat. gas

Retail sales: $5,333,000,000, 45th
Per household: $17,478, 39th
Percent increase (1987-90): 24.6%, 7th
Service indust., value (1987): $2,459,000,000, 47th
Per capita: $3,077.35, 42nd
Tourism indus., value (1989): $1,179,000,000, 42nd
Foreign exports value: $229,000,000, 49th
Per capita: $286.58, 49th
Patents per 1,000 pop.: 11.1, 11th

Travel and Transportation

Motor vehicle registrations: 783,153
Per 1,000 pop.: 980, 5th
Motorcycle registrations: 21,994
Per 1,000 pop.: 27, 12th
Licensed drivers per 1,000 driving age pop.: 997, 2nd
Deaths from motor vehicle accidents per 100,000 pop.: 26.5, 8th
Public roads & streets
Total mileage: 71,387, 28th
Rural mileage: 69,116, 24th
Urban mileage: 2,271, 43rd
Interstate mileage: 1,191, 10th
Annual vehicle-miles of travel per person: 10,427, 6th
Mean travel time for workers 16 + who work away from home: 14.8 min., 49th

Government

Registered voters (1988): 505,541
Percent of voting age pop.: 86.27%, 6th
Voter turnout (1988): 365,674
Percent of registered voters: 72.33%, 22nd
Percent of voting age pop.: 62.40%, 2nd
State legislators, total (1992): 150, 20th
Women members (1992): 31
Percent of legislature: 20.7%, 19th
Dominant party (1992): Democrats
U. S. Congress, House members (1993): 1
Increase 1983-93: -1
Revenues:
State govt.: $2,224,521,000
Per capita: $2,783.90, 16th
State & local govt.: $3,268,286,000
Per capita: $4,090.14, 20th
Indebtedness:
State govt.: $1,395,842,000
Per capita: $1,746.84, 15th
State & local govt.: $2,554,000,000
Per capita: $3,196.24, 29th

Laws and Regulations

Legal driving age: 18
Marriage age without parental consent: 18
Divorce residence requirement: 90 days

Attractions

Major opera companies (1989): 1, 30th
Per 1 million pop.: 1.24, 7th
Major symphony orchestras (1989): 7, 32nd
Per 1 million pop.: 8.65, 3rd
State appropriations for state arts agencies per capita: $0.98, 18th
State Fair in late July to early Aug. at Great Falls

Sports and Competition

NCAA sports teams, 3: Eastern Montana College Yellowjackets, Montana State Univ. Bobcats, Univ. of Montana Grizzlies
Professional teams, 4:
Baseball, 4—Butte Copper Kings (Pioneer League, Rookie Class), Alumni Coliseum; Billings Mustangs (Pioneer League, Rookie Class), Cobb Field; Helena Brewers (Pioneer League, Rookie Class), Kindrick Legion Field; Great Falls Dodgers (Pioneer League, Rookie Class), Legon Park

NEBRASKA

"For more than a century the wide Platte Valley has been the highroad to the American West. But Nebraska is more than a mere pathway...a land where the West that was wild continues to mingle with evidences of the most modern civilization...great cattle herds, nuclear reactors power modern industry...superhighways...replacing the ruts of the Oregon trail....Up-to-date cities have grown from the tracks of the Mormon wagons...some of the finest museums, music and other cultural attractions anywhere.

Frank B. Morrison

Once referred to as part of "the great American desert," Nebraska was changed into a land of vast farms through the spirit and determination of its early settlers. In the west are wheat fields as far as the eye can see. In the north-central region, huge herds of beef cattle graze on enormous ranches. In the east, corn, grain, sorghum, and other crops are grown. Nebraska is the only state to bear a nickname based on a college football team—the University of Nebraska Cornhuskers. Football at the university is so popular with the Nebraskans that on Saturdays when there is a home game, the stadium in Lincoln becomes "the third largest city in the state," after Omaha and Lincoln.

SUPERLATIVES

• Nation's first Homestead grant claimed by a Nebraskan.

• Capitol ranked among world's ten greatest buildings.

• First in U.S. alfalfa and other hays.

• World's largest concentration of meat packing and processing.

• Home of the world's largest health and accident insurance company, and the headquarters for more than 35 others.

MOMENTS IN HISTORY

• In 1699 a Navajo group returned to the Spanish Southwest, probably from the South Platte valley, and they carried trophies indicating that there were French settlers there.

• In an effort to drive the French out, in 1720 Pedro de Villasur attacked them and was killed somewhere along the Platte, perhaps at the site of North Platte or Columbus.

• The Platte is said to have been given its present name by the French brothers Pierre and Paul Mallet during their visit of 1739.

• After the region came to the United States in 1803 as part of the Louisiana Purchase, the explorers Lewis and Clark reached the mouth of the Platte on July 21, 1804.

• Lewis and Clark made their last camp in Nebraska on September 7, 1804, and continued up the Missouri River. They returned back down the river in 1806.

> **So They Say**
>
> "Arrived at the mouth of the great Platte River....passing through different channels, none of them more than five or six feet deep....spreds verry wide and ...cannot be navigated with Boats or Perogues. The Indians pass this river in Skin Boats which is flat and will not turn over."
>
> Meriwether Lewis

• The American fur trader Manuel Lisa followed the explorers and set up a fur trading operation in 1807.

• Zebulon Pike assembled 400 Indians along the Republican River, and in a ceremony of lowering the Spanish flag made them swear allegiance to the United States.

• Bellevue was founded in 1823 by Peter Sarpy as an American Fur Company post, and it proved to be the first permanent European settlement in present-day Nebraska.

• On a visit to the Oto Indian village near Papillion in 1836, the missionary Father Pierre Jean de Smet was entertained at a meal "shining with grease, a stew of buffalo tongue floating in a gravy of bear fat, thickened with wild sweet potato flour." Surprisingly, he liked it.

• Nebraska soon became a highway to the West, and more than 6,000 Mormon faithful crossed the Nebraska plains in the winter of 1846-1847 on their way to the "promised land" of Utah.

• The next major crossing of the state came with the almost endless procession of 49ers hurrying to the California gold fields, beginning in 1849.

So They Say

"The onlookers witnessed sights ranging from the laughable to the alarming. In one place six men were assisted ashore by hanging to the tail of a mule, with a rider on him....The line of wagons stretched for two miles...busy as it ordinarily does in St. Louis...."

Emigrant's journal of a 49er party crossing the Platte River.

• During the Civil War, Nebraska had a population of only about 30,000. Of these 3,307 served in the war.

• In 1862, Daniel Freeman of Beatrice was the nation's first recipient of land granted under the unique Homestead Act.

• President Andrew Johnson vetoed the Nebraska statehood bill of 1866, but Congress overrode his veto, and Nebraska became a state on March 1, 1867.

• On May 6, 1877, famed Chief Crazy Horse surrendered with 1,000 of his followers, near Camp Robinson. On September 7, 1877, he was killed because he was said to have resisted his captors.

• President William McKinley opened the Mississippi International Exposition at Omaha in 1898.

• During World War I, 47,801 Nebraskans were called into service, and 1,000 lost their lives.

• In 1934 Nebraska became unique among the states when it installed its unicameral (one house) legislature, consisting only of a senate.

• Of the 120,000 Nebraskans in World War II service, 3,830 lost their lives.

Notable Natives

Fred Astaire (Omaha, 1899-1987), dancer/actor. **Marlon Brando** (Omaha, 1924-), actor. **Henry Fonda** (Grand Island, 1905-1982), actor. **Gerald Ford** (Omaha, 1913-), U.S. president. **Howard Hanson** (Wahoo, 1896-1981), composer/conductor. **Harold Lloyd** (Burchard, 1894-1971), actor/motion picture producer. **Malcolm X** (Omaha, 1925-1965), religious leader/reformer. **Roscoe Pound** (Lincoln, 1870-1964), educator/legal scholar. **Red Cloud** (N.Cen. NE, 1822-1909), Indian leader.

General

Admitted to statehood: March 1, 1867
Origin of name: From Omaha or Otos Indian word meaning "broad water" or "flat river," describing the Platte River
Capital: Lincoln, settled 1856
Nicknames: Cornhusker State and Tree Planters State
Motto: "Equality Before the Law"
Bird: Western meadowlark
Flower: goldenrod
Fossil: mammoth
Gemstone: blue agate
Grass: little blue stem
Insect: honeybee
Rock: prairie agate
Song: "Beautiful Nebraska"
Tree: cottonwood

THE LAND

Area: 77,358 sq. mi., 16th
Land: 76,878 sq. mi., 15th
Water: 481 sq. mi., 42nd
Topography: till plains of the central lowland in the E third rising to the Great Plains and hill country of the N central and NW
Number of counties: 93
Geographic center: Custer, 10 mi. NW of Broken Bow
Length: 430 mi.
Width: 210 mi.
Highest point: 5,426 ft. (Johnson Twp., Kimball County), 20th
Lowest point: 480 ft. (Missouri River), 38th
Mean elevation: 2,600 ft., 12th

CLIMATE AND ENVIRONMENT

Temp., highest: 118 deg. on July 24, 1936, at Minden; lowest: -47 deg. on Feb. 12, 1899, at Camp Clarke
Fresh water withdrawn, per capita, per day: 6,250 gal., 4th
Endangered species: mammals, none; birds, 4—whooping crane, Eskimo curlew, American peregrine falcon, least tern; reptiles, none; amphibians, none; fishes, 1; invertebrates, 2; plants, 1

MAJOR CITIES, POPULATION PERCENTAGE INCREASE (1980-90)

Bellevue, 30,982—42.03%
Grand Island, 39,386—18.70%
Kearney, 24,396—15.30%
Lincoln, 191,972—11.66%
Omaha, 335,795—6.96%

THE PEOPLE

Population: 1,578,385, 36th
  Percent change (1980-90): 0.54%, 41st
  Per sq. mi: 20.40, 42nd
  Percent in metro. area: 48.53%, 37th
  Percent foreign born: 1.8%, 36th
White: 1,480,558—93.80%, 10th
Black: 57,404—3.64%, 34th
Native American: 12,410—0.79%, 20th
Asian, Pacific Isle: 12,422—0.79%, 37th
Other races: 15,591—0.99%, 26th
Hispanic origin: 36,969—2.34%, 27th
Percent over 5 yrs. speaking language other than English at home: 4.8%, 39th
Percent males: 48.75%, 23rd
Percent females: 51.25%, 29th
Percent never married: 24.4%, 33rd
Marriages per 1,000 (1989): 7.9, 43rd
Divorces per 1,000 (1989): 3.9, 37th
Median age: 33
Under 5 years: 119,606—7.58%, 18th
Under 18 years: 429,012—27.18%, 12th
65 years & older: 223,068—14.13%, 9th
Percent increase among the elderly: 8.5%, 50th

OF VITAL IMPORTANCE

Live births per 1,000 pop.: 15.0, 40th
Infant mortality rate per 1,000 births (1988): 9.0, 29th
Average lifetime (1979-81): 75.49, 5th
Deaths per 100,000 pop. (1988): 928.3, 17th
Causes of death per 100,000 pop. (1988):
  Diseases of heart: 321.4, 23rd
  Malignant neoplasms: 197.6, 26th
  Cerebrovascular diseases: 72.3, 9th
  Accidents & adverse effects: 38.5, 31st
  Chronic obstructive pulmonary diseases: 36.4, 20th
  Suicide: 10.4, 43rd
  HIV infection: 1.7, 38th
  Other: 87.1, 3rd

KEEPING WELL

Non-federal physicians per 100,000 pop.: 187, 35th
Dentists per 100,000 (1990-91): 73, 17th
Nurses per 100,000 (1989): 757, 15th
Hospitals per 100,000: 6.5, 5th
  Admissions per 100,000: 13,452, 28th
  Beds per 100,000: 669.10, 4th
  Occupancy rate: 61.2%, 42nd
  Semiprivate room charges per day: $209, 45th
  Average stay: 9.7, 10th
Notifiable diseases per 100,000:
  AIDS: 3.7, 44th
  Gonorrhea: 114.2, 33rd
  Measles: 6.5, 15th
  Syphillis: 2.3, 46th

Tuberculosis (TB): 1.5, 49th
Per capita spending on mental health programs (1987): $28.41, 39th
Pop. without health insur. (1991): 8.2%, 46th

Households by Type

Total households: 602,363
Percent change (1980-90): 5.49%, 45th
Family households: 415,427
Percent of total: 68.97%, 38th
Nonfamily households: 186,936
Percent of total: 31.03%, 14th
Persons per household: 2.54, 39th
Pop. living in group quarters: 47,553
Percent of pop.: 3.01%, 18th

Living Quarters

Total housing units: 660,621
Persons per unit: 2.39, 28th
Occupied housing units: 602,363
Percent of total units: 91.18%, 15th
Persons per unit: 2.48, 38th
Percent of units with over 1 person per room: 1.75%, 47th
Owner-occupied units: 400,394
Percent of total units: 60.61%, 21st
Percent of occupied units: 66.47%, 30th
Persons per unit: 2.68, 36th
Median value: $50,400, 45th
Renter-occupied units: 201,969
Percent of total units: 30.57%, 19th
Percent of occupied units: 33.53%, 23rd
Persons per unit: 2.27, 36th
Median contract rent: $282, 35th
Rental vacancy rate: 7.7%, 34th
Mobile home, trailer & other as a % of occupied housing units: 6.98%, 37th

Crime Index per 100,000

Total: 4,213, 40th
Violent: 330, 37th
Murder and nonnegligent manslaughter: 3, 43rd
Aggravated assault: 7,578, 19th
Robbery: 51, 41st
Rape: 30, 36th
Property: 3,883, 41st
Burglary: 724, 46th
Larceny, theft: 2,981, 27th
Motor vehicle theft: 178, 44th
Drug abuse arrests: 253, 26th

Teaching and Learning

Literacy (1987): 91%, 9th
Pop. 3 and over enrolled in school: 433,409
Percent of pop.: 28.7%, 12th
Public elementary & secondary schools:
Total enrollment: 271,000
Avg. class size (1987): 20, 41st
Teachers: 18,200
Percent of pop.: 1.15%, 11th
Teachers' avg. salary: $25,100, 40th
Spending per capita: $652, 43rd
Spending per pupil in avg. daily attendance: $3,874, 38th
Percent of graduates taking SAT: 10%, 41st
Combined SAT scores: 1024, 6th
Percent of pop. over 25 completing:
High school: 81.8%, 8th
College degree/s: 18.9%, 27th
Higher educa., institutions: 34
Per 100,000 pop.: 1.1, 8th
Enroll: 112,831
Percent of pop.: 7.15%, 4th
Public: 94,614
Percent of enroll.: 83.85%, 23rd
Private 18,217
Percent of enroll.: 16.15%, 29th
White non-Hispanic: 271,096
Percent of enroll.: 90.43%, 14th
Black non-Hispanic: 10,667
Percent of enroll.: 3.56%, 32nd
Hispanic: 4,692
Percent of enroll.: 1.57%, 26th
Asian/Pacific Islander: 4,991
Percent of enroll.: 1.66%, 27th
Amer. Indian/AK native: 2,050
Percent of enroll.: 0.68%, 20th
Nonresident alien: 6,278
Percent of enroll.: 2.09%, 28th
Female: 61,991
Percent of enroll.: 54.94%, 27th
Tuition, state university ('90-'91): $1,592, 30th
Public library systems: 264

Books & serial vol. per capita: 3.75, 9th
Govt. expend. per capita: $12.59, 31st
State govt.: $2.19, 34th
Local govts.: $10.40, 32nd

Law Enforcement, Courts, and Prisons

Police protection expend.: $127,663,000
Per capita: $80.90, 41st
Judicial & legal expend.: $53,831,000
Per capita: $34.11, 41st
Corrections expend.: $83,076,000
Per capita: $52.65, 40th
Police per 10,000 pop. (1990-91): 18.1, 33rd
Prisoners (state & fed.) sentenced to over 1 yr., per 100,000 pop.: 140
Percent change (1989-90): 0.35%, 45th
Death penalty: yes, by electrocution
Under sentence of death: 13, 26th
Executed (1989): none

Religion, Number and Percent of Population

Agnostic: 1,149—0.10%, 47th
Buddhist: 1,149—0.10%, 17th
Christian: 1,016,046—88.40%, 18th
Hindu: 2,299—0.20%, 3rd
Jewish: 5,747—0.50%, 27th
Moslem: NA
Unitarian: 5,747—0.50%, 6th
Other: 17,241—1.50%, 18th
None: 80,456—7.00%, 23rd
Refused to answer: 19,539—1.70%, 35th

Making a Living

Personal income per capita (1989): $12,452, 34th
Percent increase (1979-'89) (constant 1989 dollars): 7.2%, 40th
Average income per family: $37,748, 35th
Percent of pop. below poverty level: 11.1%, 34th
Percent 65 and over: 12.2%, 22nd
Cost of living, selected cities
1st qtr., 1991 (U. S. Standard=100)

Hastings	85.6
Omaha	90.4
Lincoln	90.5

Economy

Civilian labor force : 839,000
Percent of tot. pop.: 53.16%, 9th
Percent 65 and over: 4.05%, 4th
Percent females: 46.36%, 13th
Percent job growth (1980-90): 12.30%, 41st
Major employer industries:
Agriculture: 77,174—9.40%, 4th
Construction: 29,556—3.60%, 44th
Finance, insurance & real estate: 50,902—6.20%, 16th
Government: 132,181—16.10%, 22nd
Manufacturing: 107,551—13.10%, 37th
Mining: 2,095—0.3%, 30th
Service: 155,169—18.90%, 33rd
Trade: 146,959—17.90%, 34th
Transportation, communication, & public utilities: 44,334—5.40%, 22nd
Wholesale/retail: 173,905—22.5%, 6th
Unemployment rate: 2.15%, 51st
Male: 1.07%, 51st
Female: 1.07%, 51st
Total businesses (1991): 71,814
New business incorp's. (1991): 3,093
Percent of total businesses: 4.31%, 41st
Business failures (1991): 535
Percent of total businesses: 0.74%, 33rd
Agriculture farm income
Marketing (1991): $8,821,328,000, 4th
Net per operation: $34,909, 10th
Net per acre: $42, 32nd
Leading products: cattle, corn, hogs, soybeans
Av. value land & build. per acre: $562, 36th
Percent increase (1980-90): -11.50%, 34th
Govt. payments: $490,659,000, 5th
Construction, value of all: $739,000,000
Per capita: $468.20, 36th
Percent change 1989-90: 13.00%, 12th
Manufactures:
Value added: $7,450,000,000
Per capita: $4,720.01, 33rd
Value of shipments: $20,370,000,000
Per capita: $12,905.60, 18th
Leading products: foods, machinery, electric and electronic equipment, primary and fabricated metal products, transportation

equipment, instruments & related products

Mining, min. prod., value (1987): $164,000,000, 42nd

Leading products: petroleum, cement, stone

Retail sales: $10,313,000,000, 38th

Per household: $17,113, 44th

Percent increase (1987-90): 18.4%, 17th

Service indust., value (1987): $5,587,000,000, 38th

Per capita: $3,539.69, 31st

Tourism indus., value (1989): $1,509,000,000, 39th

Foreign exports value: $693,000,000, 42nd

Per capita: $439.06, 45th

Patents per 1,000 pop.: 10.7, 14th

TRAVEL AND TRANSPORTATION

Motor vehicle registrations: 1,383,846

Per 1,000 pop.: 876, 10th

Motorcycle registrations: 22,105

Per 1,000 pop.: 14, 32nd

Licensed drivers per 1,000 driving age pop.: 902, 23rd

Deaths from motor vehicle accidents per 100,000 pop.: 16.6, 34th

Public roads & streets

Total mileage: 92,403, 18th

Rural mileage: 87,451, 13th

Urban mileage: 4,952, 36th

Interstate mileage: 481, 41st

Annual vehicle-miles of travel per person: 8,843, 31st

Mean travel time for workers 16 + who work away from home: 15.8 min., 47th

GOVERNMENT

Registered voters (1988): 898,959

Percent of voting age pop.: 77.03%, 15th

Voter turnout (1988): 661,465

Percent of registered voters: 73.58%, 19th

Percent of voting age pop.: 56.68%, 14th

State legislators, total (1992): 49, 50th

Women members (1992): 9

Percent of legislature: 18.4%, 24th

Dominant party (1992): NA

U. S. Congress, House members (1993): 3

Increase 1983-93: 0

Revenues:

State govt.: $3,073,420,000

Per capita: $1,947.19, 44th

State & local govt.: $7,028,444,000

Per capita: $4,452.93, 11th

Indebtedness:

State govt.: $1,361,056,000

Per capita: $862.31, 37th

State & local govt.: $6,190,000,000

Per capita: $3,921.73, 18th

LAWS AND REGULATIONS

Legal driving age: 16

Marriage age without parental consent: 18

Divorce residence requirement: 1 yr., qualification—check local statutes

ATTRACTIONS

Major opera companies (1989): 1, 30th

Per 1 million pop.: 0.62, 27th

Major symphony orchestras (1989): 4, 42nd

Per 1 million pop.: 2.48, 43rd

State appropriations for state arts agencies per capita: $0.65, 28th

State Fair Aug. 30-Sept. 8 at Lincoln

SPORTS AND COMPETITION

NCAA sports teams, 5: Creighton Univ. Bluejays, Nebraska Wesleyan Univ. Plainsmen, Univ. of Nebraska Cornhuskers, Univ. of Nebraska at Omaha Mavericks, Wayne State College Wildcats

Professional teams, 2:

Baseball, 1—Omaha Royals (American Association, Class AAA), Rosenblatt Stadium

Basketball, 1—Omaha Racers (Continental Basketball Association), Ak-Sar-Ben Coliseum

NEVADA

"I had previously seen some beautiful valleys, but I place none of these ahead of Carson."

Horace Greeley (1859)

Every year, Nevada has enough tourists coming to the state to outnumber the population of several states. Some come only for the gambling—it is home to the world's most popular gambling and entertainment center—but many others come for the vast tracts of beautiful deserts, plains, and mountains. Nevada is a cattle- and sheep-raising state, and most of the grains grown there are used to feed livestock. Hoover Dam, on the Colorado River, created Lake Mead, one of the world's largest manmade lakes. All of this has come from the desert lands where no European was known until 1826.

Superlatives

- Two world-famed entertainment centers.
- Kept the Union solvent in the Civil War.
- Major world supplier of turquoise.
- World center of rare opals.
- World's largest open-pit copper mine.
- First large-scale reclamation program in the United States.
- Claims first use of skis in the United States.

Moments in History

- Father Silvestre Velez de Escalante may have visited the Nevada region in 1775, but records of European exploration do not begin until 1826, with the exploration of Peter Skene Ogden.
- The year 1826 is thought to be the birthdate of Dat-So-La-Lee, the Indian basketmaker, whose artistry is known worldwide.
- Walker Pass and Walker Lake are named for Joseph Walker, who brought an expedition in 1833.
- More complete records on Nevada were made by John C. Fremont, who came to the area in 1843-1844, with his guide, the famed Kit Carson.
- In 1846 the Donner party was blocked by heavy snow in what is now Donner Pass, and only about half of the party of 87 survived to reach California.
- Beginning in 1849, thousands of "49ers" crossed the bleak country, and by fall of 1850 at least 60,000 had passed through in covered wagons, on muleback and horseback, even on foot.
- In 1859 one of the world's richest silver discoveries was made in the region that became known as the Comstock, named for one of the prospectors, and Virginia City sprang up almost overnight.
- In 1862 Samuel Clemens of later fame arrived at Virginia City and took the name Mark Twain while working on the *Territorial Enterprise* poking fun at almost everyone.

> So They Say
>
> "It was ...impossible to print his lectures in full, as the cases had run out of capital I's."
>
> Mark Twain on a local judge

- By 1863 Virginia City had become the second most important city in the West, with luxurious homes, four banks, an opera house, six churches, 110 saloons, and the only elevator between Chicago and the west coast.
- During the Civil War the wealth of Nevada silver was critically important in keeping the North solvent.

> **So They Say**
> "...the gold and silver in the region...has made it possible for the government to maintain sufficient credit to continue this terrible war for the Union...."
> Abraham Lincoln

• On Oct. 31, 1864, at the urging of President Lincoln, Nevada became a state. Only a short 4 yrs. earlier, it had been a wilderness.

• New mineral finds occurred at Eureka in 1864 and Hamilton in 1869, but the wealth of the Comstock dwindled, and by 1880 Virginia City had become a sleepy village.

• In 1869 the transcontinental railroad was completed. In 1873 famed travel writer Isabella Bird left a vivid description of crossing Nevada.

> **So They Say**
> "...I sat for an hour on the rear platform of the rear car to enjoy the wonderful beauty of the sunset and the atmosphere...in the crystalline air. The bright metal track, purpling like all else in the cool distance, was all that linked one with eastern or western civilization."
> Isabella Bird

• The 1897 heavyweight championship boxing bout held at Carson City brought world attention to the state; Bob Fitzsimmons defeated James J. Corbett.

• New mineral booms occurred at Tonopah and Goldfield in 1906; Goldfield soon became a ghost town, but Tonopah continued.

• Nevada attracted little further attention until 1931, when gambling was made legal, laying the foundations for the future reputation of the state.

• The great Hoover Dam was finished in 1936.

• In 1951 the Atomic Energy Commission established the Nevada Proving Ground.

•In the late 1970s Nevada ranchers launched the "Sagebrush Rebellion," in an effort to reduce federal control of ranch lands.

• The census of 1990 revealed Nevada as the state with the largest percentage growth of population.

That's Interesting

• In order to meet a deadline for statehood, the entire constitution of Nevada was sent to Washington by telegram at a cost of $3,400.

• Virginia City was named for James Fenimore, whose nickname was "Old Virginy." He celebrated too much one night, fell and broke a bottle of whisky. Not wishing to waste the liquid he called out, "I baptize thee Virginia Town," and the name stuck.

• Mark Twain offended a local newspaper writer, who challenged him to a duel. The challenger backed out, but not before Twain had been charged with breaking the law and had to flee from Virginia City on his way to fame elsewhere.

• Many of the horses of Virginia City sported multicolored polka dots. Chemicals from the mineral crushing mills where they worked caused the unusual decorations.

• Nevada Senator William Stewart asked to see President Lincoln, who sent a note that he would see him in the morning. The president was assassinated that night and the note probably was Lincoln's last written word.

• The discovery of moccasins a foot and a half long caused archeologists to consider that Nevada might at one time have been inhabited by a race of giants.

Notable Nevadans

Samuel Langhorne "Mark Twain" Clemens (Florida, MO, 1835-1910), humorist/author. **Henry Tompkins Paige Comstock** (Trenton, Canada, 1820-1870), trapper/prospector. **Dat-So-La-Lee** (Washoe tribal lands, NV, 1829?-1925), artist/weaver. **James Graham Fair** (Belfast, Ireland, 1831-1894), mining leader/U.S. senator. **George Hearst** (Sullivan, MO, 1820-1891), businessman/public official. **John William Mackay** (Ireland, 1831-1902), mining and business leader. **William Morris Stewart** (Galen, NY, 1827-1909) lawyer/public official. **James Warren Nye** (DeRuyter, NY, 1814-1876), public official. **Sarah**

Winnemucca (Humboldt Lake, NV, c 1844-1891), Indian guide/author.

General

Admitted to statehood: Oct. 31, 1864
Origin of name: Spanish, meaning snow-clad.
Capital: Carson City
Nicknames: Silver State and Sagebrush State, Battle Born State
Motto: "All for Our Country"
Bird: mountain bluebird
Flower: sagebrush
Song: "Home Means Nevada"
Tree: single-leaf pinon

The Land

Area: 110,567 sq. mi., 7th
Land: 109,806 sq. mi., 7th
Water: 761 sq. mi., 35th.
Topography: rugged N-S mountain ranges; S area is within the Mojave Desert with the Colorado River Canyon
Number of counties: 16
Geographic center: Lander, 26 mi. SE of Austin
Length: 490 mi.
Width: 320 mi.
Highest point: 13,140 ft. (Boundary Peak), 9th
Lowest point: 479 ft. (Colorado River), 37th
Mean elevation: 5,500 ft., 5th

Climate and Environment

Temp., highest: 122 deg. on June 23, 1954, at Overton; lowest: -50 deg. on Jan. 8, 1937, at San Jacinto
Fresh water withdrawn, per capita, per day: 3,860 gal., 6th
Endangered species: mammals, none; birds, 1—American peregrine falcon; reptiles, none; amphibians, none; fishes, 16; invertebrates, none; plants, 2

Major Cities, Population Percentage Increase (1980-90)

Henderson, 64,942—166.56%
Las Vegas, 258,295—56.85%
Paradise, 124,682—47.00%
Reno, 133,850—32.85%
Sunrise Manor, 95,362—115.97%

The People

Population: 1,201,833, 39th
Percent change (1980-90): 33.39%, 1st
Per sq. mi: 10.87, 46th
Percent in metro. area: 82.87%, 11th
Percent foreign born: 8.7%, 10th
White: 1,012,695—84.26%, 27th
Black: 78,771—6.55%, 27th
Native American: 19,637—1.63%, 10th
Asian, Pacific Isle: 38,127—3.17%, 7th
Other races: 52,603—4.38%, 7th
Hispanic origin: 124,419—10.35%, 8th
Percent over 5 yrs. speaking language other than English at home: 13.2%, 13th
Percent males: 50.91%, 2nd
Percent females: 49.09%, 50th
Percent never married: 23.7%, 39th
Marriages per 1,000 (1989): 106.3, 1st
Divorces per 1,000 (1989): 11.9, 1st
Median age: 33.3
Under 5 years: 92,217—7.67%, 12th
Under 18 years: 296,948—24.71%, 39th
65 years & older: 127,631—10.62%, 44th
Percent increase among the elderly: 94.1%, 1st

Of Vital Importance

Live births per 1,000 pop.: 18.1, 8th
Infant mortality rate per 1,000 births (1988): 8.4, 41st
Average lifetime (1979-81): 72.64, 44th
Deaths per 100,000 pop. (1988): 804.0, 39th
Causes of death per 100,000 pop. (1988):
Diseases of heart: 258.3, 39th
Malignant neoplasms: 193.3, 31st
Cerebrovascular diseases: 39.5, 49th
Accidents & adverse effects: 42.7, 22nd
Chronic obstructive pulmonary diseases: 52.8, 1st
Suicide: 26, 1st
HIV infection: 6.1, 9th
Other: 70.1, 37th

Keeping Well

Non-federal physicians per 100,000 pop.: 160, 47th
Dentists per 100,000 (1990-91): 48, 46th
Nurses per 100,000 (1989): 739, 20th

Hospitals per 100,000: 2.6, 32nd
Admissions per 100,000: 10,783, 49th
Beds per 100,000: 342.64, 49th
Occupancy rate: 61.0%, 43rd
Semiprivate room charges per day: $251, 32nd
Average stay: 6.4, 43rd
Notifiable diseases per 100,000:
AIDS: 15.9, 10th
Gonorrhea: 218.8, 23rd
Measles: 20.0, 3rd
Syphillis: 33.9, 22nd
Tuberculosis (TB): 7.1, 25th
Per capita spending on mental health programs (1987): $27.67, 40th
Pop. without health insur. (1991): 18.7%, 6th

Households by Type

Total households: 466,297
Percent change (1980-90): 53.39%, 1st
Family households: 307,400
Percent of total: 65.92%, 50th
Nonfamily households: 158,897
Percent of total: 34.08%, 2nd
Persons per household: 2.53, 42nd
Pop. living in group quarters: 24,200
Percent of pop.: 2.01%, 49th

Living Quarters

Total housing units: 518,858
Persons per unit: 2.32, 38th
Occupied housing units: 466,297
Percent of total units: 89.87%, 22nd
Persons per unit: 2.51, 29th
Percent of units with over 1 person per room: 6.41%, 9th
Owner-occupied units: 255,388
Percent of total units: 49.22%, 48th
Percent of occupied units: 54.77%, 48th
Persons per unit: 2.67, 38th
Median value: $95,700, 12th
Renter-occupied units: 210,909
Percent of total units: 40.65%, 5th
Percent of occupied units: 45.23%, 5th
Persons per unit: 2.35, 25th
Median contract rent: $445, 9th
Rental vacancy rate: 9.1%, 21st
Mobile home, trailer & other as a % of occupied housing units: 16.22%, 10th

Crime Index per 100,000

Total: 6,064, 12th
Violent: 601, 21st
Murder and nonnegligent Manslaughter: 10, 17th
Aggravated assault: 7,673, 13th
Robbery: 238, 11th
Rape: 62, 5th
Property: 5,463, 12th
Burglary: 1,367, 11th
Larceny, theft: 3,503, 13th
Motor vehicle theft: 593, 17th
Drug abuse arrests: 560, 7th

Teaching and Learning

Literacy (1987): 91%, 9th
Pop. 3 and over enrolled in school: 280,411
Percent of pop.: 24.4%, 50th
Public elementary & secondary schools:
Total enrollment: 194,000
Avg. class size (1987): 26, 3rd
Teachers: 9,200
Percent of pop.: 0.77%, 49th
Teachers' avg. salary: $30,600, 21st
Spending per capita: $878, 14th
Spending per pupil in avg. daily Attendance: $4,387, 30th
Percent of graduates taking SAT: 25%, 27th
Combined SAT scores: 919, 30th
Percent of pop. over 25 completing:
High school: 78.8%, 19th
College degree/s: 15.3%, 47th
Higher educa., institutions: 9
Per 100,000 pop.: 0.5, 43rd
Enroll: 61,728
Percent of pop.: 5.14%, 34th
Public: 61,242
Percent of enroll.: 99.21%, 1st
Private 486
Percent of enroll.: 0.79%, 51st
White non-Hispanic: 541,347
Percent of enroll.: 74.23%, 41st
Black non-Hispanic: 89,218
Percent of enroll.: 12.23%, 12th
Hispanic: 48,932
Percent of enroll.: 6.71%, 8th
Asian/Pacific Islander: 32,353
Percent of enroll.: 4.44%, 5th

Amer. Indian/AK native: 2,245
Percent of enroll.: 0.31%, 32nd
Nonresident alien: 15,151
Percent of enroll.: 2.08%, 29th
Female: 34,768
Percent of enroll.: 56.32%, 10th
Tuition, state university ('90-'91): $1,275, 45th
Public library systems: 26
Books & serial vol. per capita: 1.51, 50th
Govt. expend. per capita: $23.99, 5th
State govt.: $2.58, 24th
Local govts.: $21.41, 5th

Law Enforcement, Courts, and Prisons

Police protection expend.: $195,031,000
Per capita: $162.26, 5th
Judicial & legal expend.: $96,252,000
Per capita: $80.08, 6th
Corrections expend.: $186,530,000
Per capita: $155.18, 4th
Police per 10,000 pop. (1990-91): 22.9, 13th
Prisoners (state & fed.) sentenced to over 1 yr., per 100,000 pop.: 444
Percent change (1989-90): 4.11%, 38th
Death penalty: yes, by lethal injection
Under sentence of death: 45, 16th
Executed (1989): 2

Religion, Number and Percent of Population

Agnostic: 8,144—0.90%, 14th
Buddhist: 3,620—0.40%, 5th
Christian: 773,677—85.50%, 28th
Hindu: NA
Jewish: 8,144—0.90%, 18th
Moslem: NA
Unitarian: 8,144—0.90%, 2nd
Other: 11,764—1.30%, 24th
None: 73,296—8.10%, 14th
Refused to answer: 18,098—2.00%, 30th

Making a Living

Personal income per capita (1989): $15,214, 13th
Percent increase (1979-89) (constant 1989 dollars): 7.4%, 39th
Average income per family: $43,672, 17th
Percent of pop. below poverty level: 10.2%, 41st
Percent 65 and over: 9.6%, 42nd
Cost of living, selected cities
1st qtr., 1991 (U. S. Standard=100)
Carson City 104.0
Reno-Sparks 104.7
Las Vegas 108.2

Economy

Civilian labor force : 626,000
Percent of tot. pop.: 52.09%, 17th
Percent 65 and over: NA
Percent females: 44.41%, 43rd
Percent job growth (1980-90): 53.41%, 1st
Major employer industries:
Agriculture: 7,735—1.30%, 43rd
Construction: 41,650—7.00%, 1st
Finance, insurance & real estate: 32,725—5.50%, 23rd
Government: 71,995—12.10%, 46th
Manufacturing: 29,750—5.00%, 47th
Mining: 13,890–2.3%, 8th
Service: 213,605—35.90%, 1st
Trade: 102,935—17.30%, 46th
Transportation, communication, & public utilities: 34,510—5.80%, 16th
Wholesale/retail: 116,313—19.1%, 48th
Unemployment rate: 4.95%, 36th
Male: 2.72%, 35th
Female: 2.08%, 39th
Total businesses (1991): 38,593
New business incorp's. (1991): 11,030
Percent of total businesses: 28.58%, 2nd
Business failures (1991): 545
Percent of total businesses: 1.41%, 5th
Agriculture farm income
Marketing (1991): $275,836,000, 47th
Net per operation: $27,837, 15th
Net per acre: $8, 48th
Leading products: cattle, hay, dairy products, potatoes
Av. value land & build. per acre: $201, 46th
Percent increase (1980-90): -18.95%, 39th
Govt. payments: $5,679,000, 40th
Construction, value of all: $2,256,000,000
Per capita: $1,877.13, 2nd
Percent change 1989-90: -17.45%, 34th

Manufactures:
Value added: $1,470,000,000
Per capita: $1,223.13, 51st
Value of shipments: $2,925,000,000
Per capita: $2,433.78, 51st
Leading products: gaming devices, chemicals, aerospace products, lawn and garden irrigation equipment, seismic and machinery-monitoring devices
Mining, min. prod., value (1987): $1,469,000,000, 21st
Leading products: gold, silver, diatomite
Retail sales: $9,630,000,000, 40th
Per household: $19,938, 16th
Percent increase (1987-90): 11.9%, 36th
Service indust., value (1987): $11,264,000,000, 27th
Per capita: $9,372.35, 2nd
Tourism indus., value (1989): $9,753,000,000, 6th
Foreign exports value: $394,000,000, 44th
Per capita: $327.83, 47th
Patents per 1,000 pop.: 9.5, 15th

TRAVEL AND TRANSPORTATION

Motor vehicle registrations: 853,444
Per 1,000 pop.: 710, 40th
Motorcycle registrations: 19,257
Per 1,000 pop.: 16, 27th
Licensed drivers per 1,000 driving age pop.: 910, 19th
Deaths from motor vehicle accidents per 100,000 pop.: 28.5, 3rd
Public roads & streets
Total mileage: 45,524, 36th
Rural mileage: 42,440, 35th
Urban mileage: 3,084, 38th
Interstate mileage: 545, 38th
Annual vehicle-miles of travel per person: 8,499, 37th
Mean travel time for workers 16 + who work away from home: 19.8 min., 31st

GOVERNMENT

Registered voters (1988): 444,931
Percent of voting age pop.: 57.04%, 48th
Voter turnout (1988): 350,067
Percent of registered voters: 78.68%, 6th
Percent of voting age pop.: 44.88%, 43rd
State legislators, total (1992): 63, 47th
Women members (1992): 12
Percent of legislature: 19.0%, 20th
Dominant party (1992): Democrats
U. S. Congress, House members (1993): 2
Increase 1983-93: 0
Revenues:
State govt.: $3,265,776,000
Per capita: $2,717.33, 18th
State & local govt.: $5,094,653,000
Per capita: $4,239.07, 17th
Indebtedness:
State govt.: $1,572,645,000
Per capita: $1,308.54, 22nd
State & local govt.: $4,352,000,000
Per capita: $3,621.14, 22nd

LAWS AND REGULATIONS

Legal driving age: 18
Marriage age without parental consent: 18
Divorce residence requirement: 6 wks

ATTRACTIONS

Major opera companies (1989): 1, 30th
Per 1 million pop.: 0.90, 11th
Major symphony orchestras (1989): 0, 51st
Per 1 million pop.: 0.00, NA
State appropriations for state arts agencies Per capita: $0.29, 48th
State Fair in Early Sept. at Reno.

SPORTS AND COMPETITION

NCAA sports teams, 2: Univ. of Nevada Rebels, Univ. of Nevada Wolf Pack.
Professional teams, 2:
Baseball, 2—Las Vegas Stars (Pacific Coast League, Class AAA), Cashman field; Reno Silver Sox (California League, Class A), Moana Stadium

NEW HAMPSHIRE

"Up in the mountains of New Hampshire God Almighty has hung out a sign to show that there he makes men."

Daniel Webster (attrib.)

New Hampshire was one of the leaders on the road to indipendence. The state adopted a constitution six months before the Declaration of Independence was signed. New Hampshire is a year-round tourist attraction. In the summer, visitors flock to the rugged mountains, the blue lakes, the sandy beaches, and the quiet villages. In the fall, the state is a riot of color as the leaves turn. In the winter, skiers arrive from all over the East. New Hampshire might well be nicknamed "The Preparedness State," because it has seemed to be ready for any emergency and quick to respond to opportunities.

SUPERLATIVES

- Windiest place on earth, top of Mt. Washington.
- Alpine zone unique in eastern United States.
- Home of the Concord stagecoach.
- Produced the world's first machine-made watches.
- World's largest blanket mill.
- Nation's first regular stage run, between Portsmouth and Boston.
- Cog railroad system pioneered on Mt. Washington.

MOMENTS IN HISTORY

- Martin Pring in 1603 and Samuel de Champlain in 1605 both ventured up the Piscataqua River.
- Portsmouth and Dover, each founded in 1623, are usually said to be the oldest permanent European settlements in present-day New Hampshire.
- In 1627 the great Indian leader Passaconaway (Child of the Bear) united about 17 Indian groups in the Penacook Confederacy. Near the end of his life he made a remarkable prophecy about the fate of the Indians on the continent.

> **So They Say**
>
> "The Great Spirit ...whispers me now—'Tell your people, Peace, Peace, is the only hope of your race...these forests shall fall by the axe—the pale faces shall live upon your hunting grounds, and make their village upon your fishing places!...We are few and powerless before them.' Peace...is the command of the Great Spirit...the last wish of Passaconaway."
>
> Chief Passaconaway

- In 1642 the New Hampshire region came under Massachusetts rule.
- Indian leader King Philip responded to growing white intrusion with raids beginning in 1675, and the French and Indian War led to more frightful raids on New Hampshire settlements, not ending until 1759.

• Meanwhile, New Hampshire separated from Massachusetts, and became a Royal colony in 1679.

• In 1764 the king placed the western boundary of New Hampshire along the west bank of the Connecticut River, where it remains.

> **So They Say**
>
> "The trade of the province...consisted chiefly in the exports of lumber and fish to Spain and Portugal and the Caribee Islands. By decree the mast trade was wholly confined to Great Britain. In the winter small vessels went to the southern colonies with English and West Indian goods and returned with corn and pork."
>
> Jeremy Belknap, New Hampshire historian

• Grievances over the king's stamp, the reserving of the great mast trees, and other issues had built up in New Hampshire until on Jan. 5, 1776, an independent provisional government was set up, the first in the 13 colonies.

• No Revolutionary battles were fought in New Hampshire, but New Hampshire forces played a critical role in the Battle of Bunker Hill, June 17, 1775.

• In a sense New Hampshire "created" the new nation by becoming the ninth state on June 21, 1788, meeting the requirement for nine states to ratify the constitution and put the new government into operation.

• The War of 1812 again found New Hampshire among the best prepared, with 35,000 in service and boasting 14 successful privateers.

• In the case of New Hampshire against Dartmouth College in 1819, the U.S. Supreme Court held for the college in a landmark decision upholding private property.

• The Webster-Ashburton Treaty of 1840 (negotiated by the state's native Daniel Webster) finally decided the boundary between the state and Canada.

• The only native president from the state, Franklin Pierce, took that office in 1853.

• During the Civil War, the 18th New Hampshire regiment led Union troops into Richmond, VA in April, 1865.

• After 13 years of work, in 1869 Enos M. Clough of Sunapee developed a successful horseless carriage, with both reverse and forward speeds, but the city fathers made him give it up because of the noise it made.

• Portsmouth hosted the conference arbitrated by Theodore Roosevelt, ending the Russo-Japanese War on Sept. 5, 1905.

• More than 20,000 from New Hampshire served in World War I, and 697 lost their lives.

• In 1964 New Hampshire began the first state lottery since 1894.

• A boundary dispute with Maine was decided by the U.S. Supreme Court in 1976, giving most of the disputed coastal waters to Maine.

• The tragic 1986 destruction of the space shuttle *Challenger* had particular meaning for the state, in the loss of New Hampshire school teacher Christa McAuliffe, with all of the others on board.

That's Interesting

• One of the world's notable natural features is the Old Man of the Mountain. This granite profile looms 48 ft. from chin to forehead.

• New Hampshire's legislature is the largest of all the states, with a total of 400 members. If the membership of the U.S. Congress were in proportion, it would have 100,000 members.

• Horace Greeley learned to read while his mother read to him as he sat on her lap. But he learned upside down because of the angle at which she held the book. He was able to read the Bible by age 4.

• New Hampshire's 13-mile coastline is the shortest of the Atlantic states.

Notable Natives

Lewis Cass (Exeter, 1782-1866), public official. **Samuel Portland Chase** (Cornish, 1808-1873), U.S. chief justice. **Jonas Chickering** (Mason Village, 1798-1853), piano manufacturer. **Ralph Adams Cram** (Hampton Falls, 1863-1942), architect. **John Adams Dix** (Boscawen, 1798-1879), soldier/public official. **Mary Morse Baker Eddy** (Bow, 1821-1910), founder of Christian Science.

Sam Walter Foss (Candia, 1858-1911), poet/journalist. **Daniel Chester French** (Exeter, 1850-1931), sculptor. **Horace Greeley** (Amherst, 1811-1872), reformer/political leader. **John Parker Hale** (Rochester, 1806-1873), public official. **Sarah Josepha Buell Hale** (Newport, 1788-1879), editor/author. **John Irving** (Exeter, 1942-), author. **Thaddeus Sobieski Coulincourt Lowe** (Riverton, 1832-1913), aeronaut/inventor. **Franklin Pierce** (Hillsborough, 1804-1869), U.S. president. **John Stark** (Londonderry, 1728-1822) soldier. **John Sullivan** (Somersworth, 1740-1795), soldier/public official. **Daniel Webster** (Salisbury, 1782-1852), lawyer/public official. **Benning Wentworth,** (Portsmouth, 1696-1770), merchant/public official. **John Wentworth** (Portsmouth, 1737-1820), merchant/public official. **John "Long John" Wentworth** (Sandwich, 1815-1888), editor/Chicago mayor. **Paul Wentworth** (probably NH, date uncertain-d1793), British spy. **Henry Wilson** (Farmington, 1812-1875), U.S. vice-president.

GENERAL

Admitted to statehood: June 21, 1788
Origin of name: Named in 1629 by Capt. John Mason of Plymouth Council for his home county in England
Capital: Concord
Nickname: The Granite State
Motto: "Live Free or Die"
Bird: purple finch
Flower: purple lilac
Songs: "Old New Hampshire," "New Hampshire, My New Hampshire," and "New Hampshire Hills"
Tree: paper (white) birch

THE LAND

Area: 9,351 sq. mi., 46th
Land: 8,969 sq. mi., 44th
Water: 382 sq. mi., 45th
Topography: low, rolling coast followed by countless hills and mountains rising out of a central plateau.
Number of counties: 10
Geographic center: Belknap, 3 mi. E of Ashland
Length: 190 mi.
Width: 70 mi.
Highest point: 6,288 ft. (Mt. Washington), 18th
Lowest point: sea level (Atlantic Ocean), 3rd
Mean elevation: 1,000 ft., 25th
Coastline: 13 mi., 22nd
Shoreline: 131 mi., 23rd

CLIMATE AND ENVIRONMENT

Temp., highest: 106 deg. on July 4, 1911, at Nashua; lowest: -46 deg. on Jan. 28, 1925, at Pittsburg
Fresh water withdrawn, per capita, per day: 688 gal., 40th
Endangered species: mammals, none; birds, 1—American peregrine falcon; reptiles, none; amphibians, none; fishes, none; invertebrates, 1; plants, 3

MAJOR CITIES, POPULATION PERCENTAGE INCREASE (1980-90)

Concord, 36,006—18.44%
Derry, 29,603—56.84%
Manchester, 99,567—9.49%
Nashua, 79,662—17.38%
Rochester, 26,630—23.52%

THE PEOPLE

Population: 1,109,252, 40th
Percent change (1980-90): 17.01%, 6th
Per sq. mi: 118.62, 17th
Percent in metro. area: 56.07%, 35th
Percent foreign born: 3.7%, 22nd
White: 1,087,433—98.03%, 3rd
Black: 7,198—0.65%, 45th
Native American: 2,134—0.19%, 46th
Asian, Pacific Isle: 9,343—0.84%, 33rd
Other races: 3,144—0.28%, 41st
Hispanic origin: 11,333—1.02%, 40th
Percent over 5 yrs. speaking language other than English at home: 8.7%, 21st
Percent males: 49.00%, 20th
Percent females: 51.00%, 32nd
Percent never married: 25.5%, 26th
Marriages per 1,000 (1989): 10.2, 15th
Divorces per 1,000 (1989): 4.7, 24th
Median age: 32.8
Under 5 years: 84,565—7.62%, 15th

Under 18 years: 278,755—25.13%, 35th
65 years & older: 125,029—11.27%, 39th
Percent increase among the elderly: 21.4%, 24th

Of Vital Importance

Live births per 1,000 pop.: 15.0, 40th
Infant mortality rate per 1,000 births (1988): 8.3, 43rd
Average lifetime (1979-81): 74.98, 14th
Deaths per 100,000 pop. (1988): 808.3, 38th
Causes of death per 100,000 pop. (1988):
Diseases of heart: 278.3, 34th
Malignant neoplasms: 195.2, 29th
Cerebrovascular diseases: 56.2, 37th
Accidents & adverse effects: 27.6, 51st
Chronic obstructive pulmonary diseases: 33.5, 29th
Suicide: 13.1, 21st
HIV infection: 2.2, 29th
Other: 68.2, 41st

Keeping Well

Non-federal physicians per 100,000 pop.: 226, 18th
Dentists per 100,000 (1990-91): 65, 22nd
Nurses per 100,000 (1989): 909, 6th
Hospitals per 100,000: 3.6, 17th
Admissions per 100,000: 12,468, 39th
Beds per 100,000: 446.52, 33rd
Occupancy rate: 69.1%, 15th
Semiprivate room charges per day: $304, 20th
Average stay: 6.8, 35th
Notifiable diseases per 100,000:
AIDS: 5.9, 33rd
Gonorrhea: 22.8, 46th
Measles: 0.8, 42nd
Syphillis: 3.6, 41st
Tuberculosis (TB): 1.8, 48th
Per capita spending on mental health programs (1987): $50.90, 14th
Pop. without health insur. (1991): 10.1%, 39th

Households by Type

Total households: 411,186
Percent change (1980-90): 27.30%, 5th
Family households: 292,601
Percent of total: 71.16%, 20th
Nonfamily households: 118,585
Percent of total: 28.84%, 32nd
Persons per household: 2.62, 18th
Pop. living in group quarters: 32,151
Percent of pop.: 2.90%, 23rd

Living Quarters

Total housing units: 503,904
Persons per unit: 2.20, 47th
Occupied housing units: 411,186
Percent of total units: 81.60%, 47th
Persons per unit: 2.52, 26th
Percent of units with over 1 person per room: 1.61%, 50th
Owner-occupied units: 280,372
Percent of total units: 55.64%, 39th
Percent of occupied units: 68.19%, 17th
Persons per unit: 2.80, 13th
Median value: $129,400, 8th
Renter-occupied units: 130,814
Percent of total units: 25.96%, 44th
Percent of occupied units: 31.81%, 35th
Persons per unit: 2.24, 42nd
Median contract rent: $479, 7th
Rental vacancy rate: 11.8%, 8th
Mobile home, trailer & other as a % of occupied housing units: 10.20%, 28th

Crime Index per 100,000

Total: 3,645, 46th
Violent: 132, 49th
Murder and nonnegligent manslaughter: 2, 50th
Aggravated assault: 7,624, 16th
Robbery: 27, 44th
Rape: 35, 27th
Property: 3,514, 46th
Burglary: 735, 43rd
Larceny, theft: 2,534, 44th
Motor vehicle theft: 244, 38th
Drug abuse arrests: 162, 39th

Teaching and Learning

Literacy (1987): 91%, 9th
Pop. 3 and over enrolled in school: 276,765
Percent of pop.: 26.1%, 38th
Public elementary & secondary schools:
Total enrollment: 184,000

Avg. class size (1987): 21, 35th
Teachers: 10,600
Percent of pop.: 0.96%, 33rd
Teachers' avg. salary: $29,000, 25th
Spending per capita: $827, 21st
Spending per pupil in avg. daily attendance: $5,149, 15th
Percent of graduates taking SAT: 75%, 3rd
Combined SAT scores: 921, 28th
Percent of pop. over 25 completing:
High school: 82.2%, 7th
College degree/s: 24.4%, 8th
Higher educa., institutions: 28
Per 100,000 pop.: 1.1, 12th
Enroll: 59,510
Percent of pop.: 5.36%, 29th
Public: 32,163
Percent of enroll.: 54.05%, 49th
Private 27,347
Percent of enroll.: 45.95%, 3rd
White non-Hispanic: 32,200
Percent of enroll.: 89.75%, 15th
Black non-Hispanic: 114
Percent of enroll.: 0.32%, 51st
Hispanic: 280
Percent of enroll.: 0.78%, 39th
Asian/Pacific Islander: 120
Percent of enroll.: 0.33%, 51st
Amer. Indian/AK native: 2,427
Percent of enroll.: 6.76%, 2nd
Nonresident alien: 735
Percent of enroll.: 2.05%, 30th
Female: 32,445
Percent of enroll.: 54.52%, 32nd
Tuition, state university ('90-'91): $3,110, 3rd
Public library systems: 228
Books & serial vol. per capita: 3.98, 7th
Govt. expend. per capita: $16.47, 22nd
State govt.: $2.24, 32nd
Local govts.: $14.22, 22nd

Law Enforcement, Courts, and Prisons

Police protection expend.: $118,381,000
Per capita: $106.75, 24th
Judicial & legal expend.: $64,591,000
Per capita: $58.24, 16th
Corrections expend.: $78,643,000
Per capita: $70.91, 29th
Police per 10,000 pop. (1990-91): 16.8, 37th
Prisoners (state & fed.) sentenced to over 1 yr., per 100,000 pop.: 117
Percent change (1989-90): 15.09%, 3rd
Death penalty: yes, by lethal injection or hanging if lethal injection could not be given
Under sentence of death: 0
Executed (1989): none

Religion, Number and Percent of Population

Agnostic: 9,966—1.20%, 2nd
Buddhist: 4,153—0.50%, 2nd
Christian: 650,279—78.30%, 46th
Hindu: N/A
Jewish: 8,305—1.00%, 17th
Moslem: 1,661—0.20%, 13th
Unitarian: 1,661—0.20%, 23rd
Other: 22,423—2.70%, 2nd
None: 111,287—13.40%, 4th
Refused to answer: 20,762—2.50%, 18th

Making a Living

Personal income per capita (1989): $15,959, 9th
Percent increase (1979-'89) (constant 1989 dollars): 36.7%, 4th
Average income per family: $48,115, 10th
Percent of pop. below poverty level: 6.4%, 51st
Percent 65 and over: 10.2%, 39th
Cost of living, selected cities
2nd qtr., 1989 (U. S. Standard=100)
Manchester 122.9

Economy

Civilian labor force : 630,000
Percent of tot. pop.: 56.80%, 1st
Percent 65 and over: 2.22%, 40th
Percent females: 44.76%, 40th
Percent job growth (1980-90): 36.67%, 6th
Major employer industries:
Agriculture: 8,925—1.50%, 42nd
Construction: 27,965—4.70%, 23rd
Finance, insurance & real estate: 33,320—5.60%, 21st
Government: 70,210—11.80%, 48th
Manufacturing: 143,990—24.20%, 6th

Mining: 562—0.1%, 45th
Service: 113,645—19.10%, 30th
Trade: 116,620—19.60%, 12th
Transportation, communication, & public utilities: 27,370—4.60%, 39th
Wholesale/retail: 124,525—21.7%, 21st
Unemployment rate: 5.71%, 19th
Male: 3.33%, 14th
Female: 2.38%, 28th
Total businesses (1991): 43,357
New business incorp's. (1991): 2,387
Percent of total businesses: 5.51%, 30th
Business failures (1991): 853
Percent of total businesses: 1.97%, 1st
Agriculture farm income
Marketing (1991): $143,106,000, 48th
Net per operation: $14,755, 35th
Net per acre: $89, 14th
Leading products: dairy products, greenhouse, apples, cattle
Av. value land & build. per acre: $2,260, 7th
Percent increase (1980-90): 125.10%, 2nd
Govt. payments: $1,477,000, 46th
Construction, value of all: $609,000,000
Per capita: $549.02, 23rd
Percent change 1989-90: -41.61%, 50th
Manufactures:
Value added: $5,569,000,000
Per capita: $5,020.50, 28th
Value of shipments: $9,727,000,000
Per capita: $8,768.97, 35th
Leading products: machinery, electrical and electronic products, plastics, fabricated metal products
Mining, min. prod., value (1987): $50,000,000, 46th
Leading products: sand/gravel, stone, clays
Retail sales: $11,860,000,000, 34th
Per household: $28,373, 2nd
Percent increase (1987-90): 9.7%, 40th
Service indust., value (1987): $4,525,000,000, 41st
Per capita: $4,079.33, 22nd
Tourism indus., value (1989): $1,120,000,000, 44th
Foreign exports value: $973,000,000, 38th
Per capita: $877.17, 27th
Patents per 1,000 pop.: 3.4, 46th

TRAVEL AND TRANSPORTATION

Motor vehicle registrations: 945,743
Per 1,000 pop.: 852, 15th
Motorcycle registrations: 39,533
Per 1,000 pop.: 35, 6th
Licensed drivers per 1,000 driving age pop.: 981, 5th
Deaths from motor vehicle accidents per 100,000 pop.: 14.2, 42nd
Public roads & streets
Total mileage: 14,836, 45th
Rural mileage: 12,403, 44th
Urban mileage: 2,433, 41st
Interstate mileage: 224, 47th
Annual vehicle-miles of travel per person: 8,874, 30th
Mean travel time for workers 16 + who work away from home: 21.9 min., 14th

GOVERNMENT

Registered voters (1988): 649,924
Percent of voting age pop.: 78.97%, 14th
Voter turnout (1988): 451,074
Percent of registered voters: 69.40%, 32nd
Percent of voting age pop.: 54.81%, 17th
State legislators, total (1992): 424, 1st
Women members (1992): 131
Percent of legislature: 30.9%, 6th
Dominant party (1992): Republicans
U. S. Congress, House members (1993): 2
Increase 1983-93: 0
Revenues:
State govt.: $1,922,222,000
Per capita: $1,732.90, 50th
State & local govt.: $3,504,144,000
Per capita: $3,159.02, 49th
Indebtedness:
State govt.: $3,338,474,000
Per capita: $3,009.66, 8th
State & local govt.: $4,333,000,000
Per capita: $3,906.24, 19th

LAWS AND REGULATIONS

Legal driving age: 18
Marriage age without parental consent: 18
Divorce residence requirement: 1 yr., qualification—check local statutes

ATTRACTIONS

Major opera companies (1989): 1, 30th
Per 1 million pop.: 0.90, 11th
Major symphony orchestras (1989): 5, 40th
Per 1 million pop.: 4.52, 15th
State appropriations for state arts agencies per capita: $0.46, 42nd

SPORTS AND COMPETITION

NCAA sports teams, 6: Dartmouth College Big Green, Franklin Pierce College Ravens, Keene State College Owls, New Hampshire College Penmen, St. Anselm College Hawks, Univ. of New Hampshire Wildcats
Professional teams: none

NEW JERSEY

"Like China, New Jersey absorbs the invaders."

Federal Writers Project, New Jersey

New Jersey gave the world both football and baseball, as well as Thomas Nast's Democratic donkey, the Republican elephant and Santa Claus. It was the home to at least three of the most important inventors in American history. It was here that Thomas A. Edison invented the electric light bulb, Samuel F.B. Morse the electric telegraph, and John P. Holland the submarine. Washington's famed crossing of the Delaware brought his forces to the Jersey shore. The state became the pathway of the Revolution, and suffered through four major battles. The state leads the nation in many areas of manufacture and science and has long proven that it is more than a convenient pathway from North to South.

> **So They Say**
>
> "This is a very good Land to fall with, and a pleasant land to see.".
>
> Henry Hudson

Superlatives

- Claims greatest variety of manufactured products.
- Major glass manufacturing center.
- Leader in flag manufacture.
- Chemistry industry leader.
- Newark is the national jewelry center.
- Leader in scientific/industrial research.
- World's first four-lane highway, constructed between Elizabeth and Newark.
- First U.S. charter for a railroad was granted to Colonel John Stevens of Hoboken. He operated an experimental railroad track of 630 ft. near there.

Moments in History

- Explorers John Cabot, 1497, and Giovanni Verrazano, 1524, sailed past the present-day Jersey shore.
- First record of a European on New Jersey soil belongs to Henry Hudson, in 1609.
- By 1618 the Dutch had set up a trading post at Bergen.
- New Sweden was organized on the lower Delaware in 1638.
- Johan Printz (Big Tub), a giant of 400 lbs., 7 ft. tall, took control of the Swedish settlement in 1643.
- By 1664 British power in the region was such that England took over and Elizabeth was founded in 1664.
- New Jersey became a Crown Colony in 1702, under the governor of New York.
- In 1738 New Jersey had its own government.
- William Franklin, son of Benjamin Franklin, became governor in 1763.
- Dissatisfaction with the crown led to the little-known New Jersey "tea party" on December 22, 1774.
- After the Declaration of Independence, a Provincial Congress took control and arrested Governor Franklin.
- After the Revolution reached New Jersey, the state endured four major battles and 90 minor skirmishes, becoming known as the "Pathway of the Revolution."
- General George Washington and his armies crossed and recrossed New Jersey four times.
- Washington made his famed crossing of the Delaware River to the Jersey shore, and his victory

at the Battle of Trenton at Christmas time, 1775, gave hope to the American cause.

> So They Say
> "Our hopes were blasted by that unhappy affair at Trenton."
> Anonymous British officer

• By the close of the Revolution, 17,000 New Jersey men had fought for the new country, and New Jersey was known as the Garden State for supplying war provisions.

• In 1783 Princeton was the temporary capital of the new country.

• New Jersey became the third state on December 18, 1787.

• The new constitution of 1844 granted many new rights, and slaves gained a degree of freedom in 1846.

• Divided over slavery, New Jersey nevertheless was important in the Underground Railroad movement, and after the Civil War broke out, in May 1861, the New Jersey Brigade became the first to reach Washington, D.C.'s defenses.

• By war's end 88,000 from New Jersey had been in service. Because of overcrowding and disease, thousands of Confederate prisoners died at the prison camp at Fort Delaware.

> So They Say
> "...a thousand ill, 20 deaths a day from dysentery...Thus a Christian nation treats the captives of the sword."
> Anonymous federal inspector at Fort Delaware

• The nation's first intercollegiate football game was played at New Brunswick in 1869 between Rutgers and Princeton. Rutgers won.

• Opposition to the power of big business brought reforms in the period 1910-1912, under Governor Woodrow Wilson.

• Spurred by the inventions of Thomas Edison in New Jersey, the state reigned as motion picture capital of the world until about 1916.

• During World War I, the state led in shipbuilding and production of artillery shells, and Hoboken became the major embarkation point of the war.

• The Miss America contest began at Atlantic City in 1921.

• The great George Washington Bridge was opened in 1931, and Bergen County became "the bedroom of New York."

• The days of the passenger dirigible came to an end at Lakehurst with the spectacular destruction of the *Hindenburg* in 1933.

• During World War II, among other war materiel, New Jersey was predominant in production of airplane engines and warships, and Camp Kilmer was a major debarkation center.

• During the 1940s and 1950s, a series of hurricanes—Diane, Donna, Hazel, and others—took many lives and destroyed hundreds of millions of dollars' worth of property.

• The great Meadowlands development opened in 1976 with games of major league teams.

• The 1980s were notable for the resumption of large-scale gambling at Atlantic City.

That's Interesting

• Johan Printz, governor of New Sweden, was so heavy (400 lbs.) that the gangplank almost collapsed when he arrived at his colony. The Indians called him "Big Tub."

• The first real game of baseball (played under the Cartwright rules) was played at Hoboken in 1846.

• The first derby in the country was run at Passaic in 1864.

• William Campbell, non-Indian, founded a wampum mint near Hackensack and it operated until 1889.

• When American Revolutionary heroine Molly Pitcher's husband was killed, she fought in his place at his cannon.

• Telling time was difficult until Standard Time was invented in 1883 by William F. Allen of South Orange.

Notable Natives

William "Count" Basie (Red Bank, 1904-), musician. **Aaron Burr** (Newark, 1756-1836), public official/political leader. **Grover Cleveland** (Caldwell, 1837-1908), U.S. president. **Stephen Crane** (Newark, 1871-1900), author. **James Fenimore Cooper** (Burlington, 1789-1851), author. **Joyce Kilmer** (New Brunswick, 1886-1918), poet/author. **James Lawrence** (Burlington, 1781-1813), naval officer. **Mary Ludwig Hays "Molly Pitcher" McCauley** (Trenton, 1754-1832), Revolutionary heroine. **Jack Nicholson** (Neptune, 1937-), actor. **Dorothy Parker** (West End, 1893-1967) author. **Paul Bustill Robeson** (Princeton, 1898-1976), singer/actor. **Philip Milton Roth** (Newark, 1933-), author. **Frank Sinatra** (Hoboken, 1917-), singer/actor. **Robert Field Stockton** (Princeton, 1834-1902), naval officer. **Meryl Streep** (Summit, 1949-), actress. **Albert Payson Terhune** (Newark, 1872-1942), author. **William Carlos Williams** (Rutherford, 1883-1963), poet /physician.

General

Admitted to statehood: Dec. 18, 1787
Origin of name: The Duke of York, 1664, gave a patent to John Berkely and Sir George Carteret to be called Nova Caesaria, or New Jersey, after England's Isle of Jersey
Capital: Trenton
Nickname: The Garden State
Motto: "Liberty and Prosperity"
Animal: horse
Bird: Eastern goldfinch
Colors: buff and blue
Flower: purple violet
Insect: honeybee
Song: "New Jersey Loyalty" (unofficial)
Tree: red oak

The Land

Area: 8,722 sq. mi., 47th
Land: 7,419 sq. mi., 46th
Water: 1,303 sq. mi., 27th
Topography: Appalachian Valley in the NW, Appalachian Highlands, flat-topped NE-SW mountain ranges; Piedmont Plateau, low plains broken by high ridges (Palisades) rising 400-500 ft.; coastal plain, covering three-fifths of state in SE, gradually rises from sea level to gentle slopes
Number of counties: 21
Geographic center: Mercer, 5 mi. SE of Trenton
Length: 150 mi.
Width: 70 mi.
Highest point: 1,803 ft. (High Point), 40th
Lowest point: sea level (Atlantic Ocean), 3rd
Mean elevation: 250 ft., 46th
Coastline: 130 mi., 13th
Shoreline: 1,792 mi., 14th

Climate and Environment

Temp., highest: 110 deg. on July 10, 1936, at Runyon; lowest: -34 deg. on Jan. 5, 1904, at River Vale
Fresh water withdrawn, per capita, per day: 307 gal., 48th
Endangered species: mammals, 1—Indiana bat; birds, 1—American peregrine falcon; reptiles, 2; amphibians, none; fishes, none; invertebrates, none; plants, 1

Major Cities, Population Percentage Increase (1980-90)

Elizabeth, 110,002—3.58%
Jersey City, 228,537—2.24%
Newark, 275,221—16.41%
Paterson, 140,891—2.12%
Trenton, 88,675—3.74%

The People

Population: 7,730,188, 9th
Percent change (1980-90): 4.72%, 27th
Per sq. mi: 886.29, 2nd
Percent in metro. area: 100.00%, 1st
Percent foreign born: 12.5%, 5th
White: 6,130,465—79.31%, 35th
Black: 1,036,825—13.41%, 17th
Native American: 14,970—0.19%, 45th
Asian, Pacific Isle: 272,521—3.53%, 6th
Other races: 275,407—3.56%, 9th
Hispanic origin: 739,861—9.57%, 9th
Percent over 5 yrs. speaking language other than English at home: 19.5%, 7th

Percent males: 48.33%, 38th
Percent females: 51.67%, 14th
Percent never married: 29.1%, 7th
Marriages per 1,000 (1989): 7.8, 46th
Divorces per 1,000 (1989): 3.3, 44th
Median age: 34.5
Under 5 years: 532,637—6.89%, 43rd
Under 18 years: 1,799,462—23.28%, 46th
65 years & older: 1,032,025—13.35%, 16th
Percent increase among the elderly: 20.0%, 26th

Of Vital Importance

Live births per 1,000 pop.: 15.5, 32nd
Infant mortality rate per 1,000 births (1988): 9.9, 24th
Average lifetime (1979-81): 74.00, 22nd
Deaths per 100,000 pop. (1988): 950.8, 13th
Causes of death per 100,000 pop. (1988):
 Diseases of heart: 356.1, 10th
 Malignant neoplasms: 223.5, 8th
 Cerebrovascular diseases: 54.9, 38th
 Accidents & adverse effects: 31.5, 46th
 Chronic obstructive pulmonary diseases: 29.3, 41st
 Suicide: 7, 50th
 HIV infection: 15, 3rd
 Other: 77.8, 22nd

Keeping Well

Non-federal physicians per 100,000 pop.: 266, 8th
Dentists per 100,000 (1990-91): 83, 6th
Nurses per 100,000 (1989): 691, 26th
Hospitals per 100,000: 1.5, 51st
 Admissions per 100,000: 15,182, 15th
 Beds per 100,000: 493.43, 23rd
 Occupancy rate: 81.1%, 4th
 Semiprivate room charges per day: $273, 24th
 Average stay: 11.6, 6th
Notifiable diseases per 100,000:
 AIDS: 31.9, 3rd
 Gonorrhea: 230.0, 22nd
 Measles: 6.1, 16th
 Syphillis: 56.7, 13th
 Tuberculosis (TB): 12.5, 10th
Per capita spending on mental health programs (1987): $50.62, 15th
Pop. without health insur. (1991): 10.8%, 36th

Households by Type

Total households: 2,794,711
 Percent change (1980-90): 9.64%, 31st
Family households: 2,021,346
 Percent of total: 72.33%, 13th
Nonfamily households: 773,365
 Percent of total: 27.67%, 39th
Persons per household: 2.70, 10th
Pop. living in group quarters: 171,368
 Percent of pop.: 2.22%, 45th

Living Quarters

Total housing units: 3,075,310
 Persons per unit: 2.51, 7th
Occupied housing units: 2,794,711
 Percent of total units: 90.88%, 17th
 Persons per unit: 2.64, 10th
 Percent of units with over 1 person per room: 3.89%, 18th
Owner-occupied units: 1,813,381
 Percent of total units: 58.97%, 26th
 Percent of occupied units: 64.89%, 38th
 Persons per unit: 2.87, 4th
 Median value: $162,300, 5th
Renter-occupied units: 981,330
 Percent of total units: 31.91%, 16th
 Percent of occupied units: 35.11%, 16th
 Persons per unit: 2.40, 17th
 Median contract rent: $521, 3rd
 Rental vacancy rate: 7.4%, 37th
Mobile home, trailer & other as a % of occupied housing units: 2.74%, 46th

Crime Index per 100,000

Total: 5,447, 22nd
 Violent: 648, 19th
  Murder and nonnegligent manslaughter: 6, 29th
  Aggravated assault: 6,890, 43rd
  Robbery: 301, 7th
  Rape: 30, 37th
 Property: 4,800, 24th
  Burglary: 1,017, 31st
  Larceny, theft: 2,843, 34th
  Motor vehicle theft: 940, 5th
Drug abuse arrests: 600, 4th

Teaching and Learning

Literacy (1987): 86%, 33nd
Pop. 3 and over enrolled in school: 1,867,402
Percent of pop.: 25.2%, 46th
Public elementary & secondary schools:
Total enrollment: 1,117,000
Avg. class size (1987): 20, 41st
Teachers: 79,600
Percent of pop.: 1.03%, 22nd
Teachers' avg. salary: $35,700, 9th
Spending per capita: $1,114, 4th
Spending per pupil in avg. daily attendance: $8,439, 1st
Percent of graduates taking SAT: 74%, 5th
Combined SAT scores: 913, 31st
Percent of pop. over 25 completing:
High school: 76.7%, 26th
College degree/s: 24.9%, 6th
Higher educa., institutions: 59
Per 100,000 pop.: 0.4, 48th
Enroll: 323,947
Percent of pop.: 4.19%, 48th
Public: 261,601
Percent of enroll.: 80.75%, 30th
Private: 62,346
Percent of enroll.: 19.25%, 22nd
White non-Hispanic: 225,213
Percent of enroll.: 85.54%, 23rd
Black non-Hispanic: 7,361
Percent of enroll.: 2.80%, 36th
Hispanic: 6,122
Percent of enroll.: 2.33%, 15th
Asian/Pacific Islander: 15,424
Percent of enroll.: 5.86%, 3rd
Amer. Indian/AK native: 3,854
Percent of enroll.: 1.46%, 9th
Nonresident alien: 5,304
Percent of enroll.: 2.01%, 31st
Female: 178,489
Percent of enroll.: 55.10%, 21st
Tuition, state university ('90-'91): $2,860, 5th
Public library systems: 311
Books & serial vol. per capita: 3.56, 11th
Govt. expend. per capita: $21.01, 15th
State govt.: $3.25, 15th
Local govts.: $17.76, 13th

Law Enforcement, Courts, and Prisons

Police protection expend.: $1,190,920,000
Per capita: $154.06, 6th
Judicial & legal expend.: $536,996,000
Per capita: $69.47, 9th
Corrections expend.: $823,048,000
Per capita: $106.47, 12th
Police per 10,000 pop. (1990-91): 34.5, 2nd
Prisoners (state & fed.) sentenced to over 1 yr., per 100,000 pop.: 271
Percent change (1989-90): 8.69%, 17th
Death penalty: yes, by lethal injection
Under sentence of death: 25, 22nd
Executed (1989): none

Religion, Number and Percent of Population

Agnostic: 35,584—0.60%, 19th
Buddhist: 5,931—0.10%, 17th
Christian: 5,041,117—85.00%, 33rd
Hindu: 17,792—0.30%, 2nd
Jewish: 255,021—4.30%, 2nd
Moslem: 35,584—0.60%, 2nd
Unitarian: 5,931—0.10%, 31st
Other: 47,446—0.80%, 37th
None: 326,190—5.50%, 39th
Refused to answer: 160,130—2.70%, 16th

Making a Living

Personal income per capita (1989): $18,714, 3rd
Percent increase (1979-'89) (constant 1989 dollars): 37.4%, 3rd
Average income per family: $58,468, 2nd
Percent of pop. below poverty level: 7.6%, 49th
Percent 65 and over: 8.5%, 47th
Cost of living, selected cities
1st qtr., 1991 (U. S. Standard=100) not available

Economy

Civilian labor force : 4,048,000
Percent of tot. pop.: 52.37%, 16th
Percent 65 and over: 3.29%, 11th
Percent females: 44.99%, 33rd
Percent job growth (1980-90): 21.77%, 21st

Major employer industries:
Agriculture: 42,306—1.10%, 46th
Construction: 184,608—4.80%, 22nd
Finance, insurance & real estate: 299,988—7.80%, 4th
Government: 549,978—14.30%, 32nd
Manufacturing: 669,204—17.40%, 20th
Mining: 5,066—0.1%, 46th
Service: 876,888—22.80%, 9th
Trade: 696,126—18.10%, 32nd
Transportation, communication, & public utilities: 261,528—6.80%, 4th
Wholesale/retail: 795,382—20.6%, 38th
Unemployment rate: 4.99%, 34th
Male: 2.82%, 33rd
Female: 2.15%, 35th
Total businesses (1991): 263,070
New business incorp's. (1991): 27,994
Percent of total businesses: 10.64%, 6th
Business failures (1991): 2,715
Percent of total businesses: 1.03%, 15th
Agriculture farm income
Marketing (1991): $660,160,000, 39th
Net per operation: $27,874, 14th
Net per acre: $263, 5th
Leading products: greenhouse, dairy products, eggs, peaches
Av. value land & build. per acre: $4,737, 2nd
Percent increase (1980-90): 60.74%, 7th
Govt. payments: $4,051,000, 42nd
Construction, value of all: $3,734,000,000
Per capita: $483.04, 31st
Percent change 1989-90: -34.86%, 46th
Manufactures:
Value added: $45,179,000,000
Per capita: $5,844.49, 15th
Value of shipments: $87,498,000,000
Per capita: $11,319.00, 25th
Leading products: chemicals, electronic and electrical equipment, non-electrical machinery, fabricated metals
Mining, min. prod., value (1987): $326,000,000, 35th
Leading products: stone, sand/gravel, zinc
Retail sales: $63,431,000,000, 9th
Per household: $22,579, 5th
Percent increase (1987-90): 13.4%, 31st
Service indust., value (1987): $43,571,000,000, 7th
Per capita: $5,636.47, 7th
Tourism indus., value (1989): $8,974,000,000, 7th
Foreign exports value: $7,633,000,000, 14th
Per capita: $987.43, 20th
Patents per 1,000 pop.: 2.5, 49th

TRAVEL AND TRANSPORTATION

Motor vehicle registrations: 5,652,382
Per 1,000 pop.: 731, 37th
Motorcycle registrations: 86,439
Per 1,000 pop.: 11, 39th
Licensed drivers per 1,000 driving age pop.: 914, 18th
Deaths from motor vehicle accidents per 100,000 pop.: 11.5, 48th
Public roads & streets
Total mileage: 34,252, 40th
Rural mileage: 11,750, 46th
Urban mileage: 22,502, 9th
Interstate mileage: 396, 43rd
Annual vehicle-miles of travel per person: 7,622, 44th
Mean travel time for workers 16 + who work away from home: 25.3 min., 4th

GOVERNMENT

Registered voters (1988): 4,010,790
Percent of voting age pop.: 67.49%, 33rd
Voter turnout (1988): 3,099,553
Percent of registered voters: 77.28%, 10th
Percent of voting age pop.: 52.15%, 25th
State legislators, total (1992): 120, 37th
Women members (1992): 15
Percent of legislature: 12.5%, 40th
Dominant party (1992): Republicans
U. S. Congress, House members (1993): 13
Increase 1983-93: -1
Revenues:
State govt.: $22,623,961,000
Per capita: $2,926.70, 11th
State & local govt.: $35,089,837,000
Per capita: $4,539.33, 10th
Indebtedness:
State govt.: $18,907,599,000
Per capita: $2,445.94, 11th
State & local govt.: $32,565,000,000
Per capita: $4,212.70, 13th

Laws and Regulations

Legal driving age: 17
Marriage age without parental consent: 18
Divorce residence requirement: 1 yr., qualification—check local statutes

Attractions

Major opera companies (1989): 6, 8th
 Per 1 million pop.: 0.78, 21st
Major symphony orchestras (1989): 28, 10th
 Per 1 million pop.: 3.62, 26th
State appropriations for state arts agencies per capita: $2.58, 4th

Sports and Competition

NCAA sports teams, 8: Fairleigh Dickinson Univ. Knights, Monmouth College Hawks, Princeton Univ. Tigers, Rider College Broncos, Rutgers Univ. Pioneers, Seton Hall Univ. Pirates, St. Peter's College Peacocks, The State Univ. of N.J. Rutgers Scarlet Knights
Professional teams, 7:
 Basketball, 1—New Jersey Nets (NBA), Brendan Byrne Meadowlands Arena
 Football, 3—New York Jets (AFC), Giants' Stadium, The Meadowlands; New York Giants (NFC), Giants' Stadium, The Meadowlands; New York Knights (World League of American Football), Giants' Stadium, The Meadowlands
 Hockey, 1—New Jersey Devils (NHL), Brendan Byrne Meadowlands Arena
 Soccer, 2—New Jersey Eagles (American Professional Soccer League), Cochrane Stadium; Penn-Jersey Spirit (American Professional Soccer League, American Conference), Lions Stadium

NEW MEXICO

"I think New Mexico was the greatest experience from the outside world that I ever had. It certainly changed me forever....The moment I saw the brilliant, proud morning shine high over the deserts of Santa Fe, something stood still in my soul....For a greatness of beauty I have never experienced anything like New Mexico....Just day itself is tremendous there."

D.H. Lawrence

Early explorers failed to find the fabled seven cities of gold, but the prehistoric cities of the Pueblo peoples far outshone the mythical ones. Among their more important contributions, these gave the state the nation's oldest "cooperative apartments." By contrast with its ancient history, New Mexico is the state where the atomic age became a reality. This land of sunshine is governed from the nation's oldest state capital, where visitors from around the world can experience superlative grand opera. Visitors may follow the course of the country's oldest highway, and enjoy the unique sights of Taos Pueblo and the other pueblos and enjoy the unique Indian festivals held around the state.

Superlatives

• Oldest capital city in the United States, Santa Fe.

• Oldest highway in the United States, the King's Highway.

• Yucca, the only commercially valuable state flower.

• First in production of potash.

• Leads in dry ice production from carbon dioxide wells.

• Birthplace of the U.S. livestock industry.

Moments in History

• The Pueblo people are among the most remarkable and most studied of prehistoric Americans. They developed substantial cities of stone masonry—their "skyscrapers" are noted as a distinctive contribution to world architecture. They developed great skill in weaving, created complex systems of irrigation, and domesticated turkeys. They fabricated tools, and their jewelry featured fine silverwork with turquoise. Their golden age appears to have been about 950-1200 A.D. New Mexico boasts many fascinating pueblo ruins.

• In 1536 Nunez Cabeza de Vaca and three shipwrecked companions escaped from Indian captors in Texas, and they made their way across present-day New Mexico.

• The great expedition of Francisco Vasquez de Coronado crossed present-day New Mexico in 1540.

• On July 11, 1598, wealthy Don Juan de Onate established San Juan, the first European settlement in New Mexico (the second in the United States), at the Tewa pueblo of Yugeuingge. In 1605 Onate journeyed to the Gulf of California, and he carved his signature on famed Inscription Rock.

• Don Pedro de Peralta founded Santa Fe in the winter of 1609-10.

• By 1626 the Franciscan Fathers had established 43 missions, with 34,000 Indian converts.

• Because the Spaniards treated them so harshly, in 1680 the Indians revolted under Pope, a Tewa medicine man, and they captured Santa Fe.

• The Indians ruled Santa Fe until 1692, when Governor Don Diego de Vagas recaptured it.

• Albuquerque was founded in 1706, named for the Duke of Albuquerque.

• On his expedition of 1806-07, Zebulon Pike was captured and taken to Spanish Santa Fe.

• On November 6, 1822, William Becknell brought the first wagon loads of goods into Santa Fe from the Northeast, blazing the Santa Fe Trail and pioneering trade with the states.

So They Say

On the merchants' return from Santa Fe: "....My father saw them unload...and when their rawhide packages of silver dollars were dumped on the sidewalk one of the men cut the thongs and the money spilled out and clinking on the stone pavement rolled into the gutter. Everyone was excited."

Anonymous

• During the Mexican War of 1846, U.S. forces brought New Mexico under U.S. control.

• During the Civil War, Confederate forces captured Santa Fe on March 10, 1862, but General H.H. Sibley recaptured the capital on April 8.

• The Plains Indians carried on warfare with the settlers for nearly 50 years, until Indian leader Geronimo surrendered in 1886.

So They Say

"Everything is quiet in Cimarron. Nobody has been killed for three days."

Las Vegas Gazette, commenting on the lawlessness of the frontier

• In 1901 Cowboy Jim White discovered a "hole in the ground." This proved to be a vast underground wonderland, and it became known as Carlsbad Caverns.

• On Jan. 6, 1912, New Mexico became the 47th state.

• Pancho Villa, the Mexican revolutionary, raided the border town of Columbus in 1916.

• During World War I, 17,157 New Mexicans served, and 500 lost their lives.

• The atomic age was born at Trinity Site on July 16, 1945, with the explosion of the first atomic bomb.

So They Say

"The skies above New Mexico lighted up with an eerie orange-purple glow. Those few who knew what happened looked on with awe. They understood that the world would never again be the same."

John A. Carpenter

• From 1940 to 1982 the population expanded by almost 300%, but the 1990 census indicated a much slower growth.

• In 1985 a major rating of American cities placed Albuquerque among the best places to live in the nation.

That's Interesting

• In the Four Corners region, where four states touch, visitors often sprawl out so they can say they have slept in four states at once.

• Pueblo Bonito housed as many as 1,500 people in its 800 rooms, perhaps the first "condominium."

• According to Indian lore, the buffalo unwittingly contributed to its own destruction because it was so ruthlessly hunted for food, and its sinews were used for strings for the Indians' bows.

• Just before his sentence of hanging was carried out, the outlaw Black Jack Ketchum demanded of the hangman, "Hurry it up; I'm due in hell for dinner."

• One of the principal attractions of Carlsbad Caverns is the evening flight of millions of bats. Winging their way out of the cavern entrance, the swarm of bats looks like a column of smoke.

New Mexico Notables

William H. "Billy the Kid" Bonney (New York City, 1859-1881), outlaw. **Christopher "Kit" Carson** (Madison City, KY, 1809-1868), trapper/Indian agent/soldier. **John Simpson Chisum** (Hardeman Co., TN, 1824-1868), cattleman. **Emerson Hough** (Newton, IA, 1857-1923), author. **Jean Baptiste Lamy** (Prov. of Auvergne,

France, 1814-1888), religious leader. **David Herbert "D.H." Lawrence** (Nottingham, Eng., 1885-1930), author. **Mangas Coloradas** (SW NM, c1770-1863), Apache leader. **William Henry "Bill" Mauldin** (Mountain Park, NM, 1921-), cartoonist. **Georgia O'Keefe** (Sun Prairie, WI, 1887-1986), artist. **Albert Pike** (Boston, MA,1809-1891), lawyer/soldier. **Ernest Taylor "Ernie" Pyle** (near Dana, IN, 1900-1945), journalist. **Eugene Manlove Rhodes** (Tecumseh, NE, 1869-1934), cowboy/author. **Ernest Thompson Seton** (South Shields, Eng., 1860-1946), author/naturalist. **Frank Springer** (Wapella, IA, 1848-1927), lawyer/paleontologist. **Lewis Wallace** (Brookville, IN, 1827-1905), lawyer/diplomat/soldier/author.

GENERAL

Admitted to statehood: Jan. 6, 1912
Origin of name: In the 16th century, Spaniards in Mexico applied term to land north and west of the Rio Grande
Capital: Santa Fe, settled 1609
Nickname: Land of Enchantment
Motto: *"Crescit Eundo"* ("It Grows as It Goes")
Animal: black bear
Bird: roadrunner
Colors: red and yellow of old Spain
Fish: cutthroat trout
Flower: yucca
Gem: turquoise
Songs: *"Asi es Nuevo Mejico"* "O, Fair New Mexico"
Tree: pinon
Vegetables: chile and frijole

THE LAND

Area: 121,598 sq. mi., 5th
Land: 121,365 sq. mi., 5th
Water: 234 sq. mi., 49th
Topography: E third, Great Plains, central third Rocky Mtns. (85% of the state over 4,000 ft. elevation), W third high plateau
Number of counties: 33
Geographic center: Torrance, 12 mi. SSW of Willard
Length: 370 mi.
Width: 343 mi.
Highest point: 13,161 ft. (Wheeler Peak), 8th
Lowest point: 2,842 ft. (Red Bluff Reservoir), 49th
Mean elevation: 5,700 ft., 4th.

CLIMATE AND ENVIRONMENT

Temp., highest: 116 deg. on July 14, 1934, at Orogrande; lowest: -50 deg. on Feb. 1, 1951, at Gavilan
Fresh water withdrawn, per capita, per day: 2,320 gal., 11th
Endangered species: mammals, 3—Mexican long-nosed bat, Sanborn's long-nosed bat, Mexican gray wolf; birds, 3—whooping crane, American peregrine falcon, least tern; reptiles, none; amphibians, none; fishes, 4; invertebrates, 1; plants, 7

MAJOR CITIES, POPULATION PERCENTAGE INCREASE (1980-90)

Albuquerque, 384,736—15.56%
Farmington, 33,997—8.89%
Las Cruces, 62,126—37.79%
Roswell, 44,654—12.55%
Santa Fe, 55,859—13.63%
South Valley, 35,701— –8.26%

THE PEOPLE

Population: 1,515,069, 37th
Percent change (1980-90): 13.98%, 11th
Per sq. mi: 12.46, 44th
Percent in metro. area: 48.38%, 38th
Percent foreign born: 5.3%, 16th
White: 1,146,028—75.64%, 38th
Black: 30,210—1.99%, 40th
Native American: 134,355—8.87%, 2nd
Asian, Pacific Isle: 14,124—0.93%, 30th
Other races: 190,352—12.56%, 2nd
Hispanic origin: 597,224—39.42%, 1st
Percent over 5 yrs. speaking language other than English at home: 35.5%, 1st
Percent males: 49.19%, 15th
Percent females: 50.81%, 37th
Percent never married: 25.8%, 24th
Marriages per 1,000 (1989): 8.3, 36th
Divorces per 1,000 (1989): 5.0, 20th
Median age: 31.2
Under 5 years: 125,878—8.31%, 3rd

Under 18 years: 446,741—29.49%, 6th
65 years & older: 163,062—10.76%, 42nd
Percent increase among the elderly: 40.7%, 5th

Of Vital Importance

Live births per 1,000 pop.: 18.3, 7th
Infant mortality rate per 1,000 births (1988): 10.0, 23rd
Average lifetime (1979-81): 74.01, 21st
Deaths per 100,000 pop. (1988): 691.8, 46th
Causes of death per 100,000 pop. (1988):
- Diseases of heart: 189.8, 48th
- Malignant neoplasms: 144.7, 47th
- Cerebrovascular diseases: 42, 46th
- Accidents & adverse effects: 56.7, 2nd
- Chronic obstructive pulmonary diseases: 31.3, 33rd
- Suicide: 22.8, 2nd
- HIV infection: 2.1, 33rd
- Other: 72.3, 34th

Keeping Well

Non-federal physicians per 100,000 pop.: 206, 25th
Dentists per 100,000 (1990-91): 48, 45th
Nurses per 100,000 (1989): 476, 47th
Hospitals per 100,000: 4.0, 14th
- Admissions per 100,000: 12,577, 37th
- Beds per 100,000: 435.43, 37th
- Occupancy rate: 63.2%, 38th
- Semiprivate room charges per day: $254, 31st
- Average stay: 5.9, 48th

Notifiable diseases per 100,000:
- AIDS: 7.2, 28th
- Gonorrhea: 81.5, 40th
- Measles: 6.0, 17th
- Syphillis: 14.7, 28th
- Tuberculosis (TB): 7.5, 21st

Per capita spending on mental health programs (1987): $23.78, 45th
Pop. without health insur. (1991): 21.5%, 3rd

Households by Type

Total households: 542,709
- Percent change (1980-90): 23.06%, 9th

Family households: 391,487
- Percent of total: 72.14%, 14th

Nonfamily households: 151,222
- Percent of total: 27.86%, 38th

Persons per household: 2.74, 6th
Pop. living in group quarters: 28,807
- Percent of pop.: 1.90%, 50th

Living Quarters

Total housing units: 632,058
- Persons per unit: 2.40, 26th

Occupied housing units: 542,709
- Percent of total units: 85.86%, 40th
- Persons per unit: 2.69, 8th
- Percent of units with over 1 person per room: 7.89%, 6th

Owner-occupied units: 365,965
- Percent of total units: 57.90%, 31st
- Percent of occupied units: 67.43%, 25th
- Persons per unit: 2.85, 6th
- Median value: $70,100, 24th

Renter-occupied units: 176,744
- Percent of total units: 27.96%, 30th
- Percent of occupied units: 32.57%, 27th
- Persons per unit: 2.52, 8th
- Median contract rent: $312, 29th
- Rental vacancy rate: 11.4%, 11th

Mobile home, trailer & other as a % of occupied housing units: 20.71%, 2nd

Crime Index per 100,000

Total: 6,684, 6th
- Violent: 780, 10th
  - Murder and nonnegligent manslaughter: 9, 18th
  - Aggravated assault: 8,308, 4th
  - Robbery: 115, 30th
  - Rape: 50, 11th
- Property: 5,904, 6th
  - Burglary: 1,739, 4th
  - Larceny, theft: 3,828, 9th
  - Motor vehicle theft: 337, 33rd

Drug abuse arrests: 220, 31st

Teaching and Learning

Literacy (1987): 86%, 33nd
Pop. 3 and over enrolled in school: 435,989
- Percent of pop.: 30.2%, 4th

Public elementary & secondary schools:
- Total enrollment: 316,000

Avg. class size (1987): 23, 20th
Teachers: 16,300
Percent of pop.: 1.08%, 16th
Teachers' avg. salary: $25,100, 40th
Spending per capita: $857, 17th
Spending per pupil in avg. daily attendance: $4,180, 33rd
Percent of graduates taking SAT: 12%, 34th
Combined SAT scores: 996, 15th
Percent of pop. over 25 completing:
High school: 75.1%, 33rd
College degree/s: 20.4%, 22nd
Higher educa., institutions: 28
Per 100,000 pop.: 1.5, 4th
Enroll: 85,596
Percent of pop.: 5.65%, 24th
Public: 83,499
Percent of enroll.: 97.55%, 3rd
Private: 2,097
Percent of enroll.: 2.45%, 49th
White non-Hispanic: 194,943
Percent of enroll.: 84.19%, 25th
Black non-Hispanic: 6,943
Percent of enroll.: 3.00%, 34th
Hispanic: 17,319
Percent of enroll.: 7.48%, 6th
Asian/Pacific Islander: 5,417
Percent of enroll.: 2.34%, 17th
Amer. Indian/AK native: 2,315
Percent of enroll.: 1.00%, 15th
Nonresident alien: 4,610
Percent of enroll.: 1.99%, 32nd
Female: 47,604
Percent of enroll.: 55.61%, 17th
Tuition, state university ('90-'91): $1,409, 40th
Public library systems: 68
Books & serial vol. per capita: 2.41, 29th
Govt. expend. per capita: $12.89, 30th
State govt.: $2.16, 35th
Local govts.: $10.73, 29th

LAW ENFORCEMENT, COURTS, AND PRISONS

Police protection expend.: $184,232,000
Per capita: $121.61, 20th
Judicial & legal expend.: $71,909,000
Per capita: $47.46, 27th
Corrections expend.: $148,254,000
Per capita: $97.86, 16th
Police per 10,000 pop. (1990-91): 22.1, 16th
Prisoners (state & fed.) sentenced to over 1 yr., per 100,000 pop.: 184
Percent change (1989-90): 4.35%, 36th
Death penalty: yes, by lethal injection
Under sentence of death: 2, 32nd
Executed (1989): none

RELIGION, NUMBER AND PERCENT OF POPULATION

Agnostic: 10,683—1.00%, 10th
Buddhist: 1,068—0.10%, 17th
Christian: 910,216—85.20%, 32nd
Hindu: N/A
Jewish: 7,478—0.70%, 23rd
Moslem: N/A
Unitarian: 3,205—0.30%, 15th
Other: 11,752—1.10%, 32nd
None: 106,833—10.00%, 11th
Refused to answer: 17,093—1.60%, 39th

MAKING A LIVING

Personal income per capita (1989): $11,246, 42nd
Percent increase (1979-'89) (constant 1989 dollars): 9.6%, 35th
Average income per family: $34,585, 43rd
Percent of pop. below poverty level: 20.6%, 3rd
Percent 65 and over: 16.5%, 14th
Cost of living, selected cities
1st qtr., 1991 (U. S. Standard=100)
Carlsbad 90.1
Albuquerque 101.7

Economy

Civilian labor force : 700,000
Percent of tot. pop.: 46.20%, 47th
Percent 65 and over: N/A
Percent females: 44.86%, 36th
Percent job growth (1980-90): 25.65%, 17th
Major employer industries:
Agriculture: 19,024—2.90%, 21st
Construction: 30,832—4.70%, 23rd
Finance, insurance & real estate: 25,584—3.90%, 48th
Government: 150,880—23.00%, 4th
Manufacturing: 48,544—7.40%, 44th

Mining: 15,559—2.5%, 6th
Service: 120,048—18.30%, 38th
Trade: 124,640—19.00%, 22nd
Transportation, communication, & public utilities: 30,832—4.70%, 38th
Wholesale/retail: 137,112—21.8%, 20th
Unemployment rate: 6.29%, 9th
Male: 3.57%, 6th
Female: 2.71%, 15th
Total businesses (1991): 55,334
New business incorp's. (1991): 2,713
Percent of total businesses: 4.90%, 38th
Business failures (1991): 386
Percent of total businesses: 0.70%, 38th
Agriculture farm income
Marketing (1991): $1,501,152,000, 34th
Net per operation: $26,134, 18th
Net per acre: $8, 47th
Leading products: cattle, dairy products, hay, chili peppers
Av. value land & build. per acre: $200, 47th
Percent increase (1980-90): 8.11%, 21st
Govt. payments: $58,447,000, 28th
Construction, value of all: $786,000,000
Per capita: $518.79, 28th
Percent change 1989-90: -7.31%, 26th
Manufactures:
Value added: $2,252,000,000
Per capita: $1,486.40, 49th
Value of shipments: $5,548,000,000
Per capita: $3,661.88, 49th
Leading products: foods, machinery, apparel, lumber, printing, transportation equipment
Mining, min. prod., value (1987): $4,982,000,000, 9th
Leading products: nat. gas, petroleum, coal
Retail sales: $9,378,000,000, 41st
Per household: $17,044, 45th
Percent increase (1987-90): 13.6%, 30th
Service indust., value (1987): $5,779,000,000, 36th
Per capita: $3,814.35, 28th
Tourism indus., value (1989): $2,007,000,000, 37th
Foreign exports value: $249,000,000, 48th
Per capita: $164.35, 50th
Patents per 1,000 pop.: 7.7, 21st

TRAVEL AND TRANSPORTATION

Motor vehicle registrations: 1,301,261
Per 1,000 pop.: 858, 14th
Motorcycle registrations: 33,464
Per 1,000 pop.: 22, 17th
Licensed drivers per 1,000 driving age pop.: 967, 6th
Deaths from motor vehicle accidents per 100,000 pop.: 32.9, 1st
Public roads & streets
Total mileage: 54,736, 34th
Rural mileage: 49,238, 33rd
Urban mileage: 5,498, 35th
Interstate mileage: 1,000, 17th
Annual vehicle-miles of travel per person: 10,658, 3rd
Mean travel time for workers 16 + who work away from home: 19.1 min., 36th

GOVERNMENT

Registered voters (1988): 674,826
Percent of voting age pop.: 61.29%, 46th
Voter turnout (1988): 521,287
Percent of registered voters: 77.25%, 11th
Percent of voting age pop.: 47.35%, 38th
State legislators, total (1992): 112, 39th
Women members (1992): 16
Percent of legislature: 14.3%, 35th
Dominant party (1992): Democrats
U. S. Congress, House members (1993): 3
Increase 1983-93: 0
Revenues:
State govt.: $4,730,810,000
Per capita: $3,122.50, 6th
State & local govt.: $6,211,566,000
Per capita: $4,099.86, 18th
Indebtedness:
State govt.: $1,830,328,000
Per capita: $1,208.08, 24th
State & local govt.: $4,993,000,000
Per capita: $3,295.56, 27th

LAWS AND REGULATIONS

Legal driving age: 16
Marriage age without parental consent: 18
Divorce residence requirement: 6 mo.

Attractions

Major opera companies (1989): 3, 15th
Per 1 million pop.: 1.96, 3rd
Major symphony orchestras (1989): 8, 31st
Per 1 million pop.: 5.24, 9th
State appropriations for state arts agencies per capita: $0.60, 30th
State Fair in mid-Sept. at Albuquerque

Sports and Competition

NCAA sports teams, 2: New Mexico State Univ. Aggies, Univ. of New Mexico Lobos
Professional teams, 1:
Baseball, 1—Albuquerque Dukes (Pacific Coast League, Class AAA), Albuquerque Sports Stadium

NEW YORK

"Why, if you're not in New York, you are camping out."

Thomas W. Dewing

Stretching from Niagara Falls in the west and the rugged beauty of the Adirondacks in the northeast to the culturally rich and ethnically diverse "Big Apple"—Manhattan—in the southeast, New York is a state of dramatic contrasts. Although it no longer ranks first in population or manufacturing, New York State must still rank as the "Empire State" in its combination of history, cultural institutions, notable natives, commerce, industry, finance, and international influence among others.

SUPERLATIVES

- World's most extensive deep water port.
- World's longest suspension bridge—Verrazano-Narrows.
- World center of finance.
- First in printing and publishing, garment industry, and furs.
- First in the photographic industry.
- Historical center of Indian power.
- First capital of the United States—New York City.
- World center of tourism.
- Claims world's oldest chartered city—Albany.

Moments in History

- In 1524 Giovanni de Verrazano probably was the first European to set foot on New York soil, and in that same year black Portuguese explorer Estavan Gomez may also have done so.
- In 1609 explorer Henry Hudson entered the Hudson River, sailing up as far as present-day Albany, and Samuel de Champlain found Lake Champlain.

So They Say

"We found a pleasant place between steep little hills...and from those hills a mighty, deep mouthed river ran into the sea."

Giovanni de Verrazano

So They Say

"...large lake filled with beautiful islands and with a fine country around it."

Samuel de Champlain

- Hudson's discoveries supported Dutch claims. In 1614 the Dutch built Fort Nassau, near present-day Albany, and the first settlers arrived at New York City in 1624.
- In 1664 the Duke of York sent a large fleet to take over the area for England, and the Dutch surrendered.
- The outcome of the trial of publisher Peter Zenger in 1735 was vital to the preservation of freedom of the press.
- A century of warfare between the French and British for control of the area finally ended in 1761, with the British taking full control.
- In 1775, more than a year before national independence was agreed upon, 225 residents of Coxsackie signed a declaration of independence.
- New York became one of the main Revolutionary battlegrounds, suffering 92 engagements, almost a third of the total.
- New York City fell in the battles of Long Island and Fort Washington, September and October 1776.

• The Battle of Saratoga is ranked as one of the most important in world history. The British General Philip Schuyler surrendered there on October 17, 1777.

• Indian power in western New York was broken in 1779.

• On July 26, 1788, New York became the 11th state.

• New York was the capital of the new nation when George Washington took the presidential oath on the balcony of Federal Hall, April 30, 1789.

• The steamboat era began when Robert Fulton's *Clermont* chugged up the Hudson in 1807.

• During the War of 1812, much land fighting took place along the Canadian border, and the British fleet was destroyed on Lake Champlain in 1814.

• The Erie Canal opened on October 26, 1825, bringing New York City commerce to and from the far reaches of the Great Lakes.

• New Yorkers made an important contribution to the work of the Underground Railroad, spiriting slaves to safety in Canada.

• New York forces comprised one-sixth of the entire Union army during the Civil War.

• In 1883 New York became the first state with a civil service system for state employees.

• The Statue of Liberty was dedicated in 1886.

• President William McKinley received a fatal gunshot wound at the Pan-American Exposition at Buffalo in 1901.

• New York provided 10% of the U.S. servicemen and women in World War I.

• Lake Placid hosted the winter Olympic games in 1932.

• World War II brought death to 36,483 New York men and women in U.S. uniform, and New York produced 11.3% of all that war's materiel.

• New York transportation advances continued with the opening of the New York State Thruway in 1954 and the 1959 opening of the St. Lawrence Seaway.

• In 1986 New York City celebrated the 100th anniversary of the Statue of Liberty.

That's Interesting

• A giant "prehistoric" man was uncovered at Cardiff, but the "Cardiff Giant" was found to be a hoax, one of the most notable scams of all time.

• Dutch leader Hendrick Brevoort insisted that his favorite tree be saved, and Broadway at 10th Street still swings around the site of the long-vanished tree.

• Like a giant three-dimensional jigsaw puzzle, the Statue of Liberty was assembled from parts shipped to New York in 214 packing crates.

• Growing tired of his formal dinner clothes, a wealthy Hudson River man created another style. This new garment came to be known for the man's home town—Tuxedo.

• After Washington's defeat at Long Island, patriot Mary Lindley Murray arranged for British leader Lord Howe to have tea with her, giving the Americans time to escape.

• To delay British General Burgoyne on his march through New York, General Philip Schuyler's wife herself burned the wheat fields, slowing the enemy advance.

• Samuel Wilson, Troy meat packer, was known as Uncle Sam as he furnished meat to the army in the War of 1812. His reputation increased until the "real" Uncle Sam became the U.S. symbol.

• The world's first speed limit law was passed in New York City in 1652.

• Washington Square was once a potters' field where the trees were used for hangings.

Notable Natives

Humphrey Bogart (New York City, 1899-1957), actor. **James Cagney** (New York City, 1899-1986), actor, dancer. **Millard Fillmore** (Cayuga City., 1800-1874), U.S. president. **George Gershwin** (Brooklyn, 1898-1837), composer. **Jackie Gleason** (Brooklyn, 1916-1987), actor/comedian. **Edward Henry Harriman** (Hempstead, 1848-1909), financier. **Florence Jaffray, nee Hurst, Harriman** (New York City, 1870-1967), diplomat. **Hiawatha** (Onondaga tribe?, c.1570), Indian leader. **Julia Ward Howe** (New York City, 1819-1910), author/social reformer. **Charles Evans Hughes** (Glens Falls, 1862-1948), U.S.

chief justice. **George Inness** (Newburgh, 1825-1894), artist. **Washington Irving** (New York City, 1783-1859), author. **Henry James** (Albany, 1811-1882), philosopher/author. **Henry James** (New York City, 1843-1916), author. **William James** (New York City, 1842-1910), psychologist/philosopher. **Burt Lancaster** (New York, 1913-), actor. **Herman Melville** (New York City, 1819-1891), author. **Frederic Remington** (Canton, 1861-1909), artist. **John Davison Rockefeller** (Richford, 1839-1937), industrialist/philanthropist. **Anna Eleanor "Eleanor" Roosevelt** (New York City, 1884-1962), author/diplomat/humanitarian. **Franklin Delano Roosevelt** (Hyde Park, 1882-1945), U.S. president. **Theodore Roosevelt** (New York City, 1858-1919), U.S. president. **William Henry Seward** (Florida, NY, 1801-1872), public official. **Skenandoah** (near Oneida Castle, 1706?-1816), Indian leader. **Alfred Emanuel Smith** (New York City, 1873-1944), political leader. **Elizabeth Cady Stanton** (Johnstown, 1815-1902), suffrage leader. **Barbara Streisand** (New York City, 1942-), actress, singer. **Samuel Jones Tilden** (Lebanon, 1814-1886), public official. **Martin Van Buren** (Kinderhook, 1782-1862), U.S. president.

General

Admitted to statehood: July 26, 1788
Origin of name: For Duke of York and Albany, who received patent to New Netherland from his brother Charles II and sent an expedition to capture it, 1664
Capital: Albany
Nickname: The Empire State
Motto: "*Excelsior*" ("Ever Upward")
Animal: beaver
Bird: bluebird
Fish: brook trout (brookies or speckles)
Flower: rose
Fruit: apple
Gem: garnet
Song: "I Love New York"
Tree: sugar maple

The Land

Area: 54,475 sq. mi., 27th
Land: 47,224 sq. mi., 30th
Water: 7,251 sq. mi., 8th.
Topography: highest and most rugged mountains, the NE Adirondack upland; St. Lawrence-Champlain lowlands extend from Lake Ontario NE along the Canadian border; Hudson-Mohawk lowland follows the flows of the rivers N and W, 10-30 mi. wide; Atlantic coastal plain in the SE; Appalachian Highlands, covering half the state W from the Hudson Valley, include the Catskill Mtns., Finger Lakes, plateau of Erie-Ontario lowlands
Number of counties: 62
Geographic center: Madison, 12 mi. S of Oneida and 26 mi. SW of Utica
Length: 330 mi.
Width: 283 mi.
Highest point: 5,344 ft. (Mt. Marcy), 21st
Lowest point: sea level (Atlantic Ocean), 3rd
Mean elevation: 1,000 ft., 26th
Coastline: 127 mi., 14th
Shoreline: 1,850 mi., 13th

Climate and Environment

Temp., highest: 108 deg. on July 22, 1926, at Troy; lowest: -52 deg. on Feb. 18, 1979, at Old Forge
Fresh water withdrawn, per capita, per day: 508 gal., 44th
Endangered species: mammals, 1—Indiana bat; birds, 3—American peregrine falcon, piping plover, roseate tern; reptiles, 2; amphibians, none; fishes, none; invertebrates, 1; plants, 2

Major Cities, Population Percentage Increase (1980-90)

Buffalo, 328,123— –8.31%
New York City, 7,322,564—3.55%
Rochester, 231,636— –4.18%
Syracuse, 163,860— –3.67%
Yonkers, 188,082— –3.72%

The People

Population: 17,990,455, 2nd
Percent change (1980-90): 2.40%, 35th

Per sq. mi: 330.25, 7th
Percent in metro. area: 91.08%, 7th
Percent foreign born: 15.9%, 2nd
White: 13,385,255—74.40%, 42nd
Black: 2,859,055—15.89%, 13th
Native American: 62,651—0.35%, 30th
Asian, Pacific Isle: 693,760—3.86%, 4th
Other races: 989,734—5.50%, 5th
Hispanic origin: 2,214,026—12.31%, 6th
Percent over 5 yrs. speaking language other than English at home: 23.3%, 5th
Percent males: 47.95%, 47th
Percent females: 52.05%, 5th
Percent never married: 32.1%, 3rd
Marriages per 1,000 (1989): 9.0, 29th
Divorces per 1,000 (1989): 3.3, 44th
Median age: 33.9
Under 5 years: 1,255,764—6.98%, 39th
Under 18 years: 4,259,549—23.68%, 44th
65 years & older: 2,363,722—13.14%, 20th
Percent increase among the elderly: 9.4%, 49th

Of Vital Importance

Live births per 1,000 pop.: 16.8, 13th
Infant mortality rate per 1,000 births (1988): 10.8, 14th
Average lifetime (1979-81): 73.70, 29th
Deaths per 100,000 pop. (1988): 984.5, 7th
Causes of death per 100,000 pop. (1988):
Diseases of heart: 376.2, 4th
Malignant neoplasms: 216, 12th
Cerebrovascular diseases: 54, 39th
Accidents & adverse effects: 32.1, 45th
Chronic obstructive pulmonary diseases: 31, 34th
Suicide: 6.7, 51st
HIV infection: 22.3, 2nd
Other: 92.5, 2nd

Keeping Well

Non-federal physicians per 100,000 pop.: 338, 4th
Dentists per 100,000 (1990-91): 95, 2nd
Nurses per 100,000 (1989): 798, 13th
Hospitals per 100,000: 1.7, 50th
Admissions per 100,000: 13,616, 25th
Beds per 100,000: 583.28, 11th
Occupancy rate: 86.3%, 1st
Semiprivate room charges per day: $339, 11th
Average stay: 10.2, 9th
Notifiable diseases per 100,000:
AIDS: 46.7, 2nd
Gonorrhea: 287.8, 17th
Measles: 9.4, 8th
Syphillis: 51.7, 17th
Tuberculosis (TB): 23.2, 2nd
Per capita spending on mental health programs (1987): $140.08, 1st
Pop. without health insur. (1991): 12.3%, 29th

Households by Type

Total households: 6,639,322
Percent change (1980-90): 4.72%, 46th
Family households: 4,489,312
Percent of total: 67.62%, 46th
Nonfamily households: 2,150,010
Percent of total: 32.38%, 6th
Persons per household: 2.63, 16th
Pop. living in group quarters: 545,265
Percent of pop.: 3.03%, 15th

Living Quarters

Total housing units: 7,226,891
Persons per unit: 2.49, 8th
Occupied housing units: 6,639,322
Percent of total units: 91.87%, 10th
Persons per unit: 2.62, 12th
Percent of units with over 1 person per room: 6.50%, 8th
Owner-occupied units: 3,464,436
Percent of total units: 47.94%, 49th
Percent of occupied units: 52.18%, 50th
Persons per unit: 2.86, 5th
Median value: $131,600, 7th
Renter-occupied units: 3,174,886
Percent of total units: 43.93%, 2nd
Percent of occupied units: 47.82%, 2nd
Persons per unit: 2.38, 22nd
Median contract rent: $428, 11th
Rental vacancy rate: 4.9%, 50th
Mobile home, trailer & other as a % of occupied housing units: 4.56%, 43rd

Crime Index per 100,000

Total: 6,364, 9th
Violent: 1,181, 3rd

Murder and nonnegligent manslaughter: 14, 3rd
Aggravated assault: 6,980, 39th
Robbery: 625, 2nd
Rape: 30, 38th
Property: 5,183, 15th
Burglary: 1,161, 22nd
Larceny, theft: 2,979, 28th
Motor vehicle theft: 1,043, 2nd
Drug abuse arrests: 683, 3rd

TEACHING AND LEARNING

Literacy (1987): 84%, 47th
Pop. 3 and over enrolled in school: 4,656,218
Percent of pop.: 27.0%, 28th
Public elementary & secondary schools:
Total enrollment: 2,594,000
Avg. class size (1987): 22, 28th
Teachers: 183,300
Percent of pop.: 1.02%, 25th
Teachers' avg. salary: $38,900, 3rd
Spending per capita: $1,091, 5th
Spending per pupil in avg. daily attendance: $8,094, 2nd
Percent of graduates taking SAT: 75%, 3rd
Combined SAT scores: 881, 42nd
Percent of pop. over 25 completing:
High school: 74.8%, 34th
College degree/s: 23.1%, 11th
Higher educa., institutions: 324
Per 100,000 pop.: 0.5, 42nd
Enroll: 1,040,484
Percent of pop.: 5.78%, 21st
Public: 612,934
Percent of enroll.: 58.91%, 45th
Private: 427,550
Percent of enroll.: 41.09%, 7th
White non-Hispanic: 34,178
Percent of enroll.: 93.90%, 3rd
Black non-Hispanic: 375
Percent of enroll.: 1.03%, 44th
Hispanic: 428
Percent of enroll.: 1.18%, 34th
Asian/Pacific Islander: 569
Percent of enroll.: 1.56%, 30th
Amer. Indian/AK native: 131
Percent of enroll.: 0.36%, 28th
Nonresident alien: 717
Percent of enroll.: 1.97%, 33rd
Female: 577,217
Percent of enroll.: 55.48%, 18th
Tuition, state university ('90-'91): $1,587, 31st
Public library systems: 760
Books & serial vol. per capita: 3.70, 10th
Govt. expend. per capita: $23.53, 8th
State govt.: $5.01, 7th
Local govts.: $18.52, 11th

LAW ENFORCEMENT, COURTS, AND PRISONS

Police protection expend.: $3,391,355,000
Per capita: $188.51, 3rd
Judicial & legal expend.: $1,708,393,000
Per capita: $94.96, 4th
Corrections expend.: $3,332,635,000
Per capita: $185.25, 3rd
Police per 10,000 pop. (1990-91): 25.9, 7th
Prisoners (state & fed.) sentenced to over 1 yr., per 100,000 pop.: 304
Percent change (1989-90): 7.16%, 28th
Death penalty: no

RELIGION, NUMBER AND PERCENT OF POPULATION

Agnostic: 82,385—0.60%, 19th
Buddhist: 27,462—0.20%, 11th
Christian: 10,957,263—79.80%, 44th
Hindu: 82,385—0.60%, 1st
Jewish: 947,433—6.90%, 1st
Moslem: 109,847—0.80%, 1st
Other: 205,964—1.50%, 18th
Unitarian: 41,193—0.30%, 15th
None: 878,778—6.40%, 28th
Refused to answer: 398,196—2.90%, 9th

MAKING A LIVING

Personal income per capita (1989): $16,501, 7th
Percent increase (1979-'89) (constant 1989 dollars): 31.3%, 6th
Average income per family: $50,704, 9th
Percent of pop. below poverty level: 13.0%, 21st
Percent 65 and over: 11.9%, 25th

Cost of living, selected cities
1st qtr., 1991 (U. S. Standard=100)
Binghamton 100.1
Nassau-Suffolk 152.1

Economy

Civilian labor force : 8,673,000
Percent of tot. pop.: 48.21%, 41st
Percent 65 and over: 3.42%, 9th
Percent females: 44.79%, 39th
Percent job growth (1980-90): 15.42%, 35th
Major employer industries:
Agriculture: 90,453—1.10%, 45th
Construction: 361,812—4.40%, 27th
Finance, insurance & real estate: 731,847—8.90%, 3rd
Government: 1,447,248—17.60%, 12th
Manufacturing: 1,208,781—14.70%, 33rd
Mining: 7,946—0.1%, 47th
Service: 1,915,959—23.30%, 7th
Trade: 1,389,687—16.90%, 47th
Transportation, communication, & public utilities: 452,265—5.50%, 18th
Wholesale/retail: 1,599,592—19.1%, 48th
Unemployment rate: 5.20%, 31st
Male: 3.10%, 25th
Female: 2.10%, 38th
Total businesses (1991): 605,384
New business incorp's. (1991): 63,808
Percent of total businesses: 10.54%, 7th
Business failures (1991): 5,563
Percent of total businesses: 0.92%, 19th
Agriculture farm income
Marketing (1991): $2,868,321,000, 24th
Net per operation: $17,110, 29th
Net per acre: $78, 16th
Leading products: dairy products, greenhouse, cattle, apples
Av. value land & build. per acre: $1,042, 21st
Percent increase (1980-90): 44.72%, 10th
Govt. payments: $41,242,000, 31st
Construction, value of all: $5,947,000,000
Per capita: $330.56, 44th
Percent change 1989-90: -29.59%, 43rd
Manufactures:
Value added: $85,532,000,000
Per capita: $4,754.30, 32nd
Value of shipments: $154,714,000,000
Per capita: $8,599.78, 36th
Leading products: books and periodicals, clothing and apparel, pharmaceuticals, machinery, instruments, toys and sporting goods, electronic equipment, automotive and aircraft components
Mining, min. prod., value (1987): $642,000,000, 30th
Leading products: stone, cement, salt
Retail sales: $124,479,000,000, 2nd
Per household: $18,687, 28th
Percent increase (1987-90): 18.1%, 19th
Service indust., value (1987): $114,107,000,000, 2nd
Per capita: $6,342.64, 4th
Tourism indus., value (1989): $18,301,000,000, 3rd
Foreign exports value: $22,072,000,000, 4th
Per capita: $1,226.87, 14th
Patents per 1,000 pop.: 4.0, 40th

Travel and Transportation

Motor vehicle registrations: 10,196,153
Per 1,000 pop.: 566, 50th
Motorcycle registrations: 197,935
Per 1,000 pop.: 11, 40th
Licensed drivers per 1,000 driving age pop.: 727, 51st
Deaths from motor vehicle accidents per 100,000 pop.: 12.3, 46th
Public roads & streets
Total mileage: 111,242, 12th
Rural mileage: 73,329, 20th
Urban mileage: 37,913, 4th
Interstate mileage: 1,500, 6th
Annual vehicle-miles of travel per person: 5,942, 50th
Mean travel time for workers 16 + who work away from home: 28.6 min., 1st

Government

Registered voters (1988): 8,581,276
Percent of voting age pop.: 63.66%, 41st
Voter turnout (1988): 6,485,683
Percent of registered voters: 75.58%, 15th
Percent of voting age pop.: 48.11%, 36th

State legislators, total (1992): 211, 4th
Women members (1992): 27
Percent of legislature: 12.8%, 38th
Dominant party (1992): Split
U. S. Congress, House members (1993): 31
Increase 1983-93: -3
Revenues:
State govt.: $64,252,998,000
Per capita: $3,571.50, 4th
State & local govt.: $108,692,249,000
Per capita: $6,041.66, 3rd
Indebtedness:
State govt.: $46,547,127,000
Per capita: $2,587.32, 9th
State & local govt.: $94,538,000,000
Per capita: $5,254.90, 5th

Laws and Regulations

Legal driving age: 18
Marriage age without parental consent: 18
Divorce residence requirement: 1 yr., qualification—check local statutes

Attractions

Major opera companies (1989): 39, 1st
Per 1 million pop.: 2.17, 2nd
Major symphony orchestras (1989): 67, 2nd
Per 1 million pop.: 3.73, 24th
State appropriations for state arts agencies per capita: $3.29, 3rd
State Fair in late Aug.-early Sept. at Syracuse

Sports and Competition

NCAA sports teams, 42: Adelphi Univ. Panthers, Brooklyn College Kingsmen, C.W. Post Pioneers, Canisius College Golden Griffins, Colgate Univ. Red Raiders, Columbia Univ. Lions, Cornell Univ. Big Red, Fordham Univ. Rams, Hamilton College Continentals, Hartwick College Warriors, Hobart College Statesmen, Hofstra Univ. Flying Dutchmen, Iona College Gaels, Le Moyne College Dolphins, Long Island Univ. Blackbirds, Manhattan College Jaspers, Marist College Red Foxes, Niagara Univ. Purple Eagles, Rensselaer Polytechnic Institute Engineers, Siena College, Skidmore College Thoroughbreds, St. Bonaventure Univ. Bonnies, St. Francis College Terriers, St. John's Univ. Redmen, St. Lawrence Univ. Saints, State Univ. of New York (at Albany) Great Danes, State Univ. of New York (at Binghamton) Colonials, State Univ. of New York (at Stony Brook) Patriots, State Univ. College of New York/Brockport Golden Eagles, State Univ. College of New York/Cortland Red Dragons, State Univ. College of New York/Fredonia Blue Devils, State Univ. College of New York/Geneseo Knights, State Univ. College of New York/Oneonta Red Dragons, State Univ. College of New York/Oswego Lakers, State Univ. College of New York/Plattsburgh Cardinals, State Univ. College of New York/Potsdam Bears, State Univ. of New York at Buffalo Bulls, Syracuse Univ. Orangemen, U.S. Military Academy, Union College Dutchmen, Univ. of Rochester Yellowjackets, Wagner College
Professional teams, 30:
Baseball, 15—Watertown Indians (New York-Penn League, Class A), Alex T. Duffy Fairgrounds; Jamestown Expos (New York-Penn League, Class A), College Stadium; Oneonta Yankees (New York-Penn League, Class A), Damaschke Field; Utica Blue Sox (New York-Penn League, Class A), Donovan Field; Elmira Pioneers (New York-Penn League, Class A), Dunn Field; Batavia Clippers (New York-Penn League, Class A), Dwyer Stadium; Auburn Astros (New York-Penn League, Class A), Falcon Park Stadium; Albany-Colonie Yankees (Eastern League, Class AA), Heritage Park; Syracuse Chiefs (International League, Class AAA), MacArthur Stadium; Geneva Cubs (New York-Penn League, Class A), McKonough Park; Buffalo Bisons (American Association, Class AAA), Pilot Field; Niagara Falls Rapids (New York-Penn League, Class A), Sal Maglie Stadium; New York Mets (NL), Shea Stadium; Rochester Red Wings (International League, Class AAA), Silver Stadium; New York Yankees (AL), Yankee Stadium
Basketball, 2—Albany Partoons (Continental Basketball Association), Knickerbocker

Arena; New York Knickerbockers (NBA), Madison Square Garden

Football, 4—New York Jets (AFC), Giants' Stadium; New York Giants (NFC), Giants Stadium; New York Knights (World League of American Football), Giants' Stadium; Buffalo Bills (AFC) Rich Stadium

Hockey, 8—Binghamton Rangers (American Hockey League), Broome County Veterans Memorial Arena; Adirondack Red Wings (American Hockey League), Glens Falls Civic Center; New York Rangers (NHL), Madison Square Garden; Buffalo Sabres (NHL), Memorial Auditorium; New York Islanders (NHL), Nassau Veterans' Memorial Coliseum; Capital District Islanders (American Hockey League), R. P. I. Houston Field House; Utica Devils (American Hockey League), Utica Memorial Auditorium; Rochester Americans (American Hockey League), War Memorial Auditorium

Soccer, 1—Albany Capitals (American Professional Soccer League), Bleecker Stadium

NORTH CAROLINA

"In my honest and unbiased judgment, the Go[...] will place the Garden of Eden in North Carolina when He restores it[...] earth. He will do this because He will have so few changes to make in [...] achieve perfection."

Sam Irvin, Jr.

North Carolina was the site of "mankind's single most significant event," as the Wright Brothers' first flight has been named. It also was the site of one of history's great mysteries—the disappearance of the Roanoke Island settlement. North Carolina is the "longest" state in the East, and Grandfather Mountain is said to be the world's oldest. The state's seacoast is unique in the country, and the Appalachian Mountains reach their highest levels in the state. Between the mountains and the sea lies a productive land—it is both an agricultural and a manufacturing state—of historic moment.

SUPERLATIVES

- World's first heavier-than-air flight.
- First radio SOS, sent off shores of Cape Hatteras.
- First U.S. school of forestry.
- Leader in fine furniture production.
- First in the nation in tobacco cultivation.
- Leads nation in cigarette production.

MOMENTS IN HISTORY

- During his expedition of 1540 Hernando De Soto and his large party reached the western mountains, found no riches and departed.
- After receiving rights to the North Carolina area, Sir Walter Raleigh sent captains M. Philip Amadas and [...] Barlowe to scout the area in 1584.

"We found su[...]ay the world the [...]at I think in all found." [...]e is not to be

[...]rlowe

- Raleigh responde[...]even ships which landed on Roano[...] settlement failed.
- Under John White a[...], but the other group restored the R[...] added to it. There Virginia [...]7 an- child of English parents to [...]and and John White returned to E[...]rst to the colony.
- Coming back to America [...] White found one of the great [...] continent. The colony was aba[...] trace except for two cryptic car[...] further was ever known about little [...] or the other settlers.
- Edenton was begun about 1658.
- In 1663 Charles II granted the C[...] eight "Lords Proprietors." A year later Al[...] County was founded.
- Dissatisfied with their lot, in 1677 a group o[...] Albemarle settlers led by John Culpeper took part

So They Say

"As we entered up the sandy bank, upon a tree...were curiously carved...Roman letters C R O....We passed toward th place where they were left in sun houses, but we found the houses t e down...one of the chief trees...he bark taken off, and five foot ven ground in fair capital letters, gn of CROATOAN, without any cro distress."

hite

lion," the first in the short-lived "Culpe ists. ever attempted by Ame rates, and in 1718

• The coasts were a d was killed in a the notorious pirat notable struggle.

Say

"Blackbe y toppled over dead... wounds had sapped the lif agnificent body. Ed- wa ied just as hard as he h author of The Pirates colonial North Carolina

ought out the Lords Proprietors

n in the new royal colony increased by 1765 there were 120,000 settlers.

egulators, a group protesting the injus- itsh rule, were defeated in the "Battle of ce." Although the movement collapsed in t has been called by some "the first battle Revolution."

In 1779 British Lord Cornwallis marched th, captured Charlotte, and engaged in the attles of Kings Mountain and Guilford Court House.

So They Say

"I never saw such fighting since God made me. The Americans fought like demons."

Lord Cornwallis

• North Carolina became the 12th state on Nov. 21, 1778.

• The state legislature met at the new capital city of Raleigh for the first time in 1794.

• In 1838 the government began to remove the Cherokee to the West, from their ancestral lands. On the "Trail of Tears" 4,000 died, but a few managed to escape into the mountains. Cherokee leader Tsali and all but one of his family were murdered, but finally those who remained bought a reservation, where their descendants continue to live today.

• The Aug., 1861, capture of forts Clark and Hatteras was the first substantial Union victory in the Civil War.

• On May 6, 1865, the last Confederate army in the state laid down its arms. North Carolina troops suffered the greatest losses of all the states.

• After the tragedy of Reconstruction, prosperity began to revive.

• The state took the lead in cigarette production in 1884.

• Cotton mills multiplied, and by 1900 the state had achieved leadership in production of fine furniture.

• North Carolina was the scene of "the most significant single event in the long history of mankind" when the Wright Brothers' plane lifted off the sands of Kitty Hawk on December 17, 1903.

• Eighty-six-thousand people from North Carolina served in World War I, with more than 2,400 losing their lives.

• World War II called 362,000 to service from North Carolina, with nearly 8,000 losing their lives.

• When hurricane Hazel struck in 1954, it was one of the most disastrous of such storms to strike the state.

THAT'S INTERESTING

• A prehistoric group known as Early Farmers was notable for its careful burial of dogs.

• Trader John Lawson revealed that traders looked for the Indians with the smallest mouths. The Indians filled their mouths with as much rum as they could and spit it into a container before giving up a pelt.

• Colonel Benjamin Cleveland was noted not only for his courage in the Battle of Kings Mt. but also for his weight of 450 lbs.

• The women of Edenton opposed the British tax on tea by deciding not to drink it. A teapot-shaped monument pays tribute to this decision.

• Blowing Rock is a unique natural formation. When handkerchiefs are tossed over the ridge, the currents of air waft them back.

• In the course of the Civil War, General Bryan Grimes of Grimesville had six horses shot from under him.

Notable Natives

Thomas Hart Benton (Hillsboro, 1782-1858), statesman. **Braxton Bragg** (Warrenton, 1817-1876), soldier. **Thomas Lanier Clingman** (Huntersville, 1812-1807), soldier/politician. **Josephus Daniels** (Washington, NC, 1862-1948), journalist/statesman. **Andrew Johnson** (Raleigh, 1808-1875), U.S. president. **Dolley Payne Madison** (Guilford City, 1768-1849), first lady/hostess. **James K. Polk** (Mecklenburg City, 1795-1849), U.S. president. **William Sydney "O. Henry" Porter** (Greensboro, 1862-1910), author. **Matt Whittaker Ransom** (Warren Co., 1826-1904), soldier/lawyer/legislator. **Zebulon Baird Vance** (Buncombe Co., 1830-1894), lawyer/politician. **Thomas Wolfe** (Asheville, 1900-1938), author.

General

Admitted to statehood: Nov. 21, 1789
Origin of name: In 1619 Charles I gave a large patent to Sir Robert Heath to be called Province of Carolana, from Carolus, Latin name for Charles; a new patent was granted by Charles II to the Earl of Clarendon and others—divided into North and South Carolina, 1710
Capital: Raleigh
Nickname: The Tar Heel State, Old North State
Motto: *"Esse Quam Videri"* ("To Be, Rather Than to Seem")
Bird: cardinal
Colors: red and blue
Fish: channel bass
Flower: dogwood
Gemstone: emerald
Insect: honeybee
Mammal: gray squirrel
Reptile: turtle
Shell: Scotch bonnet
Song: "The Old North State"
Tree: pine

The Land

Area: 53,821 sq. mi., 28th
Land: 48,708 sq. mi., 29th
Water: 5,103 sq. mi., 10th.
Topography: coastal plain and tidewater, two-fifths of state, extending to the fall line of the rivers, Piedmont plateau; another two-fifths, 200 mi. wide of gentle to rugged hills, southern Appalachian Mtns., contains the Blue Ridge and Great Smoky Mtns.
Number of counties: 100
Geographic center: Chatham, 10 mi. NW of Sanford
Length: 500 mi.
Width: 150 mi.
Highest point: 6,684 ft. (Mt. Mitchell), 16th
Lowest point: sea level (Atlantic Ocean), 3rd
Mean elevation: 700 ft., 35th
Coastline: 301 mi., 7th
Shoreline: 3,375 mi., 6th

Climate and Environment

Temp., highest: 110 deg. on Aug. 21, 1983, at Fayetteville; lowest: -34 deg. on Jan. 21, 1985, at Mt. Mitchell
Fresh water withdrawn, per capita, per day: 1,260 gal., 24th
Endangered species: mammals, 5—Indiana bat, Virginia big-eared bat, West Indian manatee, Carolina northern flying squirrel, red wolf; birds, 2—American peregrine falcon, red-cockaded woodpecker; reptiles, 3; amphibians, none; fishes, 1; invertebrates, 3; plants, 13

Major Cities, Population Percentage Increase (1980-90)

Charlotte, 395,934—25.50%
Durham, 136,611—35.06%

Greensboro, 183,521—17.91%
Raleigh, 207,951—38.40%
Winston-Salem, 143,485—8.80%

THE PEOPLE

Population: 6,628,637, 10th
 Percent change (1980-90): 11.29%, 16th
 Per sq. mi: 123.16, 16th
 Percent in metro. area: 56.69%, 34th
 Percent foreign born: 1.7%, 37th
White: 5,008,491—75.56%, 39th
Black: 1,456,323—21.97%, 8th
Native American: 80,155—1.21%, 14th
Asian, Pacific Isle: 52,166—0.79%, 36th
Other races: 31,502—0.48%, 36th
Hispanic origin: 76,726—1.16%, 39th
Percent over 5 yrs. speaking language other than English at home: 3.9%, 42nd
Percent males: 48.49%, 30th
Percent females: 51.51%, 22nd
Percent never married: 25.1%, 30th
Marriages per 1,000 (1989): 7.7, 47th
Divorces per 1,000 (1989): 4.9, 22nd
Median age: 33.1
Under 5 years: 458,955—6.92%, 42nd
Under 18 years: 1,606,149—24.23%, 43rd
65 years & older: 804,341—12.13%, 31st
Percent increase among the elderly: 33.3%, 10th

OF VITAL IMPORTANCE

Live births per 1,000 pop.: 15.8, 27th
Infant mortality rate per 1,000 births (1988): 12.5, 3rd
Average lifetime (1979-81): 72.96, 42nd
Deaths per 100,000 pop. (1988): 888.3, 25th
Causes of death per 100,000 pop. (1988):
 Diseases of heart: 299.4, 30th
 Malignant neoplasms: 195.8, 28th
 Cerebrovascular diseases: 73.6, 6th
 Accidents & adverse effects: 49.5, 10th
 Chronic obstructive pulmonary diseases: 32.3, 31st
 Suicide: 12.1, 29th
 HIV infection: 3.4, 24th
 Other: 76.3, 24th

KEEPING WELL

Non-federal physicians per 100,000 pop.: 204, 29th
Dentists per 100,000 (1990-91): 46, 48th
Nurses per 100,000 (1989): 617, 32nd
Hospitals per 100,000: 2.3, 38th
 Admissions per 100,000: 13,094, 32nd
 Beds per 100,000: 454.42, 32nd
 Occupancy rate: 74.9%, 11th
 Semiprivate room charges per day: $220, 40th
 Average stay: 7.2, 24th
Notifiable diseases per 100,000:
 AIDS: 8.4, 27th
 Gonorrhea: 483.9, 7th
 Measles: 0.6, 43rd
 Syphillis: 51.2, 18th
 Tuberculosis (TB): 10.0, 15th
Per capita spending on mental health programs (1987): $40.40, 21st
Pop. without health insur. (1991): 14.9%, 16th

HOUSEHOLDS BY TYPE

Total households: 2,517,026
 Percent change (1980-90): 23.20%, 7th
Family households: 1,812,053
 Percent of total: 71.99%, 15th
Nonfamily households: 704,973
 Percent of total: 28.01%, 37th
Persons per household: 2.54, 39th
Pop. living in group quarters: 224,470
 Percent of pop.: 3.39%, 10th

LIVING QUARTERS

Total housing units: 2,818,193
 Persons per unit: 2.35, 35th
Occupied housing units: 2,517,026
 Percent of total units: 89.31%, 26th
 Persons per unit: 2.51, 30th
 Percent of units with over 1 person per room: 2.89%, 28th
Owner-occupied units: 1,711,817
 Percent of total units: 60.74%, 20th
 Percent of occupied units: 68.01%, 21st
 Persons per unit: 2.62, 46th
 Median value: $65,800, 28th
Renter-occupied units: 805,209
 Percent of total units: 28.57%, 29th

Percent of occupied units: 31.99%, 31st
Persons per unit: 2.39, 18th
Median contract rent: $284, 34th
Rental vacancy rate: 9.2%, 20th
Mobile home, trailer & other as a % of occupied housing units: 18.04%, 7th

Crime Index per 100,000

Total: 5,486, 21st
Violent: 624, 20th
Murder and nonnegligent manslaughter: 11, 11th
Aggravated assault: 6,924, 42nd
Robbery: 152, 22nd
Rape: 34, 29th
Property: 4,862, 22nd
Burglary: 1,530, 7th
Larceny, theft: 3,048, 24th
Motor vehicle theft: 284, 37th
Drug abuse arrests: 376, 11th

Teaching and Learning

Literacy (1987): 86%, 33nd
Pop. 3 and over enrolled in school: 1,624,913
Percent of pop.: 25.6%, 44th
Public elementary & secondary schools:
Total enrollment: 1,096,000
Avg. class size (1987): 25, 7th
Teachers: 62,900
Percent of pop.: 0.95%, 34th
Teachers' avg. salary: $27,800, 31st
Spending per capita: $737, 33rd
Spending per pupil in avg. daily attendance: $4,386, 31st
Percent of graduates taking SAT: 57%, 16th
Combined SAT scores: 844, 48th
Percent of pop. over 25 completing:
High school: 70.0%, 43rd
College degree/s: 17.4%, 38th
Higher educa., institutions: 125
Per 100,000 pop.: 1.1, 11th
Enroll: 351,990
Percent of pop.: 5.31%, 30th
Public: 285,257
Percent of enroll.: 81.04%, 29th
Private: 66,733
Percent of enroll.: 18.96%, 23rd
White non-Hispanic: 186,541
Percent of enroll.: 82.45%, 31st
Black non-Hispanic: 31,240
Percent of enroll.: 13.81%, 10th
Hispanic: 1,302
Percent of enroll.: 0.58%, 42nd
Asian/Pacific Islander: 2,283
Percent of enroll.: 1.01%, 40th
Amer. Indian/AK native: 476
Percent of enroll.: 0.21%, 48th
Nonresident alien: 4,396
Percent of enroll.: 1.94%, 34th
Female: 197,074
Percent of enroll.: 55.99%, 14th
Tuition, state university ('90-'91): $1,112, 49th
Public library systems: 73
Books & serial vol. per capita: 1.74, 45th
Govt. expend. per capita: $14.11, 27th
State govt.: $2.71, 22nd
Local govts.: $11.40, 27th

Law Enforcement, Courts, and Prisons

Police protection expend.: $645,827,000
Per capita: $97.42, 30th
Judicial & legal expend.: $217,238,000
Per capita: $32.77, 44th
Corrections expend.: $531,094,000
Per capita: $80.12, 25th
Police per 10,000 pop. (1990-91): 21.6, 18th
Prisoners (state & fed.) sentenced to over 1 yr., per 100,000 pop.: 264
Percent change (1989-90): 6.53%, 30th
Death penalty: yes, by lethal gas or lethal injection
Under sentence of death: 81, 11th
Executed (1989): none

Religion, Number and Percent of Population

Agnostic: 15,068—0.30%, 37th
Buddhist: 5,023—0.10%, 17th
Christian: 4,550,374—90.60%, 8th
Hindu: N/A
Jewish: 25,112—0.50%, 27th
Moslem: 10,045—0.20%, 13th

Unitarian: 5,023—0.10%, 31st
Other: 85,382—1.70%, 14th
None: 241,079—4.80%, 42nd
Refused to answer: 85,382—1.70%, 35th

MAKING A LIVING

Personal income per capita (1989): $12,885, 33rd
Percent increase (1979-'89) (constant 1989 dollars): 25.4%, 14th
Average income per family: $38,064, 34th
Percent of pop. below poverty level: 13.0%, 22nd
Percent 65 and over: 19.5%, 9th
Cost of living, selected cities/county
1st qtr., 1991 (U. S. Standard=100)

Gastonia	91.2
Raleigh-Durham (Chapel Hill)	110.1
Dare County	114.9

ECONOMY

Civilian labor force : 3,401,000
Percent of tot. pop.: 51.31%, 24th
Percent 65 and over: 2.88%, 22nd
Percent females: 45.90%, 23rd
Percent job growth (1980-90): 28.18%, 15th
Major employer industries:
Agriculture: 78,288—2.40%, 31st
Construction: 169,624—5.20%, 15th
Finance, insurance & real estate: 140,266—4.30%, 41st
Government: 440,370—13.50%, 39th
Manufacturing: 890,526—27.30%, 1st
Mining: 5,186—0.2%, 35th
Service: 531,706—16.30%, 46th
Trade: 583,898—17.90%, 35th
Transportation, communication, & public utilities: 156,576—4.80%, 32nd
Wholesale/retail: 658,582—20.3%, 39th
Unemployment rate: 4.09%, 47th
Male: 1.97%, 48th
Female: 2.12%, 37th
Total businesses (1991): 209,770
New business incorp's. (1991): 11,944
Percent of total businesses: 5.69%, 27th
Business failures (1991): 1,350
Percent of total businesses: 0.64%, 43rd
Agriculture farm income
Marketing (1991): $4,924,071,000, 10th
Net per operation: $35,675, 8th
Net per acre: $16, 44th
Leading products: tobacco, broilers, hogs, turkeys
Av. value land & build. per acre: $1,325, 13th
Percent increase (1980-90): 8.70%, 20th
Govt. payments: $52,837,000, 29th
Construction, value of all: $5,227,000,000
Per capita: $788.55, 12th
Percent change 1989-90: -5.80%, 24th
Manufactures:
Value added: $57,674,000,000
Per capita: $8,700.73, 1st
Value of shipments: $116,245,000,000
Per capita: $17,536.79, 3rd
Leading products: textiles, tobacco products, electrical and electronic equipment, chemical, furniture, food products, nonelectrical machinery
Mining, min. prod., value (1987): $527,000,000, 32nd
Leading products: stone, phosphate, lithium
Retail sales: $45,756,000,000, 13th
Per household: $17,995, 34th
Percent increase (1987-90): 5.9%, 48th
Service indust., value (1987): $19,437,000,000, 15th
Per capita: $2,932.28, 44th
Tourism indus., value (1989): $6,306,000,000, 13th
Foreign exports value: $8,010,000,000, 13th
Per capita: $1,208.39, 15th
Patents per 1,000 pop.: 7.8, 20th

TRAVEL AND TRANSPORTATION

Motor vehicle registrations: 5,162,005
Per 1,000 pop.: 778, 28th
Motorcycle registrations: 57,079
Per 1,000 pop.: 8, 47th
Licensed drivers per 1,000 driving age pop.: 881, 33rd
Deaths from motor vehicle accidents per 100,000 pop.: 20.9, 19th
Public roads & streets
Total mileage: 94,690, 17th
Rural mileage: 75,445, 17th
Urban mileage: 19,245, 12th
Interstate mileage: 937, 20th
Annual vehicle-miles of travel per person: 9,460, 20th

Mean travel time for workers 16 + who work away from home: 19.8 min., 31st

Government

Registered voters (1988): 3,432,042
Percent of voting age pop.: 69.86%, 28th
Voter turnout (1988): 2,134,370
Percent of registered voters: 62.19%, 44th
Percent of voting age pop.: 43.44%, 47th
State legislators, total (1992): 170, 15th
Women members (1992): 25
Percent of legislature: 14.7%, 31st
Dominant party (1992): Democrats
U. S. Congress, House members (1993): 12
Increase 1983-93: +1
Revenues:
State govt.: $14,485,060,000
Per capita: $2,185.22, 37th
State & local govt.: $23,175,644,000
Per capita: $3,496.29, 39th
Indebtedness:
State govt.: $3,071,211,000
Per capita: $463.32, 48th
State & local govt.: $15,723,000,000
Per capita: $2,371.98, 43rd

Laws and Regulations

Legal driving age: 18
Marriage age without parental consent: 18
Divorce residence requirement: 6 mo.

Attractions

Major opera companies (1989): 4, 11th
Per 1 million pop.: 0.61, 29th
Major symphony orchestras (1989): 20, 15th
Per 1 million pop.: 3.04, 32nd
State appropriations for state arts agencies per capita: $0.76, 25th
State Fair in mid-Oct. at Raleigh

Sports and Competition

NCAA sports teams, 17: Appalachian State Univ. Mountaineers, Campbell Univ. Fighting Camels, Davidson College Wildcats, Duke Univ. Blue Devils, East Carolina Univ. Pirates, Fayetteville State Univ. Broncos, Lenoir-Rhyne College Bears, North Carolina A&T State Univ. Aggies, North Carolina State Univ. Wolfpack, Pfeiffer College Falcons, Univ. of North Carolina Tar Heels, Univ. of North Carolina 49ers, Univ. of North Carolina Spartans, Univ. of North Carolina Seahawks, Wake Forest Univ. Demon Deacons, Western Carolina Univ. Catamounts, Winston-Salem State Univ. Rams.
Professional teams, 15:
Baseball, 9—Burlington Indians (Appalachian League, Rookie Class), Burlington Athletic Field; Durham Bulls (Carolina League, Class A), Durham Athletic Park; Winston-Salem Spirits (Carolina League, Class A), Ernie Shore Field; Carolina Mudcats (Southern League, Class AA), Five County Stadium; Kinston Indians (Carolina League, Class A), Grainger Stadium; Fayetteville Generals (South Atlantic League, Class A), J. P. Riddle Stadium; Asheville Tourists (South Atlantic League, Class A), McCormick Field; Gastonia Rangers (South Atlantic League, Class A), Sims Legion Park; Greensboro Hornets (South Atlantic League, Class A), War Memorial Stadium
Basketball, 1—Charlotte Hornets (NBA), Charlotte Coliseum
Football, 1—Raleigh-Durham Skyhawks (World League of American Football), Carter-Finley Stadium
Hockey, 3—Greensboro Monarchs (East Coast Hockey League), Greensboro Coliseum; Raleigh IceCaps (East Coast Hockey League), J. S. Dorton Arena; Winston-Salem Thunderbirds (East Coast Hockey League), Lawrence Joel Veterans Memorial Coliseum Annex
Soccer, 1—(located at Raleigh-Durham) (American Professional Soccer League)

NORTH DAKOTA

"I would never have been President if it had not been for my experiences in North Dakota."

Theodore Roosevelt

"From pioneer hardships to the rich abundance of modern farms, mines, and factories in little more than a lifetime is the capsule history of North Dakota."

Arthur A. Link

North Dakota is a land where the great plains have been transformed into lake country by enormous modern reservoirs. Ancient lakes figured in the state's present by depositing the rich soil that brings agricultural abundance. North Dakota is the state where Theodore Roosevelt developed his dynamic image, and the nation dedicated its only National Memorial Park on a portion of the land he once owned. It is a state small in population but rich in such resources as the world's greatest reserves of lignite and in its wealth of tradition.

SUPERLATIVES

- Novel skyscraper capitol
- "Capital" of the lignite industry.
- First in spring wheat, rye, and flax.

MOMENTS IN HISTORY

• Pierre Gaultier de Varennes, the Sieur de La Verendrye, and his two sons arrived in present-day North Dakota in 1738 and reached the Mandan Indian village near present-day Menoken.

• By 1762 the nominal French control of the area had been turned over to the equally nominal control of Britain.

• Braving an unusually bitter winter, in 1797 the party of British scientist David Thompson visited the Mandan towns on the Missouri River.

• After the Louisiana Purchase by the United States, the first true picture of the region came with the detailed reports of the Louis and Clark expedition. They spent the winter of 1804 at what they called "Fort Mandan," near the Mandan and Arikara villages north of present Washburn. They lived in log cabins chinked with mud.

• As they left the winter camp on April 7, 1805, Lewis and Clark sent back to civilization a vast amount of information they had gathered to that point. This included numbers of new and unusual plants and animals and the most complete information on the Indian tribes yet noted.

> **So They Say**
>
> "I could but esteem this moment of my departure as among the most happy of my life. The party are in excellent health and spirits, zealously attached to the enterprise and anxious to proceed, not a whisper or murmur of discontent to be heard among them, but all act in unison, and with the most perfect harmony."
>
> Meriwether Lewis

• On their way back in 1806, Lewis and Clark stopped again to visit their Indian friends at Fort Mandan. The expedition was enormously important in keeping peace with the western Indians for many years.

• Following the Lewis and Clark expedition, fur trading posts were opened, and in 1812 William Douglas established a Scottish settlement near present-day Pembina.

• David Thompson took part in the 1818 survey of the U.S.-Canadian border.

• In 1828 the American Fur Company began Fort Union on the North Dakota side of the Missouri River, and for about 40 yrs. it remained the most important post in a vast region.

• Begun in 1857, Fort Abercrombie was the first federal stronghold in the present state.

• Dakota Territory was organized in 1861.

• Indian warfare had continued over a long period, but by 1881 most of the Sioux people had turned to reservation life.

• One of the worst of the many prairie fires swept the area on September 25, 1888.

So They Say

"...For at least 40 miles in width the fire burned off every vestige of grass unprotected by breaks. One could hardly recognize the charred land the next day. Thousands of bushels of grain were burned and many men lost all they had, grain, buildings and stock."

Newspaper account

• The first capitol's cornerstone was laid in 1883 by former president U.S. Grant.

• Theodore Roosevelt arrived in North Dakota in 1883, and became a successful and popular rancher.

• Both Dakotas became states on November 2, 1889.

• After "Honest John" Burke was elected governor in 1906, child labor laws and other modern laws were enacted.

• Of 31,269 North Dakotans who served in World War I, 1,205 lost their lives.

• In 1919 the state began operating its own businesses, banks and other formerly private enterprises, an action unique among the states.

• More than 60,000 people from North Dakota served in World War II, and 1,939 lost their lives.

• Discovery of oil in 1951 brought a new surge in the state's economy.

• Completion of vast artificial lakes and irrigation systems in the 1970s further enhanced the economy.

That's Interesting

• When he signed the statehood bills for the two Dakotas on the same day, President Benjamin Harrison would not reveal which one he signed first. Consequently no one knows which is the 39th or 40th state.

• Seventeen years before Theodore Roosevelt was elected president Medora storekeeper Joe Ferris publicly predicted the event.

• Among the state's interesting archeological discoveries are the rows of carved turtles and the rings of boulders. The turtles were thought to have pointed to water sources, and the rocks probably held down the bottoms of tepees.

• A Crow Indian drew a message in the Missouri River sand. It consisted of a cluster of dots representing U.S. troops within a circle. Then he slashed out the dots with a stick. A river captain understood the message, and carried the first news of the Custer massacre down the river to Bismarck.

• Inventor D.H. Houston named his new film Kodak, and this variation of Dakota is known around the world.

• A Portal golf course is probably the only place where a golfer might make a tee shot in the U.S. and end up in a hole in Canada.

Notable North Dakotans

Maxwell Anderson (Atlantic, PA, 1888-1959), playwright. **George Catlin** (Wilkes-Barre, PA, 1796-1872), western Indian expert/artist. **John Bernard Flannagan** (Fargo, 1895-1942), sculptor. **Peggy Lee** (Jamestown, 1920-), entertainer. **Roger Maris** (Hibbing, MN, 1934-1985), baseball player. **Theodore Roosevelt** (New York City,

1858-1919), North Dakota rancher and U.S. president. **Lawrence Welk** (Strasburg, 1903-1992), entertainer.

GENERAL

Admitted to statehood: Nov. 2, 1889
Origin of name: Dakota is Sioux for *friend* or *ally*.
Capital: Bismarck, settled 1873
Nickname: Sioux State
Motto: "Liberty and Union, Now and Forever, One and Inseparable"
Bird: Western meadowlark
Fish: Northern pike
Flower: wild prairie rose
Grass: Western wheat grass
March: "Spirit of the Land"
Song: "North Dakota Hymn"
Stone: Teredo petrified wood
Tree: American elm

THE LAND

Area: 70,704 sq. mi., 19th
Land: 68,994 sq. mi., 17th
Water: 1,710 sq. mi., 22nd
Topography: Central lowland in the E comprises the flat Red River Valley and the rolling drift prairie; Missouri plateau of the Great Plains on the W
Number of counties: 53
Geographic center: Sheridan, 5 mi. SW of McClusky
Length: 340 mi.
Width: 211 mi.
Highest point: 3,506 ft. (White Butte, Slope County), 30th
Lowest point: 750 ft. (Red River), 45th
Mean elevation: 1,900 ft., 16th

CLIMATE AND ENVIRONMENT

Temp., highest: 121 deg. on July 6, 1936, at Steele; lowest: -60 deg. on Feb. 15, 1936, at Parshall
Fresh water withdrawn, per capita, per day: 1,690 gal., 18th
Endangered species: mammals, 1—black-footed ferret; birds, 3—whooping crane, American peregrine falcon, least tern; reptiles, none; amphibians, none; fishes, 1; invertebrates, none; plants, none

MAJOR CITIES, POPULATION PERCENTAGE INCREASE (1980-90)

Bismarck, 49,256—10.72%
Dickinson, 16,097—1.09%
Fargo, 74,111—20.74%
Grand Forks, 49,425—12.93%
Minot, 34,544—5.18%

THE PEOPLE

Population: 638,800, 47th
  Percent change (1980-90): -2.18%, 47th
  Per sq. mi: 9.03, 47th
  Percent in metro. area: 40.23%, 42nd
  Percent foreign born: 1.5%, 43rd
White: 604,142—94.57%, 6th
Black: 3,524—0.55%, 46th
Native American: 25,917—4.06%, 7th
Asian, Pacific Isle: 3,462—0.54%, 45th
Other races: 1,755—0.27%, 42nd
Hispanic origin: 4,665—0.73%, 44th
Percent over 5 yrs. speaking language other than English at home: 7.9%, 22nd
Percent males: 49.81%, 6th
Percent females: 50.19%, 46th
Percent never married: 25.9%, 23rd
Marriages per 1,000 (1989): 7.3, 48th
Divorces per 1,000 (1989): 3.4, 43rd
Median age: 32.4
Under 5 years: 47,845—7.49%, 22nd
Under 18 years: 175,385—27.46%, 11th
65 years & older: 91,055—14.25%, 8th
Percent increase among the elderly: 13.2%, 39th

OF VITAL IMPORTANCE

Live births per 1,000 pop.: 16.0, 19th
Infant mortality rate per 1,000 births (1988): 10.5, 19th
Average lifetime (1979-81): 75.71, 4th
Deaths per 100,000 pop. (1988): 849.2, 31st
Causes of death per 100,000 pop. (1988):
  Diseases of heart: 308.5, 28th
  Malignant neoplasms: 192.7, 32nd
  Cerebrovascular diseases: 64.6, 21st
  Accidents & adverse effects: 35.8, 37th

Chronic obstructive pulmonary diseases: 30.4, 36th
Suicide: 10.6, 41st
HIV infection: 0.4, 51st
Other: 74.5, 28th

KEEPING WELL

Non-federal physicians per 100,000 pop.: 187, 34th
Dentists per 100,000 (1990-91): 57, 35th
Nurses per 100,000 (1989): 912, 5th
Hospitals per 100,000: 8.9, 2nd
Admissions per 100,000: 17,111, 4th
Beds per 100,000: 829.37, 2nd
Occupancy rate: 64.1%, 33rd
Semiprivate room charges per day: $230, 35th
Average stay: 13.0, 3rd
Notifiable diseases per 100,000:
AIDS: 0.3, 51st
Gonorrhea: 15.7, 48th
Measles: 0.0, 51st
Syphillis: 0.9, 50th
Tuberculosis (TB): 2.8, 40th
Per capita spending on mental health programs (1987): $41.65, 20th
Pop. without health insur. (1991): 7.6%, 49th

HOUSEHOLDS BY TYPE

Total households: 240,878
Percent change (1980-90): 5.65%, 44th
Family households: 166,270
Percent of total: 69.03%, 37th
Nonfamily households: 74,608
Percent of total: 30.97%, 15th
Persons per household: 2.55, 36th
Pop. living in group quarters: 24,234
Percent of pop.: 3.79%, 4th

LIVING QUARTERS

Total housing units: 276,340
Persons per unit: 2.31, 39th
Occupied housing units: 240,878
Percent of total units: 87.17%, 37th
Persons per unit: 2.46, 43rd
Percent of units with over 1 person per room: 1.98%, 43rd
Owner-occupied units: 157,950
Percent of total units: 57.16%, 34th
Percent of occupied units: 65.57%, 35th
Persons per unit: 2.74, 22nd
Median value: $50,800, 43rd
Renter-occupied units: 82,928
Percent of total units: 30.01%, 22nd
Percent of occupied units: 34.43%, 18th
Persons per unit: 2.18, 49th
Median contract rent: $266, 40th
Rental vacancy rate: 9.0%, 22nd
Mobile home, trailer & other as a % of occupied housing units: 12.30%, 23rd

CRIME INDEX PER 100,000

Total: 2,922, 49th
Violent: 74, 51st
Murder and nonnegligent manslaughter: 1, 51st
Aggravated assault: 7,490, 23rd
Robbery: 8, 51st
Rape: 18, 51st
Property: 2,848, 49th
Burglary: 427, 51st
Larceny, theft: 2,289, 46th
Motor vehicle theft: 133, 50th
Drug abuse arrests: 66, 50th

TEACHING AND LEARNING

Literacy (1987): 88%, 25th
Pop. 3 and over enrolled in school: 177,543
Percent of pop.: 29.1%, 10th
Public elementary & secondary schools:
Total enrollment: 118,000
Avg. class size (1987): 19, 48th
Teachers: 7,800
Percent of pop.: 1.22%, 3rd
Teachers' avg. salary: $23,000, 48th
Spending per capita: $627, 45th
Spending per pupil in avg. daily attendance: $3,581, 42nd
Percent of graduates taking SAT: 6%, 46th
Combined SAT scores: 1073, 2nd
Percent of pop. over 25 completing:
High school: 76.7%, 27th
College degree/s: 18.1%, 31st
Higher educa., institutions: 20
Per 100,000 pop.: 2.3, 1st
Enroll: 37,878
Percent of pop.: 5.93%, 18th

Public: 34,690
Percent of enroll.: 91.58%, 6th
Private: 3,188
Percent of enroll.: 8.42%, 46th
White non-Hispanic: 78,795
Percent of enroll.: 92.93%, 4th
Black non-Hispanic: 3,160
Percent of enroll.: 3.73%, 30th
Hispanic: 360
Percent of enroll.: 0.42%, 47th
Asian/Pacific Islander: 688
Percent of enroll.: 0.81%, 43rd
Amer. Indian/AK native: 139
Percent of enroll.: 0.16%, 51st
Nonresident alien: 1,648
Percent of enroll.: 1.94%, 34th
Female: 18,703
Percent of enroll.: 49.38%, 49th
Tuition, state university ('90-'91): $1,930, 19th
Public library systems: 95
Books & serial vol. per capita: 2.76, 22nd
Govt. expend. per capita: $9.98, 41st
State govt.: $2.80, 21st
Local govts.: $7.18, 41st

Law Enforcement, Courts, and Prisons

Police protection expend.: $39,504,000
Per capita: $61.82, 49th
Judicial & legal expend.: $26,623,000
Per capita: $41.66, 34th
Corrections expend.: $20,593,000
Per capita: $32.23, 50th
Police per 10,000 pop. (1990-91): 15.7, 41st
Prisoners (state & fed.) sentenced to over 1 yr., per 100,000 pop.: 67
Percent change (1989-90): 7.67%, 25th
Death penalty: no

Religion, Number and Percent of Population

Agnostic: 1,854—0.40%, 34th
Buddhist: N/A
Christian: 437,927—94.50%, 2nd
Hindu: N/A
Jewish: 1,854—0.40%, 31st
Moslem: N/A
Unitarian: N/A
Other: 2,781—0.60%, 46th
None: 7,415—1.60%, 49th
Refused to answer: 11,585—2.50%, 18th

Making a Living

Personal income per capita (1989): $11,051, 45th
Percent increase (1979-'89) (constant 1989 dollars): 2.8%, 47th
Average income per family: $33,586, 45th
Percent of pop. below poverty level: 14.4%, 17th
Percent 65 and over: 14.6%, 17th
Cost of living, selected cities
2nd qtr., 1989 (U. S. Standard=100)
Fargo 98.7

Economy

Civilian labor force : 325,000
Percent of tot. pop.: 50.88%, 26th
Percent 65 and over: 3.38%, 10th
Percent females: 45.23%, 31st
Percent job growth (1980-90): 7.07%, 46th
Major employer industries:
Agriculture: 37,128—11.90%, 2nd
Construction: 10,296—3.30%, 48th
Finance, insurance & real estate: 12,792—4.10%, 46th
Government: 60,840—19.50%, 9th
Manufacturing: 18,720—6.00%, 46th
Mining: 4,490—1.6%, 11th
Service: 60,528—19.40%, 27th
Trade: 61,776—19.80%, 9th
Transportation, communication, & public utilities: 17,160—5.50%, 19th
Wholesale/retail: 65,689—22.8%, 4th
Unemployment rate: 4.00%, 48th
Male: 2.46%, 42nd
Female: 1.54%, 49th
Total businesses (1991): 32,361
New business incorp's. (1991): 820
Percent of total businesses: 2.53%, 51st
Business failures (1991): 140
Percent of total businesses: 0.43%, 48th
Agriculture farm income
Marketing (1991): $2,556,147,000, 26th
Net per operation: $20,003, 26th
Net per acre: $223, 7th
Leading products: wheat, cattle, barley, sunflower

Av. value land & build. per acre: $348, 42nd
Percent increase (1980-90): -14.07%, 36th
Govt. payments: $533,853,000, 4th
Construction, value of all: $262,000,000
Per capita: $410.14, 39th
Percent change 1989-90: 19.09%, 8th
Manufactures:
Value added: $1,110,000,000
Per capita: $1,737.63, 47th
Value of shipments: $3,013,000,000
Per capita: $4,716.66, 46th
Leading products: farm equipment, processed foods
Mining, min. prod., value (1987): $1,220,000,000, 24th
Leading products: petroleum, coal, nat. gas
Retail sales: $4,467,000,000, 49th
Per household: $18,630, 30th
Percent increase (1987-90): 20.5%, 13th
Service indust., value (1987): $2,087,000,000, 49th
Per capita: $3,267.06, 35th
Tourism indus., value (1989): $702,000,000, 49th
Foreign exports value: $360,000,000, 45th
Per capita: $563.56, 41st
Patents per 1,000 pop.: 12.8, 6th

Travel and Transportation

Motor vehicle registrations: 629,839
Per 1,000 pop.: 985, 4th
Motorcycle registrations: 20,176
Per 1,000 pop.: 31, 8th
Licensed drivers per 1,000 driving age pop.: 879, 35th
Deaths from motor vehicle accidents per 100,000 pop.: 17.5, 26th
Public roads & streets
Total mileage: 86,517, 21st
Rural mileage: 84,706, 15th
Urban mileage: 1,811, 45th
Interstate mileage: 570, 36th
Annual vehicle-miles of travel per person: 9,251, 22nd
Mean travel time for workers 16 + who work away from home: 13.0 min., 51st

Government

Registered voters (1988): N/A
Percent of voting age pop.: N/A, NR
Voter turnout (1988): 297,261
Percent of registered voters: N/A, NR
Percent of voting age pop.: 61.54%, 5th
State legislators, total (1992): 159, 19th
Women members (1992): 23
Percent of legislature: 14.5%, 33rd
Dominant party (1992): Split
U. S. Congress, House members (1993): 1
Increase 1983-93: 0
Revenues:
State govt.: $1,810,334,000
Per capita: $2,833.96, 13th
State & local govt.: $2,470,965,000
Per capita: $3,868.14, 27th
Indebtedness:
State govt.: $872,159,000
Per capita: $1,365.31, 20th
State & local govt.: $1,856,000,000
Per capita: $2,905.45, 33rd

Laws and Regulations

Legal driving age: 16
Marriage age without parental consent: 18
Divorce residence requirement: 6 mo.

Attractions

Major opera companies (1989): 1, 30th
Per 1 million pop.: 1.52, 5th
Major symphony orchestras (1989): 3, 45th
Per 1 million pop.: 4.55, 14th
State appropriations for state arts agencies per capita: $0.41, 46th
State Fair in the 3rd week in July at Minot

Sports and Competition

NCAA sports teams, 2—North Dakota State Univ. Bison, Univ. of North Dakota Fighting Sioux
Professional teams: none

OHIO

"Ohio is the farthest west of the East and the farthest north of the South"
Louis Bromfield (attrib.)

Without a historical change, Cleveland would have been in Connecticut, and, in another twist of history, Ohio did not enter the union officially until 1953. Professional baseball got its start in Ohio. The hotdog was invented in the state, as well as floating soap (Ivory). On a more serious note, Ohio has long been one of the leaders in industry and cultural activities, home of seven native U.S. presidents, along with a near record number of other natives of world acclaim. Ohio has more than 50 accredited colleges and universities; Oberlin College, established in 1833, was the first institution of higher-education in the United States to enroll both men and women.

SUPERLATIVES

- First professional baseball team—Cincinnati Red Stockings.
- First in clay products manufacture.
- Pioneer leader in rubber products.
- World leader in machine tools.

MOMENTS IN HISTORY

- The first known European explorer in the Ohio region was the French emissary La Salle, in 1669-1670. He claimed the entire vast region west of the Alleghenies for France.
- George Croghan, who operated in the area in the mid-1700s, was the most successful in promoting British claims to the area.
- Attempting to reassert French claims, in 1749 Celeron de Bienville planted a series of six lead plates along the Ohio River.
- On Oct. 31, 1750, Ohio Company representative George Gist and his dog spent Christmas at the trading post of George Croghan, and Gist and his faithful dog explored much of present-day Ohio, winning the Indians to the British cause.
- In 1763 the French gave up all claims, and British claims were confirmed.

> **So They Say**
> "The Ohio Country is fine, rich, level land, well-timbered with large walnut, ash, sugar trees...It is well watered...and full of beautiful natural...meadows, abounding with turkeys, deer, elk and most sorts of game, particularly buffaloes. In short, it wants nothing but cultivation to make it a most delightful country.
> George Gist

- Indian uprisings under chiefs including Pontiac and Cornstalk occupied British attention during most of the period before the Revolution.

> **So They Say**
> Chief Logan had been a great friend of the white people until: "...one man, Colonel Cresap...in cold blood...cut off all the relatives of Logan...not sparing even my women and children....This called on me for revenge...I have killed many....Who is there to mourn Logan? Not one."
> Famed speech of Chief Logan

- The Revolution brought no great battles to Ohio country. Most of the British cause was carried on by Indian raids. At war's end the new nation formally claimed the western lands after the Treaty of Paris, 1783.

• The claims to Ohio by Connecticut and Virginia were settled by agreements for Ohio to include the Western Reserve and the Virginia Military Survey.

• The famed Northwest Ordinance of 1787 established government in that whole great region.

• In 1788 the first of many thousands of settlers floated down the Ohio River, and founded Marietta.

So They Say

"No colony in America was settled under circumstances more favorable. There never were people better able to promote the welfare of the community."

George Washington commenting on Marietta's founding.

• In the 12 mos. in 1788-1789, 10,000 settlers reached Ohio, most of them floating down the Ohio on flatboats, sometimes attacked by Indians or pirates.

• Indian troubles increased until in the Treaty of Green Ville in 1795 the Indians gave up much of their Ohio lands.

• In 1803 Ohio became the first state west of the Alleghenies.

• Many critical battles with British/Indian forces occurred during the War of 1812.

• One of the most decisive battles of history was Oliver Hazard Perry's victory over the British fleet at the Battle of Put-in-Bay off Ohio shores in Sept. 1813.

• The "Border War" with Michigan in 1835 was settled, giving Ohio the area around Toledo.

• In the years before 1860, perhaps more slaves were spirited through Ohio on the Underground Railroad than were so assisted in any other state

• Several attacks by Confederate raiders plagued Ohio during the Civil War, which called 345,000 Ohioans into service.

• After the war John D. Rockefeller founded the Standard Oil Company at Cleveland in 1870; National Cash Register was founded at Dayton in 1879, and, with many other industries, Ohio became one of the great industrial states.

• More than 200,000 Ohioans entered World War I service.

• In 1937 the Ohio River region suffered the worst floods in the history of the Ohio-Mississippi watershed.

• Ohioans in World War II uniform numbered 840,000.

• The Ohio Turnpike opened in 1955.

• Famed Ohio astronaut John Glenn was elected to the U.S. Senate in 1971.

That's Interesting

• A part of one of the lead claim plates buried by Bienville (see *Moments in History*) was found by small boys, and the historic relic went to a Massachusetts museum.

• If Connecticut claims in Ohio had not been settled, the present-day Ohio city might have been known as Cleveland, Connecticut.

• Technically Ohio did not legally become a state until 1953, because Congress had neglected to give its formal approval, and that was when the mistake was corrected.

• Harry M. Stevens of Niles saw a cartoon of a dachshund dog as a wiener he called his sandwich invention a "hot dog."

• The first cash register was named a "mechanical money drawer" by its inventor, James Ritty.

Notable Natives

Sherwood Anderson (Camden, 1876-1941), author. **Neil Alden Armstrong** (Wapakoneta, 1930-), astronaut. **Paul Laurance Dunbar** (Dayton, 1872-1906), poet. **Thomas Alva Edison** (Milan, 1847-1931), inventor. **Daniel Decatur Emmett** (Mount Vernon, 1815-1904), entertainer/song writer. **Clark Gable** (Cadiz, 1901-1960), actor. **James Abram Garfield** (Orange, 1831-1881), U.S. president. **John Herschell Glenn** (Cambridge, 1921-), astronaut/public official. **Ulysses Simpson Grant** (Point Pleasant, 1822-1885), U.S. president. **Zane Grey** (Zanesville, 1875-1939), author. **Warren Gamaliel Harding** (Blooming Grove, 1865-1923), U.S. president. **Benjamin Harrison** (North Bend, 1833-1901), U.S. president. **Rutherford B. Hayes** (Delaware, 1822-1893), U.S. president. **William McKinley** (Niles, 1843-1901), U.S. president. **Paul Newman**

(Cleveland, 1925-), actor. **Jack William Nicklaus** (Columbus, 1940-), golfer. **Edward Vernon Rickenbacker** (Columbus, 1890-1973), aviator/businessman. **Philip Henry Sheridan** (Somerset? 1831-1888), soldier. **William Tecumseh Sherman** (Lancaster, 1820-1891), soldier. **Robert A. Taft** (Cincinnati, 1889-1935), public official. **William Howard Taft** (Cincinnati, 1857-1930), U.S. president and U.S. chief justice. **James Grover Thurber** (Columbus, 1894-1962), humorist/cartoonist.

General

Admitted to statehood: March 1, 1803
Origin of name: Iroquois word for "fine or good river"
Capital: Columbus
Nickname: The Buckeye State
Motto: "With God, All Things Are Possible"
Beverage: tomato juice
Bird: cardinal
Flower: scarlet carnation
Insect: ladybug
Song: "Beautiful Ohio"
Stone: Ohio flint
Tree: buckeye

The Land

Area: 44,828 sq. mi., 34th
Land: 40,953 sq. mi., 35th
Water: 3,875 sq. mi., 14th
Topography: generally rolling plain, Allegheny plateau in E, Lake [Erie] plains extend S; central plains in the W
Number of counties: 88
Geographic center: Delaware, 25 mi. NNE of Columbus
Length: 220 mi.
Width: 220 mi.
Highest point: 1,549 ft. (Campbell Hill), 43rd
Lowest point: 455 ft. (Ohio River), 36th
Mean elevation: 850 ft., 31st

Climate and Environment

Temp., highest: 113 deg. on July 21, 1934 near Gallipolis; lowest: -39 deg. on Feb. 10, 1899, at Milligan
Fresh water withdrawn, per capita, per day: 1,180 gal., 29th
Endangered species: mammals, 1—Indiana bat; birds, 2—American peregrine falcon, piping plover; reptiles, none; amphibians, none; fishes, 1; invertebrates, 3; plants, 1

Major Cities, Population Percentage Increase (1980-90)

Akron, 223,019— -5.97%
Cincinnati, 364,040— -5.54%
Cleveland, 505,616— -11.89%
Columbus, 632,910—12.02%
Toledo, 332,943— -6.12%

The People

Population: 10,847,115, 7th
Percent change (1980-90): 0.46%, 42nd
Per sq. mi: 241.97, 10th
Percent in metro. area: 78.98%, 18th
Percent foreign born: 2.4%, 33rd
White: 9,521,756—87.78%, 24th
Black: 1,154,826—10.65%, 20th
Native American: 20,358—0.19%, 48th
Asian, Pacific Isle: 91,179—0.84%, 34th
Other races: 58,996—0.54%, 33rd
Hispanic origin: 139,696—1.29%, 35th
Percent over 5 yrs. speaking language other than English at home: 5.4%, 36th
Percent males: 48.18%, 40th
Percent females: 51.82%, 12th
Percent never married: 25.5%, 26th
Marriages per 1,000 (1989): 9.0, 29th
Divorces per 1,000 (1989): 4.5, 28th
Median age: 33.3
Under 5 years: 785,149—7.24%, 30th
Under 18 years: 2,799,744—25.81%, 28th
65 years & older: 1,406,961—12.97%, 22nd
Percent increase among the elderly: 20.3%, 25th

Of Vital Importance

Live births per 1,000 pop.: 15.1, 38th
Infant mortality rate per 1,000 births (1988): 9.7, 26th
Average lifetime (1979-81): 73.49, 34th
Deaths per 100,000 pop. (1988): 922.4, 20th
Causes of death per 100,000 pop. (1988):
Diseases of heart: 344.6, 14th

Malignant neoplasms: 212.1, 15th
Cerebrovascular diseases: 62.1, 27th
Accidents & adverse effects: 34.6, 42nd
Chronic obstructive pulmonary diseases: 37.5, 17th
Suicide: 11.2, 38th
HIV infection: 2.1, 33rd
Other: 73.1, 32nd

Keeping Well

Non-federal physicians per 100,00 pop.: 214, 22nd
Dentists per 100,000 (1990-91): 62, 24th
Nurses per 100,000 (1989): 749, 18th
Hospitals per 100,000: 2.1, 44th
Admissions per 100,000: 14,569, 16th
Beds per 100,000: 481.28, 26th
Occupancy rate: 67.2%, 22nd
Semiprivate room charges per day: $308, 19th
Average stay: 7.2, 22nd
Notifiable diseases per 100,000:
AIDS: 6.1, 32nd
Gonorrhea: 372.6, 11th
Measles: 5.1, 21st
Syphillis: 10.2, 33rd
Tuberculosis (TB): 3.5, 36th
Per capita spending on mental health programs (1987): $45.33, 16th
Pop. without health insur. (1991): 10.3%, 38th

Households by Type

Total households: 4,087,546
Percent change (1980-90): 6.61%, 40th
Family households: 2,895,223
Percent of total: 70.83%, 25th
Nonfamily households: 1,192,323
Percent of total: 29.17%, 27th
Persons per household: 2.59, 26th
Pop. living in group quarters: 261,451
Percent of pop.: 2.41%, 36th

Living Quarters

Total housing units: 4,371,945
Persons per unit: 2.48, 10th
Occupied housing units: 4,087,546
Percent of total units: 93.49%, 1st
Persons per unit: 2.51, 30th
Percent of units with over 1 person per room: 1.76%, 46th
Owner-occupied units: 2,758,149
Percent of total units: 63.09%, 10th
Percent of occupied units: 67.48%, 24th
Persons per unit: 2.74, 22nd
Median value: $63,500, 29th
Renter-occupied units: 1,329,397
Percent of total units: 30.41%, 20th
Percent of occupied units: 32.52%, 28th
Persons per unit: 2.27, 36th
Median contract rent: $296, 31st
Rental vacancy rate: 7.5%, 36th
Mobile home, trailer & other as a % of occupied housing units: 6.03%, 42nd

Crime Index per 100,000

Total: 4,843, 33rd
Violent: 506, 28th
Murder and nonnegligent manslaughter: 6, 27th
Aggravated assault: 7,238, 30th
Robbery: 189, 17th
Rape: 47, 15th
Property: 4,337, 32nd
Burglary: 983, 32nd
Larceny, theft: 2,864, 33rd
Motor vehicle theft: 491, 22nd
Drug abuse arrests: 91, 47th

Teaching and Learning

Literacy (1987): 89%, 17th
Pop. 3 and over enrolled in school: 2,798,226
Percent of pop.: 27.0%, 28th
Public elementary & secondary schools:
Total enrollment: 1,771,000
Avg. class size (1987): 24, 15th
Teachers: 101,600
Percent of pop.: 0.94%, 37th
Teachers' avg. salary: $31,200, 17th
Spending per capita: $720, 37th
Spending per pupil in avg. daily attendance: $4,394, 29th
Percent of graduates taking SAT: 22%, 28th
Combined SAT scores: 946, 24th
Percent of pop. over 25 completing:
High school: 75.7%, 30th
College degree/s: 17.0%, 40th
Higher educa., institutions: 154
Per 100,000 pop.: 0.6, 33rd

Enroll: 555,702
Percent of pop.: 5.12%, 35th
Public: 426,511
Percent of enroll.: 76.75%, 38th
Private: 129,191
Percent of enroll.: 23.25%, 14th
White non-Hispanic: 31,106
Percent of enroll.: 90.93%, 11th
Black non-Hispanic: 250
Percent of enroll.: 0.73%, 46th
Hispanic: 94
Percent of enroll.: 0.27%, 51st
Asian/Pacific Islander: 198
Percent of enroll.: 0.58%, 50th
Amer. Indian/AK native: 1,912
Percent of enroll.: 5.59%, 3rd
Nonresident alien: 648
Percent of enroll.: 1.89%, 36th
Female: 295,249
Percent of enroll.: 53.13%, 44th
Tuition, state university ('90-'91): $2,622, 8th
Public library systems: 250
Books & serial vol. per capita: 3.37, 16th
Govt. expend. per capita: $16.01, 23rd
State govt.: $0.68, 49th
Local govts.: $15.32, 21st

Law Enforcement, Courts, and Prisons

Police protection expend.: $1,118,397,000
Per capita: $103.11, 25th
Judicial & legal expend.: $556,584,000
Per capita: $51.31, 21st
Corrections expend.: $760,991,000
Per capita: $70.16, 30th
Police per 10,000 pop. (1990-91): 17.5, 35th
Prisoners (state & fed.) sentenced to over 1 yr., per 100,000 pop.: 289
Percent change (1989-90): 4.31%, 37th
Death penalty: yes, by electrocution (check override of lethal injection veto)
Under sentence of death: 92, 9th
Executed (1989): none

Religion, Number and Percent of Population

Agnostic: 40,237—0.50%, 27th
Buddhist: 8,047—0.10%, 17th
Christian: 6,928,786—86.10%, 26th
Hindu: 8,047—0.10%, 10th
Jewish: 56,332—0.70%, 23rd
Moslem: 32,190—0.40%, 5th
Unitarian: 8,047—0.10%, 31st
Other: 193,137—2.40%, 5th
None: 595,506—7.40%, 17th
Refused to answer: 177,042—2.20%, 23rd

Making a Living

Personal income per capita (1989): $13,461, 24th
Percent increase (1979-'89) (constant 1989 dollars): 10.3%, 31st
Average income per family: $40,813, 23rd
Percent of pop. below poverty level: 12.5%, 25th
Percent 65 and over: 10.7%, 34th
Cost of living, selected cities
1st qtr., 1991 (U. S. Standard=100)

Canton	90.7
Cincinnati	104.7
Cleveland and Columbus	105.9

Economy

Civilian labor force : 5,433,000
Percent of tot. pop.: 50.09%, 28th
Percent 65 and over: 2.69%, 27th
Percent females: 45.33%, 28th
Percent job growth (1980-90): 13.71%, 39th
Major employer industries:
Agriculture: 87,142—1.70%, 40th
Construction: 225,544—4.40%, 27th
Finance, insurance & real estate: 256,300—5.00%, 30th
Government: 676,632—13.20%, 41st
Manufacturing: 1,194,358—23.30%, 8th
Mining: 21,007—0.4%, 25th
Service: 1,050,830—20.50%, 21st
Trade: 1,030,326—20.10%, 7th
Transportation, communication, & public utilities: 251,174—4.90%, 30th
Wholesale/retail: 1,088,266—22.1%, 10th
Unemployment rate: 5.65%, 20th
Male: 3.26%, 16th
Female: 2.41%, 26th
Total businesses (1991): 341,253
New business incorp's. (1991): 17,895
Percent of total businesses: 5.24%, 36th

Business failures (1991): 2,751
Percent of total businesses: 0.81%, 29th
Agriculture farm income
Marketing (1991): $3,893,074,000, 15th
Net per operation: $8,289, 45th
Net per acre: $42, 31st
Leading products: soybeans, corn, dairy products, hogs
Av. value land & build. per acre: $1,258, 15th
Percent increase (1980-90): -27.28%, 45th
Govt. payments: $156,708,000, 19th
Construction, value of all: $6,245,000,000
Per capita: $575.73, 22nd
Percent change 1989-90: -5.13%, 23rd
Manufactures:
Value added: $80,377,000,000
Per capita: $7,409.99, 4th
Value of shipments: $177,787,000,000
Per capita: $16,390.26, 7th
Leading products: transportation equipment, machinery, primary and fabricated metal products
Mining, min. prod., value (1987): $2,663,000,000, 14th
Leading products: coal, nat. gas, petroleum
Retail sales: $73,206,000,000, 7th
Per household: $17,880, 36th
Percent increase (1987-90): 12.3%, 34th
Service indust., value (1987): $42,444,000,000, 8th
Per capita: $3,912.93, 26th
Tourism indus., value (1989): $7,253,000,000, 10th
Foreign exports value: $13,378,000,000, 7th
Per capita: $1,233.32, 13th
Patents per 1,000 pop.: 4.0, 39th

Travel and Transportation

Motor vehicle registrations: 8,410,466
Per 1,000 pop.: 775, 30th
Motorcycle registrations: 228,408
Per 1,000 pop.: 21, 18th
Licensed drivers per 1,000 driving age pop.: 888, 29th
Deaths from motor vehicle accidents per 100,000 pop.: 15.1, 40th
Public roads & streets
Total mileage: 113,600, 9th
Rural mileage: 82,172, 16th
Urban mileage: 31,428, 6th
Interstate mileage: 1,572, 4th
Annual vehicle-miles of travel per person: 8,017, 41st
Mean travel time for workers 16 + who work away from home: 20.7 min., 24th

Government

Registered voters (1988): 6,323,352
Percent of voting age pop.: 79.34%, 13th
Voter turnout (1988): 4,393,585
Percent of registered voters: 69.48%, 31st
Percent of voting age pop.: 55.13%, 16th
State legislators, total (1992): 132, 33rd
Women members (1992): 20
Percent of legislature: 15.2%, 29th
Dominant party (1992): Split
U. S. Congress, House members (1993): 19
Increase 1983-93: -2
Revenues:
State govt.: $28,515,731,000
Per capita: $2,628.88, 20th
State & local govt.: $42,541,686,000
Per capita: $3,921.94, 26th
Indebtedness:
State govt.: $11,208,531,000
Per capita: $1,033.32, 29th
State & local govt.: $23,191,000,000
Per capita: $2,137.99, 45th

Laws and Regulations

Legal driving age: 18
Marriage age without parental consent: 18
Divorce residence requirement: 6 mo.

Attractions

Major opera companies (1989): 9, 4th
Per 1 million pop.: 0.83, 16th
Major symphony orchestras (1989): 39, 5th
Per 1 million pop.: 3.58, 27th
State appropriations for state arts agencies per capita: $1.11, 13th
State Fair in mid-Aug. at Columbus

Sports and Competition

NCAA sports teams, 14: Bowling Green State Univ. Falcons, Case Western Reserve Univ. Spartans, Cleveland State Univ. Vikings,

Kent State Univ. Golden Flashes, Miami Univ. Redskins, Ohio State Univ. Buckeyes, Ohio Univ. Bobcats, The Univ. of Akron Zips, Univ. of Cincinnati Bearcats, Univ. of Dayton Flyers, Univ. of Toledo Rockets, Wright State Univ. Raiders, Xavier Univ. Musketeers, Youngstown State Univ. Penguins

Professional teams, 15:

Baseball, 5—Cleveland Indians (AL), Cleveland Stadium; Columbus Clippers (International League, Class AAA), Cooper Stadium; Toledo Mud Hens (International League, Class AAA), Ned Skeldon Stadium; Cincinnati Reds (NL), Riverfront Stadium; Canton-Akron Indians (Eastern League, Class AA), Thurman Munson Memorial Stadium

Basketball, 4,—Youngstown Pride (World Basketball League), Beeghly Center; Dayton Wings (World Basketball League), Ervin J. Nutter Center; Columbus Horizon (Continental Basketball Association), Fairgrounds Coliseum at the Ohio Exposition Center; Cleveland Cavaliers (NBA), The Coliseum

Football, 2—Cleveland Browns (AFC), Cleveland Stadium; Cincinnati Bengals (AFC), Riverfront Stadium

Hockey, 3—Cincinnati Cyclones (East Coast Hockey League), Cincinnati Gardens; Dayton Bombers (East Coast Hockey League), Hara Arena Conference & Exhibition Center; Toledo Storm (East Coast Hockey League), Toledo Sports Arena

Soccer, 1—Cleveland Crunch (Major Soccer League), Richfield Coliseum

OKLAHOMA

"The state Oklahoma most resembles is of course Texas, if only because it too does everything with color and originality, but tell an Oklahoman that his state is a dependency of Texas and he will bite your eyes out."

John Gunther

Thousands of oil and natural gas wells dot the Oklahoma landscape, and there are millions of beef cattle on its ranches. Oklahoma is the home of about a third of the nation's Indian people, who speak more than 50 languages, who have demonstrated their genius in government and diplomacy and who celebrate their notable individuals, among them Will Rogers and Sequoyah. It is the state of the "Sooners" and the "Boomers." When the Oklahoma territory was opened up for settlement in 1889, those who entered the territory to stake their homestead claims before the official time were called "Sooners." Those who entered legally at the appointed time were called "Boomers." Oklahoma is also a center of cowboy culture and preserves notable collections of western art and customs.

SUPERLATIVES

- Only county touching four states—Cimarron County.
- Former home of five separate Indian nations.
- "Oil capital of the world"—Tulsa.
- Finest collection of Western and cowboy art—Woolaroc Museum, Bartlesville.

MOMENTS IN HISTORY

- Claimed variously by Spain and France, present-day Oklahoma was the starting point of a trail to Spanish Santa Fe blazed by French traders in 1750.
- Control of the present state came to the United States in 1803 with the Louisiana Purchase.
- In 1817 Auguste Pierre Chouteau of the famed Chouteau family founded Grand Saline (Salina), first permanent European settlement in the present-day state.
- One of the most shameful episodes in U.S. history began in 1817 with the first removal to Indian Territory of scattered groups of Indians from their native lands. Formal establishment of the lands known as Indian Territory in present-day Oklahoma was decided in 1834. The resettlement process intensified with the brutal removal of the groups known as the Five Civilized Tribes. Many of those five tribes indeed were more "civilized" than their white neighbors. When Congress in 1830 ordered the resettlement of the Creeks from their ancestral lands in parts of Georgia, Alabama, Mississippi, and areas of the Appalachians, they fought back, executing Chief William McIntosh for having ceded the tribal land. But their resistance was beaten down, and they started their tragic march to Oklahoma.
- In the early 1830s the Chickasaw people were moved to Oklahoma over the infamous route that became known as the Trail of Tears.
- Forced by the federal government in 1831-1833, the Choctaw Indians trudged over the Trail of Tears. Before their removal there were about 20,000. By 1843 they numbered only about 12,000.
- By 1838 U.S. armed forces had begun the evacuation of the Cherokee people. About 15,000 were marched over the bloody Trail of Tears to Indian Territory (Oklahoma) under conditions of

extreme hardship, and nearly 4,000 perished on the way.

• The Seminole wars in Florida ended in 1842 without a surrender or peace treaty. After the war some of the few remaining Seminole agreed to move to Oklahoma, forming the fifth of the Civilized Tribes.

• The five tribes gathered in 1859 for an inter-tribal council, resulting in a progressive code of laws.

• When the Civil War came, the Five Nations embraced the Confederate cause.

• The first Civil War struggle in present-day Oklahoma was the Battle of Round Mountain near Keystone, Nov. 19, 1861.

• With the collapse of the Confederacy the Five Nations faced ruin, the forfeiture of their lands and rights. However, the skill of the Indian negotiators in the late 1860s reduced the tribal losses to some of the western Oklahoma lands.

So They Say

Their (the Indian nations') escape from Confederate losses " ..constitutes a triumph of diplomacy almost unexampled in the history of the relations between a weak and a strong people."

Anonymous

• Beginning in the 1870s more than 25 other tribes were forced to move to Oklahoma on land bought or leased by the federal government.

• The displaced Indians caused much unrest, but in 1875 George Custer defeated Indian forces in the Battle of the Washita, and most of the Indian conflict ended.

• The Five Indian nations made remarkable progress in education, government, and commerce. Oklahoma's first telephone line was built by the Cherokee in 1885.

• One of the most remarkable events in U.S. history occurred when the government opened "unassigned lands" to settlement. At high noon on April 22, 1889, thousands rushed across the border, and by nightfall the empty site of what is now Oklahoma City had become a tent community of 10,000 people. Other towns were also founded that day.

So They Say

"I saw excited men jump from the windows of crowded coaches even before the train came to a stop...and rush off to stake out claims in a field that by noon next day was a busy tent city of 10,000 people...Rivals shot it out over claim disputes."

Anonymous eye witness

• In all, ten land openings brought settlers to Oklahoma during the period 1889 to 1906.

• In May, 1890, Oklahoma Territory was created, coexisting with Indian Territory.

• Oklahoma became a state on Nov. 6, 1907, with a population of 1,414,177, including Indian Territory.

• During World War I much of the virgin land was plowed for crops.

• In the drought of the 1930s terrible dust storms swept the plowed lands and blanketed the skies. Thousands of "Okies" fled their devastated farms.

• During World War II, 13 Oklahomans won the Medal of Honor.

• In the 1970s the McClellan-Kerr Arkansas River Navigation System opened. Tulsa and Muskogee became inland "seaports."

THAT'S INTERESTING

• Because of its shape on the map, Oklahoma has been called "the nation's largest meat cleaver."

• With a mountain being defined as any elevation over 2,000 feet, Oklahoma claims that the 1,999-foot rise known as Cavanal is the world's highest hill.

• In an attempt to scalp an enemy, Chief Pawhuska pulled at the man's white hair. The man's wig came off in his hand. The chief kept this powerful "magic" the rest of his life and took the name meaning "white hair."

• More languages are spoken in Oklahoma than in Europe. Each of 55 Indian tribes has a separate language or different dialect of a language.

NOTABLE NATIVES

Acee Blue Eagle (near Anadarka, 1910-1959), artist. **Woodrow Wilson "Woody" Guthrie** (Okemah, 1912-1967), folk singer/composer. **Patrick Jay Hurley** (Indian Ter., 1883-1963), diplomat. **Karl Guthe Jansky** (Norman, 1905-1950), engineer. **Robert Samuel Kerr** (Ada, 1896-1963), political figure. **Mickey Mantle** (Spavinaw, 1931-), baseball player. **Oral Roberts** (Ada, 1918-), evangelist. **Will Rogers** (near Oologah, 1879-1935), humorist/actor/philosopher. **Maria Tallchief** (Fairfax, 1925-), dancer. **James Francis "Jim" Thorpe** (Prague, 1888-1953), athlete.

GENERAL

Admitted to statehood: Nov. 16, 1907
Origin of name: Choctaw coined word meaning red man, proposed by Rev. Allen Wright, Choctaw-speaking Indian
Capital: Oklahoma City, founded 1889
Nickname: Sooner State
Motto: *"Labor Omnia Vincit"* (Labor Conquers All Things)
Animal: bison
Bird: scissor-tailed flycatcher
Colors: green and white
Flower: mistletoe (first to select floral symbol 1893)
Insect: honeybee
Reptile: mountain boomer lizard
Song: "Oklahoma"
Stone: rose rock (barite rose)
Tree: redbud

THE LAND

Area: 69,903 sq. mi., 20th
Land: 68,679 sq. mi., 19th
Water: 1,224 sq. mi., 30th.
Topography: high plains predominate in the W, hills and small mountains in the E; the E central region is dominated by the Arkansas R. Basin and the Red R. Plains, in the S
Number of counties: 77
Geographic center: Oklahoma, 8 mi. N of Oklahoma City
Length: 400 mi.
Width: 220 mi.
Highest point: 4,973 ft. (Black Mesa), 23rd
Lowest point: 289 ft. (Little River), 34th
Mean elevation: 1,300 ft., 20th

CLIMATE AND ENVIRONMENT

Temp., highest: 120 deg. on July 26, 1934, at Tishmoningo; lowest: -27 deg. on Jan. 18, 1930, at Watts
Fresh water withdrawn, per capita, per day: 386 gal., 45th
Endangered species: mammals, 3—gray bat, Indiana bat, Ozark big-eared bat; birds, 6—whooping crane, Eskimo curlew, American peregrine falcon, least tern, black-capped vireo, red-cockaded woodpecker; reptiles, none; amphibians, none; fishes, none; invertebrates, 1; plants, none

MAJOR CITIES, POPULATION PERCENTAGE INCREASE (1980-90)

Broken Arrow, 58,043—62.31%
Lawton, 80,561—0.63%
Norman, 80,071—17.72%
Oklahoma City, 444,719—10.08%
Tulsa, 367,302—1.77%

THE PEOPLE

Population: 3,145,585, 28th
Percent change (1980-90): 3.82%, 31st
Per sq. mi: 45.00, 35th
Percent in metro. area: 59.45%, 33rd
Percent foreign born: 2.1%, 34th
White: 2,583,512—82.13%, 32nd
Black: 233,801—7.43%, 24th
Native American: 252,420—8.02%, 3rd
Asian, Pacific Isle: 33,563—1.07%, 28th
Other races: 42,289—1.34%, 22nd
Hispanic origin: 86,160—2.74%, 23rd
Percent over 5 yrs. speaking language other than English at home: 5.0%, 37th
Percent males: 48.67%, 25th
Percent females: 51.33%, 27th
Percent never married: 20.9%, 50th
Marriages per 1,000 (1989): 10.3, 13th
Divorces per 1,000 (1989): 7.1, 2nd
Median age: 33.2
Under 5 years: 226,523—7.20%, 32nd

Under 18 years: 837,007—26.61%, 16th
65 years & older: 424,213—13.49%, 15th
Percent increase among the elderly: 12.8%, 41st

Of Vital Importance

Live births per 1,000 pop.: 14.3, 44th
Infant mortality rate per 1,000 births (1988): 9.0, 29th
Average lifetime (1979-81): 73.67, 30th
Deaths per 100,000 pop. (1988): 926.3, 18th
Causes of death per 100,000 pop. (1988):
Diseases of heart: 339.6, 17th
Malignant neoplasms: 197.3, 27th
Cerebrovascular diseases: 71.1, 13th
Accidents & adverse effects: 44.2, 18th
Chronic obstructive pulmonary diseases: 37.2, 19th
Suicide: 12.8, 23rd
HIV infection: 2.4, 27th
Other: 81.6, 12th

Keeping Well

Non-federal physicians per 100,00 pop.: 162, 45th
Dentists per 100,000 (1990-91): 53, 38th
Nurses per 100,000 (1989): 468, 48th
Hospitals per 100,000: 4.4, 11th
Admissions per 100,000: 13,705, 23rd
Beds per 100,000: 477.91, 28th
Occupancy rate: 60.2%, 47th
Semiprivate room charges per day: $220, 40th
Average stay: 6.7, 39th
Notifiable diseases per 100,000:
AIDS: 6.5, 30th
Gonorrhea: 198.3, 25th
Measles: 5.5, 20th
Syphillis: 19.5, 25th
Tuberculosis (TB): 7.7, 20th
Per capita spending on mental health programs (1987): $30.50, 36th
Pop. without health insur. (1991): 18.2%, 9th

Households by Type

Total households: 1,206,135
Percent change (1980-90): 7.79%, 37th
Family households: 855,321
Percent of total: 70.91%, 24th
Nonfamily households: 350,814
Percent of total: 29.09%, 28th
Persons per household: 2.35, 50th
Pop. living in group quarters: 93,677
Percent of pop.: 2.98%, 19th

Living Quarters

Total housing units: 1,406,499
Persons per unit: 2.24, 42nd
Occupied housing units: 1,206,135
Percent of total units: 85.75%, 41st
Persons per unit: 2.50, 34th
Percent of units with over 1 person per room: 3.31%, 23rd
Owner-occupied units: 821,188
Percent of total units: 58.39%, 28th
Percent of occupied units: 68.08%, 19th
Persons per unit: 2.59, 49th
Median value: $48,100, 46th
Renter-occupied units: 384,947
Percent of total units: 27.37%, 36th
Percent of occupied units: 31.92%, 33rd
Persons per unit: 2.41, 16th
Median contract rent: $259, 43rd
Rental vacancy rate: 14.7%, 2nd
Mobile home, trailer & other as a % of occupied housing units: 11.91%, 24th

Crime Index per 100,000

Total: 5,599, 20th
Violent: 547, 23rd
Murder and nonnegligent manslaughter: 8, 21st
Aggravated assault: 7,201, 32nd
Robbery: 122, 28th
Rape: 47, 13th
Property: 5,051, 18th
Burglary: 1,447, 8th
Larceny, theft: 3,002, 26th
Motor vehicle theft: 602, 16th
Drug abuse arrests: 284, 20th

Teaching and Learning

Literacy (1987): 89%, 17th
Pop. 3 and over enrolled in school: 838,811
Percent of pop.: 27.8%, 19th
Public elementary & secondary schools:
Total enrollment: 578,000

Avg. class size (1987): 21, 39th
Teachers: 35,600
Percent of pop.: 1.13%, 12th
Teachers' avg. salary: $23,100, 47th
Spending per capita: $683, 39th
Spending per pupil in avg. daily attendance: $3,484, 44th
Percent of graduates taking SAT: 9%, 43rd
Combined SAT scores: 997, 13th
Percent of pop. over 25 completing:
High school: 74.6%, 36th
College degree/s: 17.8%, 34th
Higher educa., institutions: 48
Per 100,000 pop.: 0.9, 15th
Enroll: 173,221
Percent of pop.: 5.51%, 26th
Public: 151,073
Percent of enroll.: 87.21%, 15th
Private: 22,148
Percent of enroll.: 12.79%, 36th
White non-Hispanic: 35,155
Percent of enroll.: 83.69%, 26th
Black non-Hispanic: 4,710
Percent of enroll.: 11.21%, 13th
Hispanic: 546
Percent of enroll.: 1.30%, 31st
Asian/Pacific Islander: 710
Percent of enroll.: 1.69%, 24th
Amer. Indian/AK native: 99
Percent of enroll.: 0.24%, 43rd
Nonresident alien: 784
Percent of enroll.: 1.87%, 37th
Female: 93,238
Percent of enroll.: 53.83%, 38th
Tuition, state university ('90-'91): $1,340, 42nd
Public library systems: 106
Books & serial vol. per capita: 2.01, 38th
Govt. expend. per capita: $9.56, 43rd
State govt.: $1.87, 39th
Local govts.: $7.68, 39th

Law Enforcement, Courts, and Prisons

Police protection expend.: $251,075,000
Per capita: $79.81, 43rd
Judicial & legal expend.: $95,424,000
Per capita: $30.33, 47th
Corrections expend.: $211,305,000
Per capita: $67.17, 32nd
Police per 10,000 pop. (1990-91): 21.5, 20th
Prisoners (state & fed.) sentenced to over 1 yr., per 100,000 pop.: 383
Percent change (1989-90): 6.15%, 32nd
Death penalty: yes, by lethal injection
Under sentence of death: 98, 7th
Executed (1989): none

Religion, Number and Percent of Population

Agnostic: 9,234—0.40%, 34th
Buddhist: 4,617—0.20%, 11th
Christian: 1,989,994—86.20%, 25th
Hindu: 2,309—0.10%, 10th
Jewish: 4,617—0.20%, 40th
Moslem: NA
Unitarian: 2,309—0.10%, 31st
Other: 48,480—2.10%, 9th
None: 150,058—6.50%, 25th
Refused to answer: 96,960—4.20%, 2nd

Making a Living

Personal income per capita (1989): $11,893, 39th
Percent increase (1979-'89) (constant 1989 dollars): 3.5%, 45th
Average income per family: $35,376, 41st
Percent of pop. below poverty level: 16.7%, 10th
Percent 65 and over: 17.9%, 11th
Cost of living, selected cities
1st qtr., 1991 (U. S. Standard=100)

Prior	86.4
Tulsa	92.8
Oklahoma City	95.8

Economy

Civilian labor force : 1,540,000
Percent of tot. pop.: 48.96%, 39th
Percent 65 and over: 3.57%, 7th
Percent females: 44.48%, 42nd
Percent job growth (1980-90): 6.51%, 48th
Major employer industries:
Agriculture: 53,798—3.70%, 14th
Construction: 52,344—3.60%, 44th

Finance, insurance & real estate: 66,884—4.60%, 38th
Government: 264,628—18.20%, 11th
Manufacturing: 210,830—14.50%, 34th
Mining: 42,838—3.1%, 5th
Service: 250,088—17.20%, 43rd
Trade: 258,812—17.80%, 38th
Transportation, communication, & public utilities: 72,700—5.00%, 28th
Wholesale/retail: 294,999—21.5%, 25th
Unemployment rate: 5.58%, 22nd
Male: 3.12%, 23rd
Female: 2.47%, 22nd
Total businesses (1991): 119,162
New business incorp's. (1991): 7,073
Percent of total businesses: 5.94%, 25th
Business failures (1991): 1,827
Percent of total businesses: 1.53%, 3rd
Agriculture farm income
Marketing (1991): $3,807,582,000, 17th
Net per operation: $13,434, 40th
Net per acre: $28, 36th
Leading products: cattle, wheat, greenhouse, broilers
Av. value land & build. per acre: $513, 37th
Percent increase (1980-90): -16.45%, 38th
Govt. payments: $290,922,000, 10th
Construction, value of all: $957,000,000
Per capita: $304.24, 46th
Percent change 1989-90: 15.30%, 11th
Manufactures:
Value added: $11,889,000,000
Per capita: $3,779.58, 37th
Value of shipments: $28,010,000,000
Per capita: $8,904.54, 34th
Leading products: non-electrical machinery, fabricated metal products, petroleum
Mining, min. prod., value (1987): $8,389,000,000, 5th
Leading products: nat. gas, petroleum, coal
Retail sales: $20,218,000,000, 29th
Per household: $16,780, 46th
Percent increase (1987-90): 25.6%, 3rd
Service indust., value (1987): $10,191,000,000, 28th
Per capita: $3,239.78, 38th
Tourism indus., value (1989): $2,362,000,000, 32nd
Foreign exports value: $1,646,000,000, 32nd
Per capita: $523.27, 44th
Patents per 1,000 pop.: 5.0, 33rd

TRAVEL AND TRANSPORTATION

Motor vehicle registrations: 2,649,051
Per 1,000 pop.: 842, 18th
Motorcycle registrations: 60,838
Per 1,000 pop.: 19, 22nd
Licensed drivers per 1,000 driving age pop.: 947, 9th
Deaths from motor vehicle accidents per 100,000 pop.: 20.3, 22nd
Public roads & streets
Total mileage: 111,765, 11th
Rural mileage: 99,682, 7th
Urban mileage: 12,083, 24th
Interstate mileage: 930, 21st
Annual vehicle-miles of travel per person: 10,516, 4th
Mean travel time for workers 16 + who work away from home: 19.3 min., 34th

GOVERNMENT

Registered voters (1988): 2,199,014
Percent of voting age pop.: 91.47%, 3rd
Voter turnout (1988): 1,171,036
Percent of registered voters: 53.25%, 49th
Percent of voting age pop.: 48.71%, 33rd
State legislators, total (1992): 149, 24th
Women members (1992): 13
Percent of legislature: 8.7%, 45th
Dominant party (1992): Democrats
U. S. Congress, House members (1993): 6
Increase 1983-93: 0
Revenues:
State govt.: $7,200,626,000
Per capita: $2,289.12, 33rd
State & local govt.: $10,554,311,000
Per capita: $3,355.28, 43rd
Indebtedness:
State govt.: $3,714,198,000
Per capita: $1,180.77, 25th
State & local govt.: $8,233,000,000
Per capita: $2,617.32, 39th

Laws and Regulations

Legal driving age: 16
Marriage age without parental consent: 18
Divorce residence requirement: 6 mo.

Attractions

Major opera companies (1989): 2, 21st
Per 1 million pop.: 0.62, 27th
Major symphony orchestras (1989): 9, 28th
Per 1 million pop.: 2.79, 38th
State appropriations for state arts agencies per capita: $1.03, 15th
State Fair in the last week of Sept. at Oklahoma City

Sports and Competition

NCAA sports teams, 3: Oklahoma State Univ., Cowboys, The Univ. of Tulsa Golden Hurricanes, Univ. of Oklahoma Sooners
Professional teams, 4:
Baseball, 2—Oklahoma 89ers (American association, Class AAA), All Sports Stadium; Tulsa Drillers (Texas League, Class AA), Drillers' Stadium
Basketball, 2: Tulsa Fast Breakers (Continental Basketball Association), Expo Square Pavilion; Oklahoma City Cavalry (Continental Basketball Association), Myraid Convention Center

OREGON

"The cabins rise, the fields are sown, and Oregon is theirs! They will take, they will hold; By the spade in the mold; By the seed in the soil; By the sweat and the toil; By the plow in the loam; By the school and the home!"

Arthur Guiterman

Oregon stretches from one of the most spectacular coastlines, on the west, to Hell's Canyon, the nation's deepest, on the east. Crater Lake is the deepest in the United States and one of the loveliest. The state boasts the greatest extent of standing timber, the biggest sand dunes, and the largest geyser. Oregon was the goal of the many thousands who traveled overland to the country on the Oregon Trail. Oregon has long been a leader in sound ecological legislation and forward-looking public servants. Strange as it may seem the nation's center lies in Oregon's China Cap Mountains—center of the extended region that reaches from Guam to Maine and from Point Barrow to American Samoa.

Superlatives

• Largest reserves of standing timber.

• Leading U.S. timber producer.

• Produces most U.S. plywood.

• Leads in nickel production.

• Greatest profusion of agates.

• First pheasants in United States, in Linn County

Moments in History

• In 1543 the Spanish expedition of Bartolome Ferrello passed the present-day coast of Oregon, but it is not known how far he went to the north.

• British Sir Francis Drake may have reached as far north as the southern Oregon coast in 1579.

• The prominent promontory called Cape Blanco by Martin d'Augilar in 1603 was the first Oregon feature to be named by Europeans.

• On August 17, 1775, Bruno Heceta discovered the mouth of the Columbia River, but he could not enter because of the strong currents.

> **So They Say**
>
> "On the evening of this day I discovered a large bay....The currents and eddies caused me to believe that the place is the mouth of some great river."
>
> Bruno Heceta

• Famed English explorer Captain James Cook named Cape Foulweather in 1778.

• American Captain Robert Gray was the first white person known to have landed on present Oregon, in present-day Tillamook County, 1788. His men engaged in the first skirmish of white men with the Indians in Oregon. One sailor was killed.

• On May 11, 1792, Captain Gray became the first person to make the perilous entry into the Columbia River. He and his men sailed upstream about 15 miles and traded with the Indians, buying two salmon for one nail and a prime beaver skin for two spikes. He bought 150 rare sea otters, worth $100 each in China. Gray named the river for his ship, the *Columbia.*

• The great expedition of Lewis and Clark reached its coveted goal of the Pacific and built Fort Clatsop on Young's Bay, spending the winter of 1805-1806 there.

• Lewis and Clark returned east in 1806, leaving certificates with Indian leaders concerning their fair and hospitable treatment.

> **So They Say**
>
> "...the faithfulness, honesty, and devotion of the Indians when entrusted with any charge, as the care of horses or canoes—this character of the Indians was so marked that one can hardly avoid the conclusion that the subsequent troubles with the Indians were due largely to abuse by the whites."
>
> Anonymous

• As early as 1800 American ships controlled most of the fur trade of the northwest coast, but that trade diminished as they went into whaling.

> **So They Say**
>
> "...stately clippers of the China trade would leave New England ports, sail around Cape Horn and up to the Oregon coast. There they would trade their beads, trinkets, blankets, and a few tools or other items with the Indians for the precious sea otter, beaver and other furs. After taking on water and supplies, they would sail for China, usually stopping at the Hawaiian islands for more supplies. In China teas, spices, silks, and other goods of the Orient were acquired in exchange for furs. Sometimes as much as $250,000 was made in one voyage."
>
> Anonymous

• John Jacob Astor's Pacific Fur Company set up headquarters in 1811 and established Fort Astoria, first permanent white settlement in Oregon.

• During the War of 1812, in 1814 the British seized Astoria, but the Americans retook it in 1817.

• In 1824 the great Hudson's Bay Company took over Astoria, under the remarkable leadership of John McLoughlin.

• In 1834 the Rev. Jason Lee established a mission station and school near present-day Salem.

• In May, 1843, the settlers at Champoeg voted in favor of government by the United States and set up a provisional government of their own.

• By 1846 thousands of settlers were coming over the Oregon Trail in numbers that increased until the railroad began to take over in the 1870s.

• On Feb. 14, 1859, Oregon gained statehood.

• During the Civil War, Indian troubles plagued the new state.

• In 1877 Chief Joseph of the Nez Perce and his people took a tearful farewell as they were forced out of their homeland in Washington, Oregon, and parts of Idaho.

• The transcontinental railroad reached Portland in 1883.

• Oregon pioneered U.S. primary elections, and initiated a presidential preference in 1911.

• The Third Oregon Infantry was the first of the country's national guard to be mobilized and ready for World War I.

• The great Bonneville Dam began to transmit power in 1938.

• In one of the few Japanese attacks on the mainland during World War II, a Japanese sub shelled Fort Stevens on June 21, 1942.

• Oregon attracted so many new residents that beginning in the 1970s the state discouraged newcomers.

• The much publicized effort of cult leader Bhagwan Shree Rajneesh to establish a stronghold in Oregon failed, and he left the state in 1985.

THAT'S INTERESTING

• The Indians thought the squeaks of the wheels of the settler's wagons sounded like their words "chik-chik-chaile-kikash," and that became their name for wagon.

• At 1,996 ft., Crater Lake is the nation's deepest—and one of the most beautiful.

• Oregon's madrona tree sheds its bark as well as its leaves.

• The giant insect-eating cobra lily is another unusual form of plant life.

• Oregon students earn money for school by picking up the innumerable pine cones for seed.

• More than two centuries ago the ship *Manzanita* foundered on the coast, and beachcombers are still picking up lumps of beeswax from its cargo.

Notable Natives

Homer Davenport (Silverton, 1867-1912), cartoonist. **"Chief" Joseph** (Wallowa Valley, 1840?-1904), Indian leader. **Edwin Markham** (Oregon City, 1852-1940), poet. **Linus Pauling** (Portland, 1901-), chemist. **John Reed** (Portland, 1887-1920), journalist/political radical.

General

Admitted to statehood: Feb. 14, 1859

Origin of name: Unknown. One theory holds that the name may have been derived from that of the Wisconsin River shown on a 1715 French map as "*Ouaricon-sint*"; also, perhaps, from the Indian *"Ouragon"*

Capital: Salem

Nickname: Beaver State

Motto: "The Union"

Animal: beaver

Bird: Western meadowlark

Fish: Chinook salmon

Flower: Oregon grape

Song: "Oregon, My Oregon"

Stone: thunderegg

Tree: Douglas fir

The Land

Area: 98,386 sq. mi., 9th

Land: 96,003 sq. mi., 10th

Water: 2,383 sq. mi., 19th

Topography: coast range of rugged mountains, fertile Willamette R. Valley to E and S, Cascade Mtn. range of volcanic peaks E of the valley, plateau E of Cascades, remaining two-thirds of state, rising to the Wallowa and Blue mountains

Number of counties: 36

Geographic center: Crook, 25 mi. SSE of Prineville

Length: 360 mi.

Width: 261 mi.

Highest point: 11,239 ft. (Mount Hood), 13th

Lowest point: sea level (Pacific Ocean), 3rd

Mean elevation: 3,300 ft., 9th

Coastline: 269 mi., 8th

Shoreline: 1,410 mi., 16th

Climate and Environment

Temp., highest: 119 deg. on Aug. 10, 1938, at Pendleton; lowest: -54 deg. on Feb. 10, 1933, at Seneca

Fresh water withdrawn, per capita, per day: 2,450 gal., 10th

Endangered species: mammals, 1—Columbian white-tailed deer; birds, 3—American peregrine falcon, Aleutian Canada goose, brown pelican; reptiles, 1; amphibians, none; fishes, 3; invertebrates, 1; plants, 3

Major Cities, Population Percentage Increase (1980-90)

Beaverton, 53,310—66.79%

Eugene, 112,669—6.63%

Gresham, 68,235—106.74%

Portland, 437,319—18.79%

Salem, 107,786—20.98%

The People

Population: 2,842,321, 29th

Percent change (1980-90): 7.36%, 21st

Per sq. mi: 28.89, 41st

Percent in metro. area: 68.50%, 23rd

Percent foreign born: 4.9%, 18th

White: 2,636,787—92.77%, 12th

Black: 46,178—1.62%, 42nd

Native American: 38,496—1.35%, 13th

Asian, Pacific Isle: 69,269—2.44%, 11th

Other races: 51,591—1.82%, 21st

Hispanic origin: 112,707—3.97%, 20th

Percent over 5 yrs. speaking language other than English at home: 7.3%, 24th

Percent males: 49.15%, 16th

Percent females: 50.85%, 36th

Percent never married: 23.1%, 42nd

Marriages per 1,000 (1989): 8.3, 36th

Divorces per 1,000 (1989): 5.4, 15th

Median age: 34.5

Under 5 years: 201,421—7.09%, 35th

Under 18 years: 724,130—25.48%, 31st

65 years & older: 391,324—13.77%, 12th

Percent increase among the elderly: 29.0%, 17th

Of Vital Importance

Live births per 1,000 pop.: 15.9, 24th
Infant mortality rate per 1,000 births (1988): 8.6, 39th
Average lifetime (1979-81): 74.99, 13th
Deaths per 100,000 pop. (1988): 896.6, 24th
Causes of death per 100,000 pop. (1988):
- Diseases of heart: 281.1, 33rd
- Malignant neoplasms: 210.6, 17th
- Cerebrovascular diseases: 72.5, 8th
- Accidents & adverse effects: 45.4, 16th
- Chronic obstructive pulmonary diseases: 43.2, 5th
- Suicide: 16.9, 7th
- HIV infection: 3.6, 22nd
- Other: 79.2, 15th

Keeping Well

Non-federal physicians per 100,00 pop.: 231, 17th
Dentists per 100,000 (1990-91): 80, 8th
Nurses per 100,000 (1989): 747, 19th
Hospitals per 100,000: 2.7, 29th
- Admissions per 100,000: 11,320, 45th
- Beds per 100,000: 363.15, 46th
- Occupancy rate: 62.9%, 39th
- Semiprivate room charges per day: $338, 12th
- Average stay: 5.8, 51st

Notifiable diseases per 100,000:
- AIDS: 11.8, 17th
- Gonorrhea: 89.5, 37th
- Measles: 7.5, 12th
- Syphillis: 11.3, 32nd
- Tuberculosis (TB): 5.2, 32nd

Per capita spending on mental health programs (1987): $34.35, 29th
Pop. without health insur. (1991): 14.2%, 17th

Households by Type

Total households: 1,103,313
- Percent change (1980-90): 11.22%, 27th

Family households: 750,844
- Percent of total: 68.05%, 45th

Nonfamily households: 352,469
- Percent of total: 31.95%, 7th

Persons per household: 2.52, 46th
Pop. living in group quarters: 66,205
- Percent of pop.: 2.33%, 40th

Living Quarters

Total housing units: 1,193,567
- Persons per unit: 2.38, 29th

Occupied housing units: 1,103,313
- Percent of total units: 92.44%, 7th
- Persons per unit: 2.48, 38th
- Percent of units with over 1 person per room: 3.64%, 21st

Owner-occupied units: 695,957
- Percent of total units: 58.31%, 29th
- Percent of occupied units: 63.08%, 41st
- Persons per unit: 2.62, 46th
- Median value: $67,100, 27th

Renter-occupied units: 407,356
- Percent of total units: 34.13%, 11th
- Percent of occupied units: 36.92%, 13th
- Persons per unit: 2.33, 28th
- Median contract rent: $344, 23rd
- Rental vacancy rate: 5.3%, 49th

Mobile home, trailer & other as a % of occupied housing units: 13.16%, 21st

Crime Index per 100,000

Total: 5,646, 19th
- Violent: 507, 27th
  - Murder and nonnegligent manslaughter: 4, 41st
  - Aggravated assault: 7,086, 35th
  - Robbery: 144, 23rd
  - Rape: 47, 14th
- Property: 5,139, 16th
  - Burglary: 1,135, 24th
  - Larceny, theft: 3,545, 12th
  - Motor vehicle theft: 459, 23rd
- Drug abuse arrests: 346, 13th

Teaching and Learning

Literacy (1987): 92%, 4th
Pop. 3 and over enrolled in school: 724,233
- Percent of pop.: 26.6%, 32nd

Public elementary & secondary schools:
- Total enrollment: 469,000
- Avg. class size (1987): 23, 20th
- Teachers: 25,600
  - Percent of pop.: 0.90%, 41st
- Teachers' avg. salary: $30,800, 19th
- Spending per capita: $873, 15th

Spending per pupil in avg. daily attendance: $5,085, 17th
Percent of graduates taking SAT: 54%, 19th
Combined SAT scores: 922, 27th
Percent of pop. over 25 completing:
High school: 81.5%, 9th
College degree/s: 20.6%, 21st
Higher educa., institutions: 46
Per 100,000 pop.: 0.7, 23rd
Enroll: 166,641
Percent of pop.: 5.86%, 19th
Public: 145,327
Percent of enroll.: 87.21%, 15th
Private: 21,314
Percent of enroll.: 12.79%, 36th
White non-Hispanic: 190,920
Percent of enroll.: 77.26%, 37th
Black non-Hispanic: 48,180
Percent of enroll.: 19.50%, 6th
Hispanic: 1,138
Percent of enroll.: 0.46%, 46th
Asian/Pacific Islander: 1,699
Percent of enroll.: 0.69%, 47th
Amer. Indian/AK native: 591
Percent of enroll.: 0.24%, 43rd
Nonresident alien: 4,589
Percent of enroll.: 1.86%, 38th
Female: 88,137
Percent of enroll.: 52.89%, 46th
Tuition, state university ('90-'91): $1,906, 22nd
Public library systems: 125
Books & serial vol. per capita: 2.32, 32nd
Govt. expend. per capita: $17.01, 21st
State govt.: $1.54, 43rd
Local govts.: $15.47, 20th

Law Enforcement, Courts, and Prisons

Police protection expend.: $324,070,000
Per capita: $114.03, 22nd
Judicial & legal expend.: $155,975,000
Per capita: $54.88, 19th
Corrections expend.: $265,816,000
Per capita: $93.53, 18th
Police per 10,000 pop. (1990-91): 16.3, 40th
Prisoners (state & fed.) sentenced to over 1 yr., per 100,000 pop.: 221
Percent change (1989-90): -4.57%, 51st
Death penalty: yes, by lethal injection
Under sentence of death: 15, 25th
Executed (1989): none

Religion, Number and Percent of Population

Agnostic: 25,418—1.20%, 2nd
Buddhist: 10,591—0.50%, 2nd
Christian: 1,611,943—76.10%, 49th
Hindu: NA
Jewish: 8,473—0.40%, 31st
Moslem: 2,118—0.10%, 22nd
Unitarian: 8,473—0.40%, 8th
Other: 36,009—1.70%, 14th
None: 364,329—17.20%, 1st
Refused to answer: 50,837—2.40%, 20th

Making a Living

Personal income per capita (1989): $13,418, 26th
Percent increase (1979-'89) (constant 1989 dollars): 6.0%, 42nd
Average income per family: $39,229, 30th
Percent of pop. below poverty level: 12.4%, 26th
Percent 65 and over: 10.1%, 40th
Cost of living, selected cities
1st qtr., 1991 (U. S. Standard=100)

Klamath Falls	94.8
Bend	108.0
Portland	109.2

Economy

Civilian labor force : 1,492,000
Percent of tot. pop.: 52.49%, 14th
Percent 65 and over: 3.22%, 16th
Percent females: 44.50%, 41st
Percent job growth (1980-90): 20.40%, 23rd
Major employer industries:
Agriculture: 60,587—4.30%, 11th
Construction: 56,360—4.00%, 37th
Finance, insurance & real estate: 67,632—4.80%, 34th
Government: 195,851—13.90%, 36th
Manufacturing: 238,121—16.90%, 23rd
Mining: 2,497—0.2%, 36th
Service: 290,254—20.60%, 19th
Trade: 260,665—18.50%, 26th

Transportation, communication, & public utilities: 67,632—4.80%, 34th
Wholesale/retail: 300,948—22.8%, 4th
Unemployment rate: 5.50%, 23rd
Male: 2.88%, 31st
Female: 2.68%, 16th
Total businesses (1991): 127,176
New business incorp's. (1991): 8,375
Percent of total businesses: 6.59%, 17th
Business failures (1991): 1,304
Percent of total businesses: 1.03%, 16th
Agriculture farm income
Marketing (1991): $2,454,389,000, 27th
Net per operation: $22,446, 22nd
Net per acre: $47, 29th
Leading products: cattle, greenhouse, dairy products, wheat
Av. value land & build. per acre: $602, 35th
Percent increase (1980-90): 2.56%, 26th
Govt. payments: $89,105,000, 24th
Construction, value of all: $2,421,000,000
Per capita: $851.77, 7th
Percent change 1989-90: 1.04%, 17th
Manufactures:
Value added: $13,213,000,000
Per capita: $4,648.67, 34th
Value of shipments: $31,073,000,000
Per capita: $10,932.26, 26th
Leading products: lumber and wood products, foods, machinery, fabricated metals, paper, printing and publishing, primary metals
Mining, min. prod., value (1987): $112,000,000, 44th
Leading products: stone, sand/gravel, cement
Retail sales: $22,417,000,000, 28th
Per household: $20,159, 13th
Percent increase (1987-90): 23.3%, 8th
Service indust., value (1987): $10,120,000,000, 29th
Per capita: $3,560.47, 30th
Tourism indus., value (1989): $3,141,000,000, 28th
Foreign exports value: $4,065,000,000, 20th
Per capita: $1,430.17, 11th
Patents per 1,000 pop.: 4.4, 36th

Travel and Transportation

Motor vehicle registrations: 2,445,487
Per 1,000 pop.: 860, 13th
Motorcycle registrations: 64,088
Per 1,000 pop.: 22, 16th
Licensed drivers per 1,000 driving age pop.: 999, 1st
Deaths from motor vehicle accidents per 100,000 pop.: 20.4, 21st
Public roads & streets
Total mileage: 94,969, 16th
Rural mileage: 86,559, 14th
Urban mileage: 8,410, 30th
Interstate mileage: 727, 31st
Annual vehicle-miles of travel per person: 9,407, 21st
Mean travel time for workers 16 + who work away from home: 19.6 min., 33rd

Government

Registered voters (1988): 1,524,446
Percent of voting age pop.: 74.33%, 20th
Voter turnout (1988): 1,201,694
Percent of registered voters: 78.83%, 5th
Percent of voting age pop.: 58.59%, 10th
State legislators, total (1992): 90, 44th
Women members (1992): 22
Percent of legislature: 24.4%, 12th
Dominant party (1992): Split
U. S. Congress, House members (1993): 5
Increase 1983-93: 0
Revenues:
State govt.: $7,000,702,000
Per capita: $2,463.02, 26th
State & local govt.: $13,046,705,000
Per capita: $4,590.16, 9th
Indebtedness:
State govt.: $6,558,015,000
Per capita: $2,307.27, 12th
State & local govt.: $10,120,000,000
Per capita: $3,560.47, 24th

Laws and Regulations

Legal driving age: 16
Marriage age without parental consent: 18
Divorce residence requirement: 6 mo., qualification—check local statutes

Attractions

Major opera companies (1989): 2, 21st
Per 1 million pop.: 0.71, 23rd

Major symphony orchestras (1989): 14, 21st
Per 1 million pop.: 4.96, 11th
State appropriations for state arts agencies per capita: $0.48, 39th
State Fair in late Aug. to early Sept. at Salem

Sports and Competition

NCAA sports teams, 4: Columbia Christian College Clippers, Oregon State Univ. Beavers, Univ. of Oregon Ducks, Univ. of Portland Pilots
Professional teams, 5:
Baseball, 4—Portland Beavers (Pacific Coast League), Civic Stadium; Eugene Emeralds (Northwest League, Class A), Civic Stadium; Southern Oregon Athletics (Northwest League, Class A), Miles Field; Bend Bucks (Northwest League, Class A), Vince Genna Stadium
Basketball, 1—Portland Trail Blazers (NBA), Memorial Coliseum

PENNSYLVANIA

"Nowhere in this country, from sea to sea, does nature comfort us with such assurance of plenty, such rich and tranquil beauty as in those unsung unpainted hills of Pennsylvania."

Richard Harding Davis

To many, Pennsylvania is the most historic state, birthplace of independence and of the Constitution, and home of perhaps more historic events, with more historic firsts. It often is called the "Birth-state of the Nation." All of the hard coal in the country is mined in Pennsylvania, and Pittsburgh is famous for the production of pig iron and steel. Originally a refuge for persecuted Quakers, Pennsylvania is also home to the Amish and the Mennonites, religious groups characterized by their distinctive dress and simple lifestyle—many still speak a variation of German called Pennsylvania Dutch.

SUPERLATIVES

- Nation's first museum of art—The Philadelphia Academy of Arts.
- First natural history museum.
- First hospital—The Pennsylvania Hospital.
- First scientific society—The Franklin Institute, endowed by Benjamin Franklin.
- First circulating library.
- First medical college, founded in 1765 by John Morgan.
- First chamber of commerce.
- Greatest anthracite reserves.
- First in magnetite ore.
- First regular steamboat run.
- First steam locomotive on rails.

MOMENTS IN HISTORY

- The first known visit to the area was by Captain John Smith of Virginia in 1608.
- Henry Hudson's voyage in 1609 gave the Dutch claim to the region.
- Johan Printz established the first permanent European settlement (Swedish) in the present-day state on Tinicum Island in 1643.
- The Dutch seized the Swedish settlements in 1655, and the British took over in turn in 1664.
- William Penn arrived in Pennsylvania in October 1682, aboard the *Welcome* to take over his enormous grant to Pennsylvania and Delaware.

> So They Say
>
> "The air is sweet and clear, the Heavens serene...The country itself...is not to be despised...in some places a vast fat earth, like our best vales, in England."
>
> William Penn

- In Dec. 1862, Penn's "Great Law" became one of the first documents safeguarding life, liberty, and property through jury trial.
- The 1701 Charter of Privileges contained most of the principles of present constitutions.
- George Washington won the first skirmish of the French and Indian War, the Battle of Laurel Mountain, May 28, 1754, in present-day Fayette County.

> So They Say
>
> "The volley fired by a young Virginian (Washington) in the backwoods of America set the world on fire."
>
> Robert Walpole, British leader

• In 1755 British General Edward Braddock's major defeat left much of Pennsylvania in French hands.

• After widespread losses, the French relinquished their claims in 1763.

• As Revolutionary tensions grew, in 1769 James Smith captured Fort Bedford, first stronghold to fall to American rebels.

• The first Continental Congress meeting at Philadelphia in 1774 marked that city as a national capital.

• With the Declaration of Independence, July 4, 1776, the process of Revolution formally began. Philadelphia fell to Lord William Howe on Sept. 26, 1777.

• By the spring of 1778 the hardships of Valley Forge were left behind.

• Pennsylvania contributed to the Revolution in every way, with men, ordnance and finance, even creating the state navy in 1775.

• After the Articles of Confederation failed, delegates labored at Philadelphia from May to Sept. 1787.

• Held together mainly by the will and skill of Benjamin Franklin, they brought forth a new nation.

• On Dec. 12, 1787, Pennsylvania became the second state.

• The first wagon trip westward in 1783 pioneered the way for the vast movement of settlers to western Pennsylvania.

• During the War of 1812, Oliver Hazard Perry's eventually triumphant fleet was built in the wilds near present-day Erie.

> So They Say
>
> "But to appreciate his character, a person must have seen him, as I did, fitting out a fleet of six new vessels of war...at some hundreds of miles from the sea coast...almost abandoned by his country, toiling to fit out his fleet..."
>
> Henry Eckford, regarding Perry's building of the Great Lakes war fleet

• In the 1830s, 1840s, and 1850s Pennsylvania led the nation in science and culture.

• Pennsylvania played a key role in the Underground Railroad and gave Lincoln its vote in the 1860 election.

• Pennsylvania was the only Northern state in which a critical battle of the Civil War was fought. During the four days beginning on June 15, 1863, the Union successes in the Battle of Gettysburg marked a turning point of the war.

> So They Say
>
> "Troops under my command have repulsed the enemy's assault and we have gained a great victory. The enemy is now flying in all directions in my front."
>
> General George Mead, at Gettysburg

• In 1876, the Centennial Exposition at Philadelphia celebrated the 100th birthday of the Declaration of Independence.

• The May 1889 flood at Johnstown was one of the nation's worst disasters, with 2,200 lives lost.

• More than 660,000 Pennsylvanians served in World War I.

• The floods of 1936 were the worst in the state's history.

• The record of 1,200,000 Pennsylvania men and women in World War II service was surpassed only by New York.

• In 1972 Hurricane Agnes brought the state's worst-ever hurricane/flood damage.

• The returns from the 1990 census indicated that Pennsylvania had dropped from fourth to fifth place in population.

That's Interesting

• William Penn received the greatest land grant ever given an English subject, for which he was required to pay only two beaver skins per year to the king.

• When houses were taxed according to the number of their windows, housewives poured hot water on the tax agents from those windows, spawning the "Hot Water War."

• The carp in Lake Pymatuning sometimes crowd so closely together that the ducks walk across the backs of the fish.

• When the Ringing Rocks near Upper Black Eddy are struck, the pitch depends on the size of the rock.

Notable Natives

Louisa May Alcott (Germantown, 1832-1888), author. **Richard Allen** (Philadelphia, 1760-1831), religious leader. **Marian Anderson** (Philadelphia, 1902-1993), singer. **Maxwell Anderson** (Atlantic, 1888-1959), playwright. **Samuel Barber** (West Chester, 1910-1981), composer. **James Buchanan** (Mercersburg,1791-1868), U.S. president. **Charles Wakefield Cadman** (Johnstown, 1881-1946), composer. **Simon Cameron** (Maytown, 1799-1889), public official/political leader. **W.C. Fields** (Philadelphia, 1880-1946), entertainer/actor. **Stephen Collins Foster** (Lawrenceville, 1826-1864), composer. **Henry Clay Frick** (West Overton, 1849-1919), industrialist/philanthropist. **Henry John Heinz** (Pittsburgh, 1844-1919), industrialist. **Milton Snavely Hershey** (Dauphin Cty., 1857-1945), industrialist/philanthropist. **Grace Kelly** (Philadelphia, 1929-1982), actress. **Walter Crawford Kelly** (Philadelphia, 1913-1973), cartoonist/illustrator. **George Brinton McClellan** (Philadelphia, 1826-1885), soldier. **Andrew William Mellon** (Pittsburgh, 1855-1937), financier/art collector. **Ethelbert Woodbridge Nevin** (Edgeworth, 1862-1901), composer. **Maxfield Frederick Parrish** (Philadelphia, 1870-1966), artist. **Robert Edwin Peary** (Cresson, 1856-1920), explorer. **Mary Roberts Rinehart** (Pittsburgh, 1876-1958), author. **Charles Michael Schwab** (Williamsburg, 1862-1939), industrialist. **James Stewart** (Indiana, 1908-), actor. **John Wanamaker** (Philadelphia, 1838-1922), merchant. **Anthony Wayne** (Wayneboro, 1745-1796), soldier. **Benjamin West** (Springfield, 1738-1820), painter.

General

Admitted to statehood: Dec. 12, 1787

Origin of name: William Penn, the Quaker, who was made full proprietor by King Charles II in 1681, suggested Sylvania, or woodland, for his tract.; the King's government owed Penn's father, Admiral William Penn, £16,000, and the land was granted as partial settlement; Charles II added the Penn to Sylvania, against the desires of the modest proprietor

Capital: Harrisburg

Nickname: The Keystone State

Motto: "Virtue, Liberty and Independence"

Animal: whitetail deer

Bird: ruffed grouse

Colors: blue and gold

Dog: great dane

Fish: brook trout

Flower: mountain laurel

Insect: firefly

Slogan: You've got a friend in Pennsylvania

Tree: Eastern hemlock

The Land

Area: 46,058 sq. mi., 33rd

Land: 44,820 sq. mi., 32nd

Water: 1,239 sq. mi., 28th

Topography: Allegheny Mtns. run SW to NE, with Piedmont and coast plain in the SE triangle; Allegheny Front a diagonal spine across the state's center; N and W rugged plateau falls to Lake Erie Lowland

Number of counties: 67

Geographic center: Centre, 2.5 mi. SW of Bellefonet

Length: 283 mi.

Width: 160 mi.

Highest point: 3,213 ft. (Mt. Davis, Somerset County), 33rd

Lowest point: sea level (Delaware River), 3rd

Mean elevation: 1,100 ft., 23rd

Coastline: 0 mi., 23rd

Shoreline: 89 mi., 24th

Climate and Environment

Temp., highest: 111 deg. on July 10, 1936, at Phoenixville; lowest: -42 deg. on Jan. 5, 1904, at Smethport

Fresh water withdrawn, per capita, per day: 1,210 gal., 28th

Endangered species: mammals, 1—Indiana bat; birds, 2—American peregrine falcon, piping plover; reptiles, none; amphibians, none; fishes, none; invertebrates, 2; plants, 1

Major Cities, Population Percentage Increase (1980-90)

Allentown, 105,090—1.28%
Erie, 108,718— –8.73%
Philadelphia, 1,585,577— –6.08%
Pittsburgh, 369,879— –12.76%
Scranton, 81,805— –7.16%

The People

Population: 11,881,643, 5th
Percent change (1980-90): 0.14%, 45th
Per sq. mi: 257.97, 9th
Percent in metro. area: 84.81%, 10th
Percent foreign born: 3.1%, 25th
White: 10,520,201—88.54%, 21st
Black: 1,089,795—9.17%, 21st
Native American: 14,733—0.12%, 51st
Asian, Pacific Isle: 137,438—1.16%, 25th
Other races: 119,476—1.01%, 25th
Hispanic origin: 232,262—1.95%, 30th
Percent over 5 yrs. speaking language other than English at home: 7.3%, 24th
Percent males: 47.92%, 48th
Percent females: 52.08%, 4th
Percent never married: 27.3%, 16th
Marriages per 1,000 (1989): 7.1, 51st
Divorces per 1,000 (1989): 3.2, 47th
Median age: 35
Under 5 years: 797,058—6.71%, 47th
Under 18 years: 2,794,810—23.52%, 45th
65 years & older: 1,829,106—15.39%, 2nd
Percent increase among the elderly: 19.5%, 28th

Of Vital Importance

Live births per 1,000 pop.: 14.2, 45th
Infant mortality rate per 1,000 births (1988): 9.9, 24th
Average lifetime (1979-81): 73.58, 33rd
Deaths per 100,000 pop. (1988): 1050.1, 4th
Causes of death per 100,000 pop. (1988):
Diseases of heart: 400.6, 1st
Malignant neoplasms: 237.1, 4th
Cerebrovascular diseases: 67.3, 20th
Accidents & adverse effects: 37.6, 33rd
Chronic obstructive pulmonary diseases: 36, 22nd
Suicide: 12.4, 27th
HIV infection: 3.9, 20th
Other: 79.8, 14th

Keeping Well

Non-federal physicians per 100,000 pop.: 259, 10th
Dentists per 100,000 (1990-91): 75, 12th
Nurses per 100,000 (1989): 836, 9th
Hospitals per 100,000: 2.5, 34th
Admissions per 100,000: 15,877, 9th
Beds per 100,000: 575.29, 14th
Occupancy rate: 75.3%, 9th
Semiprivate room charges per day: $375, 6th
Average stay: 13.0, 4th
Notifiable diseases per 100,000:
AIDS: 10.1, 22nd
Gonorrhea: 258.9, 19th
Measles: 4.6, 24th
Syphillis: 64.7, 10th
Tuberculosis (TB): 6.5, 27th
Per capita spending on mental health programs (1987): $68.40, 3rd
Pop. without health insur. (1991): 7.8%, 48th

Households by Type

Total households: 4,495,966
Percent change (1980-90): 6.54%, 42nd
Family households: 3,155,989
Percent of total: 70.20%, 29th
Nonfamily households: 1,339,977
Percent of total: 29.80%, 23rd
Persons per household: 2.57, 31st
Pop. living in group quarters: 348,424
Percent of pop.: 2.93%, 21st

Living Quarters

Total housing units: 4,938,140
Persons per unit: 2.41, 25th
Occupied housing units: 4,495,966
Percent of total units: 91.05%, 16th
Persons per unit: 2.46, 44th
Percent of units with over 1 person per room: 1.84%, 45th
Owner-occupied units: 3,176,121
Percent of total units: 64.32%, 5th
Percent of occupied units: 70.64%, 5th
Persons per unit: 2.72, 28th
Median value: $69,700, 25th

Renter-occupied units: 1,319,845
Percent of total units: 26.73%, 39th
Percent of occupied units: 29.36%, 47th
Persons per unit: 2.19, 48th
Median contract rent: $322, 28th
Rental vacancy rate: 7.2%, 40th
Mobile home, trailer & other as a % of occupied housing units: 7.12%, 35th

CRIME INDEX PER 100,000

Total: 3,476, 47th
Violent: 431, 33rd
Murder and nonnegligent manslaughter: 7, 25th
Aggravated assault: 6,708, 47th
Robbery: 176, 18th
Rape: 26, 44th
Property: 3,045, 47th
Burglary: 729, 45th
Larceny, theft: 1,811, 50th
Motor vehicle theft: 506, 21st
Drug abuse arrests: 233, 28th

TEACHING AND LEARNING

Literacy (1987): 88%, 25th
Pop. 3 and over enrolled in school: 2,829,553
Percent of pop.: 24.8%, 49th
Public elementary & secondary schools:
Total enrollment: 1,663,000
Avg. class size (1987): 23, 20th
Teachers: 105,400
Percent of pop.: 0.89%, 43rd
Teachers' avg. salary: $33,300, 12th
Spending per capita: $789, 28th
Spending per pupil in avg. daily attendance: $5,670, 11th
Percent of graduates taking SAT: 67%, 8th
Combined SAT scores: 876, 45th
Percent of pop. over 25 completing:
High school: 74.7%, 35th
College degree/s: 17.9%, 32nd
Higher educa., institutions: 220
Per 100,000 pop.: 0.5, 36th
Enroll: 604,060
Percent of pop.: 5.08%, 37th
Public: 343,478
Percent of enroll.: 56.86%, 47th
Private: 260,582
Percent of enroll.: 43.14%, 5th
White non-Hispanic: 104,620
Percent of enroll.: 92.72%, 5th
Black non-Hispanic: 2,723
Percent of enroll.: 2.41%, 39th
Hispanic: 1,559
Percent of enroll.: 1.38%, 29th
Asian/Pacific Islander: 1,178
Percent of enroll.: 1.04%, 39th
Amer. Indian/AK native: 729
Percent of enroll.: 0.65%, 21st
Nonresident alien: 2,022
Percent of enroll.: 1.79%, 39th
Female: 326,472
Percent of enroll.: 54.05%, 36th
Tuition, state university ('90-'91): $3,401, 2nd
Public library systems: 445
Books & serial vol. per capita: 2.08, 36th
Govt. expend. per capita: $8.39, 45th
State govt.: $2.67, 23rd
Local govts.: $5.72, 45th

LAW ENFORCEMENT, COURTS, AND PRISONS

Police protection expend.: $1,059,360,000
Per capita: $89.16, 35th
Judicial & legal expend.: $582,915,000
Per capita: $49.06, 25th
Corrections expend.: $770,944,000
Per capita: $64.88, 34th
Police per 10,000 pop. (1990-91): 18.7, 31st
Prisoners (state & fed.) sentenced to over 1 yr., per 100,000 pop.: 183
Percent change (1989-90): 8.91%, 14th
Death penalty: yes, by electrocution
Under sentence of death: 115, 5th
Executed (1989): none

RELIGION, NUMBER AND PERCENT OF POPULATION

Agnostic: 63,608—0.70%, 17th
Buddhist: 9,087—0.10%, 17th
Christian: 7,987,326—87.90%, 19th
Hindu: 9,087—0.10%, 10th
Jewish: 154,476—1.70%, 10th
Moslem: 27,261—0.30%, 9th
Unitarian: 9,087—0.10%, 31st

Other: 208,997—2.30%, 6th
None: 445,255—4.90%, 40th
Refused to answer: 172,650—1.90%, 31st

Making a Living

Personal income per capita (1989): $14,068, 21st
Percent increase (1979-'89) (constant 1989 dollars): 18.6%, 18th
Average income per family: $42,648, 20th
Percent of pop. below poverty level: 11.1%, 33rd
Percent 65 and over: 10.6%, 37th
Cost of living, selected cities
1st qtr., 1991 (U. S. Standard=100)

Sharon	98.7
Pittsburgh	110.4
Philadelphia	127.6

Economy

Civilian labor force : 5,901,000
Percent of tot. pop.: 49.66%, 30th
Percent 65 and over: 2.91%, 20th
Percent females: 44.86%, 37th
Percent job growth (1980-90): 11.23%, 42nd
Major employer industries:
Agriculture: 83,745—1.50%, 41st
Construction: 295,899—5.30%, 13th
Finance, insurance & real estate: 329,397—5.90%, 18th
Government: 675,543—12.10%, 47th
Manufacturing: 1,122,183—20.10%, 15th
Mining: 31,396—0.6%, 20th
Service: 1,289,673—23.10%, 8th
Trade: 1,044,021—18.70%, 25th
Transportation, communication, & public utilities: 295,899—5.30%, 24th
Wholesale/retail: 1,166,867—21.5%, 25th
Unemployment rate: 5.39%, 25th
Male: 3.14%, 21st
Female: 2.25%, 31st
Total businesses (1991): 367,348
New business incorp's. (1991): 17,340
Percent of total businesses: 4.72%, 39th
Business failures (1991): 3,622
Percent of total businesses: 0.99%, 17th
Agriculture farm income
Marketing (1991): $3,503,040,000, 19th
Net per operation: $13,835, 39th
Net per acre: $91, 13th
Leading products: dairy products, cattle, greenhouse, mushrooms
Av. value land & build. per acre: $1,911, 9th
Percent increase (1980-90): 30.53%, 11th
Govt. payments: $34,364,000, 34th
Construction, value of all: $5,662,000,000
Per capita: $476.53, 35th
Percent change 1989-90: -23.03%, 38th
Manufactures:
Value added: $64,065,000,000
Per capita: $5,391.93, 19th
Value of shipments: $136,526,000,000
Per capita: $11,490.50, 24th
Leading products: primary metals, foods, fabricated metal products, non-electrical machinery, electrical machinery
Mining, min. prod., value (1987): $4,102,000,000, 10th
Leading products: coal, nat. gas, cement
Retail sales: $82,990,000,000, 6th
Per household: $18,413, 31st
Percent increase (1987-90): 12.8%, 32nd
Service indust., value (1987): $53,933,000,000, 6th
Per capita: $4,539.19, 15th
Tourism indus., value (1989): $8,664,000,000, 8th
Foreign exports value: $8,491,000,000, 12th
Per capita: $714.63, 33rd
Patents per 1,000 pop.: 4.2, 37th

Travel and Transportation

Motor vehicle registrations: 7,971,470
Per 1,000 pop.: 670, 46th
Motorcycle registrations: 173,301
Per 1,000 pop.: 14, 33rd
Licensed drivers per 1,000 driving age pop.: 840, 44th
Deaths from motor vehicle accidents per 100,000 pop.: 13.9, 44th
Public roads & streets
Total mileage: 116,508, 8th
Rural mileage: 88,164, 11th
Urban mileage: 28,344, 7th
Interstate mileage: 1,569, 5th
Annual vehicle-miles of travel per person: 7,213, 48th
Mean travel time for workers 16 + who work away from home: 21.6 min., 16th

GOVERNMENT

Registered voters (1988): 5,875,943
Percent of voting age pop.: 64.86%, 39th
Voter turnout (1988): 4,536,251
Percent of registered voters: 77.20%, 12th
Percent of voting age pop.: 50.07%, 30th
State legislators, total (1992): 253, 2nd
Women members (1992): 24
Percent of legislature: 9.5%, 44th
Dominant party (1992): Split
U. S. Congress, House members (1993): 21
Increase 1983-93: -2
Revenues:
State govt.: $27,222,929,000
Per capita: $2,291.18, 32nd
State & local govt.: $43,776,949,000
Per capita: $3,684.42, 32nd
Indebtedness:
State govt.: $10,926,401,000
Per capita: $919.60, 36th
State & local govt.: $45,728,000,000
Per capita: $3,848.63, 20th

LAWS AND REGULATIONS

Legal driving age: 18
Marriage age without parental consent: 18
Divorce residence requirement: 6 mo.

ATTRACTIONS

Major opera companies (1989): 10, 3rd
Per 1 million pop.: 0.83, 16th
Major symphony orchestras (1989): 43, 3rd
Per 1 million pop.: 3.57, 28th
State appropriations for state arts agencies per capita: $1.08, 14th
State Fair in the 2nd week in Jan. at Harrisburg

SPORTS AND COMPETITION

NCAA sports teams, 17: Bucknell Univ. Bison, Drexel Univ. Dragons, Duquesne Univ. Dukes, La Salle Univ. Explorers, LaFayette College Leopards, Lehigh Univ. Engineers, Penn State Univ. Nittany Lions, Philadelphia College of Textiles & Science Rams, Robert Morris College, St. Francis College of Pennsylvania Red flash, St. Joseph's Univ. Hawks, Swarthmore College Garnet, Temple Univ. Owls, Univ. of Pennsylvania Red & Blue Quakers, Univ. of Pittsburgh Panthers, Villanova Univ. Wildcats, West Chester Univ. Rams
Professional teams, 16: Baseball, 7—Erie Sailors (New York-Penn League, Class A), Ainsworth Field; Williamsport Bills (Eastern League, Class AA), Bowman Field; Scranton Red Barons (International League, Class AAA), Lackawanna County Multi-Purpose Stadium; Reading Phillies (Eastern League, Class AA), Reading Municipal Memorial Stadium; Harrisburg Senators (Eastern League, Class AA), Riverside Stadium; Pittsburgh Pirates (NL), Three Rivers Stadium; Philadelphia Phillies (NL), Veterans Stadium
Basketball, 2—Erie Wave (World Basketball League), Louis J. Tullio Convention Center; Philadelphia 76ers (NBA), The Spectrum
Football, 2—Pittsburgh Steelers (AFC), Three Rivers Stadium; Philadelphia Eagles (NFC), Veterans Stadium
Hockey, 5—Pittsburgh Penguins (NHL), Civic Arena; Erie Panthers (East Coast Hockey League), Erie Civic Center; Hershey Bears (American Hockey League), Hershey Park Arena; Philadelphia flyers (NHL), The Spectrum; Johnstown Chiefs (East Coast Hockey League), War Memorial Auditorium

RHODE ISLAND

"One views it as placed there by some refinement in the scheme of nature, just a touchstone of taste—with a beautiful little sense to be read with it by a few persons and nothing at all to be made of it, as to its essence, by most others."

Henry James

The smallest state, Rhode Island could be fitted into enormous Alaska 483 times. However, the smallest state has the longest official name. But it is an important industrial state, especially in textile and jewelry production. It lies on the beautiful Narragansett Bay—an arm of the Atlantic Ocean—and is a popular vacation area, to which boaters, fisherman, and other water-sports fans flock during the summer months. The big and the little have combined to weave the fascinating story of Rhode Island.

SUPERLATIVES

• Birthplace of the U.S. industrial revolution.

• World's costume jewelry center.

• Most heavily industrialized state in proportion to size.

• Birthplace of the modern poultry industry.

• Oldest synagogue in America.

• Largest unsupported dome in America, in the capitol.

• Nation's oldest indoor shopping center, at Providence.

MOMENTS IN HISTORY

• Giovanni de Verrazano made the first recorded European contact with the present-day state in 1524, at Narragansett Bay.

• In 1635 William Blackstone settled in Valley Falls, the first European settler known in the Rhode Island area.

• Providence was founded by Roger Williams in 1636 on a grant of land ceded to him by the Narragansett Indians.

> **So They Say**
>
> "Having a sense of God's merciful providence unto me called this place Providence, desired it might be for a shelter for persons distressed for conscience."
>
> Roger Williams

• Roger Williams and others founded the nation's first Baptist church in 1639.

• In 1643 Roger Williams obtained a charter for the colony.

• The first law against slavery in North America was enacted by Rhode Island on May 18, 1652.

• Beginning about 1652, Indian wars, particularly King Philip's War, plagued the colony.

• King Philip, chief of the Wampanoag Indians, was captured and executed on August 12, 1676, ending much of the Indian power in the region.

• During the French and Indian War, on July 1689, Block Island was attacked by privateers.

> **So They Say**
>
> The privateers at Block Island "...continued about a week on the island, plundering houses, stripping the people of their clothing, ripping up the beds, throwing out the feathers, and carrying away the ticking."
>
> Rev. Samuel Niles

• Rhode Islanders were quick to protest the British tax laws. On June 9, 1772, the British sloop of war *Gaspee* was captured and burned.

• Providence celebrated its own "tea party" on March 2, 1775, by burning a huge mound of captured tea. Women who insisted on their cup of tea sipped in secret, fearing their husbands' wrath.

• On May 4, 1776 Rhode Island "created the first free republic in the New World," according to the Rhode Island Development Council.

• During the Revolutionary War many Rhode Island communities were captured. Heaviest fighting in the state was the Battle of Rhode Island, Aug. 28-29, 1778.

• Opposed to the new U.S. constitution and its government, Rhode Island held out until May 29, 1790, when it became the last of the 13 original colonies to join.

• In 1824 women weavers of Pawtucket went on strike, thought to be the first in the United States by women.

• More than 24,000 people from Rhode Island served during the Civil War, with 255 dying in combat and 1,265 from disease.

• In 1876 President Rutherford B. Hayes made a historic conversation over the newly invented telephone, from Rocky Point to Providence, a distance of 8 miles.

• In 1895 the Cornelius Vanderbilt mansion, the Breakers, became perhaps the nation's most elegant private home, expanding Newport's high social position.

• World War I brought 28,817 Rhode Island men and women into the armed services.

• The 300th anniversary of its founding by Roger Williams was celebrated by the state in 1936.

• During World War II, working at Quonset Point near Davisville, the Navy Seabees designed a structure that became world renowned, named Quonset hut for the point.

• The America's Cup yacht race came to Newport in 1930. Americans lost the race for the first time, to Australia in 1983.

• The 1990 census showed a slight gain in the state's population during the preceding decade.

That's Interesting

• The smallest state has the longest official name, the "State of Rhode Island and Providence Plantations."

• Gentlemanly Indian men would serenade an Indian woman. If interested she would throw out her moccasin, then come out for an engagement walk. Less honorable braves sometimes knocked their prospective brides unconscious and carried them off.

• Samuel Gorton fled to Rhode Island after he was banished from Massachusetts for defending his maid, who had been punished for smiling in church.

• Many protests against the British tax on tea were made in Rhode Island. One man dashed around Providence crossing out the word "tea" on every sign he found.

• A lover of good jokes, Mrs. William Astor once invited Newport society to meet the Prince del Drago, who turned out to be a tiny monkey resplendent in a full dress suit.

Notable Natives

Nelson Wilmarth Aldrich (Foster, 1841-1915), politician. **Zachariah Allen** (Providence, 1795-1882), inventor. **Nicholas Brown** (Providence, 1729-1791), manufacturer. **William Ellery Channing** (Newport, 1780-1842), clergyman. **George Michael Cohan** (Providence, 1878-1942), composer. **George William Curtis** (Providence, 1824-1982), author/lecturer. **Thomas Wilson Dorr** (Providence, 1805-1854), political reformer. **Robert Gray** (Tiverton, 1755-1806), explorer. **Nathanael Greene** (Warwick, 1742-1786), Revolutionary soldier. **Stephen Hopkins** (Providence, 1707-1785), colonial adminstrator. **Napoleon "Larry" Lajoie** (Woonsocket, 1875-1959), baseball player. **Matthew Calbraith Perry** (Newport, 1794-1858), naval officer. **Oliver Hazard Perry** (South Kingston, 1785-1819), naval officer. **Gilbert Charles Stuart** (North Kingstown, 1755-1828), artist.

General

Admitted to statehood: May 29, 1790

Origin of name: Exact origin is unknown; one theory notes that Giovanni de Verrazano recorded an island about the size

of Rhodes in the Mediterranean in 1524, but others believe the state was named Roode Eylandt by Adriaen Block, Dutch explorer, because of its red clay
Capital: Providence
Nicknames: Little Rhody and The Ocean State
Motto: "Hope"
Bird: Rhode Island red
Colors: blue, white, and gold
Flower: violet
Rock: cumberlandite
Song: "Rhode Island"
Tree: red maple

The Land

Area: 1,545 sq. mi., 50th
Land: 1,045 sq. mi., 50th
Water: 500 sq. mi., 41st
Topography: E lowlands of Narragansett Basin, W uplands of flat and rolling hills
Number of counties: 5
Geographic center: Kent, 1 mi. SSW of Crompton
Length: 40 mi.
Width: 30 mi.
Highest point: 812 ft. (Jerimoth Hill), 46th
Lowest point: sea level (Atlantic Ocean), 3rd
Mean elevation: 200 ft., 47th
Coastline: 40 mi., 19th
Shoreline: 384 mi., 20th

Climate and Environment

Temp., highest: 104 deg. on Aug. 2, 1975, at Providence; lowest: -23 deg. on Jan. 11, 1942, at Kingston
Fresh water withdrawn, per capita, per day: 152 gal., 51st
Endangered species: mammals, none; birds, 2—American peregrine falcon, roseate tern; reptiles, 2; amphibians, none; fishes, none; invertebrates, 1; plants, 2

Major Cities, Population Percentage Increase (1980-90)

Cranston, 76,060—5.65%
East Providence, 50,380— –1.18%
Pawtucket, 72,644— 2.02%
Providence, 160,728—2.50%
Warwick, 85,427— –1.95%

The People

Population: 1,003,464, 43rd
Percent change (1980-90): 5.61%, 25th
Per sq. mi: 649.49, 3rd
Percent in metro. area: 92.48%, 5th
Percent foreign born: 9.5%, 7th
White: 917,375—91.42%, 17th
Black: 38,861—3.87%, 33rd
Native American: 4,071—0.41%, 27th
Asian, Pacific Isle: 18,325—1.83%, 16th
Other races: 24,832—2.47%, 12th
Hispanic origin: 45,756—4.56%, 18th
Percent over 5 yrs. speaking language other than English at home: 17.0%, 9th
Percent males: 47.98%, 46th
Percent females: 52.02%, 6th
Percent never married: 29.6%, 6th
Marriages per 1,000 (1989): 8.3, 36th
Divorces per 1,000 (1989): 3.6, 39th
Median age: 34
Under 5 years: 66,969—6.67%, 48th
Under 18 years: 225,690—22.49%, 48th
65 years & older: 150,547—15.00%, 4th
Percent increase among the elderly: 18.6%, 31st

Of Vital Importance

Live births per 1,000 pop.: 15.6, 29th
Infant mortality rate per 1,000 births (1988): 8.2, 44th
Average lifetime (1979-81): 74.76, 17th
Deaths per 100,000 pop. (1988): 979.2, 9th
Causes of death per 100,000 pop. (1988):
Diseases of heart: 353.6, 12th
Malignant neoplasms: 242, 3rd
Cerebrovascular diseases: 64, 24th
Accidents & adverse effects: 29.7, 48th
Chronic obstructive pulmonary diseases: 34.3, 26th
Suicide: 10, 45th
HIV infection: 4.2, 18th
Other: 81.7, 10th

Keeping Well

Non-federal physicians per 100,000 pop.: 273, 7th
Dentists per 100,000 (1990-91): 69, 21st

Nurses per 100,000 (1989): 935, 3rd
Hospitals per 100,000: 1.9, 47th
  Admissions per 100,000: 13,712, 22nd
  Beds per 100,000: 444.86, 34th
  Occupancy rate: 82.3%, 3rd
  Semiprivate room charges per day: $342, 10th
  Average stay: 7.3, 20th
Notifiable diseases per 100,000:
  AIDS: 8.8, 24th
  Gonorrhea: 119.6, 32nd
  Measles: 3.2, 31st
  Syphillis: 16.7, 27th
  Tuberculosis (TB): 7.5, 21st
Per capita spending on mental health programs (1987): $52.34, 12th
Pop. without health insur. (1991): 10.1%, 39th

Households by Type

Total households: 377,977
  Percent change (1980-90): 11.50%, 25th
Family households: 258,886
  Percent of total: 68.49%, 43rd
Nonfamily households: 119,091
  Percent of total: 31.51%, 9th
Persons per household: 2.55, 36th
Pop. living in group quarters: 38,595
  Percent of pop.: 3.85%, 3rd

Living Quarters

Total housing units: 414,572
  Persons per unit: 2.42, 21st
Occupied housing units: 337,977
  Percent of total units: 81.52%, 48th
  Persons per unit: 2.51, 30th
  Percent of units with over 1 person per room: 2.57%, 34th
Owner-occupied units: 224,792
  Percent of total units: 54.22%, 40th
  Percent of occupied units: 66.51%, 29th
  Persons per unit: 2.78, 17th
  Median value: $133,500, 6th
Renter-occupied units: 153,185
  Percent of total units: 36.95%, 7th
  Percent of occupied units: 45.32%, 4th
  Persons per unit: 2.23, 45th
  Median contract rent: $416, 13th
  Rental vacancy rate: 7.9%, 31st
Mobile home, trailer & other as a % of occupied housing units: 2.62%, 47th

Crime Index per 100,000:

Total: 5,353, 25th
  Violent: 432, 32nd
    Murder and nonnegligent manslaughter: 5, 35th
    Aggravated assault: 6,674, 48th
    Robbery: 122, 27th
    Rape: 25, 45th
  Property: 4,921, 20th
    Burglary: 1,271, 13th
    Larceny, theft: 2,695, 41st
    Motor vehicle theft: 954, 4th
  Drug abuse arrests: 281, 21st

Teaching and Learning

Literacy (1987): 85%, 40th
Pop. 3 and over enrolled in school: 254,635
  Percent of pop.: 26.5%, 35th
Public elementary & secondary schools:
  Total enrollment: 139,000
  Avg. class size (1987): 22, 28th
  Teachers: 9,400
    Percent of pop.: 0.94%, 36th
  Teachers' avg. salary: $36,100, 7th
  Spending per capita: $827, 22nd
  Spending per pupil in avg. daily attendance: $6,523, 6th
Percent of graduates taking SAT: 67%, 8th
  Combined SAT scores: 880, 43rd
Percent of pop. over 25 completing:
  High school: 72.0%, 41st
  College degree/s: 21.3%, 18th
Higher educa., institutions: 12
  Per 100,000 pop.: 0.3, 50th
  Enroll: 78,273
  Percent of pop.: 7.80%, 2nd
  Public: 42,350
    Percent of enroll.: 54.11%, 48th
  Private: 35,923
    Percent of enroll.: 45.89%, 4th
  White non-Hispanic: 28,952
    Percent of enroll.: 92.42%, 8th
  Black non-Hispanic: 284
    Percent of enroll.: 0.91%, 45th

Hispanic: 905
Percent of enroll.: 2.89%, 14th
Asian/Pacific Islander: 184
Percent of enroll.: 0.59%, 49th
Amer. Indian/AK native: 444
Percent of enroll.: 1.42%, 10th
Nonresident alien: 557
Percent of enroll.: 1.78%, 40th
Female: 42,750
Percent of enroll.: 54.62%, 30th
Tuition, state university ('90-'91): $2,311, 13th
Public library systems: 51
Books & serial vol. per capita: 2.74, 23rd
Govt. expend. per capita: $15.64, 25th
State govt.: $5.72, 4th
Local govts.: $9.93, 33rd

Law Enforcement, Courts, and Prisons

Police protection expend.: $122,008,000
Per capita: $121.64, 19th
Judicial & legal expend.: $65,562,000
Per capita: $65.37, 10th
Corrections expend.: $80,165,000
Per capita: $79.93, 26th
Police per 10,000 pop. (1990-91): 22.6, 14th
Prisoners (state & fed.) sentenced to over 1 yr., per 100,000 pop.: 157
Percent change (1989-90): 7.90%, 23rd
Death penalty: no

Religion, Number and Percent of Population

Agnostic: 3,889—0.50%, 27th
Buddhist: NA
Christian: 680,552—87.50%, 21st
Hindu: NA
Jewish: 12,444—1.60%, 11th
Moslem: 3,111—0.40%, 5th
Unitarian: 3,111—0.40%, 8th
Other: 5,444—0.70%, 43rd
None: 46,666—6.00%, 32nd
Refused to answer: 22,555—2.90%, 9th

Making a Living

Personal income per capita (1989): $14,981, 15th
Percent increase (1979-89) (constant 1989 dollars): 29.6%, 8th
Average income per family: $45,953, 14th
Percent of pop. below poverty level: 9.6%, 43rd
Percent 65 and over: 11.6%, 26th
Cost of living, selected cities
1st qtr., 1991 (U. S. Standard=100) not available

Economy

Civilian labor force : 516,000
Percent of tot. pop.: 51.42%, 23rd
Percent 65 and over: 3.29%, 11th
Percent females: 47.29%, 7th
Percent job growth (1980-90): 15.26%, 37th
Major employer industries:
Agriculture: 2,886—0.60%, 49th
Construction: 23,569—4.90%, 18th
Finance, insurance & real estate: 29,822—6.20%, 15th
Government: 59,644—12.40%, 45th
Manufacturing: 107,744—22.40%, 9th
Mining: 240—0.0%, 51st
Service: 107,744—22.40%, 13th
Trade: 94,276—19.60%, 13th
Transportation, communication, & public utilities: 19,721—4.10%, 46th
Wholesale/retail: 103,392—21.2%, 33rd
Unemployment rate: 6.78%, 6th
Male: 3.68%, 5th
Female: 3.10%, 6th
Total businesses (1991): 32,764
New business incorp's. (1991): 2,458
Percent of total businesses: 7.50%, 13th
Business failures (1991): 454
Percent of total businesses: 1.39%, 7th
Agriculture farm income
Marketing (1991): $70,917,000, 49th
Net per operation: $52,606, 5th
Net per acre: $558, 1st
Leading products: greenhouse, dairy products, eggs, potatoes
Av. value land & build. per acre: $5,080, 1st
Percent increase (1980-90): 101.35%, 3rd
Govt. payments: $110,000, 50th
Construction, value of all: $328,000,000
Per capita: $326.87, 45th
Percent change 1989-90: -44.50%, 51st

Manufactures:
Value added: $5,149,000,000
Per capita: $5,131.23, 25th
Value of shipments: $9,761,000,000
Per capita: $9,727.30, 32nd
Leading products: costume jewelry, machinery, textiles, electronics
Mining, min. prod., value (1987): $20,000,000, 48th
Leading products: stone, sand/gravel, gem stones
Retail sales: $7,325,000,000, 42nd
Per household: $19,276, 24th
Percent increase (1987-90): 7.4%, 45th
Service indust., value (1987): $4,372,000,000, 42nd
Per capita: $4,356.91, 17th
Tourism indus., value (1989): $621,000,000, 51st
Foreign exports value: $595,000,000, 43rd
Per capita: $592.95, 39th
Patents per 1,000 pop.: 5.5, 27th

Travel and Transportation

Motor vehicle registrations: 671,807
Per 1,000 pop.: 669, 47th
Motorcycle registrations: 23,605
Per 1,000 pop.: 23, 15th
Licensed drivers per 1,000 driving age pop.: 841, 43rd
Deaths from motor vehicle accidents per 100,000 pop.: 8.4, 50th
Public roads & streets
Total mileage: 6,111, 48th
Rural mileage: 1,523, 50th
Urban mileage: 4,588, 37th
Interstate mileage: 70, 48th
Annual vehicle-miles of travel per person: 6,999, 49th
Mean travel time for workers 16 + who work away from home: 19.2 min., 35th

Government

Registered voters (1988): 548,758
Percent of voting age pop.: 71.83%, 25th
Voter turnout (1988): 404,622
Percent of registered voters: 73.73%, 18th
Percent of voting age pop.: 52.96%, 24th
State legislators, total (1992): 150, 20th
Women members (1992): 25
Percent of legislature: 16.7%, 27th
Dominant party (1992): Democrats
U. S. Congress, House members (1993): 2
Increase 1983-93: 0
Revenues:
State govt.: $3,034,237,000
Per capita: $3,023.76, 8th
State & local govt.: $4,104,635,000
Per capita: $4,090.47, 19th
Indebtedness:
State govt.: $3,615,805,000
Per capita: $3,603.32, 3rd
State & local govt.: $4,335,000,000
Per capita: $4,320.04, 12th

Laws and Regulations

Legal driving age: 18
Marriage age without parental consent: 18
Divorce residence requirement: 1 yr.

Attractions

Major opera companies (1989): 0, NA
Per 1 million pop.: 0.00, NA
Major symphony orchestras (1989): 4, 42nd
Per 1 million pop.: 4.01, 20th
State appropriations for state arts agencies
Per capita: $1.37, 10th

Sports and Competition

NCAA sports teams, 6: Brown Univ. Bears, Providence College Friars, Rhode Island College Anchorman, Roger Williams College Hawks, Salve Regina College Newporters, Univ. of Rhode Island Rams
Professional teams, 1:
Baseball, 1—Pawtucket Red Sox (International League, Class AAA), McCoy Stadium

SOUTH CAROLINA

"South Carolina in many ways epitomizes the American South. Historically, it was central in the events that preceded the Civil War....Since the Civil War, South Carolina has endured some of the worst effects of the reconstruction era and subsequently negotiated the economic shift from agriculture to industry that has been crucial to the development of other states in the deep South."

Robert O'Brien

Two of the most important battles in the history of the United States were fought in South Carolina. The British were defeated in 1780 in the Battle of King's Mountain, which was the turning point of the Revolutionary War in the South. And in 1861, Confederate batteries bombed Fort Sumter in Charleston Harbor, beginning the Civil War. The Palmetto State is the smallest in the Deep South, and ranges from a lowland in the east, through sand hills, to the mountains in the west. Charleston, its first capital, much older than the nation, boasts a restored residential section which, with its historic homes, ironwork, courtyards, piazza, and gardens, is one of the country's most delightful.

SUPERLATIVES

• First European settlement on the North American coast—San Miguel de Guadalupe, founded in 1526 but lasted only a few months.

• First American Protestant settlement.

• Most Revolutionary battles of any state.

• First state to secede from the Union.

• First shots of the Civil War.

• Leader in vermiculite.

• First U.S. steam railroad.

• Nation's first cotton mill.

• Leader in glass fiber production.

• Nation's oldest theater building—The Street Theater on Charleston's Old Dock.

MOMENTS IN HISTORY

• San Miguel de Guadalupe, the short-lived settlement, founded at present-day Winyah Bay by Spanish Captain Lucas Vasquez de Ayllon in 1526, is said to have been the first European settlement on the coast of North America.

• Near modern Silver Bluff the destructive 1540-1541 expedition of Hernando de Soto entered present-day western South Carolina, leaving a trail of disease and misery upon its departure.

• The Parris Island settlement by Huguenots in 1652, under the leadership of Jean Ribaut, was the first Protestant settlement in America.

• Charles II granted the Carolina region to loyal friends, the Lords Proprietors, and in 1670 Charles Towne was founded. Ten years later it was moved to its present location and eventually was renamed Charleston.

• Plantations flourished after the first importation of slaves in 1670.

• Alarmed by seizure of their lands, in 1715 the Indians attacked and massacred widely in a struggle known as the Yamassee War.

• Urged on by the French, the Cherokee began attacks on western settlements, but were forced to surrender in 1761.

• Although prosperous, South Carolina resisted the despised British taxes and sent delegates to the Continental Congresses of 1774 and 1775.

• South Carolina experienced some of the fiercest fighting and suffering of the Revolutionary War, with 137 battles fought there, 103 of them without help from the other colonies.

• Francis Marion organized a guerilla group in 1780. He became known as the Swamp Fox for his brilliant raids and disappearance into the swamps.

• A quickly assembled frontier force defeated the British at the Battle of King's Mountain on Oct. 7, 1780, in a major turning point of the Revolution because it upset the British timetable.

• Another important American victory occurred on Jan. 17, 1781, at the Battle of the Cowpens.

• In Dec. 1782, British forces withdrew from Charleston.

• On May 23, 1788, South Carolina became the 8th state.

• By 1827 state leaders were threatening to nullify U.S. laws, and it appeared that South Carolina might secede from the union in opposition to high tariffs, but the tariff rates were lowered.

> **So They Say**
>
> "...they can talk and write resolutions and print threats to their heart's content. But if one drop of blood is shed there in defiance of the laws of the United States, I will hang the first man of them I can get my hands on, to the first tree I can find."
>
> Andrew Jackson on nullification

• The country's divisions over slavery deepened, and on Dec. 20, 1860, South Carolina became the first state to secede.

• On April 12, 1861, Fort Sumter in Charleston harbor was attacked. With that attack on the Union stronghold and surrender of the fort the Civil War had begun.

• The state suffered greatly during the war, and further suffering continued during Reconstruction until about 1876.

> **So They Say**
>
> "Thus began the darkest period in the State's history...from 1868 to 1874...the 'Rule of the Robbers,'...Votes in the legislature were bought. Furniture, jewelry, clothing, and groceries were purchased with public funds, while patients in the state hospital actually suffered for food, and threats were made to turn convicts out of the penitentiary because they could not be fed."
>
> South Carolina, A Guide to the Palmetto State

• The state constitution of 1895 deprived most of the state's blacks of the right to vote.

• World War I called 62,000 people to service from South Carolina, and 2,085 lost their lives.

• Ervin David Shaw of Sumter was one of the first American pilots killed in action in World War II, when 173,642 served from South Carolina.

• During the period 1940 to 1960 the port of Charleston jumped from 57th place to 14th among the nation's ports.

• In 1975 Dr. James B. Edwards became the first Republican governor since Reconstruction days.

• The census of 1990 showed an almost 11% gain in the state's population.

That's Interesting

• When the chief of an early Indian group died, his horse was buried alive with him. There were so many such burials that Indian Hill is known as a mountain.

• A group of Seewee Indians decided to take their grievances directly to the King of England. A pirate crew spotted their canoes far out to sea, and they were never heard from again.

• Corporal Jesse Gillespie was wounded, then healed in a French hospital during World War I. Meanwhile the U.S. Army had issued a death certificate. When he returned home he was made to sign an affidavit that he was not dead.

• On the way to a Lancaster cemetery, the body of Andrew Jackson's father was taken from bar to bar on a sled, until some mourner found that the body had disappeared. It turned up in a snowbank and finally reached the burial place.

• Theodosia Burr Alston, Aaron Burr's daughter, was the wife of South Carolina governor Joseph Alston. In 1812 she sailed from Charleston to New York and was never heard from again. Later a pirate confessed that she had been made to walk the plank, but this was never verified.

• The state's first steam locomotive produced such a hiss of steam that the fireman sat on the safety valve to reduce the noise, resulting in the explosion of the locomotive and death of the fireman.

• Onlookers at Beaufort Bay thought that a man named Jones had finally reached his long-sought goal of perpetual motion, as his boat dashed about the bay. However, he had hooked a sting ray, was being pulled by it and could not cut the line.

Notable Natives

James Francis Byrnes (Charleston, 1879-1972), U.S. Supreme Court justice. **John Caldwell Calhoun** (Abbeville Cty., 1782-1850), public official/political leader. **Andrew Jackson** (Waxhaw—probably in SC, 1767-1845), U.S. president. **Henry Laurens** (Charleston, 1724-1792), political leader. **Francis "Swamp Fox" Marion** (Berkeley Cty., 1732?-1795), Revolutionary soldier. **Joel Roberts Poinsett** (Charleston, 1779-1851), diplomat.

General

Admitted to statehood: May 23, 1788
Origin of name: In 1619 Charles I gave a large patent to Sir Robert Heath to be called Province of Carolana, from Carolus, Latin name for Charles; a new patent was granted by Charles II to the Earl of Clarendon and others—divided into North and South Carolina, 1710
Capital: Columbia
Nickname: The Palmetto State
Mottos: *"Animis Opibusque Parati"* ("Prepared in Mind and Resources") and *"Dum Spiro Spero"* ("While I Breathe, I Hope")
Animal: white-tail deer
Beverage: milk
Bird: Carolina wren
Wild game bird: wild turkey
Dance: the shag
Fish: striped bass
Flower: Carolina (yellow) jessamine
Fruit: peach
Gemstone: amethyst
Shell: lettered olive
Songs: "Carolina" and "South Carolina on My Mind"
Stone: blue granite
Tree: palmetto

The Land

Area: 32,007 sq. mi., 40th
Land: 30,111 sq. mi., 40th
Water: 1,896 sq. mi., 21st
Topography: Blue Ridge province in NW has highest peaks; Piedmont lies between the mountains and the fall line; coastal plain covers two-thirds of the state.
Number of counties: 46
Geographic center: Richland, 13 mi. SE of Columbia
Length: 260 mi.
Width: 200 mi.
Highest point: 3,560 ft. (Sassafras Mountain), 29th
Lowest point: sea level (Atlantic Ocean), 3rd
Mean elevation: 350 ft., 44th
Coastline: 187 mi., 11th
Shoreline: 2,876 mi., 11th

Climate and Environment

Temp., highest: 111 deg. on June 28, 1954, at Camden; lowest: -19 deg. on Jan. 21, 1985, at Caesar's Head
Fresh water withdrawn, per capita, per day: 2,040 gal., 15th
Endangered species: mammals, 2—Indiana bat, West Indian manatee; birds, 3—American peregrine falcon, wood stock, red-cockaded woodpecker; reptiles, 3; am-

phibians, none; fishes, none; invertebrates, none; plants, 11

Major Cities, Population Percentage Increase (1980-90)

Charleston, 80,414—15.24%
Columbia, 98,052— -3.14%
Greenville, 58,282—0.07%
North Charleston, 70,218—12.39%
Spartanburg, 43,467— -0.82%

The People

Population: 3,486,703, 25th
Percent change (1980-90): 10.50%, 18th
Per sq. mi: 108.94, 20th
Percent in metro. area: 60.60%, 32nd
Percent foreign born: 1.4%, 44th
White: 2,406,974—69.03%, 46th
Black: 1,039,884—29.82%, 4th
Native American: 8,246—0.24%, 39th
Asian, Pacific Isle: 22,382—0.64%, 40th
Other races: 9,217—0.26%, 43rd
Hispanic origin: 30,551—0.88%, 41st
Percent over 5 yrs. speaking language other than English at home: 3.5%, 45th
Percent males: 48.43%, 36th
Percent females: 51.57%, 16th
Percent never married: 26.4%, 21st
Marriages per 1,000 (1989): 15.5, 3rd
Divorces per 1,000 (1989): 4.2, 33rd
Median age: 32
Under 5 years: 256,337—7.35%, 27th
Under 18 years: 920,207—26.39%, 19th
65 years & older: 396,935—11.38%, 37th
Percent increase among the elderly: 38.1%, 7th

Of Vital Importance

Live births per 1,000 pop.: 15.9, 24th
Infant mortality rate per 1,000 births (1988): 12.3, 4th
Average lifetime (1979-81): 71.58, 50th
Deaths per 100,000 pop. (1988): 848.1, 32nd
Causes of death per 100,000 pop. (1988):
Diseases of heart: 293.9, 31st
Malignant neoplasms: 177.1, 41st
Cerebrovascular diseases: 74.7, 5th
Accidents & adverse effects: 55.9, 3rd
Chronic obstructive pulmonary diseases: 27.4, 44th
Suicide: 9.9, 46th
HIV infection: 3.3, 25th
Other: 62.0, 48th

Keeping Well

Non-federal physicians per 100,000 pop.: 175, 40th
Dentists per 100,000 (1990-91): 46, 49th
Nurses per 100,000 (1989): 454, 50th
Hospitals per 100,000: 2.6, 33rd
Admissions per 100,000: 13,202, 29th
Beds per 100,000: 417.30, 40th
Occupancy rate: 71.7%, 13th
Semiprivate room charges per day: $212, 43rd
Average stay: 6.7, 40th
Notifiable diseases per 100,000:
AIDS: 9.8, 23rd
Gonorrhea: 402.2, 9th
Measles: 0.1, 49th
Syphillis: 62.5, 11th
Tuberculosis (TB): 13.0, 9th
Per capita spending on mental health programs (1987): $44.42, 17th
Pop. without health insur. (1991): 13.1%, 22nd

Households by Type

Total households: 1,258,044
Percent change (1980-90): 22.14%, 11th
Family households: 928,206
Percent of total: 73.78%, 4th
Nonfamily households: 329,838
Percent of total: 26.22%, 48th
Persons per household: 2.68, 11th
Pop. living in group quarters: 116,543
Percent of pop.: 3.34%, 12th

Living Quarters

Total housing units: 1,424,155
Persons per unit: 2.45, 15th
Occupied housing units: 1,258,044
Percent of total units: 88.34%, 33rd
Persons per unit: 2.50, 34th
Percent of units with over 1 person per room: 4.06%, 15th
Owner-occupied units: 878,704
Percent of total units: 61.70%, 13th

Percent of occupied units: 69.85%, 12th
Persons per unit: 2.75, 21st
Median value: $61,1000, 31st
Renter-occupied units: 379,340
Percent of total units: 26.64%, 41st
Percent of occupied units: 30.15%, 40th
Persons per unit: 2.25, 39th
Median contract rent: $276, 37th
Rental vacancy rate: 11.5%, 9th
Mobile home, trailer & other as a % of occupied housing units: 20.14%, 3rd

Crime Index per 100,000

Total: 6,045, 14th
Violent: 977, 5th
Murder and nonnegligent manslaughter: 11, 10th
Aggravated assault: 7,352, 28th
Robbery: 152, 21st
Rape: 54, 6th
Property: 5,069, 17th
Burglary: 1,380, 10th
Larceny, theft: 3,302, 16th
Motor vehicle theft: 386, 29th
Drug abuse arrests: 430, 9th

Teaching and Learning

Literacy (1987): 85%, 40th
Pop. 3 and over enrolled in school: 913,010
Percent of pop.: 27.4%, 23rd
Public elementary & secondary schools:
Total enrollment: 627,000
Avg. class size (1987): 23, 20th
Teachers: 35,600
Percent of pop.: 1.02%, 24th
Teachers' avg. salary: $27,200, 33rd
Spending per capita: $678, 40th
Spending per pupil in avg. daily attendance: $3,731, 41st
Percent of graduates taking SAT: 58%, 15th
Combined SAT scores: 832, 51st
Percent of pop. over 25 completing:
High school: 68.3%, 45th
College degree/s: 16.6%, 42nd
Higher educa., institutions: 64
Per 100,000 pop.: 0.9, 14th
Enroll: 159,302
Percent of pop.: 4.57%, 45th
Public: 131,134
Percent of enroll.: 82.32%, 26th
Private: 28,168
Percent of enroll.: 17.68%, 26th
White non-Hispanic: 52,573
Percent of enroll.: 61.42%, 49th
Black non-Hispanic: 2,176
Percent of enroll.: 2.54%, 38th
Hispanic: 23,635
Percent of enroll.: 27.61%, 1st
Asian/Pacific Islander: 1,125
Percent of enroll.: 1.31%, 37th
Amer. Indian/AK native: 4,596
Percent of enroll.: 5.37%, 5th
Nonresident alien: 1,491
Percent of enroll.: 1.74%, 41st
Female: 90,019
Percent of enroll.: 56.51%, 8th
Tuition, state university ('90-'91): $2,317, 11th
Public library systems: 40
Books & serial vol. per capita: 1.49, 51st
Govt. expend. per capita: $10.14, 39th
State govt.: $2.30, 29th
Local govts.: $7.83, 38th

Law Enforcement, Courts, and Prisons

Police protection expend.: $289,434,000
Per capita: $83.00, 40th
Judicial & legal expend.: $96,045,000
Per capita: $27.54, 49th
Corrections expend.: $300,386,000
Per capita: $86.14, 19th
Police per 10,000 pop. (1990-91): 20.7, 25th
Prisoners (state & fed.) sentenced to over 1 yr., per 100,000 pop.: 451
Percent change (1989-90): 9.45%, 12th
Death penalty: yes, by electrocution
Under sentence of death: 46, 15th
Executed (1989): none

Religion, Number and Percent of Population

Agnostic: 5,133—0.20%, 42nd
Buddhist: 2,567—0.10%, 17th
Christian: 2,386,841—93.00%, 6th
Hindu: NA
Jewish: 7,700—0.30%, 35th

Moslem: 5,133—0.20%, 13th
Unitarian: NA
Other: 30,798—1.20%, 29th
None: 82,128—3.20%, 45th
Refused to answer: 46,197—1.80%, 34th

MAKING A LIVING

Personal income per capita (1989): $11,897, 38th
Percent increase (1979-89) (constant 1989 dollars): 20.6%, 17th
Average income per family: $36,562, 38th
Percent of pop. below poverty level: 15.4%, 15th
Percent 65 and over: 20.5%, 7th
Cost of living, selected cities
1st qtr., 1991 (U. S. Standard=100)

Lancaster	88.1
Greenville	95.1
Florence	99.7

ECONOMY

Civilian labor force : 1,724,000
Percent of tot. pop.: 49.45%, 32nd
Percent 65 and over: 2.55%, 32nd
Percent females: 47.39%, 6th
Percent job growth (1980-90): 27.41%, 16th
Major employer industries:
Agriculture: 32,860—2.00%, 35th
Construction: 98,580—6.00%, 7th
Finance, insurance & real estate: 87,079—5.30%, 27th
Government: 243,164—14.80%, 30th
Manufacturing: 430,466—26.20%, 2nd
Mining: 2,353—0.1%, 48th
Service: 251,379—15.30%, 50th
Trade: 292,454—17.80%, 40th
Transportation, communication, & public utilities: 69,006—4.20%, 44th
Wholesale/retail: 324,374—20.2%, 42nd
Unemployment rate: 4.70%, 40th
Male: 2.55%, 39th
Female: 2.15%, 36th
Total businesses (1991): 103,796
New business incorp's. (1991): 5,700
Percent of total businesses: 5.49%, 31st
Business failures (1991): 598
Percent of total businesses: 0.58%, 46th
Agriculture farm income
Marketing (1991): $1,225,396,000, 36th
Net per operation: $15,767, 32nd
Net per acre: $74, 19th
Leading products: tobacco, cattle, broilers, greenhouse
Av. value land & build. per acre: $949, 24th
Percent increase (1980-90): 5.44%, 24th
Govt. payments: $49,364,000, 30th
Construction, value of all: $2,503,000,000
Per capita: $717.87, 17th
Percent change 1989-90: -3.77%, 20th
Manufactures:
Value added: $21,075,000,000
Per capita: $6,044.39, 12th
Value of shipments: $46,734,000,000
Per capita: $13,403.49, 14th
Leading products: textiles, chemicals and allied products, machinery & fabricated metal products, apparel and related products
Mining, min. prod., value (1987): $179,000,000, 40th
Leading products: cement, stone, clays
Retail sales: $23,754,000,000, 27th
Per household: $18,685, 29th
Percent increase (1987-90): 17.2%, 22nd
Service indust., value (1987): $9,363,000,000, 31st
Per capita: $2,685.34, 49th
Tourism indus., value (1989): $3,937,000,000, 23rd
Foreign exports value: $3,116,000,000, 24th
Per capita: $893.68, 24th
Patents per 1,000 pop.: 8.6, 18th

TRAVEL AND TRANSPORTATION

Motor vehicle registrations: 2,519,737
Per 1,000 pop.: 722, 39th
Motorcycle registrations: 31,087
Per 1,000 pop.: 8, 48th
Licensed drivers per 1,000 driving age pop.: 896, 26th
Deaths from motor vehicle accidents per 100,000 pop.: 28.1, 4th
Public roads & streets
Total mileage: 64,046, 31st
Rural mileage: 54,703, 31st
Urban mileage: 9,343, 27th
Interstate mileage: 791, 27th
Annual vehicle-miles of travel per person: 9,859, 10th
Mean travel time for workers 16 + who work away from home: 20.5 min., 28th

Government

Registered voters (1988): 1,447,151
Percent of voting age pop.: 57.11%, 47th
Voter turnout (1988): 986,009
Percent of registered voters: 68.13%, 34th
Percent of voting age pop.: 38.91%, 50th
State legislators, total (1992): 170, 15th
Women members (1992): 22
Percent of legislature: 12.9%, 36th
Dominant party (1992): Democrats
U. S. Congress, House members (1993): 6
Increase 1983-93: 0
Revenues:
State govt.: $8,750,261,000
Per capita: $2,509.61, 23rd
State & local govt.: $12,559,271,000
Per capita: $3,602.05, 37th
Indebtedness:
State govt.: $3,894,367,000
Per capita: $1,116.92, 27th
State & local govt.: $9,723,000,000
Per capita: $2,788.59, 36th

Laws and Regulations

Legal driving age: 16
Marriage age without parental consent: 18
Divorce residence requirement: 1 yr., qualification—check local statutes

Attractions

Major opera companies (1989): 2, 21st
Per 1 million pop.: 0.57, 32nd
Major symphony orchestras (1989): 10, 27th
Per 1 million pop.: 2.85, 36th
State appropriations for state arts agencies per capita: $0.99, 16th
State Fair in mid Oct. at Columbia

Sports and Competition

NCAA sports teams, 9: Baptist College Buccaneers, Clemson Univ. Tigers, College of Charleston Cougars, Furman Univ. Paladins, South Carolina State College Bulldogs, The Citadel Bulldogs, Univ. of South Carolina Fighting Gamecocks, Univ. of South Carolina Rifles, Winthrop College Eagles
Professional teams, 7:
Baseball, 7—Columbia Mets (South Atlantic League, Class A), Capital City Stadium; Myrtle Beach Hurricanes (South Atlantic League, Class A), Coastal Carolina Stadium; Charleston Rainbows (South Atlantic League, Class A), College Park Stadium; Spartanburg Phillies (South Atlantic League, Class A), Duncan Park Stadium; Greenville Braves (Southern League, Class AA), Greenville Municipal Stadium; Charlotte Knights (Southern League, Class AA), Knights Castle Stadium; Sumter Flyers (South Atlantic League, Class A), Riley Park

South Dakota

"Hard work is a legacy of the generations who settled the prairie, broke the soil, built the sod houses, fought the draughts and grasshoppers and penny-a-pound price for their products. It is a legacy that even those of us who leave carry with us. All of this work has produced what may be the largest collection of powerful hands in the world."

Tom Brokaw

Visitors flock to South Dakota to see the world-famed "rock stars," the presidential faces of the Mt. Rushmore Memorial. Dakota is a land where "the great lakes" were created on barren prairie and where the Homestead Mine has produced more gold than any other, worldwide. The history of South Dakota reads like an adventure story, filled with daring fur trappers, battles between settlers and Indians, and such colorful characters as Calamity Jane, General George A. Custer, Sitting Bull, and Wild Bill Hickock.

Superlatives

• Highest point east of the Rockies—Harney Peak.

• Longest non-navigable river—James River.

• Probable origin of the ancient camel.

• World's largest portrait busts—Mt. Rushmore.

• World record total production of a single gold mine—Homestake Mine.

• Leader in bentonite production.

Moments in History

• On their expedition of 1743, brothers François and Louis-Joseph La Verendrye are the first Europeans known to have visited present-day South Dakota. On a hill overlooking the Missouri River they buried a lead plate claiming the region for France.

> So They Say
>
> "Placed by the Chevalier de La Verendrye, Lo Jost Verendrye, Louis La Londette A Miotte, the 30th March 1743."
>
> Legend on the lead plate rediscovered Feb. 16, 1913

• In 1794 Jean Baptiste Trudeau established a trading company in present-day Charles Mix County.

• On Aug. 22, 1804, the great Lewis and Clark expedition camped at present-day Elk Point; the election they held for sergeant was the first in the entire Northwest.

> So They Say
>
> "This scenery already rich, pleasing and beautiful was still farther heightened by immense herds of buffalo, deer, elk and antelopes...I do not think I exaggerate when I estimate the number of buffalo, which could be comprehended at one view to amount to 3,000."
>
> Meriwether Lewis

• Fort Pierre Chouteau (Pierre) was founded in 1831, the oldest permanently occupied European settlement in the state.

• The first "Puffing Canoe" (steamboat), the *Yellowstone,* reached Fort Pierre in 1831.

• When Father Peter John DeSmet visited the Black Hills in 1848 an Indian chief offered him a bag of glittering powder, which he recognized as gold but did not disclose to anyone, fearing for the Indian rights in the area.

So They Say

"Put it away and show it to nobody."

Father Peter DeSmet, on being offered a bag of gold dust

• Dakota Territory was created on March 2, 1861.

• During the Civil War the Santee Sioux began an uprising called the War of the Outbreak, settled in 1865 at a great council with the Indians near present-day Pierre.

• Fort Sisseton was established in 1864 at the unheard-of cost of $2 million

• The great military expedition of George Armstrong Custer entered the Black Hills in 1874, and gold was discovered by the party. A Chicago newspaper carried the news, and the rush for gold was on.

• By midsummer 1876, Dead Tree Gulch (later Deadwood) harbored 25,000 gold seekers, squatters on Indian lands. Deadwood became a rip-roaring prospecting town.

• On Aug. 2, 1876, Wild Bill Hickock was killed at Deadwood.

• The winter of 1880-1881 was the worst in history, followed by great floods, sweeping away villages.

• On Nov. 2, 1889, South Dakota became a state along with North Dakota. President Benjamin Harrison never revealed which was the 39th and which the 40th state.

• Famed Chief Sitting Bull was killed by police action in 1890 at present-day Little Eagle.

• On Dec. 28, 1890, the infamous "battle" at Wounded Knee resulted in the deaths of more than 200 Sioux men, women, and children, slain by government forces after an Indian shot an officer. This proved to be the country's last large-scale action between troops and Indians.

• After a contest between Mitchell and Pierre, the latter was chosen state capital by a vote in 1904.

• World War I called 32,719 people from South Dakota into service. It was noted that men from the state had the best health record of all who served.

• The visit of President Calvin Coolidge to the Black Hills captured world attention. On Aug. 10, 1927, President Coolidge dedicated the unfinished Rushmore Memorial. His speech there was said by some to have been the finest of a career not noted for public eloquence.

So They Say

"This memorial will crown the height of land between the Rocky Mountains and the Atlantic seaboard, where coming generations may view it for all time....On this towering wall...is to be inscribed a memorial which will represent some of the outstanding events of American history..."

Calvin Coolidge, dedicating the Rushmore Memorial

• The Great Depression was made worse by a terrible drought from 1933 through 1936. The Sioux planned to revive their rain dance, but no one remembered it.

• With the increase in gold prices in 1933, gold mining returned to the Black Hills.

• The disastrous flood of 1973 at Rapid City killed nearly 250 persons.

• A 1980 Supreme Court ruling ordered the United States to pay the Sioux Indians of South Dakota $122 million for the 1877 seizure of their lands.

• In 1981 Citicorp moved its credit card operation to Sioux Falls, and others followed, bringing many new jobs.

That's Interesting

• In the floods of 1881, a church at Green Islands was swept away intact. The story was told that it was seen floating down the river with its bell tolling.

• During the skirmish at the murder of Sitting Bull, his horse performed many of the tricks his owner had taught him as they traveled with Buffalo Bill's Wild West Show.

• On his visit to the Black Hills, President Calvin Coolidge gained a reputation as a golfer. He did not know that the greens had been altered to slope toward the holes.

• The Nystrom Bank at Wall did not close during F.D. Roosevelt's bank holiday—the only one in the country not to. No one had thought to notify the owner.

Notable Natives

Crazy Horse (Oglala Sioux tribe, 1849?-1877), Indian leader. **Ernest Orlando Lawrence** (Canton, 1901-1958), physicist. **George Stanley McGovern** (Avon, 1922-), public official. **Sitting Bull** (Hunkpapa Sioux tribe site on Grand River, 1831?-1890, Indian leader.

General

Admitted to statehood: Nov. 2, 1889
Origin of name: From the Sioux language for "Friend or Ally"
Capital: Pierre, settled 1880
Nickname: Coyote State
Motto: "Under God the People Rule"
Animal: coyote
Bird: Chinese ringnecked pheasant
Colors: blue and gold
Fish: walleye
Flower: Pasque flower
Gemstone: Fairburn agate
Grass: Western wheat grass
Greeting: "How Kola!" (Sioux greeting meaning "Hello, friend")
Insect: honeybee
Mineral stone: rose quartz
Song: "Hail, South Dakota"
Stone: Black Hills gold
Tree: Black Hills spruce

The Land

Area: 77,121 sq. mi., 17th
Land: 75,898 sq. mi., 16th
Water: 1,224 sq. mi., 29th
Topography: prairie plains in the E, rolling hills of the Great Plains in the W, the Black Hills, rising 3,500 ft. in the SW corner
Number of counties: 67
Geographic center: Hughes, 8 mi. NE of Pierre
Length: 380 mi.
Width: 210 mi.
Highest point: 7,242 ft. (Harney Peak), 15th
Lowest point: 966 ft. (Big Stone Lake), 46th
Mean elevation: 2,200 ft., 13th

Climate and Environment

Temp., highest: 120 deg. on July 5, 1936, at Gannvalley; lowest: -58 deg. on Feb. 17, 1936, at Mcintosh
Fresh water withdrawn, per capita, per day: 956 gal., 34th
Endangered species: mammals, 1—black-footed ferret; birds, 4—whooping crane, Eskimo curlew, American peregrine falcon, least tern; reptiles, none; amphibians, none; fishes, 1; invertebrates, none; plants, none

Major Cities, Population Percentage Increase (1980-90)

Aberdeen, 24,927— –3.57%
Brookings, 16,270—8.82%
Rapid City, 54,523—17.27%
Sioux Falls, 100,814—23.94%
Watertown, 17,592—12.42%

The People

Population: 696,004, 45th
Percent change (1980-90): 0.75%, 39th
Per sq. mi: 9.02, 48th
Percent in metro. area: 29.45%, 48th
Percent foreign born: 1.1%, 46th
White: 637,515—91.60%, 16th
Black: 3,258—0.47%, 47th
Native American: 50,575—7.27%, 4th
Asian, Pacific Isle: 3,123—0.45%, 50th
Other races: 1,533—0.22%, 44th
Hispanic origin: 5,252—0.75%, 43rd
Percent over 5 yrs. speaking language other than English at home: 6.5%, 29th
Percent males: 49.21%, 14th
Percent females: 50.79%, 38th
Percent never married: 24.4%, 33rd
Marriages per 1,000 (1989): 9.9, 20th

Divorces per 1,000 (1989): 3.7, 38th
Median age: 32.5
Under 5 years: 54,504—7.83%, 9th
Under 18 years: 198,462—28.51%, 8th
65 years & older: 102,331—14.70%, 7th
Percent increase among the elderly: 12.4%, 43rd

Of Vital Importance

Live births per 1,000 pop.: 15.2, 36th
Infant mortality rate per 1,000 births (1988): 10.1, 21st
Average lifetime (1979-81): 74.97, 15th
Deaths per 100,000 pop. (1988): 922.7, 19th
Causes of death per 100,000 pop. (1988):
  Diseases of heart: 364, 6th
  Malignant neoplasms: 189.9, 35th
  Cerebrovascular diseases: 73.2, 7th
  Accidents & adverse effects: 40.4, 25th
  Chronic obstructive pulmonary diseases: 33.7, 28th
  Suicide: 11.5, 33rd
  HIV infection: 0.7, 48th
  Other: 78.0, 21st

Keeping Well

Non-federal physicians per 100,000 pop.: 157, 48th
Dentists per 100,000 (1990-91): 52, 41st
Nurses per 100,000 (1989): 824, 11th
Hospitals per 100,000: 9.5, 1st
  Admissions per 100,000: 16,422, 7th
  Beds per 100,000: 779.88, 3rd
  Occupancy rate: 63.6%, 35th
  Semiprivate room charges per day: $209, 45th
  Average stay: 12.4, 5th
Notifiable diseases per 100,000:
  AIDS: 1.3, 49th
  Gonorrhea: 44.4, 42nd
  Measles: 3.3, 29th
  Syphillis: 1.0, 49th
  Tuberculosis (TB): 2.0, 46th
Per capita spending on mental health programs (1987): $30.67, 35th
Pop. without health insur. (1991): 9.9%, 42nd

Households by Type

Total households: 259,034
  Percent change (1980-90): 6.60%, 41st
Family households: 180,306
  Percent of total: 69.61%, 33rd
Nonfamily households: 78,728
  Percent of total: 30.39%, 19th
Persons per household: 2.59, 26th
Pop. living in group quarters: 25,841
  Percent of pop.: 3.71%, 6th

Living Quarters

Total housing units: 292,436
  Persons per unit: 2.38, 30th
Occupied housing units: 259,034
  Percent of total units: 88.58%, 32nd
  Persons per unit: 2.53, 24th
  Percent of units with over 1 person per room: 2.96%, 26th
Owner-occupied units: 171,161
  Percent of total units: 58.53%, 27th
  Percent of occupied units: 66.08%, 32nd
  Persons per unit: 2.71, 29th
  Median value: $45,200, 50th
Renter-occupied units: 87,873
  Percent of total units: 30.05%, 21st
  Percent of occupied units: 33.92%, 21st
  Persons per unit: 2.34, 27th
  Median contract rent: $242, 46th
  Rental vacancy rate: 7.3%, 38th
Mobile home, trailer & other as a % of occupied housing units: 13.21%, 20th

Crime Index per 100,000

Total: 2,909, 50th
  Violent: 163, 46th
    Murder and nonnegligent manslaughter: 2, 48th
    Aggravated assault: 7,831, 10th
    Robbery: 12, 49th
    Rape: 34, 28th
  Property: 2,747, 50th
    Burglary: 527, 50th
    Larceny, theft: 2,109, 47th
    Motor vehicle theft: 110, 51st
  Drug abuse arrests: 61, 51st

Teaching and Learning

Literacy (1987): 89%, 17th
Pop. 3 and over enrolled in school: 185,246
  Percent of pop.: 27.9%, 18th

Public elementary & secondary schools:
Total enrollment: 131,000
Avg. class size (1987): 19, 48th
Teachers: 8,200
Percent of pop.: 1.18%, 8th
Teachers' avg. salary: $21,300, 51st
Spending per capita: $618, 50th
Spending per pupil in avg. daily attendance: $3,312, 47th
Percent of graduates taking SAT: 5%, 48th
Combined SAT scores: 1047, 3rd
Percent of pop. over 25 completing:
High school: 77.1%, 24th
College degree/s: 17.2%, 39th
Higher educa., institutions: 19
Per 100,000 pop.: 1.1, 7th
Enroll: 34,208
Percent of pop.: 4.91%, 38th
Public: 26,596
Percent of enroll.: 77.75%, 36th
Private: 7,612
Percent of enroll.: 22.25%, 16th
White non-Hispanic: 280,786
Percent of enroll.: 79.44%, 34th
Black non-Hispanic: 49,566
Percent of enroll.: 14.02%, 9th
Hispanic: 4,803
Percent of enroll.: 1.36%, 30th
Asian/Pacific Islander: 11,400
Percent of enroll.: 3.23%, 12th
Amer. Indian/AK native: 860
Percent of enroll.: 0.24%, 43rd
Nonresident alien: 6,027
Percent of enroll.: 1.71%, 42nd
Female: 19,161
Percent of enroll.: 56.01%, 13th
Tuition, state university ('90-'91): $1,854, 24th
Public library systems: 117
Books & serial vol. per capita: 4.13, 5th
Govt. expend. per capita: $14.81, 26th
State govt.: $4.26, 11th
Local govts.: $10.56, 31st

Law Enforcement, Courts, and Prisons

Police protection expend.: $52,195,000
Per capita: $74.99, 46th
Judicial & legal expend.: $21,761,000
Per capita: $31.27, 45th
Corrections expend.: $30,526,000
Per capita: $43.86, 46th
Police per 10,000 pop. (1990-91): 14.4, 51st
Prisoners (state & fed.) sentenced to over 1 yr., per 100,000 pop.: 187
Percent change (1989-90): 7.43%, 26th
Death penalty: yes, by lethal injection
Under sentence of death: 0, NA
Executed (1989): none

Religion, Number and Percent of Population

Agnostic: 4,975—1.00%, 10th
Buddhist: NA
Christian: 467,690—94.00%, 4th
Hindu: NA
Jewish: 995—0.20%, 40th
Moslem: 1,491—0.30%, 9th
Unitarian: 1,493—0.30%, 15th
Other: 3,483—0.70%, 43rd
None: 12,439—2.50%, 48th
Refused to answer: 4,975—1.00%, 47th

Making a Living

Personal income per capita (1989): $10,661, 47th
Percent increase (1979-'89) (constant 1989 dollars): 11.7%, 27th
Average income per family: $32,818, 48th
Percent of pop. below poverty level: 15.9%, 12th
Percent 65 and over: 15.5%, 15th
Cost of living, selected cities
1st qtr., 1991 (U. S. Standard=100)
Sioux Falls 90.5
Rapid City 96.3

Economy

Civilian labor force : 360,000
Percent of tot. pop.: 51.72%, 18th
Percent 65 and over: 5.28%, 1st
Percent females: 45.83%, 24th
Percent job growth (1980-90): 15.30%, 36th
Major employer industries:
Agriculture: 48,580—14.00%, 1st
Construction: 10,410—3.00%, 51st
Finance, insurance & real estate: 15,962—4.60%, 37th

Government: 57,602—16.60%, 20th
Manufacturing: 32,618—9.40%, 43rd
Mining: 2,821—0.9%, 17th
Service: 65,930—19.00%, 32nd
Trade: 64,195—18.50%, 27th
Transportation, communication, & public utilities: 13,533—3.90%, 49th
Wholesale/retail: 69,846—21.7%, 21st
Unemployment rate: 3.61%, 49th
Male: 1.94%, 49th
Female: 1.67%, 48th
Total businesses (1991): 39,038
New business incorp's. (1991): 1,040
Percent of total businesses: 2.66%, 50th
Business failures (1991): 313
Percent of total businesses: 0.80%, 30th
Agriculture farm income
Marketing (1991): $3,264,286,000, 20th
Net per operation: $34,937, 9th
Net per acre: $28, 37th
Leading products: cattle, hogs, corn, soybeans
Av. value land & build. per acre: $337, 43rd
Percent increase (1980-90): 15.41%, 16th
Govt. payments: $286,237,000, 11th
Construction, value of all: $363,000,000
Per capita: $521.55, 27th
Percent change 1989-90: 25.17%, 5th
Manufactures:
Value added: $1,630,000,000
Per capita: $2,341.94, 44th
Value of shipments: $4,533,000,000
Per capita: $6,512.89, 41st
Leading products (1986): food & kindred products, machinery, electric and electronic equipment
Mining, min. prod., value (1987): $263,000,000, 36th
Leading products: gold, cement, petroleum
Retail sales: $4,649,000,000, 47th
Per household: $17,921, 35th
Percent increase (1987-90): 25.6%, 3rd
Service indust., value (1987): $1,934,000,000, 50th
Per capita: $2,778.72, 46th
Tourism indus., value (1989): $679,000,000, 50th
Foreign exports value: $205,000,000, 50th
Per capita: $294.54, 48th
Patents per 1,000 pop.: 17.0, 2nd

TRAVEL AND TRANSPORTATION

Motor vehicle registrations: 703,786
Per 1,000 pop.: 1,011, 3rd
Motorcycle registrations: 29,959
Per 1,000 pop.: 43, 3rd
Licensed drivers per 1,000 driving age pop.: 938, 11th
Deaths from motor vehicle accidents per 100,000 pop.: 22.0, 17th
Public roads & streets
Total mileage: 74,696, 26th
Rural mileage: 72,962, 21st
Urban mileage: 1,734, 46th
Interstate mileage: 678, 33rd
Annual vehicle-miles of travel per person: 10,041, 8th
Mean travel time for workers 16 + who work away from home: 13.8 min., 50th

GOVERNMENT

Registered voters (1988): 440,301
Percent of voting age pop.: 86.50%, 5th
Voter turnout (1988): 312,991
Percent of registered voters: 71.09%, 28th
Percent of voting age pop.: 61.49%, 6th
State legislators, total (1992): 105, 40th
Women members (1992): 26
Percent of legislature: 24.8%, 10th
Dominant party (1992): Republicans
U. S. Congress, House members (1993): 1
Increase 1983-93: 0
Revenues:
State govt.: $1,493,854,000
Per capita: $2,146.33, 38th
State & local govt.: $2,337,985,000
Per capita: $3,359.15, 42nd
Indebtedness:
State govt.: $1,787,363,000
Per capita: $2,568.04, 10th
State & local govt.: $2,274,000,000
Per capita: $3,267.22, 28th

Laws and Regulations

Legal driving age: 16
Marriage age without parental consent: 18
Divorce residence requirement: none, qualification—check local statutes

Attractions

Major opera companies (1989): 0, NA
Per 1 million pop.: 0.00, NA
Major symphony orchestras (1989): 2, 48th
Per 1 million pop.: 2.80, 37th
State appropriations for state arts agencies
Per capita: $0.50, 36th
State Fair in late Aug.-early Sept. at Huron

Sports and Competition

NCAA sports teams, 2: South Dakota State Univ. Jackrabbits, Univ. of South Dakota Coyotes
Professional teams, 2:
Basketball, 2—Rapid City Thrillers (Continental Basketball Association), Rushmore Plaza Civic Center; Sioux Falls Skyforce (Continental Basketball Association), Sioux Falls Arena

TENNESSEE

"With his good tempered easiness of manners, the Tennessean has democratic feeling of equality....Whether of farm, mountain or city, he is like the Tennessee farmer, who, after hearing Martin Van Buren speak, stepped up, took the President's hand and invited him 'to come out and r'ar around with the boys.'"

Federal Writers Project, Tennessee

Tennessee's borders touch eight other states, a record tied only with Missouri. Renowned for its scenery and natural wonders, Tennessee also has distinction in many other fields. In music it is known as the "birthplace of the blues," the home of Elvis Presley. Nashville, with its *Grand Ole Opry* and its many recording studios, is the country music capital of the United States. The land in Tennessee slopes from its impressive mountains in the east to its lowlands along the Mississippi River in the west. The state has a long military tradition, and its history includes John Sevier in the Revolutionary War, Andrew Jackson in the War of 1812, and Alvin C. York in World War I. More Civil War battles were fought in Tennessee than in any other state except Virginia.

SUPERLATIVES

- Claims the greatest variety of birds in the United States.
- First in U.S. aluminum production.
- Leader in diverse hardwood products.
- Nation's largest, oldest, and most visited national military park—Chickamauga-Chattanooga.
- Called "Birthplace of the Blues"—Memphis.
- Country music capital—Nashville.

MOMENTS IN HISTORY

- In April, 1541, the great party of Spanish explorer Hernando De Soto reached the area of present-day Memphis, and perhaps other Tennessee points.
- In 1763 Marquette and Jolliet were greeted by Indians of the Memphis area, and in the same year James Needham and Gabriel Arthur explored East Tennessee.
- Robert Cavelier, Sieur de La Salle, built primitive Fort Prudhomme in 1682.
- Spain, England and France claimed the region, but British interests seemed to prevail, and in 1757 Fort Loudoun, near present-day Knoxville, was completed.
- In 1763 the French gave up all claims to the region.
- Defying a British ban on settlement, settlers arrived. Washington County was proclaimed, and Jonesboro was laid out in 1779 as its county seat, the oldest permanent European settlement in present-day Tennessee.
- No formal battles of the Revolution occurred in present-day Tennessee, but mountain men from the eastern section took an important part in the 1780 Battle of King's Mountain, South Carolina.
- In 1780 Fort Nashborough (Nashville) was founded.
- Neglected by the central government, settlers met at Jonesboro in 1784 and set up what they called the (never-recognized) State of Franklin.
- In 1790 North Carolina gave up its claim to the region, and the federal government established a territory including present-day Tennessee.
- Indian troubles recurred in 1792.

> **So They Say**
> "News from this place is desperate. The Indians have killed whole families...You may hear the cries of some persons for their friends daily....Nothing but screams and the roaring of guns, and no man to assist me for some time."
> John Sevier, Nov. 11, 1794

• Indian troubles diminished; population increased, and Tennessee became a state on June 1, 1796.

• The earthquake of 1811, the most destructive in U.S. history, created Reelfoot Lake.

• Against their will, beginning in 1838, the Cherokee were driven from their ancestral lands in the mountain areas of Tennessee and other southern states, and suffered the terrible hardships of the "Trail of Tears" on the journey west.

• Eastern Tennessee opposed slavery, but the central and western sections favored the Confederacy, and on June 8, 1861, Tennessee joined the Confederacy, and Tennessee became a major battleground of the Civil War.

• Nashville was captured by Union forces on Feb. 23, 1862.

• By 1864 most of Tennessee was in Union hands, but there were destructive Confederate raids.

• By the end of the Civil War in 1865, 186,652 Tennesseeans had joined the Confederates, with 31,092 on the Union side.

> **So They Say**
> "The progress of seventy-five years has been wiped out by four years of war."
> Anonymous comment on the Civil War in Tennessee

• On Feb. 25, 1865, Tennessee adopted a state constitutional amendment freeing the slaves, the only state to do this by popular vote.

• After the Civil War, attacks of cholera and yellow fever took a heavy toll. The worst struck Memphis in 1878, with more than 5,000 dying.

• Nashville held the state's Centennial Exposition in 1897.

• Among the state's 91,180 serving in World War I, Sergeant Alvin York became one of the best known enlisted men, cited for outstanding bravery in that war.

• In 1925 world attention turned to Tennessee during the notorious "Monkey Trial" of Tennessee teacher John T. Scopes, who was convicted of teaching about evolution.

• Begun in 1933, Norris Dam, near Andersonville, was the first of the great projects of the Tennessee Valley Authority.

• World War II called 315,501 to service, and 7,727 of these lost their lives.

• The progress in civil rights was shadowed by the murder of civil rights leader Dr. Martin Luther King, Jr., at Memphis in April, 1968.

• In 1977 Memphis mourned the death of its favorite son, Elvis Presley.

• The 1982 world's fair at Knoxville attracted 11 million visitors.

> **So They Say**
> "Despite a great deal of adverse publicity generated by the fact that the press simply did not like Knoxville, the 1982 World's Fair was a rousing success."
> Tennessee Dept. of Tourist Development

That's Interesting

• The only known defeat of a naval force by cavalry was carried out in a Civil War raid by Confederate Gen. Nathan Bedford Forrest. On Nov. 4, 1864, Forrest's cavalry attacked the federal supply base at Johnsonville on the Tennessee River. His nearly complete destruction of the base included the fleet of 30 gunboats, transports, and barges.

• When Tennessean Andrew Jackson won the Battle of New Orleans during the War of 1812, his fans in Tennessee spread the word that he had left immediately to conquer England.

• Confederate heroine Antoinette Polk was so close to capture by Union forces that they managed to pluck a feather from her hat, but she escaped to warn Confederate troops of Union plans.

Notable Natives

John Bell (Nashville, 1796-1869), public official. **George Deforest Brush** (Shelbyville, 1855-1941), artist. **David "Davy" Crockett** (Greeneville, 1786-1836), frontiersman/public official. **David Glasgow Farragut** (near Knoxville, 1801-1870), naval officer. **Nathan Bedford Forrest** (Chapel Hill, 1821-1877), soldier. **Richard Halliburton** (Brownsville, 1900-1939), explorer/author. **Cordell Hull** (Overton County, 1871-1955), public official. **Opie Percival Read** (Nashville, 1842-1939), author. **Alvin York** (Pall Mall, 1887-1964), World War I hero.

General

Admitted to statehood: June 1, 1796
Origin of name: Tanasi was the name of Cherokee villages on the Little Tennessee River
Capital: Nashville
Nickname: The Volunteer State
Motto: "Tennessee—America at Its Best"
Animal: raccoon
Bird: mockingbird
Flower: iris
Gem: Tennessee River pearl
Insects: firefly and ladybug
Rock: limestone
Songs: "When It's Iris Time in Tennessee," "Tennessee Waltz," "My Homeland Tennessee," "My Tennessee," and "Rocky Top"
Stone: agate
Tree: tulip poplar
Wildflower: passion flower (passiflora)

The Land

Area: 42,146 sq. mi., 36th
Land: 41,220 sq. mi., 34th
Water: 926 sq. mi., 32nd
Topography: rugged country in the E, the Great Smoky Mtns. of the Unakas, low ridges of the Appalachian Valley, the flat Cumberland Plateau, slightly rolling terrain and knobs of the Interior Low Plateau; the largest region, Eastern Gulf Coastal Plain to the W, is laced with meandering streams; Mississippi alluvial plain, a narrow strip of swamp and flood plain in the extreme W
Number of counties: 95
Geographic center: Rutherford, 5 mi. NE of Murfreesboro
Length: 440 mi.
Width: 120 mi.
Highest point: 6,643 ft. (Clingmans Dome), 17th
Lowest point: 178 ft. (Mississippi R.), 29th
Mean elevation: 900 ft., 30th

Climate and Environment

Temp., highest: 113 deg. on Aug. 9, 1930, at Perryville; lowest: -32 deg. on Dec. 30, 1917, at Mountain City
Fresh water withdrawn, per capita, per day: 1,770 gal., 17th
Endangered species: mammals, 3—gray bat, Indiana bat, Carolina northern flying squirrel; birds, 3—American peregrine falcon, least tern, red-cockaded woodpecker; reptiles, none; amphibians, none; fishes, 4; invertebrates, 24; plants, 7

Major Cities, Population Percentage Increase (1980-90)

Chattanooga, 152,466— –10.06%
Clarksville, 75,494—37.82%
Knoxville, 165,121— –5.67%
Memphis, 610,337— –5.55%
Nashville, 488,374—7.18%

The People

Population: 4,877,185, 17th
Percent change (1980-90): 5.87%, 24th
Per sq. mi: 115.72, 18th
Percent in metro. area: 67.66%, 25th
Percent foreign born: 1.2%, 45th
White: 4,048,068—83.00%, 30th
Black: 778,035—15.95%, 11th
Native American: 10,039—0.21%, 42nd
Asian, Pacific Isle: 31,839—0.65%, 39th
Other races: 9,204—0.19%, 46th
Hispanic origin: 32,741—0.67%, 45th

Percent over 5 yrs. speaking language other than English at home: 2.9%, 46th
Percent males: 48.16%, 41st
Percent females: 51.84%, 11th
Percent never married: 23.2%, 41st
Marriages per 1,000 (1989): 13.2, 6th
Divorces per 1,000 (1989): 6.5, 4th
Median age: 33.6
Under 5 years: 3,33,415—6.84%, 45th
Under 18 years: 1,216,604—0.02%, 37th
65 years & older: 618,818—12.69%, 25th
Percent increase among the elderly: 19.6%, 27th

Of Vital Importance

Live births per 1,000 pop.: 15.6, 29th
Infant mortality rate per 1,000 births (1988): 10.8, 14th
Average lifetime (1979-81): 73.30, 38th
Deaths per 100,000 pop. (1988): 935.1, 16th
Causes of death per 100,000 pop. (1988):
 Diseases of heart: 327.7, 20th
 Malignant neoplasms: 201.1, 23rd
 Cerebrovascular diseases: 76.2, 3rd
 Accidents & adverse effects: 49.4, 11th
 Chronic obstructive pulmonary diseases: 35.6, 23rd
 Suicide: 13.4, 15th
 HIV infection: 2.1, 33rd
 Other: 75.9, 25th

Keeping Well

Non-federal physicians per 100,000 pop.: 212, 23rd
Dentists per 100,000 (1990-91): 59, 31st
Nurses per 100,000 (1989): 589, 34th
Hospitals per 100,000: 3.2, 21st
 Admissions per 100,000: 17,445, 3rd
 Beds per 100,000: 604.45, 10th
 Occupancy rate: 67.6%, 20th
 Semiprivate room charges per day: $183, 49th
 Average stay: 6.8, 32nd
Notifiable diseases per 100,000:
 AIDS: 7.0, 29th
 Gonorrhea: 408.6, 8th
 Measles: 1.5, 36th
 Syphillis: 89.1, 6th
 Tuberculosis (TB): 12.3, 12th
Per capita spending on mental health programs (1987): $36.46, 24th
Pop. without health insur. (1991): 13.4%, 20th

Households by Type

Total households: 1,853,725
 Percent change (1980-90): 14.50%, 21st
Family households: 1,348,019
 Percent of total: 72.72%, 9th
Nonfamily households: 505,706
 Percent of total: 27.28%, 43rd
Persons per household: 2.56, 34th
Pop. living in group quarters: 129,129
 Percent of pop.: 2.65%, 31st

Living Quarters

Total housing units: 2,026,067
 Persons per unit: 2.41, 24th
Occupied housing units: 1,853,725
 Percent of total units: 91.49%, 13th
 Persons per unit: 2.51, 30th
 Percent of units with over 1 person per room: 2.74%, 31st
Owner-occupied: 1,261,118
 Percent of total units: 62.24%, 11th
 Percent of occupied units: 68.03%, 20th
 Persons per unit: 2.66, 40th
 Median value: $58,400, 37th
Renter-occupied units: 592,607
 Percent of total units: 29.25%, 26th
 Percent of occupied units: 31.97%, 32nd
 Persons per unit: 2.35, 25th
 Median contract rent: $273, 38th
 Rental vacancy rate: 9.6%, 16th
Mobile home, trailer & other as a % of occupied housing units: 11.19%, 25th

Crime Index per 100,000:

Total: 5,051, 30th
 Violent: 670, 16th
  Murder and nonnegligent manslaughter: 10, 13th
  Aggravated assault: 6,836, 45th
  Robbery: 191, 16th
  Rape: 50, 12th
 Property: 4,381, 30th
  Burglary: 1,264, 14th

Larceny, theft: 2,545, 43rd
Motor vehicle theft: 572, 18th
Drug abuse arrests: 241, 27th

Teaching and Learning

Literacy (1987): 85%, 40th
Pop. 3 and over enrolled in school: 1,171,640
Percent of pop.: 25.0%, 48th
Public elementary & secondary schools:
Total enrollment: 822,000
Avg. class size (1987): 25, 7th
Teachers: 43,600
Percent of pop.: 0.89%, 42nd
Teachers' avg. salary: $27,100, 35th
Spending per capita: $575, 51st
Spending per pupil in avg. daily attendance: $3,503, 43rd
Percent of graduates taking SAT: 12%, 34th
Combined SAT scores: 1015, 9th
Percent of pop. over 25 completing:
High school: 67.1%, 46th
College degree/s: 16.0%, 44th
Higher educa., institutions: 87
Per 100,000 pop.: 0.5, 44th
Enroll: 226,238
Percent of pop.: 4.64%, 44th
Public: 175,049
Percent of enroll.: 77.37%, 37th
Private: 51,189
Percent of enroll.: 22.63%, 15th
White non-Hispanic: 75,157
Percent of enroll.: 83.12%, 29th
Black non-Hispanic: 12,188
Percent of enroll.: 13.48%, 11th
Hispanic: 431
Percent of enroll.: 0.48%, 45th
Asian/Pacific Islander: 740
Percent of enroll.: 0.82%, 42nd
Amer. Indian/AK native: 438
Percent of enroll.: 0.48%, 22nd
Nonresident alien: 1,471
Percent of enroll.: 1.63%, 43rd
Female: 123,108
Percent of enroll.: 54.42%, 34th
Tuition, state university ('90-'91): $1,518, 36th
Public library systems: 135
Books & serial vol. per capita: 1.56, 48th
Govt. expend. per capita: $8.01, 48th
State govt.: $2.53, 26th
Local govts.: $5.47, 46th

Law Enforcement, Courts, and Prisons

Police protection expend.: $416,825,000
Per capita: $85.47, 37th
Judicial & legal expend.: $167,842,000
Per capita: $34.42, 40th
Corrections expend.: $402,634,000
Per capita: $82.56, 24th
Police per 10,000 pop. (1990-91): 19.6, 30th
Prisoners (state & fed.) sentenced to over 1 yr., per 100,000 pop.: 207
Percent change (1989-90): -2.28%, 47th
Death penalty: yes, by electrocution
Under sentence of death: 69, 13th
Executed (1989): none

Religion, Number and Percent of Population

Agnostic: 7,321—0.20%, 42nd
Buddhist: 3,661—0.10%, 17th
Christian: 3,316,487—90.60%, 9th
Hindu: NA
Jewish: 10,982—0.30%, 35th
Moslem: 3,661—0.10%, 22nd
Unitarian: 3,661—0.10%, 31st
Other: 36,606—1.00%, 34th
None: 219,635—6.00%, 32nd
Refused to answer: 58,570—1.60%, 39th

Making a Living

Personal income per capita (1989): $12,255, 37th
Percent increase (1979-'89) (constant 1989 dollars): 17.7%, 20th
Average income per family: $36,478, 39th
Percent of pop. below poverty level: 15.7%, 13th
Percent 65 and over: 20.9%, 5th
Cost of living, selected cities
1st qtr., 1991 (U. S. Standard=100)

Chattanooga	91.9
Memphis	94.3
Knoxville	96.2

Economy

Civilian labor force : 2,397,000
Percent of tot. pop.: 49.15%, 37th

Percent 65 and over: 3.25%, 13th
Percent females: 45.18%, 32nd
Percent job growth (1980-90): 23.09%, 20th
Major employer industries:
Agriculture: 56,800—2.50%, 29th
Construction: 93,152—4.10%, 31st
Finance, insurance & real estate: 109,056—4.80%, 35th
Government: 308,992—13.60%, 37th
Manufacturing: 583,904—25.70%, 3rd
Mining: 7,707—0.3%, 31st
Service: 406,688—17.90%, 40th
Trade: 399,872—17.60%, 44th
Transportation, communication, & public utilities: 115,872—5.10%, 26th
Wholesale/retail: 480,155—21.3%, 30th
Unemployment rate: 5.21%, 30th
Male: 2.75%, 34th
Female: 2.46%, 23rd
Total businesses (1991): 151,392
New business incorp's. (1991): 8,306
Percent of total businesses: 5.49%, 32nd
Business failures (1991): 1,992
Percent of total businesses: 1.32%, 9th
Agriculture farm income
Marketing (1991): $1,977,569,000, 30th
Net per operation: $4,280, 49th
Net per acre: $30, 34th
Leading products: cattle, dairy products, tobacco, cotton
Av. value land & build. per acre: $1,052, 20th
Percent increase (1980-90): 7.79%, 22nd
Govt. payments: $70,331,000, 26th
Construction, value of all: $2,667,000,000
Per capita: $546.83, 24th
Percent change 1989-90: -14.08%, 32nd
Manufactures:
Value added: $30,245,000,000
Per capita: $6,201.32, 10th
Value of shipments: $67,404,000,000
Per capita: $13,820.27, 12th
Leading products: chemicals & allied products, food and kindred products, nonelectrical machinery, electric and electronic equipment, apparel, fabricated metal products, transportation equipment, rubber and misc. plastic products, paper and allied products
Mining, min. prod., value (1987): $661,000,000, 29th
Leading products: coal, stone, zinc
Retail sales: $32,422,000,000, 20th
Per household: $17,384, 41st
Percent increase (1987-90): 7.0%, 46th
Service indust., value (1987): $17,769,000,000, 20th
Per capita: $3,643.29, 29th
Tourism indus., value (1989): $5,530,000,000, 15th
Foreign exports value: $3,746,000,000, 21st
Per capita: $768.07, 32nd
Patents per 1,000 pop.: 8.7, 17th

Travel and Transportation

Motor vehicle registrations: 4,444,108
Per 1,000 pop.: 911, 9th
Motorcycle registrations: 80,478
Per 1,000 pop.: 16, 26th
Licensed drivers per 1,000 driving age pop.: 881, 32nd
Deaths from motor vehicle accidents per 100,000 pop.: 24.1, 11th
Public roads & streets
Total mileage: 84,639, 22nd
Rural mileage: 69,299, 23rd
Urban mileage: 15,340, 16th
Interstate mileage: 1,062, 16th
Annual vehicle-miles of travel per person: 9,577, 17th
Mean travel time for workers 16 + who work away from home: 21.5 min., 19th

Government

Registered voters (1988): 2,417,033
Percent of voting age pop.: 66.02%, 37th
Voter turnout (1988): 1,636,250
Percent of registered voters: 67.70%, 36th
Percent of voting age pop.: 44.69%, 45th
State legislators, total (1992): 132, 33rd
Women members (1992): 15
Percent of legislature: 11.4%, 43rd
Dominant party (1992): Democrats
U. S. Congress, House members (1993): 9
Increase 1983-93: 0

Revenues:
State govt.: $9,109,677,000
Per capita: $1,867.81, 46th
State & local govt.: $17,965,066,000
Per capita: $3,683.49, 33rd
Indebtedness:
State govt.: $2,618,094,000
Per capita: $536.80, 45th
State & local govt.: $14,390,000,000
Per capita: $2,950.47, 32nd

LAWS AND REGULATIONS

Legal driving age: 16
Marriage age without parental consent: 18
Divorce residence requirement: 6 mo.

ATTRACTIONS

Major opera companies (1989): 3, 15th
Per 1 million pop.: 0.61, 29th
Major symphony orchestras (1989): 12, 25th
Per 1 million pop.: 2.43, 46th
State appropriations for state arts agencies per capita: $0.81, 24th
State Fair in mid-Sept. at Nashville

SPORTS AND COMPETITION

NCAA sports teams, 11: Austin Peay State Univ. Governors, East Tennessee State Univ. Bucs, Memphis State Univ. Tigers, Middle Tennessee State Univ. Blue Raiders, Tennessee State Univ. Tigers, Tennessee Tech Univ. Golden Eagles, Univ. of the South Tigers, Univ. of Tennessee Moccasins, Univ. of Tennessee Volunteers, Univ. of Tennessee Pacers, Vanderbilt Univ. Commodores
Professional teams, 11:
Baseball, 7—Knoxville Blue Jays (Southern League, Class AA), Bill Myer Stadium; Nashville Sounds (American Association, Class AAA), Herschel Greer Stadium; Chattanooga Lookouts (Southern League, Class AA), Historic Engel Stadium; Johnson City Cardinals (Appalachian League, Rookie Class), Howard Johnson Field; Kingsport Mets (Appalachian League, Rookie Class), J. Fred Johnson Stadium; Elizabethton Twins (Appalachian League, Rookie Class), Joe O'Brien Field; Memphis Chicks (Southern League, Class AA), Tim McCarver Stadium
Basketball, 2—Memphis Rockers (World Basketball League), Mid-South Coliseum; Nashville Stars (World Basketball League) Nashville Municipal Auditorium
Hockey, 2—Knoxville Cherokees (East Coast Hockey League), Civil Coliseum; Nashville Knights (East Coast Hockey League), Minicipal Auditorium

TEXAS

"The province of Techas will be the richest state of our union, without any exception."

Thomas Jefferson

Novelist Edna Ferber labeled Texas as a giant, and she was right. The total wealth of its natural resources surpasses all the other states. As a separate country it would rank 11th in wealth among the nations. It leads the nation in total productivity, and its history retells one of the nation's most heroic events, the defense of the Alamo. Texans are friendly—indeed, "Friendship" is their state motto. Once the typical Texan was a frontier cowboy with a ten-gallon hat, but today the state's symbol might be an oil field worker or a scientist in a laboratory. Texas is still a frontier state, but this time the frontier is the space program. Perhaps it is typical and appropriate that this giant has constructed the largest of all the state capitols as a symbol of its strength.

SUPERLATIVES

- Greatest variety of flowers.
- Greatest variety of reptiles.
- Leader in helium production.
- Leader in sulphur production.
- First in petroleum refining.
- First in asphalt production.
- First in cotton production.
- Produces the most chemicals from seawater.
- Only state with five major ports.

MOMENTS IN HISTORY

• The shipwrecked party of Alva Nunez Cabeza de Vaca escaped from Indian captivity in Texas in 1528 and made an incredible journey across country back to Mexico.

• The renowned expedition of Francisco Vasquez de Coronado crossed the Rio Grande in 1541.

• First permanent European settlement in present-day Texas was Ysleta, founded in 1682.

• In the first half of the 1700s about a dozen missions became outposts of civilization in present-day Texas.

• The Sabine and Red rivers were established as northern and eastern boundaries in 1819.

• Moses and Stephen Austin established an American foothold in Texas before Moses died in the 1820s, and the American presence grew in the early 30s.

> So They Say
>
> "When young folks danced in those days, they danced....They 'shuffled' and 'double-shuffled,' 'wired' and 'cut the pigeon's wing,' making the splinters fly...."
>
> Noah Smithwick, at a wedding in 1828

• By 1835 the Americans in Texas realized that they must seek independence from Mexico, and they laid siege to the Spanish capital of San Antonio, which fell in December.

• Cruel Mexican leader Santa Anna arrived in Feb. 1836 to recapture San Antonio, finding the defenders at an old mission called the Alamo.

• Santa Ana overwhelmed and slaughtered the Alamo's defenders. Then Santa Ana captured and murdered 330 Texans at Goliad.

So They Say

"The enemy has demanded a surrender at discretion, or otherwise, the garrison are to be put to the sword...I shall never surrender or retreat—victory or death."

Alamo Commander William Barret Travis

• Texan dynamo Sam Houston led his forces eastward and lured Santa Ana into a difficult position.

So They Say

"This morning we are in preparation to meet Santa Ana. It is the only chance of saving Texas. Texas could have started 4,000 men. We will only have about seven hundred. We go to conquer." Later—"Victory is certain. Trust in God and fear not. And remember the Alamo!"

Sam Houston

• Santa Ana was defeated and captured at the Battle of San Jacinto, considered one of the decisive struggles of world history, April 21, 1836. Later that year the people held an election and chose Sam Houston as the first president of the Independent Republic of Texas.

• After ten years of independence, on December 29, 1845, Texas became the 28th state.

• As the divisions over slavery increased, Sam Houston became governor in 1859.

So They Say

"I cannot for a moment entertain that the masses of the people would be willing to precipitate the country into all the horrors of revolution and civil war. No human being could calculate the injury that would be inflicted upon mankind."

Sam Houston

• Despite Houston's objection, the state voted to secede on Jan. 28, 1861, and Houston resigned as governor.

• During the Civil War, Texas furnished enormous quantities of essential materials and food.

• Texas was readmitted to the Union on March 30, 1870, and a new constitution became law on Feb. 15, 1876.

• Between the years 1870 and 1890 ten million cattle were shipped from Texas to the nation's markets.

• The terrible hurricane at Galveston on Sept. 8, 1900, killed at least 6,000, and left 8,000 homeless.

• World War I called more than 200,000 Texans to service, and Texan E.M. House was a principal adviser to President Woodrow Wilson.

• Dallas celebrated the Texas Centennial in 1936.

• The school explosion at New London in 1937 brought death to 279 pupils, two teachers, and two visitors.

• World War II called 750,000 Texans into the armed services, and 23,022 lost their lives.

• The border dispute with Mexico was settled in 1963.

• Texan Lyndon Baines Johnson succeeded to the presidency on the assassination of President John F. Kennedy at Dallas on Nov. 22, 1963.

So They Say

"All I have I would have given gladly not to be standing here today."

Lyndon Johnson, assuming the presidency after the Kennedy assasination

• The year 1986 brought the 150th anniversary celebration of the founding of the Republic of Texas.

That's Interesting

• Texas even boasts some notable holes in the ground—Meteor Crater covers 10 acres near Odessa. The strange Hueco Tanks, where rainwater is held in natural cups carved into the granite, welcome thirsty travelers.

• In 1598, explorer Don Juan de Onate crossed the Rio Grande at present-day El Paso, bringing four purple and three yellow velvet coats, eleven pairs of satin trousers, sixteen pairs of silk stockings, and five suits of armor.

• At statehood, Texas retained the right to divide itself into five new states. This could still be done if the people wished.

• In order to get to the Alamo to join his friend Colonel Travis, James Bonham had to borrow money, only to meet the fate of the other Alamo defenders.

• It's not a shrub but a full grown tree—Texas's own shin oak, only 12 in. high.

• Fifteen thousand carloads of Texas pink granite were required to build the Texas capitol, the largest outside Washington, D.C. This material was donated by the owners of Granite Mountain, near Marble Falls.

Notable Natives

Joan Crawford (San Antonio, 1906-1977), actress. **James Frank Dobie** (Live Oak Cty., 1888-1964), folklorist/educator. **Dwight David Eisenhower** (Denison, 1890-1969), U.S. president. **James Edward Ferguson** (Temple, 1871-1944), Texas governor. **Miriam A. "Ma" Ferguson** (Bell Cty., 1875-1961), Texas governor. **John Nance Garner** (Red River Cty., 1868-1967), U.S. vice-president. **Howard Robard Hughes** (Houston, 1905-1976), industrialist/aviator/motion-picture producer. **Lyndon Baines Johnson** (near Stonewall, 1908-1973), U.S. president. **Audie Murphy** (Kingston, 1924-1971), soldier/actor. **Chester William Nimitz** (Fredericksburg, 1885-1966), naval officer. **Katherine Anne Porter** (Indian Creek, 1890-1980), author.

General

Admitted to statehood: Dec. 29, 1845
Origin of name: Variant of word used by Caddo and other Indians meaning friends or allies, and applied to them by the Spanish in eastern Texas—also written *Texias, tejas, teysas*
Capital: Austin, founded 1839
Nickname: Lone Star State
Motto: "Friendship"
Bird: mockingbird
Dish: chili
Flower: bluebonnet
Gem: topaz
Grass: sideoats grama
Song: "Texas, Our Texas"
Stone: petrified palmwood
Tree: pecan

The Land

Area: 268,601 sq. mi., 2nd
Land: 261,914 sq. mi., 2nd
Water: 6,687 sq. mi., 9th
Topography: Gulf Coast Plain in the S and SE; N Central Plains slope upward with some hills; the Great Plains extend over the Panhandle, are broken by low mountains; the Trans-Pecos is the southern extension of the Rockies
Number of counties: 254
Geographic center: McCulloch, 15 mi. NE of Brady
Length: 790 mi.
Width: 660 mi.
Highest point: 8,749 ft. (Guadalupe Peak), 14th
Lowest point: sea level (Gulf of Mexico), 3rd
Mean elevation: 1,700 ft., 17th
Coastline: 367 mi., 6th
Shoreline: 3,359 mi., 7th

Climate and Environment

Temp., highest: 120 deg. on Aug. 12, 1936, at Seymour; lowest: -23 deg. on Feb. 8, 1933, at Seminole
Fresh water withdrawn, per capita, per day: 1,230 gal., 26th
Endangered species: mammals, 4—Mexican long-nosed bat, jaguarundi, West Indian manatee, ocelot; birds, 10—whooping crane, Eskimo curlew, American peregrine falcon, Northern aplomado falcon, brown pelican, Attwater's greater prairie-chicken, least tern, black-capped vireo, golden-cheeked (wood) warbler, red-cockaded woodpecker; reptiles, 3; amphibians, 2; fishes, 7; invertebrates, 5; plants, 16

Major Cities, Population Percentage Increase (1980-90)

Austin, 465,622—34.62%
Dallas, 1,006,877—11.31%
El Paso, 515,342—21.18%
Houston, 1,630,553—2.22%
San Antonio, 935,933—19.08%

The People

Population: 16,986,510, 3rd
Percent change (1980-90): 16.25%, 7th
Per sq. mi: 63.24, 30th
Percent in metro. area: 81.64%, 14th
Percent foreign born: 9.0%, 9th
White: 12,774,762—75.21%, 41st
Black: 2,021,632—11.90%, 18th
Native American: 65,877—0.39%, 28th
Asian, Pacific Isle: 319,459—1.88%, 14th
Other races: 1,804,780—10.62%, 3rd
Hispanic origin: 4,339,905—25.55%, 3rd
Percent over 5 yrs. speaking language other than English at home: 25.4%, 3rd
Percent males: 49.25%, 13th
Percent females: 50.75%, 39th
Percent never married: 25.1%, 30th
Marriages per 1,000 (1989): 10.3, 13th
Divorces per 1,000 (1989): 5.5, 13th
Median age: 30.8
Under 5 years: 1,390,054—8.18%, 4th
Under 18 years: 4,835,839—28.47%, 9th
65 years & older: 1,716,576—10.11%, 47th
Percent increase among the elderly: 25.2%, 21st

Of Vital Importance

Live births per 1,000 pop.: 19.2, 5th
Infant mortality rate per 1,000 births (1988): 9.0, 29th
Average lifetime (1979-81): 73.64, 32nd
Deaths per 100,000 pop. (1988): 729.6, 45th
Causes of death per 100,000 pop. (1988):
Diseases of heart: 242.5, 44th
Malignant neoplasms: 153.8, 45th
Cerebrovascular diseases: 48.5, 43rd
Accidents & adverse effects: 38.8, 30th
Chronic obstructive pulmonary diseases: 24.3, 47th
Suicide: 13.4, 15th
HIV infection: 6.9, 7th
Other: 63.6, 46th

Keeping Well

Non-federal physicians per 100,00 pop.: 186, 36th
Dentists per 100,000 (1990-91): 52, 40th
Nurses per 100,000 (1989): 481, 46th
Hospitals per 100,000: 3.2, 23rd
Admissions per 100,000: 13,111, 31st
Beds per 100,000: 465.40, 30th
Occupancy rate: 60.3%, 46th
Semiprivate room charges per day: $223, 36th
Average stay: 6.2, 45th
Notifiable diseases per 100,000:
AIDS: 19.8, 7th
Gonorrhea: 254.5, 20th
Measles: 26.0, 2nd
Syphillis: 77.5, 8th
Tuberculosis (TB): 13.2, 8th
Per capita spending on mental health programs (1987): $20.53, 49th
Pop. without health insur. (1991): 22.1%, 2nd

Households by Type

Total households: 6,070,937
Percent change (1980-90): 23.17%, 8th
Family households: 4,343,878
Percent of total: 71.55%, 17th
Nonfamily households: 1,727,059
Percent of total: 28.45%, 35th
Persons per household: 2.73, 8th
Pop. living in group quarters: 393,447
Percent of pop.: 2.32%, 41st

Living Quarters

Total housing units: 7,008,999
Persons per unit: 2.42, 20th
Occupied housing units: 6,070,937
Percent of total units: 86.62%, 39th
Persons per unit: 2.70, 6th
Percent of units with over 1 person per room: 8.15%, 5th
Owner-occupied units: 3,695,115
Percent of total units: 52.72%, 45th
Percent of occupied units: 60.87%, 44th

Persons per unit: 2.85, 6th
Median value: $59,600, 35th
Renter-occupied units: 2,375,822
Percent of total units: 33.90%, 12th
Percent of occupied units: 39.13%, 9th
Persons per unit: 2.55, 7th
Median contract rent: $328, 27th
Rental vacancy rate: 13.0%, 4th
Mobile home, trailer & other as a % of occupied housing units: 10.39%, 27th

Crime Index per 100,000

Total: 7,827, 4th
Violent: 761, 11th
Murder and nonnegligent manslaughter: 14, 4th
Aggravated assault: 8,183, 5th
Robbery: 261, 10th
Rape: 52, 9th
Property: 7,065, 4th
Burglary: 1,852, 3rd
Larceny, theft: 4,305, 4th
Motor vehicle theft: 909, 7th
Drug abuse arrests: 366, 12th

Teaching and Learning

Literacy (1987): 84%, 47th
Pop. 3 and over enrolled in school: 4,805,895
Percent of pop.: 29.7%, 6th
Public elementary & secondary schools:
Total enrollment: 3,354,000
Avg. class size (1987): 22, 28th
Teachers: 202,400
Percent of pop.: 1.19%, 6th
Teachers' avg. salary: $27,500, 32nd
Spending per capita: $849, 19th
Spending per pupil in avg. daily attendance: $4,056, 37th
Percent of graduates taking SAT: 44%, 23rd
Combined SAT scores: 874, 46th
Percent of pop. over 25 completing:
High school: 72.1%, 40th
College degree/s: 20.3%, 24th
Higher educa., institutions: 172
Per 100,000 pop.: 0.6, 29th
Enroll: 901,437
Percent of pop.: 5.31%, 30th
Public: 802,314
Percent of enroll.: 89.00%, 9th
Private: 99,123
Percent of enroll.: 11.00%, 43rd
White non-Hispanic: 24,264
Percent of enroll.: 81.33%, 32nd
Black non-Hispanic: 1,079
Percent of enroll.: 3.62%, 31st
Hispanic: 634
Percent of enroll.: 2.13%, 17th
Asian/Pacific Islander: 740
Percent of enroll.: 2.48%, 15th
Amer. Indian/AK native: 2,648
Percent of enroll.: 8.88%, 1st
Nonresident alien: 468
Percent of enroll.: 1.57%, 44th
Female: 480,711
Percent of enroll.: 53.33%, 41st
Tuition, state university ('90-'91): $986, 50th
Public library systems: 478
Books & serial vol. per capita: 2.22, 33rd
Govt. expend. per capita: $9.11, 44th
State govt.: $1.17, 46th
Local govts.: $7.94, 37th

Law Enforcement, Courts, and Prisons

Police protection expend.: $1,705,197,000
Per capita: $100.38, 29th
Judicial & legal expend.: $719,988,000
Per capita: $42.38, 33rd
Corrections expend.: $1,410,975,000
Per capita: $83.06, 23rd
Police per 10,000 pop. (1990-91): 21.4, 22nd
Prisoners (state & fed.) sentenced to over 1 yr., per 100,000 pop.: 290
Percent change (1989-90): 13.68%, 4th
Death penalty: yes, by lethal injection
Under sentence of death: 283, 2nd
Executed (1989): 4

Religion, Number and Percent of Population

Agnostic: 72,904—0.60%, 19th
Buddhist: 24,301—0.20%, 11th
Christian: 10,935,604—90.00%, 11th
Hindu: NA
Jewish: 85,055—0.70%, 23rd

Moslem: 24,301—0.20%, 13th
Unitarian: 24,301—0.20%, 23rd
Other: 194,411—1.60%, 17th
None: 595,383—4.90%, 40th
Refused to answer: 194,411—1.60%, 39th

Making a Living

Personal income per capita (1989): $12,904, 32nd
Percent increase (1979-'89) (constant 1989 dollars): 6.9%, 41st
Average income per family: $40,255, 26th
Percent of pop. below poverty level: 18.1%, 8th
Percent 65 and over: 18.4%, 10th
Cost of living, selected cities
1st qtr., 1991 (U. S. Standard=100)

Amarillo	90.5
Houston	101.5
Dallas	103.7

Economy

Civilian labor force : 8,443,000
Percent of tot. pop.: 49.70%, 29th
Percent 65 and over: 2.71%, 26th
Percent females: 44.90%, 35th
Percent job growth (1980-90): 21.07%, 22nd
Major employer industries:
Agriculture: 237,660—3.00%, 20th
Construction: 411,944—5.20%, 15th
Finance, insurance & real estate: 427,788—5.40%, 26th
Government: 1,227,910—15.50%, 27th
Manufacturing: 1,180,378—14.90%, 32nd
Mining: 164,571—2.2%, 9th
Service: 1,560,634—19.70%, 25th
Trade: 1,528,946—19.30%, 18th
Transportation, communication, & public utilities: 459,476—5.80%, 15th
Wholesale/retail: 1,707,213—22.4%, 7th
Unemployment rate: 6.17%, 11th
Male: 3.21%, 19th
Female: 2.96%, 9th
Total businesses (1991): 844,821
New business incorp's. (1991): 34,571
Percent of total businesses: 4.09%, 44th
Business failures (1991): 6,976
Percent of total businesses: 0.83%, 28th
Agriculture farm income
Marketing (1991): $12,126,182,000, 2nd
Net per operation: $16,545, 30th
Net per acre: $23, 39th
Leading products: cattle, cotton, dairy products, greenhouse
Av. value land & build. per acre: $506, 38th
Percent increase (1980-90): 16.06%, 15th
Govt. payments: $777,925,000, 1st
Construction, value of all: $8,161,000,000
Per capita: $480.44, 32nd
Percent change 1989-90: -0.20%, 19th
Manufactures:
Value added: $83,630,000,000
Per capita: $4,923.32, 30th
Value of shipments: $210,584,000,000
Per capita: $12,397.13, 20th
Leading products: machinery, transportation equipment, foods, electrical and electronic equipment, chemicals and allied products
Mining, min. prod., value (1987): $40,319,000,000, 1st
Leading products: petroleum, nat. gas, cement
Retail sales: $120,459,000,000, 3rd
Per household: $19,631, 20th
Percent increase (1987-90): 17.0%, 23rd
Service indust., value (1987): $69,881,000,000, 3rd
Per capita: $4,113.91, 21st
Tourism indus., value (1989): $15,543,000,000, 4th
Foreign exports value: $32,931,000,000, 2nd
Per capita: $1,938.66, 7th
Patents per 1,000 pop.: 5.3, 29th

Travel and Transportation

Motor vehicle registrations: 12,799,815
Per 1,000 pop.: 753, 34th
Motorcycle registrations: 174,334
Per 1,000 pop.: 10, 43rd
Licensed drivers per 1,000 driving age pop.: 888, 30th
Deaths from motor vehicle accidents per 100,000 pop.: 19.1, 23rd
Public roads & streets
Total mileage: 305,951, 1st
Rural mileage: 217,175, 1st
Urban mileage: 88,776, 1st
Interstate mileage: 3,229, 1st
Annual vehicle-miles of travel per person: 9,550, 18th

Mean travel time for workers 16 + who work away from home: 22.2 min., 12th

Government

Registered voters (1988): 8,201,856
Percent of voting age pop.: 66.84%, 35th
Voter turnout (1988): 5,427,410
Percent of registered voters: 66.17%, 39th
Percent of voting age pop.: 44.23%, 46th
State legislators, total (1992): 181, 11th
Women members (1992): 23
Percent of legislature: 12.7%, 39th
Dominant party (1992): Democrats
U. S. Congress, House members (1993): 30
Increase 1983-93: +3
Revenues:
State govt.: $30,975,026,000
Per capita: $1,823.51, 49th
State & local govt.: $58,778,749,000
Per capita: $3,460.32, 40th
Indebtedness:
State govt.: $7,863,557,000
Per capita: $462.93, 49th
State & local govt.: $64,127,000,000
Per capita: $3,775.17, 21st

Laws and Regulations

Legal driving age: 18
Marriage age without parental consent: 18
Divorce residence requirement: 6 mo., qualification—check local statutes

Attractions

Major opera companies (1989): 7, 6th
Per 1 million pop.: 0.41, 37th
Major symphony orchestras (1989): 42, 4th
Per 1 million pop.: 2.47, 44th
State appropriations for state arts agencies per capita: $0.16, 51st
State Fair in mid-Oct. at Dallas

Sports and Competition

NCAA sports teams, 19: Baylor Univ. Bears, Hardin-Simmons Univ. Cowboys, Lamar Univ. Cardinals, Prairie View A&M Univ. Panthers, Rice Univ. Owls, Sam Houston State Univ. Bearkats, Southern Methodist Univ. Mustangs, Southwest Texas State Univ. Bobcats, Stephen F. Austin State Univ. Lumberjacks, Texas A&M Univ. Aggies, Texas Christian Univ. Horned Frogs, Texas Southern Univ. Tigers, Texas Tech Univ. Red Raiders, Univ. of Houston Cougars, Univ. of North Texas Mean Green Eagles, Univ. of Texas Longhorns, Univ. of Texas Miners, Univ. of Texas Broncs, Univ. of Texas Roadrunners
Professional teams, 13: Baseball, 5—Midland Angels (Texas League, Class AA), Angels Stadium; Texas Rangers (AL), Arlington Stadium; El Paso Diablos (Texas League, Class AA), Cohen Stadium; Houston Astros (NL), The Astrodome; San Antonio Missions (Texas League, Class AA), V.J. Keefer Memorial Stadium
Basketball, 4—Wichita Falls Texans (Continental Basketball Association), D.L. Ligon Coliseum; San Antonio Spurs (NBA), Hemisfair Arena; Dallas Mavericks (NBA), Reunion Arena; Houston Rockets (NBA), The Summit
Football, 3—San Antonio Riders (World League of American Football), Alamo Stadium; Houston Oilers (AFC), Astrodome; Dallas Cowboys (NFC), Texas Stadium
Soccer, 1—Dallas Sidekicks (Major Soccer League), Reunion Arena

UTAH

"...that the physical obstacles to the occupation of a region so unpromising were sufficient to discourage the most sanguine imagination and to appall the stoutest heart, the mind is filled with wonder at witnessing the immense results which have been accomplished in so short a time, and from a beginning apparently so insignificant."

Howard Stansbury

Utah is a land that was settled because no one else wanted it, and it soon blossomed under the dedication of an unusual people, the Mormons. It is a "desert" land swarming with seagulls and pelicans, where the faithful erected a monument to a bird. Its broad expanses possess some of the nation's most spectacular natural formations, many found nowhere else. Today the capital, Salt Lake City, with only 163,034 residents, is the smallest city in the country to boast a top-ranked symphony, dance company, and opera company. A fascinating land described as "wonderful, outrageous, mysterious, and strange."

SUPERLATIVES

• Bear River is the continent's longest not reaching the sea.

• Largest salt lake in North America—Great Salt Lake.

• Nation's only major east-west range—the Uintas.

• Highest and largest natural arch—Rainbow Bridge.

• Boasts 210 useful minerals.

• World center of genealogical research.

MOMENTS IN HISTORY

• Little was known of the region until Catholic fathers Silvestre Velez de Escalante and Francisco Atanasio Dominguez passed through the area in 1776, looking for a route to California. They left present-day Utah at Padre Creek. Many Spanish expeditions followed the padre's route to California.

• The winter of 1824-1825 brought Jim Bridger, the first European explorer known to have arrived at the shores of Great Salt Lake. Bridger told a tale of the terrible winter which "froze" all the buffalo there.

> **So They Say**
>
> "All I had to do was tumble 'em into Salt Lake an' I had pickled buffalo enough for myself and the whole Ute nation for years."
>
> Jim Bridger's tall tale

• In 1826 the fur business of Jackson and Sublette was organized in the region, and the great frontiersman Jedediah Strong Smith made a thorough exploration of the area.

• The "Rendezvous" of fur traders and trappers was held in 1826 at present-day Ogden. These annual gatherings in the wilderness took on a carnival atmosphere of games, singing, story telling, races, and other contests, brightened by the colorful Indian costumes and the typical frontier garb of the white participants.

• The explorations of John C. Fremont, 1843, 1844, 1845, and 1854, did much to make the region known.

• In 1845, guided by Kit Carson, Fremont crossed the central Salt Desert.

• The first permanent European style settlement was Fort Buenaventura (later, Ogden), built in 1844-1845 by Miles Goodyear.

• Driven from their three prosperous settlements in the east, the first of vast numbers of members of the Church of Jesus Christ of the Latter-Day Saints (Mormons) reached their "Promised Land" on July 24, 1847. Their leader, Brigham Young, looked out from a hill over present-day Salt Lake City, and said "This is the place"—a region so remote and forlorn he expected never again to be driven out.

> **So They Say**
> "When my husband said 'This is the place,' I cried, for it seemed to me the most desolate in all the world."
> Clara Decker Young, wife of Brigham Young

• The fall of 1847 found the Mormons ready to reap substantial crops, until a swarm of crickets threatened all. The crops were saved by the arrival of flights of seagulls, who ate the crickets and gave the Mormons their "symbol of deliverance."

• By 1849 the broad streets of Salt Lake City had been laid out; there were gristmills and sawmills run by waterpower, carding machines and other advances. That year the thousands of 49ers began to pass by on their way to the California gold fields, and the Mormons prospered by supplying their desperate needs.

• With incredible Mormon energy, by 1855 Ogden, Provo, Utah Valley, Manti, Sanpete Valley, Tooele, Nephi, Fillmore, Brigham City, Cedar City, and Santa Clara had been established in Utah, along with Las Vegas in Nevada, and Morgan, Moab, and Fort Lemhi in Idaho, all settled by the Mormons.

• From 1855 to 1860, more than 4,000 Mormon converts from Europe crossed the plains to Utah, pulling and pushing their handcarts from the eastern railheads, the only "transportation" the leaders at Salt Lake City could provide for them.

> **So They Say**
> "They are expected to walk and draw their carts across the plains. Sufficient teams will be furnished to haul the aged, infirm and those unable to walk. A few good cows will be sent along to furnish milk and some beef cattle."
> Brigham Young

• Indian warfare plagued the settlers until about 1868.

• On Jan. 4, 1896, Utah became the 45th state.

• The magnificent Rainbow Bridge was discovered in 1909.

• World War I called 21,000 Utahans to service, and the Mormon Relief Societies made substantial contributions to the starving of Europe.

• During World War II, 70,000 Utah men and women saw service.

• In 1983 the heaviest rains and snowfalls of record brought the most widespread flooding ever experienced there. Great Salt Lake rose 10 ft. in 2 yrs.

• By the late 1980s the lake level had fallen, confounding the doomsayers.

THAT'S INTERESTING

• The beautiful Seagull monument at Salt Lake City pays tribute to the bird that saved the first Mormon crops.

• The Navajo banned their ancient symbol of friendship during World War II because it resembled the Nazi swastika.

• Celebrating the completion of the first transcontinental railroad, Governor Leland Stanford of California swung his sledgehammer at the gold spike—and missed.

• Zion Narrows canyon is so narrow and deep that even in bright daylight stars are visible from the canyon bottom.

• When Bishop Whipple of Minnesota asked a Utah chief if his belongings were safe in his tent, the chief replied, "Yes, there is not a white man within a hundred miles."

• Brigham Young did not choose the Salt Lake valley for its beauty but rather because it was so desolate he thought no one would ever try to take it away from his Mormon people.

NOTABLE NATIVES

Maude Adams (Salt Lake City, 1872-1953), actress. **John Moses Browning** (Ogden, 1855-1926), inventor. **Bernard Augustine DeVoto** (Ogden, 1897-1955), author. **Marriner Stoddard Eccles** (Logan, 1890-1977), banker. **Philo Taylor Farnsworth** (Beaver, 1906-1971), engineer/inventor. **Harvey Fletcher** (Provo, 1884-1981), physicist. **William Dudley "Big Bill" Haywood,** (Salt Lake City, 1869-1928), labor leader. **John Held Jr.** (Salt Lake City, 1889-1958), illustrator/author. **Mahonri Mackintosh Young** (Salt Lake City, 1877-1957), sculptor/painter/etcher.

GENERAL

Admitted to statehood: Jan. 4, 1896
Origin of name: From Navajo word meaning "upper" or "higher up," as applied to a Shoshone tribe called Ute; Spanish form is Yutta, English Uta or Utah (proposed name Deseret, "land of honeybees," from *Book of Mormon*, was rejected by Congress.)
Capital: Salt Lake City
Nickname: beehive State
Motto: "Industry"
Bird: seagull
Flower: Sego lily
Gem: topaz
Song: "Utah, We Love Thee"
Tree: blue spruce

THE LAND

Area: 84,904 sq. mi., 13th
Land: 82,168 sq. mi., 12th
Water: 2,736 sq. mi., 16th
Topography: high Colorado plateau is cut by brilliantly-colored canyons of the SE; broad, flat, desert-like Great Basin of the W; the Great Salt Lake and Bonneville Salt flats to the NW; middle Rockies in the NE run E-W; valleys and plateaus of the Wasatch Front
Number of counties: 29
Geographic center: Sanpete, 3 mi. N of Manti
Length: 350 mi.
Width: 270 mi.
Highest point: 13,528 ft. (Kings Peak), 7th
Lowest point: 2,000 ft. (Beaverdam Wash), 48th
Mean elevation: 6,100 ft., 3rd

CLIMATE AND ENVIRONMENT

Temp., highest: 117 deg. on July 5, 1985, at Saint George; lowest: -69 deg. on Feb. 1, 1985, at Peter's Sink
Fresh water withdrawn, per capita, per day: 2,540 gal., 8th
Endangered species: mammals, 1—black-footed ferret; birds, 2—whooping crane, American peregrine falcon; reptiles, none; amphibians, none; fishes, 6; invertebrates, none; plants, 10

MAJOR CITIES, POPULATION PERCENTAGE INCREASE (1980-90)

Orem, 67,561—28.94%
Provo, 86,835—17.17%
Salt Lake City, 159,936— -1.90%
Sandy City, 75,058—43.76%
West Valley City, 86,976—19.95%

THE PEOPLE

Population: 1,722,850, 35th
Percent change (1980-90): 15.20%, 9th
Per sq. mi: 20.29, 43rd
Percent in metro. area: 77.55%, 19th
Percent foreign born: 3.4%, 23rd
White: 1,615,845—93.79%, 11th
Black: 11,576—0.67%, 44th
Native American: 24,283—1.41%, 11th
Asian, Pacific Isle: 33,371—1.94%, 13th
Other races: 37,775—2.19%, 16th
Hispanic origin: 84,597—4.91%, 16th
Percent over 5 yrs. speaking language other than English at home: 7.8%, 23rd
Percent males: 49.67%, 8th
Percent females: 50.33%, 44th
Percent never married: 25.5%, 26th
Marriages per 1,000 (1989): 10.9, 10th
Divorces per 1,000 (1989): 4.7, 24th
Median age: 26.2
Under 5 years: 169,633—9.85%, 2nd

Under 18 years: 627,444—36.42%, 1st
65 years & older: 149,958—8.70%, 50th
Percent increase among the elderly: 37.3%, 8th

Of Vital Importance

Live births per 1,000 pop.: 21.6, 3rd
Infant mortality rate per 1,000 births (1988): 8.0, 45th
Average lifetime (1979-81): 75.76, 3rd
Deaths per 100,000 pop. (1988): 545.8, 50th
Causes of death per 100,000 pop. (1988):
Diseases of heart: 175.3, 49th
Malignant neoplasms: 101.1, 50th
Cerebrovascular diseases: 40.8, 47th
Accidents & adverse effects: 35, 39th
Chronic obstructive pulmonary diseases: 22.1, 49th
Suicide: 13.6, 13th
HIV infection: 2, 36th
Other: 49.8, 49th

Keeping Well

Non-federal physicians per 100,000 pop.: 198, 31st
Dentists per 100,000 (1990-91): 74, 15th
Nurses per 100,000 (1989): 498, 44th
Hospitals per 100,000: 3.0, 26th
Admissions per 100,000: 11,042, 48th
Beds per 100,000: 324.17, 50th
Occupancy rate: 60.6%, 45th
Semiprivate room charges per day: $353, 7th
Average stay: 6.3, 44th
Notifiable diseases per 100,000:
AIDS: 5.7, 35th
Gonorrhea: 23.0, 45th
Measles: 8.5, 10th
Syphillis: 2.8, 43rd
Tuberculosis (TB): 3.0, 39th
Per capita spending on mental health programs (1987): $33.20, 31st
Pop. without health insur. (1991): 13.9%19th

Households by Type

Total households: 537,273
Percent change (1980-90): 19.66%, 17th
Family households: 410,862
Percent of total: 76.47%, 1st
Nonfamily households: 126,411
Percent of total: 23.53%, 51st
Persons per household: 3.15, 1st
Pop. living in group quarters: 29,048
Percent of pop.: 1.69%, 51st

Living Quarters

Total housing units: 598,388
Persons per unit: 2.88, 1st
Occupied housing units: 537,273
Percent of total units: 89.79%, 23rd
Persons per unit: 3.03, 1st
Percent of units with over 1 person per room: 5.51%, 13th
Owner-occupied units: 365,979
Percent of total units: 61.16%, 16th
Percent of occupied units: 68.12%, 18th
Persons per unit: 3.38, 1st
Median value: $68,900, 26th
Renter-occupied units: 171,294
Percent of total units: 28.63%, 28th
Percent of occupied units: 31.88%, 34th
Persons per unit: 2.67, 3rd
Median contract rent: $300, 30th
Rental vacancy rate: 8.6%, 23rd
Mobile home, trailer & other as a % of occupied housing units: 7.64%, 34th

Crime Index per 100,000

Total: 5,660, 18th
Violent: 284, 41st
Murder and nonnegligent manslaughter: 3, 42nd
Aggravated assault: 9,846, 3rd
Robbery: 57, 40th
Rape: 38, 26th
Property: 5,376, 13th
Burglary: 881, 37th
Larceny, theft: 4,258, 5th
Motor vehicle theft: 238, 40th
Drug abuse arrests: 190, 34th

Teaching and Learning

Literacy (1987): 94%, 1st
Pop. 3 and over enrolled in school: 610,696
Percent of pop.: 37.7%, 1st
Public elementary & secondary schools:
Total enrollment: 445,000

Avg. class size (1987): 28, 1st
Teachers: 18,300
Percent of pop.: 1.06%, 19th
Teachers' avg. salary: $23,700, 46th
Spending per capita: $738, 32nd
Spending per pupil in avg. daily attendance: $2,733, 51st
Percent of graduates taking SAT: 5%, 48th
Combined SAT scores: 1031, 5th
Percent of pop. over 25 completing:
High school: 85.1%, 2nd
College degree/s: 22.3%, 15th
Higher educa., institutions: 15
Per 100,000 pop.: 0.5, 38th
Enroll: 121,303
Percent of pop.: 7.04%, 5th
Public: 86,108
Percent of enroll.: 70.99%, 41st
Private: 35,195
Percent of enroll.: 29.01%, 11th
White non-Hispanic: 85,699
Percent of enroll.: 69.74%, 46th
Black non-Hispanic: 33,699
Percent of enroll.: 27.42%, 2nd
Hispanic: 395
Percent of enroll.: 0.32%, 50th
Asian/Pacific Islander: 783
Percent of enroll.: 0.64%, 48th
Amer. Indian/AK native: 377
Percent of enroll.: 0.31%, 32nd
Nonresident alien: 1,930
Percent of enroll.: 1.57%, 44th
Female: 59,242
Percent of enroll.: 48.84%, 50th
Tuition, state university ('90-'91): $1,524, 35th
Public library systems: 69
Books & serial vol. per capita: 2.47, 27th
Govt. expend. per capita: $15.86, 24th
State govt.: $2.22, 33rd
Local govts.: $13.64, 23rd

Law Enforcement, Courts, and Prisons

Police protection expend.: $154,229,000
Per capita: $89.51, 34th
Judicial & legal expend.: $74,222,000
Per capita: $43.08, 32nd
Corrections expend.: $107,446,000
Per capita: $62.36, 37th
Police per 10,000 pop. (1990-91): 17.7, 34th
Prisoners (state & fed.) sentenced to over 1 yr., per 100,000 pop.: 143
Percent change (1989-90): 4.81%, 35th
Death penalty: yes, by firing squad or lethal injection
Under sentence of death: 8, 28th
Executed (1989): none

Religion, Number and Percent of Population

Agnostic: 9,859—0.90%, 14th
Buddhist: 1,095—0.10%, 17th
Christian: 959,576—87.60%, 20th
Hindu: NA
Jewish: 7,668—0.70%, 23rd
Moslem: NA
Unitarian: 1,095—0.10%, 31st
Other: NA
None: 85,442—7.80%, 16th
Refused to answer: 31,767—2.90%, 9th

Making a Living

Personal income per capita (1989): $11,029, 46th
Percent increase (1979-89) (constant 1989 dollars): 4.4%, 43rd
Average income per family: $39,025, 31st
Percent of pop. below poverty level: 11.4%, 32nd
Percent 65 and over: 8.8%, 46th
Cost of living, selected cities
1st qtr., 1991 (U. S. Standard=100)

Salt Lake City	92.1
Provo-Orem	93.1
St. George	98.8

Economy

Civilian labor force : 792,000
Percent of tot. pop.: 45.97%, 49th
Percent 65 and over: NA
Percent females: 43.31%, 50th
Percent job growth (1980-90): 30.88%, 12th
Major employer industries:
Agriculture: 21,982—2.90%, 22nd
Construction: 27,288—3.60%, 44th
Finance, insurance & real estate: 36,384—4.80%, 33rd

Government: 141,746—18.70%, 10th
Manufacturing: 117,490—15.50%, 29th
Mining: 9,473—1.3%, 13th
Service: 145,536—19.20%, 29th
Trade: 147,052—19.40%, 17th
Transportation, communication, & public utilities: 48,512—6.40%, 9th
Wholesale/retail: 164,203—22.3%, 8th
Unemployment rate: 4.29%, 44th
Male: 2.27%, 45th
Female: 1.89%, 44th
Total businesses (1991): 58,156
New business incorp's. (1991): 4,973
Percent of total businesses: 8.55%, 11th
Business failures (1991): 513
Percent of total businesses: 0.88%, 24th
Agriculture farm income
Marketing (1991): $730,882,000, 38th
Net per operation: $14,365, 36th
Net per acre: $17, 43rd
Leading products: cattle, dairy products, hay, turkeys
Av. value land & build. per acre: $404, 40th
Percent increase (1980-90): -23.77%, 43rd
Govt. payments: $33,197,000, 36th
Construction, value of all: $1,271,000,000
Per capita: $737.73, 15th
Percent change 1989-90: 25.59%, 4th
Manufactures:
Value added: $6,111,000,000
Per capita: $3,547.03, 38th
Value of shipments: $13,950,000,000
Per capita: $8,097.05, 38th
Leading products: guided missiles and parts, electronic components, food products, fabricated metals, steel, electrical equipment
Mining, min. prod., value (1987): $1,952,000,000, 17th
Leading products: petroleum, coal, copper
Retail sales: $10,581,000,000, 36th
Per household: $19,501, 21st
Percent increase (1987-90): 20.1%, 14th
Service indust., value (1987): $5,521,000,000, 39th
Per capita: $3,204.57, 39th
Tourism indus., value (1989): $2,117,000,000, 35th
Foreign exports value: $1,596,000,000, 34th
Per capita: $926.37, 22nd
Patents per 1,000 pop.: 4.7, 35th

Travel and Transportation

Motor vehicle registrations: 1,205,517
Per 1,000 pop.: 699, 42nd
Motorcycle registrations: 28,172
Per 1,000 pop.: 16, 28th
Licensed drivers per 1,000 driving age pop.: 916, 16th
Deaths from motor vehicle accidents per 100,000 pop.: 15.8, 37th
Public roads & streets
Total mileage: 43,244, 37th
Rural mileage: 37,669, 36th
Urban mileage: 5,575, 34th
Interstate mileage: 938, 19th
Annual vehicle-miles of travel per person: 8,501, 36th
Mean travel time for workers 16 + who work away from home: 18.9 min., 40th

Government

Registered voters (1988): 806,934
Percent of voting age pop.: 74.85%, 18th
Voter turnout (1988): 647,008
Percent of registered voters: 80.18%, 3rd
Percent of voting age pop.: 60.02%, 7th
State legislators, total (1992): 104, 41st
Women members (1992): 12
Percent of legislature: 11.5%, 42nd
Dominant party (1992): Republicans
U. S. Congress, House members (1993): 3
Increase 1983-93: 0
Revenues:
State govt.: $4,302,275,000
Per capita: $2,497.18, 24th
State & local govt.: $6,950,036,000
Per capita: $4,034.03, 24th
Indebtedness:
State govt.: $1,790,494,000
Per capita: $1,039.26, 28th
State & local govt.: $10,010,000,000
Per capita: $5,810.14, 4th

Laws and Regulations

Legal driving age: 16
Marriage age without parental consent: 18 county

to provide premarital counseling if under 19 or divorced

Divorce residence requirement: 3 mo.

ATTRACTIONS

Major opera companies (1989): 1, 30th
Per 1 million pop.: 0.59, 31st

Major symphony orchestras (1989): 6, 39th
Per 1 million pop.: 3.51, 29th

State appropriations for state arts agencies per capita: $1.67, 8th

State Fair in Sept. at Salt Lake City

SPORTS AND COMPETITION

NCAA sports teams, 5: Brigham Young Univ., Southern Utah State Thunderbirds, Univ. of Utah, Utah State Univ. Aggies, Weber State College Wildcats

Professional teams, 4: Baseball, 1—Salt Lake Trappers (Pioneer League, Rookie Class), Derks Field

Basketball, 1—Utah Jazz (NBA), The Salt Palace

Hockey, 1—Salt Lake Golden Eagles (International Hockey League), The Salt Palace

Soccer, 1—Salt Lake Sting (American Professional Soccer League), Derks Field

VERMONT

"Up where the north wind blows just a little keener,
Up where the grasses grow just a little greener,
Up where the mountain peaks rise a little higher
Up where the human kind draws just a little nigher,
That's where Vermont comes in.."

Charles Hial Darling

Vermont is particularly known for the independent nature of its people. They were so opposed to slavery that the Georgia legislature once voted humorously that "...the whole state should be made into an island and towed out to sea." Vermonters are so "politically correct" that their legislature declared war on Germany before the United States did. It is the most sparsely populated state east of the Mississippi River. Every year, the spectacular Green Mountains attract thousands of skiers and other tourists. Farming is more important in Vermont than it is in the other New England states. Three-fifths of the state is covered by forests, and lumbering and wood processing are major industries, as are the quarrying of granite, marble, and slate. Only about 34% of its people reside in cities and towns.

Superlatives

- Claims only breed of horse produced in the United States.
- Leader in marble production.
- World granite center.
- Leader in asbestos production.
- First in maple syrup production.
- First U.S. patent issued.

Moments in History

- On July 4, 1609, during the first known European visit to present-day Vermont, French explorer Samuel de Champlain discovered the lake he named Champlain for himself.
- In 1666 French Capt. de La Motte built a fortress on present-day La Motte Island in Lake Champlain.
- To counter the French, in 1690 the English built a fort at Chimney Point.
- The outpost of Fort Dummer, begun in 1724, was the first permanent settlement in present-day Vermont.
- The 1741 proclamation of King George II of England appeared to include present-day Vermont in New Hampshire, but the boundaries were long disputed.
- In 1764, King George III set the boundary at the Connecticut River, leaving present-day Vermont in New York territory.
- Those owners of New Hampshire grants contested the New York claims, and were supported by Ethan Allen and his Green Mountain Boys. They withstood a New York attack in 1771.
- On May 10, 1775, Allen and Benedict Arnold captured Fort Ticonderoga in one of the early actions of New World revolution.

So They Say

Ethan Allen demanded the surrender of Fort Ticonderoga " '...in the name of the Great Jehovah and the Continental Congress' in spite of the fact that he held a commission from neither source."

Anonymous

• After British Gen. John Burgoyne recaptured Fort Ticonderoga on July 6, 1777, he pursued American Gen. Arthur St. Clair, and the next day the Americans defeated Burgoyne in the Battle of Hubbardton, the only battle of the Revolution fought on Vermont soil.

• The Battle of Bennington, Sept. 1777, was fought just across the New York border, but was led by Gen. John Stark and Seth Warner of Vermont; Vermont men played the most important role in this struggle.

So They Say

"There are the Red Coats and they are ours, or this night Molly Stark sleeps a widow!"

John Stark

• Indian attacks terrorized the countryside during the Revolution; the worst witnessed plundering, burning, and taking of prisoners from Tunbridge to Royalton during Oct., 1780.

• Vermont operated as an independent republic from 1777 to 1791, but this was not recognized by the Continental Congress or New York State.

• Various difficulties were settled and on March 4, 1791, Vermont became the first state added to the Union following the original 13.

• During the war of 1812, the Battle of Plattsburgh, Sept. 1814, brought U.S. control to Lake Champlain and thwarted the British invasion of Vermont.

• The state legislature was converted to the two-house system in 1836.

• Vermonters were always opposed to slavery, and Senator Jacob Collamer of Woodstock introduced Lincoln's first war powers act in 1861.

• During the Civil War, Vermont forces played a key role in the Battle of Gettysburg (July 1-3, 1863).

• Vermont's Chester A. Arthur became president in 1881.

• Montpelier native Admiral George Dewey emerged the hero of the Spanish-American War of 1898.

• Admiral Henry T. Mayo of Burlington was the principal commander of the U.S. Atlantic fleet during World War I, the fourth leading "sea dog" from inland Vermont.

• On the death of President Warren G. Harding, in the flicker of kerosene lamps at Plymouth, Calvin Coolidge took the oath of office as U.S. president, administered by his justice-of-the-peace father, Aug. 3, 1923.

So They Say

"Never before or since has a president taken the oath of office from his own father, in his own home, and under such unique surroundings. It holds an appeal, in its uniqueness and moving simplicity, to all Americans."

Vermont Board of Historic Sites

• In 1941 the good people of Vermont got so enraged at the Nazis that they declared war on Germany two months before the United States did. Of the 49,942 Vermonters who saw service in that war, 1,233 lost their lives.

• In 1985 Democrat Madelleine M. Kunin became the first woman governor of Vermont.

THAT'S INTERESTING

• In the late 1700s, school teacher Justin Morgan developed the Morgan horse, the only breed originating in the United States.

• The Indians were so devoted to the chapel they had built at Swanton that when the French were driven out the faithful Indians went with them and took the chapel apart, rebuilding it stone by stone at their new home in Canada.

• In the dispute between Vermont and New York, the Green Mountain Boys tore the roof from the home of New York supporter Benjamin Spencer. After he took an oath to support Vermont, the "boys" restored his roof.

• Although ridiculed as a do-nothing president, Calvin Coolidge had the support of many Vermonters who agreed that government should interfere as little as possible in the affairs of the people.

• James Johns of Huntington printed by hand every copy of every issue of the newspaper he published for 40 years.

• At the Haskell opera house at Derby Line the audience sits in the United States and the stage is in Canada. According to one account, a U.S. police officer had to sit in the audience and watch a wanted criminal performing on the stage.

Notable Natives

Chester Alan Arthur (Fairfield, 1829-1886), U.S. president. **Calvin Coolidge** (Plymouth, 1872-1933), U.S. president. **John Deere** (Rutland, 1804-1886), inventor/industrialist. **George Dewey** (Montpelier, 1837-1917), naval officer. **Stephen Arnold Douglas** (Brandon, 1813-1861), public official/political leader. **James fisk** (Bennington, 1834-1872), financier. **Brigham Young** (Whitingham, 1801-1877), religious leader.

General

Admitted to statehood: March 4, 1791
Origin of name: from French words *vert*("green") and *mont*("mountain"); the Green Mountains were said to have been named by Samuel de Champlain, and when the state was formed, 1777, Dr. Thomas Young suggested combining *vert* and *mont* into Vermont
Capital: Montpelier
Nickname: The Green Mountain State
Motto: "Freedom and Unity"
Animal: Morgan horse
Bird: hermit thrush
Cold-water fish: brook trout
Warm-water fish: walleye pike
Flower: red clover
Insect: honeybee
Song: "Hail, Vermont"
Tree: sugar maple

The Land

Area: 9,615 sq. mi., 45th
Land: 9,249 sq. mi., 43rd
Water: 366 sq. mi., 47th
Topography: Green Mtns. N-S backbone 20-36 mi. wide; avg. altitude 1,000 ft.
Number of counties: 14
Geographic center: Washington, 3 mi. E of Roxbury
Length: 160 mi.
Width: 80 mi.
Highest point: 4,393 ft. (Mt. Mansfield), 26th
Lowest point: 95 ft. (Lake Champlain), 28th
Mean elevation: 1,000 ft., 27th

Climate and Environment

Temp., highest: 105 deg. on July 4, 1911, at Vermon; lowest: -50 deg. on Dec. 30, 1933, at Bloomfield
Fresh water withdrawn, per capita, per day: 235 gal., 49th
Endangered species: mammals, 1—Indiana bat; birds, 1—American peregrine falcon; reptiles, none; amphibians, none; fishes, none; invertebrates, 1; plants, 3

Major Cities, Population Percentage Increase (1980-90)

Bennington, 16,451—4.02%
Burlington, 39,127—3.75%
Colchester, 14,731—16.64%
Essex, 16,498—14.63%
Rutland, 18,230— –1.12%

The People

Population: 562,758, 49th
Percent change (1980-90): 9.12%, 19th
Per sq. mi: 58.53, 31st
Percent in metro. area: 23.28%, 50th
Percent foreign born: 3.1%, 25th
White: 555,088—98.64%, 1st
Black: 1,951—0.35%, 49th
Native American: 1,696—0.30%, 33rd
Asian, Pacific Isle: 3,215—0.57%, 42nd
Other races: 808—0.14%, 47th
Hispanic origin: 3,661—0.65%, 46th
Percent over 5 yrs. speaking language other than English at home: 5.8%, 31st
Percent males: 48.95%, 21st
Percent females: 51.05%, 31st
Percent never married: 27.6%, 12th
Marriages per 1,000 (1989): 10.6, 12th
Divorces per 1,000 (1989): 4.4, 29th
Median age: 33
Under 5 years: 41,261—7.33%, 28th
Under 18 years: 143,083—25.43%, 32nd
65 years & older: 66,163—11.76%, 36th
Percent increase among the elderly: 13.7%, 38th

Of Vital Importance

Live births per 1,000 pop.: 14.0, 47th
Infant mortality rate per 1,000 births (1988): 6.8, 51st
Average lifetime (1979-81): 74.79, 16th
Deaths per 100,000 pop. (1988): 837.7, 34th
Causes of death per 100,000 pop. (1988):
 Diseases of heart: 289.4, 32nd
 Malignant neoplasms: 183.3, 38th
 Cerebrovascular diseases: 56.9, 34th
 Accidents & adverse effects: 41.8, 23rd
 Chronic obstructive pulmonary diseases: 42.2, 8th
 Suicide: 16.2, 10th
 HIV infection: 1.1, 44th
 Other: 72.4, 33rd

Keeping Well

Non-federal physicians per 100,000 pop.: 290, 6th
Dentists per 100,000 (1990-91): 71, 19th
Nurses per 100,000 (1989): 919, 4th
Hospitals per 100,000: 3.2, 22nd
 Admissions per 100,000: 11,154, 46th
 Beds per 100,000: 403.37, 42nd
 Occupancy rate: 69.7%, 14th
 Semiprivate room charges per day: $378, 5th
 Average stay: 7.3, 21st
Notifiable diseases per 100,000:
 AIDS: 3.9, 43rd
 Gonorrhea: 9.8, 51st
 Measles: 0.2, 47th
 Syphillis: 0.4, 51st
 Tuberculosis (TB): 2.3, 44th
Per capita spending on mental health programs (1987): $51.61, 13th
Pop. without health insur. (1991): 12.7%, 27th

Households by Type

Total households: 210,650
 Percent change (1980-90): 18.34%, 19th
Family households: 144,895
 Percent of total: 68.78%, 39th
Nonfamily households: 65,755
 Percent of total: 31.22%, 13th
Persons per household: 2.57, 31st
Pop. living in group quarters: 21,642
 Percent of pop.: 3.85%, 2nd

Living Quarters

Total housing units: 271,241
 Persons per unit: 2.07, 51st
Occupied housing units: 210,650
 Percent of total units: 77.66%, 51st
 Persons per unit: 2.48, 38th
 Percent of units with over 1 person per room: 1.71%, 49th
Owner-occupied units: 145,368
 Percent of total units: 53.59%, 43rd
 Percent of occupied units: 69.01%, 15th
 Persons per unit: 2.73, 26th
 Median value: $95,500, 13th
Renter-occupied units: 65,282
 Percent of total units: 24.07%, 49th
 Percent of occupied units: 30.99%, 37th
 Persons per unit: 2.22, 46th
 Median contract rent: $374, 17th
 Rental vacancy rate: 7.5%, 35th
Mobile home, trailer & other as a % of occupied housing units: 13.57%, 19th

Crime Index per 100,000

Total: 4,341, 39th
 Violent: 127, 50th
  Murder and nonnegligent manslaughter: 2, 47th
  Aggravated assault: 7,332, 29th
  Robbery: 12, 50th
  Rape: 26, 43rd
 Property: 4,214, 35th
  Burglary: 1,087, 28th
  Larceny, theft: 2,918, 31st
  Motor vehicle theft: 208, 41st
Drug abuse arrests: 86, 49th

Teaching and Learning

Literacy (1987): 90%, 14th
Pop. 3 and over enrolled in school: 145,988
 Percent of pop.: 27.1%, 26th
Public elementary & secondary schools:
 Total enrollment: 95,000
 Avg. class size (1987): 19, 48th

Teachers: 7,000
Percent of pop.: 1.24%, 2nd
Teachers' avg. salary: $28,800, 26th
Spending per capita: $921, 10th
Spending per pupil in avg. daily attendance: $5,418, 13th
Percent of graduates taking SAT: 68%, 7th
Combined SAT scores: 890, 38th
Percent of pop. over 25 completing:
High school: 80.8%, 12th
College degree/s: 24.3%, 9th
Higher educa., institutions: 22
Per 100,000 pop.: 1.1, 13th
Enroll: 36,398
Percent of pop.: 6.47%, 10th
Public: 20,910
Percent of enroll.: 57.45%, 46th
Private: 15,488
Percent of enroll.: 42.55%, 6th
White non-Hispanic: 122,964
Percent of enroll.: 77.19%, 38th
Black non-Hispanic: 31,177
Percent of enroll.: 19.57%, 4th
Hispanic: 911
Percent of enroll.: 0.57%, 43rd
Asian/Pacific Islander: 1,494
Percent of enroll.: 0.94%, 41st
Amer. Indian/AK native: 334
Percent of enroll.: 0.21%, 48th
Nonresident alien: 2,422
Percent of enroll.: 1.52%, 46th
Female: 20,667
Percent of enroll.: 56.78%, 5th
Tuition, state university ('90-'91): $4,092, 1st
Public library systems: 205
Books & serial vol. per capita: 4.14, 4th
Govt. expend. per capita: $12.06, 37th
State govt.: $4.69, 10th
Local govts.: $7.37, 40th

Law Enforcement, Courts, and Prisons

Police protection expend.: $47,678,000
Per capita: $84.69, 38th
Judicial & legal expend.: $24,768,000
Per capita: $43.99, 31st
Corrections expend.: $26,880,000
Per capita: $47.74, 44th
Police per 10,000 pop. (1990-91): 14.9, 48th
Prisoners (state & fed.) sentenced to over 1 yr., per 100,000 pop.: 117
Percent change (1989-90): 8.79%, 16th
Death penalty: no

Religion, Number and Percent of Population

Agnostic: 5,036—1.20%, 2nd
Buddhist: NA
Christian: 350,848—83.60%, 39th
Hindu: NA
Jewish: 4,616—1.10%, 15th
Moslem: NA
Unitarian: 4,616—1.10%, 1st
Other: 3,777—0.90%, 35th
None: 47,843—11.40%, 8th
Refused to answer: 2,938—0.70%, 48th

Making a Living

Personal income per capita (1989): $13,527, 23rd
Percent increase (1979-89) (constant 1989 dollars): 30.7%, 7th
Average income per family: $40,520, 25th
Percent of pop. below poverty level: 9.9%, 42nd
Percent 65 and over: 12.4%, 21st
Cost of living, selected cities
1st qtr., 1991 (U.S. Standard=100)
Montpelier (1st qtr., 1989) 127.6

Economy

Civilian labor force: 309,000
Percent of tot. pop.: 54.91%, 3rd
Percent 65 and over: 2.59%, 31st
Percent females: 46.28%, 17th
Percent job growth (1980-90): 30.60%, 13th
Major employer industries:
Agriculture: 8,526—2.90%, 23rd
Construction: 16,758—5.70%, 8th
Finance, insurance & real estate: 12,348—4.20%, 45th
Government: 37,632—12.80%, 42nd
Manufacturing: 44,688—15.20%, 30th
Mining: 790—0.3%, 32nd

Service: 66,444—22.60%, 11th
Trade: 52,626—17.90%, 36th
Transportation, communication, & public utilities: 10,878—3.70%, 51st
Wholesale/retail: 62,185—22.0%, 14th
Unemployment rate: 4.85%, 38th
Male: 2.91%, 29th
Female: 1.94%, 42nd
Total businesses (1991): 26,339
New business incorp's. (1991): 1,486
Percent of total businesses: 5.64%, 28th
Business failures (1991): 187
Percent of total businesses: 0.71%, 36th
Agriculture farm income
Marketing (1991): $433,140,000, 45th
Net per operation: $13,229, 42nd
Net per acre: $60, 25th
Leading products: dairy products, cattle, greenhouse, hay
Av. value land & build. per acre: $1,203, 16th
Percent increase (1980-90): 66.85%, 6th
Govt. payments: $3,339,000, 43rd
Construction, value of all: $352,000,000
Per capita: $625.49, 19th
Percent change 1989-90: -28.60%, 41st
Manufactures:
Value added: $3,233,000,000
Per capita: $5,744.92, 17th
Value of shipments: $5,592,000,000
Per capita: $9,936.78, 29th
Leading products: machine tools, furniture, scales, books, computer components, fishing rods
Mining, min. prod., value (1987): $90,000,000, 45th
Leading products: stone, asbestos, sand/gravel
Retail sales: $4,512,000,000, 48th
Per household: $21,223, 10th
Percent increase (1987-90): 4.8%, 50th
Service indust., value (1987): $2,178,000,000, 48th
Per capita: $3,870.22, 27th
Tourism indus., value (1989): $889,000,000, 47th
Foreign exports value: $1,154,000,000, 37th
Per capita: $2,050.62, 4th
Patents per 1,000 pop.: 3.9, 43rd

TRAVEL AND TRANSPORTATION

Motor vehicle registrations: 461,796
Per 1,000 pop.: 820, 19th
Motorcycle registrations: 17,590
Per 1,000 pop.: 31, 9th
Licensed drivers per 1,000 driving age pop.: 941, 10th
Deaths from motor vehicle accidents per 100,000 pop.: 15.6, 39th
Public roads & streets
Total mileage: 14,121, 46th
Rural mileage: 12,941, 43rd
Urban mileage: 1,180, 50th
Interstate mileage: 320, 46th
Annual vehicle-miles of travel per person: 10,373, 7th
Mean travel time for workers 16 + who work away from home: 18.0 min., 42nd

GOVERNMENT

Registered voters (1988): 348,312
Percent of voting age pop.: 84.54%, 8th
Voter turnout (1988): 243,328
Percent of registered voters: 69.86%, 30th
Percent of voting age pop.: 59.06%, 9th
State legislators, total (1992): 180, 12th
Women members (1992): 56
Percent of legislature: 31.1%, 4th
Dominant party (1992): Split
U.S. Congress, House members (1993): 1
Increase 1983-93: 0
Revenues:
State govt.: $1,592,229,000
Per capita: $2,829.33, 15th
State & local govt.: $2,279,782,000
Per capita: $4,051.09, 23rd
Indebtedness:
State govt.: $1,258,945,000
Per capita: $2,237.10, 13th
State & local govt.: $1,686,000,000
Per capita: $2,995.96, 31st

LAWS AND REGULATIONS

Legal driving age: 18
Marriage age without parental consent: 18
Divorce residence requirement: 6 mo., qualification—check local statutes

Attractions

Major opera companies (1989): 0, NA
Per 1 million pop.: 0.00, NA
Major symphony orchestras (1989): 4, 42nd
Per 1 million pop.: 7.05, 5th
State appropriations for state arts agencies per capita: $0.90, 22nd
State Fair in early Sept. at Rutland

Sports and Competition

NCAA sports teams, 4: Middlebury College Panthers, Norwich Univ. Cadets, St. Michael's College Purple Knights, Univ. of Vermont Catamounts
Professional teams, none

VIRGINIA

"Of all the states, but three will live in story,
Old Massachusetts with her Plymouth Rock,
And old Virginia with her noble stock,
And sunny Kansas with her woes and glory."

Eugene Fitch Ware

Before the Europeans arrived, Virginia was the realm of a great Indian emperor, Powhatan. During its epic years Virginia became both the "Mother of Presidents" (eight), and "Mother of the Frontier." Having given up claims to Illinois, Indiana, Ohio, Michigan, Wisconsin, and parts of Minnesota, it also is known as "Mother of the States." The state was in the forefront of the Revolutionary War, which ended when Lord Cornwallis surrendered to Washington in Yorktown. In the Civil War, more battles were fought on Virginia soil than in any other state. Virginia is a land of stately mansions, battlefields, old churches, and colonial homes.

SUPERLATIVES

• Most native presidents—eight.

• First manufacturing in the United States—in a glass factory, 1608.

• First iron furnace, 1619.

• Reaper invented, 1831.

• Leads in synthetic fiber production.

• Pioneer in tobacco farming.

• Country's first canal—built in 1790, it ran the 7 mi. between Richmond and Westham.

• Oldest daily newspaper—the Alexandria *Gazette.*

MOMENTS IN HISTORY

• Early explorers must have passed the shores of Virginia. By the 1580s the Spanish Jesuit missionaries had a mission on Aquia Creek in the Potomac region, but they were massacred by the Indians.

• On May 14, 1607, three English ships anchored in the James River and next day James Town (Jamestown) was begun, the first permanent English American settlement.

> **So They Say**
>
> The ships "...moored to the trees in 6 fathoms of water...." The Indians came "...creeping upon all foures from the Hills, like Beares with their Bowes in their mouthes." Next morning, May 15, 1607, the pioneers "...set to work about the fortifications."
>
> John Smith

• John Smith, leader of the settlement, made peace with powerful Chief Powhatan, probably with the somewhat legendary help of the chief's daughter, Pocahontas. Smith returned to England in Oct. 1609, to care for an injury.

• The 65 survivors of the "starving time" of 1609-1610 were rescued by Lord De la Warr with supplies and new settlers.

• In 1619 the colonists organized a House of Burgesses, claimed as the first democratically elected legislative body in the New World.

• After the death of Powhatan in 1618, Indian troubles began and continued until 1646 when King Opechancanough was shot.

• Nathaniel Bacon rallied the people against the government of Sir William Berkeley with "America's first declaration of independence," but he died soon after, and Berkeley hanged 20 of Bacon's followers.

• The frontiers pushed westward, and Augusta County was organized in 1738, claiming lands to the Mississippi.

• As discontent over the taxes and other acts of the government grew, Patrick Henry entered the House of Burgesses in 1765 and became a leader in opposing the government.

So They Say

"Gentlemen may cry 'Peace! Peace!' but there is no peace. The war is actually begun!....Is life so dear or peace so sweet as to be purchased at the price of chains and slavery? Forbid it. Almighty God! I know not what course others may take...but, as for me, give me liberty, or give me death!"

Patrick Henry

• On May 6, 1776, the fifth Virginia Convention declared that the colony was free and independent.

• Sponsored by Virginia, the work of George Rogers Clark in 1778 kept the western area in the hands of the colonies.

• American armies laid siege to Yorktown, and General Lord Cornwallis surrendered on Oct. 18, 1781.

• After the failure of the Articles of Confederation, Virginian George Washington presided at the convention that finally created a new government, and Virginia became the 10th state on June 25, 1788.

• On April 30, 1789, Washington became the first of the long succession of Virginians who were to hold the office of president.

• As early as 1778, Virginia had made the slave trade a criminal offense, but most Virginians supported slavery, and Virginia became the capital of the Confederacy on May 29, 1861.

• Many important battles of the Civil War were fought in Virginia until, on April 9, 1865, Gen. Robert E. Lee surrendered his exhausted forces at Appomatox Courthouse.

• On Jan. 26, 1870, Virginia once more became a sovereign state.

• The great financial and human losses of the Civil War caused many hardships, but by the 1890s prosperity was returning.

• World War I found Virginia a center of shipping, troop embarkation, ship building, and war training. Of 91,623 Virginians in service, 1,635 lost their lives.

• During the administration of Gov. Harry Flood Byrd, in 1927 the government was simplified and improved, but segregation became a law.

• World War II called 214,903 Virginians to service, and Newport News Shipyard built 185 ships for war purposes.

• Virginia's third constitution was approved in 1970, and the state elected its first Republican governor since 1886.

That's Interesting

• Virginia might be considered a midwestern state as well as eastern because it extends as far west as Detroit.

• George Washington was said to be as proud of his estate as of his public service. One of his many prizes was awarded for the largest jackass.

• The old apothecary shop in Alexandria, where Martha Washington bought castor oil in quarts, is still standing. One jokester said she probably used it to make her candy.

• As Lord Cornwallis surrendered at Yorktown, the band played "The World Turned Upside Down."

• The annual jousting tournament near Staunton is said to be the nation's oldest continuously operating sporting event.

Notable Natives

Richard Evelyn Bird (Winchester, 1888-1957), naval officer/explorer. **Willa Cather** (Winchester, 1873-1947), novelist. **William Clark** (Caroline Cty., 1770-1838), soldier/explorer. **William Henry Harrison** (Berkeley, Charles Cty., 1773-1841), U.S. president. **Thomas Jefferson** (Goochland, now Albemarle Cty., 1743-1826), U.S. president. **Joseph Eggleston Johnston** (Farmville, 1807-1891), soldier. **Henry "Light-Horse Harry" Lee** (Prince William Cty., 1756-1818) soldier/public official. **Robert Edward Lee** (Westmoreland Cty., 1807-1870), soldier. **Meriwether Lewis** (Albemarle Cty., 1774-1809), soldier/explorer/public official. **Charles Lynch** (Lynchburg, 1736-1779), planter/patriot. **James Madison** (Port Conway, 1751-1836), U.S. president. **John Marshall** (Fauquier Cty., 1755-1835), U.S. chief justice. **Cyrus Hall McCormick** (Rockbridge Cty., 1809-1884) inventor/industrialist. **James Monroe** (Westmoreland Cty., 1758-1831), U.S. president. **Pocahontas** (probably near Jamestown, 1595?-1617), Indian princess. **Peyton Randolph** (Williamsburg?, 1721?-1775), politician. **William Styron** (Newport News, 1925-1993), novelist. **Zachary Taylor** (Orange Cty., 1784-1850), U.S. president. **John Tyler** (Charles City Cty., 1790-1862), U.S. president. **Booker Taliafero Washington** (Franklin Cty., 1856-1915), educator. **George Washington** (Westmoreland Cty., 1732-1799), military leader/U.S. president. **Thomas Woodrow Wilson** (Staunton, 1856-1924), U.S. president.

General

Admitted to statehood: June 25, 1788
Origin of name: named by Sir Walter Raleigh, who fitted out the expedition of 1584, in honor of Queen Elizabeth, the Virgin Queen of England
Capital: Richmond
Nickname: The Old Dominion—Mother of Presidents
Motto: *"Sic Semper Tyrannis"* ("Thus Always to Tyrants")
Animal/Dog: fox hound
Bird: cardinal
Flower: dogwood flower
Shell: oyster shell
Song: "Carry Me Back to Old Virginny"
Tree: dogwood

The Land

Area: 42,769 sq. mi., 35th
Land: 39,598 sq. mi., 37th
Water: 3,171 sq. mi., 15th
Topography: mountain and valley region in the W, including the Blue Ridge Mtns., rolling Piedmont plateau; tidewater, or coastal plain, including the eastern shore
Number of counties: 95
Geographic center: Buckingham, 5 mi. SW of Buckingham
Length: 430 mi.
Width: 200 mi.
Highest point: 5,729 ft. (Mt. Rogers), 19th
Lowest point: sea level (Atlantic Ocean), 3rd
Mean elevation: 950 ft., 28th
Coastline: 112 mi., 15th
Shoreline: 3,315 mi., 8th

Climate and Environment

Temp., highest: 110 deg. on July 15, 1954, at Balcony Falls; lowest: -30 deg. on Jan. 22, 1985, at Mtn. Lake Bio. Station
Fresh water withdrawn, per capita, per day: 853 gal., 37th
Endangered species: mammals, 5—gray bat, Indiana bat, Virginia big-eared bat, Delmarva peninsula fox squirrel, Virginia northern flying squirrel; birds, 2—American peregrine falcon, red-cockaded woodpecker; reptiles, 3; amphibians, 1; fishes, 1; invertebrates, 17; plants, 4

Major Cities, Population Percentage Increase (1980-90)

Arlington, 170,936—12.02%
Newport News, 170,045—17.35%
Norfolk, 202,798— –2.15%
Richmond, 203,056— –7.37%
Virginia Beach, 393,069—49.91%

The People

Population: 6,187,358, 12th
Percent change (1980-90): 13.59%, 12th
Per sq. mi: 144.67, 15th
Percent in metro. area: 72.45%, 21st
Percent foreign born: 5.0%, 17th
White: 4,791,739—77.44%, 37th
Black: 1,162,994—18.80%, 9th
Native American: 15,282—0.25%, 37th
Asian, Pacific Isle: 159,053—2.57%, 9th
Other races: 58,290—0.94%, 27th

Hispanic origin: 160,288—2.59%, 25th
Percent over 5 yrs. speaking language other than English at home: 7.3%, 24th
Percent males: 49.04%, 17th
Percent females: 50.96%, 35th
Percent never married: 27.1%, 18th
Marriages per 1,000 (1989): 11.3, 8th
Divorces per 1,000 (1989): 4.2, 33rd
Median age: 32.6
Under 5 years: 443,155—7.16%, 34th
Under 18 years: 1,504,738—24.32%, 41st
65 years & older: 664,670—10.74%, 43rd
Percent increase among the elderly: 31.5%, 13th

Of Vital Importance

Live births per 1,000 pop.: 15.6, 29th
Infant mortality rate per 1,000 births (1988): 10.4, 20th
Average lifetime (1979-81): 73.43, 35th
Deaths per 100,000 pop. (1988): 791.5, 41st
Causes of death per 100,000 pop. (1988):
- Diseases of heart: 268.6, 37th
- Malignant neoplasms: 184.5, 37th
- Cerebrovascular diseases: 58.5, 31st
- Accidents & adverse effects: 37.1, 36th
- Chronic obstructive pulmonary diseases: 27.3, 45th
- Suicide: 12.6, 24th
- HIV infection: 4.3, 16th
- Other: 65.5, 44th

Keeping Well

Non-federal physicians per 100,000 pop.: 223, 20th
Dentists per 100,000 (1990-91): 59, 30th
Nurses per 100,000 (1989): 565, 37th
Hospitals per 100,000: 2.2, 42nd
- Admissions per 100,000: 12,900, 33rd
- Beds per 100,000: 473.51, 29th
- Occupancy rate: 42.3%, 51st
- Semiprivate room charges per day: $220, 40th
- Average stay: 7.0, 31st

Notifiable diseases per 100,000:
- AIDS: 11.9, 16th
- Gonorrhea: 285.2, 18th
- Measles: 1.4, 37th
- Syphillis: 34.5, 21st
- Tuberculosis (TB): 6.6, 26th

Per capita spending on mental health programs (1987): $39.44, 22nd
Pop. without health insur. (1991): 16.3%, 13th

Households by Type

Total households: 2,291,830
- Percent change (1980-90): 23.02%, 10th

Family households: 1,629,490
- Percent of total: 71.10%, 21st

Nonfamily households: 662,340
- Percent of total: 28.90%, 31st

Persons per household: 2.61, 21st
Pop. living in group quarters: 209,300
- Percent of pop.: 3.38%, 11th

Living Quarters

Total housing units: 2,496,334
- Persons per unit: 2.48, 11th

Occupied housing units: 2,291,830
- Percent of total units: 91.81%, 11th
- Persons per unit: 2.57, 17th
- Percent of units with over 1 person per room: 2.84%, 29th

Owner-occupied units: 1,519,521
- Percent of total units: 60.87%, 19th
- Percent of occupied units: 66.30%, 31st
- Persons per unit: 2.70, 33rd
- Median value: $91,000, 16th

Renter-occupied units: 772,309
- Percent of total units: 30.94%, 18th
- Percent of occupied units: 33.70%, 22nd
- Persons per unit: 2.43, 15th
- Median contract rent: $411, 14th
- Rental vacancy rate: 8.1%, 28th

Mobile home, trailer & other as a % of occupied housing units: 7.95%, 33rd

Crime Index per 100,000

Total: 4,441, 37th
- Violent: 351, 35th
  - Murder and nonnegligent manslaughter: 9, 19th
  - Aggravated assault: 7,162, 34th
  - Robbery: 123, 26th
  - Rape: 31, 35th
- Property: 4,090, 39th
  - Burglary: 731, 44th

Larceny, theft: 3,031, 25th
Motor vehicle theft: 327, 35th
Drug abuse arrests: 285, 19th

Teaching and Learning

Literacy (1987): 87%, 31st
Pop. 3 and over enrolled in school: 1,546,257
Percent of pop.: 26.1%, 38th
Public elementary & secondary schools:
Total enrollment: 1,026,000
Avg. class size (1987): 22, 28th
Teachers: 62,600
Percent of pop.: 1.01%, 26th
Teachers' avg. salary: $30,900, 18th
Spending per capita: $852, 18th
Spending per pupil in avg. daily attendance: $5,000, 20th
Percent of graduates taking SAT: 60%, 14th
Combined SAT scores: 890, 38th
Percent of pop. over 25 completing:
High school: 75.2%, 32nd
College degree/s: 24.5%, 7th
Higher educa., institutions: 83
Per 100,000 pop.: 0.6, 28th
Enroll: 353,442
Percent of pop.: 5.71%, 22nd
Public: 291,286
Percent of enroll.: 82.41%, 25th
Private: 62,156
Percent of enroll : 17.59%, 27th
White non-Hispanic: 50,910
Percent of enroll.: 82.47%, 30th
Black non-Hispanic: 2,931
Percent of enroll.: 4.75%, 27th
Hispanic: 3,408
Percent of enroll.: 5.52%, 10th
Asian/Pacific Islander: 2,559
Percent of enroll.: 4.15%, 8th
Amer. Indian/AK native: 1,043
Percent of enroll.: 1.69%, 8th
Nonresident alien: 877
Percent of enroll.: 1.42%, 47th
Female: 195,348
Percent of enroll.: 55.27%, 20th
Tuition, state university ('90-'91): $2,691, 6th
Public library systems: 90
Books & serial vol. per capita: 2.33, 31st
Govt. expend. per capita: $21.06, 14th
State govt.: $3.41, 14th
Local govts.: $17.65, 14th

Law Enforcement, Courts, and Prisons

Police protection expend.: $721,552,000
Per capita: $116.62, 21st
Judicial & legal expend.: $284,546,000
Per capita: $45.99, 29th
Corrections expend.: $593,138,000
Per capita: $95.87, 17th
Police per 10,000 pop. (1990-91): 21.1, 23rd
Prisoners (state & fed.) sentenced to over 1 yr., per 100,000 pop.: 274
Percent change (1989-90): 5.23%, 34th
Death penalty: yes, by electrocution
Under sentence of death: 40, 18th
Executed (1989): 1

Religion, Number and Percent of Population

Agnostic: 28,096—0.60%, 19th
Buddhist: 18,731—0.40%, 5th
Christian: 4,092,610—87.40%, 23rd
Hindu: 4,683—0.10%, 10th
Jewish: 51,509—1.10%, 15th
Moslem: 9,365—0.20%, 13th
Unitarian: 9,365—0.20%, 23rd
Other: 79,605—1.70%, 14th
None: 299,688—6.40%, 28th
Refused to answer: 88,970—1.90%, 31st

Making a Living

Personal income per capita (1989): $15,713, 12th
Percent increase (1979-89) (constant 1989 dollars): 25.4%, 13th
Average income per family: $46,710, 13th
Percent of pop. below poverty level: 10.2%, 39th
Percent 65 and over: 14.1%, 18th
Cost of living, selected cities/areas
1st qtr., 1991 (U.S. Standard=100)

Lynchburg	95.7
Virginia Peninsula	101.5
Richmond	112.7

Economy

Civilian labor force : 3,196,000
Percent of tot. pop.: 51.65%, 20th

Percent 65 and over: 2.85%, 23rd
Percent females: 47.50%, 4th
Percent job growth (1980-90): 34.17%, 8th
Major employer industries:
Agriculture: 70,380—2.30%, 32nd
Construction: 174,420—5.70%, 8th
Finance, insurance & real estate: 174,420—5.70%, 20th
Government: 630,360—20.60%, 6th
Manufacturing: 425,340—13.90%, 36th
Mining: 18,072—0.6%, 21st
Service: 624,240—20.40%, 22nd
Trade: 541,620—17.70%, 42nd
Transportation, communication, & public utilities: 165,240—5.40%, 21st
Wholesale/retail: 588,926—19.4%, 46th
Unemployment rate: 4.29%, 45th
Male: 2.22%, 46th
Female: 2.03%, 40th
Total businesses (1991): 193,800
New business incorp's. (1991): 16,883
Percent of total businesses: 8.71%, 9th
Business failures (1991): 2,283
Percent of total businesses: 1.18%, 12th
Agriculture farm income
Marketing (1991): $2,095,371,000, 29th
Net per operation: $10,913, 44th
Net per acre: $56, 27th
Leading products: cattle, broilers, dairy products, tobacco
Av. value land & build. per acre: $1,597, 11th
Percent increase (1980-90): 55.35%, 8th
Govt. payments: $26,616,000, 37th
Construction, value of all: $4,979,000,000
Per capita: $804.71, 11th
Percent change 1989-90: -32.36%, 44th
Manufactures:
Value added: $32,511,000,000
Per capita: $5,254.42, 23rd
Value of shipments: $61,042,000,000
Per capita: $9,865.60, 30th
Leading products: textiles, transportation equipment, electric & electronic equipment, food processing, chemicals
Mining, min. prod., value (1987): $2,664,000,000, 13th
Leading products: coal, stone, cement
Retail sales: $47,472,000,000, 11th
Per household: $20,459, 12th
Percent increase (1987-90): 8.6%, 42nd
Service indust., value (1987): $28,476,000,000, 11th
Per capita: $4,602.29, 13th
Tourism indus., value (1989): $7,827,000,000, 9th
Foreign exports value: $9,333,000,000, 11th
Per capita: $1,508.40, 9th
Patents per 1,000 pop.: 7.5, 23rd

Travel and Transportation

Motor vehicle registrations: 4,938,062
Per 1,000 pop.: 798, 22nd
Motorcycle registrations: 61,884
Per 1,000 pop.: 10, 42nd
Licensed drivers per 1,000 driving age pop.: 905, 21st
Deaths from motor vehicle accidents per 100,000 pop.: 17.4, 28th
Public roads & streets
Total mileage: 67,700, 30th
Rural mileage: 52,449, 32nd
Urban mileage: 15,251, 17th
Interstate mileage: 1,076, 15th
Annual vehicle-miles of travel per person: 9,725, 13th
Mean travel time for workers 16 + who work away from home: 24.0 min., 7th

Government

Registered voters (1988): 2,878,718
Percent of voting age pop.: 63.35%, 42nd
Voter turnout (1988): 2,191,609
Percent of registered voters: 76.13%, 13th
Percent of voting age pop.: 48.23%, 34th
State legislators, total (1992): 140, 28th
Women members (1992): 17
Percent of legislature: 12.1%, 41st
Dominant party (1992): Democrats
U.S. Congress, House members (1993): 11
Increase 1983-93: +1
Revenues:
State govt.: $13,606,679,000
Per capita: $2,199.11, 36th
State & local govt.: $21,976,846,000
Per capita: $3,551.90, 38th

Indebtedness:
State govt.: $6,082,564,000
Per capita: $983.06, 33rd
State & local govt.: $15,802,000,000
Per capita: $2,553.92, 40th

Laws and Regulations

Legal driving age: 16
Marriage age without parental consent: 18
Divorce residence requirement: 6 mo., qualification—check local statutes
State appropriations for state arts agencies per capita: $0.85, 23rd
State Fair in late Sept.-early Oct. at Richmond

Sports and Competition

NCAA sports teams, 15: College of William & Mary Tribe, George Mason Univ. Patriots, James Madison Univ. Dukes, Liberty Univ. Flames, Old Dominion Univ. Monarchs, Radford Univ. Highlanders, St. Paul's College Tigers, U.S. Marine Corps Academy, Univ. of Richmond Spiders, Univ. of Virginia Wahoos & Cavaliers, Virginia Commonwealth Univ. Rams, Virginia Military Institute Keydets, Virginia Polytechnic Institute & State Univ. Gobblers & Hokies, Virginia State Univ. Trojans, Washington & Lee Univ. Generals
Professional teams, 12:
Baseball, 9—Pulaski Braves (Appalachian League), Calfee Park; Lynchburg Red Sox (Carolina League, Class A), City Stadium; Bristol Tigers (Appalachian League, Rookie Class), Devault Memorial Stadium; Martinsville Phillies (Appalachian League, Rookie Class), English ; Tidewater Tides (International League, Class AAA), Metropolitan Park; Prince William Cannons (Carolina League, Class A), Prince William County Stadium; Salem Buccaneers (Carolina League, Class A), Salem Municipal Field; Richmond Braves (International League, Class AAA), The Diamond; Peninsula Pilots (Carolina League, Class A), War Memorial Stadium
Hockey, 3—Roanoke Valley Rebels (East Coast Hockey League), Lancerlot Sports Complex; Richmond Renegades (East Coast Hockey League), Richmond Coliseum; Hampton Roads Admirals (East Coast Hockey League), Scope Plaza

WASHINGTON

"But, however inviting may be the soil, the remote distance and savage aspect of the boundless wilderness along the Pacific seem to defer the colonization of such a region to a period far beyond the present generation (1811); and yet, if we consider the rapid progress of civilization in other new and equally remote countries, we might still indulge the hope of seeing this, at no distant time, one of the most flourishing countries on the globe."

Alexander Ross

Smallest of the conterminous states west of Iowa, Washington is a state with a split personality—the rainy lands to the west and the desert land east of the Cascade Mts. which stretch for miles without a single tree—with both sides known for their production of major crops. Ships from all parts of the world dock in the ports of Washington, and fishing fleets catch salmon, halibut, and other fish in the Pacific Ocean. Washington is a lumbering state, as well as a leader in dairy farming and flower-bulb production, cattle raising, and wheat, fruit, and vegetable crops. Grand Coulee Dam, on the Columbia River, is the mightiest piece of masonry in the world.

Superlatives

- Provides 10% of all U.S. annual timber growth.
- Produces 30% of the nation's hydroelectric power.
- World leader in apple production.
- World's largest farm reclamation project.
- First in hops, rhubarb, edible peas, and sweet cherries.
- Leader in vegetable seed production.
- Unique temperate rain forest—Olympic Peninsula.

Moments in History

- Juan de Fuca may have sailed the Washington shores in 1592, but the first recorded visit was made by Juan Perez in 1774.
- Bruno Heceta and Juan de Bodega y Quadra in 1775 were the first Europeans known to have touched present-day Washington, and they claimed the land for the King of Spain.
- Captain George Vancouver discovered Puget Sound in 1792.
- Also in 1792, U.S. Captain Robert Gray made the long-sought discovery of the Columbia River, sailed into its treacherous mouth, and landed his ship the *Columbia* at present-day Fort Columbia on May 12.
- The great expedition of Lewis and Clark made the dangerous passage down the Snake and Columbia rivers and arrived at the coast in Nov. 1805.

> **So They Say**
>
> "Great joy in camp we are in view of the Ocean, this great Pacific Ocean which we been so long anxious to see, and the roreing or noise made by the waves...may be heard distinctly."
>
> Meriwether Lewis

- The explorers began their return journey on March 23, 1806, trading with the Indians and very considerately treating their ailments.
- David Thompson established the trading post of Spokane House in 1810.

So They Say

"...The Pierced nose Indians (Nez Perce) are stout likely men, handsom women, and verry dressey in their way, the dress of the men are a White Buffalow robe or Elk Skin dressed with Beeds...Sea Shells and the Mother of Pirl hung to their hair...The women dress in a shirt of Ibex or Goat Skins which reach quite down to their anckles."

Meriwether Lewis

• Several mergers extended the Hudson's Bay Company interests in the area, and they established Fort Vancouver in 1824. It became the first permanent European settlement in present-day Washington.

• By 1828, only four years after its founding, Fort Vancouver had become a civilization in the wilderness, under the direction of Dr. John McLoughlin, who was known throughout the West for his hospitality and kindness to those in difficulty. When no one would receive the immigrant party of black traveler George Washington Bush, he allowed them to settle in Washington, although he knew it might give the Washington area to the United States, destroying his British "Kingdom."

• In 1836 Dr. Marcus Whitman established a mission called Waiilatpu, near present-day Walla Walla.

So They Say

"The fort dining hall was a noble apartment capable of seating 500 guests. A huge map of the Indian country covered the wall...the long tables began to fill. With a wave of the hand the stately governor (McLoughlin) seated his guests according to rank. Before them cut-glass and silver, with the McLoughlin coat of arms, shone side by side with modern queen's ware and rare old china...the branching candelabra sent out an odor of perfumed wax."

Eva Dye, on Dr. John McLoughlin's hospitality.

• In 1844 the remarkable party of George Washington Bush reached the region. An African-American, Bush was the wealthiest man to cross the Oregon Trail. Because blacks could not settle in Oregon, Dr. McLoughlin let them establish a settlement at Bush Prairie, doing much to establish U.S. claims to Washington.

• The rival claims of Britain and the United States appeared to be leading to war, but in 1846 the present boundaries of Washington were settled.

• In 1847 the Cayuse Indians attacked Waiilatpu and killed Dr. and Mrs. Whitman.

• Oregon Territory—Oregon, Washington, and parts of Idaho—was established in 1848, and development came rapidly.

• The relentless Indian wars came to a virtual halt in 1858.

• The cities of Vancouver, Ellensburg, Spokane, and Seattle were all swept by fire in 1889.

• On Nov. 11, 1889, Washington became a state.

• Seattle hosted the Alaska-Yukon-Pacific Exposition in 1909.

• World War I called 68,326 Washingtonians to service.

• The Golden Jubilee of statehood was celebrated in 1939.

• During World War II the super-secret installations at Richland turned out nuclear materials, and the state's production of airplanes and ships made a vital contribution to the war effort.

• Seattle (1962) and Spokane (1974) celebrated with world's fairs.

• The 1980 explosion of Mt. St. Helens was one of the worst disasters of an era.

• In 1992, experts claimed the world's largest living organism, a 1,500-acre fungus growing south of Mt. Adams.

THAT'S INTERESTING

• Point Roberts on the mainland juts out from Canada and cannot be reached by land from the rest of the United States.

• The strange Indian custom of Potlatch was observed at parties, when the host or hostess gave most of his or her possessions to the guests.

• The "Pig War" started when both the United States and Canada claimed the San Juan Islands.

The British threatened to place Lyman Cutler on trial for shooting a pig owned by a Briton. The matter was settled when arbitration gave the islands to the United States.

• Early Seattle had a shortage of females. Asa Mercer went East and persuaded eleven girls of good families to return to meet the many eligible bachelors. Several prominent families trace their roots back to the Mercer girls.

Notable Natives

Bing Crosby (Tacoma, 1904-1977), singer/actor. **Joseph "Hallshallakeen"** (near Washington, Idaho, Oregon border, 1840?-1904), Indian leader. **Mary McCarthy** (Seattle, 1912-1989), writer. **Seattle, or Seatlh** (near Seattle, 1786?-1866), Indian leader. **Minoru Yamasaki** (Seattle, 1912-), architect.

General

Admitted to statehood: Nov. 11, 1889
Origin of name: Named after George Washington; when the bill creating the territory of Columbia was introduced in the 32nd Congress, the name was changed to Washington
Capital: Olympia
Nickname: Evergreen State
Motto: *"Al-ki"* ("By and By")
Bird: willow goldfinch
Fish: steelhead trout
Flower: Western rhododendron
Song: "Washington, My Home"
Tree: Western hemlock

The Land

Area: 71,303 sq. mi., 18th
Land: 66,582 sq. mi., 20th
Water: 4,721 sq. mi., 11th
Topography: Olympic Mtns. on NW peninsula, open land along coast to Columbia R., flat terrain of Puget Sound lowland, Cascade Mtns. region's high peaks to the E, Columbia Basin in central portion, highlands to the NE, mountains to the SE
Number of counties: 39
Geographic center: Chelan, 10 mi. WSW of Wenatchee
Length: 360 mi.
Width: 240 mi.
Highest point: 14,410 ft. (Mt. Rainier), 4th
Lowest point: sea level (Pacific Ocean), 3rd
Mean elevation: 1,700 ft., 18th
Coastline: 157 mi., 12th
Shoreline: 3,026 mi., 10th

Climate and Environment

Temp., highest: 118 deg. on Aug. 5, 1961, at Ice Harbor Dam; lowest: -48 deg. on Dec. 30, 1968, at Mazama & Winthrop
Fresh water withdrawn, per capita, per day: 1,600 gal., 19th
Endangered species: mammals, 3—woodland caribou, Columbian white-tailed deer, Northern Rocky Mountain gray wolf; birds, 3—American peregrine falcon, Aleutian Canada goose, brown pelican; reptiles, 1; amphibians, none; fishes, none; invertebrates, 1; plants, none

Major Cities, Population Percentage Increase (1980-90)

Bellevue, 86,874—17.55%
Everett, 69,961—28.57%
Seattle, 516,259—4.54%
Spokane, 177,196—3.44%
Tacoma, 176,664—11.46%

The People

Population: 4,866,692, 18th
Percent change (1980-90): 15.09%, 10th
Per sq. mi: 68.25, 29th
Percent in metro. area: 81.70%, 13th
Percent foreign born: 6.6%, 14th
White: 4,308,937—88.54%, 22nd
Black: 149,801—3.08%, 36th
Native American: 81,483—1.67%, 9th
Asian, Pacific Isle: 210,958—4.33%, 3rd
Other races: 115,513—2.37%, 14th
Hispanic origin: 214,570—4.41%, 19th
Percent over 5 yrs. speaking language other than English at home: 9.0%, 19th
Percent males: 49.60%, 9th
Percent females: 50.40%, 43rd
Percent never married: 24.8%, 32nd

Marriages per 1,000 (1989): 9.2, 28th
Divorces per 1,000 (1989): 5.7, 11th
Median age: 33.1
Under 5 years: 366,780—7.54%, 20th
Under 18 years: 1,261,387—25.92%, 25th
65 years & older: 575,288—11.82%, 35th
Percent increase among the elderly: 33.3%, 10th

Of Vital Importance

Live births per 1,000 pop.: 15.8, 27th
Infant mortality rate per 1,000 births (1988): 9.0, 29th
Average lifetime (1979-81): 75.13, 10th
Deaths per 100,000 pop. (1988): 781.8, 42nd
Causes of death per 100,000 pop. (1988):
- Diseases of heart: 252.7, 41st
- Malignant neoplasms: 179.3, 40th
- Cerebrovascular diseases: 60.2, 28th
- Accidents & adverse effects: 37.5, 34th
- Chronic obstructive pulmonary diseases: 39.7, 15th
- Suicide: 15.5, 11th
- HIV infection: 4.4, 15th
- Other: 68.3, 40th

Keeping Well

Non-federal physicians per 100,000 pop.: 233, 14th
Dentists per 100,000 (1990-91): 74, 14th
Nurses per 100,000 (1989): 751, 17th
Hospitals per 100,000: 2.3, 39th
- Admissions per 100,000: 11,335, 44th
- Beds per 100,000: 324.10, 51st
- Occupancy rate: 65.5%, 26th
- Semiprivate room charges per day: $334, 15th
- Average stay: 5.8, 50th

Notifiable diseases per 100,000:
- AIDS: 13.1, 14th
- Gonorrhea: 102.9, 35th
- Measles: 7.2, 14th
- Syphillis: 17.1, 26th
- Tuberculosis (TB): 5.8, 29th

Per capita spending on mental health programs (1987): $36.37, 25th
Pop. without health insur. (1991): 10.4%, 37th

Households by Type

Total households: 1,872,431
- Percent change (1980-90): 21.51%, 12th

Family households: 1,264,934
- Percent of total: 67.56%, 47th

Nonfamily households: 607,497
- Percent of total: 32.44%, 5th

Persons per household: 2.53, 42nd
Pop. living in group quarters: 120,531
- Percent of pop.: 2.48%, 35th

Living Quarters

Total housing units: 2,032,378
- Persons per unit: 2.39, 27th

Occupied housing units: 1,872,431
- Percent of total units: 92.13%, 8th
- Persons per unit: 2.49, 36th
- Percent of units with over 1 person per room: 3.89%, 19th

Owner-occupied units: 1,171,580
- Percent of total units: 57.65%, 32nd
- Percent of occupied units: 62.57%, 42nd
- Persons per unit: 2.68, 36th
- Median value: $93,400, 15th

Renter-occupied units: 700,851
- Percent of total units: 34.48%, 10th
- Percent of occupied units: 37.43%, 12th
- Persons per unit: 2.30, 32nd
- Median contract rent: $383, 16th
- Rental vacancy rate: 5.8%, 47th

Mobile home, trailer & other as a % of occupied housing units: 11.07%, 26th

Crime Index per 100,000:

Total: 6,223, 10th
- Violent: 502, 29th
  - Murder and nonnegligent manslaughter: 5, 32nd
  - Aggravated assault: 7,537, 21st
  - Robbery: 130, 25th
  - Rape: 64, 4th
- Property: 5,721, 8th
  - Burglary: 1,263, 15th
  - Larceny, theft: 4,011, 7th
  - Motor vehicle theft: 447, 24th

Drug abuse arrests: 220, 32nd

Teaching and Learning

Literacy (1987): 92%, 4th
Pop. 3 and over enrolled in school: 1,252,312
- Percent of pop.: 26.9%, 30th

Public elementary & secondary schools:
Total enrollment: 827,000
Avg. class size (1987): 25, 7th
Teachers: 40,300
Percent of pop.: 0.83%, 47th
Teachers' avg. salary: $30,500, 22nd
Spending per capita: $966, 7th
Spending per pupil in avg. daily attendance: $4,638, 23rd
Percent of graduates taking SAT: 49%, 20th
Combined SAT scores: 913, 31st
Percent of pop. over 25 completing:
High school: 83.8%, 4th
College degree/s: 22.9%, 14th
Higher educa., institutions: 57
Per 100,000 pop.: 0.7, 26th
Enroll.: 263,278
Percent of pop.: 5.41%, 28th
Public: 227,632
Percent of enroll.: 86.46%, 18th
Private: 35,646
Percent of enroll.: 13.54%, 34th
White non-Hispanic: 56,522
Percent of enroll.: 94.98%, 2nd
Black non-Hispanic: 669
Percent of enroll.: 1.12%, 43rd
Hispanic: 490
Percent of enroll.: 0.82%, 38th
Asian/Pacific Islander: 760
Percent of enroll.: 1.28%, 38th
Amer. Indian/AK native: 229
Percent of enroll.: 0.38%, 26th
Nonresident alien: 840
Percent of enroll.: 1.41%, 48th
Female: 147,127
Percent of enroll.: 55.88%, 15th
Tuition, state university ('90-'91): $1,823, 25th
Public library systems: 70
Books & serial vol. per capita: 2.56, 26th
Govt. expend. per capita: $25.46, 4th
State govt.: $2.55, 25th
Local govts.: $22.91, 4th

Law Enforcement, Courts, and Prisons

Police protection expend.: $497,240,000
Per capita: $102.17, 27th
Judicial & legal expend.: $240,086,000
Per capita: $49.33, 23rd
Corrections expend.: $410,107,000
Per capita: $84.26, 22nd
Police per 10,000 pop. (1990-91): 16.3, 38th
Prisoners (state & fed.) sentenced to over 1 yr., per 100,000 pop.: 162
Percent change (1989-90): 15.40%, 2nd
Death penalty: yes, by lethal injection or hanging
Under sentence of death: 7, 29th
Executed (1989): none

Religion, Number and Percent of Population

Agnostic: 50,474—1.40%, 1st
Buddhist: 18,027—0.50%, 2nd
Christian: 2,779,690—77.10%, 47th
Hindu: 3,605—0.10%, 10th
Jewish: 14,421—0.40%, 31st
Moslem: NA
Unitarian: 18,027—0.50%, 6th
Other: 97,343—2.70%, 2nd
None: 504,743—14.00%, 2nd
Refused to answer: 118,975—3.30%, 4th

Making a Living

Personal income per capita (1989): $14,923, 16th
Percent increase (1979-89) (constant 1989 dollars): 10.3%, 31st
Average income per family: $43,721, 16th
Percent of pop. below poverty level: 10.9%, 35th
Percent 65 and over: 9.1%, 44th
Cost of living, selected cities
1st qtr., 1991 (U. S. Standard=100)

Wenatchee	95.4
Spokane	97.0
Seattle	115.1

Economy

Civilian labor force : 2,503,000
Percent of tot. pop.: 51.43%, 22nd
Percent 65 and over: NA
Percent females: 45.75%, 25th
Percent job growth (1980-90): 33.51%, 9th
Major employer industries:
Agriculture: 54,763—2.30%, 33rd
Construction: 116,669—4.90%, 18th

Finance, insurance & real estate: 128,574—5.40%, 25th
Government: 383,341—16.10%, 21st
Manufacturing: 373,817—15.70%, 28th
Mining: 4,000—0.2%, 37th
Service: 473,819—19.90%, 24th
Trade: 478,581—20.10%, 8th
Transportation, communication, & public utilities: 116,669—4.90%, 31st
Wholesale/retail: 501,419—21.9%, 18th
Unemployment rate: 4.87%, 37th
Male: 2.56%, 38th
Female: 2.32%, 29th
Total businesses (1991): 183,769
New business incorp's. (1991): 11,521
Percent of total businesses: 6.27%, 21st
Business failures (1991): 1,418
Percent of total businesses: 0.77%, 31st
Agriculture farm income
Marketing (1991): $3,946,524,000, 14th
Net per operation: $37,245, 7th
Net per acre: $86, 15th
Leading products: apples, dairy products, cattle, wheat
Av. value land & build. per acre: $815, 29th
Percent increase (1980-90): 10.73%, 19th
Govt. payments: $206,084,000, 16th
Construction, value of all: $4,794,000,000
Per capita: $985.06, 3rd
Percent change 1989-90: -8.00%, 28th
Manufactures:
Value added: $24,871,000,000
Per capita: $5,110.45, 26th
Value of shipments: $67,538,000,000
Per capita: $13,877.60, 11th
Leading products: aircraft, pulp and paper, lumber and plywood, aluminum, processed fruits and vegetables
Mining, min. prod., value (1987): $380,000,000, 33rd
Leading products: cement, sand/gravel, stone
Retail sales: $36,762,000,000, 16th
Per household: $19,370, 23rd
Percent increase (1987-90): 23.3%, 8th
Service indust., value (1987): $19,073,000,000, 16th
Per capita: $3,919.09, 25th
Tourism indus., value (1989): $4,451,000,000, 19th
Foreign exports value: $24,432,000,000, 3rd
Per capita: $5,020.25, 2nd
Patents per 1,000 pop.: 5.1, 32nd

Travel and Transportation

Motor vehicle registrations: 4,256,866
Per 1,000 pop.: 874, 11th
Motorcycle registrations: 119,318
Per 1,000 pop.: 24, 14th
Licensed drivers per 1,000 driving age pop.: 900, 25th
Deaths from motor vehicle accidents per 100,000 pop.: 17.0, 31st
Public roads & streets
Total mileage: 81,299, 23rd
Rural mileage: 65,039, 27th
Urban mileage: 16,260, 15th
Interstate mileage: 759, 30th
Annual vehicle-miles of travel per person: 9,183, 24th
Mean travel time for workers 16 + who work away from home: 22.0 min., 13th

Government

Registered voters (1988): 2,499,309
Percent of voting age pop.: 73.14%, 22nd
Voter turnout (1988): 1,865,253
Percent of registered voters: 74.63%, 16th
Percent of voting age pop.: 54.59%, 19th
State legislators, total (1992): 147, 26th
Women members (1992): 48
Percent of legislature: 32.7%, 2nd
Dominant party (1992): Split
U.S. Congress, House members (1993): 9
Increase 1983-93: +1
Revenues:
State govt.: $14,999,316,000
Per capita: $3,082.04, 7th
State & local govt.: $23,332,509,000
Per capita: $4,794.33, 8th
Indebtedness:
State govt.: $5,685,548,000
Per capita: $1,168.26, 26th
State & local govt.: $23,640,000,000
Per capita: $4,857.51, 8th

Laws and Regulations

Legal driving age: 18
Marriage age without parental consent: 18
Divorce residence requirement: bona fide res.

Attractions

Major opera companies (1989): 1, 30th
Per 1 million pop.: 0.21, 45th
Major symphony orchestras (1989): 19, 16th
Per 1 million pop.: 3.99, 21st
State appropriations for state arts agencies per capita: $0.46, 41st

Sports and Competition

NCAA sports teams, 4: Eastern Washington Univ. Eagles, Gonzaga Univ. Bulldogs & Zags, Univ. of Washington Huskies, Washington State Univ. Cougars.
Professional teams, 11
Baseball, 6—Tacoma Tigers (Pacific Coast League, Class AAA), Cheney Stadium; Everett Giants (Northwest League, Class A), Everett Memorial Stadium; Spokane Indians (Northwest League, Class A), Interstate Fairgrounds Stadium; Bellingham Mariners (Northwest League, Class A), Joe Martin Stadium; Yakima Bears (Northwest League, Class A), Parker Field; Seattle Mariners (AL), The Kingdome
Basketball, 2—Seattle Supersonics (NBA), The Seattle Center Coliseum; Yakima Sun Kings (Continental Basketball Association), Yakima Sundome
Football, 1—Seattle Seahawks (AFC), Kingdome
Soccer, 2—Seattle Center (American Professional Soccer League), Memorial Stadium; Tacoma Stars (Major Soccer League), Tacoma Dome

WEST VIRGINIA

"We West Virginians are very tired of being considered inhabitants of just a dominion of Old Dominion....Some inhabitants take a very strong line about this and always refer to it in conversation as 'West—By God—Virginia!' "

John Knowles

West Virginia's "birth" during the Civil War, when the region refused to secede from the Union, made it unique among the states. Its mountains have given it the loftiest average height east of the Rockies. The state contains some of the most rugged land in the country: there are no large areas of level ground, except along major rivers. Its beautiful mountain scenery and mineral springs attract many tourists. Its surface shelters an unusual variety of plants, ranging from Arctic types to those of the semitropics. Beneath the surface lie minerals, including coal, in which the state has long been a leader. This war-born state suffered terribly during the Civil War. One city changed hands an incredible 56 times. But it has been a state which always seems to bounce back from disaster.

SUPERLATIVES

- "Highest state" east of the Mississippi.
- Only state carved from another without its permission.
- Pioneer in natural gas production and leads the Eastern states.
- Noted for record sizes of individual trees.

MOMENTS IN HISTORY

- The earliest known Europeans in present-day West Virginia came with the party of Walter Austin in 1641.
- Noted for its heavy drinking, the party of Gov. Alexander Spotswood of Virginia may have staggered as far as present-day Pendelton County in 1716.
- Laid out in 1732, Shepherdstown became the oldest permanent settlement in present-day West Virginia.
- By 1753 settlers were arriving in substantial numbers.
- The French and Indian War caused great hardship, diminishing when the French lost the continent in 1763.

So They Say

"I am too little acquainted, Sir, with pathetic language to attempt a description of the people's distresses—I see inevitable destruction in so clear a light, that, unless vigorous measures are taken by the Assembly and speedy assistance sent...the poor inhabitants that are now in the Fort (Edwards) must unavoidably fall..."

George Washington on French and Indian War attacks.

- In 1774 the entire family of Mingo Chief Logan was murdered in the chief's absence.
- A battle with the Indians at Point Pleasant on Oct. 10, 1774, has been labeled by some "The first battle of the Revolution."

> **So They Say**
>
> "...in cold blood and unprovoked, cut off all the relatives of Logan, not sparing even my women and chillcren. There runs not a drop of my blood in the veins of any creature. This called on me for revenge. I have fully glutted my vengeance...."
>
> Chief Logan, who took 30 white scalps in Lord Dunmore's War.

• During the Revolution, Indian wars again erupted in 1777. A principal cause was the cold-blooded murder of Chief Cornstalk, who was on a peaceful mission.

• The Battle of Fort Henry (Wheeling) has been called the "Last Battle of the Revolution," Sept. 1782, long after war had ceased in the East.

• The most notorious episode of the growing hostility over slavery took place when "Isaac Smith" led his followers across the Potomac and captured the federal arsenal at Harpers Ferry. This, of course, was the notorious Abolitionist John Brown, who was quickly tried and executed.

> **So They Say**
>
> "Let no man pray that Brown be spared. Let Virginia make him a martyr. Now he has only blundered. His cause was noble, his work miserable. But a cord and a gibbet would redeem all that, and round up Brown's failure with a heroic success."
>
> Henry Ward Beecher

• When Virginia seceded in 1861, the West Virginia legislators voted against it but were overruled.

• The skirmish at Philippi, June 3, 1861, is considered the first land battle of the Civil War. It was important for shutting off the Confederates from the coal fields of the region.

• On two different occasions, the people of West Virginia voted to separate from Virginia, and on April 20, 1863, the wartime state of West Virginia was born by acceptance of the federal government.

• Civil War battles brought much destruction, especially to industry. The state's last major encounter of the war was the Battle of Droop Mountain, Nov. 6, 1863, but Confederate raids continued. Romney changed hands 56 times between Union and Confederate troops. Those in Union service totalled 36,530, with 7,000 in Confederate uniform.

• After much controversy, the capital was moved permanently to Charleston in 1885.

• The mine explosion in 1907 at Monongah was one of the worst in the state's history, causing 361 deaths.

• World War I called 46,648 West Virginians into the armed services, with 1,721 losing their lives.

• The state capitol burned on Jan. 3, 1921, and that same year a miners' disagreement came to be known as the Battle of Blair Mountain.

• The 1937 Ohio River floods were the worst in history, with some cities overwhelmed by water more than 20 ft. above flood stage.

• During World War II the famed Greenbrier Hotel became an internment center for enemy diplomats, then a government hospital, serving more than 20,000 patients. The state's war casualties totalled 4,865 dead.

• The state's coal production reached its all-time high in 1947, declined, then was reborn in the mid-1970s.

That's Interesting

• The West Virginia "panhandle" is so narrow that the city of Weirton stretches from border to border.

• A touring circus is said to have decided the choice of Charleston as state capital. Its supporters lured voters statewide with a flamboyant circus and won handily.

• Ann Royall became the first woman journalist to interview a president. While John Quincy Adams was swimming, she stole his clothes and would not let him out until he gave her a hearing.

• Entomologist Romeo D. Erdie gained fame for his bug factory. Uses for his model insects have ranged from exterminator ads to fine jewelry. He turned them out by millions.

• The community of Shepherdstown was on George Washington's list for choice of a national capital, but it lost out in the final selection.

• Bluefield, 2,558 ft. above sea level, is the highest city east of Denver.

• West Virginia has the only city that stretches from border to border—Weirton, located in the narrow portion of the state, wedged between Ohio and Pennsylvania.

NOTABLE NATIVES

Newton-Diehl Baker (Martinsburg, 1871-1937), public official. **Pearl S. Buck** (Hillsboro, 1892-1973), author. **Cornstalk** (Ohio-WV frontier, c1720-1777), Indian leader. **John William Davis** (Clarksburg, 1873-1955), politician. **Thomas Jonathan "Stonewall" Jackson** (Clarksburg, 1824-1863), soldier. **Dwight Whitney Morrow** (Huntington, 1873-1931), banker/diplomat. **Walter Philip Reuther** (Wheeling, 1907-1970), labor leader. **George C. Scott** (Wise, 1927-), actor.

GENERAL

Admitted to statehood: June 20, 1863
Origin of name: named by Sir Walter Raleigh, who fitted out the expedition of 1584, in honor of Queen Elizabeth, the Virgin Queen of England, becoming West Virginia when western counties of Virginia refused to secede from the United States in 1863
Capital: Charleston
Nickname: The Mountain State
Motto: *"Montani Semper Liberi"* ("Mountaineers Are Always Free")
Animal: black bear
Bird: cardinal
Fish: brook trout
Flower: big rhododendron
Songs: "West Virginia, My Home Sweet Home," "The West Virginia Hills," and "This Is My West Virginia"
Tree: sugar maple

THE LAND

Area: 24,231 sq. mi., 41st
Land: 24,087 sq. mi., 41st
Water: 145 sq. mi., 50th
Topography: ranging from hilly to mountainous, Allegheny Plateau in the W, covers two-thirds of the state; mountains here are the highest in the state—over 4,000 ft.
Number of counties: 55
Geographic center: Braxton, 4 mi. E. of Sutton
Length: 240 mi.
Width: 130 mi.
Highest point: 4,861 ft. (Spruce Knob), 24th
Lowest point: 240 ft. (Potomac River), 31st
Mean elevation: 1,500 ft., 19th

CLIMATE AND ENVIRONMENT

Temp., highest: 112 deg. on July 10, 1936, at Martinsburg; lowest: -37 deg. on Dec. 30, 1917, at Lewisburg
Fresh water withdrawn, per capita, per day: 2,810 gal., 7th
Endangered species: mammals, 3—Indiana bat, Virginia big-eared bat, Virginia northern flying squirrel; birds, 1—American peregrine falcon; reptiles, none; amphibians, none; fishes, none; invertebrates, 5; plants, 3

MAJOR CITIES, POPULATION PERCENTAGE INCREASE (1980-90)

Charleston, 57,287— –10.44%
Huntington, 54,844— –13.88%
Morgantown, 25,879— –6.25%
Parkkersburg, 33,862— –15.23%
Wheeling, 34,882— –19.01%

THE PEOPLE

Population: 1,793,477, 34th
Percent change (1980-90): -8.74%, 51st
Per sq. mi: 74.02, 27th
Percent in metro. area: 36.41%, 44th
Percent foreign born: 0.9%, 49th
White: 1,725,523—96.21%, 5th
Black: 56,295—3.14%, 35th
Native American: 2,458—0.14%, 50th
Asian, Pacific Isle: 7,459—0.42%, 51st
Other races: 1,742—0.10%, 51st
Hispanic origin: 8,489—0.47%, 51st

Percent over 5 yrs. speaking language other than English at home: 2.6%, 50th
Percent males: 48.04%, 44th
Percent females: 51.96%, 8th
Percent never married: 22.2%, 47th
Marriages per 1,000 (1989): 7.2, 49th
Divorces per 1,000 (1989): 5.1, 16th
Median age: 35.4
Under 5 years: 106,659—5.95%, 51st
Under 18 years: 443,577—24.73%, 38th
65 years & older: 268,897—14.99%, 5th
Percent increase among the elderly: 13.0%, 40th

OF VITAL IMPORTANCE

Live births per 1,000 pop.: 12.6, 51st
Infant mortality rate per 1,000 births (1988): 9.0, 29th
Average lifetime (1979-81): 72.84, 43rd
Deaths per 100,000 pop. (1988): 1055.1, 3rd
Causes of death per 100,000 pop. (1988):
  Diseases of heart: 397.1, 2nd
  Malignant neoplasms: 231.7, 5th
  Cerebrovascular diseases: 69.8, 17th
  Accidents & adverse effects: 47.7, 13th
  Chronic obstructive pulmonary diseases: 48.1, 2nd
  Suicide: 11.4, 34th
  HIV infection: 0.9, 46th
  Other: 83.2, 8th

KEEPING WELL

Non-federal physicians per 100,000 pop.: 189, 33rd
Dentists per 100,000 (1990-91): 51, 43rd
Nurses per 100,000 (1989): 605, 33rd
Hospitals per 100,000: 3.8, 16th
  Admissions per 100,000: 16,668, 6th
  Beds per 100,000: 567.33, 15th
  Occupancy rate: 64.9%, 29th
  Semiprivate room charges per day: $223, 36th
  Average stay: 7.1, 26th
Notifiable diseases per 100,000:
  AIDS: 3.5, 45th
  Gonorrhea: 82.1, 39th
  Measles: 0.3, 46th
  Syphillis: 13.7, 29th
  Tuberculosis (TB): 4.9, 34th
Per capita spending on mental health programs (1987): $22.96, 47th
Pop. without health insur. (1991): 15.7%, 14th

HOUSEHOLDS BY TYPE

Total households: 688,557
  Percent change (1980-90): 0.37%, 50th
Family households: 500,259
  Percent of total: 72.65%, 11th
Nonfamily households: 188,298
  Percent of total: 27.35%, 41st
Persons per household: 2.55, 36th
Pop. living in group quarters: 36,911
  Percent of pop.: 2.06%, 48th

LIVING QUARTERS

Total housing units: 781,295
  Persons per unit: 2.30, 41st
Occupied housing units: 688,557
  Percent of total units: 88.13%, 34th
  Persons per unit: 2.48, 37th
  Percent of units with over 1 person per room: 1.91%, 44th
Owner-occupied: 510,058
  Percent of total units: 65.28%, 1st
  Percent of occupied units: 74.08%, 1st
  Persons per unit: 2.63, 44th
  Median value: $47,900, 47th
Renter-occupied units: 178,499
  Percent of total units: 22.85%, 51st
  Percent of occupied units: 25.92%, 51st
  Persons per unit: 2.33, 28th
  Median contract rent: $221, 49th
  Rental vacancy rate: 10.1%, 15th
Mobile home, trailer & other as a % of occupied housing units: 18.61%, 6th

CRIME INDEX PER 100,000:

Total: 2,503, 51st
  Violent: 169, 45th
    Murder and nonnegligent manslaughter: 6, 28th
    Aggravated assault: 5,947, 51st
    Robbery: 38, 43rd
    Rape: 24, 47th

Property: 2,334, 51st
Burglary: 657, 48th
Larceny, theft: 1,523, 51st
Motor vehicle theft: 154, 48th
Drug abuse arrests: 88, 48th

Teaching and Learning

Literacy (1987): 86%, 33nd
Pop. 3 and over enrolled in school: 436,513
Percent of pop.: 25.2%, 46th
Public elementary & secondary schools:
Total enrollment: 310,000
Avg. class size (1987): 21, 35th
Teachers: 21,700
Percent of pop.: 1.21%, 4th
Teachers' avg. salary: $22,800, 49th
Spending per capita: $725, 36th
Spending per pupil in avg. daily attendance: $4,146, 35th
Percent of graduates taking SAT: 17%, 31st
Combined SAT scores: 926, 26th
Percent of pop. over 25 completing:
High school: 66.0%, 49th
College degree/s: 12.3%, 51st
Higher educa., institutions: 28
Per 100,000 pop.: 0.9, 16th
Enroll: 84,790
Percent of pop.: 4.73%, 42nd
Public: 74,108
Percent of enroll.: 87.40%, 14th
Private: 10,682
Percent of enroll.: 12.60%, 38th
White non-Hispanic: 273,874
Percent of enroll.: 77.81%, 35th
Black non-Hispanic: 62,032
Percent of enroll.: 17.62%, 7th
Hispanic: 2,528
Percent of enroll.: 0.72%, 41st
Asian/Pacific Islander: 5,622
Percent of enroll.: 1.60%, 29th
Amer. Indian/AK native: 3,082
Percent of enroll.: 0.88%, 17th
Nonresident alien: 4,852
Percent of enroll.: 1.38%, 49th
Female: 46,977
Percent of enroll.: 55.40%, 19th
Tuition, state university ('90-'91): $1,543, 34th
Public library systems: 98
Books & serial vol. per capita: 2.15, 35th
Govt. expend. per capita: $7.26, 49th
State govt.: $5.01, 8th
Local govts.: $2.25, 49th

Law Enforcement, Courts, and Prisons

Police protection expend.: $89,466,000
Per capita: $49.90, 51st
Judicial & legal expend.: $53,140,000
Per capita: $29.64, 48th
Corrections expend.: $46,528,000
Per capita: $25.95, 51st
Police per 10,000 pop. (1990-91): 14.6, 50th
Prisoners (state & fed.) sentenced to over 1 yr., per 100,000 pop.: 85
Percent change (1989-90): 1.89%, 43rd
Death penalty: no

Religion, Number and Percent of Population

Agnostic: 2,700—0.20%, 42nd
Buddhist: 1,350—0.10%, 17th
Christian: 1,167,664—86.50%, 24th
Hindu: 1,350—0.10%, 10th
Jewish: 1,350—0.10%, 43rd
Moslem: 1,350—0.10%, 22nd
Unitarian: 1,350—0.10%, 31st
Other: 39,147—2.90%, 1st
None: 107,992—8.00%, 15th
Refused to answer: 25,648—1.90%, 31st

Making a Living

Personal income per capita (1989): $10,520, 49th
Percent increase (1979-89) (constant 1989 dollars): 2.2%, 48th
Average income per family: $31,290, 50th
Percent of pop. below poverty level: 19.7%, 4th
Percent 65 and over: 16.7%, 13th
Cost of living, selected cities/county
1st qtr., 1991 (U.S. Standard=100)

Wheeling	92.7
Charleston	100.1
Berkeley County	104.3

Economy

Civilian labor force : 772,000
  Percent of tot. pop.: 43.04%, 51st
Percent 65 and over: NA
  Percent females: 41.84%, 51st
  Percent job growth (1980-90): -1.13%, 50th
Major employer industries:
  Agriculture: 12,036—1.70%, 38th
  Construction: 40,356—5.70%, 8th
  Finance, insurance & real estate: 29,736—4.20%, 43rd
  Government: 118,236—16.70%, 18th
  Manufacturing: 99,828—14.10%, 35th
  Mining: 36,412—5.4%, 2nd
  Service: 116,112—16.40%, 45th
  Trade: 151,512—21.40%, 2nd
  Transportation, communication, & public utilities: 47,436—6.70%, 5th
  Wholesale/retail: 145,363—21.7%, 21st
Unemployment rate: 8.29%, 1st
  Male: 5.05%, 1st
  Female: 3.37%, 3rd
Total businesses (1991): 51,655
  New business incorp's. (1991): 2,219
    Percent of total businesses: 4.30%, 42nd
  Business failures (1991): 395
    Percent of total businesses: 0.76%, 32nd
Agriculture farm income
  Marketing (1991): $330,237,000, 46th
  Net per operation: $3,915, 50th
  Net per acre: $21, 41st
  Leading products: cattle, broilers, dairy products, turkeys
  Av. value land & build. per acre: $652, 34th
    Percent increase (1980-90): -2.54%, 29th
  Govt. payments: $5,421,000, 41st
Construction, value of all: $302,000,000
  Per capita: $168.39, 51st
  Percent change 1989-90: 3.78%, 16th
Manufactures:
  Value added: $6,342,000,000
    Per capita: $3,536.15, 39th
  Value of shipments: $12,938,000,000
    Per capita: $7,213.92, 39th
  Leading products: machinery, plastic and hardwood products, fabricated metals, basic organic and inorganic chemicals, aluminum, steel
Mining, min. prod., value (1987): $5,889,000,000, 7th
  Leading products: coal, nat. gas, petroleum
Retail sales: $10,060,000,000, 39th
  Per household: $14,718, 51st
  Percent increase (1987-90): 14.6%, 28th
Service indust., value (1987): $4,874,000,000, 40th
  Per capita: $2,717.63, 47th
Tourism indus., value (1989): $1,161,000,000, 43rd
Foreign exports value: $1,550,000,000, 35th
  Per capita: $864.24, 28th
Patents per 1,000 pop.: 10.8, 13th

Travel and Transportation

Motor vehicle registrations: 1,224,947
  Per 1,000 pop.: 683, 45th
Motorcycle registrations: 22,138
  Per 1,000 pop.: 12, 36th
Licensed drivers per 1,000 driving age pop.: 916, 17th
Deaths from motor vehicle accidents per 100,000 pop.: 26.8, 7th
Public roads & streets
  Total mileage: 34,592, 39th
    Rural mileage: 31,516, 39th
    Urban mileage: 3,076, 39th
    Interstate mileage: 517, 40th
Annual vehicle-miles of travel per person: 8,596, 34th
Mean travel time for workers 16 + who work away from home: 21.0 min., 23rd

Government

Registered voters (1988): 968,619
  Percent of voting age pop.: 69.29%, 29th
Voter turnout (1988): 653,311
  Percent of registered voters: 67.45%, 38th
  Percent of voting age pop.: 46.73%, 40th
State legislators, total (1992): 134, 32nd
  Women members (1992): 28
    Percent of legislature: 20.9%, 17th
  Dominant party (1992): Democrats
U.S. Congress, House members (1993): 3
  Increase 1983-93: -1

Revenues:
State govt.: $4,435,474,000
Per capita: $2,473.11, 25th
State & local govt.: $5,752,630,000
Per capita: $3,207.53, 46th
Indebtedness:
State govt.: $2,471,073,000
Per capita: $1,377.81, 19th
State & local govt.: $6,292,000,000
Per capita: $3,508.27, 25th

Laws and Regulations

Legal driving age: 18
Marriage age without parental consent: 18
Divorce residence requirement: 1 yr.

Attractions

Major opera companies (1989): 0
Per 1 million pop.: 0.00
Major symphony orchestras (1989): 7, 32nd
Per 1 million pop.: 3.77, 22nd
State appropriations for state arts agencies per capita: $0.93, 21st
State Fair in late Aug. at Lewisburg (Fairlea)

Sports and Competition

NCAA sports teams, 3: Marshall Univ. Thundering Herd, Shepherd College Rams, West Virginia Univ. Mountaineers
Professional teams, 4
Baseball, 4—Bluefield Orioles (Appalachian League, Rookie Class), Bowen Field; Princeton Reds (Appalachian League, Rookie Class), Hunnicutt Field; Huntington Cubs (Appalachian League, Rookie Class), St. Cloud Commons; Charleston Wheelers (South Atlantic League, Class A), Watt Powell Park

WISCONSIN

"Wisconsin is the soul of a great people. She manifests the spirit of the conqueror, whose strength has subdued the forest, quickened the soil, harnessed the forces of Nature and multiplied production. From her abundance she served food to the world."

Fred L. Holmes

Wisconsin is a state of progress and leadership in many areas. Spurred by Wisconsin native Robert LaFollette, the state pioneered in progressive social legislation. It continues to lead the nation in dairy products. It produces more milk than any other state, 40% of the nation's cheese, and 20% of its butter. But manufacturing is Wisconsin's chief industry. It is a leader in the manufacturing of machinery, and produces more paper than any other state. The state's nickname (The Badger State) began with a group of burrowing miners—all adding to a state of many contrasts.

Superlatives

- First U.S. kindergarten—opened by Mrs Carl Schurz, Waterton, 1865.
- Pioneer in social legislation.
- Leads nation in dairy products.
- First in paper, paper products, and paper-making machinery.
- Smallest city with a major pro football team.
- World's oldest continuously operating radio station, WHA, Madison

Moments in History

- In 1634 French explorer Jean Nicolet became the first European in the area.
- Pierre Esprit Radisson and Medart Chouart (Sieur de Groseillier) explored in 1654-1656, opening the area to fur trade.

> **So They Say**
>
> "I liked noe country as I have that wherein we wintered Washington Island, Wisconsin; for whatever a man could desire was to be had in great plenty; viz. staggs, fishes in abundance, and all sort of meat, corne enough."
>
> Pierre Esprit Radisson, in later memoirs

- After crossing the state and pioneering a route from the east, at the mouth of the Wisconsin River, on June 17, 1673, the noted explorers Marquette and Jolliet discovered the long-sought upper reaches of the Mississippi River.

> **So They Say**
>
> As he marvelled at the Mississippi's great flow, Father Marquette felt "...a joy that I cannot express."

- Sieur Du Lhut (Daniel Greysolon) in 1678 explored the western end of Lake Superior and claimed the land in the name of France.
- With the Treaty of Paris in 1763, the British gained control.
- Augustin Monet de Langlade founded Green Bay in 1764, a thriving fur trading post, present-day Wisconsin's first permanent European settlement.
- Prairie du Chien (Prairie of the Dog) was founded in 1781 on the site of a large Indian village.

- The Treaty of Paris in 1783 gave the area to the United States, but the British continued to claim the region until after the War of 1812.
- By 1822 lead mining was in full swing in southwest Wisconsin. Many miners burrowed into the hillside like badgers, giving the "Badger State" its nickname.
- During the Black Hawk War, Chief Black Hawk fled into Wisconsin. On Aug. 2, 1832, the Battle of Bad Axe ended the Black Hawk War. Trying to escape across the Mississippi River, many of the men, women, and children were massacred.

> **So They Say**
>
> "Bad, and cruel, as our people were treated by the whites, not one of them was hurt or molested by any of my band...This is a lesson worthy for the white man to learn..."
>
> Chief Black Hawk

- In 1835 the first steamboat arrived at the trading port that became Milwaukee.
- Madison was selected as the territorial capital in 1836, although still wilderness.
- After it became the 30th state on May 29, 1848, Wisconsin attracted waves of Scandinavian, German, and other immigrants.
- In 1851 the first train chugged over new tracks, Milwaukee to Waukesha.
- Wisconsin was well prepared for the Civil War, and the state produced many wartime heroes.
- The Oct. 8, 1871 forest fire devastated the lumber town of Peshtigo, killing as many as 1,200.
- In 1890 Stephen M. Babcock developed a machine and method of testing the amount of butterfat in milk, giving a new boost to the "Dairy State."
- Robert M. LaFollette became the first native-born governor of Wisconsin in 1901, bringing many widely copied reforms.
- In 1904 fire partially destroyed the statehouse. The third capitol in Madison, the present one, was built between 1906 and 1917, as the state mobilized for World War I.
- During the Great Depression of the 1930s Wisconsin passed the first unemployment compensation legislation in 1932.
- The depression squeeze on dairy workers sparked the state's milk strikes of 1934, and thousands of gallons of milk were dumped in protest of conditions.
- World War II brought unfounded concerns about the German population in Milwaukee.
- The baseball Braves came to Milwaukee in 1953 and won the World Series in 1957.
- The opening of the St. Lawrence Seaway in 1959 brought many benefits to state ports.

That's Interesting

- Believing that he had reached China and the Far East, Jean Nicolet stepped ashore near the Winnebago village of Red Bank, shooting pistols and wearing embroidered Chinese silk robes, to the astonishment of the Indians.
- Prairie du Chien (Prairie of the Dog) was named for Chief Alim, a prominent Indian whose native name means Dog.
- Pioneer Wisconsin was so sparsely settled that Justice of the Peace Pat Kelly sometimes was forced to use trees as witnesses.

Notable Natives

Zona Gale (Portage, 1874-1938), author. **Hamlin Garland** (West Salem, 1860-1940), author. **King Camp Gillette** (Fond du Lac, 1855-1932), industrialist. **Vinnie Ream Hoxie** (Madison, 1847-1914), sculptor. **Robert Marion La Follette** (Primrose, 1855-1925), political leader. **Georgia O'Keefe** (Sun Prairie, 1887-1986), artist. **Spencer Tracy** (Milwaukee, 1900-1967), actor. **Thornton Wilder** (Madison, 1897-1975), novelist/playwright. **Frank Lloyd Wright** (Richland Center, 1867-1959), architect.

General

Admitted to statehood: May 29, 1848

Origin of name: an Indian name, spelled (Ouisconsin) and (Mesconsing) by early chroniclers, believed to mean "grassy place" in Chippewa; Congress made it Wisconsin

Capital: Madison
Nickname: The Badger State
Motto: "Forward"
Animal: badger
Bird: robin
Domestic animal: dairy cow
Fish: muskellunge
Flower: wood violet
Insect: honeybee
Mineral: galena
Song: "On, Wisconsin!"
Stone/rock: red granite
Tree: sugar maple
Wildlife animal: white-tailed deer

The Land

Area: 65,503 sq. mi., 23rd
Land: 54,314 sq. mi., 25th
Water: 11,190 sq. mi., 4th
Topography: narrow Lake Superior Lowland Plain met by Northern Highland, which slopes gently to the sandy crescent Central Plain; Western Upland in the SW; three broad parallel limestone ridges running N-S are separated by wide and shallow lowland in the SE
Number of counties: 72
Geographic center: Wood, 9 mi. SE of Marshfield. Length: 310 mi.
Width: 260 mi.
Highest point: 1,951 ft. (Timms Hill), 39th
Lowest point: 581 ft. (Lake Michigan), 41st
Mean elevation: 1,050 ft., 24th

Climate and Environment

Temp., highest: 114 deg. on July 13, 1936, at Wisconsin Dells; lowest: -54 deg. on Jan. 24, 1922, at Danbury
Fresh water withdrawn, per capita, per day: 1,400 gal., 22nd
Endangered species: mammals, 2—Indiana bat, Eastern timber wolf; birds, 3—American peregrine falcon, piping plover, Kirtland's warbler; reptiles, none; amphibians, none; fishes, none; invertebrates, 1; plants, none

Major Cities, Population Percentage Increase (1980-90)

Green Bay, 96,466—9.75%
Kenosha, 80,352—3.43%
Madison, 191,262—12.10%
Milwaukee, 628,088— -1.29%
Racine, 84,298— -1.66%

The People

Population: 4,891,769, 16th
Percent change (1980-90): 3.80%, 32nd
Per sq. mi: 74.68, 26th
Percent in metro. area: 67.42%, 27th
Percent foreign born: 2.5%, 31st
White: 4,512,523—92.25%, 14th
Black: 244,539—5.00%, 29th
Native American: 39,387—0.81%, 19th
Asian, Pacific Isle: 53,583—1.10%, 27th
Other races: 41,737—0.85%, 30th
Hispanic origin: 93,194—1.91%, 31st
Percent over 5 yrs. speaking language other than English at home: 5.8%, 31st
Percent males: 48.92%, 22nd
Percent females: 51.08%, 30th
Percent never married: 27.1%, 18th
Marriages per 1,000 (1989): 8.3, 36th
Divorces per 1,000 (1989): 3.6, 39th
Median age: 32.9
Under 5 years: 360,730—7.37%, 26th
Under 18 years: 1,288,982—26.35%, 20th
65 years & older: 651,221—13.31%, 18th
Percent increase among the elderly: 15.4%, 34th

Of Vital Importance

Live births per 1,000 pop.: 14.8, 42nd
Infant mortality rate per 1,000 births (1988): 8.4, 41st
Average lifetime (1979-81): 75.35, 6th
Deaths per 100,000 pop. (1988): 886.3, 26th
Causes of death per 100,000 pop. (1988):
Diseases of heart: 320.7, 24th
Malignant neoplasms: 202.1, 21st
Cerebrovascular diseases: 69.8, 17th
Accidents & adverse effects: 34.8, 40th
Chronic obstructive pulmonary diseases: 32.7, 30th

Suicide: 13.5, 14th
HIV infection: 1.2, 42nd
Other: 73.6, 30th

KEEPING WELL

Non-federal physicians per 100,000 pop.: 205, 28th
Dentists per 100,000 (1990-91): 73, 16th
Nurses per 100,000 (1989): 710, 24th
Hospitals per 100,000: 3.0, 27th
Admissions per 100,000: 12,863, 34th
Beds per 100,000: 485.63, 24th
Occupancy rate: 68.8%, 17th
Semiprivate room charges per day: $222, 38th
Average stay: 8.2, 14th
Notifiable diseases per 100,000:
AIDS: 4.3, 42nd
Gonorrhea: 176.6, 29th
Measles: 15.2, 4th
Syphillis: 12.7, 30th
Tuberculosis (TB): 2.0, 46th
Per capita spending on mental health programs (1987): $31.11, 34th
Pop. without health insur. (1991): 8.0%, 47th

HOUSEHOLDS BY TYPE

Total households: 1,822,118
Percent change (1980-90): 10.30%, 29th
Family households: 1,275,172
Percent of total: 69.98%, 30th
Nonfamily households: 546,946
Percent of total: 30.02%, 22nd
Persons per household: 2.61, 21st
Pop. living in group quarters: 133,598
Percent of pop.: 2.73%, 26th

LIVING QUARTERS

Total housing units: 2,055,774
Persons per unit: 2.38, 31st
Occupied housing units: 1,822,118
Percent of total units: 88.63%, 31st
Persons per unit: 2.53, 24th
Percent of units with over 1 person per room: 2.10%, 41st
Owner-occupied units: 1,215,350
Percent of total units: 59.12%, 25th
Percent of occupied units: 66.70%, 28th
Persons per unit: 2.79, 15th
Median value: $62,500, 30th
Renter-occupied units: 606,768
Percent of total units: 29.52%, 25th
Percent of occupied units: 33.30%, 24th
Persons per unit: 2.26, 38th
Median contract rent: $331, 26th
Rental vacancy rate: 4.7%, 51st
Mobile home, trailer & other as a % of occupied housing units: 7.10%, 36th

CRIME INDEX PER 100,000:

Total: 4,395, 38th
Violent: 265, 44th
Murder and nonnegligent manslaughter: 5, 36th
Aggravated assault: 7,374, 27th
Robbery: 113, 32nd
Rape: 21, 48th
Property: 4,130, 38th
Burglary: 751, 42nd
Larceny, theft: 2,963, 29th
Motor vehicle theft: 416, 28th
Drug abuse arrests: 192, 33rd

TEACHING AND LEARNING

Literacy (1987): 90%, 14th
Pop. 3 and over enrolled in school: 1,302,230
Percent of pop.: 27.8%, 19th
Public elementary & secondary schools:
Total enrollment: 792,000
Avg. class size (1987): 22, 28th
Teachers: 46,400
Percent of pop.: 0.95%, 35th
Teachers' avg. salary: $31,900, 16th
Spending per capita: $887, 13th
Spending per pupil in avg. daily attendance: $5,703, 10th
Percent of graduates taking SAT: 11%, 38th
Combined SAT scores: 1023, 7th
Percent of pop. over 25 completing:
High school: 78.6%, 21st
College degree/s: 17.7%, 36th
Higher educa., institutions: 61
Per 100,000 pop.: 0.6, 30th
Enroll: 299,774
Percent of pop.: 6.13%, 14th

Public: 253,529
Percent of enroll.: 84.57%, 22nd
Private: 46,245
Percent of enroll.: 15.43%, 30th
White non-Hispanic: 162,549
Percent of enroll.: 91.40%, 9th
Black non-Hispanic: 10,491
Percent of enroll.: 5.90%, 24th
Hispanic: 738
Percent of enroll.: 0.41%, 48th
Asian/Pacific Islander: 1,343
Percent of enroll.: 0.76%, 44th
Amer. Indian/AK native: 506
Percent of enroll.: 0.28%, 37th
Nonresident alien: 2,225
Percent of enroll.: 1.25%, 50th
Female: 163,883
Percent of enroll.: 54.67%, 29th
Tuition, state university ('90-'91): $1,951, 18th
Public library systems: 377
Books & serial vol. per capita: 3.11, 19th
Govt. expend. per capita: $21.53, 12th
State govt.: $1.97, 38th
Local govts.: $19.56, 8th

LAW ENFORCEMENT, COURTS, AND PRISONS

Police protection expend.: $601,638,000
Per capita: $122.98, 18th
Judicial & legal expend.: $243,868,000
Per capita: $49.85, 22nd
Corrections expend.: $348,578,000
Per capita: $71.25, 28th
Police per 10,000 pop. (1990-91): 21.8, 17th
Prisoners (state & fed.) sentenced to over 1 yr., per 100,000 pop.: 149
Percent change (1989-90): 8.27%, 22nd
Death penalty: no

RELIGION, NUMBER AND PERCENT OF POPULATION

Agnostic: 10,808—0.30%, 37th
Buddhist: 10,808—0.30%, 8th
Christian: 3,249,714—90.20%, 10th
Hindu: NA
Jewish: 14,411—0.40%, 31st
Moslem: 7,206—0.20%, 13th
Unitarian: 7,206—0.20%, 23rd
Other: 28,822—0.80%, 37th
None: 219,770—6.10%, 31st
Refused to answer: 54,042—1.50%, 42nd

MAKING A LIVING

Personal income per capita (1989): $13,276, 28th
Percent increase (1979-'89) (constant 1989 dollars): 9.4%, 36th
Average income per family: $40,649, 24th
Percent of pop. below poverty level: 10.7%, 38th
Percent 65 and over: 9.1%, 44th
Cost of living, selected cities
1st qtr., 1991 (U. S. Standard=100)

New London	89.2
La Crosse	94.8
Milwaukee	103.3

ECONOMY

Civilian labor force : 2,587,000
Percent of tot. pop.: 52.88%, 11th
Percent 65 and over: 2.90%, 21st
Percent females: 46.35%, 15th
Percent job growth (1980-90): 16.82%, 34th
Major employer industries:
Agriculture: 98,960—4.00%, 13th
Construction: 101,434—4.10%, 31st
Finance, insurance & real estate: 118,752—4.80%, 32nd
Government: 351,308—14.20%, 33rd
Manufacturing: 551,702—22.30%, 10th
Mining: 2,658—0.1%, 49th
Service: 472,534—19.10%, 31st
Trade: 487,378—19.70%, 10th
Transportation, communication, & public utilities: 111,330—4.50%, 41st
Wholesale/retail: 505,469—21.2%, 33rd
Unemployment rate: 4.37%, 43rd
Male: 2.55%, 40th
Female: 1.82%, 46th
Total businesses (1991): 175,870
New business incorp's. (1991): 6,994
Percent of total businesses: 3.98%, 45th
Business failures (1991): 900
Percent of total businesses: 0.51%, 47th
Agriculture farm income
Marketing (1991): $5,449,043,000, 9th

Net per operation: $15,022, 34th
Net per acre: $68, 22nd
Leading products: dairy products, cattle, corn, hogs
Av. value land & build. per acre: $867, 27th
Percent increase (1980-90): -13.65%, 35th
Govt. payments: $149,950,000, 20th
Construction, value of all: $3,412,000,000
Per capita: $697.50, 18th
Percent change 1989-90: -0.09%, 18th
Manufactures:
Value added: $37,090,000,000
Per capita: $7,582.12, 3rd
Value of shipments: $83,013,000,000
Per capita: $16,969.93, 4th
Leading products: machinery, foods, fabricated metals, transportation equipment, paper and wood products
Mining, min. prod., value (1987): $209,000,000, 38th
Leading products: stone, sand/gravel, lime
Retail sales: $36,031,000,000, 18th
Per household: $19,691, 19th
Percent increase (1987-90): 24.6%, 6th
Service indust., value (1987): $16,005,000,000, 22nd
Per capita: $3,271.82, 34th
Tourism indus., value (1989): $3,647,000,000, 24th
Foreign exports value: $5,158,000,000, 17th
Per capita: $1,054.42, 18th
Patents per 1,000 pop.: 4.0, 38th

Travel and Transportation

Motor vehicle registrations: 3,671,859
Per 1,000 pop.: 750, 35th
Motorcycle registrations: 189,102
Per 1,000 pop.: 38, 5th
Licensed drivers per 1,000 driving age pop.: 884, 31st
Deaths from motor vehicle accidents per 100,000 pop.: 15.7, 38th
Public roads & streets
Total mileage: 109,876, 13th
Rural mileage: 95,481, 8th
Urban mileage: 14,395, 20th
Interstate mileage: 640, 34th
Annual vehicle-miles of travel per person: 9,051, 26th
Mean travel time for workers 16 + who work away from home: 18.3 min., 41st

Government

Registered voters (1988): UNK
Percent of voting age pop.: UNK, NR
Voter turnout (1988): 2,191,608
Percent of registered voters: UNK, NR
Percent of voting age pop.: 61.98%, 4th
State legislators, total (1992): 132, 33rd
Women members (1992): 32
Percent of legislature: 24.2%, 13th
Dominant party (1992): Democrats
U.S. Congress, House members (1993): 9
Increase 1983-93: 0
Revenues:
State govt.: $13,387,631,000
Per capita: $2,736.77, 17th
State & local govt.: $21,766,102,000
Per capita: $4,449.54, 12th
Indebtedness:
State govt.: $6,119,267,000
Per capita: $1,250.93, 23rd
State & local govt.: $12,090,000,000
Per capita: $2,471.50, 42nd

Laws and Regulations

Legal driving age: 18
Marriage age without parental consent: 18
Divorce residence requirement: 6 mo.

Attractions

Major opera companies (1989): 4, 11th
Per 1 million pop.: 0.82, 18th
Major symphony orchestras (1989): 22, 14th
Per 1 million pop.: 4.52, 15th
State appropriations for state arts agencie per capita: $0.46, 40th
State Fair in mid Aug. at West Allis.

Sports and Competition

NCAA sports teams, 11: Marquette Univ. Warriors, Univ. of Wisconsin Phoenix, Univ. of Wisconsin Eagles, Univ. of Wisconsin Badgers, Univ. of Wisconsin Panthers, Univ. of Wisconsin Titans, Univ. of Wisconsin Rangers, Univ. of Wisconsin Falcons, Univ. of Wisconsin Pointers, Univ. of Wisconsin Yellowjackets, Univ. of Wisconsin Warhawks

Professional teams, 9:

Baseball, 5—Appleton Foxes (Midwest League, Class A), Goodland Field; Beloit Brewers (Midwest League, Class A), Harry C. Pohlman Field; Milwaukee Brewers (AL), Milwaukee County Stadium; Kenosha Twins (Midwest League, Class A), Simmons Field; Madison Muskies (Midwest League, Class A), Warner Park

Basketball, 2—Milwaukee Bucks (NBA), Bradley Center; La Crosse Catbirds (Continental Basketball Association, American Conference), La Crosse Center

Football, 1—Green Bay Packers (NFC), Lambeau Field

Hockey, 1—Milwaukee Admirals (International Hockey League), Bradley Center

WYOMING

Sept. 20, 1852—"Here we reached the dividing height between the waters of the Pacific and those of the Atlantic. One universal shout arose at the announcement of this fact; and visions of home and all its joys floated before the imagination in vivid brightness." Sept. 23—"The scenery from the 'divide' was in beautiful contrast with that of the country left behind us. Broad and grassy valleys were spread out before us, bounded by low rounded hills covered with verdure, over which ranged bands of buffalo, while little flocks of antelope bounded gracefully around us. The low bottom of the Medicine-bow, upon which we are encamped, is thickly covered with excellent grass, and the stream has an extensive fringe of willows and rose-bushes, with occasional groves of cottonwood and aspens."

Howard Stansbury

Small in population, rich in history, Wyoming lives up to its nickname of "The Equality State." It boasts the nation's first elected woman official, the first woman governor, and the greatest plainswoman of the West. It relishes such mysteries as the prehistoric Medicine Wheel. Among its notable scenic attractions, Wyoming claims the first national park (Yellowstone), the first national monument (Devil's Tower), and the first national forest (Shoshone). More than 80% of its land is used for cattle grazing, and thousands of oil wells dot the prairies. To emphasize its Western past, Wyoming celebrates with one of the most notable annual festivals, Frontier Days at Cheyenne.

SUPERLATIVES

- World's largest elk (wapiti) herd—Jackson Elk Refuge.
- Largest U.S. coal reserves.
- First "Dude Ranch"—Eaton Brothers, near Dayton.

MOMENTS IN HISTORY

- The first white explorer of record in what is now Wyoming was John Colter, who discovered Yellowstone and the Tetons in 1807.
- In 1811 Wilson Price Hunt's party crossed much of the present state.
- General William H. Ashley established a trading center on the Yellowstone River in 1822.
- Sponsored by Ashley a series of meetings known as Rendezvous gathered annually in various locations from 1834 through the 1840s. These attracted a picturesque group of trappers, traders, and Indian families, who traded furs, frolicked, and brawled uproariously.
- Wyoming's first substantial trading post was set up by Antonio Mateo in 1828, near the Powder River forks.
- In 1832 the expedition of Captain B.L.E. de Bonneville made tracks across Wyoming, pioneering parts of the Oregon Trail.
- Laramie was begun in 1834 to become the state's first permanent European-style settlement.
- During the California gold rush, in 1850 alone

more than 60,000 people and 90,000 domestic animals crossed the state.

• A period of Indian troubles extended from about 1862 to 1868, with 1865 known as "the bloody year on the plains."

> So They Say
>
> "...All were killed. Within a small space most were found, horribly mutilated. I loaded the wagons with as many of the bodies as they could contain...the soldiers being so overcome with horror as almost unable to obey orders..."
>
> Tenadore Ten Eyck, on the so-called Fetterman Massacre

• The transcontinental railroad arrived at Cheyenne in 1867, was completed two years later, and Wyoming was on the nation's mainline. Cities sprang up almost overnight.

• In 1870 the first scientific party reached Yellowstone, and its reports caused a sensation.

• On March 1, 1872, Yellowstone became the first national park.

> So They Say
>
> "All honor then to the United States for having bequeathed as a free gift to man the beauties and curiosities of Wonderland. It was an act worthy of the greatest nation."
>
> Earl of Dunraven, on establishment of Yellowstone National Park

• "Nesters" and rustlers vied for positions with the ranchers in the "Johnson County Cattle War of 1892."

• Although the Wyoming population of 62,500 was not enough to qualify for statehood, on July 10, 1890 Wyoming nevertheless became a state.

• Devil's Tower became the nation's first national monument in 1906.

• The 11,393 from Wyoming who served in World War I represented 7% of the state's population.

• The election of Nellie Tayloe Ross as governor in 1924 was a landmark in women's progress.

• The state's 75th anniversary was celebrated in 1965.

• In the elections of 1980 and 1984 Ronald Reagan won Wyoming's vote, but Democrats retained the governor's chair, as they continued to do through the early 1990s.

That's Interesting

• When the Indians saw the first two white women in Wyoming, they were astonished that such pale creatures could survive the trip, and they killed the fattest dogs to prepare a feast for their guests.

• The Indian name for Bull Lake was "the lake that roars." The strange sound comes from the action of the wind on the ice.

• The prehistoric Medicine Wheel is similar to Stonehenge in England and one in the Gobi Desert. It remains a mystery to scholars.

• The first telephone poles in Wyoming made such attractive scratching posts for buffaloes that as many as 30 of the huge animals might be seen waiting their turn to rub against one.

Wyoming Notables

James Bridger (Richmond, VA, 1804-1881), frontiersman/fur trader/scout. **Martha Jane "Calamity Jane" Burk** (Princeton, MO, 1852?-1903), frontierswoman. **William Frederick "Buffalo Bill" Cody** (Scott Cty., IA, 1846-1917), frontiersman/entertainer. **Crazy Horse** (Oglala Sioux tribe, 1849?-1877), Indian leader. **Emerson Hough** (Newton, IA, 1857-1923), author. **Thomas Moran** (Bolton, England, 1837-1926), landscape artist. **Edgar Wilson "Bill" Nye** (Shirley, ME, 1850-1896), humorist. **Jackson Pollock** (Cody, WY, 1912-1956), artist. **Red Cloud** (north-central Nebraska, 1822-1909), Indian leader. **Nellie Tayloe Ross** (St. Joseph, MO, 1880?-1977), public official. **Washakie** (Montana, 1804-1900), Indian leader. **Owen Wister** (Philadelphia, PA, 1860-1938), novelist.

General

Admitted to statehood: July 10, 1890

Origin of name: the word was taken from Wyoming Valley, PA, which was the site of an Indian massacre and became widely known by Campbell's poem, "Gertrude of Wyoming"; in Algonquin it means "large prairie place," or a Delaware Indian word, meaning "mountains and valleys alternating"

Capital: Cheyenne, founded 1867
Nickname: Equality State
Motto: "Equal Rights"
Bird: meadowlark
Flower: Indian paintbrush
Song: "Wyoming"
Stone: jade
Tree: cottonwood

The Land

Area: 97,818 sq. mi., 10th
Land: 97,105 sq. mi., 9th
Water: 714 sq. mi., 36th
Topography: the Eastern Great Plains rise to the foothills of the Rocky Mtns.; the Continental Divide crosses the state from the NW to SE
Number of counties: 23
Geographic center: Fremont, 58 mi. ENE of Lander
Length: 360 mi.
Width: 280 mi.
Highest point: 13,804 ft. (Gannett Peak), 5th
Lowest point: 3,099 ft. (Belle Fourche River), 50th
Mean elevation: 6,700 ft., 2nd

Climate and Environment

Temp., highest: 114 deg. on July 12, 1900, at Basin; lowest: -63 deg. on Feb. 9, 1933, at Moran
Fresh water withdrawn, per capita, per day: 12,200 gal., 2nd
Endangered species: mammals, 2—black-footed ferret, Northern Rocky Mountain gray wolf; birds, 2—whooping crane, American peregrine falcon; reptiles, none; amphibians, 1; fishes, 2; invertebrates, none; plants, none

Major Cities, Population Percentage Increase (1980-90)

Casper, 46,742— -8.38%
Cheyenne, 50,008—5.76%
Gillette, 17,635—45.34%
Laramie, 26,687—9.33%
Rock Springs, 19,050— -2.10%

The People

Population: 453,588, 51st
  Percent change (1980-90): -3.52%, 48th
  Per sq. mi: 4.64, 50th
  Percent in metro. area: 29.54%, 47th
  Percent foreign born: 1.7%, 37th
White: 427,061—94.15%, 9th
Black: 3,606—0.79%, 43rd
Native American: 9,479—2.09%, 8th
Asian, Pacific Isle: 2,806—0.62%, 41st
Other races: 10,636—2.34%, 15th
Hispanic origin: 25,751—5.68%, 13th
Percent over 5 yrs. speaking language other than English at home: 5.7%, 33rd
Percent males: 50.05%, 5th
Percent females: 49.95%, 47th
Percent never married: 21.7%, 48th
Marriages per 1,000 (1989): 9.7, 24th
Divorces per 1,000 (1989): 6.4, 6th
Median age: 32
Under 5 years: 34,780—7.67%, 13th
Under 18 years: 135,525—29.88%, 5th
65 years & older: 47,195—10.40%, 46th
Percent increase among the elderly: 27.0%, 18th

Of Vital Importance

Live births per 1,000 pop.: 13.9, 48th
Infant mortality rate per 1,000 births (1988): 8.9, 34th
Average lifetime (1979-81): 73.85, 25th
Deaths per 100,000 pop. (1988): 677.7, 47th
Causes of death per 100,000 pop. (1988):
  Diseases of heart: 191.9, 47th
  Malignant neoplasms: 145.7, 46th
  Cerebrovascular diseases: 48.9, 42nd
  Accidents & adverse effects: 53.2, 7th
  Chronic obstructive pulmonary diseases: 41.1, 10th
  Suicide: 16.9, 7th
  HIV infection: 0.6, 49th
  Other: 63.1, 47th

Keeping Well

Non-federal physicians per 100,000 pop.: 162, 46th

Dentists per 100,000 (1990-91): 61, 26th
Nurses per 100,000 (1989): 588, 35th
Hospitals per 100,000: 7.1, 4th
Admissions per 100,000: 12,086, 40th
Beds per 100,000: 644.86, 7th
Occupancy rate: 58.9%, 49th
Semiprivate room charges per day: $234, 34th
Average stay: 7.5, 19th
Notifiable diseases per 100,000:
AIDS: 0.7, 50th
Gonorrhea: 34.4, 43rd
Measles: 3.3, 29th
Syphillis: 2.6, 45th
Tuberculosis (TB): 1.1, 51st
Per capita spending on mental health programs (1987): $29.92, 37th
Pop. without health insur. (1991): 11.3%, 33rd

Households by Type

Total households: 168,839
Percent change (1980-90): 1.71%, 48th
Family households: 119,825
Percent of total: 70.97%, 23rd
Nonfamily households: 49,014
Percent of total: 29.03%, 29th
Persons per household: 2.63, 16th
Pop. living in group quarters: 10,240
Percent of pop.: 2.26%, 44th

Living Quarters

Total housing units: 203,411
Persons per unit: 2.23, 44th
Occupied housing units: 168,839
Percent of total units: 83.00%, 45th
Persons per unit: 2.57, 17th
Percent of units with over 1 person per room: 2.78%, 30th
Owner-occupied units: 114,544
Percent of total units: 56.31%, 37th
Percent of occupied units: 67.84%, 23rd
Persons per unit: 2.74, 22nd
Median value: $61,600, 32nd
Renter-occupied units: 54,295
Percent of total units: 26.69%, 40th
Percent of occupied units: 32.16%, 29th
Persons per unit: 2.39, 18th
Median contract rent: $270, 39th
Rental vacancy rate: 14.4%, 3rd
Mobile home, trailer & other as a % of occupied housing units: 21.24%, 1st

Crime Index per 100,000

Total: 4,211, 41st
Violent: 301, 39th
Murder and nonnegligent manslaughter: 5, 34th
Aggravated assault: 7,668, 14th
Robbery: 16, 47th
Rape: 30, 39th
Property: 3,909, 40th
Burglary: 631, 49th
Larceny, theft: 3,129, 22nd
Motor vehicle theft: 149, 49th
Drug abuse arrests: 121, 42nd

Teaching and Learning

Literacy (1987): 93%, 2nd
Pop. 3 and over enrolled in school: 134,739
Percent of pop.: 31.1%, 2nd
Public elementary & secondary schools:
Total enrollment: 96,000
Avg. class size (1987): 20, 41st
Teachers: 6,500
Percent of pop.: 1.43%, 1st
Teachers' avg. salary: $28,200, 29th
Spending per capita: $1,149, 2nd
Spending per pupil in avg. daily attendance: $5,281, 14th
Percent of graduates taking SAT: 13%, 33rd
Combined SAT scores: 980, 20th
Percent of pop. over 25 completing:
High school: 83.0%, 5th
College degree/s: 18.8%, 29th
Higher educa., institutions: 9
Per 100,000 pop.: 1.8, 2nd
Enroll: 31,326
Percent of pop.: 6.91%, 8th
Public: 30,623
Percent of enroll.: 97.76%, 2nd
Private: 703
Percent of enroll.: 2.24%, 50th
White non-Hispanic: 55,487
Percent of enroll.: 97.03%, 1st
Black non-Hispanic: 296
Percent of enroll.: 0.52%, 50th

Hispanic: 195
Percent of enroll.: 0.34%, 49th
Asian/Pacific Islander: 418
Percent of enroll.: 0.73%, 46th
Amer. Indian/AK native: 398
Percent of enroll.: 0.70%, 19th
Nonresident alien: 392
Percent of enroll.: 0.69%, 51st
Female: 17,624
Percent of enroll.: 56.26%, 12th
Tuition, state university ('90-'91): $1,148, 48th
Public library systems: 23
Books & serial vol. per capita: 4.28, 3rd
Govt. expend. per capita: $23.32, 9th
State govt.: $3.76, 12th
Local govts.: $19.55, 9th

Law Enforcement, Courts, and Prisons

Police protection expend.: $65,182,000
Per capita: $143.57, 9th
Judicial & legal expend.: $26,981,000
Per capita: $59.43, 14th
Corrections expend.: $38,300,000
Per capita: $84.36, 21st
Police per 10,000 pop. (1990-91): 28.4, 3rd
Prisoners (state & fed.) sentenced to over 1 yr., per 100,000 pop.: 237
Percent change (1989-90): 9.25%, 13th
Death penalty: yes, by lethal injection
Under sentence of death: 2, 32nd
Executed (1989): none

Religion, Number and Percent of Population

Agnostic: 1,590—0.50%, 27th
Buddhist: NA
Christian: 260,494—81.90%, 41st
Hindu: 636—0.20%, 3rd
Jewish: NA
Moslem: NA
Unitarian: NA
Other: 1,908—0.60%, 46th
None: 42,939—13.50%, 3rd
Refused to answer: 10,496—3.30%, 4th

Making a Living

Personal income per capita (1989): $12,311, 36th
Percent increase (1979-'89) (constant 1989 dollars): -7.3%, 51st
Average income per family: $37,127, 37th
Percent of pop. below poverty level: 11.9%, 28th
Percent 65 and over: 10.7%, 34th
Cost of living, selected cities
1st qtr., 1991 (U. S. Standard=100)
Casper 97.2
Laramie 97.8

Economy

Civilian labor force : 246,000
Percent of tot. pop.: 54.23%, 6th
Percent 65 and over: 3.25%, 13th
Percent females: 44.31%, 46th
Percent job growth (1980-90): -4.34%, 51st
Major employer industries:
Agriculture: 16,543—7.10%, 7th
Construction: 11,417—4.90%, 18th
Finance, insurance & real estate: 8,155—3.50%, 51st
Government: 52,891—22.70%, 5th
Manufacturing: 9,320—4.00%, 49th
Mining: 15,924—7.7%, 1st
Service: 35,882—15.40%, 49th
Trade: 41,241—17.70%, 41st
Transportation, communication, & public utilities: 18,174—7.80%, 2nd
Wholesale/retail: 43,416—20.9%, 35th
Unemployment rate: 5.28%, 28th
Male: 2.85%, 32nd
Female: 2.44%, 25th
Total businesses (1991): 26,383
New business incorp's. (1991): 1,386
Percent of total businesses: 5.25%, 35th
Business failures (1991): 161
Percent of total businesses: 0.61%, 44th
Agriculture farm income
Marketing (1991): $812,743,000, 37th
Net per operation: $22,270, 23rd
Net per acre: $6, 49th
Leading products: cattle, sugar beets, hay, barley
Av. value land & build. per acre: $153, 48th
Percent increase (1980-90): -4.97%, 32nd

Govt. payments: $33,241,000, 35th
Construction, value of all: $135,000,000
Per capita: $297.63, 47th
Percent change 1989-90: 17.39%, 10th
Manufactures:
Value added: $844,000,000
Per capita: $1,860.72, 46th
Value of shipments: $2,756,000,000
Per capita: $6,076.00, 44th
Leading products: refined petroleum products, foods, wood products, stone, clay and glass products
Mining, min. prod., value (1987): $5,847,000,000, 8th
Leading products: petroleum, coal, nat. gas
Retail sales: $2,726,000,000, 51st
Per household: $16,314, 48th
Percent increase (1987-90): 15.9%, 25th
Service indust., value (1987): $1,444,000,000, 51st
Per capita: $3,183.51, 40th
Tourism indus., value (1989): $990,000,000, 46th
Foreign exports value: $264,000,000, 47th
Per capita: $582.03, 40th
Patents per 1,000 pop.: 12.6, 8th

Travel and Transportation

Motor vehicle registrations: 528,421
Per 1,000 pop.: 1,163, 1st
Motorcycle registrations: 20,310
Per 1,000 pop.: 44, 2nd
Licensed drivers per 1,000 driving age pop.: 991, 3rd
Deaths from motor vehicle accidents per 100,000 pop.: 27.6, 6th
Public roads & streets
Total mileage: 39,213, 38th
Rural mileage: 37,261, 37th
Urban mileage: 1,952, 44th
Interstate mileage: 913, 22nd
Annual vehicle-miles of travel per person: 12,859, 1st
Mean travel time for workers 16 + who work away from home: 15.4 min., 48th

Government

Registered voters (1988): 226,189
Percent of voting age pop.: 64.44%, 40th
Voter turnout (1988): 176,551
Percent of registered voters: 78.05%, 9th
Percent of voting age pop.: 50.30%, 29th
State legislators, total (1992): 94, 43rd
Women members (1992): 23
Percent of legislature: 24.5%, 11th
Dominant party (1992): Republicans
U.S. Congress, House members (1993): 1
Increase 1983-93: 0
Revenues:
State govt.: $1,899,867,000
Per capita: $4,188.53, 2nd
State & local govt.: $2,726,590,000
Per capita: $6,011.16, 4th
Indebtedness:
State govt.: $938,236,000
Per capita: $2,068.48, 14th
State & local govt.: $2,257,000,000
Per capita: $4,975.88, 7th

Laws and Regulations

Legal driving age: 18
Marriage age without parental consent: 18
Divorce residence requirement: 60 days, qualification—check local statutes

Attractions

Major opera companies (1989): 0
Per 1 million pop.: 0.00
Major symphony orchestras (1989): 3, 45th
Per 1 million pop.: 6.32, 8th
State appropriations for state arts agencies per capita: $0.51, 35th
State Fair in late Aug. at Douglas.

Sports and Competition

NCAA sports teams, 1: Univ. of Wyoming Cowboys
Professional teams, none

OUTLYING AREAS

CARIBBEAN ISLANDS

Commonwealth of Puerto Rico: Puerto Rico is the smallest of the islands known as the Greater Antilles. The Atlantic Ocean lies to the north and the Caribbean to the south. The Dominican Republic is the neighbor to the west, and the American Virgin Islands lie to the east. Vieques is the largest of the outlying islands. The main island is mountainous, rising to massive El Yunque near the east coast. The island climate is ideal, with an average variation of climate of only six degrees. Puerto Rico is subject to hurricanes, the most destructive occurring in 1515.

Christopher Columbus reached the island in 1493, and, by early 1511, the island became the first Spanish colony in the New World. It suffered many attacks by the English. After almost 400 years of Spanish rule, Spain ceded Puerto Rico to the U.S. as a condition of ending the Spanish American War of 1898.

Puerto Ricans received U.S. citizenship in 1917, and the island became the Commonwealth of Puerto Rico in 1952. The status of its relationship to the U.S. is a matter of continuing concern, with many Puerto Ricans enjoying the benefits of the present system, others desiring statehood, and still others advocating independence.

The Land

Capital: San Juan, settled 1508
Area: 3,515 sq. mi.
Land: 3,459 sq. mi.
Water: 56 sq. mi.
Width (n/s): about 36 mi.
Length (e/w): about 100 mi.
Highest point: 4,389 ft (Cerro de Punta)
Lowest point: sea level
Mean elevation: 1,800 ft.

Symbols

Flag: three red and white horizontal stripes, with a blue triangle at the mast, bearing one white star
Song: "La Borinquena"
Motto: *Joannes Est Nomen Eius* (John is his name)
Flower: maya
Bird: reinita
Tree: ceiba

Population (1991)

Population: 3,566,000
Population density: 1,030.9 per sq. mi.
Percent urban (1990): 66.8%

Principal Cities

San Juan, Bayamon, Ponce, Carolina, Caguas, Mayaguez

Economy

Principal industries: manufacturing
Principal manufactured goods: pharmaceuticals, chemicals, machinery and metals, electric machinery and equipment, petroleum refining, food products, apparel
Principal agricultural products: sugarcane, coffee, pineapples, plantains, bananas, yams, taniers, pidgeon peas, peppers, pumpkins, coriander, lettuce, tobacco
Livestock: cattle, pigs, poultry
Minerals: mostly cement

Interesting People
Pablo Casals, Orlando Cepeda, Roberto Clemente, Dona Felisa Rincon de Gautier, Luis Munoz Marin, Luis A. Ferre, Jose Ferrer, Rita Moreno, Francisco Olier, Jose Campeche, Julio Rosado, Marshal Alejandro O'Reilly

Virgin Islands: The Virgin Islands were discovered by Columbus in 1493 and named by him in honor of the Virgins of St. Ursula. Before Columbus, the islands had been inhabited by the Siboney Indians, by the Arawak from South America (who invented the hammock), and by the fierce Carib, (whose name was given to the Caribbean).

Pirates swarmed over the islands, which have been claimed by Holland, Spain, France, England and Denmark. In 1917 the U.S. bought its present portion of the Virgins from Denmark, to keep them from falling into German hands during World War I.

In 1927 the people became American nationals; they achieved limited self-government in 1936, and their rights were expanded in 1954. Today the Virgin Islands has a republican form of government, with a governor and lieutenant governor; they elect a nonvoting member to the U.S. House of Representatives.

Geography
Capital: Charlotte Amalie, St. Thomas
Main islands: St. John, St. Thomas, St. Croix
Area: 132 sq. mi.
Land: 132 sq. mi.
Water: 0 sq. mi.
Highest point: 1,556 ft. (Crown Mt., St. Thomas)
Lowest point: sea level

Symbols
Bird: yellow breast
Flower: yellow elder or yellow trumpet (Ginger Thomas)
Song: "Virgin Islands March"

Population
Total: 101,809
Density: 771.3 per sq. mi.

Principal Cities
Frederiksted, Christiansted, Charlotte Amalie

The Economy
Principal industries: tourism (a principal source of income), rum, alumina production, petroleum refining, watch industry, textiles, electronics.
Principal manufactured goods: rum, textiles, pharmaceuticals, perfumes
Principal agricultural products: truck garden produce
Minerals: sand & gravel

Navassa: This other Caribbean island, uninhabited, lies between Jamaica and Haiti, has an area of about 2 sq. mi., administered by the U.S. Coast Guard, which operates an automatic lighthouse.
Until 1981 the U.S. laid claim to the uninhabited islands of Quita Sueno Bank, Roncador and Serrana, but the claim of Columbia to the islands was recognized in that year.

PACIFIC ISLANDS

American Samoa: This unincorporated territory of six small islands of the Samoan group is the most southerly region under U.S. jurisdiction.

The islands lie 2,600 miles southwest of Honolulu, Hawaii. The main islands are mountainous and volcanic, surrounded by coral reefs. Swain Island came under U.S. control in 1925 and is organized as a part of the Samoan group.

Native Polynesians probably reached the islands about 1000 B.C. The Dutch explorer, Jacob Roggeveen, visited the islands in 1722. The U.S., Britain and France claimed trade and other privileges in the islands, and the U.S. established a naval station at Pago Pago in 1878. The agreement of 1899 recognized the U.S. right to govern present American Samoa. In 1978, Peter Tali Coleman became the first popularly elected governor.

The islands retain much of their original Polynesian culture, clinging to the traditional lava lava garment, and *siva*, the traditional dance, is popular with both the local people and the increasing number of tourists.

Pago Pago was the the site of the popular short story *Rain* by Somerset Maugham.

Principal exports are fish products, mostly tuna, packed by leading producers. Copra, bread-fruit, yams, coconuts, bananas, oranges and pineapples are other products. The cocoa of the island is ranked among the world's best. Most of the cultivated crops are grown near the coasts. The Samoan people are known for their fine craft work, particularly tapa cloth, pounded from the bark of the paper mulberry trees. Baskets and laufala floor mats are woven from palm leaves.

Some of the multioared longboats, known as *fautasi*, are hollowed from tree trunks, reaching 40 ft. in length. Other craft are the smaller outrigger fishing boats.

Geography:
Capital: Pago Pago
Area: 77 sq. mi.
Highest point: 3,160ft. (Lata Mountain)
Lowest point: sea level

Symbols:
Motto: In Samoa, God is First
Flower: Paogo (Ula-fala)
Plant: ava
Song: "Amerika Samoa"

Population
Total: 46,773
Density: 607.4 per sq. mi.

Largest City:
Pago Pago on the Island of Tutuila

Government
Administered by the U.S. Dept. of the Interior
One nonvoting delegate to the U.S. House of Representatives

Guam: Explorer Magellan reached Guam in the Marianas chain in 1521. Spanish missionaries began colonization in 1668.

After the Spanish American War in 1898, Spain ceded the island to the U.S. Its residents are U.S. citizens, but do not vote for president.

Guam is the largest and most southern of the Marianas, with a tropical climate. Its principal manufactures are textiles and foods. The government is the principal employer, and tourism is important.

Geography
Capital: Agana
Area: 209 sq. mi.
Width (n/s): about 4 to 8.5 mi
Length (e/w): about 30 mi.
Highest point: 1,329 ft. (Mt. Lamlam)
Lowest point: sea level

Symbols
Nickname: Where America's Day Begins
Bird: Toto (fruit dove)
Flower: Puti Tai nobio (Bougainvillaea)
Tree: Ifit (Intsiabijuga)
Song: "Stand Ye Guamians"

Population
Total: 133,152
Density: 637.09

Economy
Principal industries: construction, light manufacturing, tourism, banking, defense
Principal manufactured goods: textiles, foods
Principal agricultural products: cabbages, eggplants, cucumber, long beans, tomatoes, bananas, coconuts, watermelon, yams, canteloupe, papayas, maize, sweet potatoes
Livestock: cattle & hogs/pigs

Government
Self-governing organized unincorporated U.S. territory
Governor: Elected
Legislature: Unicameral, 21 members elected biennially
U.S. House of Representatives: One elected nonvoting member

Wake Island: With its sister islands, Wilkes and Peale, is an important outpost on the route from Hawaii to Hong Kong. It formally became a U.S. possession in 1899. Administered by the U.S. Air Force, its population mainly is associated with the Air force

Midway Islands: With Sand and Eastern Island in the North Pacific, 1,150 miles Northwest of Hawaii, Midway came under U.S. control in 1867. It is administered by the U.S. Navy. The Midway cluster is occupied only by a group of military personnel.

Johnston Atoll: With Kingman Reef, this point of land occupies only about one square mile and is under the U.S. Defense Nuclear Agency.

Kingman Reef: This islet was discovered in 1874 by American explorers. Less than half a mile square, it lies south of Hawaii and is under U.S. Navy control.

Howland, Jarvis and Baker Islands: Lying more than 1,500 miles southwest of the Hawaiian Islands, these uninhabited islets are under control of the Interior Department.

Palmyra: This 4-mile-square island is privately owned and is administered by the U.S. Interior Department.

Micronesia: Several Pacific Island groups, collectively known as Micronesia, were placed under U.S. trusteeship after World War II. Their status continues to change as they move toward greater independence.

Commonwealth of the Northern Mariana Islands: An archipelago of 16 islands of the Northern Marianas archipelago, stretching for 300 miles, with a total land area of 183.5 sq. miles. Population of Chamorro descent is 43,345, concentrated on three main islands: Saipan (38,896), Rota (2,295) and Tinian (2,118). The group has been self-governing since 1978, under a constitution adopted by the people. There is a governor, with a bicameral legislature. Tourism is increasing and is the principal industry.

Federated States of Micronesia: Stretching for 1,800 miles along the archipelago of the Caroline Islands, are the four states, consisting of Pohnpei, the capital, (pop. 52,00), Kosrae (pop. 16,500), Truk (pop. 31,000), and Yap (pop. 12,000), each made up of several small islands. The island federation lies southwest of Honolulu and southeast of Guam. The population is diverse, with several languages. FSM is a sovereign self-governing state, with guarantees of defense and aid from the U.S.

Republic of the Marshall Islands: Two clusters of atolls comprise this sovereign, self-governing state. Each atoll is a cluster of a number of small islands surrounding a lagoon. The total land area is 70 square miles. Total population is 43,000, with 20,000 in the capital, Majuro. The republic is governed by the Nitijela, a parliament which serves as the executive branch. The U.S. remains responsible for defense and retains certain other responsibilities.

Republic of Palau: The 200 islands of the Caroline Island chain form the Republic of Palau. Eight are permanently inhabited, with a total population of 15,122, with 10,501 of these on the island of Koror. The U.S. recognized the constitution of Palau, and it became effective in 1980. There is a bicameral legislature. The president and vice president are elected, and they are advised by a council of chiefs.

PART II

THE STATES COMPARED

NOTE TO THE READER

The data in the following tables is listed in "Descending Numerical Order" ("Desc. Num. Order"). That arrangement applies to every column in the table.

This arrangement of data provides an opportunity for analysis of the states in unprecedented depth.

States are referred to by their postal abbreviations:

AL, Alabama
AK, Alaska
AZ, Arizona
AR, Arkansas
CA, California
CO, Colorado
CT, Connecticut
DE, Delaware
DC, District of Columbia
FL, Florida
GA, Georgia
HI, Hawaii
ID, Idaho
IL, Illinois
IN, Indiana
IA, Iowa
KS, Kansas
KY, Kentucky
LA, Louisiana
ME, Maine
MD, Maryland
MA, Massachusetts
MI, Michigan
MN, Minnesota
MS, Mississippi
MO, Missouri
MT, Montana
NE, Nebraska
NV, Nevada
NH, New Hampshire
NJ, New Jersey
NM, New Mexico
NY, New York
NC, North Carolina
ND, North Dakota
OH, Ohio
OK, Oklahoma
OR, Oregon
PA, Pennsylvania
RI, Rhode Island
SC, South Carolina
SD, South Dakota
TN, Tennessee
TX, Texas
UT, Utah
VT, Vermont
VA, Virginia
WA, Washington
WV, West Virginia
WI, Wisconsin
WY, Wyoming

THE LAND

Area, Land, Water, and Counties

Area (sq. mi.)		Land (sq. mi.)		Water (sq. mi.)		Number of Counties		Desc. Num. Order
AK	656,424	AK	570,374	AK	86,051	TX	254	1
TX	268,601	TX	261,914	MI	40,001	GA	159	2
CA	163,707	CA	155,973	FL	11,761	KY	120	3
MT	147,046	MT	145,556	WI	11,190	MO	114	4
NM	121,598	NM	121,365	LA	8,277	KS	105	5
NJ	8,722	HA	6,423	VT	366	CT	8	47
CT	5,544	CT	4,845	AZ	364	HA	5	48
DE	2,489	DE	1,955	NM	234	RI	5	49
RI	1,545	RI	1,045	WV	145	DE	3	50
DC	68	DC	61	DC	7	DC	–	51

SOURCE: U.S. Geological Survey, *Elevations and Distances in the United States*, 1989.

Length, Width, Highest /Lowest Point, and Mean Elevation.

Length (mi.)		Width (mi.)		Highest Point (ft.)		Lowest Point (ft.)		Mean Elevations		Coastline Statute (mi.)		Shoreline Statute (mi.)		Desc. Num. Order
HI	1,600	AK (N-S)	810	AK	20,320	CA	−282	CO	6,800	AK	6,640	AK	33,904	1
AK	1,480	TX	660	CA	14,494	LA	−8	WY	6,700	FL	1,350	FL	8,426	2
TX (N-S)	790	NM	343	CO	14,433	AL	Sea level	UT	6,100	CA	840	LA	7,721	3
CA (N-S)	770	NV	320	WA	14,410	AK	Sea level	NM	5,700	HI	750	ME	3,478	4
MT	630	AZ	310	WY	13,804	CT	Sea level	NV	5,500	LA	397	CA	3,427	5
NJ (N-S)	150	MA (N-S)	50	MS	806	MT	1,800	RI	200					47
CT (N-S)	110	DE	30	LA	535	UT	2,000	DC	150					48
DE (N-S)	100	RI	30	DE	442	NM	2,842	FL	100					49
RI (N-S)	40	DC	–	DC	410	WY	3,099	LA	100					50
DC	–	HI	–	FL	345	CO	3,350	DE	60					51

SOURCE: U.S. Geological Survey, *Elevations and Distances in the United States*, 1989.

Greatest Extent (mi.)

East-West		North-South		Desc. Num. Order
HI	1,600	AK	800	1
AK	900	TX	800	2
TX	775	CA	770	3
MT	580	FL	507	4
NC	520	ID	490	5
VT	90	DE	96	47
NJ	57	CT	75	48
RI	37	RI	48	49
DE	35	DC	12	50
DC	8	HI	–	51

CLIMATE AND ENVIRONMENT

Hottest and Coldest Temperatures on Record (°F)

	Hottest	*Date*	*Place*		*Coldest*	*Date*	*Place*
CA	134	July 10, 1913	Greenland Ranch	AK	-80	Jan. 23, 1971	Prospect Creek Camp
AZ	127	July 7, 1905	Parker	MT	-70	Jan. 20, 1954	Rogers Pass
NV	122	June 23, 1954	Overton	UT	-69	Feb. 1, 1985	Peter's Sink
KS	121	July 24, 1936	Alton (near)	WY	-63	Feb. 9, 1933	Moran
ND	121	July 6, 1936	Steele	CO	-61	Feb. 1, 1985	Maybell
ME	105	July 10, 1911	North Bridgton	GA	-17	Jan. 27, 1940	CCC Camp F-16
VT	105	July 4, 1911	Vermon	LA	-16	Feb. 13, 1899	Minden
RI	104	Aug. 2, 1975	Providence	DC	-15	Feb. 11, 1988	Washington
AK	100	June 27, 1915	Fort Yukon	FL	-2	Feb. 13, 1899	Tallahassee
HI	100	April 27, 1931	Pahala	HI	12	May 17, 1979	Mauna Kea

SOURCE: National Climatic Data Center, NOAA, U.S. Department of Commerce.

Monthly Average Temperatures (°F)

Highest		*Lowest*			*Temperatures (Highest*	*Lowest)*	*Spread*	*Desc. Num. Order*
AZ	105.0	AK	-21.6	AK	(71.8	-21.6)	93.4	1
NV	104.5	ND	-5.1	ND	(84.4	-5.1)	89.5	2
CA	98.8	MN	-2.9	MN	(83.4	-2.9)	86.3	3
TX	98.5	SD	1.9	NV	(104.5	19.5)	85.0	4
OK	93.9	WI	5.4	SD	(86.5	1.9)	84.6	5
MA	81.8	LA	36.2	MS	(92.5	34.9)	57.6	47
RI	81.7	CA	36.8	LA	(93.3	36.2)	57.1	48
VT	80.5	AZ	38.1	FL	(91.7	39.9)	51.8	49
ME	78.9	FL	39.9	OR	(82.6	32.8)	49.8	50
AK	71.8	HI	65.3	HI	(87.1	65.3)	21.8	51

SOURCE: National Climatic Data Center, NOAA, U.S. Department of Commerce.

Selected Cities in Which Air Quality Meets Federal Standards

AK	Juneau
AL	Mobile
AR	Fort Smith, Little Rock, North Little Rock
AZ	Tucson
CA	Escondido, Oceanside, Salinas
CO	Pueblo
CT	New Haven, Waterbury
DE	Dover, Newark
FL	Gainesville, Miami Beach, Orlando, Tallahassee
GA	Albany, Columbus, Macon, Savannah
HA	Hilo, Honolulu, Wailuku
IA	Cedar Rapids, Davenport, Des Moines, Sioux City
ID	Boise, Idaho Falls, Pocatello, Springfield
IL	Decatur, Peoria, Rockford
IN	Evansville, Fort Wayne, Gary, Hammond
KS	Overland Park, Topeka, Wichita
KY	Frankfort
LA	Kenner, Lafayette, New Orleans, Shreveport
MA	New Bedford, Quincy
MD	Annapolis
ME	Augusta
MI	Dearborn, Flint, Kalamazoo, Lansing, Livonia, Sterling Heights, Warren, Westland
MN	Duluth
MO	Independence, Jefferson City
MS	Biloxi, Gulfport, Jackson, Springfield
MT	Billings, Butte, Helena
ND	Bismarck, Fargo, Grand Forks
NE	Grand Island, Lincoln, Omaha
NH	Concord, Nashua
NM	Las Cruces, Santa Fe
NV	Carson City, Las Vegas, Reno
NY	Rochester, Syracuse
OK	Lawton
OR	Eugene, Salem
RI	Cranston, Warwick
SC	Charleston
SD	Pierre, Rapid City, Sioux Falls
TN	Chattanooga
TX	Abilene, Amarillo, Austin, Brownsville, Corpus Christi, Lubbock, McAllen, Midland, Odessa, Pasadena, Plano, Richardson, San Angelo, San Antonio, Tyler, Waco, Wichita Falls
VA	Chesapeake, Hampton, Portsmouth, Roanoke
VT	Burlington, Montpelier, Rutland
WA	Olympia
WI	Green Bay, Kenosha, Madison, Racine
WV	Wheeling
WY	Casper, Cheyenne, Laramie

SOURCE: National Oceanic and Atmospheric Administration.

Tornadoes (1953–91)

Number		*Fatalities*		*Desc. Num. Order*
TX	4,949	TX	455	1
OK	2,040	MS	346	2
FL	1,762	AL	245	3
KS	1,737	MI	236	4
NE	1,449	IN	215	5
VT	31	NJ	0	47
HI	28	OR	0	48
RI	7	RI	0	49
AK	1	UT	0	50
DC	0	VT	0	51

SOURCE: U.S. Department of Commerce, National Weather Service, National Severe Storms Forecast Center.

Earthquakes (1980–91)

Number of Earthquakes 1980–91		*Largest Magnitude (Richter scale)*		*Desc. Num. Order*
AK	10,253	AK	7.9	1
CA	6,732	ID	7.3	2
WA	615	CA	7.2	3
ID	536	OR	6.9	4
NV	398	HI	6.7	5
FL	0	FL	–	47
IA	0	IA	–	48
MN	0	MN	–	49
VT	0	VT	–	50
WI	0	WI	–	51

SOURCE: U. S. Geological Survey, National Earthquakes Information Center.

Notable Earthquakes by Magnitude

State	*Location*	*Date*	*Magnitude*
MO	New Madrid	Jan. 23, 1812	8.7
MO	New Madrid	Dec. 16, 1811	8.6
MO	New Madrid	Jan. 23, 1812	8.4
CA	Fort Tejon	Jan. 9, 1857	8.3
CA	San Francisco	April 18, 1906	8.3
MT	Yellowstone Nat. Park	June 30, 1975	6.1
MO	New Madrid	Jan. 5, 1843	6.0
NY	Massena	Sept. 5, 1944	5.9
VA	Giles County	May 31, 1897	5.8
UT	Logan	Aug. 30, 1962	5.7

SOURCE: Earthquakes in the Conterminous U.S. (1534–1991), from the map by the U.S. Geological Survey.

Endangered Species (no. of species endangered)

Total		*Mammals*		*Birds*		*Reptiles*		*Amphibians*		*Fishes*		*Invertebrates*		*Plants*		*Desc. Num. Order*
CA	64	FL	11	HI	29	FL	5	CA	2	NV	16	TN	24	FL	31	1
HI	51	CA	8	CA	10	AL	4	TX	2	CA	10	AL	21	CA	29	2
FL	45	AZ	6	TX	10	CA	3	VA	1	AZ	9	VA	17	HI	19	3
TX	43	NC	5	FL	7	GA	3	WY	1	TX	7	KY	16	TX	16	4
AL	38	VA	5	OK	6	LA	3	AL	0	UT	6	CA	10	NC	13	5
ND	4	MN	0	NV	1	UT	0	UT	0	SC	0	ND	0	OK	0	47
NJ	4	NE	0	NH	1	VT	0	VT	0	VT	0	SC	0	SD	0	48
WI	4	NV	0	NJ	1	WV	0	WA	0	WA	0	SD	0	WA	0	49
ID	3	NH	0	VT	1	WI	0	WV	0	WV	0	UT	0	WI	0	50
DC	2	RI	0	WV	1	WY	0	WI	0	WI	0	WY	0	WY	0	51

SOURCE: Report to Congress, Endangered and Threatened Species Recovery Program, U. S. Department of the Interior, U. S. Fish and Wildlife Service, Washington D.C. 20240, December, 1990.

MAJOR CITIES

Total Urban Mileage (mi., 1989)

		Desc. Num. Order
NY/NJ/NYC and Newark	35,180	1
CA, Los Angeles	24,906	2
IL, Chicago	19,319	3
TX, Houston	16,990	4
MI, Detroit	12,834	5
SD, Sioux Falls	523	47
NH, Manchester	509	48
WY, Cheyenne	366	49
VT, Burlington	311	50
VA, Virginia Beach	–	51

SOURCE: U.S. Department of Transportation.

Population, Increase/Decrease

Population		*Increase in Population, 1980–90 (%)*		*Desc. Num. Order*
NY, NY City	7,322,564	NV, Las Vegas	56.85	1
CA, Los Angeles	3,485,398	VA, Virginia Beach	49.91	2
IL, Chicago	2,783,726	AK, Anchorage	29.76	3
TX, Houston	1,630,553	NC, Charlotte	25.50	4
PA, Philadelphia	1,585,577	AZ, Phoenix	24.53	5
DE, Wilmington	71,529	KY, Louisville	–9.92	47
ME, Portland	64,358	WV, Charleston	–10.44	48
WV, Charleston	57,287	LA, New Orleans	–10.93	49
WY, Cheyenne	50,008	MI, Detroit	–14.58	50
VT, Burlington	39,127	NJ, Newark	–16.41	51

(continued on next page)

Population, Increase/Decrease (cont.)

Area		Population (sq. mi.)		Desc. Num. Order
FL, Jacksonville	758.7	NY, NY City	23,698	1
AK, Anchorage	697.7	NJ, Newark	15,766	2
OK, Oklahoma City	608.1	IL, Chicago	12,252	3
TX, Houston	539.9	MA, Boston	11,865	4
CA, Los Angeles	469.3	PA, Philadelphia	11,736	5
WY, Cheyenne	18.8	MO, Kansas City	1,057	47
RI, Providence	18.5	SC, Columbia	837	48
CT, Bridgeport	16.0	Fl, Jacksonville	837	49
DE, Wilmington	10.8	OK, Oklahoma City	736	50
VT, Burlington	10.6	AK, Anchorage	324	51

SOURCES: *Facts About the Cities*, U.S. Bureau of the Census.

THE PEOPLE

Population, Increase/Decrease

Population		*Change in Population, 1980–90 (%)*		*Population, 1990 (per sq. mi.)*		*Percentage of Pop. in Metro Area, 1990 (%)*		*Desc. Num. Order*
CA	29,760,021	NV	33.39	DC	8,925.00	DC	100.00	1
NY	17,990,455	AK	26.94	NJ	886.29	NJ	100.00	2
TX	16,986,510	AZ	25.88	RI	649.49	CY	95.74	3
FL	12,937,926	FL	24.66	CT	592.91	MD	92.84	4
PA	11,881,643	CA	20.47	MA	570.01	RI	92.48	5
ND	638,800	ND	−2.18	ND	9.03	WY	29.54	47
DC	606,900	WY	−3.52	SD	9.02	SD	29.45	48
VT	562,758	IA	−4.94	MT	5.43	MT	23.90	49
AK	550,043	DC	−5.20	WY	4.64	VT	23.28	50
WY	453,588	WV	−8.74	AK	0.84	ID	20.46	51

(continued on next page)

Racial and Ethnic Composition of the States

White (% of total population)		*Black (% of total population)*		*American Indian (% of total population)*		*Asian or Pacific Isles (% of total population)*		*Desc. Num. Order*
VT	98.64	DC	65.84	AK	15.58	HI	61.83	1
ME	98.41	MS	35.56	NM	8.87	CA	9.56	2
NH	98.03	LA	30.79	OK	8.02	WA	4.33	3
IA	96.63	SC	29.82	SD	7.27	NY	3.86	4
WV	96.21	GA	26.96	MT	5.97	AK	3.59	5
CA	68.97	SD	0.47	IL	0.19	AR	0.53	47
LA	67.28	ME	0.42	OH	0.19	MS	0.51	48
MS	63.48	VT	0.35	KY	0.16	KY	0.48	49
HI	33.35	ID	0.33	WV	0.14	SD	0.45	50
DC	29.60	MT	0.30	PA	0.12	WV	0.42	51

(continued on next page)

Population, Increase/Decrease (cont.)

Change in Metro Population, 1980–90 (%)		*Percentage of Pop. in Nonmetro Areas, 1990 (%)*		*Change in Nonmetro Population, 1980–90 (%)*		*Desc. Num. Order*
NE	51.60	ID	79.56	NC	71.20	1
AZ	36.80	VT	76.59	NV	43.06	2
FL	32.31	MT	76.09	AK	42.73	3
AK	29.89	SD	70.55	FL	37.20	4
CA	25.58	WY	70.33	HI	34.65	5
IA	0.00	RI	7.47	IL	–5.12	47
MI	–0.45	MD	7.17	NE	–5.80	48
DC	–4.86	CA	4.26	WV	–7.47	49
WY	–4.96	DC	0.00	IA	–8.10	50
WV	–9.05	NJ	0.00	ND	–8.85	51

SOURCE: U.S. Bureau of the Census, 1990.

Racial and Ethnic Composition of the States (cont.)

Other Races (% of total population)		*Hispanic Origin (% of total population)*		*Foreign Born, 1990 (% of population)*		*Over 5 Years Who Speak a Language Other than English at Home (% of population)*		*Desc. Num. Order*
CA	13.24	NM	39.42	CA	21.7	NM	35.5	1
NM	12.56	CA	25.83	NY	15.9	CA	31.5	2
TX	10.62	TX	25.55	HI	14.7	TX	25.4	3
AZ	9.08	AZ	18.78	FL	12.9	HI	24.8	4
NY	5.50	CO	12.88	NJ	12.5	NY	23.3	5
VT	0.14	MS	0.62	AR	1.1	TN	2.9	47
AL	0.14	AL	0.61	SD	1.1	AR	2.8	48
ME	0.14	KY	0.60	KY	0.9	MS	2.8	49
MS	0.12	ME	0.56	WV	0.9	WV	2.6	50
WV	0.10	WV	0.47	MS	0.8	KY	2.5	51

SOURCE: U.S. Department of Commerce, Bureau of the Census, 1990.

Indian Groups and Other Native Peoples, Reservations, and Trust Lands

AK *Regional Corporations:* Arctic Slope, N.A.N.A, Bering Straits, Doyon, Calista; Cook Inlet, Ahtna, Chugach, Sealaska, Annette Island, Bristol Bay, Koniag, Aleutian
Native peoples: Aleut, Eskimo, Athapascan, Haida, Tlingit, Tsimpshian

AL Poarch Creek

AZ Kaibab, Navajo, Hopi, San Juan Paiute, Havasupai, Hualapai, Fort Mojave, Yavapai/Apache, Tonto Apache, Colorado River, Fort McDowell, Salt River, Fort Apache, San Carlos, Cocopan, Ak Chin, Gila River, Pascua Yaqui, San Xavier, Tohono O'Odham, Papago, Yavapai, Pima.

CA Karok, Fort Bidwell, Yurok, Hoopa Valley, Numerous Small Rancherias, Round Valley, Woodfords Indian Community, Ft. Independence, Tule River, Santa Ynez, Chemehuevi, Morongo, Agua Caliente, Mission Indians, Quchan, Jamul Indian Village, Hoopa, Paiute, Yurok, Karok, Mission Bands

CO Ute Mountain, Southern Ute, Ute

CT Mashantucket Pequot

FL Seminole, Miccosukee

IA Sac and Fox, Ioway

ID Coeur'D'alene, Kootenai, Nez Perce, Shoshone/Bannock

KS Kickapoo, Potawatomi

LA Coushatta, Chitimacha

MA Wampanoag

ME Houlton Maliseets, Passamaquoddy, Penobscot

MI Keweenaw Bay, Lac Vieux Desert, Hannaville, Grand Traverse

MN Red Lake, Nett Lake, White Earth, Leech Lake, Fond du Lac, Mille Lacs, Upper Sioux, Shakopee, Lower Sioux

MS Mississippi Choctaw

MT Blackfeet, Assiniboine/Sioux, Chippewa/Cree, Fort Belknap, Salish/Kootenai

NE Santee Sioux, Winnebago, Omaha, Iowa

NV Duck Valley, Summit Lake, Winnnemucca Colony, Te-Moak, Lovelock Paiute, Pyramid Lake, Paiute/Shoshone, Goshute, Yerington, Yowba, Walker River, Duckwater, Moapa Paiute, Las Vegas Paiute, Reno Spark, Carson Colony, Dresslervile Colony, Washoe

NM Jicarilla Apache, Santa Clara, San Ildefonso, Jemez, Zia, Laguna, Navajo, Acoma, Alamo Navajo, Mescalero, Taos, Picuris, San Juan, Pojoaque, Nambe, Tesuque, Cochiti, Santo Domingo, San Felip, Santa Ana, Sandia, Canoncito, Isleta, Zuni

NY St. Regis, Tuscaroa, Tonawanda, Oneida, Onondaga, Seneca, Cattaraugus, Catuga, Oil Springs, Allegany, Mohawk

NC Cherokee

ND Turtle Mountain, Three Affiliated Tribes, Devils Lake, Sioux, Chippewa, Mandan, Arikara, Hidatsa

OK Peoria, Eastern Shawnee, Ottawa, Quapaw, Wynadotte, Seneca/Cayuga, Modoc, Miami, Kaw, Ronca, Osage, Tonkawa, Otoe/Missouri, Thlopthlocco Creek, Sac and Fox, Cherokee, United Keetoowah Band, Cheyenne/Arapaho, Iowa, Alabama/Quassarte, Wichita, Kickapoo, Absentee/Shawnee, Kiowa, Caddo, Kialegee Creek, Delaware, Apache, Seminole, Fort Sill, Apache, Citizen Band/Apache, Comanche, Chickasaw, Choctaw

OR Grande Ronde, Umatilla, Siletz, Warm Springs, Coos, Lower Umpqua, Siuslaw, Burns Paiute, Coquille, Klamath, Cow Creek of Umpaqua, Wasco

RI Narragansett

SD Standing Rock, Sisseton, Cheyenne River, Lower Bule, Crow Creek, Ogalala Sioux, Rosebud, Yankton

TX Alabama-Coushatta, Texas Kickapoo, Ysleta del Sur, Tiwa

UT Skull Valley, Northwestern Shoshoni, Ute, Goshute, Paiute

WA Swinomish, Lummi, Nooksack, Upper Skagit, Stillaguamish, Sauk Suiattle, Colville, Kalispel, Port Gamble, Suquamish, Skokomish, Puyallup, Muckleshoot, Nisqually, Yakima, Chehalis, Tulalip, Jamestown Klallam, Lower Elwha, Makah, Ozette, Quinault, Hoh, Quinalt, Squaxin Island, Shoalwater Bay

WI Red Cliff, Bad River, Lac du Flambeau, Lac Courte Oreilles, St. Croix, Mole Lake, Potawatomi, Menominee, Mohican, Winnebago, Oneida, Chippewa

WY Shoshone/Arapahoe

SOURCE: U.S. Geological Survey in cooperation with Bureau of Indian Affairs.

Gender and Marital Status

Male (%)		Female (%)		15 Years of Age and Over Who Have Never Married (% of pop.)		Marriage Rate (per 1,000 pop.)		Divorce Rate (per 1,000 pop.)		Desc. Num. Order
AK	52.70	DC	53.37	DC	47.6	HI	16.1	NV	11.4	1
NV	50.91	MS	52.18	MA	32.8	SC	15.7	OK	7.7	2
HI	50.88	AL	52.08	NY	32.1	AR	14.8	AZ	6.9	3
CA	50.06	PA	52.08	CA	30.1	ID	14.6	AR	6.9	4
WY	50.05	NY	52.05	HI	29.8	KY	13.8	WY	6.6	5
NY	47.95	WY	49.95	WV	22.2	ND	7.3	MA	2.8	47
PA	47.92	CA	49.94	WY	21.7	PA	7.2	CA (1989, 31)	4.3	48
AL	47.92	HI	49.12	ID	21.2	WV	7.2	IL (1989, 35)	4.0	49
MS	47.82	NV	49.09	OK	20.9	NV (1989, 1)	106.3	IN	NA	50
DC	46.63	AK	47.30	AR	20.7	IL (1989, 49)	7.2	LA	NA	51

SOURCE: U.S. Bureau of the Census.

Age Groups

Median Age		Under 5 Years of Age (% of pop.)		Under 18 Years of Age (% of pop.)		65 Years of Age and Over (% of pop.)		Change in Population 65 Years of Age and Over (% of pop.)		Desc. Num. Order
FL	36.4	AK	9.98	UT	36.42	FL	18.31	NV	94.1	1
WV	35.4	UT	9.85	AK	31.33	PA	15.39	AK	93.7	2
PA	35.0	NM	8.31	ID	30.63	IA	15.35	HI	64.2	3
NJ	34.5	TX	8.18	LA	30.27	RI	15.00	AZ	55.8	4
OR	34.5	CA	8.06	WY	29.88	WV	14.99	NM	40.7	5
NM	31.2	PA	6.71	CT	22.80	TX	10.11	MO	10.7	47
LA	31.0	RI	6.67	RI	22.49	GA	10.10	IA	9.9	48
TX	30.8	FL	6.57	MA	22.49	CO	10.00	NY	9.4	49
AK	29.4	DC	6.15	FL	22.15	UT	8.70	NE	8.5	50
UT	26.2	WV	5.95	DC	19.29	AK	4.07	DC	4.8	51

SOURCE: U.S. Bureau of the Census.

OF VITAL IMPORTANCE

Birth and Mortality

Live Birth Rate		*Mortality Rate for Infants Under 1 Year, 1988 (per 1,000 live births)*		*Death Rate, 1988, (per 100,000)*		*Average Lifetime in Years, 1979–81*		*Desc. Num. Order*
DC	36.8	DC	23.2	DC	1,242.1	HI	77.02	1
UT	21.6	GA	12.6	FL	1,062.4	MN	76.15	2
AK	20.7	NC	12.5	WV	1,055.1	UT	75.76	3
CA	20.7	MS	12.3	PA	1,050.1	ND	75.71	4
TX	19.2	SC	12.3	AR	1,039.8	NE	75.49	5
VT	14.0	ME	7.9	WY	677.7	GA	72.22	47
IA	13.9	MA	7.9	CO	646.8	MS	71.98	48
WY	13.9	MN	7.8	HI	553.3	LA	71.74	49
ME	13.1	HI	7.2	UT	545.8	SC	71.58	50
WV	12.6	VT	6.8	AK	393.9	DC	69.20	51

SOURCE: National Center for Health Statistics, *Statistical Abstract 1992.*

Causes of Death, 1988 (per 100,000 pop.)

Total		*Diseases of Heart*		*Malignant Neoplasms*		*Cerebrovascular Diseases*		*Accidents and Adverse Effects*		*Desc. Num. Order*
DC	1,242.1	PA	400.6	DC	263.9	AR	88.9	AK	74.4	1
FL	1,062.4	WV	397.1	FL	253.0	IA	78.1	NM	56.7	2
WV	1,055.1	FL	380.4	RI	242.0	TN	76.2	SC	55.9	3
PA	1,050.1	NY	376.2	PA	237.1	MS	76.1	MS	54.8	4
AR	1,039.8	MI	372.2	WV	231.7	SC	74.7	ID	54.6	5
WY	677.7	WY	191.9	NM	144.7	UT	40.8	CT	30.7	47
CO	646.8	NM	189.8	HI	139.3	CO	40.1	MA	29.7	48
HI	553.3	UT	175.3	CO	134.9	NV	39.5	RI	29.7	49
UT	545.8	HI	167.3	UT	101.1	HI	39.2	HI	28.7	50
AK	393.9	AK	88.7	AK	85.7	AK	16.4	NH	27.6	51

(continued on next page)

Causes of Death, 1988 (cont.)

Chronic Obstructive Pulmonary Diseases		*Suicide*		*HIV Infection*		*Other Causes of Death Not Listed*		*Desc. Num. Order*
NV	52.8	NV	26.0	DC	40.0	DC	447.4	1
WV	48.1	NM	22.8	NY	22.3	AR	263.0	2
MT	47.6	AZ	19.5	NJ	15.0	PA	255.2	3
ME	46.1	CO	18.1	FL	11.7	MA	250.2	4
OR	43.2	MT	18.0	CA	11.2	NE	250.0	5
TX	24.3	MA	8.6	IA	0.8	CO	178.7	47
DC	23.5	HI	7.9	SD	0.7	MI	164.0	48
UT	22.1	DC	7.8	MT	0.6	UT	155.9	49
HI	17.5	NJ	7.0	WY	0.6	HI	147.8	50
AK	13.5	NY	6.7	ND	0.4	AK	103.4	51

SOURCE: U.S. National Center for Health Statistics Vital Statistics of the United States, annual.

KEEPING WELL

Healthiest States (1992)

MN	1
HI	2
NH	3
WI	4
NE	5
LA	46
NM	46
MS	49
WV	50
DC	NA

SOURCE: From a subjective appraisal by National Life Insurance Co.

Physicians, Dentists, and Nurses

Nonfederal MDs, 1990 (per 100,000 pop.)		*Membership in the ADA, 1990–91 (per 100,000 pop.)*		*RNs, 1989 (per 100,000 pop.)*		*Desc. Num. Order*
DC	647	DC	151	DC	1,575	1
MA	357	NY	95	MA	1,150	2
MD	350	CT	91	RI	935	3
NY	338	HI	87	VT	919	4
CT	325	MA	83	ND	912	5
NV	160	AR	47	NM	476	47
SD	157	NC	46	OK	468	48
MS	146	SC	46	MS	465	49
ID	143	AL	46	SC	454	50
AK	141	MS	41	LA	427	51

SOURCES: American Medical Association, American Dental Association, American Nurses Association, Department of Health and Human Services.

Hospitals

Hospitals (per 100,000 pop.)		*Hospital Admissions (per 100,000 pop.)*		*Hospital Beds (per 100,000 pop.)*		*Hospital Occupancy Rate (%)*		*Semi-private Room Charges ($)*		*Average Hospital Stay (days)*		*Desc. Num. Order*
SD	9.483	DC	32,912.01	DC	1,324.93	NY	86.3	CT	456	MT	18.7	1
ND	8.923	TN	17,444.82	ND	829.37	HI	83.0	CA	453	MI	13.2	2
MT	7.759	ND	17,110.52	SD	779.88	RI	82.3	AK	407	ND	13.0	3
WY	7.055	MS	16,873.24	NE	669.10	NJ	81.1	DE	385	PA	13.0	4
NE	6.462	WV	16,668.24	MS	666.52	CT	80.1	VT	378	SD	12.4	5
RI	1.893	UT	11,041.88	AK	359.24	OK	60.2	LA	203	AK	5.9	47
CA	1.841	NV	10,783.20	CA	354.10	LA	60.2	GA	198	NM	5.9	48
MD	1.715	AK	10,774.79	NV	342.64	WY	58.9	TN	183	AZ	5.8	49
NY	1.695	HI	10,665.58	UT	324.17	AK	51.9	AR	170	WA	5.8	50
NJ	1.539	ID	10,273.46	WA	324.10	VA	42.3	MS	167	OR	5.8	51

SOURCES: American Hospital Association, Health Insurance Association of America, *Source Book of Health Insurance Data 1991.*

Notifiable Diseases (per 100,000 pop., 1990)

AIDS		*Gonorrhea*		*Measles*		*Syphillis*		*TB*		*Desc. Num. Order*
DC	122.1	DC	2,419.7	CA	41.9	DC	488.5	DC	26.9	1
NY	46.7	GA	756.7	TX	26.0	GA	142.2	NY	23.2	2
NJ	31.9	MS	555.8	NV	20.0	LA	125.1	HI	17.7	3
FL	31.3	AL	533.7	WI	15.2	FL	115.9	CA	16.4	4
CA	24.7	DE	506.3	AK	14.5	MS	96.5	FL	14.2	5
IA	2.5	ME	16.3	LA	0.2	ME	1.7	WI	2.0	47
MT	2.1	ID	15.7	VT	0.2	MT	1.3	NH	1.8	48
SD	1.3	KY	15.7	MT	0.1	SD	1.0	NE	1.5	49
WY	0.7	ND	15.7	SC	0.1	ND	0.9	ID	1.4	50
ND	0.3	VT	9.8	ND	0.0	VT	0.4	WY	1.1	51

SOURCE: Center for Disease Control, *Morbidity and Mortality Weekly Report, Summary of Notifiable Diseases*, United States, 1990.

Mental Health

	Per Capita Spending, 1987 ($)	*Desc. Num. Order*
NY	140.08	1
DE	128.61	2
PA	68.40	3
CT	68.02	4
MI	66.94	5
WV	22.96	47
MS	21.81	48
TX	20.53	49
AZ	19.76	50
ID	16.74	51

SOURCE: *Care of the Seriously Mentally Ill*, 3rd ed., 1990.

Health Insurance

	Population Without Health Insurance, 1991, (% of pop.)	*Desc. Num. Order*
DC	25.7	1
TX	22.1	2
NM	21.5	3
LA	20.7	4
MS	18.9	5
WI	8.0	47
PA	7.8	48
ND	7.6	49
CT	7.5	50
HI	7.0	51

SOURCE: U.S. Bureau of the Census.

HOUSEHOLDS BY TYPE

Households

Total Households, 1990		Change in the Number of Households, 1980–90 (%)		Family Households		Family Households (% of total)		Nonfamily Households		Desc. Num. Order
CA	10,381,206	NV	53.39	CA	7,139,394	UT	76.47	CA	3,241,812	1
NY	6,639,322	AK	44.21	NY	4,489,312	MS	74.00	NY	2,150,010	2
TX	6,070,937	AZ	43.03	TX	4,343,878	HI	73.95	TX	1,727,059	3
FL	5,134,869	FL	37.15	FL	3,511,825	SC	73.78	FL	1,623,044	4
PA	4,495,966	NH	27.30	PA	3,155,989	KY	73.63	PA	1,339,977	5
DE	247,497	IL	3.89	ND	166,270	WA	67.56	ND	74,608	47
ND	240,878	WY	1.71	VT	144,895	MA	67.41	DE	71,630	48
VT	210,650	IA	1.08	AK	132,837	CO	66.61	VT	65,755	49
AK	188,915	WV	0.37	DC	122,087	NV	65.92	AK	56,078	50
WY	168,839	DC	−1.33	WY	119,825	DC	48.91	WY	49,014	51

(continued on next page)

Housing in General

Persons per Housing Unit (from total pop.)		Housing Units Occupied (%)		Persons per Occupied Unit		Occupied Units with Over 1 Person per Room (%)		Mobile Home, Trailer, and Other (% of occupied units)		Desc. Num. Order
UT	2.88	OH	93.49	UT	3.03	HI	15.92	WY	21.24	1
HI	2.84	IL	93.25	HI	2.99	CA	12.29	NM	20.71	2
CA	2.66	CT	93.16	CA	2.79	AK	8.58	SC	20.14	3
MS	2.55	IA	93.06	AK	2.78	DC	8.25	AZ	20.08	4
IL	2.54	CA	92.83	MS	2.72	TX	8.15	MT	19.13	5
NH	2.20	NH	81.60	PA	2.46	NE	1.75	RI	2.62	47
DC	2.18	RI	81.52	FL	2.44	ME	1.72	CT	2.52	48
FL	2.12	AK	81.22	IA	2.44	VT	1.71	MA	2.27	49
ME	2.09	ME	79.26	MN	2.43	NH	1.61	HI	1.71	50
VT	2.07	VT	77.66	DC	2.31	IA	1.50	DC	1.14	51

SOURCE: U.S. Bureau of the Census.

Quality of Housing

With No Telephone (% of pop.)		Without Complete Plumbing (% of pop.)		Ascend. Num. Order
MA	2.1	CT	0.4	1
MN	2.4	FL	0.5	2
CT	2.6	MA	0.5	3
HA	2.6	NV	0.5	4
PA	2.6	NJ	0.5	5
KY	10.2	KY	2.9	47
WV	10.3	NM	3.2	48
AR	10.9	WV	3.2	49
NM	12.4	MN	3.5	50
MS	12.6	AK	12.5	51

SOURCE: U.S. Bureau of the Census.

Households (cont.)

Nonfamily Households (% of total)		Persons per Household		Living in Group Quarters		Living in Group Quarters (% of total)		Desc. Num. Order
DC	51.09	UT	3.15	CA	751,860	DC	6.87	1
NV	34.08	HI	3.01	NY	545,265	VT	3.85	2
CO	33.39	AK	2.80	TX	393,447	RI	3.85	3
MA	32.59	CA	2.79	PA	348,424	ND	3.79	4
WA	32.44	MS	2.75	FL	307,461	AK	3.76	5
KY	26.37	OR	2.52	VT	21,642	ID	2.13	47
SC	26.22	CO	2.51	ID	21,490	WV	2.06	48
HI	26.05	FL	2.46	AK	20,701	NV	2.01	49
MS	26.00	OK	2.35	DE	20,071	NM	1.90	50
UT	23.53	DC	2.26	WY	10,240	UT	1.69	51

SOURCE: U.S. Bureau of the Census.

Owner-Occupied Housing

Total Units Owner-Occupied (%)		Occupied Units Owner-Occupied (%)		Persons per Owner-Occupied Unit		Specified Owner-Occupied Units Value (in median $)		Desc. Num. Order
WV	65.28	WV	74.08	UT	3.38	HI	245,300	1
IA	65.17	MN	71.83	HI	3.19	CA	195,500	2
IN	64.60	MS	71.50	AK	2.97	CT	177,800	3
MS	64.49	MI	71.00	NJ	2.87	MA	162,800	4
PA	64.32	PA	70.64	NY	2.86	NJ	162,300	5
HI	49.23	CA	55.62	OR	2.62	WV	47,900	47
NV	49.22	NV	54.77	AR	2.61	AR	46,300	48
NY	47.94	HI	53.87	OK	2.59	MS	45,600	49
AK	45.57	NY	52.18	DC	2.50	SD	45,200	50
DC	34.87	DC	38.90	FL	2.49	IA	15,900	51

SOURCE: U.S. Bureau of the Census.

Rental Housing

Renter-Occupied Housing Units (% of total)		Renter-Occupied Occupied Units (% of total)		Persons per Renter-Occupied Unit		Median Contract Rent for Renter-Occupied Unit ($)		Rental Vacancy Rate (%)		Desc. Num. Order
DC	54.77	DC	61.10	HI	2.78	HI	599	AZ	15.3	1
NY	43.93	NY	47.82	CA	2.74	CA	561	OK	14.7	2
HI	42.16	HI	46.13	UT	2.67	NJ	521	WY	14.4	3
CA	41.20	RI	45.32	MS	2.65	CT	510	TX	13.0	4
NV	40.65	NV	45.23	AK	2.58	MA	506	LA	12.5	5
DE	25.42	PA	29.36	ME	2.20	AR	230	WA	5.8	47
MN	25.11	MI	29.00	PA	2.19	AL	229	HI	5.4	48
VT	24.07	MS	28.50	ND	2.18	WV	221	OR	5.3	49
ME	23.41	MN	28.17	DC	2.12	IA	216	NY	4.9	50
WV	22.85	WV	25.92	MN	2.08	MS	215	WI	4.7	51

SOURCE: U.S. Bureau of the Census.

TEACHING AND LEARNING

Public Elementary and Secondary Schools (1989–90)

Number of Schools		*Students (% of pop.)*		*Average Number of Students per Class, 1987*		*Teaching (% of pop.)*		*Desc. Num. Order*
CA	7,433	UT	25.60	CA	28	WY	1.43	1
TX	5,937	ID	21.36	UT	28	VT	1.24	2
IL	4,225	WY	21.16	AL	26	ND	1.22	3
NY	3,996	AK	20.36	FL	26	WV	1.21	4
OH	3,715	NM	20.33	HI	26	MT	1.20	5
NV	331	FL	14.04	WY	20	WA	0.83	47
RI	294	PA	13.92	ND	19	FL	0.80	48
HI	234	DC	13.84	SD	19	NV	0.77	49
DC	184	MA	13.78	VT	19	CA	0.70	50
DE	170	RI	13.55	DC	NA	CO	0.10	51

(continued on next page)

Educational Achievement

Illiteracy Rate Among Population 20 Years of Age and Over, 1987 (%)		*% of Grads. Taking SAT, 1991*		*Combined SAT Scores, 1990–91*		*High School Graduates 25 Years of Age and Over (% of pop.)*		*25 Years of Age and Over Who Have Bachelor's or Other Advanced Degree (% of pop.)*		*Desc. Num. Order*
UT	6	CT	81	IA	1,093	AK	86.6	DC	33.3	1
AK	7	MA	79	ND	1,073	UT	85.1	CT	27.2	2
WY	7	NH	75	SD	1,047	CO	84.4	MA	27.2	3
CO	8	NY	75	KS	1,039	WA	83.8	CO	27.0	4
ID	8	NJ	74	UT	1,031	WY	83.0	MD	26.5	5
DC	16	ND	6	IN	865	AL	66.9	NV	15.3	47
LA	16	IA	5	GA	844	AR	66.3	MS	14.7	48
MS	16	SD	5	NC	844	WV	66.0	KY	13.6	49
NY	16	UT	5	DC	840	KY	64.6	AR	13.3	50
TX	16	MS	4	SC	832	MS	64.3	WV	12.3	51

SOURCES: Altrusa International Foundation, Inc., *Literacy Needs Assessment*, College Entrance Examination Board, U.S. Department of Education, U.S. Bureau of the Census.

Pupil/Teacher Ratio, Selected Cities (1989)

MO	Kansas City	13.9
GA	Atlanta	13.9
NJ	Newark	14.2
CO	Denver	16.0
AR	Little Rock	16.1
MS	Jackson	20.2
UT	Salt Lake City	20.9
NV	Las Vegas	21.2
MN	Minneapolis	21.4
CA	Los Angeles	23.7

SOURCE: U.S. National Center for Educational Statistics.

Public Elementary and Secondary Schools (cont.)

Average Teachers Salary (annual)		Spending on Public Elementary and Secondary Schools ($ per cap.)		Current Spending Avg. per Pupil in Avg. Daily Attendance		Desc. Num. Order
AK	43,200	AK	1,566	NJ	8,439	1
CT	40,500	WY	1,149	NY	8,094	2
NY	38,900	CT	1,129	CT	7,934	3
DC	38,000	NJ	1,114	DC	7,407	4
MD	36,600	NY	1,091	AK	7,252	5
OK	23,100	AL	624	SD	3,312	47
ND	23,000	AR	621	AR	3,272	48
WV	22,800	LA	620	MS	3,151	49
AR	22,000	SD	618	ID	3,037	50
SD	21,300	TN	575	UT	2,733	51

SOURCE: Department of Education.

3 Years of Age and Over Enrolled in School

Enrolled in School (% of pop.)		Enrolled in Public School (% of those enrolled in school)		Enrolled in Private School (% of those enrolled in school)		Desc. Num. Order
UT	37.7	WY	94.4	DC	35.8	1
WY	31.1	ND	92.5	MA	28.1	2
ID	30.8	WV	92.5	RI	24.7	3
AK	30.2	NM	91.8	NY	24.0	4
NM	30.2	MT	91.5	PA	23.6	5
WV	25.2	PA	76.4	MT	8.5	47
TN	25.0	NY	76.0	NM	8.2	48
PA	24.8	RI	75.3	ND	7.5	49
NV	24.4	MA	71.9	WV	7.5	50
FL	23.5	DC	64.2	WY	5.6	51

SOURCE: U.S. Bureau of the Census.

Higher Education Institutions

Higher Educational Institutions (per 100,000 pop.)		*Enrolled in Institutions of Higher Education (% of pop.)*		*Enrolled in Public Institutions (% of pop.)*		*Enrolled in Private Institutions (% of pop.)*		*Undergraduate Tuition (1990–91) at 4-Year In-State Public Institutions of Higher Education*		*Desc. Num. Order*
ND	2.3	DC	13.29	NV	99.21	DC	84.39	VT	4,092	1
WY	1.8	RI	7.80	WY	97.76	MA	55.91	PA	3,401	2
MT	1.8	AZ	7.22	NM	97.55	NH	45.95	NH	3,110	3
NM	1.5	NE	7.15	AZ	93.98	RI	45.89	DE	2,910	4
AL	1.4	UT	7.04	AK	93.16	PA	43.14	NJ	2,860	5
CA	0.5	LA	4.42	PA	56.86	AK	6.84	ID	1,189	47
NJ	0.4	NJ	4.19	RI	54.11	AZ	6.02	WY	1,148	48
DC	0.3	FL	4.16	NH	54.05	NM	2.45	NC	1,112	49
RI	0.3	GA	3.89	MA	44.09	WY	2.24	TX	986	50
FL	0.3	AR	3.85	DC	15.61	NV	0.79	DC	664	51

SOURCES: U.S. Department of Education, National Center for Education Statistics, Federal-State Cooperative System for Public Data, July 1991, February 1992; Schantz, Nancy Borkow, *Trends in Racial Ethnic Enrollment in Higher Education: Fall 1980 Through Fall 1990, Electronic E.D. TABS*, U.S. Department of Education, Office of Educational Research and Improvement National Center for Education Statistics, Postsecondary Education Statistics Division, January 1992.

Higher Education Enrollment Breakdown (% of pop.)

White, Non-hispanic		*Black, Non-hispanic*		*Hispanic*		*Asian/ Pacific Islander*		*American Indian/ AK Native*		*Non-resident Alien*		*Female*		*Desc. Num. Order*
ME	97.03	DC	30.71	NM	27.61	HI	58.31	AK	8.88	DC	11.19	AK	59.78	1
NH	94.98	MS	27.42	TX	16.45	CA	12.16	MT	6.76	HI	6.81	KY	58.05	2
VT	93.90	LA	23.98	CA	12.57	WA	5.86	SD	5.59	MA	5.04	ME	57.91	3
WV	92.93	SC	19.57	AZ	11.19	NY	4.73	OK	5.55	OR	4.61	AR	57.20	4
NE	92.72	GA	19.54	FL	10.86	IL	4.44	NM	5.37	NY	4.55	VT	56.78	5
TX	68.52	ND	0.65	WV	0.42	AL	0.69	GA	0.22	NV	1.42	IN	52.69	47
CA	63.88	ID	0.60	KY	0.41	MS	0.64	SC	0.21	NH	1.41	CO	52.20	48
NM	61.42	UT	0.54	ME	0.34	WY	0.59	TN	0.21	NC	1.38	ND	49.38	49
DC	50.80	ME	0.52	MS	0.32	SD	0.58	PA	0.17	KY	1.25	UT	48.84	50
HI	30.00	MT	0.32	SD	0.27	MT	0.33	WV	0.16	ME	0.69	AL	48.03	51

SOURCE: Nancy Borkow, Schantz, *Trends in Racial/Ethnic Enrollment in Higher Education: Fall 1980 through Fall 1990, Electronic E.D. TABS*, U.S. Department of Education, Office of Education Research and Improvement National Center for Education Statistics, Postsecondary Education Statistics Division, January 1992.

LAW ENFORCEMENT, COURTS, AND PRISONS

Prisoners

Prisoners, 1990 (per 100,000 pop.)		*Change in Sentences of More Than 1 Year, 1989–90 (% of total sentences)*		*Under Sentence of Death (Aug. 1991)*		*Under Sentence of Death (per 500,000 pop.)*		*Executed During 1989*		*Desc. Num. Order*
DC	1,125	CT	23.17	FL	294	NV	21.6	AL	4	1
SC	451	WA	15.40	TX	283	OK	17.3	TX	4	2
NV	444	NH	15.09	CA	247	AL	13.1	FL	2	3
LA	427	TX	13.68	IL	120	AZ	11.5	NV	2	4
OK	383	AL	13.19	PA	115	FL	11.2	GA	1	5
NH	117	TN	-2.28	ND	NA	ND	NA	ND	NA	47
VT	117	DE	-2.32	RI	NA	RI	NA	RI	NA	48
WV	85	HI	-2.51	VT	NA	VT	NA	VT	NA	49
MN	72	AK	-2.99	WV	NA	WV	NA	WV	NA	50
ND	67	OR	-4.57	WI	NA	WI	NA	WI	NA	51

SOURCE: Bureau of Justice Statistics Bulletin, May 1991, *Sourcebook Criminal Justice Statistics 1990*, NAACP Legal Defense and Education Fund.

Police

Total Officers, 1991		*Police Officers, 1990–91, (per 10,000)*		*Police Officers, 1990–91, (% of pop.)*		*Male Officers, 1991*		*Male Police Officers, 1991 (%)*		*Female Officers, 1991*		*Female Police Officers, 1991*		*Desc. Num. Order*
CA	61,139	DC	74.2	DC	0.74	CA	55,052	WV	96.44	CA	6,087	DC	21.24	1
NY	46,524	NJ	34.5	NJ	0.34	NY	41,603	MT	96.17	NY	4,921	LA	19.22	2
TX	36,268	WY	28.4	WY	0.28	TX	33,007	ME	95.95	TX	3,261	ID	11.93	3
FL	30,647	MD	27.2	MD	0.27	FL	27,533	RI	95.77	FL	3,114	GA	11.65	4
IL	29,415	GA	26.3	GA	0.26	IL	26,662	NH	95.50	IL	2,753	CO	11.16	5
WY	1,289	MN	15.1	MN	0.15	WY	1,205	CO	88.84	ME	76	NH	4.50	47
ND	1,004	VT	14.9	MS	0.15	SD	947	GA	88.35	AK	66	RI	4.23	48
SD	1,000	MS	14.9	VT	0.15	ND	927	ID	88.07	SD	53	ME	4.05	49
AK	963	WV	14.6	WV	0.15	AK	897	LA	80.78	MT	50	MT	3.83	50
VT	840	SD	14.4	SD	0.14	VT	794	DC	78.76	VT	46	WV	3.56	51

SOURCE: Department of Justice, Bureau of Justice Statistics.

Crime Index (per 100,000 pop.)

Crime Index (total)		Violent Crime Index		Murder and Non-negligent Manslaughter		Aggravated Assault		Robbery		Rape		Desc. Num. Order
DC	10,774.3	DC	2,458	DC	78	DE	72,628	DC	1,214	DE	88	1
FL	8,810.8	FL	1,244	LA	17	AK	9,980	NY	625	MI	78	2
AZ	7,888.7	NY	1,181	NY	14	UT	9,846	FL	417	AK	73	3
TX	7,826.8	CA	1,045	TX	14	NM	8,308	IL	394	WA	64	4
GA	6,763.6	SC	977	MS	12	TX	8,183	CA	377	NV	62	5
PA	3,476.1	MT	159	VT	2	PA	6,708	WY	16	WV	24	47
KY	3,299.4	ME	143	SD	2	RI	6,674	ID	15	WI	21	48
ND	2,922.4	NH	132	IA	2	FL	6,567	SD	12	ME	20	49
SD	2,909.3	VT	127	NH	2	DC	6,154	VT	12	IA	18	50
WV	2,503.0	ND	74	ND	1	WV	5,947	ND	8	ND	18	51

(continued on next page)

State and Local Government Expenditure for Law Enforcement, Courts, and Prisons ($, 1989–90)

Police Protection		Police Protection (per cap.)		Judicial and Legal Administration		Desc. Num. Order
CA	4,914,911,000	DC	454.25	CA	2,619,101,000	1
NY	3,391,355,000	AK	195.92	NY	1,708,393,000	2
FL	1,904,096,000	NY	188.51	FL	793,540,000	3
TX	1,705,197,000	CA	165.15	TX	719,988,000	4
IL	1,522,440,000	NV	162.26	PA	582,915,000	5
WY	65,182,000	KY	71.60	MT	32,564,000	47
MT	64,348,000	MS	64.86	WY	26,981,000	48
SD	52,195,000	ND	61.82	ND	26,623,000	49
VT	47,678,000	AR	61.65	VT	24,768,000	50
ND	39,504,000	WV	49.90	SD	21,761,000	51

(continued on next page)

Crime Index (cont.)

Property Crime								Drug Abuse				
Index		*Burglary*		*Larceny (Theft)*		*Motor Vehicle Theft*		*Arrests for Violations*		*Difference in Arrests for Drug Abuse Violations, 1989–90*		*Desc. Num. Order*
DC	8,316	FL	2,171	DC	4,997	DC	1,336	DC	1,647	CT	1,001	1
FL	7,566	DC	1,983	AZ	4,703	NY	1,043	CA	839	TN	673	2
AZ	7,236	TX	1,852	FL	4,570	CA	1,016	NY	683	MT	274	3
TX	7,065	NM	1,739	TX	4,305	RI	954	NJ	600	KS	189	4
GA	6,007	AZ	1,670	UT	4,258	NJ	940	MD	599	SD	66	5
PA	3,045	MT	709	SD	2,109	ID	165	OH	91	GA	−17,953	47
KY	2,909	WV	657	MS	2,070	WV	154	WV	88	FL	−20,048	48
ND	2,848	WY	631	KY	1,943	WY	149	VT	86	NJ	−22,025	49
SD	2,747	SD	527	PA	1,811	ND	133	ND	66	IL	−37,124	50
WV	2,334	ND	427	WV	1,523	SD	110	SD	61	CA	−55,777	51

SOURCES: *Uniform Crime Reports 1990, Crime in the United States*, Uniform Crime Report, special run.

State and Local Government Expenditure for Law Enforcement, Courts, and Prisons (cont.)

Judicial and Legal Administration (per capita.)		*Correction*		*Correction (per cap.)*		*Desc. Num. Order*
DC	201.33	CA	4,368,817,000	DC	660.15	1
AK	163.83	NY	3,332,635,000	AK	208.92	2
HI	100.62	FL	1,466,698,000	NY	185.25	3
NY	94.96	TX	1,410,975,000	NV	155.18	4
CA	88.01	MI	958,387,000	CA	146.80	5
OK	30.33	WY	38,300,000	AR	42.94	47
WV	29.64	MT	34,227,000	MT	42.84	48
SC	27.54	SD	30,526,000	MS	41.15	49
MS	24.08	VT	26,880,000	ND	32.23	50
AR	23.82	ND	20,593,000	WV	25.95	51

SOURCE: *Government Finances State & Local Government Finances* 1990 (GF-90-5).

RELIGION, NUMBER, AND PERCENT OF POPULATION

Religious Preference (% of pop. 18 yrs. of age and over)

Christian		*Jewish*		*Moslem/ Islamic*		*Hindu*		*Buddhist*		*Unitarian*		*Agnostic*		*Other*		*None*		*Refused to Respond*		*Desc. Num. Order*
LA	94.70	NY	6.90	NY	0.80	NY	0.60	CA	0.70	VT	1.10	WA	1.40	WV	2.90	OR	17.20	DE	5.70	1
ND	94.50	NJ	4.30	CA	0.60	NJ	0.30	NH	0.50	NV	0.90	CA	1.20	NH	2.70	WA	14.00	OK	4.20	2
MS	94.20	FL	3.60	DC	0.60	CO	0.20	OR	0.50	MA	0.80	NH	1.20	WA	2.70	WY	13.50	CT	3.90	3
SD	94.00	MA	3.50	NJ	0.60	GA	0.20	WA	0.50	CO	0.70	OR	1.20	DC	2.50	NH	13.40	WA	3.30	4
AL	93.30	MD	2.80	IL	0.40	IL	0.20	MA	0.40	ME	0.60	VT	1.20	OH	2.40	CA	13.00	WY	3.30	5
WA	77.10	HI	N/A	OK	N/A	TN	N/A	ND	N/A	LA	N/A	NE	0.10	WY	0.60	MS	2.80	SD	1.00	47
CA	77.00	ID	N/A	UT	N/A	TX	N/A	RI	N/A	MS	N/A	AK	N/A	DE	0.30	SD	2.50	VT	0.70	48
OR	76.10	IA	N/A	VT	N/A	UT	N/A	SD	N/A	ND	N/A	DE	N/A	AK	N/A	ND	1.60	MS	0.60	49
AK	N/A	MT	N/A	WA	N/A	VT	N/A	VT	N/A	SC	N/A	HI	N/A	HI	N/A	AK	N/A	AK	N/A	50
HI	N/A	WY	N/A	WY	N/A	WI	N/A	WY	N/A	WY	N/A	LA	N/A	UT	N/A	HI	N/A	HI	N/A	51

SOURCE: *Religious Composition of State Population, 1990*, Research Report by The National Survey of Religious Identification.

MAKING A LIVING

Income

Income ($ per cap., 1989)		*Change in Per Capita Income, 1979–89 (%, constant = 1989 $)*		*Mean (Average) Family Income ($, 1990)*		*Below the Poverty Level 1990 (% of pop. for whom poverty status is determined)*		*65 Years of Age & Over Below the Poverty Level 1990 (% of pop for whom poverty status is determined)*		*Desc. Num. Order*
CT	20,189	CT	41.5	CT	61,458	MS	25.2	MS	29.4	1
DC	18,881	MA	37.8	NJ	58,468	LA	23.6	LA	24.1	2
NJ	18,714	NJ	37.4	AK	54,203	NM	20.6	AL	24.0	3
MD	17,730	NH	36.7	MD	53,846	WV	19.7	AR	22.9	4
AK	17,610	ME	34.1	DC	53,049	AR	19.1	TN	20.9	5
SD	10,661	ND	2.8	MT	33,358	MD	8.3	NJ	8.5	47
LA	10,635	WV	2.2	SD	32,818	HI	8.3	HI	8.0	48
WV	10,520	MT	1.5	AR	31,499	NJ	7.6	AK	7.6	49
AR	10,520	LA	−1.2	WV	31,290	CT	6.8	CA	7.6	50
MS	9,648	WY	−7.3	MS	30,769	NH	6.4	CT	7.2	51

SOURCE: U.S. Department of Commerce, Bureau of the Census.

Cost of Living Index (1st qtr., 1991, U.S. standard = 100)

Nassau-Suffolk, NY	152.1
Kodiak, AK	147.9
Hilo, HI	135.4
Anchorage, AK	135.0
Fairbanks, AK	133.7
Pryor, OK	86.4
Loveland, CO	86.2
Hastings, NE	85.6
Murray, KY	85.6
Kennett (2nd qtr., 1989), MO	83.6

SOURCE: ACCRA, American Chamber of Commerce Research Association.

THE ECONOMY

Labor Force

Labor Force, 1990		*Labor Force, 1990 (% of pop.)*		*65 Years of Age and Over, 1991 (% of civilian labor force)*		*Females in Labor Force, 1990*		*Desc. Num. Order*
CA	14,670,000	NH	56.80	SD	5.28	CA	6,387,000	1
NY	8,673,000	MN	54.95	KS	4.46	NY	3,885,000	2
TX	8,443,000	VT	54.91	IA	4.34	TX	3,791,000	3
FL	6,365,000	CT	54.42	NE	4.05	FL	2,951,000	4
IL	6,029,000	DE	54.34	MT	3.98	IL	2,712,000	5
ND	325,000	NM	46.20	AL	N/A	DC	147,000	47
VT	309,000	MS	46.01	WA	N/A	ND	147,000	48
DC	298,000	UT	45.97	WV	N/A	VT	143,000	49
AK	257,000	LA	44.48	AK	N/A	AK	117,000	50
WY	246,000	WV	43.04	AZ	N/A	WY	109,000	51

(continued on next page)

Average Annual Pay

1989 ($)		*1990 ($)*		*Change, 1989–90 (%)*		*Desc. Num. Order*
DC	32,106	DC	33,717	HI	7.1	1
AK	29,704	AK	29,946	NJ	6.2	2
NY	27,303	NY	28,873	RI	6.0	3
NJ	26,780	NJ	28,449	MA	5.8	4
MA	25,233	MA	26,689	NY	5.8	5
MT	17,224	MT	17,895	UT	3.7	47
MS	17,047	MS	17,718	NM	3.6	48
ND	16,932	ND	17,626	AZ	3.0	49
SD	15,810	SD	16,430	MI	2.5	50
CT	N/A	CT	N/A	CT	N/A	51

SOURCE: Bureau of Labor Statistics, Department of Labor.

Labor Force (cont.)

Females in Labor Force, 1990		*Difference in Employment (Job Growth) 1970–80 (%)*		*Difference in Employment (Job Growth) 1980–90 (%)*		*Difference in Employment (Job Growth) 1970–90 (%)*		*Desc. Num. Order*
DC	49.33	NV	91.17	NV	53.41	NV	193.27	1
HI	48.05	WY	74.48	FL	50.14	AZ	155.51	2
CO	47.89	AZ	72.13	AZ	48.44	FL	137.03	3
VA	47.50	CO	61.32	AK	40.53	AK	123.13	4
MD	47.50	AK	58.77	GA	36.84	CO	100.83	5
LA	44.08	IL	10.31	IA	7.04	IL	25.19	47
CA	43.54	RI	9.77	OK	6.51	PA	20.27	48
ID	43.35	PA	8.13	LA	2.46	WV	18.19	49
UT	43.31	DC	4.51	WV	−1.13	NY	17.75	50
WV	41.84	NY	2.02	WY	−4.34	DC	16.01	51

SOURCE: U.S. Department of Labor.

Unemployment (1991)

Rate (%)		*Male Rate (%)*		*Female Rate (%)*		*Desc. Num. Order*
WV	8.29	WV	5.05	MS	4.22	1
MI	7.51	MI	4.50	AR	3.44	2
MS	7.43	AK	3.89	WV	3.37	3
AK	7.00	DC	3.69	AL	3.33	4
AR	6.88	RI	3.68	AK	3.11	5
NC	4.09	MD	2.21	CT	1.79	47
ND	4.00	NC	1.97	SD	1.67	48
SD	3.61	SD	1.94	ND	1.54	49
HI	2.78	HI	1.67	HI	1.11	50
NE	2.15	NE	1.07	NE	1.07	51

SOURCE: U.S. Department of Labor.

Major Employer Industries of Population 16 Years of Age and Over (no. of workers and % of workers)

Agriculture				Construction				Finance, Insurance, Real Estate				Government				Manufacturing				Desc. Num. Order
Workers		%		Workers		%		Workers		%		Workers		%		Workers		%		
CA	429,226	SD	14.00	CA	733,838	NV	7.00	CA	899,990	CT	9.20	CA	1,924,594	DC	31.10	CA	2,256,898	NC	27.30	1
TX	237,660	ND	11.90	TX	411,944	MD	6.90	NY	731,847	DE	9.00	NY	1,447,248	AK	26.30	NY	1,208,781	SC	26.20	2
FL	143,688	IA	9.80	FL	365,207	HI	6.40	FL	437,051	NY	8.90	TX	1,227,910	MD	23.50	OH	1,194,358	TN	25.70	3
IA	140,434	NE	9.40	NY	361,812	LA	6.30	TX	427,788	NJ	7.80	FL	880,089	NM	23.00	TX	1,180,378	MI	24.90	4
MN	128,128	MT	9.10	PA	295,899	DE	6.20	IL	413,034	FL	7.30	IL	752,514	WY	22.70	PA	1,122,183	IN	24.30	5
NV	7,735	MA	0.90	WY	11,417	MI	3.50	MT	14,023	LA	3.90	RI	59,644	PA	12.10	MT	23,877	NV	5.00	47
DE	6,536	AK	0.60	SD	10,410	DC	3.30	ND	12,792	NM	3.90	SD	57,602	NH	11.80	ND	18,720	HI	5.00	48
RI	2,886	RI	0.60	ND	10,296	IA	3.30	VT	12,348	AR	3.80	WY	52,891	IN	11.80	AK	9,321	WY	4.00	49
AK	1,434	CT	0.60	AK	9,560	ND	3.30	AK	10,277	MT	3.70	DE	44,032	MO	11.70	WY	9,320	AK	3.90	50
DC	556	DC	0.20	DC	9,174	SD	3.00	WY	8,155	WY	3.50	VT	37,632	CT	11.10	DC	8,896	DC	3.20	51

(continued on next page)

Major Employer Industries of Population 16 Years of Age and Over (cont.)

Mining				Services				Trade				Transport., Commerce, and Public Utilities				Wholesale/Retail				Desc. Num. Order
Workers		%		Workers		%		Workers		%		Workers		%		Workers		%		
TX	164,571	WY	7.7	CA	2,866,122	NV	35.90	CA	2,533,818	FL	22.00	CA	650,762	AK	7.90	CA	2,922,338	FL	24.2	1
LA	52,329	WV	5.4	NY	1,915,959	DC	33.10	TX	1,528,946	WV	21.40	TX	459,476	WY	7.80	TX	1,707,213	MT	23.1	2
OK	42,838	AK	3.6	TX	1,560,634	MA	26.20	NY	1,389,687	MO	21.30	NY	452,265	GA	6.90	NY	1,599,592	HI	23.0	3
CA	39,542	LA	3.2	FL	1,353,062	MD	24.30	FL	1,317,140	IN	21.00	IL	345,138	NJ	6.80	FL	1,405,861	ND	22.8	4
KY	37,595	OK	3.1	PA	1,289,673	CT	23.70	IL	1,075,020	MI	20.60	FL	323,298	WV	6.70	PA	1,166,867	OR	22.8	5
ME	533	NY	0.1	VT	66,444	AR	16.30	ND	61,776	NY	16.90	ND	17,160	IA	4.00	ND	65,689	AK	19.2	47
DE	427	SC	0.1	SD	65,930	AL	15.70	VT	52,626	MD	16.80	DE	15,136	AZ	4.00	VT	62,185	NV	19.1	48
HI	323	WI	0.1	ND	60,528	WY	15.40	AK	42,064	CT	16.70	SD	13,533	SD	3.90	AK	47,046	NY	19.1	49
RI	240	DC	0.0	AK	44,454	SC	15.30	WY	41,241	ME	16.60	VT	10,878	DC	3.80	WY	43,416	MD	18.8	50
DC	102	RI	0.0	WY	35,882	MS	15.00	DC	28,634	DC	10.30	DC	10,564	VT	3.70	DC	36,190	DC	11.9	51

SOURCE: U.S. Dept. of Labor, Bureau of Labor Statistics, U.S. Department of Commerce, Bureau of the Census.

Business (1990–91)

Total Businesses, 1991		*New Business Incorporations, 1990*		*New Business Incorporations, 1991*		*New Businesses, 1991 (% of total businesses)*		*Change in New Business Incorporations, 1990–91 (%)*		*Desc. Num. Order*
CA	1,097,465	FL	82,172	FL	81,083	DE	138.74	UT	19.92	1
TX	844,821	NY	65,569	NY	63,808	NV	28.58	WY	18.36	2
NY	605,384	CA	39,111	CA	36,561	FL	19.49	CO	10.82	3
IL	441,411	TX	35,523	TX	34,571	HI	12.16	AK	-7.06	4
FL	415,975	DE	29,861	DE	29,887	MD	11.09	MS	5.79	5
DC	28,638	MT	1,519	VT	1,486	MT	3.58	NH	−10.90	47
WY	26,383	AK	1,345	WY	1,386	CA	3.33	WV	−12.71	48
VT	26,339	WY	1,171	AK	1,250	IA	2.69	AR	−12.85	49
DE	21,542	SD	1,078	SD	1,040	SD	2.66	RI	−18.07	50
AK	19,262	ND	860	ND	820	ND	2.53	SC	−20.37	51

(continued on next page)

Minority-Owned Businesses (1987)

Total Firms		*Black-Owned Firms*		*Firms Black-Owned (% of total)*		*Women-Owned Firms*		*Firms Women-Owned (% of total)*		*Change in Women-Owned Firms, 1982–87 (%)*		*Desc. Num. Order*
CA	1,809,300	CA	47,728	DC	28.34	CA	559,800	DC	37.67	NH	90.7	1
TX	1,025,600	NY	36,289	MD	8.88	TX	298,100	HI	35.63	NJ	85.6	2
NY	930,700	TX	35,725	MS	8.62	NY	284,900	CO	34.04	RI	80.7	3
FL	735,800	FL	25,527	SC	8.59	FL	221,400	MD	33.55	FL	76.5	4
PA	595,700	MD	21,678	LA	7.49	IL	177,100	OR	31.80	MA	76.3	5
VT	45,200	ID	94	ME	0.15	SD	13,400	ME	27.10	ID	41.6	47
ND	42,700	WY	81	ID	0.14	ND	12,700	AL	26.95	MT	39.1	48
WY	34,600	MT	77	ND	0.13	DC	11,000	TN	26.82	OK	29.5	49
DE	31,000	SD	63	SD	0.13	WY	10,800	AR	26.34	WY	28.6	50
DC	29,200	ND	57	MT	0.12	DE	9,700	MS	25.85	DC	23.5	51

SOURCE: U.S. Bureau of the Census, 1987 Economic Censuses, Survey of Minority Owned Business Enterprises, Blacks (MB87-1) and Women-Owned Businesses (WB87-1).

Business (cont.)

Business Failures, 1990		Business Failures, 1991		Business Failures, 1991 (% of total businesses)		Change in Business Failures, 1990–91 (%)		Desc. Num. Order
CA	14,466	CA	8,968	NH	1.97	NH	205.73	1
TX	6,976	TX	6,742	GA	1.76	MN	196.03	2
NY	5,563	FL	3,665	OK	1.53	RI	148.09	3
FL	5,180	NY	3,284	AZ	1.51	VT	139.74	4
PA	3,622	OH	2,262	NV	1.41	OR	120.64	5
MT	159	ND	144	WI	0.51	CO	–7.03	47
DE	158	AK	124	ND	0.43	WY	–9.55	48
AK	143	DC	100	MT	0.36	MT	–16.75	49
ND	140	DE	80	HI	0.23	IA	–47.92	50
HI	72	VT	78	IA	0.17	HI	–51.68	51

SOURCE: Dun & Bradstreet.

Number of Fortune 500 Industrials

NY	59
IL	48
CA	39
OH	37
PA	36
NM	0
ND	0
SD	0
VT	0
WY	0

SOURCE: *Fortune* Magazine, April 22, 1991.

Farm Marketing Income and Net Farm Income

Farm Marketing Income, 1990 ($000)		Farm Marketing Income, 1991 ($000)		Difference, 1990–91 ($000)		Difference, 1990–91 (%)		Net Farm Income per Operation, 1991		Net Farm Income per Acre, 1991		Desc. Num. Order
CA	19,157,859	CA	17,886,698	FL	396,841	WY	7.81	FL	68,018	RI	558	1
TX	11,831,478	TX	12,126,182	TX	294,704	OK	7.50	CA	67,531	CT	462	2
IA	10,282,269	IA	10,179,249	OK	265,595	FL	6.91	AZ	64,828	DE	307	3
NE	8,708,170	NE	8,821,328	AL	152,190	MA	6.65	DE	60,296	MA	281	4
IL	7,789,302	IL	7,508,777	WA	148,079	AL	5.39	RI	52,606	NJ	263	5
NV	323,953	NV	275,836	WI	–284,966	ID	–9.34	IN	7,155	NM	8	47
NH	143,193	NH	143,106	IN	–436,015	ME	–9.77	AK	6,371	NV	8	48
RI	71,346	RI	70,917	CO	–454,953	CO	–10.79	TN	4,280	WY	6	49
AK	26,783	AK	26,622	CA	–1,271,161	NV	–14.85	WV	3,915	AK	4	50
DC	N/A	DC	N/A	DC	N/A	DC	N/A	DC	N/A	DC	N/A	51

SOURCE: Farm Income Estimation Section, Agriculture & Rural Economy Division, U.S. Department of Agriculture, Economic Research Service, Agricultural Income & Finance, Situation and Outlook Report (AFO-46, USDA/ERS, September 1992).

Farm Real Estate, Government Payments, and Net Farm Income

Farm Real Estate Average Value of Land and Vuildings (per acre) 1990 ($)		Increase, 1980–90 ($)		Increase 1980–90 (%)		Government Payments, 1989 ($)		Government Payments, 1991 ($)		Desc. Num. Order
RI	5,080	RI	2,557	MA	136.44	TX	1,249,000,000	TX	777,925,000	1
NJ	4,737	MA	2,194	NH	125.10	IA	981,000,000	KS	697,895,000	2
CT	4,463	CT	2,076	RI	101.35	IL	762,000,000	IA	644,955,000	3
MA	3,802	NJ	1,790	CT	86.97	MN	600,000,000	ND	533,853,000	4
MD	2,512	NH	1,256	ME	73.23	KS	588,000,000	NE	490,659,000	5
NM	200	IL	–625	IN	–30.86	NH	2,000,000	CT	1,351,000	47
WY	153	IA	–710	IA	–38.59	AK	1,000,000	AK	1,285,000	48
AK	N/A	AK	N/A	AK	N/A	HI	below 500,000	HI	906,000	49
DC	N/A	DC	N/A	DC	N/A	RI	below 500,000	RI	110,000	50
HI	N/A	HI	N/A	HI	N/A	DC	N/A	DC	N/A	51

(continued on next page)

Construction Valuation by Permit

1989 ($000)		1990 ($000)		Difference, 1989–90 ($000)		Increase, 1989–90 (%)		Per Capita, 1990 ($)		Desc. Num. Order
CA	40,870,000	CA	24,480,000	CO	415,000	AK	84.38	HI	1,909.35	1
FL	17,037,000	FL	12,007,000	HI	333,000	MT	84.31	NV	1,877.13	2
NY	8,446,000	TX	8,161,000	UT	259,000	ID	32.48	WA	985.06	3
IL	8,239,000	IL	6,711,000	ID	202,000	UT	25.59	FL	928.05	4
TX	8,177,000	OH	6,245,000	AK	135,000	SD	25.17	AZ	874.98	5
ND	220,000	AK	295,000	NJ	–1,998,000	ME	–35.05	WY	297.63	47
AK	160,000	MT	282,000	VA	–2,382,000	CT	–38.10	DC	280.11	48
MT	153,000	ND	262,000	NY	–2,499,000	CA	–40.10	LA	260.90	49
DC	139,000	DC	170,000	FL	–5,030,000	NH	–41.61	MS	230.06	50
WY	115,000	WY	135,000	CA	–16,390,000	RI	–44.50	WV	168.39	51

SOURCE: Statistical Abstract of the United States 1992.

Agricultural Commodities, by State (1991)

	Leading 1991 Commodities (in order of importance)	Percentage of Total Farm Marketing Income (%)	Desc. Num. Order
IA	Hogs, corn, cattle, soybeans	91	1
VT	Dairy products, cattle, greenhouse, hay	90	2
NE	Cattle, corn, hogs, soybeans	89	3
NV	Cattle, hay, dairy products, potatoes	88	4
WY	Cattle, sugar beets, hay, barley	88	5
NJ	Greenhouse, dairy products, eggs, peaches	48	47
OR	Cattle, greenhouse, dairy products, wheat	47	48
SC	Tobacco, cattle, broilers, greenhouse	43	49
CA	Dairy products, greenhouse, cattle, grapes	42	50
DC	N/A	N/A	51

SOURCE: Farm Income Estimation Section, Agriculture and Rural Economy Division, U.S. Department of Agriculture, Economic Research Service, Agricultural Income and Finance, Situation and Outlook Report, (AFO-46, USDA/ERS, September 1992).

Farm Real Estate, Government Payments, and Net Farm Income (cont.)

Difference in Government Payments, 1989–90 ($)		*Difference in Government Payments, 1989–90 (%)*		*Net Farm Income per Operation, 1991 ($)*		*Net Farm Income per Acre, 1991 ($)*		*Desc. Num. Order*
KS	109,895,000	WA	57.32	FL	68,018	RI	558	1
WA	75,084,000	OR	48.51	CA	67,531	CT	462	2
ND	58,853,000	ID	42.68	AZ	64,828	DE	307	3
OK	55,922,000	AK	28.50	DE	60,296	MA	281	4
ID	42,250,000	OK	23.80	RI	52,606	NJ	263	5
WI	–372,050,000	WI	–71.27	IN	7,155	NM	8	47
TX	–471,075,000	NJ	–80.71	AK	6,371	NV	8	48
DC	NA	DC	NA	TN	4,280	WY	6	49
HI	NA	HI	NA	WV	3,915	AK	4	50
RI	NA	RI	NA	DC	NA	DC	NA	51

SOURCE: Farm Income Estimation Section, Agriculture and Rural Economy Division, U.S. Department of Agriculture, Economic Research Service, Agricultural Income and Finance, Situation and Outlook Report (AFO-46, USDA/ERS, September 1992).

Manufacturing, Value Added & Shipments (1990)

Value Added ($000,000)		*Value Added per Capita ($)*		*Value of Shipments ($000,000)*		*Value of Shipments per Capita ($)*		*Desc. Num. Order*
CA	149,578	NC	8,700.73	CA	293,190	DE	19,365.99	1
NY	85,532	IN	8,102.94	TX	210,584	IN	17,787.91	2
TX	83,630	WI	7,582.12	OH	177,787	NC	17,536.79	3
OH	80,377	OH	7,409.99	IL	156,675	WI	16,969.93	4
IL	70,784	CT	7,248.30	NY	154,714	IA	16,539.81	5
NV	1,470	ND	1,737.63	AK	3,676	FL	4,695.50	47
AK	1,390	MT	1,489.24	ND	3,013	HI	3,792.54	48
MT	1,190	NM	1,486.40	NV	2,925	NM	3,661.88	49
ND	1,110	HI	1,405.85	WY	2,756	DC	3,545.89	50
WY	844	NV	1,223.13	DC	2,152	NV	2,433.78	51

SOURCE: U.S. Department of Commerce, Bureau of the Census, SA92 1246, SA92 1246.

Principal Manufactured Goods (by product and state)

Product	State
Aerospace products	CO, NV
Aircraft and missiles	AZ
Aircraft engines and parts	CT
Aircraft	WA, WV
Airplane parts	AR
Aluminum	WA
Apparel and related products	SC
Apparel	AR, AZ, DE, GA (1990), KY, MS, NM, TN
Appliances	IA
Auto accessories	IA
Auto components	AR
Automotive and aircraft components	NY
Autos	DE
Basic organic and inorganic chemicals	WV
Books and periodicals	NY
Books	VT
Canned pineapple	HI
Cast iron and plastic pipe	AL (1988–89)
Chemical	NC
Chemical products	ID, IL, IN, LA (1990), MD
Chemicals and allied products	SC, TN, TX
Chemicals	AL (1988-89), AR, IA, MN, MO, NJ, NV, VA
Clay and glass products	WY
Clothing and apparel	NY
Clothing	HI
Computer components	VT
Computer equipment	CO
Costume jewelry	RI, DC
Electric and electronic equipment	CA, FL, IL, MA (1990), MD, MN, NE, SD (1986), TN, VA

(continued on next page)

Principal Manufactured Goods (cont.)

Product	States
Electric motors	AR
Electrical and electronic equipment	IN, MO, NC, TX, KY, NH
Electrical equipment	UT
Electrical machinery and equipment	MS
Electrical machinery	PA
Electronic and electrical equipment	NJ
Electronic components	ID, UT
Electronic equipment	LA (1990), NY
Electronic products	IA
Electronics and electrical equipment	CT
Electronics	AL (1988-89), AZ, RI
Fabricated metal products	ID, MA (1990), MN, NH, OK, PA, TN
Fabricated metals	MI, NJ, OR, UT, WV, WI
Fabricated steel products	AL (1988-89)
Fabrics	AL (1988-89)
Farm equipment	ND
Farm machinery	IA
Fertilizers	IA
Fish products	AK
Fishing rods	VT
Food and kindred products	IL, KS, MD, SD (1986), TN
Food and related products	MO
Food	FL
Food	GA (1990)
Food processing	MN, VA
Food products	AR, KY, MI, MT, NC, UT
Foods and kindred products	MS
Foods	AZ, CA, DE, HI, IN, LA (1990), NE, NM, OR, PA, TX, WI, WY
Furniture	AR, MS, NC, VT
Furs	AK
Gaming devices	NV
Guided missiles and parts	UT
Helicopters	CT
Home appliances	AR
Industrial machinery and equipment	MA (1990)
Industrial machinery	KS
Instruments and related products	NE
Instruments	CA, CT, MN, NY
Lawn and garden irrigation equipment	NV
Leather goods	ME
Luggage	DE
Lumber and plywood	WA
Lumber and pulp	AK
Lumber and wood products	ID, MS, OR
Lumber	AR, LA (1990), NM
Machine tools	VT
Machinery and computer equipment	CT
Machinery and fabricated metal products	SC
Machinery	AR, CA, FL, ID, IL, MA (1990), MI, NE, NH, NM, NY, OH, OR, RI, SD (1986), TX, WI, WV

Product	States
Mobile homes	AL (1988-89)
Nonelectrical machinery	KY, TN, IN, MN, NC, NJ, OK, PA
Nylon	DE
Office furniture	IA
Paper and allied products	TN, ME, WI
Paper	AR, MN, OR
Paper products	AL (1988-89)
Petroleum and coal products	MT
Petroleum	OK
Petroleum products	AR, LA (1990)
Pharmaceuticals	NY
Plastic and hardwood products	WV
Plastics	IN, NH
Poultry processing	AL (1988-89)
Primary and fabricated metal products	NE, OH
Primary and fabricated metals	AZ, CA, IL, IN
Primary metals	ID, MI, MT, OR, P
Printed material	CA
Printing and publishing	AZ, FL, GA (1990), HI, IL, KS, KY, MA (1990), MN, MT, OR, TN
Printing	NM
Processed foods	ID, ND
Processed fruits and vegetables	WA
Processed meats and vegetables	DE
Pulp and paper	WA
Railroad and aircraft equipment	DE
Refined petroleum products	WY
Rubber and miscellaneous plastic products	TN
Rubber and plastic	MI
Scales	VT
Seismic and machinery-monitoring devices	NV
Ships	AL (1988-89)
Steel	AL (1988-89), UT, WV
Stone	WY
Submarines	CT
Sugar	HI
Textiles	GA (1990), NC, RI, SC, VA
Tires	IA
Tobacco products	NC
Toys and sporting goods	NY
Transportation equipment	FL, GA (1990), IN, KS, LA (1990), MI, MO, MS, NE, NM, OH, TN, TX, VA, WI
Transportation equipment instruments	CA
Wood and paper	LA (1990)
Wood and paper products	MT
Wood products	WY

SOURCE: *World Almanac 1992*, Principal Manufactured Goods.

Mineral Industries, Value of Shipments and Receipts, 1987

	Shipments and Receipts ($000,000)	*Desc. Num. Order*
TX	40,319	1
LA	24,630	2
CA	8,693	3
AK	8,567	4
OK	8,389	5
NH	50	46
HI	31	47
RI	20	48
DE, DC	17	49[1]
DE, DC	17	49[1]
ME	8	51

[1]DC is included in DE.

SOURCE: *State and Metropolitan Area Data Book 1991,* 4th ed.

Principal Minerals (by state)

AK	Petroleum, natural gas, sand/gravel
AL	Coal, petroleum, natural gas
AR	Petroleum, natural gas, bromine
AZ	Natural gas, petroleum, coal
CA	Petroleum, natural gas, cement
CO	Petroleum, natural gas, coal
DE	Magnesium compounds, sand/gravel
FL	Phosphate, petroleum, stone
GA	Clays, stone, cement
HI	Stone, cement, sand/gravel
IA	Stone, cement, sand/gravel
ID	Silver, phosphate, gold
IL	Coal, petroleum, stone
IN	Coal, petroleum, stone
KS	Petroleum, natural gas, cement
KY	Coal, petroleum, stone
LA	Petroleum, natural gas, sulfur
MA	Stone, sand/gravel, lime
MD	Coal, stone, cement
ME	Sand/gravel cement, stone
MI	Petroleum, iron ore, natural gas, clay
MN	Iron ore, sand/gravel, stone
MO	Lead, cement, stone
MS	Petroleum, natural gas, sand/gravel
MT	Petroleum, coal, natural gas
NC	Stone, phosphate, lithium
ND	Petroleum, coal, natural gas
NE	Petroleum, cement, stone
NH	Sand/gravel, stone, clays
NJ	Stone, sand/gravel, zinc
NM	Natural gas, petroleum, coal
NV	Gold, silver, diatomite
NY	Stone, cement, salt
OH	Coal, natural gas, petroleum
OK	Natural gas, petroleum, coal
OR	Stone, sand/gravel, cement
PA	Coal, natural gas, cement
RI	Stone, sand/gravel, gem stones
SC	Cement, stone, clays
SD	Gold, cement, petroleum
TN	Coal, stone, zinc
TX	Petroleum, natural gas, cement
UT	Petroleum, coal, copper
VA	Coal, stone, cement
VT	Stone, asbestos, sand/gravel
WA	Cement, sand/gravel, stone
WI	Stone, sand/gravel, lime
WV	Coal, natural gas, petroleum
WY	Petroleum, coal, natural gas

SOURCE: Bureau of Mines, Department of Interior.

Retail Sales (1990)

Total Retail Sales ($000,000)		Retail Sales per Household ($)		Change per Household, 1987–90 (%)		Desc. Num. Order
CA	225,066	HI	31,121	LA	36.2	1
NY	124,479	NH	28,373	HI	29.4	2
TX	120,459	AK	24,533	OK	25.6	3
FL	105,304	DE	24,145	SD	25.6	4
IL	83,479	NJ	22,579	IA	25.5	5
SD	4,649	ID	16,591	GA	6.5	47
VT	4,512	WY	16,314	NC	5.9	48
ND	4,467	DC	15,360	MD	5.2	49
DC	3,815	MS	15,131	VT	4.8	50
WY	2,726	WV	14,718	CT	3.3	51

SOURCE: *State and Metropolitan Area Data Book 1991*, 4th ed.

Service Industry (1987)

Receipts from Firms Subject to Income Tax ($000,000)		Tax-Exempt Firms Revenues ($000,000)		Total Receipts ($000,000)		Total Receipts ($ per cap.)		Desc. Num. Order
CA	146,288	NY	30,583	CA	175,670	DC	23,278.96	1
NY	83,524	CA	29,382	NY	114,107	NV	9,372.35	2
TX	57,922	PA	16,475	TX	69,881	MA	6,875.68	3
FL	50,997	IL	15,201	FL	60,872	NY	6,342.64	4
IL	40,742	OH	12,973	IL	55,943	CA	5,902.89	5
MT	1,680	AK	644	MT	2,459	WV	2,717.63	47
VT	1,591	ID	594	VT	2,178	KY	2,692.32	48
ND	1,244	VT	587	ND	2,087	SC	2,685.34	49
SD	1,177	NV	536	SD	1,934	AR	2,571.97	50
WY	1,041	WY	403	WY	1,444	MS	2,185.59	51

SOURCE: *Statistical Abstract 1991*, Table 1377, *Statistical Abstract 1992*, Table 1307.

Domestic Travel Expenditures (1989)

Expenditures ($000,000)		Desc. Num. Order
CA	38,241	1
FL	24,437	2
NY	18,301	3
TX	15,543	4
IL	10,865	5
VT	889	47
DE	748	48
ND	702	49
SD	679	50
RI	621	51

SOURCE: © U.S. Travel Data Center.

Value of Exports (1990)

Value of Exports ($000,000)		Value of Exports ($ per cap.)		Desc. Num. Order
CA	44,520	AK	5,181.41	1
TX	32,931	WA	5,020.25	2
WA	24,432	LA	3,364.71	3
NY	22,072	VT	2,050.62	4
MI	18,474	DE	2,017.51	5
WY	264	NV	327.83	47
NM	249	SD	294.54	48
MT	229	MT	286.58	49
SD	205	NM	164.35	50
HI	179	HI	161.52	51

SOURCE: U.S. Bureau of the Census, U.S. Merchandise Trade, Series FT 900 December issue.

Patents (1990)

Total U.S. Patents		Persons per Patent		Patents per 1,000 Population		Desc. Num. Order
CA	7,922	MS	19,947	MS	19.9	1
NY	4,524	SD	16,976	SD	17.0	2
TX	3,176	AK	16,178	AK	16.2	3
NJ	3,090	AR	15,883	AR	15.9	4
IL	2,935	HI	13,193	HI	13.2	5
ND	50	MN	2,968	MN	3.0	47
DC	48	MA	2,847	MA	2.8	48
SD	41	NJ	2,502	NJ	2.5	49
WY	36	CT	2,174	CT	2.2	50
AK	34	DE	1,535	DE	1.5	51

SOURCE: U.S. Patent and Trademark Office.

Electric Generation, Net and Source (1989)

Net (in billions of kW)		% from Coal		% from Petroleum		% from Gas		% from Hydroelectric		% from Nuclear		Desc. Num. Order
TX	232.3	WV	99.1	DC	100.0	AK	64.6	ID	100.0	MT	75.8	1
PA	154.8	WY	98.0	HA	99.4	TX	43.0	OR	84.1	SC	60.9	2
CA	131.9	UT	97.3	RI	67.1	LA	42.6	WA	81.6	ME	59.7	3
OH	131.3	IN	96.6	MA	48.9	OK	40.3	SD	65.6	IL	59.0	4
NY	130.1	KY	93.6	NH	41.6	CA	38.9	MT	37.0	CT	57.1	5
SD	7.0	CA	0.0	MT	0.1	WV	NA	KS	NA	NM	NA	47
VT	4.8	HA	0.0	CO	0.1	KY	NA	DE	NA	UT	NA	48
AK	4.4	ME	0.0	NM	0.1	TN	NA	DC	NA	NV	NA	49
DC	0.7	VT	0.0	WA	0.1	ID	NA	MS	NA	AK	NA	50
RI	0.5	RI	0.0	ID	0.0	HA	NA	LA	NA	HI	NA	51

SOURCE: U.S. Energy Information Administration.

Energy Sources (1989)

Total (trillions of Btu)		Petroleum (trillions of Btu)		Petroleum Energy Derived (% of total)		Natural Gas (dry) (trillions of Btu)		Natural Gas (dry) Energy Derived (% of total)		Desc. Num. Order
TX	9,617	TX	4,407	HI	98.33	TX	3,763	AK	56.61	1
CA	6,202	CA	3,540	RI	74.13	CA	1,906	LA	46.65	2
PA	3,913	NY	1,777	NH	73.36	LA	1,599	OK	45.40	3
IL	3,691	FL	1,555	MA	66.07	IL	1,014	DC	44.16	4
OH	3,634	LA	1,489	ME	62.98	NY	870	TX	39.13	5
NH	229	ND	118	SC	30.68	SD	26	NH	6.11	47
SD	218	SD	111	UT	29.90	NH	14	ND	6.02	48
VT	150	RI	106	ND	22.18	VT	6	VT	4.00	49
RI	143	VT	74	WY	20.77	ME	4	ME	1.10	50
DC	77	DC	42	WV	20.34	HI	3	HI	1.00	51

(continued on next page)

Energy End-Use Consumption

Total (trillions of Btu)		Per Capita (millions of Btu)		Per Capita Change in Btu, 1988–89 (%)		Residential (trillions of Btu)		Residential (% of total)		Desc. Num. Order
TX	9,690	GA	3,115	TX	18.80	CA	1,270	CT	31.90	1
CA	7,127	AK	1,075	HI	13.20	TX	1,155	RI	31.55	2
OH	3,883	LA	804	AK	9.00	NY	1,024	NH	31.20	3
PA	3,590	WY	803	NV	8.20	IL	898	MA	30.39	4
NY	3,556	TX	570	ME	8.10	PA	867	VT	29.01	5
DE	233	MA	232	VA	0.50	AK	43	TX	11.92	47
SD	212	VT	231	GA	0.30	VT	38	WY	9.19	48
RI	206	NH	226	MO	0.30	DC	35	HI	8.36	49
DC	175	RI	206	OK	0.30	WY	35	LA	8.32	50
VT	131	NY	196	PA	0.10	HI	25	AK	7.58	51

(continued on next page)

Energy Sources (cont.)

Coal (trillions of Btu)		Coal Energy Derived (% of total)		Hydroelectric (trillions of Btu)		Hydroelectric Energy Derived (% of total)		Nuclear Electric (trillions of Btu)		Nuclear Electric Energy Derived (% of total)		Desc. Num. Order
OH	1,464	WV	68.46	WA	730	OR	43.94	IL	802	SC	34.46	1
PA	1,464	ND	68.05	OR	413	WA	40.13	SC	437	VT	26.00	2
TX	1,326	WY	64.77	CA	349	ID	34.70	PA	420	CT	25.36	3
IN	1,308	UT	50.81	NY	296	SD	22.02	CA	349	IL	21.73	4
WV	929	IN	50.17	AL	136	MT	20.67	NC	313	ME	20.44	5
AK	5	AK	0.88	DE	0	DE	0.00	RI	0	RI	0.00	47
DC	1	OR	0.74	DC	0	DC	0.00	SD	0	SD	0.00	48
HI	1	RI	0.70	KS	0	KS	0.00	UT	0	UT	0.00	49
RI	1	HI	0.33	LA	0	LA	0.00	WV	0	WV	0.00	50
VT	0	VT	0.00	MS	0	MS	0.00	WY	0	WY	0.00	51

SOURCE: *1992 Statistical Abstract,* Table 915.

Energy End-Use Consumption (cont.)

Commercial (trillions of Btu)		Commercial (% of total)		Industrial (trillions of Btu)		Industrial (% of total)		Transportation (trillions of Btu)		Transportation (% of total)		Desc. Num. Order
CA	1,244	DC	44.00	TX	5,359	LA	65.29	CA	2,774	HI	50.84	1
TX	1,027	NY	27.47	LA	2,300	WY	58.79	TX	2,150	CA	38.92	2
NY	977	CO	25.41	CA	1,839	TX	55.30	FL	1,129	FL	37.70	3
FL	659	MA	23.76	OH	1,585	WV	53.69	NY	872	NM	36.85	4
IL	643	CT	22.92	PA	1,374	AK	52.56	OH	828	AZ	35.37	5
ND	37	MS	10.72	SD	58	DC	18.86	DE	65	ND	21.32	47
WY	37	TX	10.60	NH	56	RI	17.48	SD	65	OH	21.32	48
DE	33	WY	9.71	RI	36	CT	16.67	RI	61	LA	19.56	49
SD	32	AK	9.17	DC	33	MA	15.23	VT	42	WV	18.77	50
VT	25	LA	6.84	VT	25	FL	13.89	DC	29	DC	16.57	51

SOURCE: *1992 Statistical Abstract,* Table 915.

TRAVEL AND TRANSPORTATION

Motorized Vehicles

Motor Vehicle Registrations		*Motor Vehicle Registrations per 1,000 Population*		*Motorcycle Registrations*		*Motorcycle Registrations per 1,000 Population*		*Desc. Num. Order*
CA	21,925,878	WY	1,164.98	CA	640,554	IA	62.4	1
TX	12,799,815	ID	1,046.48	OH	228,408	WY	44.8	2
FL	10,949,806	SD	1,011.18	FL	205,827	SD	43.0	3
NY	10,196,153	ND	985.97	NY	197,935	ID	41.7	4
OH	8,410,466	MT	980.09	WI	189,102	WI	38.7	5
WY	528,421	RI	669.49	VT	17,590	SC	8.9	47
DE	526,089	MA	619.27	AR	14,556	NC	8.6	48
AK	477,325	AR	615.84	AK	11,541	LA	7.1	49
VT	461,796	NY	566.75	DE	8,867	AR	6.2	50
DC	261,931	DC	431.59	DC	2,560	DC	4.2	51

SOURCE: U.S. Department of Transportation, U.S. Department of Commerce, Bureau of the Census.

Streets, Roads, Highways, and Miles Traveled

Total Rural and Urban Mileage		*People per Rural and Urban Mile*		*Rural Mileage*		*People per Rural Mile*		*Urban Mileage*		*Desc. Num. Order*
TX	305,951	DC	550.7	TX	217,175	RI	658.9	TX	88,776	1
CA	163,574	HI	270.4	KS	124,473	NJ	657.9	CA	73,922	2
IL	135,944	NJ	225.7	MN	115,189	MA	454.8	FL	48,034	3
KS	133,578	CA	181.9	MO	105,488	HI	428.4	NY	37,913	4
MN	129,397	MA	176.6	IL	103,941	CT	361.8	IL	32,003	5
AK	13,485	ID	16.1	CT	9,086	WY	12.2	DE	1,615	47
RI	6,111	WY	11.6	DE	3,829	MT	11.6	AK	1,549	48
DE	5,444	MT	11.2	HI	2,587	SD	9.5	HI	1,512	49
HI	4,099	SD	9.3	RI	1,523	ND	7.5	VT	1,180	50
DC	1,102	ND	7.4	DC	NA	DC	0.0	DC	1,102	51

(continued on next page)

Drivers, Fatalities, Travel Time and Housing Units with 2 or More Vehicles

Licensed Drivers per 1,000 Driving Age Population		*Fatalities per 100,000 Population*		*Fatalities per 100 Million Vehicle-Miles of Travel*		*Mean Travel Time for Workers 16 and Over Who Work Away from Home (min.)*		*Rate of Occupied Housing Units with Two or More Vehicles*		*Desc. Num. Order*
OR	999	NM	32.94	NV	3.36	HI	28.6	ID	67.3	1
MT	997	MS	28.99	WV	3.12	WY	27.1	WY	66.9	2
WY	991	NV	28.54	NM	3.09	SD	27.0	UT	66.1	3
MS	990	SC	28.08	MS	3.06	RI	25.3	SD	64.1	4
NH	981	AL	27.67	AR	2.87	AZ	25.1	MT	63.5	5
CO	810	CT	11.68	CT	1.46	KY	15.8	FL	49.8	47
AK	801	NJ	11.46	MN	1.45	OR	15.4	PA	49.5	48
HI	797	MA	10.05	DC	1.41	NE	14.8	MA	49.3	49
MN	754	RI	8.37	MA	1.31	MO	13.8	NY	37.5	50
NY	727	DC	7.91	RI	1.20	MD	13.0	DC	21.2	51

SOURCE: U.S. Department of Transportation, U.S. Department of Commerce, Bureau of the Census.

Streets, Roads, Highways, and Miles Traveled (cont.)

People per Urban Mile		*Total Interstate Mileage*		*People per Interstate Mile*		*Annual Vehicle-Miles of Travel per Person*		*Vehicle-Miles of Travel per Person per Day*		*Desc. Num. Order*
HI	733.0	TX	3,229	DC	50,575	WY	12,859	WY	35	1
WV	583.1	CA	2,399	HI	25,773	GA	11,229	GA	30	2
DC	550.7	IL	1,961	NJ	19,521	NM	10,658	NM	29	3
ME	492.4	OH	1,572	DE	16,248	OK	10,516	OK	28	4
KY	479.1	PA	1,569	RI	14,335	AL	10,480	AL	28	5
AZ	249.9	NH	224	ND	1,121	AK	7,233	AK	19	47
AL	239.7	RI	70	SD	1,027	PA	7,213	PA	19	48
WY	232.4	HI	43	MT	671	RI	6,999	RI	19	49
RI	218.7	DE	41	AK	505	NY	5,942	NY	16	50
TX	191.3	DC	12	WY	497	DC	5,613	DC	15	51

SOURCE: U.S. Department of Transportation, U.S. Department of Commerce, 1990 Census.

GOVERNMENT

Government Finances (1990)

State Government Total Revenue ($000)		*State Government Total Revenue per Capita ($)*		*State and Local Government Total Revenue*		*State and Local Government Total Revenue per Capita ($000)*		*Desc. Num. Order*
CA	88,703,877	AK	9,999.67	CA	147,714,787	AK	12,942.87	1
NY	64,252,998	WY	4,188.53	NY	108,692,249	DC	8,117.65	2
TX	30,975,026	HI	3,903.10	TX	58,778,749	NY	6,041.66	3
OH	28,515,731	NY	3,571.50	FL	47,069,843	WY	6,011.16	4
PA	27,222,929	DE	3,475.97	PA	43,776,949	HI	5,108.38	5
IL	24,313,085	NM	3,122.50	IL	43,541,366	CA	4,963.53	6
FL	23,868,131	WA	3,082.04	OH	42,541,686	MN	4,822.41	7
MI	23,405,004	RI	3,023.76	MI	37,183,968	WA	4,794.33	8
NJ	22,623,961	MN	3,008.36	NJ	35,089,837	OR	4,590.16	9
MA	17,034,053	CA	2,980.64	MA	26,068,621	NJ	4,539.33	10
WA	14,999,316	NJ	2,926.70	GA	24,059,769	NE	4,452.93	11
NC	14,485,060	CT	2,917.67	WA	23,332,509	WI	4,449.54	12
VA	13,606,679	ND	2,833.96	NC	23,175,644	CT	4,427.98	13
WI	13,387,631	MA	2,831.26	VA	21,976,846	DE	4,427.82	14
MN	13,161,868	VT	2,829.33	WI	21,766,102	MA	4,332.91	15
GA	13,107,914	MT	2,783.90	MN	21,098,505	CO	4,277.77	16
MD	12,194,598	WI	2,736.77	MD	19,527,566	NV	4,239.07	17
IN	11,456,232	NV	2,717.33	IN	18,168,008	NM	4,099.86	18
LA	10,096,284	ME	2,643.50	TN	17,965,066	RI	4,090.47	19
CT	9,590,710	OH	2,628.88	LA	15,561,600	MT	4,090.14	20
MO	9,343,485	MD	2,550.39	MO	15,412,201	MD	4,084.01	21
TN	9,109,677	MI	2,517.94	AZ	14,902,970	AZ	4,066.04	22
AL	9,040,995	SC	2,509.61	CT	14,555,281	VT	4,051.09	23
SC	8,750,261	UT	2,497.18	CO	14,092,653	UT	4,034.03	24
AZ	8,598,443	WV	2,473.11	AL	13,770,020	MI	4,000.30	25
KY	8,592,819	OR	2,463.02	OR	13,046,705	OH	3,921.94	26
CO	7,526,860	IA	2,422.87	SC	12,559,271	ND	3,868.14	27
OK	7,200,626	ID	2,400.80	KY	11,791,869	IL	3,809.19	28
OR	7,000,702	LA	2,392.50	OK	10,554,311	IA	3,785.37	29
IA	6,727,704	AZ	2,345.95	IA	10,511,043	GA	3,713.95	30
AK	5,500,247	KY	2,331.65	KS	9,050,852	LA	3,687.61	31
MS	5,343,972	PA	2,291.18	MS	8,150,934	PA	3,684.42	32
KS	5,135,621	OK	2,289.12	AK	7,119,136	TN	3,683.49	33
NM	4,730,810	CO	2,284.75	NE	7,028,444	ME	3,681.72	34
AR	4,511,017	AL	2,237.54	UT	6,950,036	KS	3,653.11	35
WV	4,435,474	VA	2,199.11	AR	6,346,952	FL	3,638.13	36
HI	4,325,531	NC	2,185.22	NM	6,211,566	SC	3,602.05	37
UT	4,302,275	SD	2,146.33	WV	5,752,630	VA	3,551.90	38
NV	3,265,776	IL	2,127.02	HI	5,661,258	NC	3,496.29	39
ME	3,246,033	MS	2,076.77	NV	5,094,653	TX	3,460.32	40
NE	3,073,420	KS	2,072.84	DC	4,926,602	AL	3,407.93	41
RI	3,034,237	IN	2,066.36	ME	4,520,883	SD	3,359.15	42
ID	2,417,006	GA	2,023.38	RI	4,104,635	OK	3,355.28	43
DE	2,315,578	NE	1,947.19	NH	3,504,144	ID	3,349.92	44
MT	2,224,521	AR	1,918.99	ID	3,372,524	IN	3,276.96	45
WY	1,899,867	FL	1,844.82	DE	2,949,672	KY	3,199.71	46
NH	1,922,222	TN	1,867.81	MT	3,268,286	WV	3,207.53	47
ND	1,810,334	MO	1,825.94	WY	2,726,590	MS	3,167.61	48
VT	1,592,229	TX	1,823.51	ND	2,470,965	NH	3,159.02	49
SD	1,493,854	NH	1,732.90	SD	2,337,985	MO	3,011.92	50
DC	N/A	DC	N/A	VT	2,279,782	AR	2,700.00	51

(continued on next page)

Government Finances (cont.)

State Government Total Debt Outstanding ($000)		State Government Total Debt Outstanding per Capita ($)		State and Local Government Total Debt ($000,000)		State and Local Government Total Debt per Capita ($)		Desc. Num. Order
NY	46,547,127	AK	10,063.81	NY	94,538	AK	18,851.25	1
CA	28,866,306	DE	4,470.36	CA	93,358	DC	7,282.91	2
NJ	18,907,599	RI	3,603.32	TX	64,127	DE	5,944.45	3
MA	18,714,704	CT	3,342.65	FL	53,464	UT	5,810.14	4
IL	15,262,397	MA	3,110.60	PA	45,728	NY	5,254.90	5
LA	12,770,321	HI	3,064.30	NJ	32,565	LA	5,109.04	6
OH	11,208,531	LA	3,026.16	IL	32,027	WY	4,975.88	7
CT	10,987,665	NH	3,009.66	MA	26,976	WA	4,857.51	8
PA	10,926,401	NY	2,587.32	WA	23,640	AZ	4,792.61	9
FL	9,950,071	SD	2,568.04	OH	23,191	MA	4,483.73	10
MI	9,169,639	NJ	2,445.94	LA	21,560	CT	4,378.31	11
TX	7,863,557	OR	2,307.27	MI	21,414	RI	4,320.04	12
MD	6,643,753	VT	2,237.10	AZ	17,566	NJ	4,212.70	13
OR	6,558,015	WY	2,068.48	GA	17,397	FL	4,132.35	14
WI	6,119,267	MT	1,746.84	MN	17,351	CO	4,053.55	15
VA	6,082,564	ME	1,730.68	MD	16,288	HI	3,996.47	16
WA	5,685,548	KY	1,436.89	VA	15,802	MN	3,965.85	17
AK	5,535,526	MD	1,389.48	NC	15,723	NE	3,921.73	18
KY	5,295,370	WV	1,377.81	CT	14,392	NH	3,906.24	19
MO	5,249,856	ND	1,365.31	TN	14,390	PA	3,848.63	20
IN	4,140,038	IL	1,335.22	CO	13,354	TX	3,775.17	21
AL	3,979,067	NV	1,308.54	KY	13,321	NV	3,621.14	22
SC	3,894,367	WI	1,250.93	WI	12,090	KY	3,614.64	23
MN	3,764,071	NM	1,208.08	IN	10,883	OR	3,560.47	24
OK	3,714,198	OK	1,180.77	AK	10,369	WV	3,508.27	25
RI	3,615,805	WA	1,168.26	AL	10,221	MD	3,406.49	26
HI	3,395,949	SC	1,116.92	OR	10,120	NM	3,295.56	27
NH	3,338,474	UT	1,039.26	MO	10,110	SD	3,267.22	28
GA	3,117,366	OH	1,033.32	UT	10,010	MT	3,196.24	29
NC	3,071,211	MO	1,025.95	SC	9,723	CA	3,137.03	30
DE	2,978,014	MI	986.48	OK	8,233	VT	2,995.96	31
TN	2,618,094	AL	984.77	KS	6,961	TN	2,950.47	32
WV	2,471,073	VA	983.06	WV	6,292	ND	2,905.45	33
CO	2,421,555	ID	970.62	NE	6,190	KS	2,809.60	34
AZ	2,192,956	CA	969.97	IA	5,456	IL	2,801.86	35
ME	2,125,146	PA	919.60	NM	4,993	SC	2,788.59	36
IA	1,875,183	NE	862.31	MS	4,769	ME	2,767.26	37
NM	1,830,328	MN	860.34	AR	4,612	GA	2,685.46	38
UT	1,790,494	FL	769.06	HI	4,429	OK	2,617.32	39
SD	1,787,363	IN	746.74	DC	4,420	VA	2,553.92	40
AR	1,747,048	AR	743.20	NV	4,352	AL	2,529.58	41
NV	1,572,645	CO	735.05	RI	4,335	WI	2,471.50	42
MT	1,395,842	IA	675.31	NH	4,333	NC	2,371.98	43
NE	1,361,056	AZ	598.31	DE	3,960	MI	2,303.75	44
MS	1,342,623	TN	536.80	ME	3,398	OH	2,137.99	45
VT	1,258,945	MS	521.77	MT	2,554	MO	1,975.74	46
ID	977,171	GA	481.21	SD	2,274	IA	1,964.88	47
WY	938,236	NC	463.32	WY	2,257	IN	1,962.97	48
ND	872,159	TX	462.93	ND	1,856	AR	1,961.95	49
KS	306,297	KS	123.63	VT	1,686	MS	1,853.32	50
DC	N/A	DC	N/A	ID	1,528	ID	1,517.76	51

SOURCE: Government Finances State Government Finances, 1990 (GF-90-3), Government Finances State and Local Giovernment Finances, 1990 (GF-90-5)

Voting (1988)

Total Registered on Rolls		Population Registered (% of voting age)		Voter Turnout		Rate of Registered Who Voted in the Election (%)		Rate of Voting Age Population Who Voted (%)		Desc. Num. Order
CA	14,004,873	ME	95.72	CA	9,887,065	MA	80.40	MN	66.33	1
NY	8,581,276	MN	92.28	NY	6,485,683	CT	80.39	MT	62.40	2
TX	8,201,856	OK	91.47	TX	5,427,410	UT	80.18	ME	62.15	3
IL	6,356,940	MI	87.65	IL	4,559,120	HI	79.88	WI	61.98	4
OH	6,323,352	SD	86.50	PA	4,536,251	OR	78.83	ND	61.54	5
DC	299,757	SC	57.11	DE	249,891	MS	58.37	NC	43.44	47
AK	293,871	NV	57.04	VT	243,328	AL	56.23	HI	43.02	48
WY	226,189	HI	53.85	AK	200,116	OK	53.25	DC	39.44	49
ND	N/A	ND	N/A	DC	192,877	ND	N/A	SC	38.91	50
WI	UNKNOWN	WI	UNKNOWN	WY	176,551	WI	UNKNOWN	GA	38.79	51

SOURCE: Federal Election Commission.

State Legislature (1992) and U.S. House of Representatives

State Legislatures' Total Members		Women in State Legislatures		Rate of Women in State Legislatures (%)		Control of State Legislature		Number of Representatives in the U.S. House, 1993		Loss or Gain in the U.S. House, 1983–93		Desc. Num. Order
NH	424	NH	131	AZ	34.4	AL	Dem.	CA	52	CA	+7	1
PA	253	ME	60	WA	32.7	AR	Dem.	NY	31	FL	+4	2
GA	236	VT	56	ME	32.3	CA	Dem.	TX	30	TX	+3	3
NY	211	WA	48	VT	31.1	CT	Dem.	FL	23	AZ	+1	4
MN	201	KS	45	CO	31.0	FL	Dem.	PA	21	GA	+1	5
NV	63	NE	9	LA	6.9	PA	Split	ND	1	LA	−1	47
DE	62	AL	8	MS	6.9	VT	Split	SD	1	MA	−1	48
AK	60	DE	8	KY	5.8	WA	Split	VT	1	MT	−1	49
NE	49	KY	8	AL	5.7	DC	N/A	WY	1	NJ	−1	50
DC	0	DC	N/A	DC	N/A	NE	N/A	DC	0	WV	−1	51

SOURCE: Center for the American Woman and Politics, National Conference of State Legislatures.

LAWS AND REGULATIONS

Laws and Regulations

Minimum Age for Regular Driver's License, 1989		*Marriage Laws Age Without Consent for Males, May 1, 1991*		*Marriage Laws Age Without Consent for Females, May 1, 1991*		*Residence Requirement for Divorce, May 1, 1991*		*Desc. Num. Order*
CO	21	UT[1]	18	UT[2]	18	CT	1 year*	1
GA	21	AL	18	AL	18	IA	1 year*	2
MN	19	AK	18	AK	18	LA	1 year*	3
AZ	18	AZ	18	AZ	18	MA	1 year*	4
CA	18	AR	18	AR	18	NE	1 year*	5
CT	18	CA	18	CA	18	NH	1 year*	6
DE	18	CO	18	CO	18	NJ	1 year*	7
DC	18	CT	18	CT	18	NY	1 year*	8
HI	18	DE	18	DE	18	SC	1 year*	9
IL	18	DC	18	DC	18	MD	1 year	10
IN	18	FL	18	FL	18	RI	1 year	11
IA	18	HI	18	HI	18	WV	1 year	12
KY	18	ID	18	ID	18	KY	180 days	13
MD	18	IL	18	IL	18	MI	180 days	14
MA	18	IN	18	IN	18	MN	180 days	15
MI	18	IA	18	IA	18	AZ	90 days	16
MT	18	KS	18	KS	18	CO	90 days	17
NV	18	KY	18	KY	18	IL	90 days	18
NH	18	LA	18	LA	18	MO	90 days	19
NY	18	ME	18	ME	18	MT	90 days	20
NC	18	MD	18	MD	18	WY	60 days*	21
OH[3]	18	MA	18	MA	18	AR	60 days	22
PA	18	MI	18	MI	18	KS	60 days	23
RI	18	MN	18	MN	18	ID	6 weeks	24
TX	18	MO	18	MO	18	NV	6 weeks	25
VT	18	MT	18	MT	18	AL	6 months*	26
VA	18	NE	18	NE	18	HI	6 months*	27
WA	18	NV	18	NV	18	IN	6 months*	28
WV	18	NH	18	NH	18	ME	6 months*	29
WI	18	NJ	18	NJ	18	OR	6 months*	30
WY	18	NM	18	NM	18	TX	6 months*	31
LA	17	NY	18	NY	18	VT	6 months*	32
ME	17	NC	18	NC	18	VA	6 months*	33
NJ	17	ND	18	ND	18	CA	6 months	34
AL	16	OH	18	OH	18	DE	6 months	35
AK	16	OK	18	OK	18	DC	6 months	36
AR	16	OR	18	OR	18	FL	6 months	37
FL	16	PA	18	PA	18	GA	6 months	38
ID	16	RI	18	RI	18	MS	6 months	39
KS	16	SC	18	SC	18	NM	6 months	40
MS	16	SD	18	SD	18	NC	6 months	41
NE	16	TN	18	TN	18	ND	6 months	42
NM	16	TX	18	TX	18	OH	6 months	43
ND	16	VT	18	VT	18	OK	6 months	44
OK	16	VA	18	VA	18	PA	6 months	45
OR	16	WA	18	WA	18	TN	6 months	46
SC	16	WV	18	WV	18	WI	6 months	47
SD	16	WI	18	WI	18	UT	3 months	48
TN	16	WY	18	WY	18	SD	none*	49
UT[4]	16	MS[5]	17	GA	16	WA	bona fida resident	50
MO	15	GA	16	MS[6]	15	AK	*	51

SOURCE: *Book of the States, 1991*

*Indicates qualification; check local statutes.

[1]County to provide premarital counseling if under 19 or divorced.

[2]County to provide premarital counseling if under 19 or divorced.

[3]Certain restrictions apply.

[4]Certain restrictions apply.

[5]Notice to parents if under 21.

[6]Notice to parents if under 21.

COMMUNICATIONS

Radio Broadcasting Stations (1990)[1]

Commercial AM Stations		Commercial AM Stations per 1,000,000 Population		Commercial FM Stations		Commercial FM Stations per 1,000,000 Population		Educational FM Stations		Educational FM Stations per 1,000,000 Population		Desc. Num. Order
TX	309	AK	72.7	TX	315	WY	70.5	CA	94	SD	23.0	1
CA	249	WY	70.5	CA	285	MT	61.3	NY	84	AK	21.8	2
NC	227	MT	63.8	PA	162	AK	54.5	OH	69	VT	21.3	3
FL	221	ND	53.2	NY	160	SD	47.4	IL	65	ME	16.3	4
GA	202	SD	53.2	IL	159	AR	45.9	PA	65	ND	12.5	5
NV	26	MA	11.5	VT	24	MD	8.8	RI	6	MD	3.8	47
VT	20	MD	11.1	HI	22	MA	8.3	DC	4	HI	3.6	48
RI	16	NY	9.6	DE	9	RI	8.0	HI	4	CA	3.2	49
DE	10	CA	8.4	DC	9	CT	7.3	WY	4	DE	3.0	50
DC	7	NJ	4.8	RI	8	NJ	4.5	DE	2	AZ	2.2	51

SOURCE: Federal Communications Commission.

[1] AM-FM stations that filed combined reports with the FCC are counted as both AM and FM; represents stations licensed; excludes construction permits.

Television Broadcasting Stations (1990)

Commercial Stations		Commercial Stations per 1,000,000 Population		Noncommercial Educational Stations		Noncommercial Educational Stations per 1,000,000 Population		Desc. Num. Order
TX	88	WY	24.3	TX	20	SD	11.5	1
CA	75	ND	23.5	CA	17	ND	9.4	2
FL	55	SD	20.1	KY	16	AK	7.3	3
NY	40	MT	18.8	FL	12	VT	7.1	4
OH	38	AK	18.2	MI	12	NE	5.7	5
DC	6	CT	2.4	NV	2	NY	0.7	47
NH	4	MD	2.3	UT	2	NJ	0.6	48
RI	3	NY	2.2	MT	1	PA	0.6	49
VT	3	DE	1.5	RI	1	CA	0.6	50
DE	1	NJ	0.9	WY	1	MA	0.5	51

SOURCE: Federal Communications Commission.

Newspapers (1989)

*Daily Newspapers**		*Daily Newspapers per 1,000,000 Population*		*Sunday Newspapers**		*Sunday Newspapers per 1,000,000 Population*		*Desc. Num. Order*
CA	119	WY	22.0	TX	95	OK	13.0	1
TX	104	KS	18.6	CA	67	ND	11.0	2
PA	93	SD	17.2	OK	41	WY	8.8	3
OH	87	ND	15.7	NY	37	MT	8.8	4
IN	73	OK	15.6	FL	35	NM	8.6	5
NY	71	VT	14.2	OH	33	ID	7.9	6
IL	70	MT	13.8	NC	31	AK	7.3	7
NC	54	AR	13.6	PA	30	AR	7.2	8
MI	52	IA	13.3	IL	27	KS	6.9	9
OK	49	IN	13.2	IN	21	SD	5.7	10
KS	46	WV	12.8	LA	21	TX	5.6	11
FL	45	AK	12.7	MI	21	WV	5.6	12
MO	45	NM	12.5	AL	20	MS	5.4	13
MA	42	NE	12.0	MO	19	VT	5.3	14
IA	37	ID	11.9	GA	18	LA	5.0	15
GA	36	NH	9.0	AR	17	AL	4.9	16
WI	36	MO	8.8	KS	17	NC	4.7	17
VA	34	MS	8.5	NJ	17	HI	4.5	18
AR	32	CO	8.2	TN	16	NE	4.4	19
LA	28	NC	8.1	VA	15	IN	3.8	20
TN	28	OH	8.0	WA	15	SC	3.7	21
AL	27	PA	7.8	WI	15	MO	3.7	22
CO	27	WI	7.4	MS	14	NH	3.6	23
WA	26	OR	7.0	MA	13	IA	3.6	24
MN	25	CT	7.0	MN	13	OR	3.5	25
CT	23	MA	7.0	NM	13	UT	3.5	26
KY	23	RI	7.0	SC	13	CT	3.3	27
WV	23	AL	6.7	KY	12	CO	3.3	28
MS	22	NV	6.7	AZ	11	NV	3.3	29
NJ	22	LA	6.6	CO	11	TN	3.3	30
OR	20	ME	6.5	CT	11	KY	3.3	31
AZ	19	KY	6.2	IA	10	WA	3.1	32
NE	19	IL	6.1	OR	10	WI	3.1	33
NM	19	TX	6.1	WV	10	OH	3.0	34
SC	17	TN	5.7	ID	8	DE	3.0	35
MD	14	MN	5.7	MD	7	AZ	3.0	36
ID	12	MI	5.6	MT	7	RI	3.0	37
SD	12	GA	5.6	NE	7	MN	3.0	38
MT	11	VA	5.5	ND	7	GA	2.8	39
NH	10	HI	5.4	UT	6	FL	2.7	40
ND	10	WA	5.3	HI	5	PA	2.5	41
WY	10	AZ	5.2	AK	4	VA	2.4	42
ME	8	SC	4.9	NV	4	IL	2.4	43
NV	8	CA	4.0	NH	4	MI	2.3	44
VT	8	NY	3.9	SD	4	CA	2.3	45
AK	7	UT	3.5	WY	4	NJ	2.2	46
RI	7	FL	3.5	RI	3	MA	2.2	47
HI	6	DC	3.3	VT	3	NY	2.1	48
UT	6	DE	3.0	DE	2	DC	1.6	49
DE	2	MD	2.9	ME	2	ME	1.6	50
DC	2	NJ	2.8	DC	1	MD	1.5	51

(continued on next page)

Newspapers (cont.)

*Daily Newspapers' Net Paid Circulation**		*Persons per Daily Newspapers' Net Paid Circulation*		*Sunday Newspapers' Net Paid Circulation**		*Persons per Sunday Newspapers' Net Paid Circulation*		*Desc. Num. Order*
NY	7,500,000	MD	6.7	CA	6,768,000	NH	7.3	1
CA	6,645,000	MS	6.4	NY	5,736,000	MD	7.2	2
TX	3,616,000	UT	6.0	TX	4,579,000	MS	6.8	3
PA	3,300,000	GA	5.6	FL	3,802,000	ME	6.6	4
FL	3,103,000	KY	5.6	PA	3,182,000	VA	6.4	5
OH	2,749,000	LA	5.4	OH	2,868,000	WY	6.2	6
IL	2,604,000	AL	5.3	IL	2,781,000	VT	5.6	7
MI	2,541,000	SC	5.3	MI	2,562,000	KY	5.5	8
VA	2,504,000	AZ	5.1	NJ	1,893,000	AL	5.4	9
MA	2,069,000	TN	5.1	MA	1,759,000	NM	5.4	10
NJ	1,660,000	NH	4.9	NC	1,403,000	UT	5.3	11
IN	1,542,000	ID	4.9	IN	1,355,000	SD	5.2	12
NC	1,447,000	NM	4.8	MO	1,329,000	GA	5.1	13
MO	1,252,000	WY	4.8	GA	1,270,000	KS	5.0	14
WA	1,166,000	TX	4.7	WA	1,168,000	SC	4.9	15
GA	1,155,000	NJ	4.7	CO	1,146,000	LA	4.8	16
WI	1,154,000	DE	4.6	MN	1,136,000	NC	4.7	17
CO	970,000	KS	4.6	DC	1,126,000	AZ	4.6	18
TN	965,000	MN	4.6	WI	1,108,000	WV	4.6	19
MN	948,000	NC	4.6	TN	1,073,000	TN	4.5	20
DC	881,000	HI	4.5	VA	966,000	ID	4.5	21
CT	867,000	CA	4.5	LA	885,000	WI	4.4	22
LA	777,000	AK	4.4	OK	881,000	CA	4.4	23
AL	761,000	IL	4.4	CT	829,000	HI	4.2	24
OK	741,000	VT	4.4	AZ	794,000	OR	4.2	25
IA	733,000	OR	4.3	AL	754,000	MT	4.2	26
AZ	725,000	ME	4.3	IA	733,000	WA	4.2	27
MD	712,000	NV	4.3	SC	706,000	IL	4.1	28
KY	660,000	MT	4.3	OR	674,000	IN	4.1	29
SC	658,000	OK	4.2	KY	668,000	NJ	4.1	30
OR	655,000	WI	4.2	MD	666,000	CT	4.0	31
AR	571,000	WA	4.2	AR	665,000	DE	3.9	32
KS	536,000	FL	4.2	KS	492,000	NV	3.9	33
NE	469,000	SD	4.2	NE	437,000	MN	3.9	34
WV	440,000	AR	4.1	WV	394,000	MO	3.9	35
MS	400,000	MO	4.1	MS	377,000	AK	3.8	36
NM	313,000	WV	4.1	UT	326,000	IA	3.8	37
RI	295,000	OH	3.9	NV	310,000	OH	3.8	38
ME	286,000	CT	3.8	RI	308,000	PA	3.7	39
UT	285,000	IA	3.8	NM	283,000	TX	3.7	40
NV	280,000	MI	3.7	HI	262,000	MI	3.6	41
HI	245,000	PA	3.6	ID	222,000	NE	3.6	42
NH	227,000	IN	3.6	MT	190,000	OK	3.6	43
ID	207,000	ND	3.4	ME	186,000	AR	3.5	44
MT	188,000	RI	3.4	ND	183,000	ND	3.5	45
ND	186,000	CO	3.4	DE	169,000	MA	3.4	46
SD	167,000	NE	3.4	NH	152,000	FL	3.4	47
DE	144,000	MA	2.9	AK	144,000	RI	3.3	48
VT	129,000	VA	2.5	SD	135,000	NY	3.1	49
AK	125,000	NY	2.4	VT	100,000	CO	2.9	50
WY	95,000	DC	0.7	WY	73,000	DC	0.5	51

*Data subject to copyright: Editor & Publisher Co., Inc., New Y ork, NY, *Editor & Publisher International Yearbook*, annual.

SOURCE: *Editor & Publisher International Yearbook* (annual).

ATTRACTIONS

Opera Companies, Symphony Orchestras, National Preserves, and Appropriation for State Arts Agencies

Opera Companies		*Opera Companies per 1,000,000 Population, 1989*		*Symphony Orchestras*		*Symphony Orchestras per 1,000,000 Population, 1989*		*State Appropriations for State Arts Agencies, 1990 ($ per cap.)*		*National Preserves, 1989**		*Desc. Num. Order*
NY	39	DC	3.31	CA	93	DC	11.59	HI	7.92	AZ	22	1
CA	23	NY	2.17	NY	67	AK	9.49	DC	4.61	CA	21	2
PA	10	NM	1.96	PA	43	MT	8.65	NY	3.29	NY	18	3
OH	9	AK	1.90	TX	42	CT	7.10	NJ	2.58	DC	17	4
IL	8	ND	1.52	OH	39	VT	7.05	AK	2.29	AK	16	5
RI	0	RI	0.00	WY	3	KY	2.41	CO	0.40	OK	1	47
SD	0	SD	0.00	DE	2	LA	2.08	NV	0.29	RI	1	48
VT	0	VT	0.00	HI	2	HI	1.80	LA	0.21	CT	0	49
WV	0	WV	0.00	SD	2	AL	1.70	MS	0.19	VT	0	50
WY	0	WY	0.00	NV	0	NV	0.00	TX	0.16	DE	0	51

Note: National preserves include national parks, national monuments, national lakeshores and national seashores, national rivers and wild and scenic riverways, national scenic trails, national historic sites, national military and battle sites, national memorials, national recreation areas, national parkways and national wilderness areas.

*Listed by the state that includes the major portion and/or preserve headquarters.

SOURCES: American Symphony Orchestra League, *Sterns Performing Arts Directory*, The National Parks Index (1989), National Assembly of State Arts Agencies.

NCAA and Professional Sports Teams

NCAA Schools		*Professional Teams*		*Baseball Teams*		*Basketball Teams*		*Football Teams*		*Hockey Teams*		*Soccer Teams*		*Desc. Num. Order*
NY	42	CA	30	FL	16	CA	5	CA	5	NY	8	CA	3	1
CA	24	NY	30	NY	15	FL	4	NY	4	PA	5	FL	3	2
TX	19	FL	27	CA	14	OH	4	FL	3	CA	3	MD	2	3
NC	17	PA	16	NC	9	TX	4	NJ	3	MI	3	MO	2	4
PA	17	NC	15	VA	9	IL	3	TX	3	NC	3	NJ	2	5
SD	2	HI	0	NH	0	SD	0	UT	0	TX	0	VT	0	47
AK	1	NH	0	NJ	0	VT	0	VT	0	VT	0	VA	0	48
HI	1	ND	0	ND	0	VA	0	VA	0	WA	0	WV	0	49
ME	1	VT	0	VT	0	WV	0	WV	0	WV	0	WI	0	50
WY	1	WY	0	WY	0	WY	0	WY	0	WY	0	WY	0	51

SOURCE: List from the *USA Today Sports Atlas.*

INDEXES

INDEX TO PEOPLE

INDEX TO PLACES

Index to Statistics